MW01103645

From Solidarity to Martial Law:
The Polish Crisis of 1980–1981

A Documentary History

NATIONAL SECURITY ARCHIVE
COLD WAR READERS

Series Editor
MALCOLM BYRNE

Previously published:
THE PRAGUE SPRING '68
UPRISING IN EAST GERMANY, 1953
THE 1956 HUNGARIAN REVOLUTION
A CARDBOARD CASTLE?

From Solidarity to Martial Law: The Polish Crisis of 1980–1981

A DOCUMENTARY HISTORY

Edited by
ANDRZEJ PACZKOWSKI
and
MALCOLM BYRNE

Associate Editors
GREGORY F. DOMBER
MAGDALENA KLOTZBACH

Central European University Press
Budapest New York

Published in 2007 by
Central European University Press

An imprint of the
Central European University Share Company
Nádor utca 11, H-1051 Budapest, Hungary
Tel: +36-1-327-3138 or 327-3000
Fax: +36-1-327-3183
E-mail: ceupress@ceu.hu
Website: www.ceupress.com

400 West 59th Street, New York NY 10019, USA
Tel: +1-212-547-6932
Fax: +1-646-557-2416
E-mail: mgreenwald@sorosny.org

ISBN 963-7326-84-7   cloth
978-963-7326-84-4
ISSN 1587-2416

Library of Congress Cataloging-in-Publication Data

From Solidarity to martial law : the Polish crisis of 1980-1981 : a documentary history / edited
by Andrzej Paczkowski and Malcolm Byrne ; associate editors, Gregory F. Domber, Magdalena
Klotzbach. — 1st ed.
    p. cm. — (National Security Archive Cold War readers)
    Includes bibliographical references and index.
    ISBN 9637326847
1. Poland—Politics and government—1980–1989—Sources. 2. NSZZ "Solidarnosc" (Labor organization)—History—Sources. I. Paczkowski, Andrzej, 1938– II. Byrne, Malcolm. III. Domber,
Gregory F., 1974– IV. Klotzbach, Magdalena. V. Title. VI. Series.

DK4442.F76 2006
943.805'6—dc22

2006034150

Printed in Hungary by
Akadémiai Nyomda, Budapest

Table of Contents

PART TWO—FRATERNAL ASSISTANCE

PART THREE—FROM CRISIS TO CRISIS

PART FIVE—FINAL PREPARATIONS

From Romanticism to Realism:
Our Struggle in the Years 1980–1982

It is difficult to consider the year 1980 in Poland and its consequences for the world without referring to the past of this Polish nation, exhausted by communism. After all, that year did not occur in a void. We experienced earlier outbursts that were stifled in a bloody manner by the authorities. I had December 1970 strongly etched in my heart and memory. I prayed after those events that I would be given a chance once more to fight the battle. I already understood then that one had to use different methods. It was not enough to go out into the streets and demand one's rights. We needed a more effective means to employ against the totalitarian system. And with God's help, which came at an opportune moment, and because of supernatural circumstances, August yielded just such a harvest.

I would like to call to your attention one thing that was inconceivable in those days. A Pole became pope, came to Poland, and his word became flesh. "Solidarity" was born, and its power lay in the fact that for the first time in the post-war years all social groups gathered under one banner: workers, intellectuals, artists, farmers, and the youth. We walked shoulder to shoulder, and we knew where we were heading.

The aim of the struggle in August was clear to us all. We had to weather the strike, state our main demands and obtain the approval of the authorities. We achieved this in a dreamlike way, without losses, and without internal splits. The August agreements were precisely a worker's shoe shoved in the door to freedom. We achieved as much as was possible under those circumstances. We did not intend to stop there, even though we could not enlighten the authorities about this openly. After all, the door to freedom was not entirely ajar, and our demands had not met with official approval. I knew that these demands were evolutionary in nature, that we had to continue to fight for them, and that we would be able to crack open this door, against the authorities' harsh repression, only by the sweat of our brow. I remembered that we continued to be in this country, and not another one, and that we were still a part of the Soviet bloc. We therefore played a strategic game for each sliver of freedom. We could not irritate the authorities too much. All that was left for us was constantly to wear down that stone with drops of hope and faith from August.

After the events of August 1980, Solidarity entered its own period of jubilation. But at the same time it was a period of arduous struggle, followed finally by a letdown and the night of martial law. In August, we were romantics dreaming about a Poland we needed and which we saw in our dreams. After August, more and more, we became realists, having understood what kind of Poland was possible. We were not naïve; we had to fight within the realm of our power and possibilities. It was important to maintain the spirit of the struggle so that it would not die out after what we had already accomplished. At that time, we were not interested in politics in the sense of political parties whose aim is to take over power and sweep out the group in authority. The point was rather to press for a gradual and systematic internal change in the government as it was, since the next one perhaps would be no better—which is something we learned from history.

So as not to frighten anyone too much, we first fought for acknowledgement from the authorities of social trends and the creation of a social mechanism that would protect against abuses of power, against open injustices, and against the destruction of people. Later, we wanted to take a step further. It was impossible under those conditions to think about something more, and the goals and desires we posed at the time were, after all, unattainable. With hindsight, all of this looks completely different. A new independent labor union was becoming the motor and the reason for these changes. In this way, we could become advocates of a universal, and not a narrow, cause. And this was where our power lay, because to the world we were not just another political group fighting for power for ourselves, but a movement fighting for change: a massive movement battling for freedom—"yours and ours," as time was to show.

It is difficult today to look at the times of August from the perspective of the past, of a daily struggle for those goals. During those famous "five hundred" days of 1980-1981, we were equipped, luckily, with the faith and hope of August. This was, of course, a time of trial for the Solidarity movement and the labor union, to maintain the victory of the strike and to take a step forward. It was difficult to hold, let alone open wider, the door to freedom. In August, we maintained a different stance at the shipyard. During the strike, we were the moving force; it was we who doled out the problems to be negotiated; the strike had a program and rhythm which we specified. After August, the circumstances were not up to us to the same degree; we struggled with events, which were slipping away from us. It was much more difficult to keep a tight rein on the social backlash, to prevent it from leading to a catastrophe, but at the same time skillfully to fan the flames of the drive to freedom.

The labor union was to play the thankless role of buffer between the radical demands of society and the authorities. The way to achieve this was not to burn the committees, but to build our own. I had to calm the mood at many meetings so that we would not repeat mistakes from previous outbursts, but at the same time keep the August flame high enough to give us hope and illuminate our goals. The flame was highly visible, even beyond our borders.

My role lay in appropriately feeding the flame, tossing in the right ingredients, merging ideas, and maintaining unity, while at the same time not allowing a conflagration to break out. This was nothing more than carrying out the thankless—yet at the time the only effective—doctrine of "self-limiting revolution." My drama lay particularly in the fact that I could not talk about it openly. But time blurs the details, the atmosphere surrounding the fight, and the game with the authorities. The communists had to believe that our actions and aspirations did not threaten the foundations of the system. They could not know that after taking one finger we would reach out in a moment for the entire hand under the right circumstances.

Patience and strong nerves were the conditions for success. I felt that the system was succumbing to methodical and lasting disintegration, and our task was precisely to accelerate and facilitate this discreetly, without irritating the bear. This was where our opportunity lay. The crisis of communism was becoming more and more universal, spreading to other countries of the bloc as well. Even the imposition of martial law was incapable of annihilating our determination and hopes. It was not capable of breaking us, even though we came out of it decimated and bruised.

The harsh reality of martial law also determined the adoption of an appropriate strategy. After all, it was difficult for us to maintain the mass nature of the movement underground. Organizationally, that was impossible. It was easier to work at the elite and individual level. I felt, however, that the power of Solidarity lay in the masses. I have always tried to emphasize this so that propaganda would not relegate us to the role of radicals and marginal players. The nation would not trust hecklers, as we were then called. I spoke publicly about the independence of the labor union, about its scale, about the need for dialogue between the authorities and society, so that our fight would continue to be the fight of the entire nation, if not directly then symbolically. At the same time, our union was active in secret, our underground printers carried out their tasks, and organizations supporting and maintaining Solidarity's ideas and the everyday activities of the union were sprouting near parishes.

The aim of the fight was to enable the many to identify with the struggle of the few. Underground circulation of the press and foreign broadcasting helped in this respect. And it was working. The demands for the re-legalization of Solidarity, which society identified with the aims for freedom, were heard everywhere. None of this took away from Solidarity's massive, widespread, and universal character. And the August flame lasted and led us through the next difficult years to victory. This in turn started the dominos of change falling in this part of Europe.

The costs of these systemic changes dimmed the flame, but they did not extinguish it entirely. Even now, after all these years, the universalism of the cause for which Solidarity fought is surprising. It served as a guide for inter-human coexistence across different times and epochs. It commanded a life not against someone, but in cooperation. The political classes must understand that the global epoch functions on the basis of vessels that are connected, and the misfortune and poverty of one neighbor never benefit the other. And this is both on a local and a global scale. Today, we must proceed precisely according to Solidarity's principle of cooperation and not fight one another. It is up to us what we do with our freedom.

The 21 demands raised in Gdańsk were dictated by totalitarian circumstances, and the most important demand—for free labor unions—was achieved. Then came a time of further difficult changes, grueling struggles for full freedom which entailed great costs. These costs were assigned to Solidarity, the most precious good of our generation, because we did not fold our banners at the appropriate moment. We must do everything so that "Solidarity" regains its rightful place, so that it can still serve the nation. In 1980, we were, after all, 10 million strong, so let everyone pass down their own, and our, legend.

I believe that year by year the victory of August 1980 and everything that Solidarity has accomplished have increased in stature. One needs historical distance to see this. I believe that those days of struggle, festive and ordinary, will forever be etched in the books of our national heritage because it will be easier for us to look with hope into the future. Let it also be a weapon for the young generation in the struggle with real life.

Here, important lessons come from history, and Solidarity is needed under new circumstances. We still have a lot to do. We need time so that the full and real picture of those days and the extent of the victory are taught in schools. History will defend itself, just as the truth always defends itself. I am not worried about this. I look at the past with a peaceful spirit and conscience. If I had to take this road again, I would not choose any other way, despite the price we paid and are still paying today. The taste of real freedom has no price. The time of August 1980 and the celebrations of subsequent days of freedom have helped us to feel and understand this.

Lech Wałęsa
Gdańsk, 2006

Editors' Preface and Acknowledgments

This volume pulls together documentation on the Polish crisis of 1980–1981 from a variety of archives in both East and West. The months between August 1980 when the Solidarity trade union was founded and December 1981 when Polish authorities declared martial law and crushed the nationwide opposition movement that had grown up around the union represent a pivotal moment in modern Polish and world history. Of all the populations of the Warsaw Pact member-states, Poles had always posed the greatest potential challenge to communist rule. Riots and unrest in Poznań in 1956, in Gdańsk in 1970, and in Radom in 1976 were part of a pattern of public resistance which culminated in the creation of the first independent trade union in the communist camp. The 1980–1981 period, in turn, prepared the ground for the collapse of the Soviet-dominated system in Poland.

The documents in this volume describe the events of that critical period from a variety of national and political perspectives. Transcripts of Soviet and Polish Politburo meetings, that were never intended to be made public, give a detailed picture of the goals, motivations and deliberations of the leaders of these countries at which contemporary Westerners could only guess. Records of Warsaw Pact gatherings, notes of bilateral sessions and reports to the political and military leadership of the communist camp provide additional pieces to the puzzle of what Moscow and its allies had in mind. Orders and plans for martial law highlight the level of preparation and efficiency of the crackdown. The collection includes materials from Solidarity, too. Notes and statements from top-level union meetings reflect the organization's internal dynamics and the mix of priorities of its diverse membership, while speeches by Pope John Paul II and Stefan Cardinal Wyszyński indicate the attitudes of another powerful political force, the Polish Catholic Church. From the United States' point of view, a variety of materials are included in the collection. Memoranda to the president, notes of National Security Council and other high-level interagency meetings, CIA alert memoranda, intelligence reports and State Department cables spell out American and allied efforts to predict Warsaw Pact behavior, to find ways to avert a Soviet invasion and finally to exact a cost for the crackdown when it finally came. Of particular note are three once-highly classified messages to the CIA from Col. Ryszard Kukliński, who served on the Polish General Staff and for years (until he fled the country ahead of arrest in November 1981) was one of the United States' most prized undercover sources inside the Warsaw Pact.

The volume thus represents the most varied and detailed compilation of original documentation from virtually every important national archival source on the Solidarity crisis that is available in any language.

From Solidarity to Martial Law: The Polish Crisis of 1980–1981 represents the final phase of a multinational project that originated in 1992, immediately after the collapse of the Soviet Union when the former communist archives were in an early stage of relative openness. In April of that year, the National Security Archive, a non-governmental research institute now based at the George Washington University, set about establishing a network of scholars, archivists, and human rights activists in the countries of the former Warsaw Pact with the aim of recovering the history of the communist past, officially repressed for decades, and of examining it from a multiplicity of perspectives. The methodology centered around the study of a series of crises in the region during the Cold War: the 1953 uprisings in East Germany, the 1956 Hungarian revolution, the 1968 Soviet-led invasion of Czechoslovakia, the 1980–1981 Solidarity crisis, and the 1989 collapse of communism in the region.

The first step was to locate and link together experts in each of these countries, as well as the former Soviet Union, then to initiate—or build upon—archival research activities among all available government and former communist party repositories. The project, known as the Openness in Russia and Eastern Europe Project, was able to ride a wave of extraordinary talent, enthusiasm and resourcefulness generated by the atmosphere of the times and the near universal desire in the region to come to terms with recent mutual experiences. The first organization in the region to join the Openness Project was the Institute of Political Studies (IPS) of the Polish Academy of Sciences, an institute established in part to counteract the party-based academic practices of the previous regime. IPS's lead scholarly participant in the new network was Andrzej Paczkowski, professor of history and director of research and studies at the institute.

The next step in the Project's activity was to add the "human" dimension—in effect to vivify the process—by convening international conferences on each crisis featuring major historical figures who had been at the center of these events and to encourage open discussion by ensuring a scholarly and non-polemical environment. One of the highlights of this phase of activity was the gathering spearheaded by IPS in the village of Jachranka, outside Warsaw, in November 1997. The three-day session, "Poland 1980–1982: Internal Crisis, International Dimensions," featured the following participants:

Polish communist party – First Secretaries Wojciech Jaruzelski and Stanisław Kania; Deputy Prime Minister Mieczysław Rakowski; Defense Minister Florian Siwicki; and other senior officials including Andrzej Werblan and Stanisław Ciosek.

Polish opposition – Tadeusz Mazowiecki, who later became the first post-World War II non-communist prime minister in Eastern Europe; Solidarity national spokesmen Karol Modzelewski and Janusz Onyszkiewicz; Solidarity's Mazowsze regional Chairman Zbigniew Bujak; Bronisław Geremek who later became Poland's foreign minister; Andrzej Stelmachowski, representative of Archbishop Jozef Glemp.

Soviet Union and Warsaw Pact – Viktor G. Kulikov, commander-in-chief of Warsaw Pact forces; Anatolii I. Gribkov, chief-of-staff of the Warsaw Pact forces; Georgy K. Shakhnazarov, International Department of the CPSU CC.

United States – National Security Advisor Zbigniew Brzezinski; Gen. William Odom, National Security Council staff, later director of the National Security Agency; Richard Pipes, National Security Council staff; Stephen Larrabee, National Security Council staff.

The discussions produced important new information and insights about Soviet intentions; the relationship between senior Soviet and Polish communist party officials, and particularly Moscow's attitude towards Jaruzelski; the views of the authorities towards Solidarity and vice versa; and the thinking of American officials at the time.[1] The meeting also generated new documents that were added to the public record, the most significant being pages from the notebook of Gen. Viktor Anoshkin, adjutant to Marshal Kulikov, who brought his notebook to the conference. These findings and materials are incorporated into the text and documentation in this volume.

The final phase of this project is this volume. It is the latest in a series published by CEU Press under the rubric National Security Archive Cold War Readers. Previous titles include each of the Cold War crises mentioned above and a volume on the hidden history of the Warsaw Pact. Compilations on the collapse of communism in Eastern Europe will make up the final volumes in this series.

* * *

A great many people are responsible for making the Openness Project so successful, including its latest offshoot—the current volume.

On the Polish side, the following colleagues provided fundamental contributions, most notably with respect to the November 1997 Jachranka conference: Andrzej Friszke, Paweł Machcewicz and Ryszard Żelichowski.

At the National Security Archive, Executive Director Thomas Blanton helped to shape the original idea for the Openness Project and has contributed regular guidance since then. Magdalena Klotzbach and Gregory F. Domber served as associate editors of this volume providing invaluable assistance in selecting documents, preparing front matter, conducting research and copy-editing text. Catherine Nielsen, William Burr, Robert Wampler, Vladislav Zubok and Svetlana Savranskaya contributed advice and expertise along the way. Sue Bechtel, Mary Curry and Kelly Peterman gave of their time to help organize materials and meet deadlines.

James G. Hershberg, associate professor of history and international relations at the George Washington University, helped to conceive the initial project and has contributed a steady stream of ideas and inspiration throughout. Christian

---

[1] See the Jachranka conference transcript (in Polish) in *Wejdą nie Wejdą.*

Ostermann, director of the Cold War International History Project, has also giv-en unstinting support in addition to editing the volume in this series on the 1953 East German uprisings.

Zbigniew Brzezinski was an early and particularly effective supporter of this project, to which he donated not only time and advice but documents declassified specifically at his request.

Former CIA analysts Doug MacEachin and Tom Troy contributed signifi-cantly to public scholarship on the Solidarity crisis through their own publica-tions and by pressing for the declassification of important intelligence records. Pulitzer Prize-winning author Tina Rosenberg, while a visiting fellow at the Ar-chive, filed numerous Freedom of Information Act requests which have yielded thousands of pages of State Department and other documentation. Independent scholar L.W. Głuchowski also donated records he obtained from Polish and other sources to the Archive's collections. Additional items came through the Archive's participation in the Carter–Brezhnev Project led by Brown University scholars James Blight and Janet Lang. All of these materials are available for research at the National Security Archive.

The editors, who were involved in organizing the conference "Poland, 1980–1982: Internal Crisis, International Dimensions" in Jachranka, Poland, in No-vember 1997, wish to thank the participants, scholars, translators, archivists and others who made the event possible. Among those who could not be present but whose presence was felt were Lech Wałęsa and Ryszard Kukliński. We are very grateful for the moral and substantive support they provided.

Benjamin Weiser and PublicAffairs, a member of Perseus Books, L.L.C., kindly granted permission to use translations of materials Kukliński provided to the CIA that appear in Weiser's remarkable account, *A Secret Life: The Polish Officer, His Covert Mission, and the Price He Paid to Save His Country* (New York: PublicAffairs, 2004. Copyright 2004 by Benjamin Weiser).

Translators have played a crucial role in making the new, multinational Cold War history available to a broad international audience. The following schol-ars contributed translations to this volume, for which the editors are extremely grateful: László Beke, Ruud van Dijk, Detelina Dineva, Mark Doctoroff, L.W. Głuchowski, Małgorzata Gnoińska, Christiaan Hetzner, Wanda Jarząbek, Mag-dalena Klotzbach, Paweł Machcewicz, Catherine Nielsen, Aleksandra Niemirycz, Christian F. Ostermann, Aleksandra Rodzińska-Chojnowska (who translated the original draft of the essay), Edward Rothert, Svetlana Savranskaya, Paweł Świeboda, Oldřich Tůma, David Wolff, Vladislav Zubok. In addition, we thank the anonymous U.S. government specialists who rendered the versions of Ryszard Kukliński's letters that appear in this volume (but originally for *A Secret Life*).

Our gratitude extends as well to the many archivists at institutions in Bul-garia, the Czech Republic, Germany, Hungary, Poland, Russia, Ukraine and the United States who provided guidance—and access—to some very important ma-terials. In the United States, we acknowledge the valuable contributions of the Freedom of Information Act officers at the CIA and State Department.

The editors are very grateful to the KARTA Center for permission to use photographs in their collection.

Without the generous financial support of the Open Society Institute (New York), The John D. and Catherine T. MacArthur Foundation (Chicago), The Smith Richardson Foundation (Westport, Connecticut), the Ford Foundation (New York), The German Marshall Fund of the United States (Washington, D.C.), The Committee for Scientific Research (Warsaw), and The Batory Foundation (Warsaw), this project would not have been possible.

As always, we appreciate the continued commitment of CEU Press, particularly István Bart, Péter Inkei, Linda Kunos and Aniko Kádár, to this documentary series.

Scope conditions - POS

Game theory:

Acronyms and Abbreviations

(Note: Entries are listed according to the most commonly used form, or according to the English form if not widely known in the original language.)

AFL-CIO	American Federation of Labor–Congress of Industrial Organizations
AFLD (ZBWD)	Association of Fighters for Liberty and Democracy, *Związek Bojowników o Wolność i Demokrację*
AP	Associated Press
APJ (SDP)	Association of Polish Journalists, *Stowarzyszenie Dziennikarzy Polskich*
ASS (WSW)	Army Security Service, *Wojskowa Służba Wewnętrzna*
BCP	Bulgarian Communist Party
CC (KC)	Central Committee, *Komitet Centralny*
CCTU (CRZZ)	Central Council of Trade Unions, *Centralna Rada Związków Zawodowych*
Cde.	Comrade
CIA	Central Intelligence Agency
CIP (KPN)	Confederation for an Independent Poland, *Konfederacja Polski Niepodleglej*
CMEA	Council for Mutual Economic Assistance
COMECON	*See* CMEA
CP (MO)	Citizens' Police, *Milicja Obywatelska*
CP	Communist Party
CPA (ČLA)	Czechoslovak People's Army, *Československá Lidová Armáda*
CPC (KKP)	Committee of Party Control, *Komisja Kontroli Partyjnej*
CPCC (CKKP)	Central Party Control Commission, *Centralna Komisja Kontroli Partyjnej*
CPCz	Communist Party of Czechoslovakia
CPSU	Communist Party of the Soviet Union
CPUkr	Communist Party of Ukraine
CSCE	Conference on Security and Cooperation in Europe
CSPS (OPSZ)	Center for Socio-Professional Studies, *Ośrodek Prac Społeczno-Zawodowych*
CSSR (ČSSR)	Czechoslovak Socialist Republic, *Československá Socialistická Republika*
CTO (NOT)	Chief Technical Organization, *Naczelna Organizacja Techniczna*
CUAC (CZKR)	Central Union of Agricultural Circles, *Centralny Związek Kółek Rolniczych*
CWS (KSR)	Conference of Workers' Self-Government, *Konferencja Samorządu Robotniczego*

DC (KD)	District Committee, *Komitet Dzielnicowy*
DCI	Director of Central Intelligence (U.S.)
DCM	Deputy Chief of Mission (U.S.)
DOD	Department of Defense (U.S.)
DP (SD)	Democratic Party, *Stronnictwo Demokratyczne*
EC (KW)	Executive Committee, *Komitet Wykonawczy*
EE	Eastern Europe
FC (KZ)	Factory Committee, *Komitet Zakładowy*
FMS	Foreign Military Sales (U.S.)
FNU (FJN)	Front for National Unity, *Front Jedności Narodu*
FOIA	Freedom of Information Act (U.S.)
FNA (FPN)	Front of National Accord, *Front Porozumienia Narodowego*
FRG	Federal Republic of Germany
FY	Fiscal Year
GDR	German Democratic Republic
GOY	Government of Yugoslavia
GSFG	Group of Soviet Forces, Germany
HSSS (WSNS)	Higher School of Social Studies, *Wyższa Szkoła Nauk Społecznych (PUWP CC)*
HSWP	Hungarian Socialist Workers' Party
HUMINT	Human intelligence
IFC (MKZ)	Inter-Institute Founding Committee, *Międzyzakładowy Komitet Założycielski*
ILO	International Labor Organization
IMF	International Monetary Fund
INR	U.S. State Department, Bureau of Intelligence and Research
ISTU	*See* NSZZ
IUS (NZS)	Independent Union of Students, *Niezależne Zrzeszenie Studentów*
JCS	Joint Chiefs of Staff (U.S.)
KGB	Committee for State Security (USSR), *Komitet Gosudarstvennoi Bezopasnosti*
KIK (CIC)	Clubs of Catholic Intelligentsia, *Kluby Inteligencji Katolickiej*
KOK	Homeland Defense Committee, *Komitet Obrony Kraju*
KOR	Committee for Workers' Defense, *Komitet Obrony Robotników*
KSS	Committee for Social Self-Defense, *Komitet Samoobrony Społecznej*
LOA	Letter of Offer and Acceptance (U.S.)
MD (OW)	Military District, *Okręg Wojskowy*
MFA	Ministry of Foreign Affairs
MFG (WOP)	Military Frontier Guards, *Wojska Ochrony Pogranicza*
MHCP (KGMO)	Main Headquarters of the Citizens' Police, *Komenda Główna Milicji Obywatelskiej*
MIA (MSW)	Ministry of Internal Affairs, *Ministerstwo Spraw Wewnętrznych*

MITS (MHWU)	Ministry of Internal Trade and Services, *Ministerstwo Handlu Wewnętrznego i Usług*
MKR	Interfactory Workers' Committee, *Miedzyzakładowy Komitet Robotniczy*
MKS	Interfactory Strike Committee, *Miedzyzakładowy Komitet Strajkowy*
MND (MON)	Ministry of National Defense, *Ministerstwo Obrony Narodowej*
MS (GM)	Minister's Secretariat, *Gabinet Ministra*
MSW	*see* MIA
NATO	North Atlantic Treaty Organization
NC (KK)	National Commission, *Komisja Krajowa*
NCC (KKP)	National Coordinating Commission, *Krajowa Komisja Porozumiewawcza*
NMC (MRN)	National Municipal Council, *Miejska Rada Narodowa*
NSC	National Security Council (U.S.)
NPA (NVA)	National People's Army (GDR), *Nationale Volksarmee*
NSZZ	Independent Self-Governing Trade Union, *Niezależny Samorządny Związek Zawodowy*
NVC (WRN)	National Voivodeship Council, *Wojewódzka Rada Narodowa*
OMB	Office of Management and Budget (U.S.)
OSD	Office of the Secretary of Defense (U.S.)
PA (WP)	Polish Army, *Wojsko Polskie*
PAS (PAN)	Polish Academy of Sciences, *Polska Akademia Nauk*
PB	Politburo
PES (PTE)	Polish Economic Society, *Polskie Towarzystwo Ekonomiczne*
PLP (PPP)	Polish Labor Party, *Polska Partia Pracy*
PPA (LWP)	Polish People's Army, *Ludowe Wojsko Polskie*
PPA (PAP)	Polish Press Agency, *Polska Agencja Prasowa*
PPO (POP)	Primary Party Organization, *Podstawowa Organizacja Partyjna*
PPP (PSL)	Polish Populist Party, *Polskie Stronnictwo Ludowe*
PPR (PRL)	Polish People's Republic, *Polska Rzeczpospolita Ludowa*
PR	Polish Radio, *Polskie Radio*
PRC	People's Republic of China
PRC	Policy Review Committee (U.S.)
PSR (PKP)	Polish State Railways, *Polskie Koleje Państwowe*
PUWP (PZPR)	Polish United Workers' Party, *Polska Zjednoczona Partia Robotnicza*
RA (ZR)	Regional Board, *Zarząd Regionalny*
RFE	Radio Free Europe
RGS (SOK)	Railway Guard Service, *Służba Ochrony Kolei*
RMH (WKR)	Regional Military Headquarters, *Wojskowa Komenda Rejonowa*

RTV	Radio-Television, *Radio-Telewizja*
RYU (ZMW)	Rural Youth Union, *Związek Młodzieży Wiejskiej*
SB	Security Service, *Służba Bezpieczeństwa*
SCC	Special Coordination Committee (U. S.)
SED	Socialist Unity Party (GDR), *Sozialistiche Einheitspartei Deutschlands*
SF (PGR)	State Farm, *Państwowe Gospodarstwo Rolne*
SIGINT	Signals intelligence
SPD	Social Democratic Party (FRG), *Sozialdemokratische Partei Deutschlands*
SSA (WSW)	Security Service of the Army, *Wojskowa Służba Wewnętrzna*
STA (SNT)	Scientific-Technical Association, *Stowarzyszenie Naukowo-Techniczne*
SUPS (SZSP)	Socialist Union of Polish Students, *Socjalistyczny Związek Studentów Polskich*
TASS	Soviet News Agency, *Telegrafnoe Agentstvo Sovietskogo Soyuza*
SSOM (TNOiK)	Scientific Society of Organization and Management, *Towarzystwo Naukowe Organizacji i Kierownictwa*
TGO	Local Operational Groups, *Terenowe Grupy Operacyjne*
U.K.	United Kingdom
U.N.	United Nations
UNSC	United Nations Security Council
UPP (ZSL)	United Populist Party, *Zjednoczone Stronnictwo Ludowe*
UPW (ZLP)	Union of Polish Writers, *Związek Literatów Polskich*
USA	United States of America
USAF	U.S. Air Force
USC	United Strike Committee, *Ob'edinyonnyi Zabastovochnyi Komitet*
USG	U.S. Government
USPY (ZSMP)	Union of Socialist Polish Youth, *Związek Socjalistycznej Młodzieży Polskiej*
USSR	Union of Soviet Socialist Republics
VC (KW)	Voivodeship Committee, *Komitet Wojewódzki*
VDC (WKO)	Voivodeship Defense Committee, *Wojewódzki Komitet Obrony*
VE	Voivodeship Exchange
VHCP (KWMO)	Voivodeship Headquarters of the Citizens' Police, *Komenda Wojewódzka Milicji Obywatelskiej*
VLKSM	All-Union Leninist Communist Youth Union (Komsomol), *Vsesoyuznyi Leninskii Kommunisticheskii Soyuz Molodyozhi*
VMS (WSW)	Voivodeship Military Staff, *Wojewódzki Sztab Wojskowy*
VMU (NJW)	Vistula Military Units, *Nadwiślańskie Jednostki Wojskowe*
VOA	Voice of America

VPCC (WKKP)	Voivodeship Party Control Commission, *Województwa Komisja Kontroli Partyjnej*
VRCP (ORMO)	Voluntary Reserves of the Citizens' Police, *Ochotnicza Rezerwa Milicji Obywatelskiej*
WP	Warsaw Pact
WRON	Military Council for National Salvation, *Wojskowa Rada Ocalenia Narodowego*
WSOP	Firefighters' Academy, *Wyższa Szkoła Oficerów Pożarnictwa*
WZD	General Assembly of Delegates, *Walne Zebranie Delegatów*
YAF	Yugoslav Armed Forces
ZOMO	Mechanized Detachments of Citizens' Police, *Zmotoryzowane Odwody Milicji Obywatelskiej*

Abbreviations Used in Citations

AAN	Archive of Modern Records (Warsaw), *Archiwum Akt Nowych*
AIPN	Archive of the Institute of National Remembrance (Warsaw), *Instytut Pamięci Narodowej*
A ÚV KSC	Archive of the CC CPCz, Prague, *Archiv Ústředního Výboru Komunistické Strany Československa*
BMZP	German Federal Archives—Temporary Military Archives, Potsdam, *Bundesarchiv—Militärisches Zwischenarchiv Potsdam*
CA MSW	Central Archive of the Ministry of Internal Affairs (Warsaw), *Centralne Archiwum Ministerstwa Spraw Wewnętrznych*
FBIS	Foreign Broadcast Information Service
FOIA	Freedom of Information Act
IPN	Institute of National Remembrance (Warsaw), *Instytut Pamięci Narodowej*
MOL	Hungarian National Archives, *Magyar Országos Levéltár*
PÚV	Presidium of the CC, *Předsednictvo Ústředního Výboru*
RGANI	Russian State Archive of Contemporary History, *Rossiskii Gosudarstvennyi Arkhiv Noveishchei Istorii*
SAPMO-BArch	Foundation for the Archive of Parties and Mass Organizations of the Former GDR under the Federal Archival Service (Berlin), *Stiftung "Archiv der Parteien und Massenorganisationen der ehemaligen DDR" im Bundesarchiv*
TsDAGOU	Central State Archive of Social Organizations of Ukraine, *Tsentral'nyi derzhavnyi arkhiv gromad'skikh organizatsii Ukraini*
ZPA	Central Party Archive of the SED (Berlin), *Zentrales Parteiarchiv der SED*

Chronology of Events

1945–1968

February 4–11, 1945: At the Yalta Conference, Roosevelt, Churchill and Stalin reach agreement on demarcation of the Polish–Soviet border and support for the mainly pro-Soviet Lublin government.

July 17–August 2, 1945: The Potsdam Conference sets Poland's western border at the Oder and Neisse rivers, placing areas of former East Prussia, including the Baltic port city of Gdańsk, under Polish sovereignty.

December 1948: The Polish United Workers' Party (PUWP) is formed by merging the communist and socialist parties. Bolesław Bierut heads the new entity, having previously replaced Władysław Gomułka as secretary general of the communist party.

January 25, 1949: The Council for Mutual Economic Assistance (CMEA) is established to coordinate the economic policies of the communist states.

March 5, 1953: Joseph Stalin dies.

May 14, 1955: The Warsaw Pact is established in the Polish capital with Poland as a key member.

February 14–25, 1956: At the XX Congress of the CPSU, Nikita Khrushchev delivers a secret speech denouncing Stalin and declaring a more moderate approach to Soviet foreign policy. The speech has far-reaching effects in Eastern Europe, contributing to major outbreaks of unrest in Poland and Hungary later in the year.

March 12, 1956: Polish party leader Bierut dies.

June 28, 1956: Workers at the Stalin engineering works in Poznań protest against deteriorating economic conditions. Over the next two days, at least 70 people are killed in street fighting.

October 1956: The "Polish October" witnesses the PUWP's reassessment of Stalinism, communist leader Władysław Gomułka's return to political power, cardinal Stefan Wyszyński's return from internal exile, and the dramatic confrontation between Polish and Soviet leaders in Warsaw concerning alleged anti-Soviet developments in the country.

March 1968: Student protests break out in Poland and are violently suppressed.

August 20–21, 1968: Soviet-led Warsaw Pact forces invade Czechoslovakia, replacing Alexander Dubček and putting an end to the "Prague Spring." Two Polish armored divisions take part in the invasion. Gen. Wojciech Jaruzelski is Poland's minister of defense and Gen. Florian Siwicki is in command of the Polish invasion forces.

1970s

December 13, 1970: The Polish government raises prices of staple foods by as much as 36 percent, sparking widespread worker protests. Gomułka orders police and soldiers to crush the "counter-revolution" leading to the December 16 shooting of workers in front of the Lenin Shipyard in Gdańsk. On December 20, Gomułka is replaced as first secretary by Edward Gierek. The events of December 1970 are later considered the most important precursor to the Solidarity period.

June 26, 1976: Following unexpected food price hikes averaging 60 percent, Polish workers again stage nationwide strikes. The crisis marks the beginning of a "nosedive" for Gierek and the Polish leadership. No combination of schemes succeeds in changing the course of the economy. Meanwhile, the population begins to organize and raise fundamental demands of the leadership.

September 23, 1976: The Workers' Defense Committee (KOR) is formed.

October 16, 1978: Karol Wojtyła, archbishop of Kraków, is elected Pope. The initial Soviet reaction is mostly surprise.

June 2–10, 1979: Pope John Paul II visits Poland and is greeted by massive crowds at every stop on his itinerary (among them: Warsaw, Częstochowa, Gniezno, Kraków, Auschwitz).

December 25, 1979: The Soviet Union launches the invasion of Afghanistan.

1979: For the first time since World War II, the Polish economy shrinks by 2 percent. The growing level of foreign debt—reaching some $18 billion by 1980—is the major problem facing the regime.

1980

February 11–15, 1980: At the PUWP's Eighth Congress, Gierek is reelected first secretary.

July 1, 1980: The Polish government increases the price of some consumer goods, including meat, without advance notice. The deregulation of some meat prices causes as much as a 60-to-90-percent hike. The decision to raise prices, based in part on a miscalculation of public discontent, is later seen as the beginning of the end of the Gierek regime.

July 2, 1980: Strikes for compensatory wage increases break out throughout Poland. Strikers are generally appeased with salary hikes of between 10 and 15 percent. However, as soon as a strike is settled in one factory, another begins. This pattern continues throughout the month.

July 11–20, 1980: Strikes take place in Lublin, situated along the rail link connecting East Germany and the Soviet Union.

July 19–August 3, 1980: The Soviet Union hosts the Summer Olympics, which the United States and several other Western countries boycott.

July 31, 1980: Gierek arrives in the Crimea for an annual visit with Soviet leader Leonid Brezhnev. He stays for two weeks until the strikes in Gdańsk break out.

August 14, 1980: Workers in the Lenin Shipyards in Gdańsk go on strike. Initial demands include the reinstatement of fired workers, including Wałęsa and Anna Walentynowicz; a 2,000-złoty wage increase; normal pay for workers on strike; a written statement promising no reprisals; and government approval to erect a monument in memory of workers who died in the December 1970 strikes. Wałęsa became the leader of the strike. The PUWP Politburo decides that Gierek should be summoned back from the Crimea as soon as possible.

August 15, 1980: With strikes involving thousands of workers in Gdańsk alone and spreading to other cities, the PUWP Politburo holds continuing emergency sessions. The Polish leadership begins to prepare a series of moves to clamp down on the unrest.

August 16, 1980: The director of the Lenin Shipyard and the local party leader agree to local strikers' demands. However, strikers appeal to continue the walkout until negotiations are complete in all striking factories.

August 16, 1980: In the Ministry of Internal Affairs a special staff for Operation "Summer-80" is created.

August 17, 1980: The Pope sends a letter to cardinal Wyszyński in which he sides with the striking workers. Wyszyński calls for peace.

August 17, 1980: A general strike begins in Szczecin.

August 17–18, 1980: The Inter-Factory Strike Committee (MKS), consisting of 13 persons, is formed to coordinate the strikes, with Wałęsa as its leader. The Committee, representing the strikers of Gdańsk, Gdynia, and Sopot, draws up a list of 21 demands, including: the right to form independent trade unions, a guaranteed right to strike, guaranteed freedom of expression, and the adoption of measures to address the national economic crisis.

August 18, 1980: A State Department spokesman declares that Poland's difficulties are "a matter for the Polish people and the Polish authorities to work out."

August 22, 1980: The first issue of the strike bulletin, *Solidarność*, is printed in the Lenin Shipyard.

August 22, 1980: Deputy Premier Kazimierz Barcikowski travels to Szczecin and makes contact with the MKS.

August 23, 1980: Deputy Premier Mieczysław Jagielski, as head of the governmental delegation, begins to negotiate with the Gdańsk MKS.

August 24, 1980: The Fourth Plenum of the PUWP CC decides to dismiss Premier Babiuch, Deputy Premier Tadeusz Pyka, and trade union chief Jan Szydlak from the Politburo. By now, strikes have spread to many major industrial centers, and 253 factories.

August 24, 1980: Józef Pińkowski replaces Babiuch as prime minister. He later promises to implement the Gdańsk, Szczecin, and Jastrzębie agreements.

August 25, 1980: The CPSU CC Politburo establishes a commission consisting of Mikhail A. Suslov (chair), Andrei A. Gromyko, Yurii V. Andropov, Dmitrii F. Ustinov, Konstantin U. Chernenko, Mikhail V. Zimyanin, Ivan V. Arkhipov, Leonid M. Zamyatin, and Oleg B. Rakhmanin. Later known as the Suslov Commission, it is charged with closely following the crisis in Poland and advising the Politburo on possible measures to take.

August 25, 1980: Carter sends letters to Thatcher, Giscard and Schmidt underlining American interests in recent developments in Poland, and initiating an exchange of views on the situation. The letters also note the possibility of Soviet intervention, and lead to State Department consultations with European governments over contingency plans in that eventuality.

August 27, 1980: Soviet Ambassador to Warsaw Boris Aristov delivers a letter to Gierek spelling out Moscow's increasing anxiety over the situation in Poland, and hinting at the need to crush the opposition. Gierek reportedly tells Aristov he is unsure whether Polish soldiers would be willing to shoot at workers.

August 27, 1980: The Polish government requests more U.S. grain credits. U.S. officials handle the request cautiously in order to avoid "provoking" the Soviets.

August 30, 1980: Polish authorities and representatives of the Szczecin Inter-Factory Strike Committee sign the Szczecin Agreement. Currently, 700 industries are on strike throughout Poland.

August 30, 1980: During a plenary session, the PUWP CC approves signing the Szczecin and Gdańsk Agreements.

August 31, 1980: Wałęsa and Jagielski sign the Gdańsk Agreement in the shipyard. Its essential points include the unprecedented concession of allowing independent trade unions; the right to strike without reprisals; the right to "freedom of expression;" pay increases; improved working conditions; Saturdays off; and Sunday Masses broadcast over the loudspeakers.

September 1, 1980: In a campaign speech, Carter reacts to the Polish accords, stating that the American people have been "inspired and gratified by the peaceful determination with which [Polish workers] acted under the most difficult of circumstances." These are his strongest comments to date on the Polish crisis.

September 1, 1980: Pravda publishes an article under the byline "Alexei Petrov" that is critical of the Gdańsk Agreement but differentiates between the strikes and "anti-socialist" elements.

September 3, 1980: The Silesian coal fields strike ends with the Jastrzębie Agreement.

September 3, 1980: In a report, "On Theses for the Discussion with Representatives of the Polish Leadership," the CPSU CC Politburo lays out its critique of the Gdańsk Agreement. They call for a "counterattack" and at the same time offer financial help to Poland.

September 3, 1980: Brzeziński meets with CIA Director Stansfield Turner and voices concern over a possible Soviet invasion of Poland on the grounds that the recent agreements between the Polish government and workers have dramatically undermined the regime. Brzeziński orders a paper on the prospects for an invasion.

September 3, 1980: Lane Kirkland, head of the AFL-CIO, tells Muskie that the union is planning to make a $25,000 donation to the Polish strikers. U.S. officials, worried that the move could be "deliberately misinterpreted" by Moscow, telephone the Soviet and Polish ambassadors to deny U.S. government involvement.

September 4–12, 1980: Soviet–East German joint military exercises take place in the GDR. Although previously planned, the maneuvers are widely broadcast on East bloc television.

September 5–6, 1980: The Sixth Plenum of the Central Committee convenes. Kania replaces Gierek as first secretary.

September 10, 1980: Francis Meehan is nominated as U.S. ambassador to Poland.

September 12, 1980: Carter announces $670 million in credits for Poland in 1980–1981, a boost from $550 million in fiscal year 1979–1980.

September 17, 1980: Delegates from 35 independent trade unions decide to register as the Independent Self-Governing Trade Union (NSZZ) "Solidarność." Wałęsa becomes chairman of the new union's Provisional Coordinating Commission.

September 19, 1980: CIA Director Turner sends Carter an "Alert" memo noting that "Soviet military activity detected in the last few days leads me to believe that the Soviet leadership is preparing to intervene militarily in Poland if the Polish situation is not brought under control in a manner satisfactory to Moscow."

September 21, 1980: The first holy mass is broadcast on Polish radio.

September 22, 1980: The first meeting of Solidarity's National Coordinating Commission (KKP) is held in Gdańsk.

September 23, 1980: The high-level Special Coordination Committee (SCC), a sub-group of Carter's National Security Council, assesses the probability of Soviet military intervention in Poland and potential Western deterrence measures. CIA Director Turner notes that Moscow is undertaking preparations similar to those it undertook in Czechoslovakia in 1968. The group is unanimous that the Poles would fight if invaded.

September 24, 1980: Wałęsa and a delegation of the NCC applies in court for the Solidarity union's legal registration. On the same day, the first meeting takes place between the premier and his deputies with Wałęsa and a NCC delegation.

September 25, 1980: Leszek Moczulski, leader of the Confederation for an Independent Poland, an illegal political party, is arrested.

September 27, 1980: Pravda publishes another "Alexei Petrov" article portraying the issue in the context of East–West confrontation. Western forces are accused of "inciting anti-socialist actions in the PPR" and attempting to "drive a wedge in its relations with the fraternal states of the socialist commonwealth."

October 3, 1980: Solidarity holds a one-hour "warning strike" to protest government delays in implementing the August agreements, particularly on pay increases.

October 4–6, 1980: The second round of the Sixth Plenum of the PUWP CC calls for the full implementation of the August agreements. Further personnel changes also occur in the CC and Politburo.

October 22, 1980: Jaruzelski orders the Polish General Staff to update plans for martial law on a nationwide scale.

October 23, 1980: The U.S. Special Coordination Committee (SCC) approves "a series of specific steps designed to penalize the Soviet Union severely in the event of military intervention."

October 24, 1980: The registration of Solidarity is delayed by the Warsaw Provincial Court because there is no language recognizing the Party's leading role in the state, nor a promise not to threaten Polish alliances. Solidarity refuses to change the wording and threatens to call a general strike if the registration is not processed by November 12.

October 24, 1980: The CPSU Secretariat expresses "utter dismay" at the finding of a top-secret report that "work stoppages and other negative incidents" have "substantially increased" throughout the USSR since August, apparently due to the events in Poland. The prospect that worker unrest will destabilize the rest of the bloc, and particularly the Soviet Union, is one of Moscow's central concerns throughout the crisis.

October 27, 1980: In Toruń, representatives of seven party organizations from factories and one from a local university participate in the first meeting of the new "horizontal movement." The movement later represents a threat to the traditional Party structure by establishing stronger contacts among local and regional groupings.

October 29, 1980: At a CPSU Politburo meeting, Gromkyo declares that "we simply cannot and must not lose Poland" under any circumstances. At the same meeting, Brezhnev remarks: "Perhaps they really should introduce martial law."

November 8, 1980: Kania mentions that although martial law would be the last resort, the Politburo needs to consider this option and be prepared to exercise it.

November 9, 1980: Solidarity's NCC approves a compromise statute for the union.

November 10, 1980: The Polish Supreme Court registers Solidarity, ruling that it is a legally independent organization and need not refer to subservience to the PUWP in its charter. Solidarity responds by withdrawing its strike threat.

November 12, 1980: Jaruzelski informs a session of the Homeland Defense Committee (KOK) that the drafts of plans and legal documents for martial law are not yet fully ready.

November 14, 1980: Wałęsa and Kania hold their first meeting.

November 18, 1980: Brzeziński informs the secretary of state that the president has decided the U.S. should "prepare for a full rescheduling of Poland's hard currency debt in 1981 and coordinate our position on this matter with other major creditors, while not making any new financial commitments to Poland."

November 21, 1980: Jan Narożniak, a volunteer for the Mazowsze branch of Solidarity, is arrested in connection with the discovery of a secret document on methods of prosecuting anti-socialist activity at Mazowsze's headquarters. The "Narożniak Affair" sparks calls by some opposition figures for measures such as a parliamentary investigation into the legality of government actions following the events of December 1970 and June 1976.

Late November 1980: The Soviet leadership reportedly begins to covertly seek a new PRL leadership composed of hard-liners.

November 25, 1980: The CIA issues an "Alert" memo noting that the Polish leadership is facing "the gravest challenge to its authority since the strikes on the Baltic Coast ended in August."

November 26, 1980: After brief strikes in Warsaw, Narożniak is released from custody.

November 26, 1980: East German leader Erich Honecker sends a letter to Brezhnev urging an emergency meeting of Warsaw Pact leaders to "work out collective measures to assist the Polish friends in overcoming the crisis." He warns, that "any delay in acting [...] would mean death—the death of socialist Poland."

November 28, 1980: The governments of the NATO countries warn that Russian intervention on the territory of Poland will prompt serious political and economic sanctions against the Soviet Union.

December 1, 1980: First Deputy Chief of Staff of the Polish Army Tadeusz Hupałowski and Gen. Franciszek Puchała fly to Moscow to familiarize themselves with details of Soviet plans for maneuvers with the Warsaw Pact. Soviet Marshal Nikolai Ogarkov informs them that the plans call for 15 Soviet divisions, two Czechoslovak divisions, and one GDR division to be ready to cross the Polish frontier on December 8, 1980.

December 3, 1980: Carter sends a hotline message to Brezhnev conveying his intention not to exploit events in Poland but also warning of the negative impact on relations if the Soviets choose to resort to force. His concerns are based on high-level intelligence, including satellite imagery and information from CIA spy Ryszard Kukliński, that leads senior U.S. officials to believe a Soviet-led invasion may be imminent.

December 5, 1980: Leaders of the Warsaw Pact convene in Moscow for an extraordinary session to discuss how to deal with the crisis in Poland. The

Soviet participants, including Brezhnev and Ustinov, also meet separately, one-on-one, with the Polish representatives, Kania and Jaruzelski. After Kania promises Brezhnev there will be no change to the "constitutional order," the Soviet leader responds: "Okay, we will not go in."

December 5, 1980: Solidarity's National Coordinating Commission issues a statement noting the absence of any strikes in the country and declaring that none are planned.

December 7, 1980: Carter decides to send another hotline message to Moscow that includes the warning that any intervention into Poland would merit the transfer of advanced weaponry to the People's Republic of China.

December 9, 1980: NATO allies meet to discuss possible actions in the event of a Soviet intervention. Contingency plans include increasing defense spending, closing Western ports to Soviet vessels, halting credits to both Poland and the Soviet Union, recalling ambassadors, and boycotting the Conference on Security and Cooperation in Europe (CSCE) talks.

December 10, 1980: Polish poet Czesław Miłosz receives the Nobel Prize for literature.

December 14, 1980: Rural Solidarity holds its first congress in Warsaw. The main subject is registration of their union.

December 16, 1980: On the tenth anniversary of the December 1970 strike, a martyrs' memorial is dedicated in front of the Lenin Shipyard in Gdańsk. An extraordinary group of national figures attends, including government and party officials.

December 25–26, 1980: Polish Foreign Minister Józef Czyrek flies to Moscow to meet with the Soviet leadership. At the conclusion of the talks, the Poles issue a communiqué stating that Brezhnev "expressed confidence" that the PUWP leadership would be able to accomplish its tasks.

End 1980: By the end of this year, Poland's debt has reached $23 billion.

1981

January 1, 1981: The Politburo ratifies a decision introducing three work-free Saturdays this month.

January 2, 1981: The peasants' occupation-strike begins in Rzeszów, Nowy Sącz and Ustrzyki with demands of registration of free peasant union.

January 13–20, 1981: Wałęsa leads a delegation to visit Pope John Paul II.

January 20, 1981: Ronald Reagan is inaugurated president. Reportedly, the Polish crisis dominates the new administration's for virtually the entire year.

January 21, 1981: Unsuccessful talks take place between Wałęsa, Geremek, Mazowiecki and Pińkowski on the subject of work-free Saturdays. The government proposes creating a mixed commission which would include representatives from both sides, and would be responsible for reaching an agreement.

January 24, 1981: Solidarity, upset with government delays in keeping the Gdańsk Agreement, has its members take Saturday off. A mass boycott occurs in major enterprises throughout the country, with the exception of the mining and metallurgy industries.

January 28–February 6, 1981: Strikes break out in many areas, including a general strike in Bielsko-Biała Voivodeship which not even Wałęsa's presence can bring to an end.

Early February 1981: Eighteen Soviet generals arrive in Poland, ostensibly to check the army's state of preparation for the Soyuz-81 exercises.

February 3, 1981: Solidarity calls off the one-hour strike that had been planned to show unity with the farmers in Rzeszów after the government agrees to negotiate with Rural Solidarity.

February 5, 1981: In terms of the economy, the Politburo concludes that 1980 was the worst year since 1945 with drops in production, exports and imports. Poland's debts are increasing and food shortages persist.

February 8, 1981: Kania informs the Politburo about his meeting with Wyszyński in which the cardinal declared that the Church does not want political power and does not wish to make labor unions look like Catholic organizations.

February 9–10, 1981: At the Eighth Plenum of the PUWP Central Committee, Defense Minister Jaruzelski is appointed prime minister, replacing Pińkowski. This is seen as a victory for Party hard-liners who had been demanding harsh measures against the workers.

February 10, 1981: The Supreme Court denies Rural Solidarity's application to register as a union, but determines it could register as an "association." Wałęsa urges the group to accept the decision.

February 11–12, 1981: The Sejm approves Jaruzelski as prime minister. He appeals to the nation for "90 days of peace" without strikes.

February 12, 1981: Meeting in Gdańsk, Solidarity's National Commission warns its members that because of the uncontrolled strikes the union is threatened with being broken up into many regional organizations which would mean "the destruction of our movement."

February 16, 1981: The Council of Ministers issues a resolution regarding free Saturdays, a forty-hour work week, and an eight-hour work day. This is a direct outgrowth of negotiations with the Solidarity trade union.

February 16, 1981: Thirty-eight Polish Defense and Ministry of Internal Affairs officials conduct a secret war game to simulate the introduction of martial law. Several conclusions come from the exercise, including that the element of surprise would be paramount; therefore the Sejm cannot be notified.

February 19, 1981: The Rzeszów Agreement ends the peasants' occupation-strike. The government agrees to pass legislation protecting peasants' private property and recognizing private farming as a legitimate economic activity.

February 19, 1981: The students' strike in Łódź comes to an end; the minister of education decides to register the Independent Union of Students.

February 19, 1981: A Soviet–Polish trade and credit protocol for the year 1981 is signed on terms beneficial to Poland.

February 23, 1981: The CPSU's 26th Party Congress takes place. Kania leads the Polish delegation. Brezhnev refers to the Polish situation in his report, saying that anarchist, anti-socialist elements, with the help of outside powers, are pushing Poland towards destruction. He declares that the Warsaw Pact will not abandon Poland in her struggle against such elements.

February 27, 1981: The U.S. government agrees to a four-month deferral of $88 million in debts owed by Poland to the Agricultural Department's Commodity Credit Corporation.

March 1981: U.S. officials begin to discuss expanding covert action against Soviet interests in Eastern Europe. But only after the declaration of martial law in December, according to former senior CIA official Robert Gates, do clandestine operations increase significantly.

March 4, 1981: At the Kremlin, Jaruzelski and Kania present the Soviets with plans for imposing martial law. Jaruzelski explains that the "key to the solution" is to gain popular confidence in the government and the party. He writes later that the Soviet leaders received their explanations coolly.

March 4, 1981: The CPSU concludes its XXVI Congress with a statement that re-invokes the language of the "Brezhnev doctrine" in calling for the protection of the "Socialist commonwealth."

March 8–9, 1981: A peasant congress takes place in Poznań.

March 10, 1981: Wałęsa and Jaruzelski meet.

March 17, 1981: The Soyuz-81 Warsaw Pact maneuvers begin in Poland.

March 19, 1981: In the course of being expelled from the provincial assembly building in Bydgoszcz, two Solidarity leaders and one member of the farmers' union are badly hurt by Security Service (SB) officers. The "Bydgoszcz Crisis" is the first incident of violence against Solidarity.

March 21, 1981: Jaruzelski appoints a committee to investigate the events in Bydgoszcz. But as early as the next day, the PUWP accuses Solidarity of provoking the incident and initiating "mass neurosis."

March 22, 1981: At a Politburo meeting, Olszowski and Grabski use the occasion to press once again for either a state of emergency or martial law.

March 22, 1981: The second meeting takes place between Wałęsa and Jaruzelski, this time in strict secrecy.

March 23–24, 1981: At the Solidarity National Coordinating Committee meeting, heated arguments take place over whether to call an immediate strike. Members adopt Wałęsa's proposal to call a four-hour warning strike for March 27, and a general strike for March 31 if the authorities do not adequately respond to the workers' demands.

March 24, 1981: Warsaw Pact Commander-in-Chief Viktor Kulikov announces that ongoing Warsaw Pact maneuvers will be extended.

March 26, 1981: Jaruzelski meets with Cardinal Wyszyński.

March 27, 1981: From 8:00 a.m. to noon, the nationwide four-hour "warning strike" takes place; it is the largest strike in the history of communism, and proves that Solidarity is capable of bringing the country to a halt.

March 27, 1981: Jaruzelski meets with Kulikov and KGB Deputy Director Vladimir Kryuchkov; they discuss a plan for introducing martial law.

March 27, 1981: Kania and Jaruzelski sign key documents laying out basic guidelines for the introduction of martial law as well as general plans of activity for political and administrative organs and the military.

March 28, 1981: Cardinal Wyszyński meets with Wałęsa and a delegation from Solidarity; he appeals to them to act with moderation.

March 28–29, 1981: U.S. officials believe martial law may be invoked during this weekend. Contingency plans are drawn up accordingly.

March 29, 1981: The Ninth Plenum of the PUWP CC accepts a general statement of compromise with Solidarity.

March 30, 1981: The Polish government reaches agreement with Solidarity. As part of the "Warsaw Agreement," the government concedes to demands regarding police brutality, but postpones decisions on Rural Solidarity and on the issue of political prisoners. The government also acknowledges mishandling the Bydogoszcz incident. In return, Wałęsa agrees to postpone the general strike scheduled for March 31. While the agreement temporarily relieves tensions in the country, it prompts a major split within the union—what Wałęsa later calls "the breaking point" for the organization.

March 30, 1981: Brezhnev and Kania speak on the telephone. Kania complains that Polish hard-liners are criticizing him. The Soviet leader responds: "They acted correctly. They should not just have criticized you but taken a cudgel to you. Then perhaps you would understand." (See Document No. 39)

March 31, 1981: The White House, in a show of support for Poland's continued domestic "restraint," initiates a draft program of rewards.

April 1, 1981: The first issue of *Solidarity* weekly comes out.

April 2, 1981: Deputy Prime Minister Jagielski and Vice President George Bush meet to discuss U.S. non-intervention in Polish internal affairs and the sale of dairy products, at concessionary prices, to Poland.

April 3, 1981: Reagan sends a "strongly worded" message to Brezhnev warning against any extension of Soyuz-81 maneuvers into an invasion of Poland.

April 3, 1981: The Soviet Union promises Poland financial aid worth $1.3 billion.

April 4, 1981: Kania and Jaruzelski depart Warsaw for an unannounced, secret meeting with Yurii Andropov and Dmitrii Ustinov in an abandoned railway car in the Belorussian forest. While not conceding to Soviet demands immediately to institute martial law, the Poles promise "to restore order with our own forces."

April 7, 1981: In an address to the Czechoslovak Party Congress, Soviet leader Brezhnev says that the PUWP should be able "to give a fitting rebuff to the designs of the enemies of the socialist system." His failure to endorse the Polish leadership is seen as a warning to Kania and Jaruzelski.

April 7, 1981: The latest round of Warsaw Pact maneuvers comes to an end.

April 7, 1981: Kania proposes to create a Council for National Salvation consisting of leading government and party officials, Cardinal Wyszyński, Wałęsa and others.

April 9, 1981: Andropov and Ustinov report to the Politburo that at their secret meeting Kania and Jaruzelski were extremely tense and nervous. While he notes that others in the Polish Politburo such as Olszowski and Grabski have taken a "firmer" position than the current leadership, Andropov stops short of advocating replacement of the two top leaders.

April 19–25, 1981: The Pope and Vatican Secretary of State Cardinal Casaroli meet three times with the Soviet ambassador who tells them Moscow believes the situation in Poland has stabilized and urges continued efforts to restrain the workers.

April 21, 1981: On the basis of domestic and political considerations, the Reagan administration decides to lift the grain embargo on the Soviet Union.

April 23–24, 1981: Mikhail Suslov pays an unscheduled visit to Warsaw.

April 27, 1981: The U.S. and 14 other industrialized countries agree to a partial rescheduling of Poland's government-to-government debt.

April 29, 1981: The PUWP Central Committee meets for its Tenth Plenum and decides to hold an Extraordinary Party Congress on July 14–18.

May 10–17, 1981: A Solidarity delegation, headed by Lech Wałęsa, visits Japan. Wałęsa later leads a delegation to Switzerland. In both countries, Wałęsa establishes contacts with international labor organizations.

May 12, 1981: The Supreme Court registers Rural Solidarity.

May 13, 1981: The Pope is shot by Turkish would-be assassin Mehmet Ali Agca. The question immediately arises in the West whether the Soviets or their allies, notably the Bulgarians, were behind the attack.

May 15, 1981: Brezhnev, Honecker and Czechoslovak leader Gustáv Husák meet in Moscow and decide to try to remove Kania or possibly both Kania and Jaruzelski from the Polish leadership.

May 28, 1981: Cardinal Wyszyński dies.

May 28, 1981: The "Katowice Forum," a group of hard-line party members, publishes a heated attack on Kania's policies. The group warns of the effects of "Trotskyite-Zionism," nationalism, clericalism and anti-Sovietism. TASS publishes a positive report on the article.

June 1, 1981: The representatives of 35 voivodeship militia organizations create the Founding Committee of the Trade Union of Militiamen.

June 2, 1981: During a Politburo meeting, Kania reports on a phone conversation with Brezhnev, who again has expressed major dissatisfaction with the situation in Poland and advised paying particular attention to the army, the police and the mass media.

June 4, 1981: The Katowice Forum "suspends" itself temporarily, but similar views continue to be pressed by the "Grunwald Patriotic Union."

June 5, 1981: The CPSU Central Committee meets in Moscow to discuss the Polish crisis and to prepare a formal letter to the Polish CC which warns of the danger facing the country and declares that the Soviet Union will not permit any attacks on socialist Poland.

June 6, 1981: The U.S. agrees to begin talks in preparation for arms control negotiations with the USSR.

June 9–10, 1981: The PUWP CC calls its Eleventh Plenum to discuss the June 5 letter from the CPSU CC. Party Secretary Grabski uses the letter to attack Kania's leadership. However, Kania survives thanks to support from Jaruzelski and the military.

June 16, 1981: In a policy reversal, the U.S. announces an agreement "in principle" to sell weapons to the People's Republic of China.

June 27–29, 1981: The 25th anniversary of "Poznań June" is commemorated.

July 3–5, 1981: Gromyko meets with Kania and Jaruzelski in Warsaw. They discuss the agenda for the PUWP Extraordinary Congress as well as a restatement of the Soviet position concerning Poland.

July 7, 1981: Józef Glemp, Archbishop of Warmia, is named Primate of Poland.

July 8, 1981: NATO ambassadors meeting in Brussels conclude there is no imminent danger of a Soviet intervention in Poland.

July 11, 1981: Jaruzelski meets with Primate Glemp.

July 14–19, 1981: The ground-breaking PUWP Extraordinary (Ninth) Congress takes place in Warsaw. Ninety percent of the delegates, recently elected, are attending their first Congress. They insist on a variety of new procedures, including direct election of the first secretary by secret ballot—a privilege previously reserved for the Politburo. Kania eventually wins reelection on July 18 with 1,311 votes; his rival, Kazimierz Barcikowski, gets 568 votes. Western analysts see his reelection as showing the Party's support for his policy of balancing popular demands for more reforms with Soviet requirements for stricter controls. Gierek and several followers are ousted from the Party. Only four of the previous eleven Politburo members gain reappointment—Kania, Jaruzelski, Barcikowski, and Olszowski.

July 15, 1981: In his speech before the PUWP, Soviet delegation leader Viktor Grishin sums up the Kremlin stance toward Poland. It is "the job of the Polish Communists themselves... to extricate their country from the crisis. At the same time, our Party and the Soviet people cannot be indifferent to matters concerning the fate of socialism in a fraternal socialist country."

July 24, 1981: A 20-percent cut in meat rations for the following months is announced by the government. Protests erupt throughout Poland, while the government concerns itself with an anti-Solidarity campaign.

July 24–26, 1981: Solidarity's National Commission meets in Gdańsk for an extraordinary conference. Pressures emerge from Solidarity's members to move beyond "pure" trade union activity to adopting demands for authentic self-government in order to save the "sinking ship."

July 31, 1981: The Sejm passes the Censorship Act. Originally promised by the government for the end of November 1980, it is the first legislation arising from the Gdańsk Agreement to be passed and stipulates fundamental changes from past censorship practices.

July 31, 1981: Gen. Czesław Kiszczak, chief of military intelligence and counterintelligence, and one of Jaruzelski's closest collaborators, is appointed minister of internal affairs.

August 12, 1981: Solidarity publishes an "Appeal to union members and the whole society" which faults not only the Gierek leadership but the entire administrative system for the growing economic crisis. It calls for a "democratic reconstruction" of administrative institutions, from local councils to the Sejm, through democratic elections. Wałęsa declares at a press conference: "We find ourselves at a crossroads."

August 14, 1981: Kania and Jaruzelski meet with Brezhnev in the Crimea. Brezhnev warns, "it is still possible to mobilize the masses and to counter the counter-revolution. But soon it may be too late. You state yourselves that you are faced with an extraordinary situation. Why not take extraordinary, tough measures?"

August 27, 1981: The U.S. government signs an agreement with the Polish government that will delay the repayment of 90 percent of debts owed in 1981 for five-to-eight years.

September 4, 1981: Soviet naval maneuvers commence in the southern Baltic, including the Gulf of Gdańsk.

September 5–10, 1981: Solidarity's First National Congress takes place in Gdańsk, attended by almost 900 delegates. On September 8, the Congress sends a message of support to pro-independent union workers throughout the Soviet bloc. Both Soviet and Western press reaction is that the union has gone too far.

September 13, 1981: At a session of the Homeland Defense Committee, with Kania in attendance, representatives of the military and the Ministry of Internal Affairs declare that all preparations for martial law have been completed. The decision whether to introduce martial law is delayed.

September 15, 1981: Kukliński learns of a leak of information to Solidarity (apparently relating to martial law), and sends a dispatch to the CIA: "Due to the investigation in progress, I have to stop providing daily information about the situation…" He continues to smuggle out updates on the final martial law plans until early November.

September 16, 1981: PUWP leaders proclaim that Solidarity is in violation of the Gdańsk Agreements and has, by its actions, become a spearhead of political opposition to the Party. The proclamation declares that the state will take whatever action is necessary to defend socialism. This is the worst propaganda attack as of yet, as tensions rise.

September 17, 1981: Kania and Jaruzelski meet with Glemp who reportedly agrees to try to prevent KOR from exerting influence on Solidarity.

September 18, 1981: The CPSU CC promulgates a declaration about the situation in Poland demanding that the Polish leadership act immediately against any anti-Soviet outbursts by the public.

September 24, 1981: Jaruzelski tells the Sejm that army units will assist the Ministry of Internal Affairs in maintaining law and order.

September 25, 1981: The Sejm approves the Bill on Workers' Self-Government, adopting wording far closer to Solidarity's preferences than Kania's. It is said to be the first time in Poland since 1947 that parliament has directly and publicly gone against the wishes of the party leader.

September 26–October 7, 1981: The Solidarity National Congress meets for its second "round." Wałęsa is reelected to the leadership position but in general the attitude of the Congress reflects a view more radical than Wałęsa's. The Congress adopts a wide-ranging Program for a self-governing republic consisting of eight chapters and 37 "theses" covering everything from Solidarity's definition to its attitudes toward economic reform, social policy, self-governance and other issues.

September 30, 1981: Politburo member Albin Siwak informs branch trade union representatives that a six-man Council for National Salvation has been established with Jaruzelski and Kiszczak at its head. Special police and security units are set up to deal with possible political disturbances.

October 16–18, 1981: The Fourth Plenum of the PUWP Central Committee meets and on October 18 accepts Kania's resignation as first secretary. The vote is 104 in favor of his resignation and 79 against. Jaruzelski replaces him (only four participants vote against his appointment) while continuing as prime minister and minister of defense. Party members who are also members of Solidarity are told to choose which organization they wish to remain affiliated with. Jaruzelski proposes a ban on strikes.

October 18, 1981: Polish authorities extend conscription by two months for soldiers scheduled to become reservists in November.

October 19, 1981: Brezhnev calls Jaruzelski to congratulate him on his appointment as first secretary. He takes the opportunity to urge him to take "decisive measures."

October 21, 1981: Jaruzelski meets Cardinal Glemp and discusses the need for continued cooperation between church and state.

October 23–25, 1981: The Polish government dispatches military operational groups *(wojskowe grupy operacyjne)* into the countryside under the official pretext of helping rural administrators procure food and prepare for the winter.

October 26, 1981: A strike at the high school of engineering in Radom takes place, eventually spreading nationwide. (See next entry.)

October 28, 1981: A one-hour nationwide strike takes place. Jaruzelski, in a speech to the Fifth Plenum of the PUWP CC meeting the same day, claims that the strike did not receive unanimous support from the workers.

October 28, 1981: The U.S. signs a contract to provide Poland with $29 million worth of surplus dairy products, and plans another $50 million in food aid for 1982.

November 2, 1981: In an interview with *Der Spiegel,* Brezhnev offers to cut Soviet missile deployments if Pershing and Cruise missiles are not deployed in Europe.

November 4, 1981: Jaruzelski, Wałęsa, and Glemp hold an unprecedented summit dealing largely with the formation of a "Front of National Accord." But the talks go nowhere.

November 4, 1981: Solidarity's National Commission declares its distrust of the concept of a "Front of National Accord," and demands the creation of a Social Council for the National Economy *(Społeczna Rada Gospodarki Narodowej)* as well as changes in electoral laws.

November 7, 1981: Kukliński is smuggled out of the country on a U.S. transport plane.

November 10, 1981: Poland formally applies for membership in the IMF and the World Bank. The Soviet Union does not object.

November 11, 1981: Military operational groups are dispatched to some 500 of the largest factories in the country.

November 17, 1981: Solidarity and the government agree to hold their first substantive talks in over three months. The areas to be discussed are: economy, winter preparations, media access, and the neutralization of local conflicts.

November 18–19, 1981: Nine Soviet General Staff and Warsaw Pact officials travel to Warsaw, primarily to review documentation on implementing martial law, and to discuss the situation after Kukliński's escape.

November 21, 1981: The Soviet Politburo approves transmission of an oral message from Brezhnev to Jaruzelski warning against making concessions to the "enemies of socialism," and against allowing agreements to become "ends in themselves." The group decides to invite a Polish delegation to Moscow for December 14–15.

November 24, 1981: Kulikov and Gribkov arrive in Warsaw for talks with Jaruzelski.

November 25, 1981: Reagan authorizes a food donation of $30 million to the Polish people.

November 25–December 2, 1981: A sit-in demonstration takes place at the Firefighters' Academy in Warsaw. The academy is subordinated to the Ministry of Internal Affairs.

November 27, 1981: Military operational groups are deployed in all voivodeships.

November 27, 1981: At a Politburo meeting, Jaruzelski states that the occupation strike in the Firefighter's Academy in Warsaw "has to be solved in a radical way."

November 27–28, 1981: The Sixth Plenum of the PUWP Central Committee issues a declaration that a continued increase in social tensions may lead to a threat to national security. Jaruzelski announces a Politburo decision to instruct the government to demand an Extraordinary Powers Bill, seeking legislation to permit banning strikes in an emergency. This clearly repudiates the August 1980 agreements.

December 1, 1981: The price of alcohol rises sharply—vodka by about 75 percent, domestic wines by 80 percent, imported wines by 40 percent. Car insurance also goes up.

December 2, 1981: ZOMO troops break into the Firefighters' Academy in Warsaw to end the week-long occupation strike. Their action represents the largest use of force since the Bydgoszcz crisis.

December 3, 1981: Prompted largely by the previous day's ZOMO action, an emergency session of Solidarity's Presidium and regional chairmen in Radom issues an official statement accusing the regime of secretly preparing to attack the union, and threatening a 24-hour strike if the Sejm passes Jaruzelski's Extraordinary Powers Bill.

December 5, 1981: The mood at a PUWP Politburo meeting, according to Jaruzelski, is "funereal." A majority reluctantly approves granting Jaruzelski authority to order martial law at his discretion.

December 5, 1981: Talks take place between Glemp and Wałęsa.

December 6, 1981: The Mazowsze branch of Solidarity calls for "a day of protest against the use of force to solve social conflicts" on December 17, to mark the anniversary of the suppression of riots in the Baltics in 1970.

December 6, 1981: The government accuses Solidarity of violating its agreements and launching a power struggle. Radio Warsaw broadcasts a tape of the Radom meeting of December 3, in which various union leaders can allegedly be heard discussing being "prepared to overthrow the authorities." Solidarity claims that the passages have been taken out of context.

December 7, 1981: During a telephone conversation with Jaruzelski, Brezhnev warns him to take appropriate measures before it is too late.

December 7, 1981: Marshal Kulikov together with his staff arrives in Poland.

December 7, 1981: The Homeland Defense Committee orders the appointment of military commissars *(komisarze wojskowi)* in all factories, offices, and state institutions.

December 7–8, 1981: U.S. Commerce Secretary Malcolm Baldrige indicates that the United States will support Warsaw's bid to join the IMF, will grant $740 million in additional credits for food and agricultural products, and continue to delay debt repayments.

December 8, 1981: The CPSU CC Politburo meets, arriving at a set of "instructions" regarding actions to be taken in Poland. No transcript of this crucial session has yet been released.

December 8, 1981: Conferences take place involving all voivodeship first secretaries and chiefs of voivodeship militia commands.

December 9, 1981: Andropov speaks to former Polish Minister of Internal Affairs Mirosław Milewski, asking him what measures the leadership intends to take and when. Milewski says he does not know about Operation X and its timeframe.

December 9, 1981: Glemp receives a delegation from Solidarity.

December 9, 1981: A meeting of the Military Council of the Ministry of Defense, consisting of the most senior officers in the Polish military, takes place.

December 10, 1981: CPSU CC Politburo members discuss Poland in detail, reiterating grave concerns but, according to the transcript, concluding that there can be no introduction of Soviet troops.

December 11–12, 1981: Solidarity's National Commission meets in Gdańsk. The agenda reflects a radical attitude and heated rhetoric. Wałęsa watches as the commission takes the drastic measures of calling for free elections for parliament and for a national referendum on Jaruzelski and his government.

December 12, 1981: Jaruzelski telephones Brezhnev but is told the Soviet leader is indisposed. He is put through to Suslov. The substance of their conversation is disputed: Soviet officials later say Jaruzelski asked for Soviet assistance in case the operation failed; Jaruzelski maintains he wanted to be sure Moscow considered the operation an internal Polish affair.

December 12, 1981: Within hours of the Jaruzelski–Suslov conversation, Ustinov calls the Polish leader. According to Jaruzelski, the purpose of the call is to stiffen his resolve for the operation.

December 12, 1981: By 2:00 p.m., Jaruzelski gives orders to proceed with Operation X.

December 12, 1981: At 3:45 p.m., the Ministry of Internal Affairs sends a cable to all voivodeship militia commands with orders to initiate "Operation Synchronizacja."

December 12, 1981: At 11:30 p.m., the first stage of introducing martial law begins. Special militia and army units take over all means of communication.

December 13, 1981: Beginning at midnight on December 12, ZOMO units start rounding up Solidarity activists as well as other figures, including Gierek. At 3:00 a.m., Wałęsa is awoken and taken away. During the first night and day, several thousand activists are arrested.

December 13, 1981: At 1:00 a.m., an extraordinary session of the Council of State convenes, approving (with only one dissenting vote) decrees on the implementation of martial law.

December 13, 1981: At 6:00 a.m., Jaruzelski goes on national radio to announce martial law. "Our country has found itself at the edge of an abyss," he declares. "Poland's future is at stake: the future for which my generation fought." He accuses Solidarity leaders of "acts of terrorism" and states that "famine," "chaos," and "civil war" would be the result if the situation were allowed to deteriorate further. Over 20 martial law decrees are initiated suspending such rights as free association and freedom of the press. Strict curfews are instituted, mail service is suspended, key economic enterprises are militarized, and the mass media are restricted to one government channel. Travel by the population is curtailed and public meetings are banned.

December 13, 1981: Leaders of Solidarity who avoided being put in jail organize regional strike committees (for example, Władysław Frasyniuk in Wrocław, Andrzej Słowik in Łódź, and the National Committee in Gdańsk Shipyard lead by Solidarity Vice President Mirosław Krupinski).

December 13, 1981: Kiszczak and Siwicki report to the Politburo that the implementation of martial law is progressing according to plan, and 70 percent of those targeted for arrest are in jail; Jaruzelski informs the leadership that Brezhnev telephoned to present congratulations.

December 13, 1981: The Kremlin sends a brief statement to the leaders of several socialist countries, including Cuba and Vietnam, expressing approval of martial law and asking for support to the Polish comrades.

December 13, 1981: In a sermon broadcast over the radio, Glemp appeals for non-violent resistance and describes martial law as a "lesser evil."

December 14–28, 1981: During this period, resistance by workers and members of Solidarity takes several forms. Strikes take place in more than 250 factories and many institutions (such as universities). Special units of the Army and ZOMO stage some 50 attacks on factories and street demonstrations (among other instances in Nowa Huta, Kraków, Wrocław, Szczecin, Gdańsk, and Świdnik). The army and militia block access to the main cities. Approximately 80,000 soldiers, 1,600 tanks and 1,800 armored vehicles are involved in these operations. The strongest resistance takes place in Silesia where nine workers are shot at the "Wujek" coal mine on December 16. ZOMO troops, with army and tank support, attack some 10 coal mines as well as the Katowice steelworks. The last strike is crushed on December 28 (at the "Piast" coal mine). The official death toll as a result of clashes with police is eventually placed at 17. While brutally efficient in its implementation, the "state of war" is later described as a pyrrhic victory for both Polish authorities and the Kremlin.

December 14, 1981: A committee to help the detained and their families under the protection of Archbishop Glemp is established in Warsaw.

December 14, 1981: Speaking with John Paul II by telephone, Reagan offers condolences for the people of Poland.

December 16, 1981: Marshal Kulikov departs Poland.

December 17, 1981: The first underground newspaper, *Wiadomości (News)*, is published in Warsaw.

December 18, 1981: Pope John Paul II sends a letter to Jaruzelski.

December 23, 1981: Condemning Polish government actions, President Reagan imposes economic sanctions, including suspending all government-sponsored agricultural and dairy shipments. Humanitarian aid will continue.

December 23, 1981: The NATO countries meet to discuss their options for a response to the declaration of martial law.

December 24, 1981: Polish courts hand down the first sentences (3–5 years in prison) to members of strikes committees.

December 29, 1981: In a White House statement, President Reagan announces that due to the role of the Soviets in the Polish crisis, the United States will take a more aggressive stance in relations with the USSR.

1982

January 3, 1982: Jaruzelski writes a letter to Soviet leaders expressing gratitude for their fraternal assistance but requesting confirmation of previously agreed deliveries of oil and gas products. Jaruzelski advises that he has also asked Hungary, the GDR, Bulgaria, Romania, and Czechoslovakia for basic agricultural and industrial goods.

January 4, 1982: In a meeting with EEC diplomats, Jaruzelski criticizes U.S. sanctions as "interference in Poland's internal affairs." However, EEC members issue a communiqué promising not to undermine the U.S. action.

January 9, 1982: Jaruzelski meets with Glemp.

January 10–12, 1982: Foreign Minister Czyrek travels to Moscow for meetings with Gromyko and Suslov, the first official encounters between high-ranking Poles and Soviets since martial law.

January 19, 1982: The Polish government announces a possible four-fold increase in food prices as of February 1, and severe meat shortages, due to poor delivery by farmers.

January 26, 1982: Wałęsa is formally interned.

April 28, 1982: The Polish government releases 800 internees and lifts several martial law restrictions, including the nationwide curfew.

October 8, 1982: The Sejm adopts a new law on trade unions, which dissolves all unions—including Solidarity—that existed prior to December 13, 1981.

December 31, 1982: Martial law is officially suspended at midnight.

1983

July 21, 1983: Effective at midnight, Polish authorities officially terminate martial law.

The Polish Crisis: Internal and International Dimensions

by Andrzej Paczkowski and Malcolm Byrne

When Poland's rulers suddenly raised meat prices nationwide on July 1, 1980, no-one expected that the decision would touch off a chain reaction that would undermine the foundations of the Polish communist system by the end of the decade. Yet, this is exactly what happened, and although historians disagree as to what (or who) played the decisive role in ultimately toppling communism, there is no question that what is often described as the "Polish crisis of 1980–1981" made a significant contribution. In fact, the Polish crisis did not finally end until the second half of 1988, when the communist authorities recognized that there was no solution other than to begin profoundly reforming the system. This, of course, led within months to a total systemic transformation—to the creation of a democratic state and a market economy.

The 1980–1981 period was therefore only the first phase in a long-term process. But it retains crucial significance because it was precisely at this juncture that an alternative political force to the communist party emerged and took shape—the "Solidarity" trade union.

Without the creation of that alternative institution, it probably would have proven impossible to shift from merely reforming the system to transforming it. It is also highly plausible that without the changes that occurred in Poland the communist system would not have been rejected in other Central-East European countries, including the German Democratic Republic, in 1989. The loss of control over this region and the unification of Germany were, in turn, decisively important for the collapse of the Soviet Union in 1991, and thus for the end of the Cold War.

The "Polish crisis" is therefore relevant not only as the prologue to an important fragment of European history, but as a model for how an internal crisis can affect international politics, and ultimately as a reference point for analyzing the final implosion of the communist system.

THE POLISH CASE

In many respects, Poland differed from other Soviet bloc states. Naturally, each had its own characteristic features, but in our opinion three distinct attributes are fundamentally important for comprehending the character of the events of 1980–1981: the strikes, the Church, and the opposition.[1]

---

[1] For the historical context to these events, see Paczkowski, *The Spring Will Be Ours.*

The Strikes. Starting in 1956, a number of economic strikes took place that turned into revolts which the authorities quickly stifled but which greatly affected the ruling Polish United Workers' Party (PUWP). This was the case when unrest in Poznań in June 1956, preceded by a strike, polarized the party leadership and created acute social tensions, which were alleviated only by a combination of changes at the pinnacle of power and by basic transformations in economic policy and other spheres of national and state life. Although those changes were part of a general scheme of de-Stalinization, the "Poznań incidents," as they were enigmatically termed at the time, acquired added drama because the workers' revolt inherently undermined the party's Marxist–Leninist justification for governing "in the name of the working class."

Much less profound but just as immediate were the effects of strikes and street riots in December 1970 in a number of towns along the Baltic coast—Gdańsk, Gdynia, Elbląg and Szczecin—which responded to a drastic hike in food prices. PUWP leader Władysław Gomułka, who in 1956 had won enthusiastic approval from most of Polish society for facing down a direct threat of intervention from Moscow,[2] was ousted from power. In order to calm public anger the authorities made him a scapegoat, but the very fact that an authoritarian leader had been relegated to political non-existence because of an event that could be described as a "revolt of inferiors" convinced the public that such revolts could be effective.

A similar protest took place in 1976, centering mainly in the city of Radom. This time, the riots were put down without resort to the army (which in the past had led to dozens of fatalities). Nonetheless, the possibility of strikes spreading across the country was curbed only by the virtually instantaneous reversal of the price hikes that once again had been the original cause of the unrest. Not a single head "rolled," but the authorities were forced to retreat once more, yielding to pressure from the streets by abandoning an important policy decision. Consequently, Edward Gierek, who in 1970 had replaced Gomułka as party first secretary, found his authority seriously impaired.

To this list of disturbances we could add the students' strikes, which broke out in March 1968, and which prompted sharp factional infighting within the power elite. This high-level bickering led to the dismissal of several top PUWP leaders and weakened Gomułka's position. The March events were also evidence that the intelligentsia had lost faith not just in this particular group of leaders, but to a considerable degree in the system itself. Confrontations between crowds and security forces broke out on many other occasions (for example, in 1960 and 1966), mainly against the background of conflicts over the building of churches or after major religious demonstrations.

All these facts reinforced the belief that the party's authority was based on brute force, that its legitimacy was enfeebled, and that one only had to "press

---

[2] See, for example, Głuchowski, *Poland 1956,* 38–49. For earlier, very emotional but detailed analyses, see among others, Lewis, *A Case History of Hope* and Syrop, *Spring in October.*

harder" to win concessions. Although it would be hard to prove that these experiences had somehow accumulated in the public mind, it should be stressed that the leaders of the greatest strikes in the summer of 1980—in Gdańsk and Szczecin—included participants from the 1970 outbreaks (respectively, Lech Wałęsa and Marian Jurczyk). For the workers, the most important tactical lessons from those earlier experiences were that occupation strikes were more effective than street demonstrations, and that a representative group had to be created to conduct negotiations with the authorities. Finally, it was important for protest leaders not to be satisfied with on-the-spot concessions, but to establish a permanent organization that would take care of long-term demands—a trade union.

The authorities also learned their lessons. After the experiences of December 1970, Gierek realized that the use of force—especially the army—would only escalate a crisis, which would end with bodies in the streets, divisions among top party leaders, and personal blame being assigned for destabilizing the state and worsening the plight of the victims. Gierek knew perfectly well that no one would come to his rescue. He could recall that in 1970 Moscow never lifted a finger to protect Gomułka. In a certain sense, Gierek was "disarmed" in advance, and his room to maneuver significantly confined.

Other communist states in Central-Eastern Europe also witnessed powerful social disturbances during those years, including the Hungarian national uprising of 1956 and the "Prague Spring" of 1968. Each event was crushed by a Warsaw Pact invasion followed by months of widespread passive resistance. Even the June 1953 revolt in East Germany involved a far greater number of participants than the "Polish seditions" of the period.[3] All of these events, however, were one-time occurrences. By striking so directly at the system's institutional bases and undermining Soviet international standing, these outbreaks prompted an acute military reaction by a superpower determined to wield complete control over the region. The societies of those countries were consequently "pacified" for years as a result of the number of victims, the extent of material losses, and the feelings of helplessness and hopelessness brought about by the brutality of the repression. No one seriously contemplated repeating those experiences—not least the superpowers. Certainly, Moscow did not relish the idea of mounting military invasions of those countries. Intervention was always the last option for the Kremlin, although, as happened during the Solidarity crisis, hard-line East European leaders were eager for the Red Army to march. From the very first crisis in East Germany in 1953, the United States recognized how limited their ability was to counter any Soviet military move.

The Polish uprisings prior to 1980 never reached the broad scope of the earlier East European crises. They focused entirely on domestic issues, with no apparent implications for the Soviets' international position or the integrity of the

---

[3] For information on these earlier crises, see: Ostermann, *Uprising in East Germany, 1953*; Békés, Byrne, and Rainer, *The 1956 Hungarian Revolution*; and Navrátil *et al*, *The Prague Spring '68*.

Warsaw Pact. And to a certain extent they were effective, since they led to changes in the communist party leadership, a reorientation of economic policy, and an expanded range of political liberties. Furthermore, the Poles accomplished all of that without provoking a Warsaw Pact invasion. This particular form of protest therefore became a kind of permanent element in the relationship between the Polish authorities and society for the rest of the 1980s.[4]

The Church. A second distinctive Polish trait was the position and role of the Catholic Church, which, despite regular attempts by the authorities from 1949–1955, was never subjugated to the state as occurred in the Soviet Union and other communist countries. Although the Church did not engage in political activity in the strict sense, it offered a widely accepted alternative ideology and worldview to communism. This stemmed from the Church's deep roots in Polish society, extending back to its role during the period when the Polish state temporarily ceased to exist (1795–1918). The emergence of an almost universally Catholic, and virtually mono-ethnic, population after World War II enhanced its position, and official policies to propagate atheism made little progress. Another factor was the leadership, beginning in 1949, of Primate Stefan Wyszyński, an outstanding personality and an extremely skillful and "unyielding" politician. Paradoxically, the communists themselves contributed to the Church's growing importance: whenever state and party authorities experienced instability at the top, the leadership—Gomułka in 1956 and Gierek in 1970—reached out for ecclesiastical support in restoring public calm. Such help was always forthcoming.

Gomułka, however, never felt obliged to express gratitude for the assistance, and from 1959–1966 he declared war on the Church (a *sui generis kulturkampf*), an act which produced the opposite of its intended effect, consolidating millions of believers around the Church hierarchy.[5] Gierek never dared to opt for open confrontation. Still, mobilization of the faithful continued, in part because the regime insisted on keeping up various forms of official harassment, and in part because the Church enjoyed unfettered freedom in carrying out its pastoral activities.

For the majority of Poles, the ultimate spiritual authority was Primate Wyszyński, whose standing was even more considerable after both Gomułka and Gierek quite rapidly spent the social trust they had enjoyed when they came to power. Wyszyński and many other high-ranking Church dignitaries looked favorably on the democratic opposition that emerged in 1976; some priests directly supported hunger strikes held in churches and delivered ceremonial Masses on national holidays. The Church also defended victims of official repression in the wake of the 1976 strikes, and acted as a protective umbrella for Catholic intellectual activities

---

[4] Strikes and revolts also took place in other countries (for example, the miners' strike in Jiu, Romania, in 1977) and even in the Soviet Union (the revolt in Novocherkassk in 1962), but these were isolated cases.

[5] For details, see Diskin, *The Seeds of Triumph.*

4

which cropped up, for example, following a compromise reached between Go-mułka and Wyszyński in Autumn 1956. As a result, the authorities tolerated independent clubs set up by the Catholic intelligentsia and allowed the weekly *Tygodnik Powszechny* to be published. The only paper of its kind in the communist camp, it operated under censorship, to be sure, but not under direct central party control.

In a word, the Church over time became both a player in the growing crisis and a mediator of sorts between much of society and the communist-run state. But the institution's prominence rose dramatically and permanently in October 1978 when a Pole, Cardinal Karol Wojtyła of Kraków, was elected Pope. In a single moment, John Paul II became both a national hero and a spiritual leader, and Primate Wyszyński became his vicar. The Pope's June 1979 pilgrimage to Poland is seen almost universally as a turning point for the country as millions of Poles greeting the pontiff suddenly became aware of their own strength. At the same time, they understood the relative helplessness of the authorities, who put on a bold front during the visit but for all practical purposes had already lost the battle for the people's soul.

The Opposition. The third distinguishing feature in Poland was the democratic opposition's character and range. Although opponents of the system (dissidents) existed in the 1970s in the Soviet Union, Czechoslovakia, Romania and Hungary, nowhere were they capable of reaching the same level of organization or ability to conduct such dynamic activity as in Poland. At the very outset of the Polish crisis, organized opposition elements became involved in helping people who were arrested or harassed for their participation in the 1976 strike. The largest group, formed in September of that year, was known as the Committee for Workers' Defense (*Komitet Obrony Robotników*, or KOR). Despite rivalries between different organizations—some gave greater importance to national traditions and independence, others to civil liberties and improved living conditions—they foreshadowed, in some sense, the pluralistic political scene of the future, and attracted a determined and overwhelmingly young following. From 1976 to 1980, at least 100 illegal periodicals appeared in print, hundreds of books and brochures were published, and a number of opposition events and ceremonies drew thousands of participants, including many workers. The Free Trade Unions were founded in 1978 (the most active ones being, not accidentally, in Gdańsk), and KOR began issuing the periodical *Robotnik* ("The Worker").

By establishing a link between workers and intellectuals, the opposition had crossed the boundaries of the "intelligentsia ghetto."[6] This development disturbed the authorities. But, again, their range of options was by now more limited. In particular, fear of provoking a negative reaction from Western countries, to whom Poland was increasingly in debt, led Gierek to avoid drastic measures.

[6] See Bernhard, *The Origins of Democratization in Poland.*

5

Obviously, the most active opposition members were harassed, dismissed from jobs, had typewriters confiscated, and so on. But generally no harsher punishments occurred.[7]

The three factors listed above—the tradition and experiences surrounding strikes, the Catholic Church's strength and independence, and the impact of the opposition—fundamentally influenced the character and direction of the tidal wave of events that swept across Poland in summer 1980. Naturally, these were not the only elements at work. Social moods proved to be crucial for the development of future events. The lack of reliable research and analysis for the period makes it hard to be precise, but dissatisfaction clearly began to grow significantly by 1976 at the earliest.[8] Complaints proliferated about the hardships of daily life including long lines for consumer goods and commodity shortages, and the conviction spread that the power elite was corrupt. The population talked about communist party leaders as "the owners of People's Poland." They were particularly critical of their tendency to vacillate and their unwillingness to take drastic steps to improve conditions. To some extent, these leadership failings grew out of fears about the likely attitude of the West and a sense of loss of control over events, but in the opinion of a number of historians they also reflected, importantly, a weakening of ideological motivation among most of the communist elite.[9] This seriously undermined the determination to act whenever difficult, risky, or unpopular decisions had to be made.

SUMMER 1980

For a variety of reasons then, a surge of strikes swept across the country beginning July 1. In some towns, such as Lublin, they reached the scale of a general strike. The party leadership reacted by offering blandishments—mainly by raising wages and bonuses—but once a strike ended in one factory, it flared up in others. The authorities took these developments extremely seriously, sometimes sending high-level ministers to hold talks. Their greatest sources of anxiety— even more than the inherent political threat—were the inflationary effect of higher wages and the prospect of further declines in consumer supplies.[10] Not until a few weeks later, when the strikes reached the Gdańsk docks on August 14, did their perspective change. In a new development, the organizers of the work ac-

---

[7] One exception occurred in mid-1977, centering around the arrest of several members of KOR (among them Adam Michnik and Jacek Kuroń), but they were released after only a few weeks in jail.

[8] The Gierek-era "economic miracle" *de facto* came to an end slightly earlier, but 1976 revealed clear symptoms of discontent (for example, the tide of strikes in June) and produced a symbol of the failure of the regime's economic policy—the introduction of sugar rationing.

[9] For an interesting analysis, see Taras, *Ideology in a Socialist State*.

[10] See Document No. 1.

6

tions at the Lenin Shipyards in the Baltic port city included activists from the illegal Free Trade Unions and KOR.[11] From that moment on, the PUWP's supreme decision-making body, the Politburo, began to meet daily to discuss the situation. Gierek, who was on his annual vacation with Soviet Communist Party leader Leonid Brezhnev in the Crimea, hurried home. Within two days, on August 16, the Ministry of Internal Affairs issued an order to prepare Operation "Summer-80," a plan for suppressing the strikes.

Meanwhile, the Lenin Shipyard set up a strike committee headed by Lech Wałęsa, who had been removed from the shipyard in 1976 but maintained contacts and continued to be one of the most dynamic of the Free Trade Unions' activists. On August 18, dock workers from Szczecin joined the strike, creating an identical organizational structure. Thus the main urban areas along the Baltic coast—one of the most important industrial agglomerations in the country—became the site of a large-scale general occupation strike led by organized representative bodies.

The strike committees immediately prepared lists of demands. The Gdańsk list contained 21 items, the Szczecin list 36. The first point on each was almost identical, calling for the creation of free trade unions independent of the government. For practical purposes this was a qualitative shift, even though workers in Szczecin had formulated a similar demand in December 1970. At that time, independent unions were only a secondary demand, and when street rioting broke out all negotiations were rendered moot. In 1980, both sides acted more cautiously. Workers did not take to the streets, the authorities decided not to use force, and negotiations were entrusted to the highest echelon. Mieczysław Jagielski, who went to Gdańsk, and Kazimierz Barcikowski, who went to Szczecin, were both vice premiers and members of the Politburo.

For two weeks, Poland witnessed a highly complex game involving a host of issues.[12] On August 24, the party leadership applied the tried-and-true tactic of scape-goating, as several senior officials were dismissed: the prime minister and various other ministers, Politburo and Central Committee (CC) Secretariat members, and the head of the official trade union organization. With Gierek's personal participation, an intensive propaganda campaign gravely threatened a "fourth partition" of Poland—a clear reference to a possible Soviet military intervention. The authorities also sought support from the Church, and Wyszyński met Gierek the same day at the latter's request. Meanwhile, the Ministry of Internal Affairs continued preparations already underway to set up blockades and mount assaults against striking workplaces. Every means at the ministry's disposal was placed in "full readiness." Even field hospitals were set up. The plan devised by the Sum-

---

[11] A protocol from a Politburo session held the same day noted the presence of "anti-socialist elements" among the workers. See Włodek, *Tajne dokumenty*, 23–28, especially 24.

[12] For the text of the final agreements from Szczecin and Gdańsk, see Document Nos. 6 and 7, respectively.

mer-80 operations staff envisaged a total blockade of the shipyard; handing control of the ports, which had gone on strike together with the docks, to the Polish Navy; making arrests; even disrupting talks with the strike committees.

From the very beginning, the workers had the support of the democratic opposition. Leaflets and illegal news-sheets were circulated (one edition of *Robotnik* was issued in tens of thousands of copies), and information was supplied to the foreign media, predominantly the U.S.-run Radio Free Europe, which was one of the main channels for news about events in Poland. When security forces arrested the principal labor leaders as soon as the strike broke out, advisers representing intellectuals as well as young workers from illegal publishing houses and print shops appeared in the shipyards, which already had hard-to-obtain office equipment (printing machines, copiers, paper) and intra-shipyard broadcasting facilities.

As August wore on, strikers along the coast showed mounting determination. They had broad local support and knew that work stoppages were gradually spreading to factories and industrial centers elsewhere. In contrast to the July strikes, the actions at the end of August were not only based on economic concerns. In every case, slogans proclaimed solidarity with the strikers in Gdańsk and Szczecin, making it hard to put down each outbreak simply by proposing higher wages locally.

The work actions generated high emotional tension, to which the workers tended to respond by treating religious symbols and the Pope as *sui generis* defense shields—embellishing factory gates with pictures of the Madonna, portraits of John Paul II and papal or Marian flags. Holy Mass was a regular event at strike locations and strikers went to confession in large numbers. No reliable public opinion studies exist from this period, but pieces of information passed on by the security apparatus and PUWP to the highest authorities show that the overwhelming majority of society supported the strikers.[13]

The institutional Church, following previous practice, appealed for reconciliation. This was possible only in an "atmosphere of peace and inner order," according to a communiqué from the Main Council of the Episcopate of Poland on August 26.[14] The sermon read by the primate on the same day[15] called for work to continue and for maintaining "professional responsibility." Some of the strikers, and even certain priests, expressed disappointment at the "passive attitude of the Polish Episcopate towards the fundamental matters [facing] the Polish nation."[16] But Wyszyński upheld the Church's image as a mediator. The mission conducted by his special envoy in the Gdańsk Shipyard was distinctly conciliatory.

---

[13] Minutes of the PUWP CC Politburo Meeting, August 30, in: Włodek, *Tajne Dokumenty*, 90–92.

[14] For the full text, see *Zapis wydarzeń*, 295–296.

[15] Document No. 3.

[16] *Zapis wydarzeń*, 393. See also Document No. 3.

The Soviet and Western governments—the so-called "external actors"—quickly made their concerns known about the unfolding crisis.

The Kremlin clearly understood the significance of what was happening in Poland.[17] On August 21, Moscow presented Gierek with a letter expressing anxiety over developments, and on August 25 set up a special Politburo commission headed by chief ideologist Mikhail Suslov and including Foreign Minister Andrei Gromyko, Defense Minister Dmitri Ustinov, and the head of the KGB, Yurii Andropov, among others.[18] The first problem the commission discussed was the eventuality of deploying Red Army units in Poland. The possibility of Polish armed forces going over to the "counter-revolution" also came up. On August 27, Soviet Ambassador to Warsaw Boris Aristov presented Gierek with an official statement reminding Poles of the need to act decisively—defined as eliminating the strikes through force. From the very beginning, a pattern developed where Moscow applied ever increasing pressure on Polish leaders to take the necessary steps to crush the new movement. Just in case, the Kremlin took steps to prepare for military action, placing four Soviet divisions on full combat alert on August 28.[19]

The West was also anxious. In the United States, Poland had risen in priority under the Carter administration. Encouraged by his Polish-born national security adviser, Zbigniew Brzezinski, the new president made Poland his first overseas state visit at the end of 1977. The White House ordered an early review of U.S. policy toward Europe, which led to a decision to sharpen the traditional policy of differentiating among the nations of Eastern Europe by promoting closer ties to regimes, like Poland's, which either pursued more liberal internal policies or enjoyed relative independence from the Soviet Union.[20] After the 1979 invasion of Afghanistan, Poland's significance in the U.S.–Soviet confrontation grew. As recently as July 11, 1980, Brzezinski had offered assurances to Polish leaders that they could count on American help.[21] As much as U.S. officials rooted for Solidarity, the spreading unrest inspired anxiety as well as anticipation. The union's creation presaged either a dramatic expansion of domestic democratic activity or, at the other end of the spectrum, a major crackdown, possibly involving a So-

---

[17] See, for example, Document No. 9.

[18] Document No. 2.

[19] Document No. 5.

[20] See Presidential review memorandum, "Comprehensive Review of European Issues," PRM/NSC-9, February 1, 1977. President Carter formally adopted this policy by signing Presidential Directive 21 on September 13, 1977; see Brzezinski, *Power and Principle*, 296–297.

[21] Warsaw was informed of Brzezinski's position by Mieczyslaw Rakowski, a CC member and chief editor of the influential weekly *Polityka*, who was in Washington at the time. Włodek, *Tajne Dokumenty*, 601; Rakowski, *Dzienniki polityczne 1979–1981*, 205.

viet-led intervention. The experiences of Hungary in 1956 and Czechoslovakia in 1968 were still vivid in everyone's minds.

Therefore, at the first signs of unrest, U.S. intelligence began systematically covering events in the country and reactions from Moscow.[22] By late July, the CIA had already reported on the possibility of expanding strikes, potentially leading to a broader confrontation and, if Polish armed forces proved as unreliable as analysts expected, an outside intervention.[23]

On August 27, President Jimmy Carter turned to the leaders of Great Britain, West Germany and France, declaring that Poles should resolve their own problems without outside intervention, a pointed reference to the Soviet Union.[24] The same day, French President Valery Giscard d'Estaing sent a personal message to Gierek expressing hope that Poland would be "capable of finding solutions to its problems in accordance with the wishes of the nation."[25] It is hard to know whether, or to what extent, the appeal had any impact on the Polish leadership.

A NEW FORCE

Finally, on August 27, the PUWP leadership recognized the need to compromise on the strikers' demands for free trade unions, and turned to Moscow with a request for "consultation with the allies."[26] The issue was becoming increasingly urgent because the strikes were spreading even further—more than 700,000 workers had walked off the job—and mines and steel mills had stopped functioning. The Kremlin kept silent, and the Polish leadership decided that no further delay was possible. On August 30, a plenary session of the Central Committee accepted, with two abstentions, the historic agreements that were signed that same day in Szczecin, and on August 31 in Gdańsk. Despite the compromise that ended the conflict, the party leadership resorted to a well-honed socio-political ploy: on September 5, Gierek resigned and with Soviet approval was replaced by Stanisław Kania who, as Central Committee secretary responsible for the security apparatus, had played a key role in all decision-making up to that point.[27]

On September 17, not quite three weeks after the historic agreements,[28] representatives of more than 30 inter-factory strike committees from all over Po-

---

[22] For a detailed insider account of the intelligence process, see: MacEachin, *U.S. Intelligence and the Polish Crisis*, and Brzezinski, "A White House Diary," 32–48. Also, see Document Nos. 10, 20, 23 and 24.

[23] Mac Eachin, *U. S. Intelligence and the Polish Crisis,* 3, 11.

[24] Document No. 8.

[25] Włodek, *Tajne Dokumenty,* 83.

[26] Document No. 4.

[27] Gierek himself believed he was dismissed because of a conspiracy by his closest co-workers, and that Kania had played an important, even a key role. See Rolicki, *Edward Gierek*, 190–224.

[28] The authorities signed additional agreements with the miners' strike committee in Jastrzębie on September 3 and with workers at the Katowice Steel Works on September 11.

land met in Gdańsk and decided to create the Independent Self-Governing Trade Union (ISTU) "*Solidarność.*" The meeting established the union's National Co-ordinating Commission and elected Lech Wałęsa as chairman. The process begun in July was thus completed. A legal organizational structure on a national scale, totally outside the control of the communist party and the state administration, had come into being. This was a truly radical breakthrough in the public life of a communist country where the ruling party—regardless of whether they were in a totalitarian phase or, as most researchers suggest, in an authoritarian phase post-1956—had always exercised complete control over all social organizations, determining their statutes, budgets, elections, and activities. Most importantly, Solidarity reached out to Poles across all segments of society, especially the so-called "large industrial working class," which the communists regarded as their main base of legitimacy and support (even though workers made up less than half of the party's membership).[29]

The problem for the party was not just the emergence of an organization of this kind, but one of its size, scope and dynamics. Solidarity's growing dimensions were crucial to determining the authorities' strategy. From the PUWP's viewpoint the situation was extremely complex. The union came into being at a time when the impetus to strike was high throughout the country, fed by a sense of euphoria over a string of unprecedented victories.[30] As a result, by October Solidarity had about 3 million members, and by December almost three times that number. 89 percent of respondents in public opinion polls backed the organization, with 58 percent expressing "decisive" support.[31] Once Solidarity's numbers reached a certain level, it became impossible to count on easily suppressing such a large organization.[32] Furthermore, this great mass of the population was organized regionally rather than by hierarchical branches. This would ensure their continuing power in case disputes arose between individual worker groups. A major asset for Solidarity was Wałęsa himself—a 37-year-old electrician and true "man of the people" who became a global celebrity in the role of David regularly outwitting the vastly more powerful Goliath.

Almost all the democratic opposition groups joined Solidarity. Their activists, either in the role of advisers or formal union functionaries, played an im-

---

[29] Sułek, "The Polish United Workers' Party," 504.

[30] In many locations strikes continued or new ones broke out whenever the workers worried that the signed agreements would ignore them. The September wave of strikes was just as large as the one at the end of August but much less spectacular since it encompassed mainly smaller towns and centers and was not accompanied by the same high emotion. The first "branch" strikes took place in October (by railway workers and the health service, among others). Although as a rule these did not involve mass absenteeism but rather hunger strikes or the occupation of buildings by relatively small groups acting in the name of a wider community, they contributed to maintaining tension.

[31] Adamski, *Polacy '81*, 92.

[32] For an example of the PUWP leadership attempting to come to grips with this realization, see Document No. 13.

portant and sometimes indispensable part in organizing Solidarity's structures and in holding successive talks with state and party authorities. By the end of September, the organizational core of other autonomous unions had already been formed: Rural Solidarity and the Independent Students' Union. Over the course of several months, a number of other professional associations, such as the highly influential journalists' and writers' unions, elected new leaders and freed themselves from PUWP control. Dozens of social organizations followed suit. Satellite political parties[33] and the pro-government Catholic association also exhibited greater independence. This new "plague" even infiltrated the party itself, whose members, in a move unthinkable just weeks before, joined Solidarity on a mass scale.[34] The supporters of radical change within the party and of governmental and political reforms, recruited mainly from the intelligentsia, also started to organize themselves outside the statutory party structures[35]; resignations from the party occurred in unprecedented numbers.[36]

The conviction by opponents of the communist system that society as a whole found itself in opposition was certainly exaggerated, but considering the size of Solidarity the view was understandable. After all, the vast Catholic Church with its developed hierarchy, institutions, social experience and charismatic leader was also opposed to communism. The alliance with the Church reinforced Solidarity's role in a significant way and made the authorities' struggle with the union more difficult.

Originally, the PUWP leadership cherished the hope that it would be able to harness Solidarity's expansion and influence at least some of its activists. To that end, it initiated various campaigns, a media blackout on information, for example (especially television), and blocked access to offices and telephone lines. As an added deterrent, the courts famously delayed Solidarity's registration.[37] None of these steps accomplished the desired outcomes; in fact, they may have given the population extra stimulus to challenge the authorities. A case in point was

---

[33] In Poland, as in some other communist states, other parties (the Democratic Party and United Populist Party) existed alongside the communist party, and officially formed a coalition with the PUWP. In reality, however, they were completely dependent on the communist party and only during periods of destabilization (as in 1956) did they attempt to expand their autonomy. This was similar to the case of the three Catholic politically-oriented organizations which were allowed to exist.

[34] According to general estimates, about a million Party members, i.e. one-third of the total, joined Solidarity.

[35] For example, the first meeting of the so-called "horizontal structures" movement was held on October 27 in Toruń; for details on horizontal structures, see: Hahn, *Democracy in a Communist Party*.

[36] By July 1981, about 300,000 members left the party, or approximately 10 percent of the total membership. For references to various reactions to these developments inside Poland and among the Warsaw Pact allies, see Document Nos. 11 and 13–16, among others.

[37] Document No. 12.

an impressive one-hour strike on October 3, called to protest the court's refusal to register the union. The success of that move showed not only that the union enjoyed extremely broad support, but that it was able to organize at a very high level. When the authorities finally allowed Solidarity to register on November 10, it was obvious that with its unique form, size and leadership—all substantially influenced by opposition activists—the union constituted an entirely alien entity within the communist system. It was therefore impossible to expect that normal pressure and persuasion tactics would be enough to subjugate a multi-million member organization that had grown spontaneously out of a core of profound and far-reaching social opposition.[38] Extraordinary measures were now needed. The choices were either to work towards fully democratizing the political system and overhauling the economy, or to liquidate—or at the very least assert full control over—Solidarity.

PHASE ONE: IN THE PRESENCE OF ALLIES
(DECEMBER 1980–MARCH 1981)

For space reasons, we will forego an analysis of why the PUWP leadership did not try to make permanent and profound changes to the system. There is no doubt that the party's top layers were psychologically, intellectually and politically unprepared for that approach. Also, the atmosphere was unfavorable, both in the Kremlin and on the international scene, especially after the Soviet intervention in Afghanistan in December 1979.[39] For practical purposes, Solidarity could only be subdued after its structures had been dismantled and its leaders removed. The only effective "extraordinary solution" that might work would be a proclamation of martial law.[40] That option was discussed in the Politburo at the end of August,[41] but it was rejected after members concluded it would be impossible to implement in the environment created by the ongoing wave of strikes. After August 31 and the creation of Solidarity, the situation did not change. The union enjoyed nearly universal support, and a large portion of society was in a state of mobilization. On November 8, the Politburo discussed what to do in case of a general strike, which Solidarity had threatened to declare if the union was

---

[38] See, for example, Document No. 13.

[39] As with every intensification of the East–West confrontation, the invasion strengthened conservative tendencies within the communist parties, but most importantly within the Soviet Union itself. Any attempt at internal reforms was subject to immediate attacks from orthodox ideologues.

[40] At the time Polish law did not foresee "an exceptional state," but only "martial law," which could be introduced for the defense or security of the state, according to Article 33 of the Constitution. The concept of "state security" could have been interpreted more broadly, recognizing that it was undermined not only by external threats but also by domestic events. Nevertheless, there was no statute to regulate the functioning of martial law.

[41] See, for example, Document No. 4.

not legally registered. A proposal to proclaim martial law was tabled. General Wojciech Jaruzelski, then minister of national defense, again noted that it would be impractical to execute martial law "in relation to millions of strikers."[42] Although some of the party leadership advocated taking radical steps, Kania spoke for the majority: "we support a struggle waged with the aid of political measures," but "we must take into consideration other variants as well."[43]

Moscow and the leaders of other East European communist states saw the situation differently. East German party chief Erich Honecker in particular pressed for tough action.[44] On November 26, at a time of renewed tensions in Poland, he wrote a formal letter to Brezhnev expressing distrust of the "Polish comrades" and proposing "joint measures," by which he undoubtedly meant Warsaw Pact military backing for the Polish security apparatus.[45] Honecker and the other allies also had another motivation: economics. The Soviets, in seeking ways to support the Poles, wanted to include economic aid, which was going to entail squeezing the allies, too.[46] The Kremlin approved Honecker's suggestion.

Polish authorities indeed considered other "variants." By no later than October 10, the General Staff set to work devising alternative approaches to resolving the crisis. By October 22, they had prepared a text entitled, "Proposal Regarding the Introduction of Martial Law for Reasons of State Security and the Underlying Consequences of Introducing Martial Law," which was discussed at a November 12 session of the Committee of National Defense, then the highest political-military entity in the government.[47] The Ministry of Internal Affairs also initiated preparations. But all of these were merely introductory steps. Decrees and resolutions had to be drafted to develop a suitable logistical foundation, to stockpile equipment, and to provide training. At high-level political meetings in late 1980, Polish leaders expressed the view that confrontation was both unavoidable and necessary, but, as Kania put it, neither the timing nor the immediate cause could be accidental.[48]

The CIA continued to produce regular assessments of the situation and Moscow's likely reactions. In mid-September, intelligence analysts began to report on Soviet military and civilian activities in the western USSR suggesting early preparations for mobilization.[49] Director of Central Intelligence Stansfield Turn-

---

[42] Włodek, *Tajne Dokumenty*, 169.

[43] *Ibid.*, 153.

[44] This activity was so far-reaching that in Autumn 1980 the Stasi set in motion an Operational Group in Warsaw, with branches in several Polish towns. Its main task was not in fact counter-intelligence "protection" of the Embassy and consulates, but the accumulation of information about the situation in Poland with the aid of a network of secret collaborators.

[45] Document No. 18.

[46] Document No. 17.

[47] Paczkowski and Werblan, *On the Decision to Introduce Martial Law*, 11.

[48] Włodek, *Tajne Dokumenty*, 185.

[49] See, for example, CIA, National Intelligence Daily, "Military Activity," September 13, 1980, and the discussion in MacEachin, *op. cit.*, 12–13.

14

er predicted to the high-level Special Coordination Committee (SCC) that the Soviet invasion force would require at least 30 divisions.[50] Other Agency analysts expected the Soviets to ratchet up the pressure on Warsaw by holding putative exercises in and around Poland. The trick was how to differentiate between warning moves and the real thing.

Because Polish and Russian military archival records are still mostly inaccessible to scholars, it is impossible to say for sure whether the "Soyuz-80" military maneuvers, which the Warsaw Pact announced on December 8 would take place on Polish territory, were simply exercises or preparations for an invasion. More recent testimony by high-level participants has added little to our understanding.[51] What is certain is that on December 2 a Polish officer brought to his superiors in Warsaw copies of a map from Moscow showing the location of armies during the maneuvers.[52] We also know that Czechoslovak Army representatives conducted an inspection of the terrain in Silesia where their troops were to be stationed.[53] Arrests presumably would have been made and some Solidarity links would have been de-legalized as Soviet, Czechoslovak, East German, and Polish troops concentrated on large cities and industrial complexes.

A critical moment in the crisis came at a meeting of Warsaw Pact leaders in Moscow on December 5.[54] The Kremlin had neared the breaking point of its patience with Warsaw. Some of the other members of the Pact were even more impatient. GDR leader Erich Honecker had demanded the meeting out of concern that the Polish events might have some spillover effect in East Germany, undermining SED rule. The Czechoslovak, Hungarian and Bulgarian representatives joined in expressing their fears; only Romania warned against an intervention— even using the actual term, unlike the others.

But in the end, the decision was made to hold off, at least for the moment. Several factors probably came into play. Poland played a vital role in the Warsaw Pact and it was considered important to maintain the unity and integrity of the socialist camp. In 1956 and 1968, Moscow had chosen invasion for those very reasons. But Poland's population had always been particularly anti-Soviet and difficult to control. Apprehension over the prospect of violent resistance and bloodshed was considerable. Also, times and circumstances had changed. The

---

[50] Document No. 10.

[51] One of the most important discussions between "veteran" former officials took place during a conference at Jachranka, Poland, November 8–10, 1997. Among others, Jaruzelski, Kania, Marshal Victor Kulikov, commander of the Warsaw Pact armies, Zbigniew Brzeziński and his former military aide, Gen. William E. Odom, attended. Several leading members of Solidarity also took part. For a transcript of the conference, see: *Wejdą nie Wejdą.*

[52] The map's existence has been mentioned by Jaruzelski and Kania as well as by Gen. Tadeusz Hupałowski and Col. Ryszard Kukliński, but despite numerous searches a copy has never surfaced in the Polish archives.

[53] Tůma, "The Czechoslovak Communist Regime," 8–10.

[54] Document No. 22.

Soviet Union was in an advancing state of decline; its leadership was aged and less able to contemplate taking radical measures. Besides, the Soviets were already deeply involved in Afghanistan and making another large-scale political and military commitment was hard to envision. The Kremlin was left to place all hopes on an internal Polish solution. In these circumstances, Kania may have helped his own cause, convincing his colleagues that Poland would take care of its own house.[55] Indeed, Kania did shore up plans for facing the crisis, as he indicated for example in his speech to the Ministry of Internal Affairs in early January 1981.[56] "Even if angels entered Poland," he said, "they would be treated as bloodthirsty vampires and the socialist ideas would be swimming in blood."[57]

In Washington, U.S. officials watched events unfold with rising alarm. American spy satellites showed unusual activity all around Poland: tank columns and artillery in northern Czechoslovakia, soldiers stockpiling ammunition and unfolding hospital tents near the border with the USSR, and dwindling civilian traffic along the border with East Germany.[58] On December 3, the CIA issued an "Alert Memorandum" describing "highly unusual or unprecedented" Soviet military preparations and warning that an invasion was possible although not yet definite.[59] Even more compelling evidence came from a highly placed spy Washington had inside the Polish General Staff, Col. Ryszard Kukliński.[60] Kukliński's responsibilities, which included drawing up options for a crackdown on Solidarity and acting as liaison to senior Soviet military officers, gave him unparalleled access to martial law plans and high-level military thinking through the Warsaw Pact's joint structures. At this critical time in late 1980, Kukliński apprised U.S. officials, based on information that was available to him, of the disturbing possibility of a Soviet military move on Poland.

The U.S. government took immediate action. On December 2, President Carter sent messages to the Western allies as well as to the leaders of China and India.[61] The following day, he contacted Brezhnev on the hotline, then four days later sent another letter to Western European leaders reiterating the basic need for a firm and coordinated response. Brzezinski telephoned the Pope to discuss the situation.[62]

---

[55] This appears to have been the Kremlin's view. See Document No. 25.

[56] Document No. 26.

[57] See Jane E. Perlez, "Poland '80–'81."

[58] See Brzezinski, *Power and Principle*, 465–468; Dobbs, *Down with Big Brother*, 56–59.

[59] Document No. 20.

[60] For details on Kukliński, see Weiser, *A Secret Life*. In preparing this highly detailed account, Weiser had extraordinary access to Kukliński, whom he interviewed extensively, as well as to many of his secret communications with the CIA while operating for several years under cover in Poland.

[61] Cable from Warren Christopher to U.S. Embassies in London, Paris, and Bonn, "Polish Situation," containing text of Carter letter, December 2, 1980.

[62] Document No. 23; Brzezinski, *Power and Principle*, 466–467; Gates, *From the Shadows*, 168.

But while U.S. officials genuinely worried about the fate of the Polish people and wanted to fend off widespread bloodshed, a broader strategic consideration lay at the heart of their concerns. Some officials, believing Poland might not be the ultimate objective, feared a Warsaw Pact move into Western Europe.[63] As far-fetched as that might seem today, many in the West believed the Soviets to harbor aggressive ambitions on that scale. U.S. concerns jumped sharply after the Soviets invaded Afghanistan, a move which bolstered the conviction of some that Moscow's real target was the warm-water ports of the Persian Gulf. If the Red Army had moved in that direction, and even more certainly if they had launched a military attack on Western Europe, the result may have been direct conflict between the superpowers, with a possibility of the clash going nuclear.[64]

When the Polish crisis broke out, Brzezinski ordered that a paper be prepared describing the Lyndon Johnson administration's response to Czechoslovakia in order to avoid repeating similar mistakes.[65] This was a reasonable step to take. But despite the analogies sometimes made between the internal situations in Poland in 1980–1981 and in Czechoslovakia in 1968, there were many more differences than similarities, which bear mentioning here. In the first place, the Prague Spring was an attempt at reform "from above," carried out by senior party activists headed by the general secretary, who had strayed from the Moscow-approved model. Other members of the Warsaw Pact saw this as a clear threat to the integrity of the Soviet bloc. In Poland, changes took place through direct social pressure "from below," and were opposed by the party leadership, albeit not very effectively. In December 1980, nothing indicated that the Polish party would succumb to "Dubčekization." It seemed more probable that the Soyuz-80 maneuvers mirrored the "Šumava" exercises in Czechoslovakia in the second half of June 1968. The purpose of the latter maneuvers was to pressure the Prague leadership to act firmly against "counter-revolutionary elements" in the country.[66] They were also conducted without Czechoslovak armed forces' participation, whereas in Poland the Kremlin would not have considered an armed intervention without the cooperation of the Polish military.

The retraction of, or more accurately the decision not to launch, Soyuz-80 in December did not mean that Moscow had abandoned the idea of a military assault against Solidarity. The Polish leadership saw the issues differently. Both the

---

[63] Document No. 23.

[64] James G. Hershberg pointed out the United States' real fears focusing on a Western European invasion at "Global Competition and the Deterioration of U.S.–Soviet Relations, 1977–1980," Conference #3 of the Carter–Brezhnev Project, Fort Lauderdale, Florida, March 23–26, 1995.

[65] Brzezinski, *Power and Principle*, 430.

[66] Another purpose was to conduct reconnaissance of the terrain prior to eventual intervention ("fraternal assistance"), since no Soviet troops had been in Czechoslovakia since December 1945. The Soviet command was well acquainted with Polish territory; about 10,000 Soviet soldiers had been stationed there since 1945.

General Staff and the Ministry of Internal Affairs kept up preparations for martial law, which included attempts at the top political levels to anticipate Solidarity's intentions and plans.[67] But the Ministry of Internal Affairs advised against a "mass attack" for the time being since it might yield "unpredictable consequences [...] and basic difficulties in controlling the situation by our forces."[68] The ministry proposed focusing on localized confrontations, and carrying out "a repressive campaign against the most aggressive anti-socialist elements." The almost unending social tensions, over issues such as whether Saturdays would be work days, were the reason Solidarity remained mobilized. Every confrontation, even a localized one, therefore had the potential to escalate into a broader conflict, which was exactly what almost everyone at the time hoped to avoid.[69]

The chief spokesperson for this cautious approach was Kania, as expressed at the allied summit on December 5 and in other remarks afterwards.[70] Moscow or, at any rate, the Soviet marshals were more impatient. At a Politburo session where Leonid Zamyatin, the head of the CPSU CC's International Information Department, reported on his January 16, 1981, visit to Poland, Marshal Ustinov declared: "We have to apply constant pressure on the Polish leadership." He announced that maneuvers were being planned for March, but said that they "should be enhanced" in order "to let them know that our forces are ready."[71] Preparations in Poland were in fact accelerated, either at local initiative or after information came from Moscow about the exercises. Also, in a very important shift at the top, Jaruzelski, who already held the post of minister of national defense, was nominated to become prime minister as well on February 12. Consolidating leadership positions this way was unusual even in communist countries, but it followed the thrust of Soviet suggestions from at least September 1980 to "intensify attention to the army," and "enlist [] army command cadres to work in the party and economic sphere."[72]

On February 16, 38 members of the General Staff, the Ministry of Internal Affairs, and the Secretariat of the National Defense Committee, along with a PUWP CC propaganda specialist, conducted an "inter-ministerial decision game devoted to the activity of the authorities and the state administration during the

---

[67] See Document Nos. 26 and 30.

[68] *Ocena sytuacji wewnętrznej w kraju i propozycje działań resortu spraw wewnętrznych* (An Assessment of the Internal Situation in the Country and Proposals for the Activity of the Ministry of Internal Affairs), December 22, 1980. See Raina and Zbrożek, *Operacja Lato-80*, 106–112; quoted on 111.

[69] At least partly for this reason, the regime and senior Solidarity advisers occasionally met privately for informal communications in a less politically charged atmosphere. See, for example, Document No. 33.

[70] Document Nos. 22 and 26.

[71] Document No. 29. See also Document No. 28.

[72] Document No. 9.

preparation and introduction of martial law."[73] The basic conclusion was that the game "demonstrated the advanced, although not quite total, degree of state preparedness in case of the necessity to introduce martial law." The authors of the summary claimed that the least promising time for declaring martial law would be a period of "intensified tensions, especially occupation strikes." They also calculated that the departments would require 72 hours after a political decision was made to initiate martial law.

Not quite a month later, on March 15, a joint session of the senior leadership of the Ministry of Internal Affairs and the General Staff, held at Jaruzelski's request, once again deliberated on the state of preparations.[74] Both the ministry and the army were "with respect to legal forms, the use of force and resources, and the introduction of internment operations" considered "competent in principle" for the introduction of martial law. The participants noted that plans for a propaganda campaign, which was regarded as vital for success, had not yet been completed. They also discussed follow-on scenarios and related activities. The most likely outcome was the "Third Variant," which predicted a general occupation strike and street demonstrations, including "attacks on party and administration buildings." In those cases, the group determined that "assistance from the Warsaw Pact is not ruled out." The Soviets agreed with these conclusions on March 16, the day before the start of the maneuvers Ustinov had announced in January.

On March 19, a major incident took place in the city of Bydgoszcz when a special police platoon broke into a meeting of the local prefecture, where Solidarity representatives were arguing for the registration of Rural Solidarity, and assaulted the group. Three Solidarity activists were among the injured. The unprovoked attack sparked the biggest internal crisis since the previous August. Solidarity declared a four-hour strike alert, the transfer of central and regional union authorities to factories, and plans for a general strike "until victory" was reached, if the perpetrators went unpunished. Because the assault closely tracked the concept of the MIA's localized confrontations, the authorities may have planned it to spark the "repressive campaign" noted above, by targeting "the most aggressive anti-socialist elements" while Warsaw Pact armies were on maneuvers inside Polish territory.[75] Gaps in the documentary record make it impossible to be sure, but in either case the Bydgoszcz crisis became one of the most important domestic flashpoints of the 1980–1981 period.[76]

---

[73] Undated document (issued prior to 19 February), "Meldunek w sprawie międzyresortowej gry decyzyjnej" (Report Concerning the Inter-Ministerial Decision Game). For a detailed presentation of this document, see Paczkowski, *Droga do mniejszego zła*, 137–139.

[74] Document No. 36.

[75] For details see: Paczkowski, "Wydarzenia bydgoskie," 33–42. There are many premises for believing that the "forceful ejection from the hall," which led to the assault, was commissioned or carried out with the consent of high-ranking authorities, although it is by no means obvious that their purpose was provocation.

[76] See, for example, Document No. 37.

The union's immediate reaction to Bydgoszcz and society's show of support—including hundreds of local PUWP organizations—forced Kania and Jaruzelski to scrutinize the prospects for martial law more critically than the army and security forces had. Despite speedy planning by the General Staff, mobilization by the minister of internal affairs, and the visit of high-ranking KGB representatives in Poland, the party leadership decided that martial law should be delayed. Cardinal Wyszyński, who was seriously ill, asked both sides for moderation,[77] and published a letter from the pope in which he "prayed for conciliation."[78] The dominant point of view within Solidarity, supported by Wałęsa, was also a moderate one, partly influenced by regular hints from the authorities that a Warsaw Pact military intervention was inevitable in the event of a general strike. Ultimately, the government and the union signed an agreement on March 30 calling off the strike in return for temporary legal status for Rural Solidarity, among other provisions.

For Moscow and its allies, the March events created growing consternation. The Soviet media railed against Solidarity's counter-revolutionary acts and the union's supposed Western inspiration while student unrest, scattered labor protests and general disorder seemed to be steadily on the rise. The Poles' failure to clamp down after Rural Solidarity's first conference on March 9, and again after the four-hour warning strike on March 27, followed by their "capitulation" on March 30 were all signs to the Kremlin of disturbing passivity.[79] With few options available, they decided to raise the pressure even further on Kania and Jaruzelski.

For the United States, the March events seemed to foreshadow a crisis of the same magnitude as the December emergency. CIA assessments since the end of 1980 kept the White House on the alert for "extended, but controlled, conflict" noting that despite the risks the Soviets "are in fact willing to intervene militarily."[80] This view comported with those of the new president. Ronald Reagan entered the White House in January 1981 convinced of Moscow's aggressive intentions and determined to pressure the Kremlin over Poland.[81] Still, the new

[77] During a meeting with Solidarity representatives on March 28, the primate said that "the situation is menacing [...] if we were to strain the point by proposing our postulates we could regret the consequences." *Krajowa Komisja Porozumiewawcza*, 30.

[78] Włodek, *Tajne Dokumenty*, 629.

[79] In addition to the discussion in Document No. 39, there is a helpful summary of Soviet press accounts during this period in Michta, *Red Eagle*, 161–163. See also Document No. 35 for the views of key ally Erich Honecker of East Germany.

[80] Document No. 31.

[81] CIA official Robert Gates wrote that the Polish crisis "dominated [Reagan's] foreign policy agenda from Inauguration Day nearly until Christmas" (Gates, *From the Shadows*, 227–239). The new secretary of state, Alexander Haig, sent Foreign Minister Gromyko the first of several warning letters just four days after Reagan took office, and four days after that held his first press conference to highlight the situation in Poland. (Cynkin, *Soviet and American Signaling*, 84–85; *The New York Times* January 30 and February 2, 1981.)

administration wanted to avoid a wider confrontation, and chose not to increase covert operations inside the country right away.[82] This was partly a matter of timing. By March, while Reagan was sanctioning similar counter-Soviet policies around the world, the White House was receiving new information from CIA informant Ryszard Kukliński and various "technical" sources (satellites and electronic intelligence) that martial law might be imminent and could be accompanied by a Soviet intervention.

The "Warsaw Agreement" on March 30 therefore was a surprise to the Americans, who immediately began drawing up plans for economic support to Poland. This was a pattern both the Carter and Reagan administrations followed throughout the crisis: rewarding restraint by Poland's leaders through food aid and debt rescheduling, while fine-tuning contingency plans in case of a crackdown and warning Moscow not to intervene, as Reagan did again in early April.[83] U.S. officials were still convinced the crisis was not over, only that the Soviets and their Polish allies had not yet decided on the final timing of an intervention.[84]

Almost immediately after the Warsaw Agreement, the Soviet Politburo decided to try again to get Kania and Jaruzelski to commit to strong measures. They summoned them to a secret meeting with Andropov and Ustinov, the heads of the two "power ministries," on the night of April 3 along the Polish–Soviet border (the eastern side). The Soviets were not encouraged by what they saw as a continuing display of excessive caution, but they recognized that they had to tolerate the current leadership in Warsaw. The Politburo's only conclusions after hearing the report of the meeting[85] had to do with applying pressure on Polish opinion by threatening interruptions in gas and oil supplies, and "working" on Poland's hard-liners (Stefan Olszowski, Tadeusz Grabski).

In effect, the Soviets were passing the initiative into Polish hands. A remark Marshal Kulikov made to senior East German military officers in early April backs this up. Kulikov declared that "the common goal should be to solve the problems without the deployment of allied armies into Poland.[86] Further on, he added: "If they cannot do so alone and then ask for help, this would be a different situation from one in which troops had been deployed from the outset." Obviously, at this point in the crisis the Brezhnev team agreed with Kania and Jaruzelski's position—that martial law should be a domestic operation.

---

[82] CIA Director William Casey, the administration's leading proponent of "rolling back" perceived Soviet gains, decided the risks in Poland at the time were too great and that the AFL-CIO was already doing a "first-rate" job on its own (Gates, *From the Shadows*, 236–237).

[83] Gates, *From the Shadows*, 230–231. See also Cynkyn, *Soviet and American Signaling*, 106–111. Cynkyn provides an exhaustive catalog of superpower actions and responses throughout the period.

[84] Document No. 40.

[85] Document No. 43.

[86] Document No. 41.

PHASE TWO: BY ONE'S OWN HAND (APRIL–DECEMBER 1981)

Despite periods of relative calm, Poland for all practical purposes remained in a state of permanent mobilization from summer 1980 onwards. The state authorities, local administration and boards of enterprises fielded a constant tide of social claims. Some of the disputes occurred on a national scale, such as Saturdays-off (in January), registration of the Independent Students' Union (in February) and Rural Solidarity (in May). Other issues were local, for example the purging of corrupt voivodeships or the handing over of state buildings for social uses. Numerous clashes broke out in factories. Often, the incidents spread. This was a function of the system of centralized power, where almost every significant issue required resolution or approval at the highest levels, and also of the fact that the name "Solidarity" was applied literally—to encompass the concept of unity within other enterprises, regions, or the union as a whole. Appeals for "social peace" by the authorities—even Jaruzelski, who initially enjoyed a level of popular trust—went unheeded. The Solidarity leadership went through similar problems. Lech Wałęsa and the Church found it more and more difficult to dampen public expectations for action and to make progress toward compromise.

As a rule, agreements were made on the spot, and when they dealt with general problems (such as the registration of the farmers' union) they did not completely eradicate the sources of tension. The ruling group showed no inclination to pursue systemic solutions, and made concessions only under enormous social pressure, treating them essentially as gestures or using them to try to deceive the opposition.[87] Both sides distrusted each other deeply.

A critical factor that shaped the social mood was the deepening economic breakdown and deteriorating material circumstances, as seen in the ever more limited supplies of food and basic articles. The ultimate consequence of this was the introduction of a food rationing system. Coupons for meat and sausages appeared on April 1, 1981, and for butter and grain products as of April 20. In time, rationing covered other commodities including such "sensitive" items as alcohol and cigarettes. Serious purchasing problems surfaced even after initial reductions in allotments, which provided new grounds for protest. From early in the crisis, a sizable segment of society, including the leaders of Solidarity, believed that this state of affairs stemmed not so much from official ineptitude as from a deliberate tactic of "starving society" to make it more submissive and to prove Solidarity's subversive role. Party and government propaganda placed the fault for the breakdown of the market entirely on Solidarity and on strike-induced "anarchy."[88]

---

[87] Talk of "framing" people, and other popular jargon entered into regular Solidarity discourse.

[88] For one expression of Solidarity's stance, see Document No. 32. Some Soviet leaders were willing to allow expanded Western economic aid, even though it increased Poland's dependence on the West. See Document No. 38 for a discussion of some of these considerations in the Kremlin.

The natural reaction for the reformists under the circumstances was to "flee forward"—to articulate new theories, but mainly to have Solidarity's elite try to come up with a new systemic alternative.[89] The basic point of departure was a February 1981 document entitled "Trends of Union Activity in the Current Situation Facing the Country" (*Kierunki działania Związku w obecnej sytuacji kraju*). It consisted of several programmatic theses, and on March 17 led to the creation of the so-called Enterprise Organization Network, which promoted the establishment of workers' self-government. The idea of self-government became the basic organizing element in the union's strategic conception. Its goal was to "extract" the workplace from the *nomenklatura*[90] system and the control of the PUWP organizations, but also to create a "Socioeconomic Chamber" in the Sejm with broad economic powers,[91] and to grant autonomy to local and regional self-governments.

From the moment Solidarity appeared it was clearly something more than a trade union. The February program declared outright that it was "the main guarantee of the process of renewal. There is no other social force in Poland which could replace it in this undertaking."[92] This awareness of a historical mission received its fullest expression in a program entitled "The Self-Governing Republic," (*Samorządna Rzeczpospolita*), adopted during a Solidarity Congress in September 1981. In contemporary terms, this was an idea for a "third path" between collective socialism (communism) and liberal capitalism. In the course of a single year after its creation, Solidarity had gone from being an organization channeling spontaneous protests (strikes) to a quasi-political party proposing an alternative to the current system.

For the PUWP, Solidarity and the gamut of organizations acting largely under its guidance were not the only problem. The party also had to deal with a rebellion in its own ranks. The so-called "horizontal movement," which came about in Autumn 1980 advocating circumventing Leninist top-down authority structures, never produced a national association but it was active among the intelligentsia and particularly influential with certain media outlets. The movement gained momentum at the PUWP Central Committee's Ninth Plenum at the end of March when the CC chose the date for an Extraordinary Party Congress[93] and initiated multi-rung elections of delegates. At a conference in Toruń in mid-April the hori-

---

[89] Document No. 57.
[90] The *nomenklatura* patronage system first came into being in the Soviet Union and was introduced into Poland in 1950. It ceded to communist party committees from the Politburo to the regional level authority to decide who would fill the top posts in all areas of social life, management and the economy. At the turn of the 1970s and 1980s, about 700,000 positions—from prime minister to speaker of the Sejm to factory foreman—were filled in this way.
[91] Jakubowicz, *Bitwa o samorząd 1980–1981*, 80.
[92] Quoted in Holzer, *"Solidarność" 1980–1981*, 191.
[93] The previous congress was held in February 1980, although according to the statute they were supposed to take place every five years.

23

zontalists tabled a draft of their own proposals aimed at opening up the internal procedures of the party and breaking the grip of the top leadership. They proposed allowing lower-level party units to elect their own leaders and place delegates at party conferences through open nominations and secret ballots, a process they demanded be replicated at the national level. The Kremlin understood the destabilizing potential of these internal pressures, and regularly criticized the Polish leadership for allowing the movement to come into existence.[94]

In some ways, a more potent internal party threat was the attempt to create a second, hard-line, wing of the PUWP. This group, which became known as "reinforced concrete," took on particular significance because its energies were directed squarely at replacing the Kania-Jaruzelski team. Their efforts began in mid-May after the creation of the Katowice Party Forum, an alliance of deeply conservative party members from Upper Silesia, whom many Poles suspected had Moscow's discreet backing. Within several weeks, as many as a dozen similar "discussion clubs" had sprung up, and the hard-line weekly, *Rzeczywistość*, had made its appearance. In contrast to the horizontalists, who did not have direct contacts with any members of the PUWP leadership, the new hard-line formations constituted an unofficial base for some of the highest party authorities, which threatened the Kania-Jaruzelski team.[95]

Regardless of the actual impact of both wings, their very existence testified to the gradual dissolution of one of the party's fundamental principles—the idea of "democratic centralism" devised by Lenin. The PUWP as a whole was no longer under the direct control of its leaders. Without guaranteed support from their own rank and file, the leadership knew that any harsh measures against Solidarity would create an additional hazard and were virtually guaranteed to fail.[96] PUWP loyalists understood they had to reestablish order within their own organization, a step that would require convening a new party congress. Available documents and published reminiscences of party leaders are not entirely clear, but after the March 30 agreement the party elite apparently sensed that Solidarity was losing its impetus and that social moods were slowly evolving—i.e. that the union was gradually losing support. They concluded that a final assault should be delayed until the optimal moment—when the party, the army, and the Ministry of Internal Affairs[97]

---

[94] Document Nos. 47 and 50.

[95] Discussion of hard-line alternatives can be found in Document No. 49. For much of this period, however, the Kremlin saw no realistic alternative to Kania and Jaruzelski. See, for example, Document No. 45.

[96] This is one of the conclusions of a PUWP CC study of Solidarity in mid-August. See Document No. 59.

[97] One of the troubling developments for the PUWP was the emergence of various independent tendencies among the Citizens' Police (CP) after the Bydgoszcz incident. Many officers protested the assignment of blame entirely to the CP. They then raised the idea of organizing their own union representation. The founding convention of the CP union took place on June 1 and was attended by more than 500 delegates from all over Poland. But the Ministry reacted quickly and smothered the movement.

were fully prepared, and when the enemy was weakened even further from internal disputes and diminished public backing.

Meanwhile, Moscow's consent to having the Poles "stifle the counter-revolution" by themselves did not mean that the Kremlin had complete trust in Kania and Jaruzelski, nor that they simply accepted the continual postponement of martial law. The established tactic, as Brezhnev himself put it to the Politburo on April 16,[98] was not to "build up their nervousness so that they lose heart" but at the same time to exert "constant pressure." He expressed similar views a few days earlier at the Czechoslovak party congress.[99]

Hoping to raise the ante, on June 5 the CPSU Central Committee presented a letter to their Polish counterparts that was severely critical of their leadership.[100] The letter arrived prior to the planned PUWP Central Committee plenary session. Its direct impact is not entirely clear but the hard-liners—Grabski, Olszowski, Andrzej Żabiński and Stanisław Kociołek—proceeded to attack Kania, first at a Politburo session on June 6 and several days later during a break at a broader Central Committee session.[101] Despite its intensity, the attack broke down. A grass-roots reaction in the form of telegrams from a number of party organizations that were supportive of Kania and Jaruzelski, and the two leaders' combined rejoinders to their critics succeeded in facing down the challenge. If the letter had singled out Kania as the only guilty party, the whole situation might have evolved differently. But Jaruzelski had strong support from the generals on the Central Committee, which carried significant weight with the other members, and Kania benefited from that. Both men were also helped by fears of a split within the leadership. Ultimately, the campaign, sometimes described as "the red putsch," failed, although the two leaders continued to face exasperation from the Kremlin.[102]

Another pressure point on the Kania–Jaruzelski leadership came at the Party Congress of July 14–21.[103] As a sign of Soviet concern, Foreign Minister Andrei Gromyko traveled to Warsaw in early July to discuss the event and to remind the two leaders about the danger of the "counter-revolutionary threat."[104] The day before the Congress, the Soviets announced that joint naval maneuvers would take place in the Baltic Sea. The move prompted U.S. Secretary of State Alexander Haig to warn about the "unacceptability of Soviet direct or indirect intervention into the internal affairs of the Polish people," a remark duly noted by the

[98] Document No. 44.
[99] Document No. 42.
[100] Document No. 50.
[101] Document No. 51.
[102] Document No. 53.
[103] For a U.S. analysis of the Congress and its impact, see CIA Special Analysis, "Poland: Beyond the Congress," July 23, 1981.
[104] Włodek, *Tajne Dokumenty*, 423–424; Jaruzelski, *Hinter den Türen der Macht*, 197. See also Document No. 55.

Polish Politburo.[105] At the Congress, Kremlin apprehensions were substantially borne out. Ninety percent of the delegates, many belonging to both the party and Solidarity, were freshly elected and attending their first national assembly, thanks to new selection procedures acquiesced to by the leadership. The new crop immediately had an impact. After a secret ballot, seven of 11 former Politburo members failed to win reelection. Not all the hard-liners lost, however. Enough managed to hang on at all levels to ensure at least a deadlock on major issues of national strategy.[106] Nonetheless, Kania emerged from the Congress with new strength, effectively relegating his adversaries on both sides—horizontalists and hard-liners—to the margins. Reluctantly, Moscow recognized this reality and resolved to continue working with him, at least for the time being.[107]

Preparations for proclaiming martial law without participation of Warsaw Pact armies could therefore go forward without serious obstacles from the so-called "impatient" ones, although Moscow continued to send reminders. The Poles, however, were able to declare that progress was being made. A National Defense Committee meeting chaired by the prime minister and held on June 16 could claim that "the basic stage of the conception-planning work was completed."[108] Events such as the special meeting of Solidarity's National Coordinating Commission in late July, where the union voted to shift its focus from workplace management issues to genuine self-government, helped to increase Warsaw's impetus for action.[109] Drafts of decrees, Sejm resolutions, and even press communiqués were readied in coordination with the Ministry of Justice and the General Prosecutor's Office. At the end of August, the KGB secretly began printing notices in Moscow in anticipation of official announcements about martial law.

Ironically, during this period American intelligence analysts generally believed that the Soviets had rejected martial law. By May, there was a sense that Moscow wanted to give the Poles the chance to work things out for themselves, but that the increasing trend towards liberalization would back the Soviets into a corner and force an invasion. Moreover, analysts actually believed that the only chance martial law would be declared was if the Poles invoked it on their own—not in tandem with Moscow. Presuming that Polish leaders were fundamentally opposed to a Soviet intervention, they argued that Warsaw would act unilaterally to keep society under control and thereby deny Moscow a pretext to invade. As the State Department's Bureau of Intelligence and Research put it in mid-June:

---

[105] United Press International, July 19, 1981; Cynkin, *Soviet and American Signaling*, 140–141; Włodek, *Tajne Dokumenty*, 429.

[106] Three seats on the new Politburo were taken up by hard-liners—Stefan Olszowski, Albin Siwak, and Mirosław Milewski.

[107] Document Nos. 56 and 58.

[108] Paczkowski and Werblan, *On the Decision to Introduce Martial Law*, 7.

[109] Document No. 57. The meeting took place from July 24–26, immediately after the PUWP Extraordinary Congress. Negotiations with the government in the weeks after the session led to public recriminations and heightened tensions.

So much for Kuklinski

"As tensions mount, Jaruzelski might additionally invoke a state of emergency or some variant of martial law in order to gird the nation against a threatened Soviet invasion."[110] It is interesting to note that in the weeks leading up to the PUWP congress, U.S. intelligence did not identify Solidarity as the root cause of Soviet apprehensions. Instead, they predicted that reformist gains at the Congress, and particularly Kania's expected outmaneuvering of his opponents, would so undermine Soviet prospects for controlling the Polish party that the pressure to intervene with force might be too great.[111]

Before summer's end, Moscow had already lost patience again with Warsaw. Events repeatedly confirmed for the Kremlin their view that the PUWP was failing to assert the necessary authority.[112] The beginning of a Solidarity congress in Gdańsk on September 5, and more specifically a provocative "Appeal to the Working People of Eastern Europe" formulated at the congress, infuriated the Soviet leadership.[113] They responded by publishing a letter of their own to all the communist countries, which, although it did not quite amount to a no-confidence vote in the Polish leadership, could well have been read that way.[114] Brezhnev's abrasive tone with Kania in subsequent conversations underlined the point, although interestingly the Kremlin demurred when East Germany's Erich Honecker called for him to be replaced by hard-liner Olszowski.[115] The Soviets did resort to other tactics. In mid-September, they announced that Poland should anticipate cuts in raw material supplies, implying that the reductions would take place if martial law were not imposed.[116] Demonstrations of force also occurred. The Soviet Army and Navy's "Zapad-81" maneuvers in the Eastern Baltic and Belorussia were the largest since World War II, and generated more warnings and admonitions from Washington. It was no accident that the exercises began

---

[110] Document No. 52.
[111] See the discussion of U.S. intelligence views during this period, and the relevant citations to declassified CIA documents, in MacEachin, *U.S. Intelligence and the Polish Crisis*, 132–135.
[112] Document No. 60.
[113] Document No. 61. The impact on Soviet citizens of the events in Poland and of the emergence of Solidarity has not yet been systematically examined. According to initial studies, this influence was most discernible in the republics adjoining Poland. (See Document No. 48.) For analysis, see Kramer, *Soviet Deliberations During the Polish Crisis*, 24–34. See also Kramer, "The Soviet Union, the Warsaw Pact, and the Polish Crisis," 6–11.
[114] Document No. 63. Other Eastern European central committees also sent letters to the Polish comrades closely approximating the one written by Kádár on September 17 (Document No. 66).
[115] Document Nos. 64 and 67.
[116] Moscow's decision stemmed mainly from a growing crisis in crude oil and gas production; the curbs were to affect all communist countries not paying in "hard" currency. So far, research has not resolved whether this was outright blackmail or a more routine warning.

27

on the eve of the Solidarity congress, with the aircraft carrier *Kiev* anchored off the Polish coast where it could be seen from some delegates' hotels.

Both Moscow and East Berlin, although the East Germans probably even more intently, maintained contacts with Polish hard-liners, the so-called "healthy forces." Brezhnev and his Moscow colleagues, however, gave no sign that they would support anyone for the role of a "Polish Bilak."[117] Apparently, they reserved that option for the most extreme circumstances. On the other hand, Moscow believed it was very important to populate the PUWP apparatus, especially the middle-ranks, almost entirely with hard-liners who would pressure the leadership along the lines set down by Moscow.[118]

Meanwhile, work on martial law in Warsaw had been completed, and on September 13 a session of the National Defense Committee confirmed that all legal and technical issues, with the exception of minor details such as tracking down missing equipment, had been prepared.[119] Although the political leadership rejected the military's proposal for an immediate crackdown, none of the attendees doubted that martial law would have to be introduced.[120] The main problem was choosing the moment. The necessary conditions included not only a reason (or pretext) that the general public would find convincing, but a set of circumstances where at least a sizeable share of society would accept a radical campaign against Solidarity. In autumn, social moods began to shift more steadily in the authorities' favor. Public opinion studies showed that the union led by Wałęsa was supported by about 71 percent of respondents as compared to 89 percent a year earlier, while the proportion declaring "decisive support" dropped from 58 to 33 percent.[121] Although the number of those who believed that Solidarity alone was responsible for the crisis was still minimal, the share of those who divided the blame on both sides had grown to 40 percent.[122]

Government propaganda, which continued to benefit from the trend in public opinion, now threatened the onset of a "winter catastrophe" in the form of hundreds of thousands of unheated apartments, and even deaths from the cold and starvation. The campaign blamed Solidarity, portraying it as anarchistic and irresponsible. Orders from the central authorities directed the Security Service

---

[117] Prior to the 1968 invasion of Czechoslovakia, Czechoslovak communist party Presidium member Vasil Bilak delivered a secret "letter of invitation" to the Soviet leadership requesting intervention to rescue Czechoslovakia from counter-revolution. (After the invasion, normalization was carried out by Gustáv Husák, not by Bilak or any of the group that had asked Moscow for help.) See Document No. 67 for Honecker's views.

[118] Not all the allies saw Kania the same way. See Document No. 68 for a more nuanced and positive description from a Hungarian perspective.

[119] Document No. 62.

[120] Document No. 69 gives an indication of some of the kinds of preparatory work the Polish leadership had undertaken to that end.

[121] Adamski, *Polacy '81*, 92.

[122] *Ibid.*, 86.

"to place the enemy in a difficult or compromising situation," and especially to "demonstrate that he is irresponsible, quarrelsome, and is leading the country to ruin."[123] An analysis of the clashes and strikes of autumn 1981 shows that some of them were probably provoked, while the security services most likely tried to prolong others.[124]

Both sides grew more aware that conflict was inevitable, a sense heightened significantly during the PUWP's Fourth Plenum of October 16–18. At this pivotal session, the party leadership dismissed Kania as first secretary and replaced him with Jaruzelski. The transfer of power took place not only with Soviet consent but probably at their initiative. Jaruzelski now held all the key posts in the state—prime minister, chairman of the National Defense Committee, and minister of national defense—as well as the leading party position.[125] Brezhnev was clearly pleased, although not all of his fears disappeared.[126] Within 10 days of making a congratulatory phone call to Jaruzelski on his new appointment, Brezhnev and his colleagues were already finding new reasons to worry.[127]

For many Solidarity activists, Jaruzelski's appointment meant that the communist party had effectively ceased to exist as a fundamental factor in the system, and that it was no longer realistic to think about direct participation in the power apparatus. Around the country the concept spread of ousting the PUWP from its position of authority over the workplace and introducing the notion of an "active strike." This meant that all products manufactured during the strike would be at the disposal of the strike committee or workers' self-government. More and more urgent demands were heard for instituting local self-government and parliamentary elections, and for allowing Solidarity to participate. The idea took hold to establish a Social Council for National Economy, which would have management functions *vis á vis* the government, but also would incorporate the right to take the initiative on legislative matters. Even Vice-Premier Mieczysław Rakowski, regarded in Moscow (and by PUWP hard-liners) as a social democrat, and therefore politically suspect, recognized this idea as "an attack against the structures of the state, actually aimed at toppling the constitutional system" in order to create "in its place a totalitarian 'Solidarity' dictatorship."[128]

A counter-proposal mentioned a Front of National Accord, which PUWP leaders in autumn 1980 had hoped would be a formula for drawing Solidarity

---

[123] Document No. 70.

[124] Paczkowski and Werblan, *On the Decision to Introduce Martial Law*, 15.

[125] It could be added that the military appeared both in the central party apparatus and in its state counterpart. By way of example, in 1981, ministerial posts were granted to Gen. Czesław Kiszczak, the heretofore head of military intelligence (minister of internal affairs), Gen. Czesław Piotrowski (minister of mining), Gen. Tadeusz Hupałowski (minister of administration), and Gen. Michał Janiszewski (head of the Office of Council of Ministers).

[126] Document No. 71.

[127] See Document No. 72.

[128] Rakowski, *Czasy nadziei i rozczarowań*, 279.

into various communist-controlled institutions. Now the idea was given wider publicity, and on November 4 a meeting of the "big three" took place: Jaruzelski, Primate Józef Glemp and Wałęsa.[129] The available historical record on the preparations for martial law confirms the impression that both the resurrection of the idea of the Front and the propaganda barrage surrounding it were meant mainly to camouflage the work done by the General Staff and the Ministry of Internal Affairs over the previous year.[130] Even if the proposal on the Front was sincere, it was no longer in line with the aspirations of Solidarity, which rejected it.

The Front initiative did not for a moment slow down technical preparations for a crackdown.[131] These included prolonging military conscription by two months and dispatching several hundred military groups to permeate enterprises and offices all over the country. Nor did the Front get in the way of legal or propaganda arrangements, such as passing a resolution in the Sejm to cover a possible grant to the government of extraordinary powers.

In mid-November, nine high-ranking Soviet General Staff officers appeared in Poland to check on near-term readiness for a crackdown. One of their main objects of interest was the escape of Col. Kukliński on November 7. A few weeks earlier, Polish authorities learned that their plans for martial law had leaked. Only a small circle of officials knew the details of those plans, and Kukliński understood he would very quickly come under close scrutiny. In an elaborate covert operation, the CIA smuggled him and his family to West Germany, and from there to the United States. His reporting during September[132] and October, prior to his extraction, and undoubtedly his lengthy debriefings in the U.S., gave American officials a detailed picture of how the crackdown would unfold (see below). The Americans did not expect, however, that his escape would create obstacles to the introduction of martial law.[133]

The immediate events that led up to martial law began on November 24, when students at the Firefighters' Academy in Warsaw went on strike. Since the academy was supervised by the Ministry of Internal Affairs, the strike, which Solidarity supported, was seen as an attack on one of the ministries responsible

---

[129] For the Soviets' wary reaction, see Document No. 73.

[130] Kazimierz Barcikowski, whom the Kremlin regarded as the leader of the "reformists," told the Politburo on November 10 that they had "to demonstrate a readiness to invite 'Solidarity' to the Front of National Accord but not to facilitate it. The invitation should be linked with certain conditions that would influence the inner differentiation of 'Solidarity'." See Włodek, *Tajne Dokumenty*, 520.

[131] See, for example, the Ministry of Internal Affairs' plan of action, Document No. 74.

[132] See, for example, Document No. 65.

[133] A note in the Polish military archives indicates that the authorities limited themselves to "correcting the part of the contents of the documents with which he could have been familiar." See Central Army Archive, vol. 1813/92/2. For examples of transmissions sent by Kukliński see Document Nos. 21, 46, and 65. Kukliński's debriefings to the CIA after his escape to the West remain secret.

did 3 provoke 'crisis'?

for national security. On December 2, special ZOMO[134] internal security units burst into the school building and crushed the strike. Solidarity treated the event as a "dress rehearsal" for an attack on the trade union. At an extraordinary session in Radom on December 3–4, the expanded union leadership approved a resolution threatening a general strike if the Sejm passed a pending bill granting extraordinary security powers, or if the authorities launched an assault against the union.[135] The resolution also mentioned holding democratic elections for local self-government. Meeting in an atmosphere of high tensions, the participants made little attempt to control their emotions. A member of the union's National Commission who was also an agent for the security services secretly taped the session and, after suitable editing, some of the more intemperate statements were broadcast on radio and television and presented as proof that Solidarity was preparing for a bloody coup.[136]

The Politburo met the day after the Radom session. In a summary of the debate, Jaruzelski declared, "The crisis has reached its peak. The counter-revolutionary forces have bluntly revealed their intentions. We must make use of this fact."[137] The group expressed unanimous support for martial law, albeit not with equal enthusiasm. Still, the political decision was made, and according to the schedule, "zero hour" would come in three days.

The Church continued to try to mediate, but, by all the evidence, it was too late. Solidarity clearly underestimated the authorities' determination and potential to crack down. Although the union leaders had access to some information about army and Ministry of Internal Affairs preparations, it was not always precise. Beyond that, many leading activists believed that if the union simply pressed harder, the PUWP leadership would make concessions, at least partial ones. Participants at a National Commission session on December 11–12 insisted that "Solidarity had found itself at an impasse,"[138] but despite some conciliatory comments, including from Wałęsa, the majority chose to press several purely political demands, including free elections for Parliament and a referendum (either nationwide or within Solidarity) on Jaruzelski and his government.

This dramatic move is often seen as the final step that pushed the authorities to declare martial law, but in fact Jaruzelski had already made up his mind. On December 7, he spoke with Brezhnev, who still seemed uncertain what to expect. After all, three days earlier Jaruzelski had lobbied a meeting of Warsaw Pact de-

---

[134] ZOMO, the Mechanized Detachments of Citizens' Police [*Zmotoryzowane Odwody Milicji Obywatelskiej*], was one of the Polish regime's main internal security units. Considered more reliable than the army, ZOMO forces played a central role in martial law planning and execution.

[135] Document No. 78.

[136] For a very different insight into Solidarity's disposition at the time, particularly the divisions among its membership over how to proceed, see Document No. 77.

[137] Document No. 80.

[138] Holzer, *"Solidarność" 1980–1981*, 230.

31

fense ministers to deliver a public warning to the Polish people that an intervention might be imminent; Moscow might easily have read this as another tactic to avoid direct measures.[139] Nevertheless, there were signs of movement. Nikolai Baibakov, the head of Gosplan, the Soviet economic planning agency, traveled to Poland, as did Marshal Kulikov once again. Locally, the voivodeship party committee secretaries and their highest officer cadres held what turned out to be final consultations.[140]

Despite their uncertainty, the Soviets apparently never made a formal decision to involve Warsaw Pact armies in the implementation of martial law. As late as December 10, just three days before Day "X", the Politburo debated the matter.[141] Because Jaruzelski continued to refuse to pin himself down to a date, some Kremlin leaders began to see his behavior as deceitful. On two of the most contentious issues surrounding the entire crisis—whether Moscow was prepared to invade and whether Jaruzelski opposed or sought such an intervention—the discussion at this key meeting seems clear. The Polish leader had insisted that he needed to be sure of Soviet military backing in case plans went awry, and the Kremlin was even more adamant that such support would not be forthcoming. These points are reinforced by one of the more remarkable documents in this collection—the notes of Marshal Kulikov's adjutant, Lt. Gen. Viktor Anoshkin, which reflect a conversation with Jaruzelski on December 11.[142]

Despite Moscow's apparent unwillingness to intervene, select Soviet units, along with Czechoslovak and East German forces deployed along the Polish frontiers and troops stationed permanently in Poland, were placed on full alert. The final decision came early Saturday afternoon, December 12,[143] after a brief talk between Jaruzelski, Suslov, and Ustinov, while the Solidarity National Commission was in the midst of a debate. At 3:40 p.m., ciphered telegrams went from the Ministry of Internal Affairs' central offices to all voivodeship militia commands announcing implementation of operation "Synchronisation" *[Synchronizacja]*. The General Staff was instructed to initiate operations at 11:30 p.m.[144] The die was cast.

PHASE THREE: "DO NOT LOOSEN THE CLAMPS ON THE ENEMY"[145]

Planners, implementers, victims, observers and historians universally agree that the Polish authorities executed martial law "to perfection." On the one hand, this

---

[139] Document No. 79.

[140] Document No. 83.

[141] Document No. 81.

[142] See Document No. 82 and accompanying headnote for more details.

[143] The intention was to implement martial law on a day when the factories were not operating.

[144] Document No. 84.

[145] Quotation from Gen. Florian Siwicki at a Politburo session on December, 22, 1981. See Włodek, *Tajne Dokumenty*, 579.

was a consequence of deploying overpowering force under cover of complete surprise, and, on the other hand, it was a function of the circumstances surrounding Solidarity. A large-scale democratic organization with a highly self-assured leadership, the union had no real opportunity to prepare itself for this kind of assault.[146]

According to available data, the operation involved about 70,000 soldiers, more than 30,000 Ministry of Internal Affairs functionaries, more than 40,000 reservists, 1,750 tanks, about 1,900 armored vehicles, more than 9,000 cars, several squadrons of cargo aircraft and helicopters, and several score warships blocking access to ports.[147] The regulations decreed under martial law beginning on the morning of December 13 were draconian.[148] They included a night-time curfew; the cutting of domestic and international telephone communications; the closing of gas stations; curtailment of freedom of movement; a ban on all gatherings; closure of frontiers, including airports; limits on bank withdrawals; the introduction of summary jurisdiction, and expansion of the reach of military courts. Regardless of the date of proclamation, all of these legal decisions became binding from the day martial law was introduced. Furthermore, state radio and television restricted broadcasting to a single channel each, most newspaper and periodical publications were suspended (only three central and seventeen regional dailies continued to appear), and all university and school classes were suspended.

In a speech broadcast over the radio at 6:00 a.m, and on television at 10:00 a.m. on December 13, Jaruzelski announced the establishment of a Military Council of National Salvation (WRON), composed of at least ten generals. The harsh nature of the regulations and rulings, along with the official declaration that the army had taken over supreme power, rendered Poland a country under siege, giving grounds for the saying that a "Poland–Jaruzelski war" had broken out.

The timing of the meeting of Solidarity's National Commission on the night of December 12 made it easy for the authorities to arrest most of the union's leading national and regional activists, including Wałęsa, in a single operation. Those who "survived" embarked on new kinds of activity.[149] After reaching their home towns, regional activists (such as Zbigniew Bujak from Warsaw, Andrzej

---

[146] See Document No. 85 for a detailed rundown of the first day's events from the PUWP Politburo viewpoint.

[147] Over the course of several weeks, tanks and armored vehicles traveled a total of 1.5 million kilometers. All data can be found in Paczkowski, *The Spring Will Be Ours*, 448. See also Document No. 95.

[148] For a list of basic decrees and directives, see Tadeusz Walichnowski, ed., *Stan wojenny w Polsce. Dokumenty i materiały archiwalne, 1981–1983*, 24–75.

[149] See Document Nos. 85 and 88 for PUWP and CIA assessments of Solidarity's plans and activities immediately after martial law.

Słowik from Łódź, Mieczysław Gil from Kraków and Władysław Frasyniuk from Wrocław) became the heads of local strike committees, while members of the NCC Presidium took refuge in the Gdańsk Shipyard and created the National Strike Committee. On the afternoon of December 13, they proclaimed a general strike. Because of the disruption in communications, that proclamation did not reach the entire country, but strikes broke out spontaneously nonetheless. According to Ministry of Internal Affairs estimates, strikes occurred in about 200 workplaces, including almost all the largest and most important locations—coal mines, steel-works, ports, shipyards, and large metallurgical factories.

The army and the police, including anti-terrorist units, blockaded almost 150 striking factories.[150] In many cases, they attacked under cover of tanks when workers refused to end their strikes and leave the workplace. In several instances, they opened fire on the protestors. The largest number of casualties was at the "Wujek" coal mine in Silesia where nine men were killed. Sometimes, for example at the Katowice Steelworks, the police and army had to "clear the terrain" repeatedly. This particular phase of the "state of war"—the liquidation of strikes—lasted about a week, although in a number of coal mines strikers organized underground sit-ins that lasted several days.[151] Street demonstrations took place in certain towns, but the basic mode of resistance, as in the summer of 1980, was the occupation strike. Eventually, the leaders and many of the strikers (about 4,000 in all) were arrested, with the first trials taking place on Christmas Eve. Many more were fired from their jobs (about 2,000 from the "Piast" mine in Silesia alone).

The martial law campaign was divided into some 20 operations. Most were "technical," aimed at gaining total control over the country and intimidating the public. Others, such as those code-named "Fir" and "Maple," grew out of a strategy intent on splitting up and subjugating Solidarity. Operation Fir consisted of detaining more than 6,000 union activists and members of opposition groups in 24 internment centers.[152] Operation Maple involved holding "warning talks" and inducing activists to sign pledges disavowing "hostile activity." Anyone who refused was to be interned. About 6,300 "talks" took place, leading to the detention of more than 400 individuals. There is no doubt, based on Ministry of Internal Affairs documents, that the purpose of the operations was to isolate "anti-socialist forces" and "cleanse" Solidarity, ultimately replacing the internees with peo-

---

[150] Mounting a military response was entrusted to military commissars (more than 8,000 officers, most of them on active duty). The military took over numerous posts in the administration, including 13 voivodes and vice-voivodes, 11 ministers or secretaries of states, and nine leaders of PUWP voivodeship committees. At the same time, hundreds of persons were discharged from office. About 500 were ejected from the party (generally at lower levels).

[151] The last to end their strike were the workers at the "Piast" mine (on December 28).

[152] Internment was often used instead of arrests since it did not require a formal indictment or a court sentence, only an administrative decision.

ple who would agree to bring the union under regime control and creating a new, thoroughly "people's Solidarity."[153]

Although in the first few weeks after December 13 a number of regional activists declared their loyalty to the authorities in the media, that concept was finally abandoned. The reasons are hard to pinpoint; it may have been because the numbers were too small. Wałęsa's refusal to comply complicated matters, although his "breakdown" was expected eventually. It is also possible that the authorities believed they had succeeded in crushing the union. In any event, Solidarity's place was temporarily taken over by a strong underground movement.

Following the logic of the situation and aware of its mission, the Church, following Jaruzelski's expectations, did not call on the workers to resist or on society to enter the battle. "The martial law period requires special wisdom, peace, and a sensible heart," Primate Glemp said in a sermon to students in Częstochowa who had already gathered by 9:00 a.m. on December 13 in response to the declaration.[154] His words were echoed by John Paul II, who, after an Angelus blessing, declared, "Polish blood cannot be shed [...] Everything possible must be done to peacefully build the future of the Homeland."[155] Glemp put the Church's stand even more precisely in an evening sermon delivered in Warsaw: "The authorities are of the opinion that the exceptional nature of martial law is dictated by higher necessity, and that it is the choice of a lesser evil." Assuming that the Church would demand "to set free citizens who had been unjustly detained," he concluded on a dramatic note: "It does not matter whether someone accuses the Church of cowardice, temporization, the calming of radical moods [...] I shall appeal even if I were to walk barefoot and plead on bended knee: do not embark upon a battle waged by a Pole against a Pole. Do not sacrifice your heads, brothers, workers, and employees of large enterprises, because the price of a head cut off will be very low."[156]

No one can say whether and how those appeals influenced prevailing social moods. Even though fragments of the primate's sermons were broadcast on radio, some of the workers at larger enterprises went on strike nonetheless. True, there were only a few skirmishes, but more because the strikers were drastically outnumbered than because of the primate's appeal. It is noteworthy that none of the Church's public statements included appeals to the martial law authorities, only general entreaties to society. In time, Church representatives, especially the

[153] Paczkowski and Werblan, *On the Decision to Introduce Martial Law*, 13. Secret collaborators were to help take over links with Solidarity. Their recruitment was intensified in spring 1981.

[154] Raina, *Jan Paweł II*, 46. The primate was informed about the introduction of martial law at about 4 a.m. by Kazimierz Barcikowski, member of the Politburo and co-chairman of the Joint Commission of the Government and the Episcopate. For his account, see Barcikowski, *U szczytów władzy*, 311–312.

[155] Document No. 87.

[156] Raina, *Jan Paweł II*, 52.

pope,[157] called more emphatically for respecting human rights, freeing detainees, abolishing martial law restrictions, and returning to a dialogue. They may have realized that Jaruzelski's forces were intent on wide-scale repression, but relatively little outright persecution. At any rate, the correspondence between Jaruzelski and the Pope, and gestures such as allowing Vatican special envoy Archbishop Luigi Poggi to meet with the interned Wałęsa, show that the communist authorities were very interested in not aggravating relations with the Church. This was standard practice whenever they found themselves in dire circumstances.

The PUWP leadership and the administrators of martial law were pleased with the course of events.[158] True, Jaruzelski was aware of the fact that, as he put it in military style, "we had won the first battle, but not the campaign (a feat which would require several months)." He estimated that winning the war would take ten years.[159] Nonetheless, he believed in a final victory. The main source of his faith was the fact that the worst case had been avoided—resorting to direct help from the Warsaw Pact armies. At one of the first post-December 13 Politburo sessions, he stressed the need to counter propaganda claims that martial law had been imposed from the outside: "This offends us. We alone made the decision, realized it and are responsible for it."[160]

FOREIGN REACTIONS

Despite Poland's importance to the United States and the commitment of American intelligence assets to cover events there, the crackdown on Solidarity took U.S. policy-makers completely by surprise.[161] Unless we count the fragmentary information which the Warsaw correspondent of Agence France-Presse managed to send to Paris via Vienna, the first official, albeit imprecise, information about the suppression was forwarded in a classified telegram to the State Department at 2:10 a.m. Warsaw time on December 13.[162] A few minutes later, at about 8:15 p.m. in Washington, this cable reached the Department's Eastern European Desk and the National Security Council. The first meeting held in the White House Situation Room was attended by, among others, Vice President George Bush, White House Chief of Staff James Baker, and Prof. Richard Pipes, a member of the NSC staff with responsibility for Poland. At 3:00 a.m. Warsaw time, the news

---

[157] Document No. 90.
[158] Document Nos. 85, 86 and 91.
[159] PUWP CC Politburo minutes of December 22, 1981, in Włodek, *Tajne Dokumenty*, 585.
[160] *Ibid.*, 587.
[161] See the discussion in MacEachin, *U.S. Intelligence and the Polish Crisis*, 179–193.
[162] For a detailed chronology of events and Western reactions during the course of the first 24 hours of martial law, see Meretik, *La nuit du Général*. A Polish edition was published under the title *Noc generała* (Warszawa: Wydawnictwo "Alfa", 1989).

Betrayal?

was passed to Secretary of State Haig, who was in Brussels at the time.[163] At 4:20 a.m.—10:20 p.m. EST—the State Department issued a brief communiqué saying that there was no news about Soviet Army movements, which had been their chief worry throughout the crisis. At about 5:00 a.m., Colonel Yvan Gujon, the French military attaché in Warsaw, returned from night rounds of the city and wired to Paris that, at least up till that moment, the military units he had observed in the streets of the Polish capital did not include a single Soviet soldier. Jaruzelski confirmed this in his radio speech at 6:00 a.m., which was repeated hourly during the day. In that speech, the chairman of the WRON made no mention of allied assistance. Obviously, this was the most important single piece of information from the standpoint of the world community, since to a great extent the absence of Soviet forces limited the international significance of the events.

Washington, of course, had been well aware of the preparations for martial law for many months, mainly thanks to Ryszard Kukliński.[164] Assessments had also come from the embassy,[165] and the CIA and DIA had produced a steady flow of analyses throughout the preceding period.[166] Nevertheless, top-level policy-makers failed to draw the conclusion that martial law was imminent. A variety of factors help to explain this. As author Tina Rosenberg points out, the CIA—along with many Soviets and even Poles themselves—did not quite believe the Polish Army had the capability to carry out the operation on its own. More broadly, the United States and its allies attached far greater importance to the eventuality of a Soviet intervention.[167] For over a year, spanning two administrations, the U.S. government had consistently prepared for the worst-case scenario of an invasion, in part because they assumed that resistance by the Polish leadership would force Moscow to act alone or risk losing Poland to the West.[168] As a result, Washington made no substantive preparations for an internal crackdown.

According to former CIA chief Soviet analyst Douglas MacEachin, the U.S. failure to prepare for martial law was due not to a lack of intelligence, as some officials asserted at the time, but to inadequate use of available information. Washington had extraordinary access to what the Poles, and to a significant de-

---

[163] The president spent the weekend away from the White House and the secretary of defense was returning to Washington from Europe by plane. Chancellor Helmut Schmidt was paying a visit to Erich Honecker, and the French prime minister had left Paris for the weekend. Naturally, none of this had any significance for the decision made by Jaruzelski.

[164] Document Nos. 46 and 65.

[165] See, for example, Telegram from U.S. Embassy Warsaw to State Department, "Martial Law—An Unpromising Option," September 19, 1981.

[166] See, for example, U.S. Defense Intelligence Agency Intelligence Appraisal, "Poland: Martial Law," November 4, 1981.

[167] Rosenberg, *The Haunted Land*, 208.

[168] Document No. 52.

gree the Soviets, were thinking. Granted, Kukliński's sudden departure in early November shut down the most valuable single source of information, but the Polish colonel had already provided a substantial amount of data and unusually precise insights into Warsaw's planning of the operation before his escape. Furthermore, numerous other reports from September and October, including press accounts, indicated the strong possibility that the Poles would resort to internal repression.[169]

If U.S. officials did know about the existence of these plans—and they certainly did—this raises the important question of why they did not spread the word immediately to Solidarity, or confront the Polish leadership and demand that they refrain from the use of force. Jaruzelski has since written that he took American silence, for example during a late November meeting with U.S. Ambassador Francis J. Meehan (after Kukliński's departure), for tacit acquiescence to his plans.[170] The argument may be self-serving but the question is still a logical one, especially given that the *ex post facto* rationalization by some American officials that they did not want to provoke futile resistance by Solidarity is contradicted by contemporaneous documentation. Alexander Haig's December 1 memo to President Reagan, for example, virtually demands action in the face of Poland's "potentially catastrophic economic crisis" and the possible "re-imposition of an inflexible Soviet-style communist dictatorship."[171]

On December 13, after morning consultations by phone, the foreign ministers of the four Western powers met in the study of the NATO secretary general. They confirmed once more that the Soviet Army was not taking part in the operations in Poland, and acknowledged, as Haig expressed it at a subsequent press conference, that "the Polish nation should find a way for overcoming current difficulties by itself." Once again, a rift opened between the allies. At a time when Washington was setting up a more determined, albeit sensible and at any rate non-military reaction, the social-democratic governments of Germany and France expressed reservations and indicated they did not intend to go beyond verbal declarations. According to a later analysis, the reactions in Bonn "were highly cautious and reserved."[172] As did Primate Glemp, a considerable segment of the Western European political elite saw martial law as a "lesser evil," which could be accepted "with open relief."[173] Opposition party views were much more decisive, but they were of little importance apart from the moral support they

---

[169] MacEachin provides a chronology of evidence available at the time, which he describes as "the *minimum* that could have been presented" to policy-makers, not including any additional information that remains classified in U.S. government files. See *U.S. Intelligence and the Polish Crisis*, 184–186. (Emphasis in the original.)

[170] See the discussion of these questions in Rosenberg, *The Haunted Land*, 204–210.

[171] Document No. 75.

[172] Bingen, *Die Polenpolitik*, quoted from the Polish edition, *Polityka Republiki Bońskiej wobec Polski*. Kraków: Kwadrat, 1997, 201.

[173] *Ibid.*, 201. The West German chancellor exemplified this reaction.

offered for Solidarity. Even on the Western side of the Atlantic, Jaruzelski was sometimes perceived almost as provident.[174] An article in the *Washington Post* on December 14 followed the symptomatic headline, "Poland's Last Chance."

Nevertheless, the United States decided to act quite rapidly by introducing economic sanctions against Poland on December 23 and, in an unusual move, against the Soviet Union, which Washington branded an accomplice to the crackdown.[175] The State Department considered the measures to be very firm. Be that as it may, not much more could be done apart from dispatching letters to Jaruzelski and Brezhnev,[176] cajoling the allies to stiffen their response—as Haig did more than once—and intensifying public criticism and propaganda measures such as President Reagan's participation in the "Day of Solidarity with the Polish Nation" on January 30, 1982. In time, these forms of overt support were accompanied by assistance for the Solidarity underground.

The Soviet camp accepted martial law with even greater relief than Chancellor Schmidt. Brezhnev not only rushed to congratulate Jaruzelski, but at an unscheduled meeting of the Politburo decided to impose this official reaction on every state within Moscow's immediate sphere of influence.[177] In his speech, he implored the comrades—including from Cuba, Mongolia, Vietnam and Laos—"to render political and moral support as well as [...] economic assistance." The December 13 telephone call from the "old man in the Kremlin" was followed by a call from János Kádár who decided to help Poland.[178] Satellite leaders in East Berlin, Prague, and Sofia followed suit. Apart from food assistance, Budapest, at Jaruzelski's request, also offered something which might be described as "technical," or psychological, assistance by sending a delegation to Warsaw to acquaint the Poles with Hungarian experiences "in the struggle waged against a counter-revolution" and for the sake of "socialist consolidation," dating from the period after the 1956 national uprising.[179]

For all practical purposes, these were symbolic gestures. Only the Soviet Union had the capacity to render substantial tangible aid. The Kremlin did authorize certain kinds of assistance, even though they were well aware that the USSR

[174] Document No. 89.
[175] The U.S. suspended shipments of food articles and fodder, restricted fishing rights, suspended Polish airline flights, and stopped providing credits. Eventually, the sanctions encompassed scientific exchanges and put on hold most-favored-nation trade status. In 1982, Polish–American trade dropped to about one-third of previous levels. On January 11, 1982, the NATO Council of Ministers also passed a declaration calling for, among other things, member states to initiate sanctions.
[176] Document No. 92.
[177] Document No. 86. The list of Warsaw Pact states did not include Romania.
[178] Tischler, *I do szabli*, 204.
[179] Document No. 93.
[180] Document No. 94. At the same time, Poland was not granted "respite" from its military and armament purchases, which from 1982–1985 grew by 12–13 percent annually. See Kaliński, *Gospodarka Polski*, 207.

was already virtually at the limit of its possibilities.[180] The Soviet economy was already entering a difficult period and the added burden would be substantial. Furthermore, the Kremlin still harbored reservations about Jaruzelski who they continued to see as much too "soft," but they were ultimately satisfied with his main accomplishment. At any rate, there was no talk of replacing him as leader, and there were no negative reactions in Moscow when he soon reshuffled his own colleagues, including both "liberals" and hard-liners, in the leadership.

Poland continued to experience turbulent street demonstrations until autumn 1982, resulting in numerous deaths and the arrests of thousands of demonstrators and Solidarity activists, whose union had been officially "delegalized." But while the political underground continued to be active and to consolidate its structures, this particular phase of the "Polish crisis," which had begun in July 1980, came to an end.

CONCLUSION

This was the conclusion of a phase, but not of the problems that Polish, and indirectly, Soviet communists had to face. Jaruzelski and the majority of his team chose not to use extreme measures against their opponents as their predecessors had done between 1944–1956. True, the repression affected thousands of people, but it was far from the level of mass terror of the Stalinist period. The authorities did not attack the Catholic Church either, and the Church maintained its position as an intermediary between the powers-that-be and the opposition. Taking harsher steps would have required a "re-Stalinization" not only in Poland but in the Soviet Union—something neither Warsaw nor Moscow was prepared to do. Jaruzelski believed that regaining control over society would be possible via less drastic measures and through the imposition of martial law itself: that is, by demonstrating the power he had at his disposal he could discourage the majority of society from supporting the opponents of communism, and could facilitate the gradual rebuilding of trust in the party. The desire to end Poland's international isolation expeditiously and to reduce the effects of economic sanctions imposed by the United States also influenced his decision considerably. He fully understood that radical actions would have long-term negative effects on Poland's international relations.

As a result of this political line, Solidarity was seriously weakened and an enormous number of members left the union, choosing not to assume the risks of illegal activity. Nonetheless, the union was not completely destroyed and underground structures were very quickly put in place. In line with the experiences of 1976–1980, when an illegal democratic opposition existed in Poland, and of 1980–1981, when a massive social movement consciously disavowed the use of force, the underground centers (with minor exceptions) carried out no terrorist activities and made no call for direct struggle, but instead concentrated on a long-term propaganda campaign aimed at deepening the de-legitimization of the system. These actions were even more effective since the need to use the military to control the situation was convincing evidence that the system was based on force and bayonets, something that was hard to construe as a "positive phenomenon."

Moreover, it was clear that without basic reforms or the possibility of obtaining aid (or loans) from abroad it would be impossible to dig the economy out of its deep crisis. This generated an unfavorable attitude within a large segment of society, including people who stopped supporting Solidarity, toward those in power, and toward communism as it was manifesting itself. The stance of a substantial number of Poles was also shaped by two charismatic personalities: by Wałęsa who was "crowned" with the Noble Peace Prize (1983), and even more importantly by John Paul II who visited Poland twice (1983 and 1987) and succeeded in strengthening the national spirit in a way that was antagonistic toward the system. Therefore a kind of stalemate emerged: Solidarity was unable to threaten the authorities, while Jaruzelski's team was unable to either heal the economy or destroy Solidarity.

In this situation, the United States became an increasingly active force on the Polish stage, for which it eventually found support from some of its allies (mainly from Great Britain's Margaret Thatcher, and to a lesser degree from France and West Germany). On the one hand, Washington supported Solidarity by providing financial assistance that was crucial to maintaining underground activity and by sustaining a propaganda and informational presence (thanks to RFE, among others). On the other hand, Washington promised Jaruzelski that it would lift sanctions and support Poland in its attempts to acquire loans, on the condition that the Polish leadership liberalize the system, release political prisoners and resume talks with Solidarity. However, Jaruzelski's minor concessions (freeing Wałęsa from prison in 1982 and granting partial amnesties in 1983 and 1984) did not satisfy Washington.[181]

Meanwhile, the Soviet Union, which was in a state of deepening economic difficulty and lacked energetic leadership (having lost three consecutive party first secretaries from 1982–1985), had nothing to offer Poland—either economic aid or a model for overcoming the crisis. Aside from advising the Poles on multiple occasions to limit the influence of the Church, collectivize agriculture and crush Solidarity and the intellectual opposition, in reality the Kremlin could not provide an alternative to Jaruzelski, and whether they liked it or not they had to accept his policy choices. The Polish leader's room to maneuver with respect to Big Brother had unexpectedly widened.

The situation gained a new dynamic when, in 1985, Mikhail Gorbachev ascended to the top ranks of the Soviet leadership. Gorbachev believed that in order to climb out of the deepening economic trough, which was costing Moscow the "next generation" arms race they believed was being imposed by Reagan,

---

[181] For a more detailed explanation of the situation after 1981, see Paczkowski, "Playground of the Superpowers," 372–401.

a shift in foreign policy as well as a move toward internal reform were needed. While Moscow's goal of warmer relations with Washington gave Jaruzelski hope that Poland would also become a beneficiary of renewed détente, Gorbachev's reformist attempts allowed the Poles to experiment with the economy. Gorbachev even encouraged these moves. Therefore, Jaruzelski's team felt supported both by Moscow in its efforts to seek unconventional solutions for the economy and by Washington in its respect for human rights and for democratizing the system through consent to the active involvement of independent organizations—most importantly Solidarity. The issues were in fact related. The PUWP leadership was aware that economic reform would not succeed unless Poland could at least partially remove the noose of international debt (it already totaled more than 30 billion dollars), and could obtain new loans. This was of course impossible without agreement from the United States.

It may be said that while Polish communist leaders were still psychologically (politically, ideologically, etc.) dependent on Moscow in real terms—for instance, in the economic sphere—they were also becoming ever more dependent on Washington. This is well illustrated by the fact that by promising to lift the last economic sanctions, the Americans forced Jaruzelski to declare a universal amnesty covering every political prisoner (other than those few who were charged with attacking and killing a policeman). The Poles announced the amnesty on September 11, 1986, a date many historians consider to be the beginning of the changes which ultimately led to the system's transformation and the fall of communism. However, before this final conversion took place, three more years would pass, during which Jaruzelski and his colleagues continued to try to maintain full control over the implementation of the planned reforms. They even considered applying the "Chinese way"—through gradual but deep economic reform, with the least possible change in the political sphere. However, the chances of adopting that approach were never more than slight: there was no Solidarity equivalent in China, only a weakly organized opposition movement consisting mainly of students, and the country was not as dramatically in debt as Poland.

In summer 1988, communists (more precisely Jaruzelski and the majority of his administration) decided to accede to the increasing pressure from the economy, Solidarity and the West, and engage the enemy in negotiations. This is how the Round Table talks came to be. Those talks ended on April 6, 1989, with an agreement that anticipated not only the renewed legalization of Solidarity but also the holding of partially democratic elections. Solidarity won those elections and Jaruzelski raised no objections. At this point, the main forces on the Polish political stage (Solidarity, PUWP, the Church) and both superpowers were interested in change, but with guarantees that they would be evolutionary and peaceful in nature. The establishment of a coalition government with a premier chosen from Solidarity (Tadeusz Mazowiecki) in September 1989 signified the effective end of the "Polish crisis" that had begun in summer 1980. That made it one of the longest crises of the 20th century. And its termination was reaffirmed during the last four months of this *Annus Mirabilis* by the subsequent collapse of the communist system in other countries of Central-Eastern Europe. The motherland of the World Proletariat—the Soviet Union—had a slight chance of surviving the loss of this cluster of allies, which had been a cornerstone of the empire it had begun to construct in 1944–1945. But it did not take advantage of the opportunity, and in 1991 the USSR ceased to exist. The Cold War ended with a bloodless *de facto* victory for the West in the form of democracy and a liberal economy. One can be sure that it would not have ended in this way—or perhaps would not yet have ended at all—had Polish officials not declared the fateful rise in the price of "meat products" on July 1, 1980.

PART ONE

The Birth of Solidarity

Document No. 1: Protocol No. 13 of PUWP CC Politburo Meeting

July 18, 1980

The first strikes of the summer of 1980 broke out on July 1, 1980. From the start, events unfolded at a pace that the government proved unable to contain. No sooner was one work stoppage resolved than another would begin. On July 11, a more serious general strike began in Lublin, a city on the strategic rail line between East Germany and the Soviet Union. The action, which continued for several days, posed a direct threat to Warsaw Pact communications, and finally prompted the PUWP CC Politburo, at this session, to focus more intently on the spread of labor unrest.

Protocol No. 13
of the Politburo Meeting on July 18, 1980

The meeting was opened by Cde. E. Gierek. He proposed that Cde. S. Kowal-czyk[1] report on the situation in the country.

The situation in Lublin has not changed. There are signs of improvement; some buses are running. The majority of buses stopped running at 16:00.

Cde. Jerzy Łukaszewicz[2]: Normal work rhythm in the country, except for one department in Stalowa Wola.

In Lublin a large variety of institutes are on strike, starting with "Herbapol," the rail junction, communications and municipal transport. Threats that water and power supply [workers] will go on strike tomorrow. Some buses resumed their work in the afternoon. Negotiations on operation of rail services came to nothing. Smaller institutes will be shut down if negotiations produce no results.

The PUWP VC can call on the *aktiv* from institutes which have stopped work-ing. The party does not exist in the institutes which went on strike.

Two rumors:
– tomorrow there will be a rally at the time of the opening of the Olympic Games;
– Polish State Railways District Board [offices] have been seized.

They were given use of radio network and press.
Group of CC employees:

Until today we have not provided assistance in organizing [market] supplies. A mood of determination ever since Lublin did not receive support from the state.

---

[1] Stanisław Kowalczyk was Minister of Internal Affairs.

[2] A Central Committee secretary responsible for propaganda.

State—communication with the First Secretaries of the VC.

Cde. Józef Pińkowski: Engineering industry—Kraśnik—brief stoppage in the toolshop [...] Stalowa Wola—discussion in the toolshop—300 persons.

Chemical industry—operating, except in Lublin.

Rail and public transport services—operating, except in Lublin.

During the first ten days of July panic buying of food in Łódź, Konin, Poznań, Bydgoszcz, Wrocław, and Chełm.

Meeting at the PSR junction—they are supposed to consider proposals. Dęblin—ultimatum until July 25.

Cde. Tadeusz Pyka: Reported on steps taken by the government departments which are examining and partly settling the demands of work crews, basically within the limits of the means which have so far been designated.

Cde. Edward Gierek: The industry needs a campaign to increase economic efficiency. We cannot accept excessive demands because if we do, the situation will spread around the entire country. On the positive side is the fact that for the moment the situation is tense only in Lublin and Stalowa Wola. More stoppages may occur. That has to be taken into account. The most disturbing situation is in rail services. This is a strategic strike. Lublin is located on the supply route for the Soviet armed forces in the GDR. If this persists, we should expect questions from the Soviet comrades. The possibility of militarization may be considered, but it would be hard to enforce. Allowing the Polish Railways District Board, post offices, and telegraphs to be taken over would have very serious implications.

Perhaps in these circumstances we should appeal to people who are honest. The Lublin Voivodeship[3] is no worse than others. There was a proposal for the premier to appear on television [to speak] to the people of Lublin. But that also creates tensions—no limits can be set. The premier should be kept in reserve.

Proposal for a Politburo letter.

Cde. Henryk Jabłoński: How do we get the letter across? Perhaps through the press?

Cde. Alojzy Karkoszka: Authorize the press. Secure government facilities with all means.

Cdes. Jerzy Łukaszewicz, Karkoszka, Werblan: Announce the composition of a commission, or at least the chairman.

Cde. Stanisław Kania: It should be a government commission.

Cde. Edward Gierek: Proposed that Cde. Mieczysław Jagielski be the chairman.

Cde. Władysław Kruczek: The letter should contain something concrete.

Cde. Wojciech Jaruzelski: Tell [them] what kind of threats to the nation are created by stoppages.

Cde. Stanisław Kowalczyk: Ensure law and order. There are a great many rumors; try to track down their sources; discount nothing. The public buildings are

---

[3] A voivodeship is a province.

concentrated. In the VC and other buildings it is necessary to concentrate the *aktivs* which could mount a defense.

Recorded by:
Jerzy Wójcik

[Source: Zbigniew Włodek, ed., Tajne Dokumenty Biura Politycznego. PZPR a "Solidarność," 1980–1981. [*Hereafter,* Tajne Dokumenty.] *(London: Aneks, 1992) pp. 37–42. Translated by Edward Rothert.]*

Document No. 2: Extract from Protocol No. 210 of CPSU CC Politburo Meeting

August 25, 1980

Although brief, this document records a significant moment—the creation of the special Politburo commission to investigate the outbreak of unrest in Poland. Named after its head, ideology secretary Mikhail Suslov, the commission became the focal point for the Soviet leadership in formulating its understanding of the nature of the Polish events and in considering how to respond.

[…]

ON THE QUESTION OF THE SITUATION IN THE POLISH PEOPLE'S REPUBLIC

1. Adopt the information from Cde. L. I. Brezhnev on the circumstances unfolding in the Polish People's Republic.

2. Form a Commission of the CC Politburo consisting of: Cdes. M. A. Suslov, (chairman), A. A. Gromyko, Y. V. Andropov, D. F. Ustinov, K. U. Chernenko, M. V. Zimyanin, I. V. Arkhipov, L. M. Zamyatin, O. B. Rakhmanin.

Instruct the Commission to follow attentively the circumstances unfolding in the PPR and inform the Politburo systematically about the situation in the PPR and about possible measures from our side. Submit proposals to the CPSU CC Politburo as necessary.

[Source: RGANI, Fond 89, Opis 42, Delo 22. Published in Dokumenty: Teczka Susłowa [Documents: The Suslov Dossier] [hereafter, Teczka Susłowa], (Warsaw: Interpress, 1993), p. 12. Translated by Malcolm Byrne for the National Security Archive.]

Document No. 3: Cardinal Wyszyński's Sermon at Jasna Góra Following the Outbreak of Strikes, with Reactions

August 26–28, 1980

In an important speech on August 26, Cardinal Stefan Wyszyński, the highly influential primate of Poland, acknowledged the workers' general discontent but did not support strikes as an appropriate course of action. Wyszyński, along with many of his generation, feared that unrest could develop into a broader uprising along the lines of the Warsaw insurrection of 1944 or the crises of 1956 and 1970, which might provoke violent suppression by the authorities. This kind of statement bolstered the Church's standing among the party leadership as a restraining force, and exerted significant influence with moderates such as Wałęsa. But it also shocked some protestors who hoped for a much more forceful statement of support from Church leaders. Following the sermon are two examples of reactions to Wyszyński's remarks. The first is from Father Hilary Jastak, a popular priest with close ties to the strikers. The second records a meeting Wyszyński held with shipyard workers from Gdynia who desperately sought clarification about his views after his sermon was presented in distorted form in the Polish media.

EXCERPTS OF SERMON BY CARDINAL STEPHAN WYSZYŃSKI

A short while ago, the father general read a letter sent by the Holy Father, John Paul II, on the occasion of today's festivities. Obviously, the Holy Father is very concerned that we should be aware of his presence with us and of his prayers among us. This is why I also received in Warsaw a special and personal handwritten letter from the Holy Father in which he refers to the holiest mother who has been given for the defense of our nation.

[…]

We have our historic experience that she is there for the protection of the Polish nation. This is the experience of centuries. This is the special incentive for us, the Poles, when working and toiling; we know that she is there for our defense. But people who are being guided by this spirit also know that it is at the same time an incentive for our actions, for our daily work, the daily toil—that she is there to help. This is why, children of God, we know that Jasna Góra is, in the opinion of the nation and in our history, a kind of fortress, a kind of watchtower, a kind of fortified castle, where we are attaining calm, attaining stability, where we come down, where we begin to reflect soberly from the viewpoint of our duties, tasks, and maybe also rights.

And thus, when everybody's eyes are turned toward Jasna Góra, it is generally known that it is impossible to raise one's hand against Jasna Góra. This is a mystery of the ages, some special grave of divine providence which has been in operation here for six centuries. But when we face this historical experience, when we know that when all is said and done it is so, that even when all the lights seem to have gone out for our nation, in the words of the great enemy and invader who attacked both the nation and the Church in Poland many years ago, then she remains—the Black Madonna of Jasna Góra.

However, let us remember that an effective defense of the people through the Holy Mother also requires efforts on our part.[4] The defense which we expect on many occasions, and at the last moment, cannot mean passively waiting for help from heaven.

In order to deserve the protection of the Holy Virgin it is necessary to fulfill our duties in everyday living, duties which rest on everybody's shoulders, duties which rest on our families, on every one of our families, duties which rest on our public life, on our professional life, and on our working life. The better we perform these duties, everyday duties, the more, my beloved children, we can rest assured that help will come. What is more, the better and the more consciously we perform our everyday duties, with a sense of our responsibility for the nation, the more justified and the better grounded are our rights, and then in the name of these rights we can also make demands. Otherwise it is impossible.

[...]

I emphasize and repeat, and I will go on repeating this during these joint reflections, that with this [sense of responsibility] is linked a sense of duty which has to be performed. With this will be linked also the sense of truth which we gain in our everyday life. There thus exists a common responsibility. Why? Because none of us is without sin, none of us is free of guilt, and thus the guilt is also common to us all. And it can assume various forms.

For instance, guilt resulting from the violation of personal human rights, which is linked with the moral and social deformation of man, guilt resulting from the failure to defend our rights, which we should do as men—always, however, inasmuch as we carry out [our] duties; and there may exist and there can be a lack of that awareness, a kind of passivity and insensitivity to the common good, to public good, the good of the family, the nation and the state. Sometimes, the concern for personal interest, concern for professional interests, may take the upper hand over the interests of higher categories such as the interest of families and the interest of the nation. Our national and civic maturity requires that we should have a sense of responsibility not only for our personal matters but also for the nation as a whole.

[...]

We have come here to recall some issues, as behooves the servants of the Church who follow the example of Christ. We have come to speak of what should be respected and what should be done in order that peace and order return to our country.

---

[4] The original translation renders the last phrase as "of our party," but "on our part" seems more in line with the context of this paragraph.

I would like to start, first of all, from a duty which rests on the shoulders of all of us, every single one of us, priests and bishops, fathers and families, representatives of the various communities living in our country.

The duty which rests on the shoulders of the whole nation and on the authorities which have assumed responsibility at this stage for the development of national life and for the proper use of the hard-won freedom in the interests of our country. This is one element which, for the sake of public peace, prosperity and normal development of our life as a nation and state, should not be infringed.

The second element is the order of family life [...] Linked with this prime position of family and of human life, as well as of economic order, will be the task—a family task—of the upbringing of the nation, both personal and social. In other words, the task of giving young Poles such directions in life that they should enter public activities as well as social and professional activities with, first of all, a sense of duty, and second, an awareness of their rights within their country [...]

And now the third element: the order of social and professional life. The life of the family and that of a state are organized in such a way that certain tasks are allocated. In the family there are the tasks performed by the mother which the father will not be capable of performing, and there are tasks of the father which are beyond the mother, and there are tasks which they must both perform. Yet even in a family, there develop tasks of the elder brothers and sisters toward their younger siblings, which means that there is a range of tasks. These tasks are conditioned not only by purely economic requirements, but also by moral postulates, and thus to some extent by religious postulates. Therefore, the Church hallows various professional groups.

[...]

When I was traveling here this morning from Warsaw, I was looking at the fields. Some had been harvested and plowed. Others are full of maize-sheaves and in others the maize has still not been cut. Of course, this can depend also on climatic conditions in the whole area. Nevertheless, this is connected with the conscientiousness of working and with the good quality of work. We know that when there is not good work then the best economic system will be unsuccessful and we will only multiply debts and borrowing. And all this will be eaten up straightaway because there is no prosperity without work. And even though man has the right to leisure, and even though, sometimes when there are no other means, man has the right to make his stance known—even if this is by refusing to work—we nevertheless know that this is a very expensive argument, an argument so expensive that they burden the whole national economy and affect the life of the nation, family and every person in some negative way or other.

Professional work is not only an economic element but it is also a social, moral element, and [it] is an element in spiritual formation. If this spiritual formation is deepened, then all the national economy stops limping. And so, my beloved, it is work and not inactivity which is the ally of man, his ally in his personal life, in family and domestic well-being and in national prosperity. The harder and more conscientiously we work, the less we will borrow.

[…]

You, dear mothers, you know how sometimes your daughters who want to be smartly dressed ask so much of you: Dear mother, give me this and that and yet another thing. And you, too, you do not satisfy these needs at once. You reply: All right, my child, I appreciate and understand this, but you must wait a while. It is sometimes also the case in public life that we have to wait. Do not forget that we are a nation which is still building its prosperity. Remember, children of God, that we have recovered our fatherland and achieved our freedom through ruins. As a newly appointed bishop of Warsaw, I went to my cathedral on heaps of rubble. Today I travel on a smooth road.

Reborn Poland has rebuilt its losses, rebuilt Warsaw, Gdańsk, Wrocław, Poznań, and many other towns which were in ruins, with patience and work. But this did not take place overnight.

We must constantly have leading circumspection, called in Latin, *prudentia gubernativa*, or circumspection of management. And we know that in the great toil of the reconstruction of Poland much has been done in the Fatherland, but much more still remains to be done, and we must multiply the efforts of work, [and] deepen its moral level and sense of professional responsibility in order to bring about proper order.

This, children of God, is a concise and short—maybe not so short—examination of the national conscience which we are making in front of her, who has been given to defend our nation.

Let us defend ourselves, and others will defend us. And let us defend ourselves by fulfilling our duty; when we fulfill it, we will have even greater claims to demand our rights.

[…]

[Source: U.S. Foreign Broadcast Information Service (FBIS) Daily Report— Eastern Europe, Vol. II, No. 168, (FBIS–EEU–80–168), August 27, 1980, pp. G–26–31.]

Father Prelate Hilary Jastak
Memorandum to the Primate of Poland

August 27

[...]

Having been a priest in the region of Gdynia for several decades as well as having steady contact with the people of Gdynia and the entire area of Kaszuby and Pomorze and having shared its everyday worries, having participated in its experiences, I permit myself to present honest information about the situation. I am forced to do so, not only from an obligation to the faithful, but also—and perhaps most importantly—because of the uneasiness caused by the stance Church dignitaries have taken towards the striking workers who are supported by the entire Polish society without any exception. [...] Generally, the attitude of the workers only arouses inspiration and recognition, and no one among us who has experienced the situation in this very place for many days now has any doubt that there is no threat of rash actions coming from the side of the striking workers. [...]

Due to the fact that the Bishop of Chełmno[5] is residing in Pelplin and the governor of Gdańsk cancelled all automobile transportation for private persons, and the Rev. Bishop has not yet arrived in Gdynia to check the actual state of affairs, I find myself in a special position since the workers think that the title of the prelate, His Holiness, represents the Church hierarchy, and they generally turn to me with various and complex matters. They are looking for moral and spiritual support in the Church, which for centuries has been the mainstay of being Polish; such support must absolutely be granted to them.

Given the above-mentioned circumstances, all of the faithful, and I personally, are surprised at the passive attitude of the Polish Episcopate towards these fundamental matters [facing] the Polish nation. The society of the coast and all of us are awaiting instructions from the Polish Episcopate to conduct prayers, special supplications for domestic peace and for a just resolution of the demands presented by the workers to the authorities of the PPR. The passivity of the Polish Episcopate in the matter of the workers is ever more painful due to the fact that one of the demands[6] of the strikers [...] is access to the mass media for representatives of all faiths. It seems to be a bitter irony that the right to free speech in the mass media, which was achieved at the cost of worker victims, and which Your Eminence utilized on August 26, 1980, was turned against those same workers. The society of the coast reproaches Your Eminence for his lack of words of encouragement, such as were found in the address by Father John Paul II.

* * *

[5] Bishop Zygfryd Kowalski.
[6] The word as printed in *Gazeta Wyborcza* is "zadań," which means "tasks," but "żądań"—"demands"—is more likely the intended term.

The Strike Committee of the Paris Commune Shipyard in Gdynia
Minutes of meeting in Warsaw with Cardinal Stefan Wyszyński

August 28

Having made assurances about the adherence of the people of the coast to the Church and to Poland, the delegates simultaneously asked His Eminence to take a position on the way the sermon was delivered by His Eminence on August 26, 1980, at Jasna Góra. The form in which the sermon was published in the PPR mass media caused turbulent controversies and misunderstandings in society. His Eminence warmly thanked "the faithful children of the Motherland" for the adherence, sacrifice, and trust which they bestow on the Holy Mother, the Church, and its priests. He also stated that only now had he obtained a full, objective, and honest picture of what was occurring in Poland and on the Gdańsk coast.

Referring to the matter of the sermon, which has caused so many misunderstandings, he explained that its content was not authorized, it is not integral and also that the author was not asked to consent to its publication in the PPR mass media.

[Source: Gazeta Wyborcza, *August 23, 2000, p. 16. Translated by Małgorzata Gnoińska for the National Security Archive. For the full text of Jastak's memorandum and protocol of the workers' visit, see* Zapis Wydarzeń. Gdańsk – Sierpień 1980. Dokumenty, *Red. Andrzej Drzycimski, Tadeusz Skutnik (Warszawa: Nowa, 1999), pp. 392–399.]*

Document No. 4: Protocol of PUWP CC Politburo Meeting

August 27, 1980

By this time, the PUWP Politburo had begun meeting almost daily. During the session recorded here, it was not yet clear whether the authorities would decide to use force against the strikers. All possibilities were discussed, and the debate was characterized by considerable candor. Although the option of force was always in the background, the focus of this meeting was on how to use propaganda to convince the population of the need to avoid a catastrophe. On at least this one point—the fear of widespread bloodshed—certain segments of the communist elite and Solidarity shared common views, particularly after the events of December 1970 (see the Chronology). While they searched for a solution, the Politburo also began looking for a scapegoat, which they soon found in party First Secretary Edward Gierek.

[…]

AGENDA

The socio-political situation in the country

Cde. S. Kania: The situation is fluctuating, for better or worse, but actually for worse. The main problem is our attitude toward the chief political issue: establishment of a political organization for separate trade unions. This issue appeals to workers. They think that new unions will guarantee a sense of strength in dealings with the authorities and the ability to force through various demands by means of strikes. Not only the opponents hide behind the slogan of F.T.U. [free trade unions]—it is also supported by a large portion of the striking crews. Mass enrollments and money collection have already begun. There are reports that two Western union organizations have donated sums of money.

At present the strikes are mainly in solidarity with Gdańsk in order to force a decision on us.

Our stance ought to be firm, though it might be fraught with serious consequences. For this reason a joint declaration of the party and its allies needs to be published today (Supplement No.1). Other measures such as sanctions by the prosecutor's office against people engaging in anti-socialist activities also need to be taken; it is about Poland. The organizers (Michnik, Kuroń, Moczulski) are being detained for 48 hours. Consideration is also being given to the possibility of capturing the Northern and Świnoujście ports. This task cannot be assigned to the army. Whether it can be carried out by the CP [Citizens' Police] is being explored. This is not a simple and easy matter; we must also be aware of the lurking consequences. Even if the ports are captured, what then? Who will man them? Skilled personnel will be needed.

An active, firm, and tactful influence should be exerted in restricting the possibilities for people to gather outside the shipyard gates. Entering the shipyard by force is unrealistic; it would do little good and could lead to bloodshed.

It appears that strict censorship control is necessary (today *Sztandar Młodych,* under the headline "What do the workers want?" published all the demands—the publication of this article was brought about by an employee of the CC Press Department).

Cde. J. Waszczuk: Part of the *Sztandar Młodych* pressrun was stopped in Warsaw. The censorship mechanisms were made more strict; we will strengthen them. But it also needs to be made known that criticism is on the rise within journalistic circles. Critical comments often come from very committed people who are now trying to whitewash themselves in the eyes of society and join the ranks of those favoring renewal. We will counter this tendency, but we have to accept that it is, and will be, no longer possible to preserve the previous model of the press. At the same time boundaries which cannot be crossed must be drawn. The press is under great pressure. There has to be a safety-valve which will become a medium for dialogue between the party and society. Our previous work contains a certain flaw. In propaganda, we are concentrating mainly on the demands, but we ought to address also other, more general subjects and be fully aware that today only concrete, radical actions—and not appeals—count.

Consideration might be given to a return to proven, positive methods as was the case with the Citizens' Tribunal after the Sixth Congress; they demand it, and rightly so. Perhaps, without waiting for the Sejm, a member of the government (e.g. Cde. Grabski) should appear on TV and clarify certain matters.

The position we have taken so far on the issue of new t[rade] u[nions] is correct, but at some point there may arise a need to propose something else. We might, for example, consider dissolving the present trade unions and holding new elections. In some places we will win them, in others we will lose. This is, of course, risky, but risk is necessary today. Today we have not only strikes but a process of the breakdown of the state, which is rapidly spreading and deepening. This is not only connected with the strikes. That is why we have to act quickly; because each day for us is a day lost.

Cde. H. Jabłoński: I have discussed the situation with three District Committee Secretaries (Hebda, Gadomski, Dąbrowa). They say that the *aktiv* is disappointed, that it regrets we do not engage in polemics, and that it is not equipped with arguments.

Public opinion has to be prepared to accept a declaration because to a lesser or greater extent it is not on our side but the strikers'. It is we who should be informing society, not the enemy. We already decided once that we had to take issue publicly with selected demands, to indicate that they were demagogic and harmful. And what about that? We are not doing anything. We are waiting. I agree with Cde. Kania that a declaration should be published today, but society is not yet ready to accept it. At the least, we must finally present a minimal, yet concrete, government program for tackling the problems.

Cde. S. Olszowski: We must continue to stand by our position on the trade unions issue: we are in favor of their renewal, but within a class framework. I would fear dissolving the present unions; we have already had bad experiences with dissolving the Polish Youth Union. A battle line might also run between the new unions and us. I reaffirm that we should adhere unyieldingly and immutably to the position we have taken on the trade unions issue. I believe that the new chairman of the CCTU should appear on TV with a good speech. I also propose that a member of the PB—I even put myself forward—appear on TV and clarify what these new unions are all about; expose them. Tell the workers that we want union renewal, elections where they consider it necessary; that we are not afraid of criticism, but that unions are their concern, not that of outside auxiliaries; and that the party responsible for the country cannot agree to the formation of an anti-socialist structure, no matter who does or does not want it. Point out the dangers involved (the ČSSR, Hungary).[7] In 1974 good material for a trade union law was almost ready; it might be worth going back to.

I believe that the declaration needs more work, that it requires consultation with the allies, and that it should be ready for the right moment, when other measures fail.

Cde. W. Kruczek: To decide on the dissolution of the CCTU and new elections would be disastrous. In this struggle we stand no chance of winning over the class unions. We in the leadership must be aware that millions of people will line up against us. Cde. Olszowski's appearance on TV should be preceded by an appearance by a member of the government who would publicly declare what the government is going to do. Such a government declaration is urgently needed. A declaration lacking arguments ends up as an appeal.

Cde. A. Karkoszka: I consider the most important and urgent matter to be a concrete response to the Gdańsk demands. The case has to be stated exhaustively on TV. If a demand is reasonable, agree to its implementation both in Gdańsk and country-wide; if it is unreasonable, say so and explain why we reject it. We have to work on this in the CC departments instead of just deliberating. This is one of the ways of retaining solidarity with Gdańsk.

Another pressing matter to be solved is free trade unions. It requires public clarification because people do not know what it is all about. Therefore I support Cde. Olszowski's proposal to appear on TV, precisely in the spirit in which he suggested, and let it be today, while tomorrow we place good articles in the press explaining this matter. We might also consider deeper involvement in the trade unions issue on the organizational and legislative levels, and say what we can offer in exchange for free trade unions.

Propaganda—so far it is operating without a plan. Various measures need to be set in motion, perhaps even an interview with [Lech] Wałęsa. The public must also

---

[7] This is a reference to the crises in Czechoslovakia in 1968 and in Hungary in 1956, in which Soviet-led forces invaded those countries to restore communist control.

be prepared for stricter repression against the villains. We also need a general plan of action for offensive propaganda (meetings, talks with the *aktiv* and members). The *aktiv* is also trying to clear itself and is throwing mud, but it has to go to the members, downward, and dispel the mood of frustration.

A number of economic decisions have to be made quickly to lend credence to government actions, e.g. economic incentives—the wages fund, employment, the system of banking incentives, incentives for anti-investment production.

The matter of convening the Sejm: if we convene [the Sejm], it should be used to present the situation seriously, and possibly to make a decision on the necessity of cutting short the strikes, and to respond to the demands. Adopting such a position would allow them to save face and give us breathing space.

We can capture the port but not get it to work again. The crowd outside the shipyard has to be handled by police measures. I do not recommend entering the shipyard by force. If even after our serious declaration the strike organizers do not calm down, use stronger arguments against them. Consider preparations for removing them.

Cde. A. Werblan: The majority of proposals deserve support. I think, however, that today and tomorrow public opinion has to be prepared propaganda-wise for the fact that the situation has changed. Tomorrow there could be a TV appearance by Cde. Olszowski. Later an article in the press on the demands, a critical analysis of them, and excerpts from Cde. Jagielski's speech in Gdańsk. Present some sort of specific government proposals. A demonstration of strength on the coast, but not just that. We might also consider the possibility of dismissing the government commission. The declaration—keep working on it and agree on its content with the allies.

Trade unions—remain committed to upholding the previous structure and be ready for its renewal in any form. Do not be afraid even of personnel changes. Even if one of the industrial unions slips out of our hands but remains within the present structure, it will not be a disaster.

I would favor meetings between members of the leadership and voivodeship *aktivs*.

I am not sure whether we should make an effort to put in motion transport and distribution under conditions of a general strike. The society must feel and understand the price that has to be paid.

Do not make a declaration today. That is the last resort and the timing of its publication must be right.

We must also weigh the possible reaction of the adversary to our harder line—there could be a spreading of strikes, but then again unrest might subside a little. Therefore, we need to have a plan for every contingency. In our actions we are banking too one-sidedly on success; we do not take defeat into account.

Accepting a law on the suspension of strikes is possible, but how to make sure that it is followed through? If there is no such possibility, it would be wrong to accept it. Besides, there would be great difficulties passing such a law in the Sejm. This has to be taken into consideration.

Cde. E. Gierek: What about accepting a law about the suspension of strikes which would apply only to port and municipal transportation workers? That would make sense if we could be sure of its implementation.

Cde. Z. Grudzień: In the voivodeship we are succeeding at mobilizing an ever wider *aktiv*. We had two minor stoppages, but the situation is under control. There are many wage-related petitions. The government is firmly in the saddle. Economic administration is functioning smoothly. The repercussions of Wyszyński's sermon[8] have varied; it made a bigger impression among the intelligentsia; the *aktiv* is judging it critically.

I share Cde. Olszowski's opinion on the trade unions issue. We must, in principle, maintain our previous position because the consequences could be incalculable. The unions will not be the end of the matter; the party will be next. The public must be told quickly which demands we have accepted, and which we reject and why. We have to engage our opponents in principled talks from a class standpoint. Let society know what our stance is. Let's not diffuse our energy on all the strikes. If the command center is in Gdańsk, that is where we should concentrate. We ought to avoid the use of threats in publications, and instead stress that the authorities are aiming to find a solution. We must gather a group of 20–30 journalists and instruct them to write polemical articles, clarifications, and reminders that there are failures but also successes. Unmask KOR and other opponents.

Consider having talks with some of the intellectuals who signed the appeal; they can be won over.

Is it necessary to involve the high authority of the Sejm for the purpose of unblocking the ports? Perhaps a State Council resolution would be enough. Also, a deputy premier should not appear on TV if the program to be presented is a modest one; a minister or even deputy minister will be enough.

Cde. Olszowski's TV appearance could be tomorrow.

Unified work by the voivodeship party apparatus is essential.

The declaration could be published tomorrow, after the propaganda groundwork has been laid.

Adopt a bolder course of isolating the elements that are against us.

Cde. J. Pińkowski: What measures can possibly be used to bring the situation under control: 1) a political fight, 2) administrative measures, 3) force.

The most important is the first measure. The second can only be employed when we are able to execute decisions. The third is also feasible, but as a last resort. Since the means of propaganda are in our hands, we have to intensify the political fight, strengthen propaganda, explain, and polemicize. People are not quite sure what the free trade unions slogan is all about. We need to explain, lucidly and convincingly, what we mean by renewal of the unions. We must also speak publicly about other demands, which of them we considered and took care of, which are demagogic, and which cannot be taken into consideration at all.

---

[8] Document No. 3.

Cde. J. Pińkowski reports on the decisions made today at the Council of Ministers meeting: additional meat imports, the freezing of meat prices until autumn 1981, reintroduction of sugar coupons, establishment of an institution for cost-of-living studies, price controls, improvement in coal supplies, and the appointment of a working group under the chairmanship of Cde. Kopeć for the ongoing distribution of supplies and raw materials. The ports: 124 ships are riding at anchor in the roads, and 480,000 tons of bulk cargo is waiting to be unloaded. Reopening of the ports is a very urgent matter. Details of the progress of farm work. I am preparing a speech for the Sejm. An initiative could be elicited from the group of union representatives (including those from the coast) to submit to the Sejm a thesis on the trade unions.

Tomorrow is pay-day. What should we do? Should we make advance payments for periods of strikes or vacations? In what amount? Or pay nothing? That requires a decision.

Cde. W. Jaruzelski: We are suffering material and moral losses. We have to display our good will. In accordance with the appeal by the intellectuals, we have acted with forethought and made concessions; now it is their turn to meet us halfway. A propaganda offensive and a credible speech about controversial economic and political matters are necessary. The new CCTU chairman, Jankowski, should appear on TV, followed by other party and government representatives. The attempts to settle accounts with the local party and union *aktiv* must be counteracted. It [the *aktiv*] must feel that we are with it. The economic consequences of the strike, the catastrophe threatening the economy, and even the specter of hunger must be emphasized. The immediate consequences for the population [must be emphasized as well]. Life will become increasingly hard during a strike.

Apply various forms of pressure:

– cordon off the shipyard against random gatherings;

– take a tougher line with Wałęsa, not only negotiate but also warn that they have embarked on a stage which saddles them with responsibility for the public peace.

Get across to the population that if the strike drags on, we will be unable to ensure supplies because stocks are running out. This activity can be undertaken and repercussions should be observed. Force can be used, but what repercussions will that have? A spontaneous solidarity movement might spread under the banners of "hands off Gdańsk." Navy ports are handling cargoes and this can be extended if the Ministry of External Trade and Shipping considers it necessary. The port can be taken by force, but then it has to be opened; otherwise it makes no sense. Engaging the military in the operation is tantamount to the use of weapons; then the troops cannot withdraw. The CP is trained for such operations; it has batons and gas and does not need to use weapons. Society must be prepared for such measures and must be fully aware of the consequences.

I propose that in the talks with the party *aktiv* Wyszyński's TV appearance be explained as follows: over the past ten years the state has been offering to cooperate with the Church in raising the morals of society. We have not changed course but merely accepted the Church's offer.

Cde. Z. Kurowski: Our weakness is our inability to anticipate developments and make decisions. Today we have nine flashpoints. We need to calmly evaluate the situation that is developing and that could result in a general strike, and foresee what we will do in such a situation. We need somehow to stop the rising tide of sympathy for the adversary. [We have to] engage in brave dialogue with society; defend the credibility of the first secretary's speech on August 18 and, on top of that, have a plan for government action.

A resolute, principled stand on the chief demand is needed.

Prepare Jankowski's TV appearance well.

The party *aktiv* demands guarantees that such a situation will not happen again.

Talk about the centers of subversion—prepare a group of journalists for polemics and a trenchant tone.

The party—what should be done to mobilize it, to explain the situation and indicate the limits of concessions? The *aktiv* fears that it will go into battle and we will leave it on its own.

I propose that today or tomorrow the first secretary hold a teleconference with voivodeship committee first secretaries; evaluate the situation and give guidelines for action.

We need to have an advance plan for what we will do after publication of the declaration. The appearance by Wojna was well received by intelligentsia circles.

Cde. E. Gierek: Our position is clear on the t[rade] u[nions] issue. The voivodeship party *aktiv* seems to have enough arguments. But it is not about talking, but about action.

The decisions of the Council of Ministers are correct; they have to be implemented.

Pay 40 percent of advance payment for the period of the strike.

Restrict the number of foreign journalists on the coast. Postpone the commencement of the school year on the coast and in Wrocław; the date will be set by the school board.

Restrict reporting of strikes and the glorification of strikers [...] Jankowski's speech—to be decided. Tomorrow, an article on trade unions in *Trybuna Ludu*. The party's position on this matter will be presented by Cde. Olszowski tomorrow on TV.

Cde. S. Kania: A TV broadcast in the Wojna spirit is needed today.

Cde. Z. Kurowski: There is a report from the Warsaw Committee that the situation in the capital is becoming tense and is threatening to explode.

Teleconference with first secretaries of the VC at 18:15 (Supplement No. 2). PB session tomorrow. August 28, at 11:00.

B. Ł.

[Source: Rzeczpospolita, *August 26, 1995, pp. 13–15. Translated by Paweł Świeboda.]*

Document No. 5: CPSU CC Politburo Commission Order to Enhance Readiness of Military Units for Possible Use in Poland

August 28, 1980

Within days of the establishment of the Suslov Commission (see Document No. 2), the Soviet Politburo, as this Top Secret memorandum testifies, had already taken steps to prepare a contingent of Red Army forces for use in Poland, should the need arise. Such was the level of Moscow's alarm at this stage of the unfolding crisis. Other documentation and memoirs substantiate the conclusion that the Soviets undertook broad military planning in order to be prepared for an intervention, even though no such action ever took place. Shortly after these orders were implemented, the affected divisions returned to their previous readiness state, but future activities by the Soviet military imply that the Kremlin was at a minimum ready to contemplate the use of armed force to support the Polish leadership in its crushing of the opposition at least until the political situation began to ameliorate starting around mid-1981.[9]

Special Dossier
Top Secret

CPSU CC

The situation in the PPR remains tense. The strike movement exists on a nation-wide scale.

Taking account of the developing situation, the Ministry of Defense requests permission, for purposes of creating a group of forces in the event military aid is provided to the PPR, in the first instance to bring three tank divisions (one from the Prib.MD, two from the BMD[10]) and one motorized (Prik.MD[11]) rifle division to full combat readiness by 18:00 on 8/29.

To bring these divisions to full strength, requisition from the national economy up to 25,000 reservists and 6,000 vehicles, including 3,000 in exchange for the vehicles taken from these forces because of the [needs of the] harvest, without which the divisions will be unable to raise their mobile reserves. The need to fully staff the divisions at the expense of national economic resources exists be-

---

[9] For an analysis of Soviet thinking on this issue, see Mark Kramer, "'In Case Military Assistance is Provided to Poland:' Soviet Preparations for Military Contingencies, August 1980," *Cold War International History Project Bulletin* No. 11, (Winter 1998), 102–109.

[10] The Baltic Military District and the Belorussian Military District.

[11] The Transcarpathian Military District.

cause they are maintained at reduced strength during peacetime, and in order to successfully fulfill their tasks in connection with their introduction onto the territory of the PPR it will be necessary to work out combat synchronization with them beforehand over the course of 5–7 days.

Regarding a further exacerbation of the situation in Poland, it will also be necessary to bring the standing divisions of the Baltic, Belorussian and Transcarpathian Military Districts to a state of wartime readiness, and if the main forces of the Polish Army take the side of the counter-revolutionary forces, it will be necessary to increase our group of forces by 5–7 divisions. For these purposes, authorize the Ministry of Defense to plan to call up as many as 75,000 more reservists and 9,000 more vehicles.

In total, it will be necessary in this case to requisition from the national economy up to 100,000 reservists and 15,000 vehicles.

A draft CPSU CC resolution is attached.[12]

M. Suslov   A. Gromyko   Yu. Andropov   D. Ustinov   K. Chernenko

[Source: Dmitrii Volkogonov Collection, Reel 18, Container 27, at the National Security Archive. Translated by Malcolm Byrne for the National Security Archive.]

---

[12] The attachment has not yet been declassified.

Document No. 6: The Szczecin Agreement

August 30, 1980

Within days of occupying the Gdańsk and Szczecin shipyards, workers at both locations began compiling sets of demands to present to the authorities. Two weeks of negotiations followed with no assurance that the authorities would refrain from the use of force, to which they had resorted during previous labor outbreaks. In fact, the Polish party leadership was at a loss as to how to resolve the situation. They sent high-level negotiators to both locales but at the same time hard-liners pressed for a crackdown. Party First Secretary Edward Gierek and others at first believed that the strikes were the work of pockets of radicals but eventually recognized that they represented the views of the vast majority of workers.

Although the strike at the Warski Shipyard in Szczecin started later than the action at Gdańsk, the Szczecin agreement was the first of the two historic accords to be signed. Starting with a list of 36 demands posted on the shipyard gates on August 18, the two sides negotiated in relative isolation and with virtually none of the fanfare that accompanied the activities in Gdańsk. The original demands included the creation of independent political parties, but that was soon scrapped and the final scope of the agreement was limited largely to workers' rights and privileges, which were essentially folded into the Gdańsk document. Nonetheless, the signing of the accord in Szczecin was an unprecedented event in the communist camp.

As a result of the discussions and of an examination of the submitted proposals and demands, the following settlement has been reached:

Self-governing labor unions, which will be socialist in character, in keeping with the Constitution of the Polish People's Republic, will be established on the basis of the opinions of experts and in accordance with the following principles:

As soon as the strike is over the strike committees will become workers' committees, which will organize—as necessary—general, direct, and secret elections to the ruling bodies of union organizations. Work will continue on preparing the law, the statutes, and other enactments provided for by Article Three of [International Labor Organization] Convention 87. A suitable work schedule will be devised for this purpose.

The government will work out a specific program to supply the market with food and will publish this program nationally by 31 December 1980.

It is explained that there will be a gradual raise in the pay of all employee groups—primarily the lowest wages. The principle was accepted that wages will be increased in individual enterprises and branch groups. The increases will be made in keeping with the specific conditions of trades and branches and will raise earnings by a single pay step or by suitably increasing other components of step or group classification. White-collar workers in factories will have their pay raised by a single step increase in their wage group.

The level of the so-called social minimum will be determined and announced to the public by 31 December 1980. After analysis of the state's budget potential, the lowest pensions and annuities will be raised to the necessary level as of 1 January 1981.

The principle was accepted that employees who have lost their health in the performance of their duties in their place of work will receive [in other jobs] wages not lower than those previously received. In keeping with the agreed principle, by 30 September 1980 the government will present the Sejm with proposals for replacing Articles 217 and 218 of the Labor Code.

An analysis of the state's ability to grant a monthly allowance to women on three-year maternity leave will be carried out by 31 December 1980. The level of that allowance will also be fixed by that date. Also by 31 December 1980, the government will submit to the Sejm draft proposals to modify Article 186 of the Labor Code concerning the above problem.

Family allowances for all occupational groups will be made equal to those of military and militia employees. The equalization should be accomplished in three equal annual installments, the first coming on 1 January 1981.

It was explained that the Human Rights Convention and the Helsinki Final Act had been printed by the publishing agencies of the Polish People's Republic and that they will be published again in the form of brochures.

Employees on strike, and especially their elected representatives, will not be subjected to any punishment and will not be victimized in any other way for any part they took in the general strike situation, with the exception of common crimes.

It is asserted that political activists will not be subjected to punishment if their activity does not strike in a criminal manner at the socialist system and the basic interests of the Polish People's Republic, and if they do not commit common criminal acts.

Organizations can be formed in accordance with the laws of the Polish People's Republic.

It is noted that the dialogue between the Roman Catholic Church and the state is proceeding successfully. Greater access co the mass media will be made possible.

A plaque will be embedded near the main gate [of the Szczecin Shipyards] commemorating the victims of the December 1970 events. The form of the tablet and the inscription will be agreed upon with the shipyard management, the Szczecin city architect, and a mixed commission appointed by the government of the Polish People's Republic.

The deadline for completion is 17 December 1980.

It is agreed that further improvement in the health service of Poland is necessary, especially in the supply of medicines and in standardizing payments for medicine for the insured.

Free medicine for the disabled, pensioners, railway men, and the military will be continued.

It is necessary to slow down increases in the prices of staples by increasing controls over both the state and private sectors and, in particular, by ending so-called surreptitious price increases.

The principle was accepted that sales of food in all shops run by enterprises and institutions will be based on the same principles.

Improvements in meat supplies for the population will be introduced by 31 December 1980.

Also by 31 December 1980, a program will be presented for improving meat supplies for the population and for eventual rationing of meat through a coupon system.

The Pewex shops will not sell domestically produced staple goods that are in short supply.

Necessary measures will be taken to explain the reasons for the present situation. Necessary proposals in that regard will be publicized nationwide, and in the future responses to existing irregularities will be prompt and effective.

It is very important to improve supplies to all work establishments (state and cooperative establishments).

Workers dismissed for strikes between 1970 and 1980 will be reinstated as individual applications are considered separately by managements and unions.

Methods of curtailing censorship operations in the Polish People's Republic will be presented by 30 November 1980.

The principles and methods of implementing the program to institute free Saturdays or to cut working hours in some other way will be prepared and presented by 30 November 1980.

The government will present a program to resolve the housing problem and guarantee that the waiting period [for apartments] is not longer than five years.

The principle was accepted that employees who are failures in executive positions should be transferred to lower, not to equal, jobs.

Travel allowances will be increased as of 1 January 1981. Proposals in this regard will be presented by the government by 30 September 1980.

Only employees who have distinguished themselves in their jobs and only those who are compelled to change jobs for health reasons should be sent to schools for outstanding workers and vocational courses at the cost of their factories. In consultation with factory managements, the labor unions will select workers for such schools and courses.

The state authorities will draw up, by 31 December 1980, a new charter for shipyard workers which will contain solutions to social problems and other solutions listed in the charter concerning all workers employed within the shipyards.

During the strike the workers on strike may be given advance payments amounting to 40 per cent of their individual actual wages. When work is resumed, workers will receive, for the period of the strike, 100 per cent of their individual actual wages [i.e., the remaining 60 per cent].

The agreement concluded will be fully publicized by the local mass media (the press, radio, and television) and will be transmitted in its entirety to PAP for publication in the information services.

FINAL DECISIONS

As a result of the work done by the government commission and the Interfactory Strike Committee in Szczecin, an agreement has been drawn up and signed.

The chairman of the Council of Ministers will appoint a mixed commission composed of representatives of government, workers, and voivodeship authorities (five persons each). The commission will be chaired by a representative of the government. One deputy chairman will be a representative of the workers and the other will be a representative of the voivodeship authorities. The three will constitute the commission's presidium.

The task of the commission will be to supervise implementation of the agreement and to keep factory personnel informed of the commission's work and of the implementation of the agreement.

In the event of questions being disputed, the two sides must consult one another in the presidium or in the full commission before they take any step whatsoever.

The Interfactory Strike Committee appeals to all workers in factories to make every effort to make good as soon as possible the losses suffered by the national economy through work stoppages.

For the Interfactory strike Committee: (1) Marian Jurczyk, Chairman of the Interfactory Strike Committee; (2) Kazimierz Fischbein, Deputy Chairman of the Interfactory Strike Committee; and (3) Marian Juszczuk, Delegate of the Interfactory Strike Committee.

For the Government Commission: (1) Deputy Premier Kazimierz Barcikowski; (2) Andrzej Żabiński, PUWP Politburo candidate member and Central Committee secretary; and (3) Janusz Brych, First Secretary of the PUWP Voivodeship Committee in Szczecin.

[Source: Glos Pracy and Zycie Warszawy, September 2, 1980. Translated by Radio Free Europe and published in William F. Robinson, ed., August 1980: The Strikes in Poland, (Munich: Radio Free Europe Research, October 1980), pp. 416–419.]

Document No. 7: The Gdańsk Agreement

August 31, 1980

A true landmark in post-war Eastern Europe, the Gdańsk agreement established the legal right of workers to form unions independent of the communist party, to conduct strikes without fear of reprisals, to speak out publicly on national issues and to produce their own publications. The workers' delegation made compromises, to be sure, including acknowledging the "leading role" of the party, disavowing intentions to act as a political party, and agreeing not to "impair[] the existing system of international alliances"—that is, the Warsaw Pact. But the accord directly undercut party control over a key segment of Polish society and set a precedent for the potential further erosion of communist authority, not just in Poland but throughout the Soviet-led alliance.

The government commission and the Interfactory Strike Committee, after having investigated and considered the 21 demands by the strikers on the Baltic Coast, established:

Regarding Item 1 which demanded the acceptance of free labor unions, independent of the party and employers, which stems from Convention No. 87 of the International Labor Organization on the freedom of labor unions, ratified by the PPR, the government commission and the MKS established:

1. Labor union operations in the PPR have not risen to the expectations of the workers.

The necessity is acknowledged of creating new, self-governing labor unions, genuinely representing the working class. Nobody is to be denied the right to remain in the existing union, and in future there will be the possibility for the two unions to cooperate.

2. Establishing new, independent, self-governing labor unions, the MKS states that they will abide by the principles stated in the PPR Constitution. The new unions will defend both the social and the material interests of the workers and have no intention of playing the role of a political party. They are based on the principle of the collective ownership of the means of production—the essence of socialism in Poland. Acknowledging the leading role of the PUWP in Poland, and not impairing the existing system of international alliances, the new unions wish to provide the working people with the appropriate means of control, freedom of opinion, and protection of their interests.

The government commission states that the government will guarantee and provide full respect for the new unions' independence and self-management, both as far as their organizational structure and their functioning on all levels are concerned. The government will grant the new unions the full possibility of carrying out the basic functions [of unions] in defending workers' interests, and realizing their material, social, and cultural needs. At the same time, it guarantees that the new unions will not be subjected to any discrimination.

3. The establishment and functioning of independent self-governing unions is in agreement with Convention No. 87 of the International Labor Organization on the freedom of labor unions and the protection of union rights, and No. 98 on the right to organize and conduct collective negotiations, both of which Poland has ratified. The size of union and staff representative bodies will require appropriate changes in legislation. In view of the above, the government commits itself to initiate these changes in the law, especially regarding unions, workers' self-government, and the Labor Code.

4. The strike committees are granted the opportunity to form factory workers' representative bodies, such as workers' committees, workers' councils, or committees establishing the new self-governing labor unions.

The Interfactory Strike Committee, as the constituent committee of these unions, has the right to choose freely the form [it wishes], one union or a coast-wide association.

The constituent committees will operate until the new authorities have been elected.

The government commits itself to creating conditions conducive to the registration of the new labor unions outside the Trade Union Central Council (TUCC).

5. The new unions should be given the genuine right to pass public judgment on key decisions determining the standard of living of the population, including the principles governing division of the national income into consumption and accumulation, the division of the social consumption fund for various purposes (the health services, education, and culture), fundamental principles governing remuneration and policy governing wages, especially the automatic adjustment of wages due to inflation, long-term economic plans, investment policy and price changes. The government commits itself to ensure conditions conducive to the implementation of these functions.

6. The Interfactory Strike Committee establishes a socio-professional work center whose main function is an objective analysis of worker conditions, the living standard of the working people, and methods of representing worker interests. The center will make expert appraisals of the wage and price index and suggest forms of compensation. It will also publish the results of its surveys. Moreover, the new unions will have their own publications.

7. The government will guarantee respect for Point 1 of the Law on Labor Unions of 1949, which says that workers and employees are guaranteed the right voluntarily to form free labor unions in Poland. The new unions will not be included in the TUCC. It is assumed that the new law will uphold this principle. At the same time, the government will ensure that MKS representatives or constituent committees or any other workers' representative bodies have the right to participate in preparing this law.

Regarding Item 2 demanding "the right to strike and security for strikers and supporters," it was agreed:

The new law on labor unions will guarantee workers the right to strike. The law should define the conditions for announcing and organizing a strike, methods of settling disputes, and responsibility for violations of law. Article Nos. 52, 64, and 65 of the Labor Code cannot be applied to strikers. Until the laws have been enacted, the government guarantees strikers, as well as their supporters, personal security and preservation of agreed-upon working conditions. As for Item 3, which reads "upholding the freedom of the press, opinion, and publications guaranteed in the PPR Constitution, no reprisals against independent publications are to be taken and the mass media are to be made accessible to representatives of all faiths," it was agreed that:

1. Within three months, the government will present draft resolutions to the Sejm on controls over the press, publications, and entertainment based on the following principles: Censorship should protect the interests of the state. This means protecting state and economic secrets, whose scope will be more closely defined by law, the security of the state and its vital international interests, protection of religious beliefs while at the same time protecting the beliefs of nonbelievers, and banning texts harmful to public morals. The draft resolution would also include the right to appeal decisions of the office controlling the press, publications, and entertainment before the Supreme Administrative Tribunal. The law will be put into force by amendment of the Code of Administrative Procedure.

2. With regard to their religious functions, denominational groups will be given access to the mass media as part of the agreement on substantive and organizational questions between the state authorities and interested denominational groups.

The government will provide radio coverage of Sunday Mass as part of the thorough adjustment with the Episcopate.

3. The Radio, TV, the press, and publications should serve the expression of the heterogeneity of ideas, views, and opinions. The above organizations should operate under social control.

4. The press, just as citizens and their organizations, should take advantage of the accessibility of public documents, especially administrative ones, socioeconomic plans, etc. published by the government and its administrative units and organizations. All exceptions to this rule will be defined by statute in accordance with Item 1.

As far as Item 4 is concerned:

A. Former rights should be restored to people dismissed from employment in the aftermath of the strikes of 1970 and 1976 and to students expelled from universities for their beliefs.

B. All political prisoners, including Edmund Zadrożyński, Jan Kozlowski, and Marek Kozlowski, should be released.

C. Reprisals for beliefs should be prohibited.

It was established:

A. To investigate the grounds for dismissal [applied] after the strikes in 1970 and 1976 in all reported cases; wherever irregularities are found, the workers should be reinstated if they so wish, with consideration given to all qualifications they have acquired in the meantime. The same procedure will be observed in the case of expelled students.

B. The cases of the people mentioned in Item B will be examined by the Minister of Justice who, within two weeks, will devote proper attention to the matter; where the persons mentioned have been imprisoned, they will be released until legal procedures can be completed.

C. An investigation of the legality of temporary detentions will be undertaken, and those listed in the appendix will be released.

D. Full respect for the freedom of expression in both public and professional life should be strictly observed.

– Regarding Point 5, which reads: "Disseminate through the mass media information on the establishment of the InterFactory Strike Committee and publish its demands," it was established:

The above demand will be satisfied through publishing this protocol in the national mass media.

– Point 6, which reads: "Undertake real measures to get the country out of the crisis through (a) broadcasting full information on the socioeconomic situation; (b) enabling all circles and social strata to take part in discussions of the reform program," it was established:

We find it essential that work on economic reform should be expedited. The authorities should define and publish the basic assumptions of this reform within the next few months. Broad participation in public discussions on reform should be made possible. The labor unions should participate, especially in those portions dealing with bills on socialist economic organizations and on worker self-management. The economic reform should be based on the substantially increased independence of enterprises and on the real participation in management of workers' self-government. Appropriate legislation should guarantee the unions' freedom of operations, as defined in Point I of the agreement.

Only a society that is aware of problems and has a firm understanding of reality can initiate and realize a program of bringing order into our economy. The government will substantially enlarge the scope of socioeconomic information accessible to society, the unions, as well as economic and social organizations.

The Interfactory Strike Committee stipulates, moreover:

That real prospects be created for the development of peasant family farming—which is the basis of Polish agriculture;

That all sectors of agriculture be given equal access to all means of production, including land; that conditions be created for the revival of rural self-government.

Regarding Point 7, which reads: "Pay all striking workers the equivalent of vacation salary for the strike period, the money to be taken from the TUCC fund," it was established:

Employees of the factories on strike will receive an advance payment of 40 percent of their salary for the strike period, and after they return to work they will obtain a settlement for the remainder, up to 100 percent of their normal salary, calculated according to vacation pay, on the basis of an 8-hour work-day.

The Interfactory Strike Committee appeals to all factory crews associated with it to endeavor, after the strike is over, in cooperation with enterprise management, work establishments and institutions, to raise productivity, to save on materials and energy, as well as to heighten their sense of duty at each workplace.

Regarding Point 8, which reads: "Raise the basic salary of each worker by 2,000 zloty per month as compensation for the rise in prices to date," it was established:

Gradual increases for all working groups will be made especially to the lowest-paid groups. It was agreed in principle that salaries would be increased within individual plants and branches. The raises are and will be made according to specifications governing trades (professions) and branches, with the aim being to raise each salary by one pay table [*tabela*] or by appropriately increasing other components of the pay or the workers' grade. In the case of white-collar workers in industrial enterprises, their salaries will be raised by one grade in their personal standing on the wage scale. The currently discussed pay increases are to be carried out by the end of September, in conformity with the branch settlements.

After having analyzed all the branches, the government, in agreement with the unions, is to present a program of pay increases by 31 October 1980 that will go into force as of 1 January 1981 for those earning the least, with particular attention to families with many children.

Regarding Point 9, which reads: "Guarantee automatic pay increases concurrently with increases in prices and a decline in the value of money," it was established:

It was accepted as necessary to stop the rise in prices of general-use articles by intensifying controls over both the socialized and private sectors, and especially by stopping so-called surreptitious price increases.

In agreement with the government decision, studies will be made on the cost of living. They will be carried out by the unions and scholarly institutions. By the end of 1980, the government is to have prepared rules for compensation for the rising cost of living, which will be submitted for general discussion and, having been approved, will be implemented. These rules are to take into consideration the problem of the "social minimum."

Regarding Point 10, which reads: "Keep the domestic market fully stocked with food articles, and export solely and exclusively the surplus;" Point 11, which reads: "Do away with commercial prices as well as hard currency sales in so-called internal export;" Point 13, which reads: "Introduce rationing for meat and meat products by issuing ration cards until the market situation is corrected," it was established:

Supplies of meat must be improved by 31 December 1980 by increasing the profitability of agricultural production, restricting the export of meat to the bare minimum, and importing additional quantities of meat. At the same time, a program for improving meat supplies, including the possibility of eventual rationing, will be presented.

It was agreed that Pewex shops will not sell scarce, locally-produced goods. By the end of this year the nation is to be advised about the decisions and actions taken on the question of market supplies.

The Interfactory Strike Committee demands the closing of commercial shops, and putting into order and standardizing prices for meat and meat products at a median level.

Regarding Point 12, which reads: "Introduce the principle of hiring managerial personnel according to [professional] qualifications, not party membership, and do away with privileges for the Citizens' Police, the security service, and the party apparatus by equalizing family allowances and putting an end to special sales for them, etc.

It was decided to accept the demand that administrative personnel be chosen according to qualifications and competence from among both party and nonparty members. A program to equalize family benefits for all professional groups of workers will be presented by the government by 31 December 1980. The government commission affirms that [on the premises of the Citizens' Police, security service, and party apparatus] there will only be workers' buffets and cafeterias, just as in other offices and places of work.

As for Point 14, which states: "To lower the retirement age for women to 50 and for men to 55 or to entitle anyone to a pension who has worked in the PPR for 30 years for women and 35 years for men," it has been decided that:

The government commission considers this demand impossible to fulfill at present, with the current economic and demographic situation in the country as it is. The matter may be put up for discussion in the future. The Interfactory Strike Committee demands that this matter be carefully examined by 31 December 1980 and regard given to the possibility of making the retirement age 5 years earlier for those employed in strenuous occupations (30 years for women and 35 years for men, and in the case of very strenuous work by at least 15 years). This should only occur when a worker requests it.

Regarding Point 15, which states: "To equalize annuities and pensions paid according to the 'old book' to the level of pensions paid now," it has been decided that:

The government commission declares that the lowest pensions will be raised annually according to the country's economic possibilities as well as with regard to raising the minimum wage. The government will present a program for implementing this demand by 31 December 1980. The government will prepare proposals to raise the lowest pensions and annuities to a so-called "social minimum" set on the basis of findings by appropriate institutes, which findings will then be made public and submitted to the unions to be checked. The Interfactory Strike Committee emphasizes the extraordinary urgency of this matter and upholds its demand that pensions and annuities figured the "old" and the new way be equalized and that in calculating them the rise in the cost of living be taken into account.

In the matter of Point 16, which states: "Improve working conditions for the health service which will ensure better medical care for the working people," it has been decided that:

It has been recognized as imperative to increase the health service's executive power so far as investments are concerned, to improve the supply of drugs by importing more raw materials, to increase the pay of all employees of the health service (revising the wage scale for nurses) and to prepare urgent government programs to improve the nation's health. Other efforts in this field are to be found in the appendix.

Addendum to Point 16:

1. To introduce a "Charter of Rights for Health Service Employees."

2. To guarantee supplies for the sale of an adequate amount of protective cotton clothing.

3. To refund health service workers for the purchase of work clothes from the material expenditure fund.

4. To provide a guaranteed wage fund that would make it possible to reward all those who have performed outstanding work in accordance with theoretical possibilities.

5. To set up funds for additional payments upon the completion of 25 and 30 years of work.

6. To establish additional payment for work under difficult or harmful working conditions, and to introduce additional pay for shift work by non-medical employees.

7. To restore additional payment to those attending patients with infectious diseases or to those handling contagious biological material and to increase pay for nurses on night duty.

8. To recognize spinal diseases as occupational for dentists.

9. To allocate good quality fuel to hospitals and nurseries.

10. To recognize additional payment for years of service to nurses without secondary school diplomas, to bring them up to the [earnings] level of graduate nurses.

11. To introduce a seven-hour work day for all skilled workers.

12. To introduce free Saturdays without the requirement of making up the time.

13. [To have] Sunday and holiday duties be paid by a 100 per cent increase in wages.

14. To make medicine available free of charge to health service workers.

15. To make possible a partial refund of housing loans from the social fund.

16. To increase the allocated apartment space for health service workers.

17. To make it easier for nurses living alone to be allotted apartments.

18. To change the award fund into salary for a 13th month.

19. To provide a six-week vacation to health service workers after 20 years of service and to make it possible for them to receive an annual paid vacation for health reasons, as is enjoyed by teachers.

20. To give people working for their M.D. degrees four-week vacations and those working for specialized degrees two-week vacations.

21. To guarantee a doctor the right to a day off after night duty.

22. To give workers in nurseries and kindergartens a five-hour schedule, as well as free board.

23. To introduce the allocation of automobiles for basic health service workers and a mileage limit or lump-sum refund for business travel.

24. Nurses with higher education should be recognized and paid the same as other workers with higher education.

25. To create specialized trained repair groups in the ZOZs [factory health centers] to protect health service buildings from further deterioration.

26. To increase the per-capita standard allowance for medicines for hospital patients from 1,138 zloty to 2,700 zloty, since the latter is the actual cost of treatment; and to increase the nutrition allowance as well.

27. To set up a system of food vouchers for the bedridden.

28. To double the number of ambulances—this being a real need today.

29. To [take steps] to guarantee the purity of air, soil, and water, especially coastal sea water.

30. Along with being provided with new housing developments, citizens must also be provided with health centers, pharmacies, and nurseries.

Regarding Point 17, which reads: "Guarantee a sufficient number of places in nursery schools and kindergartens for the children of working women," it was decided that:

The commission fully agrees with the content of this demand. By 30 November 1980 the voivodeship authorities are to present an appropriate program.

Regarding Point 18, which reads: "Introduce three-year paid maternity leave to care for the infant," it was decided that:

By 31 December 1980, in cooperation with the unions, an analysis of the national economy's possibilities will have been made, and the duration and amount of the monthly allowance for women taking advantage of the present unpaid maternity leave for the purpose of raising their infants will be set.

The Interfactory Strike Committee demands that consideration be given in the above analysis to the introduction of an allowance amounting to the full salary during the year immediately following the delivery, and 50 percent during the following year, the sum to be no less than 2,000 zloty a month. This should be done gradually, beginning in the first half of 1981.

Regarding Point 19, which reads: "Shorten the waiting time for apartments," it was decided that:

By 31 December 1980, the voivodeship authorities are to present a program to improve the housing situation designed to shorten the waiting period for allocations. The program will be submitted for broad discussion among the voivode-ship inhabitants, as well as consultations with the appropriate organizations (Society of Polish Town Planners, Association of Architects of the Polish Republic, Chief Technical Organization, etc.). The program should also consider making use of the existing housing material factories, as well as further expanding the industrial base of the construction industry. Analogous steps will be taken across the country.

Regarding Point 20, which reads: "Raise the per diem from 40 zloty to 100 zloty, as well as set [family] separation allowances," it was established:

As of 1 January 1981, travel and separation allowances will be increased. The government is to present appropriate proposals concerning the matter by 31 October 1980.

Regarding Point 21, which reads: "In general give everybody Saturdays off. Compensate those employees in enterprises operating around the clock and those who work according to the four-shift system, with longer vacations or other paid days off," it was decided that:

By 31 December 1980, ways and means to realize the program to introduce paid free Saturdays, or other ways to regulate shortened working time, will have been prepared and presented. The program is to take into consideration increasing the number of paid free Saturdays in 1981. Other steps to be taken in this sphere are included in the appendix containing the Interfactory Strike Committee's demands.

Having reached the above agreements, the following [points] were also decided upon: the government hereby commits itself to:

Guarantee the personal safety and previous work conditions of those taking part in the current strike, as well as of those aiding the strikers;

Within the framework of the ministry, consider specific branch problems presented by the personnel of all those united in the Interfactory Strike Committee;

Publish without delay the full text of the protocol of the present agreement through the national mass media (press, radio, television).

The Interfactory Strike Committee commits itself to ending the strike on 31 August 1980, at 1700 hours.

Addendum to Point 21:

1. Change the Council of Ministers' decree concerning the method of calculating vacation pay as well as sickness benefits for those working under the four-shift system. At present, an average of 30 days is used (while they work 22 days in a month). This method of calculation decreases the average day's wages during short sick leaves and lowers the vacation equivalent.

2. We demand regularization, by one legal act (a Council of Ministers' decree), of the principles governing calculation of earnings for periods of absence from work in individual cases. The obscurity of the rules at the moment is used against the workers.

3. The lack of Saturdays off for workers on the four-shift system should be compensated for by additional days off. The number of days granted in the four-

shift system is higher than anywhere else, but they serve as additional periods of rest after exhausting work, not as real days off. The administration's argument that such compensation should be granted only after the number of working hours in both systems has been made the same does not seem justified.

4. We demand all Saturdays off every month as is the case in other socialist countries.

5. We demand removal of Article 147 from the Labor Code, which permits extending the work day to 9 hours a day in a week preceding additional days off, as well as Article 148. At the moment, we have one of the longest working weeks in Europe.

6. Upgrade the importance of agreements concerning remuneration by introducing appropriate changes in the Labor Code. [These should specify] that changes in individual [salary] grading or in other components of pay, as well as a change in the method of payment (from daily wage to piecework), require notification by the employer [...] One should also introduce the principle that the system under which individuals are classified for purposes of setting piecework rates be required to cover basically all types of work performed by the worker. It is also necessary to systematize the ways in which young workers are made use of, in keeping with their qualifications, so that the above settlement does not become an additional obstacle to their professional advancement.

7. Employees working the night shift should be granted up to a 50 per cent supplement, if under the daily wage system, and 30 per cent more real pay, if under the piecework system.

The above resolutions are to be examined by the government by 30 November 1980.

The MKS Presidium	The Government Commission
Chairman Lech Wałęsa	*Chairman* Mieczysław Jagielski, Vice Chairman of the Council of Ministers of the PPR
Vice Chairman Bogdan Lis	
Vice Chairman Andrzej Kołodziej	
Members Lech Badkowski Wojciech Gruszewski Andrzej Gwiazda Stefan Izdebski Jerzy Kwiecik Zdzisław Kobyliński Henryk Krzywonos Stefan Lewandowski Alina Piekowska	*Members* Zbigniew Zieliński, PUWP CC Secretariat member Tadeusz Fiszbach, Chairman of the Gdańsk Voivodeship People's Council Jerzy Kołodziejski, The Gdańsk Voivode

Jozef Przybylski
Jerzy Sikorski
Lech Sobieszek
Tadeusz Stanny
Anna Walentynowicz
Florian Wisniewski

* * *

[Source: Głos Pracy *and* Życie Warszawy, *September 2, 1980. Translated by Radio Free Europe and published in William F. Robinson, ed.,* August 1980: The Strikes in Poland, *(Munich: Radio Free Europe Research, October 1980), pp. 423–434.]*

Document No. 8: President Carter's Letter to Allies on Poland

September 1, 1980

Developments in Poland had been a concern for American officials since the first signs of unrest in Lublin in mid-July. Tension levels jumped a month later with the Gdańsk shipyard strike, and remained high even after the signing of the August agreements between labor groups and the government, which while signaling at least a temporary truce inside Poland, also raised the chances that Moscow might react to the implicit weakening of regime authority with the use of force. President Jimmy Carter's August 27 letter to European allies spells out these concerns and attempts to produce a unified response in the event of a Soviet military move.

Department of State Outgoing Telegram
[…]
SUBJECT: PRESIDENTIAL LETTER ON POLAND
1. S - Entire Text
2. Following for your personal information only is text of letter the president sent August 27 to Thatcher, Giscard and Schmidt.
3. Begin Text.
Events in Poland are of such importance that I would like very much to have your personal assessment of them, and also to share mine with you.

Because these events involve a sizable country in the very center of Europe which inevitably plays an important role in the present communist system, what is going on in Poland could precipitate far-reaching consequences for East–West relations and even for the future of the Soviet bloc itself. In my view we in the West have adopted the correct position: to be sympathetic to Polish efforts to reform the system but to urge also restraint by all parties concerned, and particularly to stress that the matter is for the Poles themselves to resolve, without any foreign interference. My administration has been very careful not to say or do anything that could be seized upon by the Soviets as a pretext for intervention, and I know that this has been your position as well.

The best outcome from every standpoint would involve accommodation between the authorities and the Polish people, without violence. Such an accommodation could well transform the character of the Polish system, leading possibly to a more liberal and democratic mode. We must of course be concerned about possible Soviet reactions to the events in Poland, but at the moment, it appears that Mr. Gierek has at least Soviet acquiescence for his course of action. My impression is that the majority of Poles also favor evolutionary changes without recourse to violence, and I am heartened by the conciliatory approach adopted publicly by the Pope and Cardinal Wyszyński.

Certainly the economic side of the Polish situation is also important for us to consider. Poland will undoubtedly continue to want economic and financial assistance from the West. I believe our aid should be designed to encourage the Poles to undertake a more fundamental and systematic reform of their economic system. I would very much welcome your thoughts on this problem, which also has relevance to the problems faced by other Eastern Europeans as well.

I also wanted to take this opportunity to inform you of our latest contacts with the Polish ambassador in Washington, Spasowski, a senior man who had previously served as deputy minister of foreign affairs. Spasowski has been in to see Warren Christopher twice in the last several days. [...]

Ed Muskie has had the opportunity this week to discuss Poland with Jean Francois-Poncet and Hans-Dietrich Genscher. I think it is extremely important for us to keep in touch as the situation in Poland develops. I look forward to hearing from you, and hope that we can also keep in close touch at working levels.

Sincerely,
Jimmy Carter
End Text.
[...]

[Source: FOIA release from the State Department, on file at the National Security Archive, "Soviet Flashpoints" collection.]

Document No. 9: CPSU CC Politburo Report on Topics for Discussion with the Polish Leadership

September 3, 1980

This document is a catalogue of Moscow's main concerns over Poland. Addressed to Brezhnev and three other senior Politburo members (Andropov, Gromyko and Rakhmanin) for their approval, the report contains a listing of urgent measures for the Polish leadership to take in the wake of the agreements at Gdańsk and Szczecin reached just days before. The Soviets understand the need to go on the defensive, but also make clear here that it is now time to take control and restore the authority of the communist party—a theme that would be replayed relentlessly over the coming months. Three days later, a PUWP plenum replaced Party leader Edward Gierek with Stanisław Kania.

Concerning Point 38 of Prot. No. 213
To be transmitted to its destination
by the KGB in encrypted form

1. *Provide a precise evaluation of the situation and adopt a clear position in connection with the agreement with the so-called "United Strike Committees" (USC) in Gdańsk and Szczecin.*

 – The agreement with the PPR government, approved by the PUWP CC plenum, is a high political and economic price to pay for the "resolution" it achieves. Of course, we understand the conditions which required you to make such a difficult decision. The agreement essentially signifies the legalization of the anti-socialist opposition. An organization is emerging which aspires to spread its political influence across the entire country. The complexity of the struggle with it consists in particular in the fact the oppositionists masquerade as defenders of the working class and as workers.

 The agreement does not eliminate the root causes of the crisis events; moreover, now the resolution of the pressing problems of the Polish economy and Polish society has become more complicated.

 Insofar as the opposition aims to continue the struggle to achieve its goals and the healthy forces of the Party and society cannot consent to the regression of Polish society, the compromise that has been reached will most likely only be temporary. One must also take into account that the opposition, not without reason, is counting on help coming from outside.

 2. Under the pressure of anti-socialist forces, who have managed to confuse significant strata of the working class, the PUWP has been forced to go on the

83

defensive. *Now the task consists of preparing a counter-attack and recovering the positions that have been squandered among the working class and the people.*

In this counter-attack, while demonstrating political flexibility, one should utilize all the possibilities of the ruling party, its strong healthy core, the state authorities, and the mass social organizations with the necessary reliance on progressive sections of the working class and, if necessary, use reasonable administrative means.

The party must provide a principled political evaluation of the August events and also hasten the elaboration of its own action program, including matters concerning improvement of the life of workers.

3. *It is necessary to attach primary importance to strengthening the leading role of the party in society.*

The current political crisis has severely weakened the party's influence and authority among the working class. In such conditions it is necessary to take all possible measures relating to its organizational and ideological unity, and to the restoration of its influence and authority.

Among other concrete recommendations, the following may be noted:

– On an urgent basis undertake measures to increase the fighting spirit of all party organizations while taking into account the lessons of the political crisis. Resolutely remove all people who are clearly alien to the party, according to the specific conditions that currently exist in the country.

– As soon as possible, hold a plenum of the Central Committee that will propose a precise and positive program along the main policy directions. In particular, the plenum should weaken to the maximum extent the significance of the demands of the strike committees in Gdańsk and Szczecin in the eyes of the workers. In accordance with the materials of the CC plenum, convene broader PUWP plenums at the level of military district, city and communal committees, meetings of the party *aktivs*, and of party [organizations] at enterprises.

– Consider the possibility of convening a party congress at which a thorough action program for the party would be put forward, new directives for the five-year plan affirmed, and necessary changes in the leading organs introduced.

– For heightening the fighting spirit of the party in rural areas it seems advisable to strengthen organizationally the PUWP communal committees which, after the administrative reforms (in 1975), perform the role of regional committees.

– Examine the question of assigning experienced political workers from the Polish army to work in leadership positions in the party organs.

4. *For restoring the broken party ties with the working class, carry out a fundamental revival of trade union activities.* Do everything not to permit the dissolution or self-dissolution of existing trade unions (CCTU) and their organizations. As soon as possible, hold the next regular 9th Polish trade union congress, and make its top priority the task of bringing the trade unions as close as possible to the workers and earning their complete trust.

– Take on the defense of the fundamental principles of the trade union movement in the conditions of socialist society. Utilize some of the acceptable proposals from the agreement with the USC, and at the same time take all steps to limit and neutralize the actions of the most dangerous articles in the agreement. Undertake major initiatives of a socialist character which could increase the authority of the trade unions.

– Improve the morale of the cadres of the professional organizations by bringing in progressives who enjoy respect of others. Carry out elections for the trade union *aktivs* before they do so in the so-called "self-managed" trade unions.

– Direct our efforts toward limiting the activities and influence of the so-called "self-managed" trade unions among the masses, accomplishing this task predominantly by means of the appropriate mobilization of social opinion. Actively insert people devoted to the party into the so-called "self-managed" trade unions.

5. *With regard for the dangers created by the activities of the anti-socialist forces, carry out necessary measures by the state organs to strengthen socialist law and order.*

– Intensify attention to the army, paying special attention to the military-political preparation of personnel. Utilize the possibility of enlisting army command cadres to work in the party and economic sphere as well.

– Take necessary measures to unmask political figures and the intentions of opposition ringleaders.

6. *In the sphere of mass media and propaganda, concentrate efforts on further strengthening the party leadership and control over their activities.* This is especially necessary when the question of "curbing censorship" and expanded access to the mass media by the anti-socialist forces and the Church have come up as a practical matter.

– In these conditions one must sharply define the parameters of what is permissible, having openly declared that according to the law on the press any statements against socialism are prohibited.

– Take necessary measures to staunch the heavy torrent of anticommunist periodicals, film and television productions in the PPR by securing strict control over sources of information originating in Poland, including the activities of bourgeois journalists.

– Strengthen party control over the work of the central and local press and over the leaders of editorial collectives, above all television and radio.

– Through the mass media demonstrate that the events in Poland have not been triggered by shortcomings of the socialist system but by mistakes and miscalculations, as well as by certain objective causes (natural disasters, etc.). Through the media actively and broadly counteract anti-Polish and anti-Soviet attacks by hostile propaganda.

– Objectively represent the economic advantages for Poland of broad cooperation with the USSR and other fraternal countries. Rebut the widely circulated slander that one of the causes of the current difficulties in supplying the Polish population with consumer goods is supposedly their shipment to the socialist countries.

*   *   *

Having expressed a number of considerations on the critical situation that has arisen in the PPR, we would like to direct the attention of our Polish friends once more to the advice and suggestions Cde. L. I. Brezhnev offered during the discussions in the Crimea with E. Gierek both in 1979 and especially on July 31, 1980, as well as in his letter to the PUWP CC of August 21 of this year.

The following suggestions given by Cde. L. I. Brezhnev on July 31 are especially important under current circumstances:

– Across a broad front, carry out work aimed at cultivating socialist internationalism; decisively block all attempts to use nationalism to spread anti-socialist and anti-Soviet sentiments and to distort the history of Soviet–Polish relations and the nature of cooperation between the USSR and PPR;

– Deploy relentless counter-propaganda against attempts to blur the class content of socialist patriotism under the slogan "all Poles in the world are brothers," and to idealize Poland's pre-revolutionary past;

– In the political struggle with anti-socialist elements do not go on the defensive but conduct a consistent offensive against them.

September 3, 1980

[Source: RGANI, Fond 89, Opis 66, Delo 37. Published in Teczka Susłowa, *(Warsaw: Interpress, 1993), pp. 14–26. Translated by Malcolm Byrne for the National Security Archive.]*

Document No. 10: Special Coordination Committee, Summary of Conclusions, "Meeting on Poland," with Attachment

September 23, 1980

By late September 1980, signs of a possible Soviet invasion of Poland were becoming more ominous for Washington. National Security Adviser Zbigniew Brzezinski consequently began convening meetings of the Special Coordination Committee (SCC), made up of the president's most senior advisers on international affairs, to decide what to do. Four days before the session recorded below, CIA Director Stansfield Turner had prepared an "Alert" memorandum for the president declaring that in his view the Soviet leadership was preparing for a possible military move into Poland, although he believed Moscow was currently divided on how to act, and would probably give newly appointed Polish leader Stanisław Kania a chance to reestablish party authority.[13]

One of the interesting aspects of American thinking at this point was the extent to which discussion harkened back to previous history in the region. For example, Brzezinski in particular insisted on reviewing U.S. policy surrounding the Soviet invasion of Czechoslovakia in 1968, in order to be sure not to miss any lessons for discouraging Moscow from intervening once again. At the same time, the administration felt it was important not to do anything that "might give the appearance to the Soviets that we were trying to stir up the pot," according to the summary below. This choice of wording was almost identical to that voiced under the Eisenhower administration during the crises in Eastern Europe of 1953 and 1956.[14]

[...]

SUMMARY OF CONCLUSIONS

Dr. Brzezinski opened the meeting by asking the DCI to begin with a briefing on the recent intelligence and give his assessment of the probability of Soviet military intervention.

The DCI stressed two points:

– Kania had not yet turned the corner on controlling events. The unrest was spreading.

---

[13] See Robert M. Gates, *From the Shadows: The Ultimate Insider's Story of Five Presidents and How They Won the Cold War*, 163–164.

[14] See the relevant volumes in this CEU Press series: Christian F. Ostermann, *Uprising in East Germany: The Cold War, the German Question and the First Major Upheaval behind the Iron Curtain* (2001); and Csaba Békés, Malcolm Byrne and János Rainer, *The 1956 Hungarian Revolution: A History in Documents* (2002).

– The Soviet military were taking some steps similar to those they took in the Czech crisis in 1968. However, they had not yet made up their mind to invade Poland.

If an invasion were to occur, he estimated that it would take thirty divisions and that we would have two to three weeks warning time. After the first week we would know they were mobilizing. He felt, however, that unless the situation deteriorated drastically, they would not take any action until after the middle of October when crops had been harvested.

There was a general consensus that the Poles would fight if the Soviet Union intervened militarily, but it was unclear how organized the resistance would be.

The question was raised whether there was anything we could do beyond what we are doing to prevent Soviet military intervention. Dr. Brzezinski noted that in his view there were three things that would deter the Soviets:
– Strong West European reaction;
– Strong Polish resistance to any invasion;
– Fear of a Chinese reaction, especially closer U.S.–Chinese military cooperation.

In regard to the Chinese, he pointed out that there was a danger that like Wilhelmian Germany before World War I, the Soviets by their actions might create the very encirclement that they wanted to avoid.

There was general agreement that it would be useful for Schmidt and Giscard to make clear to the Soviets the consequences of any military action, and to involve some of the smaller allies, such as Belgium and Holland, where the sentiment against Soviet intervention was high. It was agreed that the NSC should draft a Presidential letter which would be cleared with State and OSD and that the situation in Poland should be discussed when Muskie met with the Quad [ripartite] foreign ministers. It was further agreed that the letter from the President to Giscard and Schmidt would not be sent until after the issues had been discussed in the Quad.

The discussion then turned to the conflict between Iran and Iraq and the prospects of military intervention there and any linkage with Poland and Eastern Europe. Dr. Brzezinski cautioned against linking Poland and Southwest Asia. We did not want to give the Soviets the impression that they have a free hand in Eastern Europe. He emphasized there was an important distinction between Iran and Iraq on the one hand and Poland on the other. In the case of Iran and Iraq [two lines excised].[15] We should try to forestall Soviet intervention in both cases.

There was general agreement that we should not approach Yugoslavia or Romania because this might give the appearance to the Soviets that we were trying to stir up the pot.

---

[15] State asked that a note be entered into the record that silence on the question of [two and 1/2 lines excised]. [Footnote from the original.]

In conclusion, it was agreed that three actions would be undertaken.
– Muskie should raise Poland with his peers in the Quad and with Gromyko.
– We should draft a message to Schmidt and Giscard on Poland.
– We should review the public warning by President Johnson to the Soviets in the aftermath of the 1968 Czech crisis to see if it had any applicability to the current crisis.

* * *

[Attachment to the Original]

NATIONAL SECURITY COUNCIL

Action   September 22, 1980
Memorandum for: Zbigniew Brzezinski
From: Steve Larrabee
Subject: SCC on Poland, Tuesday, September 23, 1980
                            10:45 a.m.

The purpose of the SCC is to review the current intelligence on Soviet troop movements and the state of our contingency planning. A more comprehensive PRC on Friday will look at longer term political-economic questions such as debt-rescheduling, IMF, and other possible credits, etc.

I. *Soviet Reaction and Preceptions [sic]:* I recommend you begin the meeting by asking CIA to review recent Soviet military movements near the Polish border and their implications, and to update the Alert Memorandum issued last Friday (Tab A).
   Key Questions
   Military
   – What have the Soviets done to increase the readiness of their forces to undertake an invasion?
   – What are the probable Soviet motivations behind these moves?
   – What other moves can we expect from the Soviets in the near future (signs to watch for, etc.)?
   Political
   – What has been the Soviet political and propaganda approach to developments in Poland?
   – What would be the political indicators of a deterioration in the Soviet eyes? At what point would they conclude that things have spiraled out of control?
   – How close to the threshold do we think they are?
   Intelligence
   – How good is our intelligence relating to developments in Poland?
   – HUMINT

– SIGINT
– Imagery
Is there anything we could or should do to improve it?

II. *U.S. Policy: Contingency Planning*: State has been working on a contingency paper (on a close-hold basis) outlining our response to (1) signs of an imminent Soviet invasion, and (2) actual Soviet invasion. Ask State to review the state of our contingency planning.
   Key Questions
   – *Public Statements*: Should we issue a new public statement or warning?
   – *Allies*: What is the status of our consultations with the allies? Should we intensify our discussions and/or planning?
   – *Soviets*: At what point do we go to the Soviets? Should this be unilateral or jointly with the allies?
   – *Neutrals*: Should we intensify consultations with neutrals such as Yugoslavia, Romania, Finland?
   – *United Nations*: Should we initiate request to UNSC to forestall an intervention? If so, how and when?
   – *NATO*: Should we increase the alert status of NATO forces in Europe? When? Should we consider naval activities in the Baltic at some point?
   – *Pope*: Should we consult with the Pope? If so, how and when?

[Source: FOIA release from the National Security Council, on file at the National Security Archive, "Soviet Flashpoints" collection.]

PART TWO

Fraternal
Assistance

Document No. 11: Transcript of Bulgarian (BCP CC) Politburo Meeting

October 21, 1980

The Polish crisis raised alarms among the leaders of the other countries of the Soviet bloc who worried about the corrosive effects on socialism generally, and more specifically in their own countries. At this Politburo meeting, Bulgaria's leaders discuss what they see as the causes of the crisis and whether it is likely to infect their population. Couched in jargon, much of their analysis centers around the inadequate state of communist education and standards in Poland. Various leadership failures are noted as well as the problem of interference by the forces of imperialism. Although the participants voice concerns that Bulgaria may be the next target of imperialism, they are also fairly brimming with confidence in the validity of their own approach to the challenges facing their country. Interestingly, Bulgarian leader Todor Zhivkov apparently later took the initiative to encourage hard-liners in the Polish leadership to take certain actions, which even the Kremlin thought was going too far (see Document No. 43).

Stanko Todorov: Comrade Zhivkov, Comrades, the developments in Poland are a fact with a lasting and strong impact not only on socialism in that country, but on world socialism, too. That is why we are acting properly when we analyze their nature and causes and draw for ourselves the appropriate conclusions.

The document we are discussing today—Comrade Todor Zhivkov's letter to the Politburo—meets all the requirements of a true, profound class analysis and contains serious measures befitting a party like ours, for the improvement of our work in all spheres of life.

And now, in the additional statement he has [just] made, Comrade Zhivkov calls attention still more definitely to the main conclusions we have to draw for ourselves from these developments—how to improve our work—with which I am in full agreement.

The Polish comrades' underestimation of the class approach, the distortions in the management of the economy, connected with the excessive centralization and bureaucratization of public life, the incorrect notions of democracy and the mistaken liberalism, brought to a crisis the level of trust in the party and led to the disintegration of the political system of the socialist order in some spheres. And that happened in a country where the party has been in power for more than three decades. It is our duty, together with the Communist Party of the Soviet Union and the other fraternal parties, to do all we can to help surmount the crisis more quickly in the People's Republic of Poland. That is certainly going to be a rather difficult and long process, and more serious clashes with anti-socialist forces in that country may not be avoided.

When someone makes a mistake and suffers a defeat, it is our first obligation to look to our own house, to analyze our work critically and [also look] critically at ourselves, to draw lessons from mistakes, to look for better decisions. That is the purpose of today's talk and of the measures we are going to approve.

For us the overall conclusion that follows from an analysis of the Polish events is that we are going in the right direction, and that the April line[1] of the party ensures our progressive development. Our experience and the experience of the Soviet Union show that crises appear only where Marxist–Leninist principles are broken or disregarded, or nothing is done with regard to negative tendencies and unsolved problems.

Life has confirmed the vitality and the historical validity of the April line of the party. But it has shown something else extremely important: this line has to be fought for, to be kept clean and unblemished, and the road toward its consistent application must be continuously cleared. This is how our party has acted in all the [past] 25 years, and this is how it is acting now. We did not close our eyes to the difficulties and the unsolved problems; we did not sidestep the contradictions, but solved them with an adherence to principles and a sense of class and national responsibility. For this, courage and historical initiative were necessary. These qualities are inherent in our first secretary, Comrade Todor Zhivkov.

[…]

Alexander Lilov: […] [These] are, in my opinion, the particularly important matters in the letter, which the Politburo must now stress.

First. [There must be] no underestimation of the consequences the Polish events are having and may have in the other socialist countries, including this one. No underestimation whatsoever! I am not speaking of the direct threat of similar events in our country. There is no such danger and such a conclusion would be incorrect. The situation in this country—in the party, among the people, in the economy, culture, etc.—is different.

We are speaking, on the one hand, of a serious attention to the political, economic, cultural and other problems and occurrences, [to their] accumulation, to the contradictions, etc., that our own socialist development raises and that must duly be solved, removed, etc., in order to exclude the possibilities and the causes of such crises.

We are doing this and we shall have to do it in the future—efficiently, calmly and thoroughly.

We are speaking, on the other hand, of some later and more lasting repercussions of the Polish events. Things go deeper and are more dangerous than the rise in wages and the market, although they are also a big problem. The goals they set for themselves are different. And the main one among them [indicates] that the development of socialism is being sought in another way, towards other aims and towards other processes.

---

[1] Following the April (1956) Plenum of the Bulgarian communist party.

We are speaking, lastly, of more concrete things, too. They were presented very clearly and categorically in the additional considerations[2] we have just heard. That is why it would be a mistake to underestimate these things and to demonstrate haughtiness or [give] justifications.

There are no conditions in our country [conductive to the] Polish events, and the entire purpose is that there not be such objective conditions in the future, either—this is the essential thing.

Second. We have the correct policy, and on the whole we are successfully carrying it out in life. This is a very important and very necessary conclusion, and it stands in contrast to the Polish events.

We have the correct economic policy, which provides a stable base for the development of the country and for solving [the problem of] living standards for our people. We have the correct social policy, which does not lend itself to the Polish phenomena.

We have the right cultural policy, which rallies our intelligentsia around the policy of the party and drives it forward in the development of our culture.

These are the main reasons for stability in our country. Life confirms this policy. The people support this policy.

There are certainly things to be done. The unresolved questions have been put correctly: for instance, supplying markets, services, debts, quality and housing; but we already have real possibilities not only for setting these tasks for ourselves but also for carrying them out successfully. Both what the letter contains and what Comrade Zhivkov has just stated [and which is] connected with the further economic and cultural development of Bulgaria, are extremely important.

The main thing, though, is that the party has a correct general line and, on this basis, a clear and correct policy by reason of which we are successfully solving difficulties, and failings are surfacing in the particular spheres of the party and the state. This is not propaganda, this is the great political fact which we must depend on resolutely in order to move in the right direction from now on as well.

Third. I think that we should note not only our correct and clear policy but also the fact that *we have a sound party, rallied around the April line, around the Central Committee with Comrade Zhivkov at the head; and in the Politburo we have a united political leadership for the party.*

I think that this conclusion, reached in the letter, has exceptionally great significance in the current period. The most terrible and most disturbing thing in Poland now is the paralysis—I would say the demoralization—of the party and of the party leaders, the denial of faith to the cadres, the lack of unity among the leaders, the backstage [dealing] and the squaring of accounts among the Polish party leaders. This poses an extremely great threat to the Polish party.

---

[2] The text of Todor Zhivkov's considerations was not included in the document. The phrase "additional considerations," often used in party life and documents, has been translated literally here.

Whereas in our country we see:

– Maturity on the part of the party in regard to the developments and the problems in Poland. All of us, often or less so, have traveled around the country in recent months and the main impression we have been getting from the local party organizations, from the cadres both in the counties and in the center, is of a mature attitude towards the Polish events.

– Faith of the cadres in our party, in our leaders.

– Unity of the generations—old, middle-aged and younger people.

– Unity among our leaders, in the Central Committee, in the Politburo, in the Secretariat.

– An atmosphere of trust, of comradeship, of respect.

[…]

Alexander Lilov: […] *The fourth conclusion,* which should be particularly strongly stressed, is the formulation in the letter that *now the platform for our work must be preparation for the XII Congress, mobilization of the party, the cadres and the people to fulfill the plan and the five-year period, and a nation-wide emulation for an appropriate meeting of the congress.*

[…]

It is upon this positive platform that we must step now and not go into the Polish affairs as if they were an end in themselves. That is precisely the way to [ensure] a normal situation and work now for more successful development of the country, for further raising living standards, and for achieving further calm and stability in our country.

[…]

Particular attention must be paid to questions connected with fulfilling the December program and supplying the market. We have to bear in mind that in a rather direct and definite way we have promised a good market for our people—not only through the December program and a number of other decisions, but also by last year's rise in prices. And we must try to keep this promise and generally to keep our promises, since I do not see any alternative, the more so as in our country a new working class is developing, a new intelligentsia of experts in various fields who have begun to remember these promises and to take an interest in the way they are being kept. Their patience is not boundless. We really have to set about ensuring, on the basis of what Comrade Zhivkov has stated, a stable and well supplied market.

[…]

Ivan Mihailov: […] It is true that […] imperialism and the counter-revolutionary forces draw serious conclusions from the past events, which have not brought results. That is why now they are applying new, much more flexible and dangerous tactics. In Poland they succeeded in joining into a united front the dissident groups, a segment of the intelligentsia, the church and a part of the working class, including a certain portion of the members of the party, as a result of which, as Comrade Zhivkov has rightly assessed, a serious class conflict is coming to a head there. Why? Because the standard of Marxist–Leninist education, the socialist patriotism and internationalism of the working people and particularly of the working class and of the youth are not equal to the task. It can be seen in the strikers' demands which are difficult to fulfill and are [also] contrary to the Leninist principles of management of the national economy and of building a socialist society. Private consumer interests prevail, not public interests, which would settle, in today's state of the economy in Poland, many of the people's individual interests, too. The existing influence of the church and the religious consciousness of a huge part of the population are a serious obstacle to success in Poland's development on the road to socialism. There are virtually two ideologies in existence—the socialist and the church one. [There is a] preponderance of the church which is constantly posing the question of participation in state government and of settling problems from the point of view of the Gospel, of turning back to the distant past when the church had a dominant and leading position in the state.

The Polish party and state leaders have to take into consideration where the seeds will fall, which they are trying to sow in order to escape the present difficult position, and how they will be able to bear good fruit. This is a very important and essential question. The present political climate will not easily contribute in a favorable way. In Polish society there are still elements of anti-Sovietism, a remnant of Poland's past history. It is known that after the October revolution the Soviet authorities decided to grant independence to the Polish people. But it was not appreciated highly enough then. The bourgeois public of the time and the bourgeois government judged the Soviet authorities [to be] on a level with [tsarist] autocracy. That is why in 1920 Poland took part in the international capitalist intervention against the Soviet government. Until the Second World War, Poland was at the center of anti-Sovietism and the Polish border with the Soviet Union was the most active one in the fight against the Soviet Union. During that period many Poles emigrated to the capitalist world. According to some reports, there are now about 12 million Poles in the United States; in France more than 120,000 people; there are Poles, too in the other capitalist countries in Europe, with which the Polish population maintains, through family ties, connections and correspondence, and from which it obtains foreign currency, parcels, etc. [Zbigniew] Brzezinski and [Secretary of State Edmund] Muskie are Poles.

Todor Zhivkov: These Poles play an enormous part. The Pope—a Pole, Brzezinski—a Pole, the French minister—a Pole. For the Pole these are Poles, heroes.

Ivan Mihailov: All Polish emigrants are against the Soviet Union, against socialism. This circumstance cannot but influence the consciousness of today's Polish population living in Poland. Even the several hundred thousand casualties the Soviet army suffered for Poland's liberation from Nazi occupation are insufficiently valued. Along these lines, Marxist–Leninist and ideological education in Poland and education in the spirit of socialist internationalism, as well as love and allegiance to the Soviet Union, will be rendered very difficult. Evidently, the current party and state leaders will run into a number of difficulties, bearing in mind both the church influence and the fact that a large part of the membership of the PUWP are [religious] believers and because of that are lacking a sufficiently socialist conscience; and also [bearing in mind that] a large part of the youth are believers.

[...]

Krustyu Trichkov: [...] In Poland there is an underestimation of the role of the party; an underestimation of the class approach, of the management of the economy and the needs of the working people. The enemy forces act without hindrance from anyone. Liberalism towards the enemy and towards anti-socialist forces is being manifested, and a mistaken form of democracy is being slavishly supported.

Measures have not been taken to reorganize the rural economy on a socialist basis.

Helplessness with regard to the church is being manifested.

Todor Zhivkov: Total corruption.

[...]

Grisha Filipov: [...] That is why I think it would be right, on the basis of this document[3] and the discussion led in the Politburo, to find an opportunity to conduct talks once more with the Soviet comrades with a view to taking the initiative for the collective elaboration of our actions and the rendering of collective assistance to the Polish comrades. In my opinion such an approach is necessitated by the fact that in Poland there is not just a certain kind of crisis but, as Comrade Zhivkov has pointed out in the report, there is a new, very dangerous form of counter-revolution, prepared and carried out by a very experienced and strong hand, by a strong center. It is also disturbing that the Polish United Workers' Party does not see a way out of the present situation. The period of temporizing, wandering, and uncertainty of action continues, by reason of which the party is losing its position among the working class and among the population. There are differences among the party leaders in regard to the main directions of party activities by reason of which, instead of advancing against the reactionary forces, the general line of the party is being bespattered and the slanderous campaign against sound leading cadres is being tolerated.

At the same time the enemies are acting in a more offensive and clever manner; they are constantly improving the forms and methods of their work, and are taking the initiative into their own hands.

With regard to this, Comrade Zhivkov has rightly pointed out that the process now developing in Poland is in actual fact already on the brink of an open conflict and that we, as communists, must lend assistance to the Polish United Workers' Party, so that it can correctly find its way in this conflict and bring the fight to a victorious end. This is even more necessary because of the fact that it is not only a question of Poland and the fate of socialism in Poland. There is a much broader plan of action on the part of the international reactionary forces against

---

[3] Todor Zhivkov's letter to the Politburo.

the unity of our camp, a plan that is directed towards an alteration of the balance of power in Europe and the world in favor of the new military strategy of American imperialism.

Todor Zhivkov: They say that the second country will be Bulgaria.

Grisha Filipov: In this connection Comrade Zhivkov has quite rightly pointed out that the first lesson for all our parties from the Polish events must be [the following] one: similar events, regardless of the specific conditions in the People's Republic of Poland, are also possible in other socialist countries, if a proper political line is not consistently carried out, if the ties of the party with the masses are not constantly strengthened, and if a class approach is not implemented in solving the urgent problems of social and economic development.

That is why we absolutely correctly, as political leaders, discuss the Polish events on a broad basis not only in order to have a clear assessment of the situation in Poland, but as a socialist country, as a part of the socialist community, to make the necessary conclusions and assessments from a national viewpoint, too.

We can point out, with a feeling of pride, that real socialism in Bulgaria has strong roots, that it is developing in a stable way and in an ascending line. As a result of the consistent implementation of the April line of the party, such events as those which have already shaken up Poland several times or events such as those which Hungary and Czechoslovakia went through earlier[4] are not possible in our country. And in this respect the plans of world counter-revolutionary forces are not realistic if they are making plans [for] Bulgaria to be the next country in which a crisis will be brought about. The Bulgarian People's Republic is universally recognized not only by friends, but also by enemies. And we must be proud of that. Foes and enemies openly declare that the Bulgarian People's Republic is a firm stronghold of genuine socialism and an example of a creative and dynamic socialist construction, where the working people are confident of their future. The people in our country see these real achievements and in no way will they allow their achievements to be encroached upon.

[...]

Stoyan Mihailov: [...] On the whole, the Polish events are an example of the success of imperialist tactics in producing a gradual erosion in real socialism.

I think that there are two possible variants: the maximum variant—[the opposition] takes a greater and greater number of positions in social and political life, leading to an explosion or to an instant when the whole situation will turn out to be in their hands and we won't be able to help; the second variant—Poland turns into an amorphous, revisionist country, a worse version of Yugoslav. I think these are the two extremes to which the anti-socialist forces in Poland are leading.

Todor Zhivkov: But the one and the other may merge.

Stoyan Mihailov: I would like to pose a few questions with regard to that.

---

[4] That is, in 1956 and 1968, respectively.

I think that, on the basis of the Polish events, the question of inter-party relations among the fraternal parties arises. It turns out that we are putting out the fire, but we did not prevent it. Why did it turn out like that? Here is a big problem. It means there is something still underdeveloped in the relations among the fraternal parties. Perhaps we boast too much and when we say some things to each other face to face, we take offense. And that means our relations are still not completely communist ones. I think that relations among the fraternal parties should be of such a kind that when we notice certain shortcomings, we are able to tell each other about them and the respective comrades would not take offense. But we haven't yet reached this stage of development in our relations. Now, for instance, despite your attitude, collective measures are still not taken. What are we waiting for? We are waiting for the situation to become irreparable.

[...]

I am not speaking of intelligence work. I think we should analyze in depth the development of the other countries, too. I am not speaking of intelligence, I am speaking of analysis of the economic and ideological processes. I think that is what we should reflect on in regard to this question. Besides, I do not know to what extent we have a scientific team which analyzes the development both of the other countries and of other regions. We should have precise information; what we reveal to the public is a different matter. But we have to be clear about the real processes that are taking place in the other socialist countries.

[...]

[Source: Bulgarian Central State Archive, Fond 1B, Opis 66, Folder 2617a; Transcript from the BCP CC Politburo held October 21–25, 1980. Translated by Detelina Dineva.]

Document No. 12: Solidarity National Coordinating Commission Statement on Union Registration

October 24, 1980

This statement by Solidarity's National Coordinating Commission followed a War-saw court ruling to delay registration of the union. The authorities, ever indecisive about how to handle Solidarity, tried to postpone a decision by creating barriers such as refusing to legalize the organization, and insisting that the union accept the authority of existing institutions such as the party (see next document). For many within the country's leadership the easiest decision was to try to dissolve Solidar-ity and take on a number of smaller unions instead. The NCC did nothing to make the party's conundrum any easier, remaining firm in its demands and calling for a general strike if registration were not granted by November 12. The Polish Supreme Court finally complied on November 10.

STATEMENT

The National Coordinating Commission of the Independent Self-Governing Trade Union Solidarity, assembled in Warsaw on October 24, 1980, states the following:

Today the Voivodeship Court of Justice, after an open hearing, issued a decision based on which the registration of our Union was declared, [but] at the same time it introduced amendments to our statute in an arbitrary and unilateral way. The Court crossed out the paragraphs of our statute which referred to the right to strike and added statements in the nature of a political declaration. These changes were made despite the unequivocal declaration of the wishes of authorized representatives of the Union. We have been waiting for the registration of our Union for a month. We consider it to be an obvious and indispensable condition of the post-strike agreements and at the same time [a condition] which flows entirely from existing legislation. The statute submitted by us, fully in accord with the law, was subjected to unlawful mutilation in a way that is without precedent in the history of Polish Justice and without the consent of the Founding Committee. We consider this fact outrageous.

At the hearing, the representatives of our Union clearly stated our stance for the record, which is that the bilateral commitments concluded in the agreement of August 31, 1980, in Gdańsk should be fully and mutually respected. The arbitrary change of our statute by the Court is a unilateral impairment of that agreement, of all principles of the social accord, and of the dialogue between the authorities and society. It is also a violation of the fundamental principle of trade union freedom, guaranteed both in the 87th Convention of the International Labor Organization and in Polish legislation. Finally, it is an expression of the decline of the Court's authority and its independence. We do not and will not agree to interference of this kind, which violates the principle of independence and self-government of our Union. We have declared many times that we want to decide our own affairs. We firmly reiterate that now.

In our work we will adhere to the Statute which we agreed to, without the amendments introduced by the Court. At the same time, we disagree on legal grounds with the decision of the Voivodeship Court of Justice which in part introduced changes to our Statute, and we declare that we will not accept [the amendments].

We demand full respect for the law. The Court decision strikingly draws attention to the issue of legal violations, which were omitted in declarations on the renewal of public life. The conduct of the Court makes the fight for observance of law and judicial independence an issue of direct interest to our Union.

The authorities bear full responsibility for sustaining social tensions around the issue of Solidarity's registration.

Warsaw, October 24, 1980
National Coordinating Commission
NSZZ Solidarity

[Source: U Źródeł Solidarności. Czerwiec-Październik 1980 *(Warszawa: Centrum Dokumentacji I Analiz NSZZ "Solidarność," [underground publication], 1984), pp. 81–82. Translated by Aleksandra Niemirycz.]*

Document No. 13: Protocol of PUWP CC Secretariat Meeting

October 25, 1980

This wide-ranging discussion by the CC Secretariat reflects the leadership's escalating concerns about the deteriorating position of the party, and the untenable state of the economy. The meeting took place against the background of a court ruling the previous day to delay Solidarity's legal registration because its charter made no reference to the leading role of the party or to guarantees not to threaten Poland's international alliances. Solidarity refused to make any changes and threatened a general strike if the registration process was not swiftly completed (see previous document). Within the Secretariat, there was general agreement that the party's authority had suffered dramatically while Solidarity's standing was steadily on the rise. Although no mention is made of a need to resort to force, two days earlier Defense Minister Jaruzelski, who did not attend this meeting, gave orders to update plans for martial law on a nationwide scale.

[…]

AGENDA

1. The current socio-political and economic situation in the country.

   Cde. Stanisław Kania

   At today's meeting of the CC Secretariat, I propose to discuss the following subjects:

   1. Forecast of development of the political, social and economic situation in the most immediate period, precisely defining actions and decisions which should be undertaken; taking into account the complexity of this situation various aspects and elements of the forecast have to be recognized, e.g., the political situation, the activity of new trade unions, the activity of Solidarity.
   2. The situation in the youth movement, with particular emphasis on the issue of universities and other circles.
   3. Penetration of the countryside by anti-socialist forces. We are dealing with attempts by those forces to create political structures. Ways of counteracting these tendencies therefore have to be considered.
   4. The situation among the intelligentsia, in artists' circles, among journalists; considering that the situation in these groups is complex, divisions are taking place within them, organizational-personal moves have to be considered.
   5. The economic situation of the country, including the difficulties in agriculture and in the market, the supply of potatoes and coal. Our forthcoming activities in that domain have to be discussed.

6. The state of the party; evaluation of the processes and tasks executed by the party and those which lie ahead. Counteraction has to be applied against occurrences of demagogy and anarchy and the willingness of certain comrades to concede to proposed ideas of immediate party elections, which would be based on the free and impulsive choice of delegates in institutes and social circles.

7. Activity of hostile groupings.

Cde. Władysław Kruczek: Comrade Brych identifies the direction in which the situation is evolving and what our enemies are threatening us with. We are accused of being in a defensive position. We said we were not going to step back and we are stepping back. Corrections will be forced upon us and they will move ahead. What kind of a situation is it where Wałęsa has to come and calm Ursus[5] to make them work? This is anarchy. Our comrade did not go, but Wałęsa did.

Cde. Andrzej Werblan: If you could calm Ursus, we would have sent you.

Cde. Władysław Kruczek: This is already anarchy because it is hard to imagine the normal functioning of the institutions. An evaluation of the current situation needs to be attempted, where we are and where we are going. Anti-socialist forces are pressuring us, e.g. a group arrived and protested in front of a court and therefore they will come to the Supreme Court as well. They demand a meeting with Cde. Pińkowski. They are pressing us against the wall. We therefore have to say what the limits of our concessions are. We are only dealing with materials concerning comrades, although this is not the most important state matter. I perceive a danger in that they will peacefully come here as well.

Cde. Stanisław Kania: I believe that it cannot be that some comrades are only asking questions while others are to respond.

Cde. Mirosław Milewski: In a decisive way, it was recommended that amendments be introduced to the Solidarity statute. It is hard to say whether crews know what is going on; most workers do not know what introducing amendments is about or what the leading role of the party is about. Pressure to register Solidarity was enormous. At the last meeting, out of 42 Solidarity delegates only two voted to introduce the amendments. Solidarity is enjoying wide support. A significant role is played by the Mazowsze Union of Solidarity which is the author of the statement against introducing amendments by the Court. It would be desirable for somebody to speak on television and say what is behind the amended statute, and what the opponents of these amendments desire.

The decision was a surprise for both the foreign centers and the crews. The registration of the statute with amendments eliminated opinions on two options for a solution: rejection of the statute or consent to the one presented by Solidarity. Wałęsa will make a final decision on the position taken by the Court only on October 27, at 10:00. As far as the opinion of the socialist countries is concerned,

---

[5] This may refer to Wałęsa's appearance at a packed soccer stadium at the Ursus plant on the occasion of Solidarity's registration on September 24, 1980.

104

the view prevails that the authorities did not bow to the pressure and solved the situation well. In six voivodeships, leaflets are being distributed with the statement of Solidarity which is a reaction to the registration of the statute with amendments. In Gdańsk, support will be given to that statement. It is anticipated that they will soon begin publishing their version of the statute, that is, without amendments, and that there will be more support for Solidarity's text. Solidarity is considering the appropriateness of, among other things, hunger strikes, organization of rallies, boycotts of purchasing press, payments for the radio and television bills. Fewer warning strikes are anticipated, but more from Solidarity. Yesterday, Wałęsa calmed the situation; he advised to consider taking a position. Solidarity is genuinely popular in the factories; they have about five million members, although they themselves speak about seven million. Seeds of the Solidarity structure also appear in the countryside. In the Grojec region, about 10 cells of Solidarity were created. About 17,000 students belong to independent student union. Extremist groups are few, but they attack heavily.

The situation among the intelligentsia is considered good. In Solidarity, there are mainly quasi-intelligentsia elements, hurt by life, dissatisfied. Maybe they should be given the possibility to express themselves more broadly. Among these groups there are also many critical voices toward Wałęsa and Solidarity, e.g. in Kraków.

Foreign correspondents interpreted the Court decision as shocking. In their reactions, different voices are heard; the main capitalist countries are not interested in inflaming the situation. The CIC circles are shocked. Mazowiecki is against the decision; Siła-Nowicki protested against any offense toward the Court. As far as the youth is concerned, a better army draft than in previous years has been recorded. The Church behaves in a loyal fashion and calms [the situation]. Three tendencies can be observed among the anti-socialist forces:

1. extremists–(e.g. Kuroń) who will aim at confrontation,
2. moderates–(Confederation for an Independent Poland),
3. and those who are winning the social-welfare issues.

Developments indicate that a confrontation might occur. We might have to deal with occupations of union buildings and with illegal wildcat strikes. We must act consistently, but if we move head-on, confrontation could be sparked. It is proposed not to give permissions for rallies, visual propaganda will be eliminated, involve the VRCM, eliminate demonstrations. A plan of action in case of confrontation is being prepared. It anticipates isolating the enemy, calling upon reserves, a state of increased readiness in the resort apparatus. The situation will be clearer the day after tomorrow, but assessments suggest that they will not go ahead with a general strike. Detention of Kuroń and the extremists is possible, but an immediate confrontation and strikes could follow.

Cde. Stefan Olszowski: A fundamental question arises: what does our opponent intend to threaten us with? Above all, a formal or de facto creation of a two-party system. Solidarity will aim at the formation of a force equal to that of the party. Questions about the electoral law arise; attempts to push the party to worse positions are apparent.

We are formulating the policy of line division, separation of intellectual group of leaders from Solidarity. The results are poor but we managed to destabilize Kuroń's position. It is still necessary to strike and repeat arguments. Voivodeships need to analyze whether parts of Solidarity could be drawn to our side, divided into two, three centers. We need to nurture newly registered trade unions. Action should focus on diffusion.

I do not draw the same conclusions as Cde. Kruczek from the letter of the Szczecin comrades, but it needs to be taken into account. The worst situation is in Gdańsk. Situation in the Voivodeship Committee in Gdańsk is also difficult.

We ought to respond to the letter of Cde. Rakowski. Views on the psychology of the bunker cannot be proclaimed. We might have to deal with a confrontation, with the most difficult conversation with the working class.

As far as the economic prognosis is concerned, there are many reasons to be worried. A war situation could be experienced on the market. We have imported what we could. However, voivodeships poorly carry out their market tasks [such as] purchasing of products. Potatoes should be purchased and coal sensibly distributed.

Cde. Andrzej Werblan: I have little to say on economic matters and this is the more important half of our problems. The society blames the party for such state of affairs. The political situation is emerging against this background and it reveals the lack of improvement of the political situation. Therefore, we should prevent the situation from worsening and facilitate its slow improvement.

The political situation at the segment which I deal with has worsened. Generally, the situation in schools of higher education is better than we had expected. It is, however, worsening, because a student political organization is emerging and does not want to be a trade one. It is moving toward an ideological-didactic organization. This does not promise good future.

The SUPS defends itself well, presents its activity, and is already advanced in that process. The SUPS is an organization stronger than an independent union. Academic self-governing bodies are emerging and will ensure order. Criticism is present among the academic workers' circles and also elements of responsibility for the functioning of universities; some are taking constructive positions. It does not hinder, however, the process of steering the independent union by KOR.

In the immediate period, the position of academic organizations needs to be made more constructive. A consultation of rectors and secretaries of the academic party committees will soon be held in order to discuss the demands which have been raised at the universities. Taking a position toward the demands of the youth is a more difficult matter.

The PAS assembly was a more serious occurrence. Criticism was expected because it is difficult to imagine that a non-party Academy would be more moderate than the Sixth Plenum of the CC. What prevailed in the proceedings was their anti-PUWP nature; all party members lost elections, even Żółkiewski and Markiewicz. As a result, groups which emerged have a non-party character. It was hard to insert support for the party into the declaration while support for

Solidarity was expressed twice. Prof. Groszkowski in his presentation stated that he was ashamed of the PAS for agreeing to serve as vice-chairman of the State Council. The electoral law passed by the PAS is advantageous; the Mother's Commission was preserved in it as well as the principle that the chairman can be elected with two thirds of the votes. Since the PUWP has 40 percent of votes, no person unfavorably disposed toward us can be elected. A non-party person should be the chairman of the PAS, e.g. Prof. Geysztor.

Declarations in favor of Solidarity will have an effect on the spreading of its influence at the expense of the PTU, in particular part of the senior staff will join Solidarity. An equilibrium model at the universities will be difficult to sustain and will require more efforts. Further extension of new unions should be expected. The key issue will be to establish a position within the new unions. Uniformity is currently manifested, [but] with the party's assistance differences might become apparent. We should dispute the anti-socialist standpoint and win influence in the grass-root sections of Solidarity. We are dealing with registered unions the struggle should therefore be conducted for the second point of the statute. This tactic ought to be applied for the next two months. [Although] there can be no capitulation at the ideological platform, in politics we ought to be moderate.

We must improve the condition of the party members, many are on the verge of a desperate assessment of the party. Among other things, former chairman deputy of the CC Department, a member of the PAS, stated in private conversations that the party's property needs to be secured because possibly in three months we will have to join the opposition.

A new emerging danger is pressure to hold elections for the Sejm and a change of the electoral law. There is a letter to the Deputy Marshal of the Sejm Skibniewska, there are demands in the regions which may emerge in the Sejm, deputies are pressured, e.g. in the Lower Silesia. Cde. will hold talks on this issue. If the pressure is too large, maybe we should go for a compromise. Could this be the sideline to which we could retreat?

The issue of Jaroszewicz's responsibility for economic policy is being raised.[6] Should not the Politburo establish a Commission? The Seventh Plenum of the CC would take a position on the question of P. Jaroszewicz's political responsibility which is not less than seven comrades who left the CC.

Cde. Kazimierz Barcikowski: Our information about the situation is characterized by the fact that old information presented a good picture while new information concerns bad things, and this affects our perception of reality. However, people live their normal lives and work; although [the situation is] worse one cannot see bad things on the streets. The party functions normally, although at a higher speed. Methods of assessing the reality need to be considered. Today,

---

[6] Piotr Jaroszewicz was prime minister from December 1970 until February 1980 when he was dismissed for his part in the country's economic problems.

economic problems are predominant. Everything needs to be looked at in the context of the party and trade unions. Cde. Milewski spoke about five million members of Solidarity. The Organizational Department determined how many members are in the party; it is estimated that it is half of the workers. We recommended to party members that they join the new trade unions. But a question arises, whether we have party members in Solidarity, or Solidarity members in the party. We have to re-evaluate our attitude toward Solidarity. First of all, fears of it have to disappear. The party is threatened with a schism, and this would be the worst thing possible. An institute director has to cooperate with Solidarity. The situation of the first secretary of the PPO is difficult in an institute in which frequently 90 percent of party members are in Solidarity, and he is outside. Conclusions drawn from that:

1. The fact of registration should be accepted as a method of functioning in Solidarity. Their commissions, committees are not based on election, but on screams at gatherings, usurping ones. We should be interested in elections within Solidarity. They are demanding elections in the party, but do not organize elections themselves. In institutes, there are no types of *aktiv* other than the party and union. A young *aktiv* does not mean the Kuroń type of *aktiv*. Solidarity has a small *aktiv*, so it favors directing large groups. This situation should be therefore reversed.

2. There is a necessity of inclining the whole party toward meetings and conversations. Mazowsze did not engage in talks with the authorities. We do not have a cooperation platform with the Solidarity center in Gdańsk. Proposals for creating institutional contacts with Gdańsk ought to be put forward. Gdańsk is not eager for this, but we must find that contact. The platform for contacts between the Government and Solidarity Union has to be determined. Otherwise, Wałęsa will appear in various places in the country. Cde. Kruczek is worried that Wałęsa puts out a strike, but that he puts out a strike is a good thing. This is what we need.

The pressure for elections in the party is the worst thing. The issue of settling accounts is being raised: 1968, 1970 the question of responsibility (of Cyrankiewicz, Jaroszewicz, Gierek). We have to pull ourselves away from that. Jaroszewicz was fortunate that he departed at the Eighth Congress. But this question cannot be left unanswered. At least a last name, decided upon by the Commission or the CPCC, has to be floated by the propaganda. But the Sejm needs to be protected from changes.

Cde. Stanisław Kania: These matters are of substantial importance.

Cde. Władysław Kruczek: Criminal settlement is demanded.

Cde. Andrzej Werblan: We should decide whether this should be a penal or political settlement, e.g. examining in the CPCC until removal from the party.

Cde. Kazimierz Barcikowki: In economic matters, payments for strikes and enforcement of new pay rises should be stopped. We have gone through a wave of strikes already; we will still face sporadic strikes.

As far as the hunger-strike of the railway workers is concerned, they are not interested in serious talks but in showing that the authorities have to concede. However, does Cde. Zajfryd always have to speak on television? Would not a director or a statement in the press be enough? Insanity emerges and we cannot fan the feeling that we are treating it seriously.

I propose not to pay for strikes if they are not called by unions. Talks with engineers in vacation resorts should not be conducted, either.

We should decide how party committees should undertake individual and offensive actions. New inspiration should be sought. The subject matter of the Seventh Plenum has been somewhat worn out. We should use the announced Seventh Plenum for the economic sphere and we must explain to the *aktiv* our attitude toward Solidarity. The Cde. has proposed a session of the *aktiv* on the socio-economic situation of the voivodeship with an explanation of our position toward Solidarity and cooperation with it. We should conduct work with party members on the basis of guidelines on agricultural policy and also explain our position in the press. The sessions with the participation of CC members should be held next week. The fight about registering Solidarity will continue and they will have to explain to us why they do not want a leading role.

We will carry out further personnel changes in five voivodeships. Recently, the question of Gdańsk was raised.

Cde. Józef Pińkowski: It is easier for us to determine what Solidarity will do than [to determine] our own actions. There will be further pressure for us to withdraw from the court recommendations, but we cannot withdraw. Solidarity will want to have a nationwide structure.

It is observed that there is a part of the society which supports both Solidarity and the Sixth Plenum of the CC. Solidarity favors renewal. Therefore, polarization has to be pursued and the line of division has to be shown: renewal and the opponents of renewal; who is for, who is against; but also state what kind of renewal is at stake, what can harm that renewal.

Cde. Andrzej Werblan: So a two-front battle has to be conducted.

Cde. Józef Pińkowski: It has to be explained that one could be in favor of renewal and harm that renewal at the same time. Changes have already taken place since the Sixth Plenum, e.g. at the VC plenum in Opole, the workers in particular showed how solving things should be approached. The workers felt more secure and their statements were not worse than those of professors. Also at the Economic Reforms Commission, Cde. Gajewski from the "Warszawa" steelworks freely presented a plan of action; hence the activists are increasing. These workers need to be involved in cooperation, because their authority is increasing. We should more often present ourselves as the whole leadership.

The remaining personnel changes need to be completed, so that all segments work properly; also in the administration. party members have to declare themselves, so that Solidarity would be behind us. Some will return their membership cards, but select a good *aktiv* from the remaining ones. Power also has to be demonstrated through rallies and articles. We should think about such meetings. If the opponent uses slogans, we should display slogans as well.

Stagnancy is being observed in propaganda and ideology; the *aktiv* needs ideological nourishment. Recently, the central press organs have been working a little better. However, the local organs leave much to be improved, e.g. in Opole the Wrocław radio and press center is received negatively.

Pressures for the possibility of enforcing pay rises have been observed. There is a myth that members of Solidarity increase productivity. Meanwhile, the shipyard industry is the worst performer; it does not meet daily targets and is six billion złoty behind. "Jastrzębie" says that they are currently extracting as much as before because the statistics were false, but they extract less. Heavy industry where Solidarity is strongly based has the worst results. In three months we lost 70 billion złoty, including a part of market production. It should be decided whether a special issue of the notebook should be prepared to show the *aktiv* these occurrences.

Positive forms of coexistence with the new unions should be found. Our leadership should be sustained there and drawn into co-responsibility, but they have after all a demagogic platform. We should decide how to come up with a plan for 1981 because there could be opposition from Solidarity to the CWS.

Cde. Stanisław Kania: Maybe co-optation of the Solidarity leadership to the CWS in an institute should be considered.

Cde. Józef Pińkowski: The issue concerns institutes, but also the voivodeship level. The establishment of plenipotentiaries of the Council of Ministers or joint Government–Solidarity commissions for cooperation with Solidarity should be considered. At the central level, Solidarity participates in the Council on Reform. In cultural matters, an institution for cooperation with the Government should be formed. Sectoral unions also have to be strengthened at the central level. The matter of work-free Saturdays is to be discussed by the Government with trade unions, including Solidarity. Hence, new structures should be established and managed.

There is a difficult situation in the state and economic administration. There is pressure on the authorities, e.g. railway workers who do not accept pay rises as part of the Gdańsk agreement; railway workers' demands are estimated at an additional six to nine billion złoty. The accepted principles need to be observed and no pay rises granted. The hunger strike at the railway can transform into paralysis of the railway system, which is being signaled by minister Zajfryd. The question arises as to whether Cde. Jagielski should talk to Wałęsa about the railway workers issue.

There is a complex situation in the market. We purchase [too] few potatoes. There are problems with coal. We have to give five million tons to the socialist countries. If we do not give Austria coal, they will withhold our dollar loan. On the meat question, a voucher rationing system is proposed; also for butter, oils and sugar. We may produce 1,200,000 tons of sugar this year. The industry experiences problems with supply and cooperation. There is a lack of cooperative supply of 35 billion złoty. Supplies and coal distribution control have to be carried out in the communes; there are too many receipts, hence there might be abuses.

110

defeated by internal pluralism (handwritten)

We need 350 million złoty in foreign currency for purchases; they do not send us anything in this situation. Aid from socialist countries could solve some of the problems for us. We expect a lot from the talks with Baibakov.[7]

The spirit of the directors of work institutes has to be raised; the Cde. proposes to convene sessions in ministries with the participation of CC secretaries (with referrals from ministers).

The health problem has to be taken off the agenda for the forthcoming meeting. Instead, information about the situation in agriculture and the supply of agricultural products should be provided.

Cde. Stanisław Kania: Good proposal.

Cde. Jerzy Waszczuk: When evaluating the situation, society expresses its longing for peace and order. There are also negative occurrences such as a decrease of trust in the authorities (in the period of the Sixth Plenum, 30 percent of the respondents in a poll by the Center for Public Opinion Research of the Polish Radio had a positive view; currently [it is] only nine percent). The impact of Solidarity will grow because there is a conviction that Solidarity will organize social life better than the party.

A fight with the anti-socialist elements needs to be conducted: a simple one through publicizing persons and their biographies, but also a more complex one, [expressing] views and giving our positive riposte. We need a clear ideological platform, with defined boundaries. Currently, there is a variety of views from the left to the right in the party—the platform to be worked out would consolidate the party. Wider intellectual support for the party is also needed.

Strengthening the leadership role of the party is currently the most important matter but our arguments in this domain are not convincing. The concept of the leadership role of the party in the present phase needs to be elaborated in practical ways: to profoundly substantiate the role of the party and of socialist democracy (not just that a bourgeois opposition party cannot exist).

A platform of political understanding needs to be shaped by presenting the rightfulness of the party and joining forces against anarchy; those who are in favor of the rightfulness of the state, against extremists—open the press forum for them.

The situation in three circles is of great significance.

1. *Journalists.*

Two hundred and fifty party members are delegates for the APJ Congress. The situation in this circle is complex. We have good chief editors, but the situation is worse within the journalists' ranks. There is embitterment, a feeling of moral guilt, demands for guarantees against manipulation, ensuring the right to personal views (they claim they are creators). The association is to defend these guarantees. There is a need to correctly draw the boundaries for the creative character of this occupation. A meeting with the delegates for the APJ Congress—mem-

[7] Nikolai Konstantinovich Baibakov was chairman of Gosplan, the Soviet state planning agency.

bers of the party—is planned for October 28 of this year. There is a group of extremists within the journalists' circle which is putting forward the idea of a meeting without party members.

2. *Writers.*

The date of the congress has been successfully moved to the end of December. The Woroszylski group wanted to hold a congress at an earlier stage. There is a 100-person KOR group among the writers. We have influence among 200 writers in Warsaw and in the regions. An open meeting of UPW members will take place on November 3 of this year. We are trying to form an alliance with Catholic writers and hold talks with less active KOR members. Within writers' circles, an attempt is being made to boycott the governing board, which would include party members. Our side proposes to attract proponents of a governing board that exists today.

3. *Artists.*

A complex situation has emerged also in that circle. We do not have influence among young artists. The prospect for tomorrow is terrifying. We produce 30 films annually and have 120 directors in the Youth Association. A young writer also does not have a chance to publish a book, and there are about 300 of them. Therefore, the problem of self-fulfillment and maturing of young artists is being brought up. Hence emerges the rage of this youth in the process of breaking up the existing structures.

Cde. Zdzisław Kurowski: Youth organizations have always had an impact on a third of all the youth.

Cde. Tadeusz Grabski: The situation is getting worse since the Sixth Plenum of the CC; the popularity of Solidarity is on the rise. The political situation will worsen in the nearest future. The disorganization of economic life is becoming apparent. Solidarity wants to throw the government to its knees, to hold it on a leash; there is pressure on the electoral law, threats of manifestations and demonstrations. The Cde. does not exclude complications. We will say "no" at some point if there are to be clashes and disturbances. The decision about a confrontation does not have to come from us. The issue is being taken up by Honecker and Bil'ak.[8]

The party should be strengthened; we will not recover three million members, but maybe one to one-and-a-half million. Go for the stratification of Solidarity. Their program has met with resistance in the Katowice voivodeship. We have to explain what they understand by renewal, e.g. doctors from Bielsko-Biała will grant sick leave to everybody (this is sabotage).

---

[8] Erich Honecker was the East German party leader and Vasil Bil'ak a member of the CPCz Presidium. Both were hardliners who favored harsh action against the Polish opposition.

We cannot concede with regard to pay rises in the railway industry. The program of railway workers is absurd; they will not be gentle toward us. We should go for elections in Solidarity in order to have a partner in setting plans. Involve them in the discussion concerning work-free Saturdays, the voucher rationing system, etc.

Cde. Zdzisław Kurowski: The processes of reorienting ways of thinking need to be accelerated. In the party, there is clarity with respect to what people from behind Solidarity aim at; there is no such clarity in society. One should think over what statements they will promote and how to fight them. They talk about: elections in the party, electoral law (also party members). Anxiety is growing that the authorities "on their knees" cannot execute power well. We should invest in strengthening discipline. There is a widespread view that renewal has to do with Solidarity and not with the party. We should discuss what should be done for the party to gain credibility. We will not provide information only about negative occurrences. We will recommend:

1. preparing the *aktiv* to explain registration;
2. explaining that we will have a different attitude toward Solidarity after its registration. Inclusion in the statute is necessary to gain trust in Solidarity. Those who do not want that inclusion do not want that trust. We are dealing with a new stage of the struggle for the political image of the workers' movement. The party wants to take over the initiative for renewal in work institutes.

The following should be explained:

1. the issue of a congress—how we want to hold it and what the envisaged role of the party is;
2. the program and what is going to be in it;
3. reform of the educational system, the system of speedy information; introduce new slogans into political work.

The Cde. supported the proposal concerning the program of improving the economic situation, preparing the 1981 plan, and meeting with segments of workers' self-government.

Cde. Stanisław Gabrielski: The situation among the youth is complex. There is a longing for spiritual and moral values. Questions arise: what is socialism, how to interpret it, how to interpret the leading role, socialist democracy, why there cannot be a second party? Young people travel abroad, they watch, study the problems. They do not like ideological subjects because actual problems are avoided during their course. Therefore there is a need to develop clubs of Marxist thought. Eighty percent of the youth declare themselves to be believers. Therefore, clubs of rationalist and religious studies need to be revived. In some circles unorganized youth constitutes about 80 percent. A key has to be found to the intellectual leaders of the youth.

More attention needs to be paid to the socialization of the youth movement, the numbers of paid jobs have to be reduced, more young workers have to be introduced into the *aktiv*. Conditions need to be created for the emergence of youth movement leaders, 40-year-olds should not be in the youth movement. A vision of the young generation needs to be shown, a social vision of our system. Disintegrating processes are taking place in the youth movement; there is criticism of the Federation; there should be more of a partnership within it. The USPY Federation was an empty organism. Approaching the rural youth with a program is an urgent task. A RYU revival is taking place.

The ideological front at the universities does not engage in actual problems. The SUPS is worried by the situation in the Gdańsk circles. People talk about Gdańsk socialism, about socialism with a human face. A process of SUPS cooperation with new trade unions should develop.

Cde. Zbigniew Zieliński: The Cde. shares the views of Cdes. Barcikowski and Kurowski regarding the political situation. Political affairs are intertwined with economic [affairs]. The Gorzów example is so far an isolated one. In "Elan" in Toruń an attempt to call the CWS has been rejected. An economic forum has been called and it went well. The situation in the "Diwilana" in Łódź is similar.

Contacts with new trade unions should be sought on the self-government platform. Workers' councils, e.g. in Ursus, were dominated by Mazowsze, 50 percent of workers need to be selected to the revived CWS's. Good workers need to be appointed as chairmen of the CWS's. However, changes in the CWS code of practice are not to be recommended.

There is a lack of management of supplies for production in the country. The registration of reserves is taking place (e.g. in the Ministry of Light Industry). In the coal mining industry incomplete teams worked on a work-free Saturday and Jastrzębie did not begin to work. In Legnica voivodeship, a return to the four-brigade system is being prepared (coalminer five days, coalmine six days).

There is a shortage of fuels; supplies from Iraq are not coming; [there is] a shortfall of 25,000 tons of fuel. A few-days-long ban on car usage is being contemplated.

Staff intimidation has not been overcome yet; sector consultations need to be held and administration needs to be revived.

Cde. Józef Pińkowski: Proposes engaging in talks with the USSR on the question of making surpluses of petroleum (about 400,000 tons) available to us.

Cde. Jerzy Wojtecki: The influence of Solidarity among peasants in the southeastern regions of the country is increasing, also in the Gdańsk voivodeship. Forty thousand peasants belong to Solidarity. The guidelines on agricultural policy are too general. Rural self-government needs to be developed, supplies granted, and statutes of agricultural associations presented for discussion; also the Congress of the CUAC should be accelerated. We are dealing with pressures to restore old systems in the countryside cooperative movement. Discussion is continuing on the profitability of production; this has not been achieved due to milk prices since January 1; the costs of changes that are being proposed will not be small. The fodder balance is bad because potato collections are below 30 million tons. Meat production will fall by over 250,000 tons. In the countryside, voices in favor of reactivating the RYU, mainly from the UPP, are becoming active. Hence, the autonomy of rural youth needs to be shaped and the UPP activated. The party is practically not operating in the countryside. The UPP is proceeding in its own way and it is said that its solutions are better. Tomorrow the UPP plenum will take place. The draft of the propositions was also unacceptable because it contained, among other things, criticism of the economic-financial system of the state, and demanded the establishment of peasant trade unions. In the Gucwa report, these statements have been eliminated. As far as the joint PUWP CC and UPP CC [Chief Committee] document is concerned, it contains the fundamental statement that a peasant is the constant element of economic policy. Discussions should be held with the VC, the commune leaders, and secretaries of the commune committees to stop the policy of not selling land to peasants and transferring it to the SF's, which lease it to peasants. At the Sejm, agricultural issues have to be considered, and, in particular, more needs to be said about the agricultural supplies than in the Guidelines.

Cde. Stanisław Kania: We are dealing with advantageous transformations in party organizations, institute and voivodeship committees, with the youth's readiness to fight for principles. This was discussed at the session of the VC's first secretaries. It is good that the existing dangers were exposed. If we do not define limits, it will be indispensable to be aware of the real grounds on which we act and the direction in which the situation will develop. The situation is characterized by distrust toward the authorities and demands for their credibility. The enemy's activity is developing against this background. Solidarity's activity is a source of difficulties, which are also influenced by the current situation in the country. There is substantial linkage between the adversary and Solidarity, with students and with peasants. There are threats in artist circles, in the mass media (e.g. the Wrocław center); there is pressure to eliminate censorship.

Phenomena in the socio-economic sphere are complicated in nature. Truly dramatic situations are taking place in the market, e.g. in the supply of potatoes or coal. It could be balanced in the statistics; we can determine who is guilty, but there is no coal in reserve. Supplies in institutes are poor; they [institutes] may even stop working. For agriculture, this is the worst year of this decade. The fear of what is going on today might influence the situation next year, e.g. sowing seeds, lack of fertilizers and potatoes.

The party is embittered and disarmed. There is severe criticism of neglects, vehement pressure for elections based from the PPO to Congress, elections to the Sejm (voices from the bottom and from the middle). And this might already concern the position of the authorities. The intentions of those who talk about the Congress and elections are diverse and the adversary is interested in power. The market in particular could be an explosive element. If we do not improve the situation in those areas, our fight with the adversary will not be effective.

The weak side of the Secretariat discussion was the lack of organizational proposals for the format of our activity.

1. There is a need to prepare a set of endeavors making the VI Congress line more concrete on the scale of the Politburo and the CC Secretariat, which I am requesting for the third time. If it is true that confidence in the authorities is falling, this is because there is too much whining that few things have moved forward. In the course of the next few days, a plan with names and dates needs to be drawn up; we should discuss what should occur each day. There has been talk about the need for changes at the leading positions of the national councils; three weeks have passed since the Sixth Plenum and there are no facts. Things are similar with respect to economic moves; here we are also late by two weeks. These matters are being prepared by Cdes. Z. Kurowski, Z. Zieliński, T. Grabski.

Cde. Zdzisław Kurowski: All things have been worked out; we only lack information.

Cde. Stanisław Kania: It cannot be that things have been set and nothing is happening, nothing comes out of it for us; no tasks have been set in the defined time-frame. We must demand concrete decisions from the CC Departments and voivodeship committees, and any marginal strike or hunger strike puts us off track. A group of VC secretaries should be invited and we should demand their plans. Currently, there is a lot of talk, but few concrete moves. Previously, it has also not been words but practice that has gone wrong. The government has worked on such a plan; it is good that it is ready. It has been decided that on Wednesday, October 29, a plan will be ready. Instructions for the directors of the CC Departments will be issued by the secretaries.

2. There is a need to define the lines of agreement and division. It is a simplification to say that it is only about Kuroń and Mazowiecki. Demagogy comes first. Our propaganda on the state of the functioning of the economy is vague. The situation is dramatic, but this issue does not function in the [sphere of] propaganda (e.g. in daily broadcasts on the radio) while the presentation of this state of affairs would be sobering. We must carry out a defense of ideological values; they need to be defended not only by means of peaceful arguments, but also arguments in case of threats, when they want to undermine fidelity to socialism.

It was recommended that in the ideological section groups of people be separated for the fight for socialist awareness against demagogy, for the leading role of the party.

3. A lot of attention is required on our side in ensuring provisions for the population. Analyze whether this could be done without consultation with Solidarity. If there are mixed opinions on this matter, then they will always find something to make the situation more difficult.

It was proposed that we consider the proposal as to who should be consulted on the voucher rationing option. Concrete conclusions need to be presented for the forthcoming meeting of the Politburo.

Cde. Władysław Kruczek: It will want to eliminate the export of meat.

Cde. Stanisław Kania: A rationing system will be proposed.

On Monday, October 27, Cde. J. Wojtecki will present concrete steps on the purchases of potatoes for the population, even with a proposal to raise their price.

At the Politburo meeting, there should be a presentation on how the population was actually supplied with heating fuel for the winter.

4. Regarding party issues, first of all, ideological boundaries need to be defined. On the one hand—the pro-party position, on the other—extraneousness. It ought to be contemplated whether an article should be published or a statement made on that matter. The verification policy is wrong, but a purification of the party is needed. Today, it would be hard to say who is to verify whom, e.g., at the Copernicus University the best would be eliminated. The possibility of dissolution of some of the PPO's, e.g. in Towimor, is not to be excluded.

It was decided that a resolution should be undertaken on the question of belonging to the party, the ideological position, and defense of party members. A draft of the resolution will be prepared by a team led by Cdes A. Werblan, W. Kruczek, and Z. Kurowski.

5. Party staff. Party members need to be quickly freed of accusations. The preceding activity of the CPCC is weak in this domain. The innocent should be defended from attacks (example of Cde. Waligórski from Poznań). It is good that following Cde. Pińkowski's intervention, a paper was issued on the matter of single family homes. Dealing with this matter ought to be the most important task for the CPCC.

6. The situation in the party varies from one voivodeship to another. The information apparatus of the Organizational Department should be restructured. It is not appropriate geographically and poor in reporting about the party's activities. Endangered points should be presented separately and observed as the situation evolves (Gdańsk, Wrocław); and more discipline should be introduced.

7. The leadership's contact with basic party organizations is weak; we benefit little from it. The issue of visits and statements of the Buro members should be considered; it should be reported on television and in the press; the provision of information by the leadership concerning the internal problems of the party, the economy, ideology and the market should be managed. Cycles of such statements should be planned.

Cde. Jerzy Waszczuk: We must get ready for statements on subjects planned in advance. A plan of such statements is being prepared (two statements and four articles in the press).

Cde. Stanisław Kania:

1. Information about the current situation in the country should be prepared for the Politburo meeting on October 28 of this year—Cde. Kazimierz Barcikowski.

2. The issue concerning Piotr Jaroszewicz. I suggest that the issue be passed on to the CPCC for consideration and evaluation of his responsibility. This

should be resolved together with the issue of Edward Gierek. In an article on the slander of the decade, M. Rakowski proposes that the Sejm examine the positive and negative sides of the decade. The issue is important, but should be the subject of evaluation during preparations for the Ninth Congress of the party and during the course of the Congress itself.

Cde. Andrzej Werblan: Proposed to put together a white book of responsibility and a proposal to create CC working groups.

Cde. Zbigniew Zieliński: The comrade informed that over 100 journalists came to Wrocław.

Cde. Jerzy Waszczuk: This is a conference of journalists called by Solidarity before the APJ Congress.

Cde. Zbigniew Zieliński: The journalists intend to describe the hunger strike of the railway workers.

Cde. Jerzy Waszczuk: The problem of supporting the Wrocław radio station was taken up; the deputy head of the Press, Radio, and Television Departments of the CC; Cde. T. Zaręba and Cde. Bajdor from the Radio Committee were sent there. Tapes were examined and reports prepared in favor of the strikers, and were released with the consent of the Secretary of the VC, Cde. Siuda. The VC is opposed to shutting down the radio station; influence can still be won within it, although the talks have not been skillfully conducted so far and there was an incident with the film.

Cde. Stefan Olszowski: Our attitude toward the tax on price increases should be presented once again in *Gazeta Robotnicza*.

Cde. Stanisław Kania: What is our attitude toward Solidarity in the APJ?

Cde. Jerzy Waszczuk: Solidarity has inconsiderable influence among journalists; however, a larger amount among the radio technicians. They were told that their role can be of a social-welfare character and not involve interference with the program. They accepted this verbal declaration. We have an additional option in case of difficulties: the General Staff center (in the Palace of Culture) with a military staff and two military newspapers are on the alert to print. There is a field plan. One and a half thousand out of 8,000 radio and television workers belong to Solidarity, among whom 1,200 are technicians.

Cde. Stanisław Kania: There has to be a response to the initial attempts to take action.

Cde. Stefan Olszowski: The third program of the radio is penetrated by Solidarity.

[Source: AAN, PUWP CC, 2254, pp. 342–370. Translated by Paweł Świeboda.]

Document No. 14: Transcript of Bulgarian (BCP CC) Politburo Meeting

October 25, 1980

Poland's "fraternal allies" in the Warsaw Pact reacted with varying degrees of concern to the August strikes and their aftermath. Bulgaria's Todor Zhivkov, traditionally a close adherent to the Soviet line, was not as vocal as some of his fellow leaders but clearly took a hard-line stance toward the crisis. At the heart of the Bulgarian leader's concerns is the possible spread of popular disaffection to other member-states of the bloc, with potentially far-reaching consequences. Although these discussions frequently blame Western interference for such crises, several interesting and candid points are raised below about the mass scale of the internal opposition in Poland and the restraining role being played by Western countries.

[...]

Petŭr Mladenov: [...] A few words about Poland. Everything said in comrade Zhivkov's letter is principled and true. The counter-revolutionary forces in Poland are, to our great regret, on an active offensive. These counter-revolutionary forces have already become conscious of their own strength. The continuous retreat of the PUWP and its leaders and our silence, comrade Zhivkov—I have in mind our silence as a community, as the Warsaw Pact, since we are writing something and saying something—gives the counter-revolutionary forces in Poland confidence that they can achieve right away, at this stage, something more. At the same time fear of an internal reaction on the part of the [security] forces, such as the militia, is observed among them. It turns out that the militia is a detachment of 70,000 people armed with modern weapons, including machine-guns, armored carriers etc. These are arms which can be used not only in street actions, but also to fight a battle.

Todor Zhivkov: Plus the workers' detachments.

Petŭr Mladenov: This is the internal militia. Their leaders have said they are ready to act, but a political decision is needed. Someone has to decide that. By the way, I think that there is a fear among the counter-revolutionary forces of a certain reaction on the part of the army or the militia. Fear is being shown concerning eventual outside interference. And at the same time I think that it is correct to see that the West, too, is afraid of a conflict on a large scale.

Alexander Lilov: Through Poland it may well be possible.

Petŭr Mladenov: At the moment the Western countries such as the Federal Republic of Germany, and both the USA and France, if you like, are playing a restraining role in regard to the extremes of the counter-revolution in Poland.

119

So that it can be noted that the internal counter-revolutionary forces, on the one hand, exult, and on the other hand show signs of nervousness for the future.

There is the following question: sometimes we compare what is happening in Poland with what happened in Czechoslovakia. I think there is an essential difference. It is true that the aims are more or less the same. But the essential difference, in my opinion, is in the fact that while in Czechoslovakia, Jiři Pelikan and [Alexander] Dubček came out as separate heroes and personalities, here the masses in their millions came out. This is the essential difference. They are already speaking of eight million Solidarity with their trade unions.

About the PUWP's stand. For me, at least, there are many unclear things. I agree with what Comrade Zhivkov has written and analyzed. I do not know how it will seem to you, it may be very exaggerated, but it seems to me that everything that is happening in Poland at the moment is with the consent of the senior party leadership of Poland. What they call renewal is, in my opinion, a search for a new model of socialism. What does renewal in the Polish way mean? It is a search for a new model of socialism, a model that will differ from what we understand by socialism. We say that maybe they will be [inclined] towards the Yugoslav model. I am afraid that they will not go towards the Yugoslav model, they are rather seeking a model that would get them near to Sweden or to Austria under [Chancellor Bruno] Kreisky, a model which would have pluralism in the sphere of politics and of ideology. They will not go towards de-nationalizing the factories and plants. Those will remain state [property]. There are such in America, too. But that is no longer socialist property.

By the way, all that will lead to a change of the character of the party. And it is heading for that. In my opinion in Poland there are essential deviations from the theory and practice of socialism. It is clear that the ideological basis for communism is Marxist philosophy. People who believe in God, i.e. who profess idealism, could easily become members of their party. Apparently radical changes will also occur in the character of their party.

I think that the Politburo should authorize Comrade Zhivkov to write a letter to Comrade Brezhnev, to the Politburo of the Central Committee of the CPSU, which would comprise our analysis and a suggestion for an eventual meeting— bilateral or multilateral for a start. Further, it should aim for a search for an internal solution in Poland. Perhaps it is right for them to be advised,[9] or more precisely, for a state of emergency to be introduced. I do not know if there are forces there that can introduce it. It is correct to undertake a massive denunciation of the forces of reaction and counter-revolution and [to also undertake] a general offensive. It should contribute to the introduction of discipline in the party.

Stanko Todorov: The trouble is that the party does not regard what is happening as the act of reactionary forces.

---

[9] As written in the original. It is also possible, though not probable, that the phrase might mean: "for them to ask advice".

Petûr Mladenov: Perhaps further they will have to solve the question of the church, of agriculture etc. The question here lies in this—are there internal forces which can accomplish this? We are the Politburo and we can say: if there are no internal forces, we must be ready for an intervention. If we leave Poland, we will have to be ready to leave the German Democratic Republic, too; we will have to be ready for a war on a large scale.

Todor Zhivkov: First Romania and Yugoslavia, then the German Democratic Republic. I said to Stambolic: after Poland come Romania and Yugoslavia, and then the German Democratic Republic.

Petûr Mladenov: I think we have to act quickly, that we missed the most opportune moment. America is on the eve of elections. Unfortunately the elections have come, they are tomorrow, the day after tomorrow. When America is on the eve of elections, it is paralyzed; before elections there is no one to decide. [...]

Dobri Dzhurov: [...] Personally I think that help for the Polish comrades could be expressed by sending the assessments and conclusions our Politburo made in its meetings on [October] 21 and now, which have been presented in the main in Comrade Zhivkov's two letters to the PUWP Politburo.

[...]

In the second place, we ought to acquaint the CPSU and the fraternal parties with our assessments and conclusions with an emphasis on our anxiety over the further worsening of the situation in Poland. I think that in this respect we ought by no means to be slow. Things there are going headlong [down] a steep slope and any delay may confront us with a new, additional situation that will be more difficult than the one we are now discussing. [...]

Ognyan Doinov: [...] That is why the assessment that no country or party is insured against events similar to the ones that have developed in Poland is very correct. Certainly, they can unfold in a different manner for each country, but, lest such events happen, precisely the work our party did and all of its efforts during previous years have been extremely necessary and urgent.

Now, of course, there are no real conditions in our country for [having] concrete fears of the [possible] effect of the Polish events on the life of our party or on the life of our working people, although we see particular adverse processes in neighboring Yugoslavia. There, however, they do not play the liberal as in Poland, but have arrested 300 people. [...]

I think, however, that Comrade Zhivkov very rightly puts the problems of our party, of our party and state leadership, at the center of our attention. I went through [it] and I see that in the report 12 pages have been allotted to the situation in Poland and more than 60 pages to our practical work. And this is not accidental, because we, together with the other socialist countries, will do what we can, will render our international assistance, [will demonstrate] our solidarity with the Polish working people. But we must seriously turn back to the problems our party has to solve, particularly on the eve of the Twelfth Congress. [...]

Lyudmila Zhivkova: [...] I think it will be right, as comrade Petûr Mladenov has also pointed out, [for] comrade Todor Zhivkov to take the initiative and write a letter to Comrade Brezhnev and pose the question either of an international meeting of party and state leaders of the socialist countries, or of a bilateral meeting. Obviously the socialist countries must make a collective decision on how to act further in connection with the developments in Poland.

Naturally, at that meeting and [also] when working out a collective decision, it will be judged which of all possible variants is the most expedient in order [for us] to be able to really help the party and the state leadership of Poland to control and gain command of the situation, which is increasingly revealing random tendencies and occurrences. It is obvious there is no leading force there to gain command of the situation, to create prerequisites and conditions for all unresolved problems and questions in the development of Poland to be correctly solved, and at the same time for the social and political life of that country to return to normal without departing from party policy or from the main principles on which socialist society is built.

No doubt the problems and questions of Polish society today, the difficulties the Communist party and socialist development in Poland are facing are a serious reason for a lesson to be learned by the socialist countries. All socialist countries will draw a lesson that will be a lesson for the whole socialist order, for the whole socialist community, for further forms and methods [to follow] in the conditions under which this community has to develop, and for its part in the development of international processes and international occurrences. [...]

Todor Zhivkov: [...] It has once more been suggested that we take the initiative with regard to the Polish events. I fully agree with this. The ambassador of the Soviet Union in our country, who is a member of the Central Committee, is not in the country now. He will return perhaps today or tomorrow. On Monday I will meet with him and after that meeting it will be decided what I am to do. Perhaps he will inform [us] of some things.

I think that the Secretariat of the Central Committee should very seriously draw an overall conclusion from the speeches made here at the two meetings of the Politburo, extract the questions raised and draw conclusions. Some questions have to be put to the Secretariat for a decision, to the Council of Ministers or to the State Council, and others may be put to the Politburo.

Comrades, *the main conclusion* we ought to draw—there are many conclusions—is that we should *change the style and methods of [our] work*.

[...]

[Source: Bulgarian Central State Archive, Fond 1B, Opis 66, Folder 2617a; Transcript from the BCP CC Politburo held October 21–25, 1980. Translated by Detelina Dineva.]

Document No. 15: Transcript of CPSU CC Politburo Meeting

October 29, 1980

*Throughout the crisis, the Polish and Soviet leaderships were in regular commu-
nication, occasionally including face-to-face meetings. This Soviet Politburo session focused on preparations for such a meeting on October 30 with party leader
Kania and Prime Minister Józef Piñkowski. Several important points are raised
here that appear continuously throughout this period. Brezhnev and others discuss
the prospect of declaring martial law to restore order, seemingly unclear only as to
the timing of the decision. Defense Minister Dmitri Ustinov, one of the members of
the Politburo's commission on Poland, declares that Soviet forces are in full combat
readiness if needed—raising the question later of whether Moscow ever seriously
considered deploying the military. The participants also bring up the unwelcome tendency of Poland's leaders to vacillate and shy away from firm action, another theme
throughout the crisis. The Soviet leaders point to signs of Jaruzelski's lack of resolve,
which would bedevil the Kremlin in coming months, although at this stage no one is
yet calling into question the Poles' commitment to the party or to Moscow. Finally,
the group pays considerable attention to the likelihood that Poland will ask for various forms of additional economic aid from all the socialist states, which will place a
considerable burden on the already stretched donor countries.*

[…]

1. Materials for the friendly working visit of Polish leaders to the USSR.

Brezhnev: Tomorrow First Secretary of the PUWP CC Cde. Kania and Chairman of the PPR Council of Ministers Cde. Piñkowski will arrive in our country. The Commission consisting of Cdes. Suslov, Gromyko, Andropov, Ustinov,
Chernenko, Zimyanin and Rusakov has presented materials for discussion with
the Polish leaders. I have attentively read these materials. I consider that the
comrades have answered all the fundamental questions. Perhaps someone has
observations to make; if so, let us please discuss them.

Ustinov: I also have carefully read the materials that have been prepared.
I consider that they are of high quality and cover all the questions. The most important thing is that all the questions here have been put very sharply, just as they
should be put to the Polish leaders.

Brezhnev: There is truly a fully raging counter-revolution in Poland, but statements in the Polish press and by the Polish comrades say nothing about this;
nothing is being said about the enemies of the people. But you know it is the
enemies of the people, the direct accomplices of the counter-revolution and the
counter-revolutionaries themselves who are speaking out against the people.
How can this be?

Andropov: Really, there is no direct formulation either in the press, on the radio or on television of the problem that there is evidence of counter-revolution in Poland. Even the Polish leaders do not talk about it.

Gromyko: The mass media are also hushing up this question.

Andropov: Instead of exposing anti-socialist elements, the Polish press is placing heavy emphasis on the inadequacies in the CC leadership, etc. One must speak directly about the enemies of the Polish socialist system. Anti-socialist elements like Wałęsa and Kuroń want to take power away from the workers. The Polish leaders should have said that openly, but we do not see that anywhere in the Polish press.

Brezhnev: The Sejm is already beginning to take it away from them, but they speak as though the army stands with them. Wałęsa travels from one end of the country to the other, from city to city. Everywhere they bestow honor on him, but the Polish leaders hold their tongues and the press and television also do not come out against these anti-socialist elements. Maybe it really will be necessary to introduce martial law.

Andropov: I believe that the facts testify to the Polish leaders' lack of understanding of the seriousness of the current situation.

Ustinov: I absolutely agree with the text of the materials prepared by the comrades. Our Polish friends conduct many conversations but they make no sense whatsoever. You know, it's gone so far that Wałęsa and others of his minions have occupied the radio station in Wrocław. As a matter of fact, they are duplicating Gierek's style in their work. You know, they have not imprisoned anybody, they have not punished any of the enemies of the working class.

Brezhnev: In Yugoslavia not long ago there was a small strike, but they reacted to it seriously. They arrested 300 people and threw them in prison.

Ustinov: If martial law is not introduced, then things will become very complicated and will get even more complicated. There is vacillation in the army. But our Northern Group of Forces is prepared and in a state of full battle readiness.

Gromyko: We must speak to our Polish friends firmly and sharply. They must say all of this to the people in the first instance, so that the people will understand the full acuteness of the current situation, because now they are criticizing Gierek, the CC and the party. However, at the other extreme the anti-socialist elements, who are literally unbridled, are given a free hand.

As far as Cde. Jaruzelski is concerned, of course he is a trustworthy person but nonetheless he is now beginning to talk somehow without passion. He is even saying that the troops will not move against the workers. On the whole, I think we must talk to the Poles about all of this, and very sharply.

Brezhnev: When Jaruzelski spoke with Kania about who should play the leading role, he flatly refused to become first secretary and recommended that Kania be first. That also says something.

Gromyko: I believe that all the basic questions have been formulated correctly in the prepared materials. As for the introduction of a state of emergency in Poland, that must be seen as a move aimed at preserving revolutionary gains. Of course, it might not be introduced immediately and, even better, not right after the return of Cdes. Kania and Pińkowski from Moscow. We should wait for a period, but it is necessary to direct them towards that end, and we will have to fortify them. We cannot lose Poland. In the battle with the Hitlerites, while liberating Poland, the Soviet Union sacrificed 600,000 of its soldiers and officers and we cannot permit a counter-revolution.

Of course, Cdes. Kania, Jaruzelski and Pińkowski are honorable and devoted comrades. When I had a conversation with them in Warsaw, they felt keenly about everything that was being discussed. Kania was even literally shaken to the core. At the same time, he enjoys substantial trust in the party.

Brezhnev: The anti-socialist elements have let themselves go to such an extent that they are repudiating the decisions of the Warsaw voivode court with respect to the judgments it has made on the registration of the "Solidarity Union." Further, they are acting threateningly concerning the opinion of the deputies of the Sejm. What is next?

Suslov: In my opinion, the prepared materials are of good quality. Everything has been considered. Today's leaders of the PPR are not sufficiently strong people but they are honorable, the best of the leadership core. True, Olszanski does poor quality work. Moczar is a leftist; he can do a lot of harm. They must initiate a counter-attack and not go on the defensive. Such a position is reflected in the materials we are reviewing today.

Brezhnev: They must have self-defense detachments.

Andropov, Suslov, Ustinov state that such a step is essential. Defense detachments should be created and should even be mobilized in the barracks, and possibly armed in advance.

Suslov: At one time we wrote a letter to Gomułka so that he would not take up arms against the workers, but in reality they did not respond to our influence then. At that time the Polish leadership used weapons.

Ponomarev: The documents that have been prepared for discussions with the Polish leaders are consistent; everything here is practical. Our alarm is strongly expressed in the materials. We must bring this alarm to the attention of the Polish leaders.

Gromyko: Perhaps we should give these materials to the Polish leaders.

Andropov: If we distribute them, it cannot be ruled out that they will wind up with the Americans.

Brezhnev: That could well happen.

Rusakov: Let them listen attentively to Leonid Ilyich and take notes.

Grishin: Leonid Ilyich, you must begin the discussion and express our unease. Then let them respond. The documents that have been prepared are good.

Tikhonov: Of course, Leonid Ilyich, you must begin your presentation according to this material and set forth everything that is written here. We are inviting them here in order to express our alarm at the situation in Poland. Everything concerning all questions has been stated very well in the materials. Currently in Poland there is evidence of activities by counter-revolutionary elements. Let them say what is happening, why they have allowed this; let them explain. Communists are leaving the party, in fear of anticommunist elements. That is how far this has already gone.

Rusakov: I believe that everything has been considered in the document, but Kania may pose certain other questions that are not considered in these materials. One such question is about cadres. In particular, they will apparently raise the question of removing Jabłoński, Werblan, Kowalczyk and Kruczek from the Politburo. But it must be said that Kruczek is of some use. He is an authoritative comrade, and in the past was a trade union figure.

A second question Cde. Kania might raise is about multilateral assistance to Poland from the socialist countries. The point is that Kania opposes such assistance. I say this because in the materials Cde. Baibakov has mentioned international assistance to Poland, but the Polish comrades say they do not have the same situation as in Hungary or in Czechoslovakia.[10]

One other question may arise. The Poles do not have especially good relations with certain neighboring socialist countries, for example with the GDR. Earlier, Poland and the GDR had a so-called visa-less regime. Taking advantage of this, Polish citizens went to the GDR and bought up produce and food products. The German comrades believe it is necessary to put an end to this system of visa-less border crossings, but the Poles of course oppose this. What should we do about it? I think that we should not get involved in this matter. Let them resolve the issue themselves. Everything else that is written in the document is good.

Chernenko: The materials that have been prepared by the Commission are comprehensive. They define the important, fundamental questions to which we must call the attention of the Polish comrades. In addition, the questions are posed very sharply. The current stark situation and the need to take drastic measures against the anti-socialist elements are addressed directly.

Kirilenko: The strikes began three months ago and they have not subsided in the least. We have done a great deal for Poland, we have given them everything and offered advice so that they might properly resolve the questions that have arisen. So far they have not enlisted the military in the struggle with the anti-socialist elements, and in fact they are not exposing them, as the comrades have correctly stated here. Currently, things are going poorly with the youth. The Komsomol as such is practically non-existent. There are also no youth detachments. Perhaps the military should be disguised and set loose among the working masses. Without a doubt communists must be mobilized as a first priority. Kania's strange inertia is becoming more and more incomprehensible to the leaders of the socialist countries. For example, when I held discussions with Husák and other Czech leaders, they expressed surprise at such behavior. The Czech comrades cited examples where they came out decisively against the strike initiators at one of the enterprises. And it produced the expected results.

[10] This is a reference to the events of 1956 in Hungary and 1968 in Czechoslovakia.

Gorbachev: I believe that the Politburo acted very properly in inviting the Polish leaders to Moscow for discussions. The Polish friends should speak openly and decisively. As long as they do not take necessary measures and assume some kind of defensive stance, they will not last long and could get tossed out themselves.

You, Leonid Ilyich, should begin the discussion. The text, in my opinion, is very good, I have no observations to make. It contains all the ideas which must be expressed to the Polish friends. Then, after your discussion we can hear them out. Then, perhaps some positions will emerge about which we should speak and exchange views.

Baibakov: If during the discussions Kania and Pińkowski raise questions about the economy, it should be noted that we received a letter from the Polish side on this matter. We were given instructions by the responsible comrades and we are preparing proposals for providing economic assistance. What can we provide? We can of course promise to extend credit in the amount of 280 million rubles, then give [additional] credit in the amount of 150 million rubles. This is short-term credit which they need now to pay off interest on loans. Further, we can say that we can increase fuel supplies somewhat in 1981, for example by 500 million rubles. Perhaps it will be possible to agree to cut back on imports of goods from Poland by approximately 250 million rubles, and overall in this way we will end up providing assistance in the amount of roughly 1 billion rubles. I think that nevertheless we may have to prepare letters to the fraternal parties. We have already written letters saying that we will have to supply them with somewhat less oil and petroleum products next year, that we will have to sell the petroleum products ourselves and transfer the money earned to the Polish People's Republic so that they can acquire what they need. We will have to withhold oil from all countries except Cuba, Mongolia and Vietnam. As far as grain, we have already decided on an amount of 500,000 tons; more than that we cannot give. Perhaps we will have to give some cotton and add 200,000 tons of diesel fuel. Further, we will obviously need to tell them that our economists will provide aid to Polish organizations in developing their national economic plan and in locating a way out of the impasse in which Poland finds itself—that is, some internal measures will need to be taken to facilitate this exit. We will address the socialist countries concerning a certain decrease in petroleum product supplies in connection with the events in Poland. Of course, they will all object, that is for sure. But what is to be done? We have no other way out and we will apparently have to use the one we have.

Brezhnev: What is the cost of oil now on the world market?

Baibakov: The cost of one ton of oil is 150 rubles, but a ton of benzine and a ton of diesel fuel cost 190 rubles each.

Arkhipov: In the memorandum there are economic questions. I think that in the discussion with Kania on these questions we must speak in a general way. We are preparing a piece of work, a draft has already been reviewed by my office today. We will work on it a little more and show it to N. A. Tikhonov. But it seems to me that in any case we should not give them oil and petroleum products because they cannot absorb them. There are strikes at their factories and plants, they are squandering fuel, and therefore it is better for us to sell them and give Poland the cash.

Rusakov: There was a letter from Cde. Kania on economic questions. They are asking us to elaborate an economic conception for the further development of the Polish economy and a way out of this impasse. I think that you, Leonid Ilyich, should give the reply to Kania that our comrades are working on these materials and will be providing this assistance.

Brezhnev: Evidently we should adopt the materials that have been presented and consider it advisable to be guided by our delegation in the negotiations with the Polish friends.

All: Correct.

[Source: RGANI, Fond 89, Opis 42, Delo 31. Translated by Malcolm Byrne for the National Security Archive.]

Document No. 16: Transcript of CPSU CC Politburo Meeting

October 31, 1980

As a follow-on to the previous document, this record of a Soviet Politburo session recaps a meeting the day before between Soviet leaders and Poland's Kania and Pińkowski. Brezhnev and his colleagues are pleased with most of the results of the meeting, which aimed at stressing the danger of the situation facing Poland while simultaneously boosting the Poles' confidence in their ability to deal with it. But other issues clearly raised concerns. For one, Kania underscored how heavily Poland depended on the West for economic aid. For another, he left the clear impression that while the Poles apparently had a plan for cracking down, if need be, they were nowhere near ready to implement the operation—as Brezhnev pointed out.

[...]

2. Toward the results of the visit to the USSR of First Secretary of the Polish United Workers' Party Cde. S. Kania and Chairman of the PPR Council of Ministers Cde. J. Pińkowski.

Brezhnev: We can say definitively that our meeting with the new Polish leaders was timely. Events in Poland are taking such a turn that if we waste time and do not correct the Polish comrades' position, then before we know it we will be facing a critical situation that will demand extraordinary and, one might say, painful measures.

The Polish comrades did not hide their alarm about the intensified activities of the anti-socialist forces. But when the subject turned to measures in the struggle with the counter-revolution, vacillation crept into their utterances.

They declared that Poland is bound by debts hand and foot. All imports from the West are based on credit, and the functioning of many enterprises and the condition of the domestic market depends upon them. Poland's economy has become dependent primarily on the West. In these conditions, our Polish comrades believe, any exacerbation of the situation in the country could create grounds for the capitalists to refuse further deferment of credits and Poland, in Kania's words, would be brought to its knees.

We asked Kania directly whether the party has a plan in case of an emergency in which an open threat to people's power arises. He said that there is a plan for that event and that they know who will have to be arrested and how to employ the army. But to all appearances they are not prepared to take such steps and are putting them off for the indefinite future.

I will not repeat the entire content of our discussions. The notes from the talks have been circulated and the comrades can acquaint themselves with them if they have not yet managed to do so.

As we said at the last session, the goal of the meeting with the Polish comrades was twofold. On the one hand, it was to help them understand the full depth of the danger and induce them to take more drastic actions. On the other hand it was to encourage them and reinforce their faith in their own strength and possibilities. I think that the talks were useful on both counts.

Kania, as I already said, displayed a definite reserve, at least on the question of introducing a state of emergency. As for other measures we proposed, he declared that he agrees with them. We also had a complete mutual understanding on the evaluation of the causes of the crisis and the scope of the counter-revolutionary threat.

Kania assured me that upon returning to Warsaw he will acquaint the PUWP CC Politburo with our point of view. They took meticulous notes of everything we said. True, Kania mentioned one reservation—that he would not inform certain members of the Politburo fully since he fears an intelligence leak to the West. It is important for the Polish leadership not to permit talk about the fact that they are acting on Moscow's orders.

As far as Kania and Pińkowski personally are concerned, they left a decent impression with me and apparently others who participated in the talks; these are serious, thoughtful people. It is clear what they are worth as political leaders and they can only be judged by their deeds.

The comrades will probably agree that at the moment we have done everything required of us on the Polish question. But of course we must stay on the alert. Conditions in Poland are literally in danger of exploding.

What ought to be accelerated is the provision of whatever economic aid we can [supply] that will enable the Poles to persevere in this difficult time. However hard it is for us, we must do this. Let us agree that all necessary proposals should be presented at the next session of the Politburo.

Perhaps Nikolai Aleksandrovich [Tikhonov] and other comrades wish to add to my report?

If not, then let us approve the results of the talks that have been held.

Andropov, Suslov, Kirilenko, Chernenko, Tikhonov state that the Polish leaders' invitation to come to the CPSU CC for a discussion was timely and crucial.

Brezhnev: There is a motion to approve the discussion.

All: Correct.

Tikhonov: Poland's economic situation is very serious. They are shouldering a large debt. They must now repay debts of roughly 500 million dollars. Beyond that, they are asking for a 150 million dollar turnover. We will prepare proposals.

Brezhnev: Prepare these proposals for the next session of the Politburo.

Tikhonov: Very well.

Arkhipov: We will prepare proposals jointly for the provision of aid to Poland and an appeal to the leaders of the fraternal countries for your signature, Leonid Ilyich.

Brezhnev: I think that these should not be linked. The appeal should be sent sooner.

Gromyko: I think that without a doubt they do not need to be linked. By the way, I will say a few words about the course of the negotiations. During the negotiations, Cdes. Kania and Piṅkowski said nothing about past policies, about Gierek's policy. They spoke about what is going on now and what they need.

Andropov: Thanks to this discussion the Polish comrades have begun to understand better their own situation. Upon his arrival in Warsaw, Cde. Kania said at the airport that he was very satisfied with the meeting with Leonid Ilyich and that Leonid Ilyich devoted his exclusive attention to the needs of Poland.

Brezhnev: They are afraid to mention the word counter-revolutionary. But listen to what Cde. Semenov reports from Bonn. He reports on a conversation with one of the Polish officials. Here, as you see, he speaks directly about an armed uprising in the PPR. How are the Polish comrades unable to understand the simple truth, that there is counter-revolution all around them?

Andropov: This is truly a serious observation. It requires thorough verification.

Ustinov: In any case, we must be very vigilant.

Chernenko: The discussion with the Polish comrades helped them to open their eyes to the actual situation that exists in Poland, and to evaluate conditions realistically and from the party's viewpoint. This will of course help them to be more energetic with respect to the measures they intend to take against the anti-socialist elements and to defend the gains of the socialist order.

[Source: RGANI, Fond 89, Opis 42, Delo 35. Translated by Malcolm Byrne for the National Security Archive.]

Document No. 17: Letter from Leonid Brezhnev to Erich Honecker

November 4, 1980

Following discussions with the Polish leadership and within the Soviet Politburo (see Document Nos. 15 and 16), the Kremlin decided it was vital to provide Poland with extra economic aid to help address one of the underlying problems facing the communist regime there. Moscow fully understood that this would cause hardships for the other satellite states that would have to give up some of their share of Soviet assistance in order to help Poland. That awareness is apparent in this personal appeal from Brezhnev to East German leader Erich Honecker to agree to a substantial cut in Soviet oil deliveries in 1981 in the name of "fraternal solidarity." The latter was already anxious about the crisis and its implications for the GDR. Honecker soon became a leading proponent of armed intervention in Poland.

[...]

Dear Erich!

After discussing the matter in the Politburo we decided to write to you and Comrades G. Husák, J. Kádár and T. Zhivkov with regard to an important, even extraordinary matter.

Recently, as you well know, we received Cdes. S. Kania and J. Pińkowski in Moscow. The situation in their country is extremely difficult. An acute need arises for all of us to help Poland survive the current crisis.

You know very well the political situation in the PPR. Counter-revolution is advancing and practically grabbing at the party's throat. At a recent meeting with the Polish friends we shared our considerations about the need to break the tide of events and to launch our own offensive against the forces of counter-revolution. We will inform you further about this meeting. In these conditions the situation in the economy acquires immense importance, and now it is near catastrophic. Further aggravation of the situation in Poland threatens to inflict grave damage on the entire socialist commonwealth. Therefore it is our internationalist, I would say our class, duty to do everything in our power not to allow this to happen.

I would say right away that we are assuming the main burden in this matter. In spite of our own economic problems, which I have reported to you, we judged it necessary to provide considerable financial and economic assistance to Poland by way of giving resources in freely convertible currency and by way of additional supplies of a number of goods and products.

But one cannot avoid certain contributions from other fraternal countries. When we weighed and discussed this issue, we, of course, understood well that it was not a simple matter. Therefore we wanted to come up with a solution that would minimally affect the fulfillment of your internal plans, one that you would be able to shoulder.

Specifically, we suggest cutting back somewhat on oil supplies to a number of the countries of the socialist commonwealth, the idea being to sell this oil on the capitalist market and to transfer the resulting currency on behalf of certain countries to Poland, in order to allow it to alleviate in part its critical financial situation and purchase some vitally needed foodstuffs and other products.

As for the GDR, if you agree, then the amount of oil supplies from the Soviet Union could be cut back in 1981 by 600–650,000 tons from the agreed level, all this without touching the level of supplies of German products to the Soviet Union.

I am asking you, Erich, to treat this suggestion with empathy. I am certain that this manifestation of fraternal solidarity will allow our Polish comrades to weather this difficult hour.

With communist greetings,

L. Brezhnev

[Source: SAPMO-BArch, ZPA, J IV 2/202–550. Translated by Vladislav Zubok.]

Document No. 18: Letter from Erich Honecker to Leonid Brezhnev

November 26, 1980

For weeks, East German concern had been building that events in Poland could spill across their shared border unless extreme action was taken to stem the crisis. In late November, SED leader Erich Honecker made the case to Brezhnev for an urgent meeting of Warsaw Pact party leaders to confront Poland's Stanisław Kania. Honecker was already on record saying to Kania's hard-line colleague, Stefan Olszowski, that bloodshed, while a last resort, was sometimes called for. In this letter to Brezhnev, Honecker pleads that to delay would mean the death of socialist Poland. The Soviet leader accedes to the entreaty and a momentous meeting eventually takes place on December 5 (see Document No. 22).

Esteemed Comrade Leonid Ilyich!

The Central Committee of the SED has discussed the current situation in Poland, and we have come to the unanimous conclusion that there is an urgent need for a meeting of the general secretaries and the first secretaries of the communist parties of our community of states. We believe that we should discuss the emerging situation in the People's Republic of Poland in order to work out collective emergency measures to assist our Polish friends in overcoming the crisis that, as you know, is escalating day after day.

Unfortunately, it already can be said that the visit of the Polish comrades to Moscow and the timely good advice to them has not had any decisive influence on the situation in Poland, which we all had been counting on.

According to information we have received from various channels, counter-revolutionary forces in the People's Republic of Poland are on the constant offensive,[11] and every delay is equivalent to death—the death of socialist Poland. Yesterday, our joint measures would have possibly been premature; today they are essential; tomorrow they could already be too late.

It would be advisable that we meet in Moscow for a day right after the Conference of the CC PVAP, whose decisions we believe will not significantly change the development of events in Poland.

---

[11] Among the events in this period that would have provoked Honecker's consternation was the so-called Narożniak affair, in which a volunteer in the Mazowsze branch of Solidarity, Jan Narożniak, was arrested on November 21 after the discovery in his apartment of a secret document from the general prosecutor's office calling for the fabrication of evidence against Solidarity. The Mazowsze branch demanded wide-ranging investigations into the general prosecutor's office that went beyond the August agreements, and threatened large-scale protests unless the authorities released Narożniak and the government employee who had leaked him the document.

As far as I know, Comrades Husák and Zhivkov have also expressed the desire that we urgently meet to discuss this issue. It would be best to do that next week. We believe that collective advice and possible assistance from Comrade Kania's allies can only help.

We ask you, esteemed Leonid Ilyich, to understand our extraordinary concern about the situation in Poland. We know that you also share these concerns.

With communist greetings,

E. Honecker
General Secretary of the SED CC

[Source: SAPMO-Barch ZPA, J IV 2/2-1868, B. 5–6. First published in Michael Kubina and Manfred Wilke, "Hart und kompromißlos durchgreifen:" Die SED contra Polen 1980/81: Geheimakten der SED-Führung über die Unterdrückung der polnischen Demokratiebewegung. *(Berlin: Akademie Verlag, 1994), pp. 122–123. Translated by Catherine Nielsen for the National Security Archive.]*

Document No. 19: Report of the Czechoslovak Army Chief of Staff to the Minister of National Defense

December 3, 1980

With the partial opening of the archives of Poland's neighbors following the collapse of the Warsaw Pact, it has become possible to view events through the eyes of their leaders, at least to a degree, and to understand developments in more detail in cases where Polish or Soviet sources are lacking. Although records of top-level Czechoslovak party discussions of the Polish crisis were apparently destroyed, numerous important files still exist, including this summary of a Warsaw Pact exercise planned for early December 1980 which generated serious alarm in the West because it was believed to be a pretext for a Soviet-led invasion of Poland (see Document Nos. 20, 21 and 23). There is no indication in the document below that this was the case, and of course no invasion ultimately took place. However, it is interesting to note that the Soviets revealed to their East European counterparts only those parts of the exercise directly relevant to their participation. This is confirmed by a similar document from East Germany which shows that the CPA and the NVA learned only what Soviet military leaders decided they needed to know, and were otherwise in the dark about Moscow's ultimate intentions. [12]

Respected Comrade,

Marshal of the Soviet Union N. V. Ogarkov, chief of the general staff of the USSR Armed Forces, with the participation of Gen. Col. Abolins, vice chief of the General Staff, and Gen. Col. Tiereshchenko, first vice chief of staff of the Soviet Armed Forces, provided clarification of the planned exercise. Present were Gen. Col. [Horst] Štechbart, commander of the NVA Land Forces of the GDR, and Armed Forces Gen. [Tadeusz] Hupałowski, first vice chief of the General Staff of the PPA. The plans assume carrying out two exercises. The first is a huge divisional tactical exercise independently carried out on each division's home territory and on the territory of the Polish People's Republic over a period of 5–6 days. The second is a command-and-control field exercise with communications equipment and partly-deployed forces on PPR territory. Four-to-five divisions of the Soviet Army (of the Baltic, Belorussian and Carpathian Military District and the 31st Tank Division of the Central Group of Soviet Forces) will take part in both exercises. From the other armies: one division from the NVA of the GDR, four divisions of the PPA and two tank divisions of the CPA [Czechoslovak People's Army].

---

[12] For a discussion of this point and the state of Czechoslovak archival sources on this period, see Oldřich Tůma, "The Czechoslovak Communist Regime and the Polish Crisis 1980–1981," 60–76.

Divisional tactical exercises will be carried out in two phases. The first phase will be carried out independently on each division's home territory over two-to-three days (see map). Following the completion of the divisional tactical exercises, both tank divisions of the CPA shall gather together near the border with the Polish People's Republic.

An order from the General Staff of the USSR Armed Forces will set the date and time for crossing the state border into the territory of the PPR (the 1st tank division along one axis, the 9th tank division along two axes—see map[13]).

The issuing of this order from the General Staff of the USSR Armed Forces initiates the second phase of the tactical exercise. The CPA in coordination with one division of the PPA (the 11th tank division) will operate in the Zagan exercise area, where both exercises will take place, under the control of the CPA in coordination with the Wrocław Military Circle's operational group.

Following the realization of the tactical exercise, the CPA and PPA divisions will move to the allotted places on the territory of the PPR (see map[14]).

Following a short rest (1 day), the second exercise will begin—a command-and-control field exercise with communications equipment and partly-deployed forces.

[...]

More detailed preparations for the second exercise will likely take place between December 8–10, 1980.

In conclusion, Marshal Ogarkov noted that at the present time the exercise is merely prepared. Its execution, including the timing of the exercise, will be decided by the political leadership. This allied action will probably be announced in accordance with the Helsinki Final Act, though with less than the 21 days notice specified.

Respected Comrade, I am also including at this time a draft information bulletin for the CPCz CC general secretary and president of the CSSR and, provided that you have no objections to its content, I would like to ask you to sign it.

[Source: Investigation Commission of the House of Representatives of the Czech Republic (copy in the possession of Oldřich Tůma); published in the Cold War International History Project Bulletin, *Issue 11 (Winter 1998), pp. 67–68. Translated by Oldřich Tůma.]*

---

[13] Map not printed.
[14] Map not printed.

Document No. 20: CIA Alert Memorandum, "Poland"

December 3, 1980

By early December, Warsaw Pact forces were mobilizing at various locations near the Polish border (see Document No. 19). As this Alert Memorandum indicates, U.S. intelligence was fully aware of this activity, finding it "highly unusual or unprecedented for this time of year." Washington's information came principally from satellite imagery and a prized HUMINT (human intelligence) source inside the Polish General Staff, Col. Ryszard Kukliński (see Document No. 21).

Alert Memorandum

Poland

There are indications that the Soviets are increasing preparations for an invasion of Poland. Recent military activities in and around Poland are highly unusual or unprecedented for this time of year. We are aware of preparations for an imminent unscheduled joint services exercise involving Soviet, East German, Polish, and possibly Czechoslovak forces. This could be designed to intimidate the Polish leadership and population, but in view of other military activity in the western USSR it could also serve as a cover for an intervention. The unusual closing of large areas of East Germany along the East German–Polish border between 30 November and 9 December is probably related.

A substantial buildup of forces could now be under way in the western military districts of the USSR. [1.5 lines excised] we do not know the status of most of the ground forces that would be used to invade Poland. We infer from the pattern of mobilization activity in the few divisions [half-line excised] that additional mobilization or training activity is likely to be taking place undetected. There might be very little warning time prior to an invasion.

On balance, this activity does not necessarily indicate that a Soviet invasion is imminent. We believe that these preparations suggest, however, that a Soviet intervention is increasingly likely.

[Source: FOIA release from the CIA, on file at the National Security Archive, "Soviet Flashpoints" collection.]

Document No. 21: Message from Ryszard Kukliński on Impending Warsaw Pact Invasion

December 4, 1980

One of the most remarkable stories of the Polish crisis is that of Ryszard Kukliński, a colonel on the Polish General Staff and an extraordinarily valuable informant for the CIA. For more than a decade, he passed thousands of pages of highly classified data on Soviet and Warsaw Pact military systems, plans and intentions to the United States.[15] During the Solidarity crisis, as part of a small circle of planners for martial law, he was able to provide remarkable access to Polish and Soviet preparations for a crackdown. As below, he often signed his notes with the code name Jack Strong. This particular communication, in which he warns of a possible Soviet-led invasion coming within four days, helped produce one of the most tension-filled moments of the crisis. Incorporating specific details such as the size and composition of the invading force, his information raised alarms in Washington and prompted President Carter to take forceful measures to try to avert a military intervention.

As it happened, Kukliński's information on this occasion was not entirely correct. The Warsaw Pact leadership had been contemplating an invasion but decided to wait until an upcoming special meeting in the Soviet capital (see Document No. 22) before arriving at a final decision. The imprecision was hardly Kukliński's fault. He had based it on information from Polish military colleagues who had just returned from high-level meetings in Moscow. Rather, the incident, like others during the period, provided an indication of just how difficult it could be accurately to assess an adversary's true intentions.

Very Urgent!

Dear Friends,

On the instruction of Defense Minister Jaruzelski, Gen. Hupałowski and Col. Puchala agreed in the General Staff of the U.S.S.R. Armed Forces in Moscow to plan for introducing (under the pretext of exercises) the troops of the Soviet Army, the Army of East Germany and the Czech Army to Poland. From prepared plans which were presented to them for viewing and partial copying, it is apparent that three armies consisting of 15 Soviet Army divisions, one army comprised of two Czech divisions and the staff of one army and one division from East Germany are to be sent to Poland. Altogether, the group of intervening forc-

---

[15] For the most complete biography of Kukliński, see Benjamin Weiser, *A Secret Life: The Polish Officer, His Covert Mission, and the Price He Paid to Save His Country* (New York: Public Affairs, 2004). Based in large part on interviews with Kukliński and on officially-granted access to CIA information, the book is an extraordinary account of the full range of Kukliński's secret activities.

es in the first phase will consist of eighteen divisions. An additional four divisions are to be attached to the armies of Czechoslovakia and East Germany (the Polish 5th and 11th Armored and the 4th and 12th Mechanized Divisions). Readiness to cross the Polish borders has been set for 8 December.

At the present time, representatives of the "fraternal armies" in civilian disguise are carrying out reconnaissance of marching routes, training areas and regions of future actions. The Czechs and East Germans are to operate in the Western part of the country, while the Central and eastern parts of Poland fall to the troops of the Soviet Army.

The operational scenario for the intervention foresees a regroupment of troops into all main training areas of the Polish forces and the conduct of live-fire exercises there, and then, contingent on how the situation develops, the blockading of all larger and industrial cities in Poland. From laconic and imprecise statements of highly placed military figures, it appears that the political decision on this matter was made much earlier and the leadership (Kania and Jaruzelski) was not put under pressure at the present time.

General Siwicki under pressure of his deputies has attempted to influence the Minister of Defense in the direction of opposing the endeavors of the allies, but that terribly trembling servant of Moscow has not even permitted discussion of this topic. At yesterday's extraordinary meeting of the Military Council, the Minister of Defense presented assignments to military districts and branches of services commanders. The leadership of the General Staff is hurriedly working out details of implementing the plans for intervention. [...]

[Jaruzelski's] partial buckling under pressure from Siwicki and Molczyk can only have the aim of throwing a smoke screen up against the judgment of those who could someday accuse [him] of national treason. [...]

In conclusion, with bitterness, I must report that as much as a small group of generals and officers of the Polish Armed Forces privy to the planning of the intervention are dispirited and crushed, there hasn't even been thought of military opposition by Polish forces to the military action of the Warsaw Pact. There are even statements that the very presence of such a large force on Polish territory can lead to increased calm.

Jack Strong

[Source: Originally published in Polish in Tygodnik Solidarność *50 (325), December 9, 1994. Translation from Benjamin Weiser,* A Secret Life: The Polish Officer, His Covert Mission, and the Price He Paid to Save His Country, *(New York: PublicAffairs, 2004), pp. 219–221. Copyright 2004 by Benjamin Weiser. Reprinted by permission of PublicAffairs, a member of Perseus Books, L.L.C.).]*

Document No. 22: Minutes of Warsaw Pact Leadership Meeting in Moscow

December 5, 1980

December 1980 represented one of the peaks of the Polish crisis, a time when Soviet intervention seemed most likely to occur. Senior American officials who had access to the intelligence from Polish Col. Ryszard Kukliński were especially alarmed because his information about military action being initiated on December 8 was so precise (see Document No. 21). Signs of heavy military preparations detected by satellites lent further weight to these suspicions. In fact, the participants at this landmark meeting of Warsaw Pact Party leaders in Moscow made no such decision. Despite the concerns expressed by Erich Honecker and Todor Zhivkov about the unraveling situation, the group resolved to give Kania another chance to clamp down on the opposition once and for all. In a private meeting between Brezhnev and Kania, however, the Soviet leader warned in plain language that the alliance would intervene if any "complications" ensued.[16]

(Start: 11:00 a.m.)

Leonid Ilyich Brezhnev: Dear Comrades! I warmly welcome you, our allies in the Warsaw Pact, our friends, in the name of the Politburo of the CC of the CPSU, and thank you for your speedy and positive response to the invitation for the meeting.

[…]

There are also events in Poland, difficult and alarming ones. This is the main question. We understand the great concerns of Comrade Kania and of all our political friends who are in a difficult situation.

The crisis in Poland concerns, of course, all of us. Various forces are mobilizing against socialism in Poland, from the so-called liberals to the fascists. They are dealing blows against socialist Poland. The objective, however, is the entire socialist community.

As we all know, the Polish comrades only recently held the Seventh CC Plenum. Perhaps we will ask them to provide us with information about this work. They will probably also not mind discussing, here in the circle of friends, measures, the implementation of which could result in overcoming the crisis and in strengthening socialist Poland.

---

[16] See the account quoting Kania's memoir in Michael Dobbs, *Down with Big Brother: The Fall of the Soviet Empire*, 60–64.

I think the comrades will agree with me that Comrade Kania will speak first. Then the other comrades will have the opportunity to speak.

We should agree on procedures for our consultation. What proposals do we have regarding the chairman?

Todor Zhivkov: I think we should not chair our meeting today in alphabetical order. Since our meeting will only have two sessions, I would propose that the Soviet delegation as hosts chair this meeting.

Leonid Ilyich Brezhnev: Are there objections? Thank you, comrades, for your confidence. [...] Comrade Kania now has the floor.

Stanisław Kania: Dearest Comrade Leonid Ilyich! Dearest Comrades! It is difficult for me to speak to you here today as a representative of the leadership of the Polish party. This is not only difficult because it is the first time that I speak to you, the party leaders, in this circle, but it is also difficult for us as representatives of the Polish leadership to speak here and before our compatriots at home; it is difficult to speak to you here in particular because the main sources of the political crisis that has gripped our country are concentrated at the level of our party. The crisis is also the topic of our meeting today, which we interpret as an expression of internationalist concerns about the situation in our country.

Our situation is indeed very complicated. There are great dangers to socialism. The dangers pose themselves in the economic field and bring anarchy and counter-revolution into our country.

We are quite conscious what responsibility we carry for our party, for our workers' class and for the Polish people to resolve this crisis effectively. We are also aware of the internationalist responsibility for the socialist camp and the international communist movement.

We are an important and inseparable part of the socialist community of states, and we know that the situation in Poland is also causing various complications for our neighbors. We know very well that we ourselves must lead the country out of this difficult situation. This is our responsibility, and we are convinced that we have a real chance for the resolution of these tasks.

We keep in constant contact with the leadership of the CPSU and very much appreciate your views and advice, which you have given us, Comrade Leonid Ilyich. We realize the fundamental importance of your view of our difficulties, and it conforms to our opinion on the causes of the problems that are occurring in Poland.

For the second time, your name stands for sensitivity not only for a class-conscious assessment but also for the national peculiarities and for the situation in Poland. [...]

What are the causes of the crisis? This is not the first, but one of several profound crises in Poland. We had the year 1956 and the bloody events in Poznań, with the ensuing changes in the leadership of the party and the great wave of revisionism in Poland. There was the year 1968, the well-known incidents by students, but there were dramatic, bloody events in 1970 as well, in December of that year, along the coast. In 1976, major incidents were staged in Radom and Ursus in connection with the preparation for price increases.

Today's crisis affects the working class, but also other segments of the population, and the crisis is of a mass character. Young people are proving to be particularly active, especially young workers, technicians and engineers, and this crisis has lasted for a long time. The strike phase is behind us, but the crisis persists, and we are affected by the results on a daily basis. The situation has become demoralizing because one cannot hand out more than one produces.

The crisis has also created new structures which are not of our making, in particular the new labor unions which create a lot of difficulties for us and pose an attempt by the enemy of socialism in Poland to test us.

There are various causes for [these] concerns, and questions can indeed be asked whether the estimate of the conflict in Poland is correct, whether we are on the right track for getting out of this crisis.

We completely agree with Comrade Leonid Ilyich that it is necessary to analyze more thoroughly the anatomy of these occurrences which have led to the crisis, of all the mechanisms which have caused the subversion of the party, the government, and even the economy of the country and which have allowed enemy forces, the forces of counter-revolution, to penetrate the working class.

Despite the various difficulties, we are of the opinion that our estimates accord with the reality of the situation. The main reason for the problems was dissatisfaction among the workers. There were, of course, real reasons for this dissatisfaction. That was the reason for the mass character of the strike movement. There were strikes in many major Polish plants, even in those which can look back to a long revolutionary tradition.

The party proved to be extremely weak in the ideological field. We were faced with the results of a policy which ignored the class character of society. The slogan of the achievement of modern socialist society was proclaimed much too early. This took place at a time when individual farmers in Poland still constituted the majority in the countryside, and in the 1970s, private enterprise spread over large parts of the trade business as well as other areas of the economy. [...]

Looking back today at these difficulties in the situation, we believe that the use of political measures for the resolution of strike conflicts was a correct decision. Other solutions and other decisions could have provoked an avalanche of incidents and led to a bloody confrontation, the results of which would have affected the entire socialist world. Despite the difficult problems, it seems to us that there was no other resort than to compromise on the question of permitting the establishment of the new labor union. [...]

What to say about the period after the great wave of strikes? How should it be evaluated? It has been a period of very hard political battle, a difficult period for the party. The new union, Solidarity, developed out of the strike committees, not at the initiative of the workers but at the initiative of anti-socialist elements. But by and large, this organization was supported by the workers throughout the entire country, and it is popular nationwide since the workers achieved social benefits through the strikes.[17] [...]

Foreign imperialist diversion centers have shown great activity and even aggressiveness towards Poland, in particular the radio station "Free Europe," the centers of reactionary emigration, which have supported anti-socialist actions by means of propaganda and by giving financial support to Solidarity. We have protested sharply against this, and there are certain positive results, a certain withdrawal of enemy forces.

[...]

We have, of course, lost some of our prestige in the eyes of party activists due to these compromises. Even if a certain state of criticism has been reached, we nevertheless managed to isolate some of the anti-socialist elements. The public did not react very agreeably to this. A situation occurred in which it was necessary to put into effect a number of repressive measures, including administrative measures.

Created by the Politburo, a group operates at the direction of the premier which is preparing a series of different measures. This includes among other things the question of introducing martial law in Poland. Actually, under our constitution we only have the option of declaring martial law.

[The group] is also preparing an operation with the aim of arresting the most active functionaries of the counter-revolution.

It also has developed guidelines for communications in case of emergency, and the same for the mass media, the newspapers, railroads and (automobile) transport facilities in general.

We will also create special groups of particularly trustworthy party members which, if necessary, can be armed. We have selected 19,000 such party members and are of the opinion that we will have about 30,000 by the end of December.

Information on these preparations has in part fallen into the hands of leading officials of the counter-revolution.

The assessment of the Seventh Plenum has further toughened our policy. We think that it has created a more favorable atmosphere for a counteroffensive than previously existed.

[...]

[17] Although it is not recorded here, Kania, in discussing Solidarity, slipped into some disparaging language about the union and its most visible leader. According to János Kádár's presentation on the summit to the Hungarian Politburo, the Polish leader referred to Wałęsa as a "sly half-wit" who headed a movement influenced by "extremists" whom Kádár characterized as "anarchists and terrorists." (Report to HSWP CC Politburo from Department of International Relations, December 8, 1980. MOL, Department of Documents on the Hungarian Workers' Party and on the Hungarian Socialist Workers' Party, 288. f. 5/815. ő.e., pp. 17–28. Published in the *Cold War International History Project Bulletin*, Issue 11 (Winter 1998), pp. 79–83. Translated by László Beke.)

We have to become active, on all fronts. Most important is the internal unity of the party, its stamina, its influence on the working class. These are the main pre-conditions of taming the counter-revolutionary forces.

The course of events might naturally confront us with the necessity to implement other measures, measures not limited to the political confrontation which we have expected, but measures of confrontation associated with repressive measures. Believe me, comrades, that in that case we will have sufficient determination with respect to the counter-revolution to defend socialism and the socialist position in Poland.

Todor Zhivkov: Dear Comrades! In consideration of the nature of our meeting, I would like to address some key questions and explain the views of our party with regard to the situation in Poland. [...]

What is our estimate of the situation in Poland, our general estimate? For five months now, events have been shaking Poland, which causes us great concern. We all understand that what is happening there is above all a Polish question and concerns the development of socialism in Poland. But we also understand quite well that it is not solely a Polish question. The developments in Poland concern all socialist countries, the entire socialist community. [...]

The general estimate of the situation has two aspects, I think. The first one concerns the question of what is actually happening in Poland, of what the character of the processes are which are taking place there, what the causes are, and what forces are behind these events.

A second aspect is the answer to the question of what the situation in this country actually is, what the reality of the situation is, what the main danger is.

It is important, for example, if we take the first—and we have no chance or time to analyze this very thoroughly, we will be able to do that later—to give the first estimate now. This is even more important given that other political forces are actively trying to force their estimate on the public. The Eurocommunists, for example, talk about the historical events in Poland and about the necessity for all socialist countries to go through this development. Yugoslavia is massively spreading its own interpretation of the Polish events, as if they were new evidence on the correctness of the Yugoslav way and the Yugoslav brand of socialism. Not to mention the Western countries, which attentively and actively watch and react to the Polish events. They are spreading the opinion that the Polish events have proved again that the political and economic system of socialism is not viable.

Our general opinion is that we are dealing with a very serious political and economic crisis in Poland which on the one hand was caused by policy flaws under the current leadership of the Polish party and government, and on the other hand by the plans and activities of anti-socialist forces which without doubt have for quite some time been active within and outside of Poland.

What concerns us is that there is no clear and reasonable estimate, and there is no program for a way out of the situation that has developed. Our opinion is that the lack of such a program is one of the reasons why change is only occurring very slowly here. There has up to now not been a mobilization of forces to the fullest extent possible. It is lacking! Defensive actions are being continued. There are even certain steps back from the political plan.

We understand the necessity of compromises but one should clearly look ahead and consider for what purpose one makes these compromises and where they might lead. As long as no major changes occur, until the party seizes the initiative we cannot at all speak of a turn of events.

What is our opinion on the ways out of this situation? We think that the solution has to be found in the People's Republic of Poland itself. One should work out various options which are appropriate for the situation, and our Polish comrades should be ready to apply these options in the country by means of the forces of the Polish United Workers' Party and the Polish People's Republic. Our estimate is to the effect that such possibilities exist at this very moment.

Secondly, in our opinion, the Polish party should try and consistently pursue going on the offensive. Of course, the Polish comrades know best which possibilities and ways exist for such an offensive. But some aspects should also be viewed from our point of view. There is, for example, a certain degree of fatigue in view of the events of the last five months, which, of course, affects the social situation of the people. There is the prospect that the economic situation and the situation of the workers will further deteriorate. One should state very clearly who is to blame for this and who creates obstacles. One cannot go on strike endlessly, one cannot live endlessly on credit, and one cannot demand a better life without improving production. This should be stated quite clearly.

There are healthy forces—the army, security forces, and the larger part of the party and population. These are forces that the party and state organs can rely on. While it is indeed necessary in today's situation to be flexible, too, it is also right to defend the socialist position in the current situation with greater certainty and greater vigor. [...] I would like to address briefly the question of strategic goals the class enemy is pursuing and the eminently important strategic dangers which result from the events in Poland.

It seems that the West hardly harbors any illusions of changing the social order in Poland in such a way that Poland would leave the Warsaw Pact and pull back to the extent that it would change the political landscape. Of course, the enemy has done and is doing everything to effect a change in the social system and the economic system in our countries, among them Poland. But now the strategic plan of the West is clearly to put a different system into practice in Poland which diverges from real socialism and heads in the direction of liberal socialism, a model which then could pose an example and provoke changes in the social order in other countries of the socialist community.

Imperialism is pursuing its policy of interference in internal Polish affairs, and is accompanied by massive propaganda drums about an alleged intervention by the Soviet Union and the other countries. Nationalist feelings are being stirred, attempts to hide the class character of the events, to cover up the counter-revolution, and to extol friends as foes and vice versa.

146

I want to state quite frankly: to our mind, there is at this moment a real chance of a change in the social order in Poland. We should not underestimate this! If we had to give a strictly class-based estimate now, we would have to say that the possibilities of a political approach, which the Polish comrades have taken thus far, have been exhausted. In our opinion, the situation in Poland is clear and no further clarification is required. [...]

János Kádár: Dear Comrades! [...] For us, the views of the Polish comrades on the situation in their country are very important. Of course, we base our own evaluation of the political situation above all on the opinion of the Polish comrades and also on the publications in the Polish press, on the international press and on our own experience. [...]

How could one describe the Hungarian position on this question?

Before I address this question, I would like to make one more remark. I fully agree with Comrade Zhivkov and would like to express the view that imperialist propaganda concerning Poland, which is also broadcast to Hungary, implies that the other European socialist countries are equally nervous and concerned about the Polish events, claiming that we fear, as they say, the Polish pest. They declare that this could also undermine our order, etc.

I would like to say the following about that in order to avoid any misunderstandings: for the Hungarian Socialist Workers' Party and for the Hungarian people, a number of concerns exist in the current period of socialist construction. We have our own problems and worries, we are struggling with them, and we will resolve them in the appropriate manner.

In consideration of this I would like to state nevertheless: as far as we are concerned, the Polish events are of little concern to us in terms of domestic politics. We do not fear any great disruption in connection with them. But our party, our government, our entire people are particularly concerned about the Polish question in international terms, and this is of concern to us all. [...]

What do we have to be aware of? It will to a certain degree surely be helpful for the Polish comrades to know what the mood is in our countries. They should know.

When we got the first news about the strikes on the coast, there were certain reactions [in Hungary]. I am speaking now not about party members and the party leadership but about the man in the street, thus *de facto* about the ideologically and politically less qualified masses. The first reaction was as follows: what do the Polish comrades think they are doing? To work less and earn more? Then it was said: what do the Polish comrades think they are doing: they want to strike and we are supposed to do the work? I must frankly state here that this is what the feeling was. These feelings were there although everybody knows that there exists a historical friendship between our two nations. [...]

Now, further on our attitude. We are in complete solidarity with the Polish communists, with the PUWP, with the Polish working class, and—in the traditional sense of the word—with the Polish nation. We would like the Polish comrades to solve their problems by themselves, to find a socialist solution of the problem under the leadership of their party. This is our attitude, which we publicly announced in parliament.

We cannot, of course, determine the tasks of the Polish comrades and have no intention of doing so. Nevertheless, I would like to state a few things. We think that, in their current struggle, the Polish comrades should focus on maintaining the leading role of the party and the socialist, constitutionally-determined social order as well as the political system in Poland. This includes the mass media, radio and TV. These media are integrally linked to the question of power, and I welcome Comrade Kania's words on this subject.

The third, central task is, it seems to me, the defense and the protection of the Warsaw Pact.

I would like to address one other point here. As other fraternal parties represented here, we maintain very broad international contacts with organizations, parties etc. Practically every week we entertain visitors. In the course of the last week, representatives of a number of fraternal parties were with us; we had a meeting with the Yugoslavs; and in the context of peaceful coexistence we met last week with capitalists as well. What I state here as the Hungarian position is the same thing which we presented in our conversations with the respective partners, be it Latin American communists or any imperialist representatives; everywhere we state the same thing as I am doing here.

About ten days ago, a meeting with the British foreign minister [Lord Carrington] took place, and last week, [Hans-Jürgen] Wischnewski, the deputy chairman of the Social-Democratic Party in West Germany, was here at the request of [West German Chancellor Helmut] Schmidt. I categorically told the Yugoslav comrades as well as Wischnewski and the British foreign minister the following: Our position is that this is an internal Polish question which has to be resolved by the Poles; that we were in solidarity with the Poles; but I also stated that there were certain limits to this. I cannot put it any other way for the gentlemen. Poland is not for sale, and Poland could not be bought. Poland cannot be detached from the Warsaw Pact. This is what I stated and I declared that I was deeply convinced that there were strong forces in Hungary which held the same opinion and would not permit this to happen. That is how I represented my point of view and that is how I told them, in order to let them know what they have to expect.

The British asked: What does this mean? Is this the end of détente? I said: no, but if these limits are reached, then détente would really be over. He said yes and then shut up. The West German representative reacted similarly.

Recently, we have used certain exchanges of opinion and consultations, and we are asked: well, if you had to give us advice, would you recommend that we act as you did? I would like to address this very frankly.

As far as the Hungarian party is concerned, we have neither authority nor ambitions to give advice to anybody or to consider ourselves a model. But at the same time, we ascribe importance to the great revolutionary experiences of all fraternal parties. We think consultations such as today's are very important, and let me add:

You cannot copy or mechanically transfer revolutionary experience. This does not work. And whenever I talk about our position, about our attitude, it is in friendship that I would like to state what the Polish fraternal party should do or what we would do if we were in its place.

To my mind it is now of decisive importance to maintain the position since withdrawal, the slippery slope downward, has not yet ended. One has to get one's act together and go on the offensive.

The second thing I would say is the following: The decisive thing is that there is an unequivocal, decisive socialist platform for future developments. And this has to happen right away. While you now have a program, it has to become more consistent.

Comrade Kania spoke of the plenum, of re-elections in the basic organizations. I am glad to hear you say that the plenum would have to be postponed a bit further; because I think without a precise platform one cannot conduct a good plenum; then one cannot elect good leading organs in the local organizations, since one does not know exactly which of the cadres are good and which are bad.

When we stewed ourselves in our own bitter juice in 1956, we dealt with this question in this way. When I asked people: Is this person still alive? Does he work? I was often told: I have known him for 30 years. I responded: 30 years is not enough. Tell me how he acted last week. People change their behavior in such situations.

For this, you need a program, so that everybody can determine his attitude towards the party and its program. You have to start at the top.

We do not want to interfere in the internal affairs of the Polish party, but our own experiences tell us: in critical times the most important organ for party unity and action is the Central Committee, the highest organ. If there is a clear program and unity in this organ, everything is set. But if there are 20 different opinions in the CC, nothing will come of it. [...]

As far as we know, the Polish party now has 3.5 million members. I know that the situation there is somewhat odd. One should probably not conduct purges now, but unfortunately the events themselves have resulted in such a purge. It is not important what the membership numbers are; it is instead important how many people participate in the struggle, how many adhere to your program.

Put another way: there is no point in trying to achieve party unity based on compromise at any price. We need a clear platform, which will serve as a rallying point and a purging device. I think such a program could easily be used to set oneself apart from certain things, to distance oneself from the mistakes of the previous leadership very clearly and decisively, not just in words but also in deed and action.

This is one aspect. I will neither praise Gierek nor insult him. While one has to distance oneself, I would like to state, comrades, that the entire party, the entire country, is now looking for scapegoats, and it will again lead you nowhere to spend most of your time calling people to account.

I am reminded again of 1956. Initially, we completely ignored Rákosi,[18] we distanced ourselves from him and other comrades, quickly distanced ourselves politically from their policies, and we postponed the calling-to-account until 1962. I am not arguing that the Party Control Commission should not do its work now, but it should not be the primary focus of your work. It cannot be that the entire party now preoccupies itself with this. People will have to know: once we regain our strength, we will call to account those responsible. It is now important that the people's government build a socialist Poland and protect the constitution.

The second thing we need is the following: we have to watch very carefully what the limits are in great [public] speeches. One should now be able to defend the fundamental order of the republic, even in party matters, and the party members will vote. What function they will serve within the party is a matter for the party, not for the entire nation. The communists first need to establish order within their own ranks. We do not need some democratic forces for that. Therefore this has to be the limit.

For example, when people are arrested and then set free again, there will again be discussions about the work of the militia. Even in the Western press it has been stated that no country on earth could permit such things to happen at all. This is not a matter of ideological argument but a matter of legal order, which has to be upheld throughout the country.

In order to make clear the limits of democratizing [*Demokratismus*], you have to have a program and be determined to do certain things.

Certain events, for example, took place without bloodshed. This is of course not a small matter. It has to be evident that the Polish party and the Polish government are not exactly looking for confrontation. They above all are not out to have people shot. But the defense of certain things has to be guaranteed—a defense by all means. And this has to become evident. This is the best way to avoid bloodshed. Because if it is clear that every means possible will be employed, bloodshed will be avoided. This is the best solution. [...]

Finally, I would like to say the following: there are other effects in Hungary. I do not want to tell you what a depressed state of affairs we were in during the months from October to December 1956, thus during the decisive hours. We were very pessimistic, but our foreign comrades supported us. Above all the Soviet comrades came to our aid and told us—I well remember this, this is not just propaganda—you now need a reasonable policy. You are stronger than you think! And the Polish comrades should know this too: in reality, the forces of socialism in Poland are stronger than they appear at first superficial glance. Within a short time, positive decisions should be reached. Once again: you are stronger than you think. [...]

---

[18] Mátyás Rákosi was the Stalinist Hungarian party leader from 1945 till July 1956 when he was replaced at Moscow's behest. After putting down the revolution in early November 1956, the Soviets chose Kádár over Rákosi to lead the reconstituted Hungarian Socialist Workers Party. See Békés, Byrne and Rainer, *op. cit.*

Erich Honecker: Dear Comrades! [...] These consultations were urgently necessary in view of the developments in the People's Republic of Poland. The events in our neighboring country Poland greatly worry the leadership of our party, the communists, the citizens of the German Democratic Republic. Nobody who cares for the cause of peace and socialism can be indifferent to what is happening in the PPR. [...]

We fully share the opinion that the survival of socialism in Poland is in acute danger. We recently spoke to comrades Kania, Żabinski, Olszowski and others about this and pointed out that it was necessary to put an end to these developments. At the same time, we provided Poland in this difficult situation with major material support. [...] The citizens of our republic are also aware of the huge amount of aid for Poland [that has come] from the Soviet Union, the ČSSR and other socialist countries. Our people are well aware of this. But there are many questions as to what exactly has improved since the Sixth Plenum of the PUWP CC. Workers, members of the intelligentsia and others have expressed their disappointment that the visit by comrades Kania and Pińkowski with Comrade Brezhnev did not live up to their expectations.[19]

We fully agreed with the results of this Moscow trip. Comrade Kania assured us on November 8 that the PUWP leadership would not withdraw one more step. But then there was the decision of the Supreme Court of the PPR which revised the decision of the Warsaw court.[20] Party and government once more retreated from the counter-revolutionary forces. This resulted in a rapid escalation of counter-revolutionary activities and a massive deterioration of the situation. This was a major setback for all those who had hoped that the PUWP would master the problems. This is the main reason for the widespread discussions of the current situation in Poland within our party and among our people and for the growing serious concerns about socialism in Poland which marks these discussions.

There is obviously no disagreement among us about the fact that capitulation to the strike committees in Gdańsk, Szczecin and Jastrzębie has already been a mistake. But we do not want to judge this here. The fact is that following this capitulation, the enemy of the government sensed a chance to spread the strike and riots throughout the country. While weeks ago the strikes were confined above all to social demands, more recently political slogans have come increasingly to the fore.

The decision of the Supreme Court prevented a general strike, but Solidarity proved that it could initiate strikes at any time and thus blackmail the party and government. It even managed to force the liberation of people who had clearly been proved to have committed crimes. Yes, it even gained the assurance that it would be allowed to enter into negotiations on security matters. Such conces-

[19] The meeting took place in Moscow on October 30–31, 1980. See Document Nos. 15 and 16.
[20] On November 10, the Polish Supreme Court ruled that Solidarity was legally independent and not subservient to the PUWP.

sions inevitably will undermine the authority of the party, of the state and its organs. This has to worry everybody who is faithfully committed to the cause of socialism.

I was in Austria at the time of the Supreme Court deliberations. Kirchschläger and Kreisky[21] asked my opinion about the events in Poland. We agreed, despite differing class positions, that Poland would be able to manage its affairs. Then, in the midst of a conversation with Kirchschläger, the news of the Supreme Court decision arrived. Honestly, I would never have been able to conceive such an idea: the party becomes an appendix to the statute. I had gone to Vienna, basing my assumptions on what Comrade Kania had said. As many others, I never expected such a result.

As the current events show, the leadership of Solidarity and the forces behind it, especially KOR, are consistently following a well-known counter-revolutionary strategy. Taking advantage of a wave of strikes, they established their organization. In the form of a union, today they already have a legal political party. Their blackmail tactics have now resulted in a direct struggle for political power. The counter-revolutionary leaders, as Comrade Kania has stated, do not hide the fact that their objective is the elimination of the PUWP as the leading power [and] the elimination of socialist achievements. Initially, the strike organizations prevented anti-socialist and anti-Soviet slogans. Today they feel strong enough to pay homage to Piłsudski[22] and to attack the Soviet Union, the GDR, the ČSSR and the other fraternal socialist countries. As the facts prove, they are about to inflame a nationalist, anti-socialist hysteria.

Dear Comrades! One can hardly ignore that the events in Poland are for the main part the result of a coordinated plan of the internal and foreign counter-revolution. It is a part of the imperialist policy of confrontation and increased diversion against the socialist countries. It is important to recognize that the PUWP is confronted with an irreconcilable enemy. In order to defeat the counter-revolution, we think one needs an unambiguous concept, an unambiguous policy of the party, from top to the bottom.

You will not get anywhere with an endless discussion of mistakes, to our mind. I would like to state that the damage from the propaganda of failures is much higher than any propaganda of success. In any case, you cannot permit a situation in which the truth is suppressed in public. This truth is that socialism, its shortcomings and mistakes notwithstanding, has brought the Polish nation great achievements, that not the Polish United Workers' Party but the leaders of Solidarity and the people who direct them are responsible for the current situation. Of course, one has to differentiate between a manipulated worker and anti-socialist forces, but one also has to say clearly who the enemy is. [...]

---

[21] Austrian President Rudolph Kirchschläger and Chancellor Bruno Kreisky.
[22] Marshal Józef Piłsudski (1867–1935), revered by many Poles as a champion of Polish independence—including from Tsarist and Soviet rule.

Dear Comrades! We have to assume that unfortunately the situation in the PPR has developed to a point where administrative measures are necessary in addition to political measures in order to destroy the counter-revolutionary conspiracy and stabilize the government. As you well know, we also had a difficult situation in the German Democratic Republic.[23] Back then we still had an open border with the Federal Republic of Germany. The imperialists were instigating the fall of the workers-and-peasants' power from without and counted on the counter-revolution from within. We therefore had to act quickly. We combined political with administrative measures. We made a public appeal to the party members and functionaries of our party, to all who were committed to the defense and strengthening of the workers-and-peasants state. Within a short time we managed to isolate the counter-revolutionary forces from the workers and defeat them.

It was stated here rightfully that the revolution could develop peacefully or in a non-peaceful manner, as we all know. As a communist you have to be ready to consider both options as the situation demands, and to act accordingly at the decisive moments. If the workers-and-peasants power, the government, is at risk, if it has to be protected from counter-revolutionary forces which are determined to go all the way, then there remains no other choice than to deploy the security organs of the workers-and-peasants state. This was our experience in 1953. This became evident in the events of 1956 in Hungary, about which Comrade Kádár spoke, and of 1968 in the ČSSR.

The representatives of the various groups, which now are mushrooming in Poland, state as a cover-up of their true intentions that their objective is the "democratic renewal of socialism" in Poland. But the opposite is the case. NATO and the EC declare quite frankly that this is a matter that falls under their protection.

I can remember quite well the conversation with Dubček on the occasion of the Dresden meeting in 1968[24] when I got him from the airport and took him to his residence. In the course of one hour, Dubček tried to convince me that what was happening in the ČSSR was not a counter-revolution but a "process of democratic renewal of socialism." What happened later, everybody knows. The Czechoslovak comrades under the leadership of Comrade Husák have composed a document about this that taught us a lot.

We are of the opinion that the PUWP has sufficient healthy forces in order to solve the urgent tasks, based on the announcement of the Central Committee of

---

[23] On June 17, 1953, workers in East Berlin began a protest over production quotas that quickly spread to the rest of the GDR incorporating other segments of society and much broader political demands in the process. Soviet and East German authorities resorted to violence to put down the uprising, the first of its kind in the Soviet bloc. See Christian F. Ostermann, *op. cit., passim.*

[24] The Dresden conference of March 23, 1968, was one of a series of Warsaw Pact leadership meetings designed to pressure the Czechoslovak party leadership to put an end to the Prague Spring. See the stenographic account of the meeting in Jaromír Navrátil et al, eds., *The Prague Spring '68*, (Budapest: CEU Press, 1998), pp. 64–72.

the Polish United Workers' Party, its directives and a clear plan. As we know, the PUWP has available reliable forces in its security organs, and we are convinced that the army as well will fulfill its patriotic and internationalist duty. This is how we understood the declaration of the Military Council of the Ministry for National Defense of the PPR, which was published after the Seventh Plenum of the CC of the PUWP. In addition, there is the possibility of arming the healthy forces, about which Comrade Kania spoke here, within the party and among the workers. We agree with Comrade Kania that there can be no further step in retreat in the current situation. Only through the struggle against the counter-revolution can the party unite its members and functionaries [and] all class-conscious workers and lead them to success.

We in the German Democratic Republic are situated along the line that separates us from the Federal Republic and NATO. On a daily basis, we feel how the imperialist enemy is trying to transfer the counter-revolutionary activities from Poland to our country as well. The TV stations of the FRG, which can be received in our republic, have never before reported so much on Poland and have never shown so much interest in the events in Polish factories. They have associated this for five months now with the call to do the same thing as is now happening in Poland. They describe the developments in the PPR as an example of "democratic reform" and "necessary changes" in all socialist countries. That is why we were forced to tell our party clearly what we thought of the developments in our socialist neighbor country. I stated in a speech before the party activists in Gera that insurmountable limits have been set on the counter-revolution west of the Elbe and Wera. This was not only understood well on our side. Our party takes a class-conscious view of events in Poland. This also concerns measures on the temporary limitation of cross-border traffic.

Dear Comrades! We have gathered here in order to consult collectively on possible support by the fraternal countries, which might be useful to Comrade Kania and all the comrades in the PUWP in strengthening the people's power in Poland. Our party and our people have great expectations with regard to this meeting.

Never before has our party felt so closely connected with the PUWP as in these difficult days and weeks. In this vein we have given orientation to the members of our party. We remain in solidarity with the fraternal Polish people and its party, the Polish United Workers' Party. And we are convinced: the cause of socialism will win.

Thank you for your attention.

Nicolae Ceauşescu: Esteemed comrades! [...] There are difficulties in some socialist countries. This is true for the events in Poland. This should give us a reason to analyze the situation very seriously, to solve all problems, the problems of socialist and communist construction, through collaboration among the socialist countries, based on our own strength. This is all the more important now that we approach the conclusion of the five-year plans and are passing to a new phase of economic and social development for the years 1981 to 1985.

I think I am not wrong in assuming: if we had analyzed the problems of the construction of socialism in our countries more frequently and thoroughly, we would have been able to avoid even the events in Poland. One has to assume that the cooperation of the socialist countries, the successful construction of socialism and communism, is of special importance to our countries, but at the same time to the maintenance of socialist principles throughout the world, the entire international situation, the policy of détente, peace and national independence. The socialist countries should demonstrate that they can indeed solve complex problems in the appropriate manner, that socialism provides a firm basis for economic development. One can say that socialism is quite capable of overcoming the appearances of an economic crisis and of giving the people greater independence and economic stability.

In the context of our discussions, it was emphasized that the events in Poland stand at the center of attention of the communist parties and of the people of our community of states as well as all communist parties and progressive forces in the world. The entire international public is also watching these events. There is no doubt that differing interpretations exist and different possibilities of analyzing the events.

But one can only say one thing: There is the concern and indeed the desire to have these problems resolved by the Poles themselves and to avoid them damaging the policy of détente, peace and cooperation. [...]

I would like to state initially that the Romanian Communist Party, our Central Committee and the Romanian people, are of the opinion that the problems in Poland should be solved by the PUWP, the Polish working class, the Polish people in complete unity and based on the assumption that it is necessary to assure the socialist development of Poland, to strengthen the economic base of Poland's independence and sovereignty and the material wealth of the Polish people, and to strengthen the cooperation between the socialist countries.

It is not the time now (and there is no reason) to have a thorough discussion about the reasons for this development. One thing is clear: economic difficulties have exerted a strong influence on developments. As is evident from the decisions of the Plenum, today's state of crisis was also caused by certain mistakes which happened in the implementation of socialist principles and the leading role of the party, in securing the unity of the working class and the broad masses of the people. [...]

Comrade Kania has correctly stated—and this is also evident from the Plenum of the Polish United Workers' Party—that attention has been called to the intensification of the activities of anti-socialist, counter-revolutionary elements in the country. To our mind, today's state of affairs could have been avoided if greater determination had been demonstrated previously. Even if there is dissatisfaction, you could have prevented the current dangerous course of events through greater determination. [...]

We do not want to interfere here in the internal events of Poland. The PUWP, the Polish working class and the Polish people as well as all the progressive forces in Poland know that they have to find the appropriate ways to overcome this situation, develop the economy, increase the standard of living, based on socialist construction and according to conditions in Poland.

Everything should be done in order to have an unambiguous orientation, to develop a program which makes it clear how the problems are to be solved—a program which the broad masses of the people will understand well and which becomes the action program of the working class above all. One cannot imagine overcoming the current crisis without such a political program, which involves the working class and the people. [...]

We also do not understand how it was possible for so-called independent free unions to be established. But they are a reality today, and you indeed have to take them into consideration. One ought to act in a way that the unity of the workers and the unity of the unions—based on socialism—are regained. But for this purpose, you will need a clear policy and an unambiguous program even in this area, and that will take some time. [...]

I would like to underline again that the Polish comrades will have to do everything—it is their great international and national obligation—to assure socialist construction on their own. One can also not neglect the fact that the possibility of an external intervention would pose a great danger for socialism in general, for the policy of détente, and for the policy of peace. That is why we should give the Polish comrades all-out support to allow them to fulfill the tasks of securing the socialist construction of Poland on their own and in their own ways, which they indeed have. [...]

Gustáv Husák: Dear Comrades! [...]

You can sense great concern about current events in Poland in our party and our people. This is not just because we are immediate neighbors—we have a common border of some 1,300 kilometers, and this is, by the way, our longest border—but also because the threat to socialism in Poland constitutes a threat to our joint interests.

We in Czechoslovakia underwent a complicated process of development as well, when the counter-revolution went on the counteroffensive in our country, when the danger of civil war in the ČSSR arose, and when there was a deadly danger to socialism. Comrade Kádár has reminded us of the events in Hungary in 1956, and Comrade Honecker has spoken about the events in the GDR.

The events which took place 12 years ago in Czechoslovakia still live in our memories, and in watching the events unfold in Poland today, we compare them to our own experience, even though we, of course, recognize the differences in time and circumstances.[25]

But all these events in Hungary, in the GDR, in Czechoslovakia and now in Poland are characterized by a common goal on the part of the anti-socialist, counter-revolutionary forces which want to roll back socialism in Poland and detach these countries from the socialist camp. [...]

[25] See Jaromír Navrátil et al, *op. cit.*, *passim*.

In our country, dissatisfaction also grew among the people, and we had to eliminate deformations, mistakes and shortcomings within the party as well as within society. [...]

The imperialists quickly realized that an excellent opportunity had been given in Czechoslovakia to reach their long-term goal of destabilizing socialism. What took place there in those summer months in 1968 had long been prepared by imperialist circles and various reactionary, anti-socialist forces. This is also what has happened this summer in Poland.

The enemy has drawn conclusions from the events in Poland and in the ČSSR. He proceeded differently in the ČSSR than in Hungary, and he drew his conclusions from the events in the ČSSR. He now acts differently in Poland than he did in the ČSSR. He takes advantage of social dissatisfaction, of economic shortcomings, and tries to win over the masses by social demagoguery and to direct them towards anti-socialist actions, towards actions against the party.

As it was, in bourgeois propaganda the ČSSR became the best model for the democratic reform of socialism, that is, socialism with a human face. The ČSSR was held up to all other socialist countries as a model. Even the pope prayed for this process, for the rebirth of Czechoslovakia, and for Dubček as well; and if anything bad was done in the socialist countries, our country was pointed out as an example. As Comrade Honecker said, the same thing happened in Czechoslovakia. Now they would like to export Poland's crisis to the ČSSR, the GDR and the other countries. We, of course, have introduced all necessary measures against this, and as far as we are concerned, there is no reason to be concerned. [...]

The situation [in Czechoslovakia in 1968] culminated to the point at which we could not fight off the attack of the counter-revolution by ourselves. In order to prevent a civil war and to defend socialism, the socialist fraternal countries were asked for internationalist support. This is our view of the situation back then. This support prevented the detachment of the ČSSR from the socialist camp. It gave the party the chance to solve the problems. The ČSSR economy had been disrupted. The internal market, the economy and the entire structure of society had been shaken and shattered, and the party had been torn apart.

It took great efforts to repair the damage that had been done. The CPCz managed to do this after 1969 thanks to the help of the other fraternal countries. I am not reminding you of our experience in order to argue for extreme and radical solutions, I do this in order to demonstrate that due to the inconsistency of our previous leadership it was necessary to go for an extreme solution in the interests of defending socialism.

Following the installation of the new leadership, it became clear that the enemy, which had maintained it would completely support the people and the party, actually had a petit-bourgeois attitude. We uncovered the counter-revolution and its representatives, precisely with the goal of showing the people what they had been after. We juxtaposed this with the progressive program of our party. As a result, our people have completely supported the Marxist-Leninist program of our party and have defeated the counter-revolution.

We know, dear comrades, that these problems of which I have spoken were of a different sort. It seems to me that the PUWP has a better leadership today than we in the ČSSR had back then. But the question of decisiveness and determination to solve the problems energetically remains acute.

With my contribution, dear comrades, I wanted to show in what creeping manner the counter-revolution acted in the ČSSR and what experience our party underwent. The developments of recent years show that you need a Marxist-Leninist party to defend socialism adequately and to defeat the opportunist, counter-revolutionary and revanchist forces. You need firm unity, courage, and determination for the solution of the most complicated problems and to avoid departing from the correct point of view. One needs to have a clear, consistent program and on that basis mobilize the communists.

[...]

Leonid Ilyich Brezhnev: Permit me as well to make a few remarks. Dear Comrades! [...]

The Polish events worry us in particular. We for the most part have talked about Poland. It pains us to see fraternal Poland going through a profound, difficult crisis. The crisis could have been avoided. It could have been suppressed and turned around in its initial phase, prior to the negative turn of events. But this did not happen.

In the course of the past four years, we asked questions about the alarming tendencies in the People's Republic of Poland in our talks with Comrade Gierek. This summer in the Crimea, I emphasized again that a decisive political fight against the anti-socialist elements was necessary. In response, we were told that nothing of special concern was happening, that there was no opposition, and that the PPR and the party were in control of the situation. What happened? Was it carelessness, hubris? Were certain ambitions the cause? I do not know.

And now the crisis, as we can see, has developed into a difficult question, not for Poland and its communists alone. The crisis hurts the entire socialist community, the international communist movement. It could have a negative impact on the general balance of power. [...]

The situation, which the comrades have described here, demands a different way of thinking and acting. One has to realize that the counter-revolution is oriented towards real conditions as they exist today. It would not risk, and would not have risked, raising itself against the government, if the Polish United Workers' Party had been mobilized completely in the face of events, if its actions had been characterized by determination and toughness.

This might sound too sharp or too harsh. But it would be completely justified to say that the crisis throughout the country accords with the crisis within the party. [...]

One month ago, we spoke at length with comrades Kania and Pińkowski. The topic of conversation was the situation as it had developed. We completely agreed on the evaluation of the situation and the determination of ways to overcome the crisis. We assumed that there was no room for retreat. We had to turn the course of events around and not wait until the enemy had the party with its back against the wall. In a word: the Polish comrades themselves had to go on the offensive against the counter-revolution and its intellectual heads. The Polish comrades and we were of the opinion that the core of the matter and the most important thing was to restore the fighting spirit of the party, to restore unity in its ranks and to mobilize all units of the party. We were all of the opinion that the PUWP could rely on the healthy forces within the nation, the army, the militia, and the state security organs as well as on that part of the union that remained faithful to the party.

As far as I know, the comrades of the other fraternal parties share our point of view.

As you know, Comrade Kania has explained that the situation has gotten worse and could not be stabilized. [...]

The comrades here have emphasized that a bitter class struggle is occurring in Poland. What is lacking? The objective is clear: Socialism must be defended! It is also clear from where the danger is emanating. The enemy's scheme has become fairly evident, and it is clear which positions he intends to take during the next steps. There is most likely a center which directs the actions of the counter-revolution and which coordinates the various departments' tactics and strategy within and outside of Poland. [...]

Particularly acute is the problem of the mass media. Unfortunately one has to admit that the situation most recently has not worked in favor of the PUWP.

As far as the army is concerned, it would be wrong to assume that events have not left any traces there. Through various channels, among others the Polish Church, obstinate attempts are being made to neutralize and subvert the armed forces.

We are not exaggerating at all on the question of responsibility, but instead are basing our views on the information of the Polish friends. During the entire crisis we have shown full understanding for the Polish comrades' [desire] to solve the crisis by political means. We do not favor taking extreme measures without extreme circumstances, and we understand the caution. But this is certain: should the enemy assume power, he would not hold back like that. From experience we know that the enemy, once in power, immediately takes extreme measures in order to eliminate the party and destroy socialism. He is after all no longer discreet in his choice of weapons: Unauthorized occupation of plants, of universities, administrative buildings, the nerve centers of transport and media, which affect the vital interests of the Warsaw Pact organization. Are these legitimate weapons? And the dishonoring of honest workers, of communists by forcing them to join Solidarity, the increasing incidents of ridiculing people in military uniforms, the incidents of sabotage in the distribution of food stuffs and consumer goods, in the transport of Polish newspapers, the cases of hiding food which further worsen the situation, and the uncontrolled import of foreign currencies, typewriters and TVs into Poland, not to speak of the threat to life to which communists and their families have been subjected. One can certainly not say that the opposition has held back, and hence the ongoing confrontation.

The reserve of the Polish party is interpreted by the opposition as a sign of weakness and indetermination, as a loss of faith in the [party's] own capabilities and power. The Supreme Court has annulled the decision of the Warsaw court and registered Solidarity. Wałęsa has drawn the conclusion that one can press further. I brought Gierek to power and I deposed him, and I can also bring the new leadership down, if I want to, he declared in an interview. This is the tone in which such things are already being discussed!

It would be unforgivable not to draw any basic conclusions from such a difficult text. It is our duty not to mince words. A terrible danger hovers over socialism in Poland. The enemy has managed to open a rift between the party and a major segment of the workers.

The Polish comrades have thus far not found a way to open the eyes of the masses, showing them that the counter-revolution intends to throw out not only the communists but also the best elements of the entire nation.

The strategic point is that the Polish comrades have to state harshly and confidently: No step back, only forward! Hence the lost positions have to be regained one after another. One has to secure the restoration of the leading role of the PUWP, one has to go on the offensive.

I have already mentioned our talks with Comrade Kania and Pińkowski. Unfortunately, nowhere near all the measures for normalizing the situation in Poland, which we talked about, have been implemented. Today these measures are even more acute and less avoidable. That is the conclusion one can draw from an analysis of the work of the Plenum of the PUWP CC. Based on the decisions of this Plenum, the Polish friends could do a lot for the improvement of the situation within the party as well as within society.

The task of all tasks is to strengthen the party organizationally, to increase its fighting capabilities. It seems to us that one has to sharply pose the question of maintaining the norm of democratic socialism within the party, the Leninist norms and methods of the party. [...]

Our experience proves—and the CPSU has gone through many trials in its history—that in extraordinary circumstances it can be helpful to establish a special commission of CC delegates who have full plenipotentiary power. They should be deployed wherever they can be helpful to the country, wherever vital areas are concerned.

[...]

Comrade Kania and others have talked about the Polish Church. Hence I will be brief. It is clear to us that a confrontation with the Church would only worsen the situation. But with this in mind we should influence as far as possible the moderate circles within the Catholic Church in our direction and keep them from closely allying themselves with the extreme anti-socialist forces and those who desire the fall of socialism in Poland and to take over power.

I repeat once again and once more: It is extremely important to restore control over the mass media. To let the mass media slip out of party control would mean to hand the enemy a very sharp weapon. We know that this is one of the greatest problems for the PUWP. [...]

A lot of correct things have already been said here about the intentions and actions of the imperialist reaction. The West does not limit itself to watching events in Poland unfold, it is directly involved. There are probably certain connections between the attempts of the international reactionary forces to launch an offensive on the position of the socialist system and an activation of the counter-revolution in Poland. I sense this in our contacts with the U.S. and other capitalist countries. We have unequivocally warned them against interference in internal Polish affairs. We have made it clear to them that neither Poland's communists nor the friends and allies of Poland would allow them to tear Poland out of the socialist community. It has been and will be an inseparable member of the political, economic and military system of socialism.

Comrades! Officially the situation in Poland is not termed an emergency. But in reality it is! Of course, the formal act does not matter. Hence the Polish comrades are acting correctly when they prepare for extraordinary measures. Intermediate steps have to be taken immediately since there is no time until the start of the counteroffensive. Tomorrow it will be more difficult than today to cope with the counter-revolution.

The situation with the lines of communication, especially the railroads and harbors, merits extreme attention. An economic catastrophe threatens Poland in the event of a stoppage at the transport facilities. It would constitute a blow against the economic interests of a number of socialist states. I repeat: In no case can we allow the security interests of the Warsaw Pact countries to be endangered due to transportation difficulties. A precise plan has to be developed as to how army and security forces can secure control over the transportation facilities and main communications lines, and this plan has to be effectively implemented. Without declaring martial law it is useful to establish military command posts and introduce patrolling services along the railroads.

[Concluding remarks regarding public communiqué.]

End of the Meeting: 15:30.

[Source: SAPMO-BArch, J IV 2/2 A-2368. First published in Michael Kubina and Manfred Wilke, "Hart und kompromißlos durchgreifen:" Die SED contra Polen 1980/81: Geheimakten der SED-Führung über die Unterdrückung der polnischen Demokratiebewegung. (Berlin: Akademie Verlag, 1994), pp. 140–195. Translated by Christian F. Ostermann.]

Document No. 23: Minutes of U.S.
Special Coordination Committee Meeting

December 7, 1980

Two days after the critical Warsaw Pact leadership meeting, President Carter and his aides remained in doubt about Soviet intentions regarding Poland. According to CIA source Ryszard Kukliński, an intervention was set to take place the following day, but at the NSC meeting summarized below, the president indicated that it was unclear whether this would in fact happen. Still, the administration intended to take measures to try to forestall any such possibility. These included certain low-profile military moves, a range of political and economic actions and a major attempt—including another presidential message to allies, the text of which is included here—to persuade the Western allies to join forces in the enterprise.

Summary of Conclusions

An SCC meeting, chaired by Dr. Brzezinski, followed by an NSC meeting, chaired by the President was held on December 7 to discuss the U. S. response to Soviet preparations for a possible military intervention in Poland.

The NSC agreed to issue a White House statement warning of preparations for a possible Soviet intervention in Poland expressing hope that such an intervention would not take place, and stressing the very adverse consequences for U. S.–Soviet relations of any Soviet military intervention in Poland.

The purpose of the statement was to raise world consciousness about the possibility of a Soviet intervention in Poland, either through a surreptitious insertion of forces or through a full scale military invasion. It was hoped that such a statement might provoke a denial and help to deter any intervention.

The *President* approved the texts of messages to Chancellor Schmidt, President Giscard d'Estaing and Prime Minister Thatcher, informing them of our actions. Similar messages were also sent to the Italians, Canadians, Japanese, as well as Secretary General Luns of NATO and U. N. Secretary General Waldheim. It was agreed that Secretary [Edmund] Muskie would also call Waldheim personally.

The *President* briefed Senators Cranston and Stevens and Congressmen Rhodes and O'Neill[26] on the current developments in Poland and U. S. actions. He informed them that he was issuing a statement, which he read. He pointed

---

[26] Alan Cranston (D-Calif.) and Ted Stevens (R-Alaska) were their parties' assistant leaders (whips) in the U.S. Senate. John J. Rhodes (R-Ariz.) was House minority leader and Thomas J. ("Tip") O'Neill, Jr. (D-Mass.) was Speaker of the House.

out that our action was based on our monitoring of Soviet military preparations. We had conflicting reports from the Summit[27] and did not really know whether the Soviets were trying to move in or exactly how they would do it. It could be through open aggression or under the guise of maneuvers. The complicating factor was that Brezhnev planned to go to India on December 8. At the moment he was in Tashkent. We were consulting with our Allies and had also notified Richard Allen, who would brief Governor Reagan as soon as he had left church. We were also sending messages to Giscard, Thatcher and Schmidt, as well as to the Italians, Japanese, Canadians, U. N. and NATO, informing them of our actions and why we were undertaking them.

The *President* then read the White House message to the congressional leaders. He noted that, due to a fortunate coincidence of circumstances, Secretaries [Harold] Brown and Muskie would be meeting with their Allied counterparts in Brussels next week. He pointed out that a Soviet move into Poland would reduce Soviet readiness-time for an attack upon Western Europe by a week. However, we did not expect an attack on Western Europe. If the Soviets intervened militarily, some bloodshed was likely, but it was unclear how much. We did not intend to get involved militarily, but we did intend to take a number of political and economic measures. Unfortunately, the more we did unilaterally, the less the Europeans were likely to do.

The *President* also asked Secretary Brown to outline the military measures we had taken. *Secretary Brown* stated that we were doing some things unilaterally, mostly in the area of logistics. However, we were not taking high-visibility personnel moves. SACEUR had asked for authority to take certain preparatory measures but he had not asked for authority to actually implement them. We could do some other additional things such as adding F-15s or moving some divisions to Europe. We were reluctant to do these, however, before first pressing the Allies. In sum, we were doing some things unilaterally, but these were not high-profile things.

The *President* summed up the discussion by stressing that we did not know whether the Soviets would go in. Our first goal was to keep them out. Secondly, we did not know how they would go in, whether under the guise of maneuvers or by means of a full scale invasion. Thirdly, the Poles would probably resist.

* * *

---

[27] A reference to the Warsaw Pact summit of December 5. See Document No. 22.

December 7, 1980

Message to Schmidt, Giscard, Thatcher, Trudeau, Luns, Forlani, Frazier, Suzuki, Waldheim [...]

Preparations for Soviet intervention in Poland appear to be essentially completed. Further, we have some evidence which indicates that the Soviet Union has made the decision to intervene with military force and that the entry into Poland by a substantial Soviet force, possibly under the guise of a joint maneuver, may be imminent.[28] This may be accompanied by widespread arrests by Polish security forces. We cannot be confident that this is the case, but the probability is sufficiently high that in my view Western nations should take whatever steps they can to affect Soviet decision-making and thus try to prevent the entry of Soviet forces into Poland.

Accordingly, I am issuing the following statement at 2:00 p.m. today Washington time. I trust that you will be able to issue similar statements soon. Such statements will demonstrate to the Soviets the resolve of the Western Alliance and will serve to warn the Polish people of the serious nature of the current situation.

[...]
End Text.
Sincerely,
Jimmy Carter

[Source: FOIA release from the National Security Council, on file at the National Security Archive, "Soviet Flashpoints" collection.]

---

[28] In other declassified versions of this message, this sentence and the next were excised presumably because the information came from Kukliński.

Document No. 24: CIA Situation Report, "Poland"

December 8, 1980

After a feverish weekend of attempts to determine whether an invasion of Poland was imminent, the CIA, as reported in this document, was prepared only to say that the Warsaw Pact, primarily consisting of Soviet forces, was "ready for military intervention." Agency analysts admitted that "we are not able to predict when the combat forces will begin moving into Poland." Part of the problem was the presence of heavy cloud cover over Poland which obstructed the view of U.S. spy satellites. By the date of this document, of course, Soviet-led forces were already scheduled to have entered Poland, according to martial law planner Ryszard Kukliński. But the leaders of the Warsaw Pact had already decided to postpone any military action for the time being (see Document No. 22).

Situation Reports

Poland

We estimate that the Warsaw Pact, with predominantly Soviet forces, is ready for military intervention in Poland. We are not able to predict when combat forces begins moving into Poland. Warsaw Pact military preparations have advanced to the point where some 15–25 divisions now could be ready for a military intervention in Poland.

President Brezhnev and Foreign Minister Gromyko arrived in New Delhi today for an official visit and will return to Moscow on Thursday. The Soviets are less likely to intervene while Brezhnev is out of the USSR, but we cannot rule out the possibility that they will.

Military Preparations

[One paragraph, 10 lines, excised]

[Two lines excised] evidence of mobilization activity and preparation of forces in East Germany, Czechoslovakia, and all three western military districts of the USSR. We have not detected any substantial mobilization activity by Polish or Soviet forces in Poland.

In East Germany, [two lines excised] Seven Soviet divisions opposite West Germany appear to have gone on alert since Wednesday, possibly in anticipation of Western reactions. Soviet divisions in Germany are maintained at high manning levels in peacetime and do not require mobilization of reservists. Troops in some East German units have had their leaves restricted, and increased states of readiness have been imposed.

In Czechoslovakia, elements of one Soviet and three Czechoslovak divisions moved out of their garrisons over the weekend. Two other Czechoslovak divisions were preparing for deployment on Saturday. [Two lines excised]

Mobilization activity has been observed at four Soviet divisions in the western USSR—two in the Baltic and two in the Carpathian Military Districts. [Half line excised] truck convoys in the southwest portion of the Baltic Military District also suggests logistics support units have been mobilized. Another division in the Belorussian Military District also may be preparing to move.

Before the Soviet invasion of Czechoslovakia in 1968, the Soviets moved airborne troops from their garrisons to departure airfields and assembled transport aircraft from other regions of the USSR at airfields where they could more directly support military operations in Eastern Europe. [Four lines excised]

We have not detected increased readiness levels of Soviet strategic rocket forces or naval forces. This could be implemented on short notice, however, just before an intervention was initiated. [Half line excised]

[Source: FOIA release from the CIA, on file at the National Security Archive, "Soviet Flashpoints" collection.]

166

Document No. 25: Transcript of CPSU CC Politburo Meeting

December 11, 1980

Following the December 5 Warsaw Pact leadership meeting, the Soviet Politburo was upbeat about the prospects for Poland. As indicated in this transcript, the Kremlin was impressed by Kania's presentation at the earlier meeting and the general expectation was that he would take to heart the advice offered to him by the other alliance leaders. Tellingly, in his summary, Mikhail Suslov mentions the speeches of several Soviet bloc leaders but omits any mention of the calls by Erich Honecker and Todor Zhivkov for imminent military action. At the Politburo session below, the effusive praise heaped on Brezhnev was characteristic of this period when the aging leader was in a poor state of health and often ceded practical authority to various of his colleagues.

[…]

1. On the results of the meeting of leaders of the Warsaw Pact member-states in Moscow on December 5, 1980.

Suslov: All the comrades have read the communiqué that was published in the press. It must be said that the decision to hold the meeting of leaders of the Warsaw Pact member-states was absolutely timely. A very thorough exchange of opinions took place at the meeting. The state representatives and first secretaries of the communist and workers' parties provided thorough reports. It must be said that the speech by Cde. Kania was on the whole interesting *[soderzhatel'nyi]*. Of course, it could have been more pointed on certain questions. However, if one is to look at Cde. Kania's speech as a whole, then in comparison with the speech he delivered to the Politburo at the plenum in his own country it was more self-critical, sharper and more correct. Most importantly, the Polish comrades understand the great danger that hangs over Poland, and they recognize the great harm of the actions of the anti-socialist elements who represent a great threat to the socialist gains of the Polish people. Cde. Kania now discusses Poland's economic conditions more soberly, its obligations to the capitalist countries, the provision of aid.

It must be noted that in his speech Cde. Kania leveled a relatively more decisive attack against the anti-socialist elements and noted that there would be no retreat and no indulgence toward the anti-socialist elements. At the same time, he noted that the Polish United Workers' Party, the Polish people, its healthy forces, its armed forces, the organs of state security and the police, which support the PUWP, will be able to deal with and normalize the situation by their own means.

The speeches of all the other comrades contained advice to the Polish friends on how to act, and how decisively one must attack the anti-socialist elements. Cde. Husák, for instance, provided quite a number of examples from the experience of 1968 when the CPCz CC had to carry on a stubborn battle with the rightist elements. Cde. Kádár also spoke about the statements by counter-revolutionary elements in 1956 in Hungary when he had to take harsh administrative measures in order to destroy the counter-revolution. Cde. Ceauşescu, true to his tradition, spoke more about independence, sovereignty and non-interference in internal affairs, and so on.

The brilliant speech of L. I. Brezhnev was received with great interest and attention. It was very balanced and contained all the necessary instructions for the PUWP and the Polish comrades, and as the Polish comrades themselves said later, L. I. Brezhnev's speech inspired them. The leaders and representatives of the other parties also evaluated Cde. Brezhnev's speech very highly.

In a word, I consider that the results of the meeting of the leaders of the member-states of the Warsaw Pact should be approved, along with the activities of the delegation of the Soviet Union headed by L. I. Brezhnev.

Andropov: The meeting was conducted on a very high level. Of course, the main thing was the speech of Leonid Ilyich, which set the tone for the entire meeting.

Ustinov: The presentation by Leonid Ilyich did not leave a single question unclear. It was clear to everyone what the Polish comrades should do and how they should act.

Gromyko: Just as the Polish comrades did, the other participants at the meeting also left very satisfied with the results of this meeting. They received a necessary supply of energy and instructions on all questions related to the situation in Poland.

Politburo members Cdes. Grishin, Kirilenko, Pel'she and CPSU CC Secretary Cde. Rusakov also expressed their opinions on this question.

Resolved: to approve the activities of the USSR delegation at the meeting of leaders and member-states of the Warsaw Pact headed by General Secretary of the CPSU CC, Chairman of the Presidium of the USSR Supreme Soviet Cde. L. I. Brezhnev.

Suslov: I believe that we should publish the resolution in the press approving the results of the meeting.

Cde. Suslov reads out the draft resolution: adopt the results of the meeting of leaders of member-states of the Warsaw Pact, and also the activities of the delegation of the Soviet Union at this meeting headed by Cde. L. I. Brezhnev.

All: Correct, agreed.

Suslov: Then there is a proposal to publish the resolution tomorrow in the press.

[Source: RGANI, Fond 89, Opis 42, Delo 59. Translated by Malcolm Byrne for the National Security Archive.]

PART THREE

From Crisis
to Crisis

Document No. 26: Protocol of Meeting of Leading *Aktiv* Members of Ministry of Internal Affairs

January 5, 1981

This protocol excerpt reproduces comments Kania made to a meeting of the leading aktiv of the Ministry of Internal Affairs. It provides a good summary of the latest wave of preparations for a crackdown that got underway after the December 5, 1980, Warsaw Pact meeting in Moscow. After winning a temporary reprieve from outside intervention at that session, Kania uses this gathering to transmit political instructions to SB agents in various areas. He minces no words about the seriousness of the "threat" facing the country, although he indicates that violent crackdowns are not the answer—because of both the domestic and international repercussions. The most important lesson from his standpoint is to be well prepared, which by his definition includes mounting a major propaganda operation in advance, among other measures, and leaving nothing to chance.

[...]

Comrade S. Kania stated that the speeches at the conference were concentrated around the matter of how to act effectively, and in what manner to win over the allies for the struggle. This is very essential because the people's authority has not been in such a difficult situation for many years and it has not conducted such a struggle. In this situation, difficult tasks stand before the Ministry of Internal Affairs since it is the major party and people's authority expert in the political struggle.

The problems that stand before the party and the people's authority are very complex; from an appraisal of the situation, however, a fundamental consequence emerges, that an onslaught does not resolve anything. Serious threats exist in the country, a very sharp class struggle on a wide front is rolling along, there is talk about counter-revolutionary activities. These matters are treated in a document discussed at the conference. Both in the document and in the discussions KOR is exposed as the steering force against socialism. However, examining the current situation and the existing crisis it is necessary to consider that we have in fact a number of crises in the country: impaired social trust, a blooming of enemy activities, an extraordinarily difficult situation in the domestic market, a very difficult situation in production, and difficulties with foreign trade (exports do not cover imports). In order to exist it is necessary to borrow, this and next year, 10 billion dollars; however, that will cause a further drop in the national income. That is also why, in our internal actions, we must take into account the kind of repercussions they may engender in the West. Of course, this is not about apprehensions in the face of repercussions in the mass media. In the situation in which our country finds itself, particular significance is gathered with Poland acquiring credits in the USSR in the amount of 2 billion złoty. To this, supplies of petroleum from the USSR have arrived valued at 450,000 dollars—secured at the cost of other socialist countries. However, our country needs 10 billion dollars. Both in our society and in the working class a feeling has arisen that it is still possible to put forward additional economic demands, that further means exist which can be divided among society.

All the crises mentioned above make our situation uncommonly complicated, and the adversary sees this.

Our doctrinal foundation comes down to this, that we must resolve the existing situation; it may not be quickly, but surely this itself is necessary and possible. The speaker expressed that this is the position of the Politburo and he presented such a position during the last talks in Moscow.

Objectives to clear up the difficult situation must be carried out on a wide front, and the role of the MSW in them is very essential. The party authorities highly appraise the "political form" of the MSW. The ministry's apparatus must, however, be conscious of the threat, and in educational work it is necessary to recall history more often. In the present situation educational work with functionaries is taking on a constantly greater meaning. The situation is constantly more complicated and certain phenomena cannot be related to 1949.[1]

The complicated phenomenon in our time is NSZZ Solidarity. There is a serious workers' current in it, with the participation of many thousands of working people, with the participation of many party members. This last fact can have a positive influence on the further activities of Solidarity. However, it is necessary to take under consideration that this also creates a threat of negative influence on the party organizations.

There is also a counter-revolutionary thread in Solidarity—KOR.

In Solidarity the danger is this—that this is a movement of young people. They are characterized by much aggression and limited susceptibility to the restraining influence of both the party and the Church. This is a current of disturbance carrying with it great danger.

Another dangerous matter is the attempt to organize Rural Solidarity. This is in fact an attempt to create a new PPP—only more dangerous. This action should be opposed. Presently it appears that in regions where the party went for fighting the farmers' circles and dismantling its self-organization, this paid off, since the slogans concerning establishing Solidarity do not find a hearing there.

In further declarations the speaker touched on certain aspects of the matter of the youth and cultural circles. He stated that in August and September serious anxieties existed as far as the beginning of the academic year. However, the situation in this area is presenting itself better than expected. To be sure, at the

[1] 1949 marked the beginning of a period of intensified Sovietization of Poland, including the purge of Władysław Gomułka as a "rightist deviationist" and the appointment of Soviet Marshal Konstantin Rokossovskii as defense minister.

SUPS Congress there were expressions, for instance, against the leading role of the party, applause for speakers indicating such demands; however, for the proposal in this matter, with 400 present, only five persons voted.

Positive advances are occurring in the USPY; there is also no indication that anti-socialist centers are being formed in the womb of that organization. The party wants to keep the USPY as an organization for the entire generation of working youth.

It is necessary to refer to the youth problem with great concern, even more so that it comes up against such problems and difficulties as, for instance, a shortage of apartments. It is necessary that the MSW organs keep the youth in mind and guard them against anti-socialist elements.

Discussing the matter of the situation in cultural circles, he expressed the view that the elections at the last UPW Congress cannot be ill-judged and treated as lost. To be sure, there were wrong pronouncements at the Congress and the majority present were against socialism; however, a few party writers entered into the Executive structure, and five relentless KOR representatives were not selected.

The party will, with all its might, strengthen the party's front in literature. It is also necessary to remember that on our side there are better writers, there are stronger pens.

Touching on the matter of the atmosphere prevailing at present, he emphasized that the characteristic feature is a higher consciousness of the existing threat to the country. Looking at it from this point of view, the Seventh Plenum was already different, and meetings presently taking place are different. Our opponents overextended the cord of anti-socialist slogans (the rail strike, the Narożniak affair[2]). Advantages also pass to us from these facts: society caught sight of the trouble makers and the prudent authorities.

The decisions, which were taken in relation to the existing facts in a specific situation, were correct.

Because we stood before the threat of a general strike, in the existing situation the terrain and moment of confrontation were unsuitable. At the moment, increasing "soberness" is asserting itself among non-party persons, and also the Church.

In further comments, the speaker stated that the Church and Episcopate have drawn profits from the existing tension, because they were able to acquire the position of defenders of welfare matters.

However, the key matter for the future of the country is the situation in the party—in its ranks the consciousness of a threat has risen. Indicating the trumps which we gained in the course of arranging and resolving matters of conflict up to the present, the speaker added to them that we have come out of the conflict without using force, that in the general assessment the authorities have shown themselves to be reasonable, that we can treat the Church as a tactical ally.

[2] See footnote 11 on p. 134.

At the present moment, it is necessary to realize that the West is interested in stability in Poland, so that it does not come to a dangerous explosion. At the time of the last meeting in Moscow, points of view were expressed that the reason the West is not interested in an explosion in Poland is because it treats it as an incubator of germs with diversionary functions directed against the countries of the socialist community.

Moving to unsettled proposals, including also proposals about the work of the MSW, he indicated that a correction to the situation in the country may follow as a result of an attack on the opponent, as well as obtaining the trust of the working class on the basis of facts, and the internal strengthening of the party.

The rebukes included in the presentations addressed at the mass media were correct. It is necessary to state, however, that at these centers changes for the better have occurred, expressed in the decline of bad publications. However, there is a continued sense of a shortage of good articles. In the area discussed, the MSW has a serious role to fulfill by furnishing suitable materials and inspiration, which might contribute to the realization of a correct publications policy. The Politburo has recognized as necessary the appointment of a discretionary group of journalists who will investigate the activities of anti-socialist groups and the changes occurring in them, as well as to publish suitable studies and articles.

In our solutions and plans, however, it is not possible to exclude confrontation with the anti-socialist forces. The Politburo assigned a team, which is studying a different variety of operations, including the introduction of Martial Law.

The operations conducted by the Ministry of Internal Affairs are proper. The intentions and operations of the Main Headquarters of the CP are proper. [...]

The realization of the intentions included in the program will influence the state of discipline, and also (relating to the fight against speculation, parasites, and the like) awaken the sympathy of society. Simultaneously there is a need to place stress on popularizing those operations of the organs that will awaken the sympathy of society.

In the study documents there is a need to take into account different activities with an operational character. At the same time, it is not only about obtaining good information, but also about having influence on different cells.

It is also necessary to consider an appropriate organizational arrangement, as well as the regrouping of forces. The situation in the country is diverse. There are centers of future danger, from which there are no concrete threats at present. It is necessary to weigh cadre matters thoroughly at the Ministry [of Internal Affairs], and to move cadres suitably so that discreet and dynamic persons can be directed during the most threatening period. Indeed, retreat by the authorities has reached its limit; however, decisions must be prudent and they should by taken after making allowances for and taking advantage of all contingencies. Prudence also demands that the matter of control be at the highest levels of experienced functionaries.

In conclusion, he acknowledged that the conference should be treated as a workshop.

174

The Comrade Minister [Mirosław Milewski] thanked the first secretary [of the PUWP], Comrade Barcikowski, Comrade [Michał] Atlas, as well as those gathered at the conference and declared that the Ministry will consciously fulfill the tasks that will be presented to them.

Beginning of conference 13:30.
End of conference 18:00.

[Source: Operacja "Lato-80". Preludium stanu wojennego. Dokumenty MSW, *Peter Raina, Marcin Zbrożek (Pelplin: Bernardinum, 2003), pp. 127–130. Translated by L.W. Głuchowski for the National Security Archive.]*

Document No. 27: CPSU CC Instructions to the Soviet Ambassador Concerning Lech Wałęsa Visit to Italy

January 14, 1981

In mid-January 1981, Solidarity leader Lech Wałęsa made a highly publicized visit to Italy that included an audience with the pope and meetings with Italian labor organizations. The Soviets understood the tremendous opportunity the trip presented for Solidarity to generate even broader global support for its cause, particularly in Western Europe, where the Soviets were engaged in their own efforts to score propaganda points on the eve of Ronald Reagan's inauguration as president of the United States. These two documents represent the Kremlin's effort to try to limit Solidarity's reach and undercut the public relations value of the visit. It clearly irked the Kremlin that Wałęsa was even allowed to travel abroad. In the Soviet Union and most other countries of the Warsaw Pact, much stricter limitations on individual travel were the norm. Wałęsa's presence in Italy did indeed generate wide attention, particularly his four-hour audience with the pope. But in fact he made an effort to depoliticize the visit, showing a degree of caution that contrasted with the numerous strikes Solidarity carried out during his absence.

RESOLUTION OF THE SECRETARIAT OF THE CPSU CC

On instructions to the Soviet ambassador in Italy in connection with L. Wałęsa's trip to Italy

1. Affirm the text of instructions to the Soviet ambassador to Italy (attached).
2. Send a copy of the appeal to the leadership of the PCI to the Central Committee of the Polish United Workers' Party.

CC Secretary

[…]

The Soviet Ambassador

Meet with Cde. Berlinguer[3] or his surrogate, and state the following:
(For Warsaw, convey to Cde. Kania, or his designee, the text of the following telegram, which was transmitted to Rome.)

---

[3] Enrico Berlinguer (1922–1984) was head of the Italian Communist Party. A sharp critic of the Soviet invasion of Afghanistan, he was a public supporter of Solidarity and had warned Moscow of the "gravest consequences" of a military intervention in Poland (*The New York Times*, December 11, 1980, p. 7).

"In connection with the trip to Italy begun by L. Wałęsa, leader of the Polish trade union 'Solidarity,' the CPSU CC would like to impart its views.

"At present, the leaders of Solidarity and those who stand with them are aiming to proceed down the path of exacerbating the socio-political situation in Poland, and intensify its pressure on the leadership of the PUWP and the government, having consolidated in its platform all who strive to weaken the party's position and its leading role in the country. That is exactly how matters stand with Solidarity's declaration on the introduction of a five-day work week, which spilled over into an attempt to switch to open confrontation with the position of the PUWP. This supports our evaluation, which is familiar to you from the CPSU CC appeal to the PCI[4] leadership, that counter-revolutionary attacks on the very foundations of socialism in the PPR have begun to assume ever greater prominence in the activities of Solidarity.

"The political plans and actions of Solidarity are constantly being manifested, leading to a deterioration of the economic situation in Poland and the shattering of the foundations of socialist society. It is well-known that the economic situation in Poland is extremely difficult. In these conditions, the further intensification of demands that do not take account of the real state of the economy, not to mention labor disruptions, could lead at a minimum to still greater disorganization in the economic life of the country. It is typical that government representatives explained to Solidarity leaders in detail that an immediate and complete transition to a five-day workweek [instead of] a gradual transition over the next five-year period, as planned by the government, could entail a drop in living standards of 8–9 percent, and lead to a significant decrease in the volume of industrial production, including consumer goods. The fact that Solidarity ignored that warning and in spite of it tried to organize practically a general strike with demands for the immediate introduction of a five-day work week, indicates that the leaders of that organization seek neither an improvement of the situation of the working class and of all workers, nor the defense of their real interests, but the further weakening of the party's position and the creation of a situation that would be fraught with a new and dangerous exacerbation of the conflict.

"This union currently constitutes a genuine force. Moreover, it does not represent a unified organization in an ideological or political sense. Serious disagreements appear in its midst between individual leaders and regional groups, a number of which openly dissociate themselves from the activity of the anti-socialist elements and occupy a strong position in the central leadership of Solidarity.

"Within the Wałęsa delegation are representatives of the so-called KOR (Committee for the Defense of Workers), an organization with an obviously anti-socialist character: [Andrzej] Gwiazda, [Anna] Walentynowicz and [Karol] Modzelewski are well-known for their openly anti-communist and anti-Soviet sentiments. It is entirely probable that these people are trying to use Wałęsa's visit

[4] Italian Communist Party.

to Italy not only to advertise Solidarity and their own personal views, but also, based on so-to-speak 'international support,' to undertake new attacks on socialism in Poland.

"We would like to direct your attention to the fact that the complexity of the ideological-political conditions in Poland is caused in part by the fact that different forces attribute directly contradictory connotations to the slogan 'renewal.' Some—the PUWP and its allies—understand it to mean an affirmation of the principles of socialism and a resurrection of Leninist norms of party life, but others have in mind the erosion and splintering of the socialist order. This duality of concrete substance, which is wrapped up in the slogan 'renewal,' is being used by opponents of the party and socialism in Poland to mask their real positions and intentions.

"Proceeding from the above, it is obvious that the interests of the Polish people and the interests of the PUWP and its course toward socialist renewal would be served by the neutralization on your part of attempts by Wałęsa and his circle to use his visit to Italy for anti-communist, anti-socialist and anti-Soviet purposes.

"At present, support for the current political line of the leadership of the Solidarity union, which, acting legally in Poland, aims in addition to undermine its constitutional order, would effectively signify support for its struggle against the PUWP.

"Taking account of all the stated conditions, we consider it our duty to bring this to the attention of the PCI leadership."

Telegraph upon implementation.

* * *

On instructions to the Soviet ambassador in Italy in connection with L. Wałęsa's trip to Italy

From January 14–18, 1981, at the invitation of local trade unions, a delegation from Solidarity (18 persons) led by L. Wałęsa, which will also include representatives of the political opposition who maintain anti-socialist tendencies (cipher telegram from Warsaw, spec. no. 15 of January 7, 1981).

According to existing evidence, the bourgeois parties and means of mass communication intend to make broad use of the visit of this delegation to Italy to discredit the socialist order in the Polish People's Republic (PPR), to support the line aimed at shaking, and in the end eliminating the socialist achievements in Poland. Toward these ends, the organization of a reception for members of the delegation is planned at a rather high trade union and political level. Aside from audiences with the pope in the Vatican, there are plans for L. Wałęsa and his delegation to be received by the leadership of the United Trade Union Federation VIKT-IKPT-IST, and to organize meetings with workers' collectives. Notwithstanding an initial decision to refuse to meet with L. Wałęsa, the leadership of

178

the Italian communist party up till now has taken a vacillating stance and does not exclude the possibility of these or other contacts with him.

We would consider it expedient to address the leadership of the Italian communist party, which occupies a strong position in the Italian trade union movement and wields significant influence in political circles in its country.

In this connection, one could give instructions to the Soviet ambassador in Italy concerning a meeting with E. Berlinguer or his designee, in the course of which the attention of the PCI leadership could be focused on the need to take all possible steps to ensure that the visit of L. Wałęsa to Italy does not lend support to the line of the political opposition which maintains anti-socialist tendencies.

It would be expedient to send a copy of the appeal to the PCI leadership to the PUWP CC.

The draft resolution of the CPSU CC is attached.

[Source: RGANI, Fond 89, Opis 43, Delo 49. Translated by Malcolm Byrne for the National Security Archive.]

Document No. 28: PUWP CC Report on Leonid Zamyatin's Visit to Katowice

January 16, 1981

Beginning in early 1981, a steady stream of Soviet delegations visited Poland representing different institutions: the CPSU CC, the military and the KGB, among others. Of course, the most important were the visits by high officials, such as Leonid Zamyatin, the head of the CC's Department of International Information and a member of the so-called Suslov Commission on the Polish crisis. This meeting took place in Katowice, one of the centers of the PUWP hard line and home to Politburo member Andrzej Żabiński. These sessions were a kind of reconnaissance mission for the Kremlin, a chance to discover, for example, who in the PUWP might support stronger measures against Solidarity. Żabiński was seen by Moscow as one possible alternative to Kania. This report below is from the Polish side. See also Document No. 29 for the CPSU Politburo discussion of Zamyatin's findings.

REPORT

From the visit to Katowice of a Soviet group with comrade L. M. Zamyatin on January 16, 1981

Program: Meetings at *Trybuna Robotnicza,* PR&TV, and with the leadership of the Voivodeship Committee chaired by Comrade A. Żabinski.

The comrades from Katowice presented the political-economic situation honestly and firmly, putting great stress on the program and ways of overcoming the crisis.

The delegation very much liked the way of thinking and concepts for solutions presented by A. Żabinski and other comrades.

Comrade Zamyatin emphasized several times, outside of official meetings as well, that he did not understand why the party did not act firmly to isolate the enemy. According to him this is particularly needed in the mass media.

Local authorities have to receive not only instructions for such action, but also assistance and constant encouragement from the central authorities.

During the course of all meetings Zamyatin spoke directly after the host's statement, expressing, in various forms, the following views and suggestions:

1. The criticism of mistakes which has taken place in the open public for several months in Poland produces only negative effects, deepens the crisis, and reduces the faith of the working class in the leadership's ability to take the nation out of the crisis. Criticism without a program is harmful.

2. Solidarity by its mere existence deepens the crisis in Poland. It adds to the mistakes made by some comrades in the late 1970s. A group of intelligen-

tsia, also party intelligentsia, is assisting the enemy by supporting its demagogy which aims at destabilizing the situation in Poland. "The impression of improvement in the standard of living has long been created in Poland by giving people money with insufficient backing. This occurrence has been particularly pronounced during recent months." Those who organized pay rises together with those who received them resort to criticism that the increases are not reflected in the supply of goods. So, everything turns against the authorities once again. This is a method of fighting socialist power in Poland preconceived by the staffs (including foreign ones).

3. In Poland, the enemy does not attack, it rarely even undermines the leading role of the party, but by organizing strikes (warning, hunger, solidarity and general ones), destabilizing the market and ridiculing the authorities it proves that the party is not prepared to govern.

4. You announce reforms and introduce changes in governance; you initiate discussions about it and make a lot of noise in the press, radio and television, but you do not agitate in favor of work or against chaos and strikes.

5. The enemy wants to weaken Poland, reduce its role in the socialist camp, weaken our community, weaken the Warsaw Pact, and reduce the effectiveness of the fight for peace and détente. "They (imperialists) know that they cannot defeat us militarily, they cannot physically violate our borders, because this would meet with decisive resistance. They have therefore chosen another (undeclared) war, a war of ideological sabotage." Zamyatin repeated twice the statement by [President] Carter that currently they do not need missiles as much as they need new means to carry out a psychological war. (Currently, three radio stations have larger significance than ten missile complexes.)

Lately, over 6,000 well-prepared specialists—wise enemies hired by RFE—have been working against us. They want to lead to our dissolution from the inside by taking advantage of Polish ideological weaknesses.

Therefore, the fundamental problem lies in the educational and ideological work of the party, which is also being carried out by the mass media, in which, unfortunately, things are not going well as far as understanding political and ideological matters; there is a lot of turmoil.

6. "We share the opinion of your leaders that Poland has been, is, and will be a socialist country, and that it will be an indisputable part of the socialist camp. We believe that you are able to solve your problems on your own because although some persons in your party have made mistakes, the party itself is pure and strong."

7. Zamyatin repeated a number of times that by organizing strikes, Solidarity is fulfilling the will of those who support it, who send it millions of dollars—various yellow unions or foundations of the Seidel[5] type.

8. For the first time, he evaluated in strongly negative terms the ideological-political decay among the youth, mainly students; they lack combativeness. He

---

[5] Presumably a reference to the Munich-based Hanns Seidel Foundation, a conservative-leaning political foundation associated with the Christian Social Union.

referred to the example from the 15th of this month when at the U.W. [University of Warsaw], in the presence of 1,000 students, the party and socialism were attacked, the Soviet Union was slandered and hence alliances were undermined, and nobody had the courage to take up the fight with the enemy; (this allegedly took place during a closed showing of the film "Workers '80").[6]

9. Also for the first time, he put forward a proposition that KOR is not a Polish phenomenon but an instrument for the struggle with socialism created by foreign centers of sabotage.

10. Both at the PR&TV as well as at the VC, he described extensively the sabotage activities of foreign correspondents and radio-television stations permanently accredited and occasionally resident in Poland. He accused Polish authorities of making it easier and even helping them in this sabotage activity. He discussed the recent interviews of Kuroń, Michnik and Gwiazda with the foreign press.

He blamed the authorities for allowing such facts and not holding responsible both those who conduct interviews and those being interviewed. "These people are after all fighting with the authorities and the party."

11. At the PR&TV, he asked those present at the meeting whether they did not notice that "things have become worse in Poland since that discussion and criticism began. You even have to purchase potatoes, and you used to export them. Nowadays, peasants instead of concentrating on food production are fighting to establish Solidarity. What is going to happen when they do establish it?"

12. He once more referred to the matter of debt as an inappropriate policy of the past. He said that we have accumulated a debt of 28 billion dollars, mainly in France and the FRG. "Do not count on the fact that they will be willing to give you new loans again and all that in exchange for nothing." The Soviet Union has, since the beginning of the crisis, that is in the course of the last several months, given Poland aid exceeding 2 billion dollars *gratis*.

Poland is a factor for economic destabilization in the CMEA. Poland is a source of tension in all of Europe where the danger of confrontation has always existed and is becoming more realistic in the situation that is emerging. Stating sometimes that Poland has been and will be a socialist country you do not focus on what this means in practice, that it is also a matter of continued struggle for the preservation of peace in which Poland together with the entire socialist camp has participated actively for the last 30 years.

In the VC, Zamyatin said among other things:

13. Our leadership is wondering whether the Poles have done everything to destroy the opponent who hides behind the back of the working class. What is happening in Poland is not just an ideological and political struggle anymore; it is a battle for positions in the economy, for positions of power. It is an opposition

[6] "Robotnicy '80", a documentary film about the Gdańsk strikes and birth of Solidarity directed by Andrzej Zajączkowski and Andrzej Chodakowski.

which has so far used demagogy; it puts the authorities in a difficult situation. Thirty-six people from KOR are not doing it themselves; there are other forces behind them.

14. The political work in the mass media is a weak aspect of the PUWP. Central TV cannot be a medium for dissemination of one's own views, the views of individual journalists or groups. The program produced there does not demonstrate engagement; it is not convincing. We have been told on TV that they want to proceed step-by-step, explain things; but the enemy is acting broadly, rapidly, and on all fronts. The party must analyze the situation in the mass media.

15. The Solidarity leadership may soon begin to play a similar role to that of the leadership of "the yellow Trade Unions in capitalist countries." This will be the beginning of a diarchy. Allowing Solidarity to publish its own newspaper will create a very bad situation in the country. "You are not able to control what they are already publishing, you are not getting rid of leaflets, you are giving them paper, so what is going to happen when they get a weekly?"

At the end, he reported on Cde. Brezhnev's conviction that the Poles are doing everything to eliminate the impact of the enemy on Poland and her neighbors. He stressed that Cde. Kania and the leadership enjoy the full confidence of Cde. L. Brezhnev.

Apart from official talks, Cde. Zamyatin expressed his astonishment and indignation that we allow the massive, illegal publication of bulletins, leaflets, newspapers and books which contain hostile texts. "That we are not able to understand," he said.

During the course of the talks and official discussions, there were attempts to clarify the problems raised by the comrades.

[Source: AAN, PUWP CC, 3982, pp. 20–25. Translated by Paweł Świeboda.]

Document No. 29: Transcript of CPSU CC Politburo Meeting

January 22, 1981

In the previous document, Polish party officials give a detailed account of the volley of criticisms leveled at them by Leonid Zamyatin, head of the CPSU CC International Information Department during his January 13–20 visit to Poland. In the transcript below, the Soviet Politburo discusses Zamyatin's conclusions about the situation in Poland. He notes that there is still a degree of unity among the leadership and that the party is making serious attempts to come to grips with the variety of problems facing the country. On the other hand, he affirms that Solidarity has a membership of several million and that they represent "a major force." The PUWP, he adds, no longer has "a genuine creative connection with the people" and the workers have legitimate grievances. Lack of control over the mass media is a particular sore point. The Politburo briefly discussed the problems Zamyatin's trip highlighted, then approved a decision to instruct various CC departments and government agencies to make proposals for the Politburo Commission on Poland to consider. The following month, a working group of the Commission recommended ratcheting up the pressure on the Polish authorities to reassert party control over the crisis.

[…]

8. About the visit of the delegation of CPSU party officials led by Cde. L. M. Zamyatin to Poland.

Zamyatin: A gradual process of increasing activity by party organizations is taking place in Poland now. Confidence in their own power is growing among the party organizations. The party has conducted the first tests, but it has not reached the apex of these tests yet. Currently they are talking about so-called "free Saturdays" and Rural Solidarity. These are the questions over which, obviously, very serious arguments will arise. It is important to note that the PUWP has an understanding with the United Peasants' Party on these issues. The difficulty of the Polish situation lies not only in the fact that the enemy, whom we must fight decisively, is acting, but also in the fact that under pressure of past mistakes the party has lost a genuine creative connection with the people. The working class has many reasons for dissatisfaction. This is especially typical for young workers, who have not experienced any hardships yet. This is precisely what Solidarity has capitalized on.

Now the Polish working people are putting forward the slogan of renewal of socialist life, i.e. a return to Lenin's norms in the party and the state.

As far as Solidarity is concerned, it is not homogeneous in its composition. By the way, one has to say that this is the main force with which the PUWP has to deal right now. In Wałęsa's opinion, he has ten million people in Solidarity right now. The PUWP CC believes that there are six million there. The counter-revolutionary forces are organizing around the Committee for Workers' Defense, the so-called KOR. Those are Kuroń, Michnik, Gwiazda, Lis, Walentynowicz— altogether approximately 40 people. Solidarity is now essentially a political party, most actively hostile to the PUWP and the state.

In addition, Wałęsa's group, supported by the bishops, represents a major force. If one looks at the situation in Poland right now, it is characterized by a certain stepping up of the role of the party, of its concrete actions. This, of course, leads in turn to increasing tensions because the counter-revolutionary forces have their own plans; they are striving for power, but they see that the counteraction that the PUWP is putting up, does not give them the possibility to implement their plans.

Today, Poland has branch trade unions, with approximately 6.5 million members. [Our] friends think about uniting them in a federation and minimizing the role of Solidarity's most militant wing using political methods. They intend to cut KOR away from Solidarity. The PUWP CC is currently involved in forming a third trade union, the so-called autonomous trade union. Of course, this work is primarily being conducted in those party organizations and at those enterprises where the actions of Solidarity are strong. The PUWP is actively working on the problems of rebuilding trust among the masses.

As far as the young people are concerned, the independent youth union covers approximately 13 percent of them. Constant discussion is going on among the young people. One can see the results of the absence of teaching of Marxist–Leninist sciences in higher education.

As far as mass media are concerned, their current state does not fit the requirements of the moment. The party is undertaking measures to bring some order and to take control of the situation. But it is still far from any normalization. The majority of newspapers are not under party control yet. On TV the state of affairs is especially poor. Ideological erosion as a consequence of a weakening of party educational work among the masses, the neglected state of this work in the mass media—this is the state of affairs in Poland. For instance, on TV and radio, the problem is that even though we replaced the leadership, the main mass of employees, i.e. those who prepare materials directly, sympathize with Solidarity. The country exists in a state of permanent discussion [taking place] in party organizations and at enterprises. This discussion is carried on in the mass media as well, where they often argue about the Polish model of socialist society, about liberalization, revision of Marxism–Leninism, about pluralism in political life, and so on.

What measures would bring order to the Polish People's Republic? In our opinion, the persistent pressure on the party and the instructions given to the Polish friends force them to reform their work actively, including work in the mass media. The understanding is growing that if the party lets the media go completely from under its control, it would not be able to win the struggle for influence over public opinion in the country.

I had a conversation with Cde. Kania. He spoke about the situation in the country. [Our] friends believe that they should not rush to convene the congress now. In our opinion, we should not send many delegations to Poland, but rather send highly qualified comrades as members of delegations who would be able to respond to questions, [in a way that] would represent the point of view of the CPSU CC. Overall, understanding of the necessity to display firmness in the struggle against the enemy has been growing among the leadership, but so far mainly in the political sphere. One cannot say that there is no unity within [the leadership], that it is split; everybody is working under the influence of the first test of forces from the changes that are happening. The wave of demands to "settle accounts" with the former leadership is subsiding. [Our] Polish friends assured [us] that they had enough decisiveness in the struggle against the enemy, that there was no place to retreat any longer. Cde. Kania asked to pass on his gratitude to L. I. Brezhnev and to all the Politburo members for all the help the Soviet Union provides to Poland. One has to note that our ambassador to the PPR, Cde. Aristov, is conducting great work and informs the Central Committee correctly about the things that are happening [in Poland].

Gromyko: We should exchange opinions about the situation in Poland in more detail. We need next steps of some kind. We need to have an uninterrupted process of influence. Maybe [more] meetings with the Polish friends are necessary. Where? We should think about that. We should not discount the danger posed by Solidarity. Solidarity is a political party of an anti-Soviet character. This thought should be constantly instilled in the Polish leadership. The situation with keeping secret the questions being discussed is especially poor there. Everything that was discussed at the Politburo becomes known to a wide circle of the population the next day. The Polish friends, our recommendations notwithstanding, do not want to apply extraordinary measures; this thought, in essence, is entirely missing among them. For example, they decided to clear the trade union sites that were occupied by Solidarity representatives, but the secretary of the voivodeship military district did not follow the PUWP's instructions, and did not return these sites.

Zamyatin: Andrei Andreevich, this happened in two military districts.

Andropov: Today we received a telegram from Warsaw that the reaction to Cde. Zamyatin's trip to Poland was positive. The visit was useful, the delegation did good work. I think that we should entrust Cdes. Rusakov and Zamyatin with preparing proposals that we could subsequently consider at the Commission on Poland.

Rusakov: We have a lot of influence with our Polish friends. One should note that Leonid Ilyich talks with Kania about all issues almost every week. I think this is the most important thing, because in his conversations Leonid Ilyich touches upon all the issues in a tactful manner, and at the same time impresses on Kania seriously how he should act. Our organizations—the MFA, the KGB and the Defense Ministry—have designated representatives with whom we could deal on a permanent basis and decide questions on Poland.

Kirilenko: I think that so far there has not been any serious revival in Poland. Maybe it is only the beginning.

Zamyatin: When I spoke about the revival of work in the PUWP, I had in mind the party organizations' site visits, conversations in work collectives, and so on.

Ustinov: Cde. Kulikov has been to Poland recently. Cde. Kulikov's impression was that there had not yet been a serious breakthrough in Poland. We have to apply constant pressure on the Polish leadership, and nourish it constantly. We plan to conduct [military] maneuvers in Poland in March. It seems to me that we should raise the level of these maneuvers, i.e., in other words, to let them know that our forces are ready.

Suslov: Of course, our main task should be to support the Polish leadership in the measures they are implementing, and at the same time to apply the necessary pressure. Now, by Cde. Zamyatin's visit we have let them know in a serious fashion how they should deal with the mass media. This is their weakest point, and here we should help them. We should also look at what they are preparing for the Congress, what changes to the Charter, and which economic issues they raise. It is true that we should send only able people to Poland.

The decision was adopted: to approve the visit of the CPSU delegation led by Zamyatin to Poland. To instruct CC departments, the MFA, the KGB and the Defense Ministry to prepare appropriate proposals taking into account the exchange of opinions at the Politburo session for discussion by the Commission on Poland.

[Source: RGANI, Fond 89, Opis 42, Delo 36. Translated by Svetlana Savranskaya for the National Security Archive.]

Document No. 30: Supplement No. 1 to PUWP CC Politburo Protocol No. 657 Analyzing the Intentions of Solidarity

January 26, 1981

This paper, submitted by a CC department for use in a Politburo discussion of Solidarity's likely future activities, is interesting for two main reasons. First, it fills a gap in the historical record since there is nothing from the Solidarity side in this time period to indicate what the union's leadership was planning to do. Second, far from being a bland, bureaucratic analysis of the situation, it offers an interesting insight into the ideological slant of the Polish leadership.

Circulated by order of Cde. T. Grabski to PB members, deputies, CC Secretaries and Secretariat members, January 20, 1981

For the PB meeting on January 21, 1981, point 1[7]

Intentions and anticipated directions of activities of the NSZZ Solidarity in 1981.

1. *The framework of activity of the NSZZ Solidarity*
As of the beginning of 1981, the NSZZ Solidarity is in a phase of transforming itself from a massive social movement, which is intensively being created, into an organization with institutionalized structures and forms of activity. This is a complex process, in which the following occurrences and tendencies are becoming apparent:
  - differences between the particular regional IFC's, leadership groups, and grass-roots members of the union;
  - enormous social expectations associated with the activity of the union are not always reflected in the actual feasibility of their fulfillment;
  - a noticeable divergence of tendencies and immediate and long-term objectives on the part of the two main forces inspiring the activity of Solidarity—the Church and KSS-KOR.

Leadership groups from the union and their advisers are interested in extending the period of formation and stabilization of structures, which makes it possible to justify the lack of a positive program for action and organizational chaos.

---

[7] This date is stamped on the document. The document was discussed twice—at the Politburo sessions of January 21 and 26. See Protocols 63 and 65 from these dates in Zbigniew Włodek, ed., *Tajne Dokumenty,* 232–254.

KSS-KOR is increasingly openly taking advantage of Solidarity's existence to propagate its own anti-socialist views, gain new supporters, and acquire both a reputation and material resources abroad.

The Church envisions in Solidarity the possibility to extend its influence among the working class; stop the processes of secularization in intelligentsia and youth circles; widely popularize the propositions of Christian social doctrine; secure educated social layers for [use in] actions initiated by the Catholic hierarchy and associations; and strengthen its position in the country and in the state. The Church has a moderating impact on the extremist elements of the union and acts as an intermediary between the authorities and Solidarity.

Both the Church and KSS-KOR attach significant expectations to the NSZZ Solidarity. This fact is a source of rivalry and contradiction between them.

Leadership groups—and to a larger extent the membership masses—of the NSZZ Solidarity still do not have their own program of activity. Attempts to elaborate one signify the use of proposals offered by Church and KSS-KOR experts who also try directly (i.e. using their own propaganda tools) and indirectly (i.e. with the assistance of their members and sympathizers in various mass media in the country and abroad) to build Solidarity's reputation, and popularize its activists and objectives. Acting on that platform, the conviction has been successfully disseminated that the line along which events are unfolding in our country results from the activities of two centers: the state authorities (identified with the PUWP) and the NSZZ Solidarity (portrayed as a trustee of the nation's will).

NSZZ Solidarity advisers are convincing the leadership groups of the union that time will be to their advantage when they are able to:

– avoid widespread and fundamental confrontation with the authorities;

– spur social tensions—in different regions of the country and in different domains—with the frequency necessary to maintain Solidarity members in readiness to act and test their personnel in action.

In this case, the low operational capacity of the authorities is assumed, as well as their inclination: to get involved in solving even inconsiderable conflicts, and to lose sight of the main trends of the union's activity.

2. Anticipated activities of the NSZZ Solidarity

Taking into account the current situation in the union, it can be presumed that its activity will focus on strengthening its impact on crews at large industrial institutes, and expanding the network of linkages with social organizations, associations, clubs, etc., which are not formally tied to Solidarity. This joint action aims at establishing [...] the union's agencies in the cities and the countryside, and in youth and creative arts intelligentsia circles. [It will] consistently demand the implementation of agreements signed in Gdańsk, Szczecin, and Jastrzębie. Delays and deviations from obligations undertaken will be used to attack the authorities.

There are signs that the NSZZ Solidarity will aim, on a social platform, for:

– the introduction of a 40-hour and a 5-day work week;

- the improvement of market supplies;
- the prompt introduction of voucher rationing of meat and fats and changes in the norms proposed for the benefit of pregnant women and children;
- a demand for increased social security;
- the establishment and guarantee of minimum welfare;
- the elimination of inequities in living standards;
- substantial growth of the hospital, sanatorium, and vacation resort system as well as full supply of medicines;
- the correction and elimination of striking wage imbalances between different professional groups, more frequently and strongly utilizing the slogan of social justice.

With the inspiration of the advisers to the Church and KSS-KOR, the NSZZ Solidarity will grant support to the newly created social organizations (student and peasant ones) and establish contacts with unions and associations which already exist.

Since the last [few] weeks, the NSZZ Solidarity has been showing increasing interest in the youth movement and the processes accompanying the renaissance of the various mutations of the cooperative movement. There are growing tendencies to widen various, non-institutionalized forms of the dissemination of knowledge. The concept evolved to establish circles of combatants who were not members of the UFFD which would be linked to Solidarity. One may conclude that Solidarity intends to tie itself to nearly all social organizations that function in the country. On the other hand, where such attempts are deemed to fail, or where success is doubtful or far in the future, it creates new social institutions.

Solidarity will continue to publicize the view that the authorities are not fulfilling the obligations undertaken in the "social agreement" and that they are delaying the execution of agreements related to the limitation of censorship, that the Church and Solidarity should be granted full access to the mass media. Solidarity will also shape the forms of pressure [exerted] on the press, radio and television in order to publish materials with contents desired by the union.

In the near future, the union may undertake a series of actions, and in particular it may aim to:
- strengthen and widen the social base of the union in the scientific, creative arts, education, and cultural circles, among students and the health service; pronounce the independence of Polish academia; intensify efforts leading to the vindication of academic staff deprived of the possibility of engaging in pedagogic activity after 1968;
- launch a campaign for changes in the local, workers', and village self-governments; and use it to antagonize society against the authorities and the party;
- become more active in the course of the campaign before the Ninth Congress of the PUWP, with the intention of exerting influence on the results of elections of delegates for the Congress and discrediting—mainly in the moral sphere—the party and party apparatus activists;

- undermine and question the leadership and guiding role of the party in social practice, encourage widespread self-criticism, and demand that the actual and presumed mistakes of the party members be cleared;
- after the Ninth Congress, take into account its results, demand that the current
tenure of the Sejm and national councils be shortened in order to accelerate
new elections and introduce amendments and changes to the Constitution;
- raise the concept of a so-called "generational battle" within the ranks of the
party and suggest that young members equate to progress while old *aktiv*
members are dogmatists, conservatives, demoralized and corrupt people;
- win over certain members of the party executive at all levels, support them,
emphasize the liberalism of those who in various forms will give way to the
union's influence;
- create a state of psychological threat among the party leadership, administrative and economic personnel, and periodically undertake actions leading
to changes in different posts; create the impression that Solidarity is making
the decisions about meaningful personnel changes;
- undertake the discrediting of functionaries of the CP [Citizens' Police], SB,
and policing services;
- attempt to neutralize the army by addressing patriotic feelings, propagate
the slogans "the army with the people" and "December no more,"[8] inspiring
draftees—the embers of Solidarity—to work among active-duty soldiers;
- maintain tensions and uncertainty within society;
- usurp exclusively to themselves the right to the only correct interpretation
of moral norms, the law and international conventions, and in case of their
presumed violation, the right to threaten a strike action.

On the international level, the activities of Solidarity may proceed along two
paths: the union, with increasing energy, will demand full autonomy in developing its own "foreign policy" in contacts with various trade unions, especially
from the capitalist countries, establishing representation for the NSZZ in the ILO
in order to obtain moral and propaganda support; simultaneously, however, the
demand will most likely be raised to include Solidarity in delegations participating in international talks and conferences.

Considering the intentions and anticipated trends of NSZZ Solidarity's activity, it should be taken into account that public opinion views the establishment
of new trade unions, and particularly Solidarity, as a positive development. They
[new trade unions] are treated as a force making possible the renewal of life in
our country, a guarantee of workers' rights and a stimulator of democracy.

Analyses carried out by the Institute of Fundamental Problems of Marxism–
Leninism show that this is a healthy, widely accepted social movement which
brings hope for improved functioning of the social system, constituting at the
same time a shield against its deformations. Public opinion also expresses the

---

[8] A reference to the strikes of December 1970.

conviction that "healthy trade unions are the basis of law and order in our country," that they are a force capable of preventing subsequent mistakes and distortions. The above view is dependent, however, on the wisdom of the people who will lead this movement—such an opinion is expressed by 80 percent of the respondents.

Taking into consideration the intended and anticipated trends of activity of the NSZZ Solidarity, it is essential to prepare detailed plans for political and organizational moves which will aim to:

– counteract the integration of interests of KSS-KOR, the Church and selected segments of the NSZZ Solidarity, by, among other means, demonstrating the negative effect of the activity of KOR members for the interests of Solidarity and the Church;

– take advantage of contacts with the Church in order to strengthen the social order, the family and respect for work;

– weaken the influence of KOR members on Solidarity by presenting them as enemies of socialist renewal and opponents of social stabilization who favor anarchy;

– take over the initiative by party organizations in large industrial institutes, and hence seize the monopoly for shaping public opinion and atmosphere from "Solidarity;" collect and settle justifiable motions and demands from the [work] crews;

– engage in an extensive discussion on implementing socialist principles of social justice, democratization of life and economic reform;

– take on, in political and propaganda work, the problem of economic stabilization, law and order, and demonstrate the threat of anarchy, lawlessness and demagogy;

– consolidate the social forces participating in the process of socialist renewal.

Warsaw, January 1981
Socio-Vocational Department
PUWP CC

The following materials were used to prepare this analysis:
NSZZ Solidarity materials, institute press, sociological studies of the IPPM-L, Catholic press ("Weekly Universal," "Trends"), "Annex," "Hornet," "Culture" (Parisian), RFE broadcasts, "Voice of America" and other sources.

[Source: AAN, PUWP CC, V/163, pp. 406–412. Translated by Paweł Świeboda.]

Document No. 31: National Intelligence Estimate (NIE 12.6–81), "Poland's Prospects over the Next Six Months"

January 27, 1981

Since the 1950s, National Intelligence Estimates (NIEs) have been considered the most authoritative judgments of the U.S. intelligence community on a given national security issue. NIEs cover major developments in important areas of the world, identifying significant trends, assessing such factors as the capabilities and vulnerabilities of foreign nations, and attempting to forecast their implications. This particular estimate represents the consensus view on the prospects for Poland during the first half of 1981. In hindsight, it is remarkably accurate. It is also measured in tone, which contrasts notably with the level of concern that prevailed in the Reagan administration during this period.

The document reviews the Warsaw Pact meeting of December 5, 1980, (see Document No. 22), correctly concluding that Kania gained a second chance—even though Moscow viewed events as going decidedly downhill—largely because the Kremlin recognized the high costs of intervention and of having to shoulder Poland's economic burden. The estimate also captures the range of attitudes that existed among the East European satellite regimes. On the Polish side, it rightly predicts that the army, whose reliability is suspect, would not be able to carry out a major crackdown without help from other security forces. The only apparent point of disagreement among the NIE's contributors is whether it would be possible to distinguish between genuine invasion preparations by the Red Army and routine annual military exercises if the forces involved totaled fewer than 30 divisions.

NIE 12.6–81

[…]

Key Judgments

The present crisis in Poland constitutes the most serious and broadly based challenge to Communist rule in the Warsaw Pact in more than a decade. Recurrent confrontations between the regime and the unions have moved Poland ever closer to the edge of Soviet military intervention. The main factors sustaining the protracted crisis—persistent union demands, factionalism in the Solidarity leadership and indiscipline in the union ranks, the continuing erosion of party authority, and the fact that Solidarity represents a massive emotional rejection of the way the party has managed the country—are contributing to an increasingly anarchic situation which no single authority seems capable of controlling.

Although some issues are more susceptible to solutions than others, we see no prospect for the resolution of basic tensions between the workers and the regime in the months ahead. No coherent regime strategy has yet emerged to limit workers' political demands and to stem the consequent erosion of the party's authority.

Because of a poor harvest, lower labor productivity, a shorter workweek, and ongoing economic drift, economic conditions in Poland will continue to deteriorate over the next six months. If deterioration is moderate—as Polish planners hope—economically inspired civil disturbances seem unlikely in the next six months. But a swift and steep decline in living standards—capable of triggering civil disorder that could cause Soviet intervention—cannot be ruled out. This could happen, particularly if Poland (a) cannot meet its massive hard currency debt service obligations, (b) defaults, as a result, on its hard currency loans, (c) is therefore unable to borrow to finance a trade deficit, and (d) thus sharply reduces imports from the West, with serious adverse effects on production and consumption. To meet its financial obligations and keep imports at a satisfactory level, Poland will require aid from Western governments.

Party leader Kania apparently continues to enjoy Soviet support. But in an environment of continuing political instability time is working against him. Under such conditions his personal support from the Soviets and from within the Politburo will diminish. Cognizant of this liability, Kania will feel increasingly compelled in the interest of preserving his own position to initiate more forceful measures to quell domestic turmoil, and to head off conservative criticism that his "leniency" is perpetuating instability.

To limit the scale of confrontation, the regime may seek to appear more conciliatory on issues with which there is widespread labor identification and support, such as the five-day, 40-hour workweek, or to fragment opposition on such national issues by advocating locally negotiated solutions. In addition, it will probably continue the periodic show of limited force against local protests, calculating that such firmness will have a restraining effect nationally. The potential for escalation is high in a strategy of limited confrontation, given the regime's diminished negotiating flexibility and probably Soviet insistence that it stand firm in the event of confrontation.

Solidarity's national leadership has come increasingly under the influence of its more militant members. But regime efforts to factionalize the leadership, and thereby dilute its national authority, have thus far failed. While internal disputes will continue to characterize the leadership, we believe that in future confrontations it will pull together rather than pull apart.

While we believe that the Soviets will not allow the present deteriorating situation to continue indefinitely, we doubt they have established a timetable for Kania. It is their continuing assessment of Polish events and Kania's reaction to them that will decide whether the Soviets forbear, increase pressure, or use military force. Moscow retains several options short of military intervention to induce moderation by workers and stronger actions by the regime—another change in leadership, heavier political pressure, as well as a number of demonstrative military measures short of intervention.

The Soviets' reluctance to intervene militarily derives above all from the enormous costs they probably anticipate in eliminating Polish armed and passive resistance, and in reestablishing a politically and economically viable Poland. Additional disincentives are the political and economic price they anticipate they would pay in their relations with Western nations, with the Third World, and within the international Communist movement.

Whatever the Soviet perception of the costs of intervention, they will quickly fade into secondary considerations if the Soviets see their vital interests threatened. Developments that would pose such a threat include:

– A breakdown of internal order in Poland.
– A frontal assault on the regime's authority, such as a general strike of some duration to which the regime did not respond decisively.
– Indications that the Polish regime was becoming unwilling or unable to meet its Warsaw Pact commitments.

Barring such developments, Moscow will continue to give Kania time, but little additional leeway to maneuver and make concessions. We believe that the Soviets are less confident than when Kania won his December 5 reprieve that he can in fact bring the situation satisfactorily under control. The trend is decidedly negative from the Soviet perspective.

In comparison with the October–November 1980 period, the chances are greater that the Polish regime will respond with force, probably at Soviet urging, if faced with a major confrontation such as a prolonged general strike or the threat of such a major confrontation. Coercion would be used in a way designed to minimize the escalation of violence. But the difficulties of manipulating force in such a tense situation are enormous, and the probability of an eruption of violence would be high.

We seriously doubt the Polish Army's dependability if called upon to quell large-scale violence, and we believe similar doubts prevail in the Polish leadership. In any case, we do not believe the Polish Army alone would be capable of containing the situation. The introduction of regular Polish military forces under such circumstances would run a high risk of bringing about the intervention or Soviet forces.

The size of any Soviet intervention force would depend upon Moscow's assessment of likely resistance from the Polish Army and population. We estimate that, if the Soviets foresaw the possibility of significant, organized resistance from the Polish armed forces, they would intervene with a force of at least 30 divisions. We believe they could ready such a force and activate all of the necessary communications in 10 to 14 days. If the Soviets were to undertake the kind of intervention they apparently planned in November–December under the guise of a joint exercise, we estimate an intervention force of some 20 divisions could be readied within about a week. A substantially smaller force involving some half dozen divisions (or more, depending on the extent to which the Soviets draw on ready divisions from their forces in East Germany and Czechoslovakia) could be readied in about two to three days, but we think it unlikely, given the possibility of resistance, that the Soviets would actually intervene with such a small force.

It is possible that a pattern of negotiation will develop between regime and unions which will subdue the level of confrontation, and that under such circumstances the regime could gain the upper hand by pursuing a cautious policy designed to undermine the union's strength. It is difficult to believe, however, that such a policy could succeed given the volatile situation in Poland and diffusion of the authority of both the party and the union. Indeed, we believe Soviet pressure on the Polish regime will increase, and that if the pattern of domestic confrontation continues, the trend is toward ultimate intervention.

DISCUSSION

I. *Introduction*

1. Six months after an increase in food prices sparked strikes throughout Poland, and spawned an organized workers opposition, the country's political and economic stability continues to be precarious. The brief periods of relative domestic calm which have punctuated tensions between the Kania leadership and the unions mask an inherently unstable situation. Indeed, the trend has been one of continuing economic and political demands by Solidarity or its local chapters, and the diffusion of political authority away from the party, fed in part by serious political divisions within the party itself. The present crisis constitutes the most serious and broadly based challenge to Communist rule in the Warsaw Pact in over a decade, and recurrent confrontations have moved Poland ever closer to the edge of Soviet military intervention.

2. That threat tempers the behavior of both workers and regime, but it may not be decisive in inducing cooperation and warding off an intervention. The main factors which now sustain the protracted crisis—persistent union demands, factionalism in the Solidarity leadership and indiscipline in the union ranks, the continuing erosion of party authority, and the fact that Solidarity represents the massive, deep-seated, and emotional rejection of the way the party has managed Poland—are contributing to an increasingly anarchic situation which no single authority seems capable of controlling.

II. *The Present State of Play in Poland*

3. Soviet military activity in late November and early December made the threat of intervention more credible to both the workers and the regime. This belief by key actors inside and outside of Poland, heightened by Soviet warnings to the Polish leadership and by public U.S. warnings to the USSR, chastened the Poles. The Polish Church and the Pope assumed an unequivocal position in urging moderation and restraint on Polish workers. The national Solidarity leadership, acknowledging the gravity of the situation, declared a six-week strike moratorium. The party appealed for restraint and professed its willingness to negotiate and compromise. Thus, the widely perceived threat of military intervention and

the temporary convergence of interests it created—together with the diversion of the holidays and the greater, if temporary, availability of foodstuffs—resulted in a period of calm lasting four to five weeks.

4. Since early January the government has taken a harder line in dealing with the unions, but has only generated more resistance. Labor groups, increasingly under the influence of militant elements pressed their demands which, together with the hardening of the party's position, reintroduced the tensions that have dominated the past months. Two issues—demands for registration of a private farmers union called 'Rural Solidarity,' and the introduction of a five-day, 40-hour workweek—now provide the focus of internal tensions. In calibrating its response the party must tread the narrow line between preserving its own eroding political authority and staying within the bounds of Soviet tolerance, and responding to worker demands in a way that placates but minimizes actual concessions. Although some specific issues are more susceptible to solutions than others we see no prospect for the resolution of basic tensions between the workers and the regime in the months ahead. No coherent strategy has yet emerged to limit workers' political demands and to stem the consequent erosion of the party's authority.

III. *The Worsening Economic Situation*

5. Domestic economic conditions in Poland will continue to deteriorate over the next six months, and throughout 1981, even if Poland receives the foreign financial and economic assistance it is clearly counting on. The modest economic reform measures introduced at the beginning of this year will have little impact in the near future (and probably will not significantly affect economic performance even over the long run). Polish officials predict a decline in GNP in 1981, following decreases in 1980 and 1979. Contributors to the anticipated drop in 1981 include the repercussions on food production of previous poor harvests, lower labor productivity, the shorter workweek and lighter work regimen in the mines, and lack of leadership control over the economy.

6. Despite the enormous 1981 payments of principal (about $7.5 billion) and interest (about $2.8 billion) that Poland must make on its $25 billion debt—accumulated over the last 10 years because of an over ambitious development program heavily dependent on imports from the West—Warsaw was forced to abandon the pre-strike priority accorded to improving its balance of payments. Instead, it is trying to maintain living standards, or at least minimize their decline, in order to forestall public disorder.

7. This objective requires Poland to continue to run large current account deficits. To prevent the decline in coal production from reducing domestic consumption, for example, Warsaw has sharply cut coal exports even though coal is Poland's major earner of hard currency. Largely because of its emphasis on preserving production for domestic use, Poland appears to have run another large hard currency trade deficit last year—at least $1.5 billion—and is likely to run an even larger one this year—perhaps $2 billion. With interest payments on its

steadily rising debt also growing, the current account deficit was at least $3.6 billion in 1980 and will be over $4.0 billion in 1981.

8. Taking other steps to free resources for use in personal consumption and in consumer-oriented investment programs, Warsaw has also

- announced that it will continue steep cuts in total investment initiated two years ago while raising capital outlays in agriculture, in housing, and in health, education, and cultural facilities;
- raised food subsidies by 40 percent in 1981 to permit higher prices for farmers while keeping retail prices stable;
- substantially increased money income for all segments of the population, with total 1981 personal income to rise by 18 percent, almost twice as fast as in 1979 and 1980.

9. Even if these plans are carried out, however, Polish consumers face a bleak year. Although the regime hopes to increase slightly the overall supply of consumer goods in 1981, it has warned that food supplies will fail. Most worrisome of all is a drop in the availability of meat; production will fall at least 10 percent in 1981 following estimated 5-percent decrease in 1980. Imports are expected to compensate for only a small proportion of the decline in meat production.

10. Living standards will rise marginally at best over the next six months, and are more likely to drop. Economically inspired civil unrest remains a possibility, despite the regime's retreat from austerity measures. The population, however, has shown considerable tolerance for economic hardship in recent months—in large measure, it appears, because of the new leadership's (a) candid admissions that past mismanagement and corruption have left the economy a shambles, (b) promises of actions that it maintains will bring about a rejuvenation of the economy, and (c) partial satisfaction of some of the population's political-social aspirations—for example, formation of Solidarity—which has created a temporary willingness to tolerate economic hardships. Consequently, economic hardship per se, short of a swift and drastic deterioration in living standards, seems unlikely to trigger widespread public disorder over the next several months.

11. Such a rapid deterioration cannot be ruled out, however, particularly if Poland does not receive substantial foreign financial and economic assistance. Poland must not only roll over principal payments as they fall due but must also find new funds both to pay interest on its Western debt and to permit continuation of hard currency trade deficits. If Poland cannot obtain the necessary financing and defaults on its loans, the country would be forced to balance its hard currency trade by sharply cutting imports. The impact on consumption and production would be severely disruptive, possibly triggering civil disturbances.

12. Despite the rapidly diminishing confidence of Western banks, Poland stands a good chance of rolling over much of the principal coming due, since banks evidently prefer such refinancing to outright default. But Western banks are likely to provide the new loans Poland requires to finance interest and trade deficits only if they receive government guarantees. Thus, if Poland is to avoid drastic curtailment of its purchases from the West, it will require prompt finan-

cial assistance from either Western governments or the Soviet Union, and probably from both. Large-scale assistance may be required very soon, since Poland's current account deficit in the first quarter alone is likely to be on the order of $1 billion. Substantial Soviet aid has already been granted but not nearly enough to meet Poland's 1981 needs.

13. Poland has been candid about its need for credits and has been scrambling to line up assistance since September. It has already received more than $2 billion in aid, part of it in hard currency, from the USSR (some of which was used in 1980) and perhaps a few hundred million dollars from other East European countries. Warsaw has also requested more than $10 billion in various types of aid from Western governments, notably bilateral reschedulings and government credits. Western countries have been generally sympathetic in considering Polish appeals because of the contribution aid can make to both political stability and the interests of Western exporters. Poland has failed to win hard-and-fast pledges of large amounts of assistance, however, largely because of the inability of Western countries to fashion a common plan for aiding Warsaw, but also because of Western doubts that Poland will ever put its finances in order.

IV. *Key Actors: Their Nature and Equities*

The Party

14. One key to Poland's short-term future is whether party leader Kania or any subsequent leader can reestablish the integrity of the party as an institution of effective political control. The evolution of Solidarity as a competing center of authority and the deterioration of party cohesion have proceeded hand-in-hand: some party members have resigned, many have taken up simultaneous membership in Solidarity;[9] some local party bodies have defied directives from the party center; and the freedom with which the party's past role and mistakes and the nature of its political authority have been questioned have led, not surprisingly, to widespread demands from within the party, and particularly from its lower echelons, for its decentralization.[10]

[9] Some of these have done so in an attempt by the party to penetrate Solidarity. [Footnote from the original.]

[10] It is probable that the longer instability in the country persists, the greater such demands will become. Therefore, ending the labor strife is related to the success of the party leadership in consolidating the party itself. Contrary to the Leninist norm under which binding policies and elections of party officials are decided at the top, demands for decentralization include changing the party statutes to provide for electing party officials for fixed terms by secret ballot, barring party officials from simultaneously holding government positions, initiating binding policies from below, and holding the top leadership accountable for its performance. We believe that demands for internal party democratization will be opposed by the party leadership, beyond superficial changes instituted for tactical reasons. Mindful of its self-preservation and the limits of Soviet tolerance, the party leadership not only will refuse to support such decentralizing changes, but also will work to restore an essentially orthodox, hierarchical party organization. [Footnote from the original.]

15. Kania's first political imperative is to consolidate his own political position within the Politburo and within the party as a whole. Under the banners of "reform" and "renewal," and an anticorruption campaign, a purge has been set in motion, apparently sponsored by Kania, which is not only a struggle for reform but also strategy to rid the party of his political opponents. Kania has encountered stiff resistance from the numerous middle- and lower-level party officials, and from within the largely Gierek-appointed Central Committee, for whom "renewal" would mean certain loss of their privileges and even expulsion or worse. Kania's efforts to reconstruct the party—within parameters that Moscow will tolerate—will not succeed, however, so long as he remains incapable of purging the party of these elements. He must proceed with more deliberate speed in purging the obdurate elements, as well as in reining in those in the rank and file—where nonetheless much of his support lies—who are pressing for far-reaching reforms as the pending extraordinary party congress approaches. The fact that the congress, initially slated for late March or early April, has reportedly been postponed to mid-May suggests that preparation for it is running well behind schedule.

16. It is difficult to assess the current constellation of forces in the Politburo except to say (a) that there probably prevails an uneasy consensus around Kania which derives from a shared interest in his near-term success in calming the situation and (b) that no organized opposition to Kania by individuals or groups has yet surfaced.[11] Whether this consensus will last will depend upon Kania's success in bringing the domestic situation under control. A crucial factor, however, is Soviet support for Kania; it is unlikely that he would be unseated without the acquiescence or support of the Soviets. While Kania apparently continues to enjoy Soviet support, he may not do so indefinitely. Indeed, in an environment of continuing political instability, time is working against him and, under such conditions, his personal support from the Soviets and from within the Politburo will diminish. Cognizant of this liability, Kania will feel increasingly compelled in the interest of preserving his own position to initiate more forceful measures to quell domestic turmoil, and to head off conservative criticism that his "leniency" is perpetuating instability.

17. It is partly for these reasons that Kania's strategy for dealing with labor opposition has hardened.[12] His room for maneuver between the Soviets and the continuing demands of the workers, has narrowed considerably as a result of So-

---

[11] At the same time, some Politburo members are powerful figures in their own right and probably command some personal support from within the party. Two such figures are Olszowski and Moczar. Olszowski is reported to be a likely replacement for Kania should the Soviets withdraw their support from the present party leader. [Footnote from the original.]

[12] This was evident in the 10 January speech of Kania in which he denounced "anti-socialist" elements and "counter-revolutionaries" who were urging formation of the Rural Solidarity farmers union. It appears doubtful that the pending court case on the legal status of Rural Solidarity will culminate in its registration. The expulsion of demonstrators at the Nowy Sącz Town Hall on 11 January—under the threat of police force to end a sit-in—is a further indication of the party's generally harder line. [Footnote from the original.]

viet admonitions surrounding the December 5 Warsaw Pact meeting. We believe that the Polish leadership perceives that the Soviets will use force if Warsaw is unable to demonstrate progress toward the restoration of party control and the limitation of Solidarity's role. Kania is probably unsure of how much time the Soviets will allow him. The hope—which may be ill-founded—is that an increasingly assertive policy, combined with the heightened awareness of the Soviet military threat, will force Solidarity to lower its demands, and weaken the movement by creating divisions within the leadership, and between it and the rank-and-file. All the same time, Kania must obtain a modicum of trust by the workers; he will therefore seek to avoid any all-out confrontation, to continue to advocate reform, and to appear at least minimally responsive to popular demands. In addition, the regime may hope that a purge of the party prior to the Extraordinary Congress, and the announcement of economic and political reforms, will win for it an additional increment of trust among labor and the Solidarity leadership.

18. To limit the scale of confrontation, the regime may seek to appear more conciliatory on issues with which there is widespread labor identification and support, such as the five-day, 40-hour workweek, or to fragment opposition on such national issues by advocating locally negotiated solutions. In addition, it will probably continue the periodic show of limited force against local protests, calculating that such firmness will have a restraining effect nationally. It is unlikely that such a strategy can succeed, because of the frequently overlapping nature of local and national issues and the potential for local issues to receive the support of the national Solidarity leadership. Furthermore, the potential for escalation is high in a strategy of limited confrontation, given the regime's diminished negotiating flexibility and probable Soviet insistence that it stand firm in the event of confrontation.

Solidarity and the Workers

19. Solidarity is an unwieldy aggregation of 6 to 10 million Polish workers born of years of frustration and a shared sense of economic and social grievance. The average Solidarity member is probably motivated above all by a desire to improve his standard of living. His goals, improved pay and emoluments, tend to be immediate and his time horizon short. Solidarity is not an organization whose members share a common goal of political reform, and its leadership has refrained from articulating a program of political reform. Indeed, rank-and-file Solidarity demands for general political liberalization have been notable for their absence over the past chaotic months, except as they effect the workers' right to strike on behalf of material demands.

20. Inevitably, however, Solidarity's economic objectives have resulted in demands that have been essentially political.[13] In addition, the workers have de-

---

[13] For example, the October–November dispute over the registration of Solidarity that focused on the union's formal recognition of the party's leading role, the threatened strike in late November over two workers arrested for allegedly pealing a secret government document, and pending demands for the further relaxation of censorship and the imposition of restrictions on the security forces. [Footnote from the original.]

veloped a fierce pride in their organization and its ability to pressure the authorities—this in itself marks a profound change in Polish political life. It is likely that some in the labor movement harbor ambitions for fundamental political changes (which may stand in contradiction to one another) but have held back from developing a political program in order to fend off charges that, ultimately, Solidarity aspires to become a political opposition. Furthermore, as Solidarity's political weight has grown and as its gains have altered the nation's political climate, other groups have been encouraged to organize and to seek the regime's recognition as legitimate interest groups with the right to participate in what is becoming an increasingly pluralistic political system.

21. Solidarity's national leadership consists of some 50 individuals elected on a regional basis, many of whom apparently identify closely with local labor grievances, a factor which may explain the divisiveness that besets the national body. Not surprisingly, the leadership—the National Coordinating Commission headed by Lech Wałęsa—is beset by dissension over goals, tactics, and philosophy. There are moderates around Wałęsa who generally favor avoiding confrontation, limiting demands to economic issues, and emphasizing organization and consolidation of the movement. But there are also militants, who favor a policy of more direct pressure to prevent the regime front backsliding, and a third type who are more receptive to the regime's position than Wałęsa. But the composition of each grouping seems to be constantly shifting depending on the issue. At both the national and the regional levels Solidarity continues to draw upon the support of groups of experts consisting of dissident intellectuals associated with the Committee for Social Self-Defense (KSS), with the movement for Civil and Human Rights (ROPCO), members of the legal profession, and advisers from the Catholic laity, some of whom act as emissaries from the episcopate. As open advocates of political liberalization and as longstanding critics of the regime, some of the dissidents have been publicly criticized as "anti-socialists" by both the regime and the Soviets. Thus far, however, Wałęsa has refused to see them as political liabilities, although he clearly wants to avoid identifying Solidarity with KOR or its political reformist point of view.

22. The divisions in the Solidarity leadership and the inclusion of political dissidents create political vulnerabilities which the regime has attempted to exploit. But regime efforts to factionalize the Solidarity leadership, and thereby dilute its national authority, have thus far failed. A sense of common cause and a realization of the dangers of succumbing to factionalism have bound the union leadership together during past crises, despite its divisions. At the same time, to maintain unity, and to preserve his own leadership position, Wałęsa and other moderates have had to accommodate the harder line, as evidenced during the January dispute over the free Saturday issue. The question for the next few months is how the Solidarity leadership will behave as the regime toughens its stand. While internal disputes will continue to characterize the leadership, we believe that in future confrontations it will pull together rather than pull apart.

23. The ability of the national leadership to control the Solidarity rank-and-file is limited. In some instances Solidarity members have persisted in local protest actions in defiance of the entreaties of the national leadership. This situation increases the danger that confrontational positions assumed by local Solidarity chapters will burgeon into national confrontation because of the perceived need by the national leadership to support its constituents or risk serious divisions within the movement. Rank-and-file discipline and retention of worker loyalty over time also depend on what progress Solidarity is able to achieve on workers' material demands (for example, on food, wages, and work hours). Given the economic disorder, however, and the widely recognized problems associated with meeting these demands in the next few months, it is unlikely that disappointment over consumption expectations will test rank-and-file loyalty in the national leadership over the next six months.

24. We expect that the near-term future will witness recurrent confrontation. Solidarity is likely to press the regime for implementation of the accords that settled last summer's strike wave. Solidarity is mindful of the regime's hardened position and its narrowed room for concession and, unless provoked (for example, by increased use of regime force or arrests of Solidarity members), is unlikely to press such political demands as the curtailing of police practices. The Solidarity leadership is aware of the fragility of the internal situation and that the regime will seek to use the fact of Soviet pressure to attenuate union demands and to elicit a more conciliatory policy. But it is also sensitive to the fact that a prolonged general strike would be perceived as a frontal challenge, and it will cross this Rubicon only as a last resort. We would foresee this as a response to regime actions that threatened the viability of Solidarity as an organization. Work actions such as the one-hour national strike on 3 October or selected boycotts are the tactics more likely to be adopted over the next few months. We believe that faced with a prolonged general strike, the regime would feel it necessary to respond coercively to demonstrate its control and to preserve its own political position.

The Church

25. Since the Communist takeover the Polish Catholic Church has fiercely and successfully defended its independence and retained the loyalty of the country's overwhelmingly Catholic population. With the election of a Polish Pope, John Paul II, and his triumphant visit in June 1979, the Church has significantly enhanced its effectiveness as a political force. But it has always used its influence cautiously—usually behind the scenes—and has extended its support to the government in times of national crisis.

26. In early December, sensing that Soviet military intervention was increasingly likely, both Cardinal Wyszyński, the Polish Primate, and Pope John Paul II ended a somewhat ambiguous period of silence to urge calm and to ease the pressure on the regime. This is a position to which the Church now appears com-

mitted and which could be a decisive factor in future confrontations. We can expect to see the Church play a more outspoken role in urging moderation in future confrontations. In the present situation, the Church hierarchy has lent its support both to Solidarity and to the Kania regime, but has avoided committing itself to an alliance with either.

27. But the regime can retain the support of the Church only so long as it eschews the use of force. In addition, the Church has particular interests and will pose demands of its own—greater access to the media, church construction, expanded clerical and religious education, etc.—and therefore has a natural interest in encouraging a progressive, if cautious, liberalization, and in exacting its own political price from the regime for its support.

28. Under the impact of the prolonged crisis, not even the episcopate has escaped internal dissension. Some elements of the clergy—especially the younger members—have questioned the wisdom of the strong support Cardinal Wyszyński was seen to have extended to the regime apparently at the expense of Solidarity. But the episcopate is likely to remain united under Wyszyński, who enjoys strong papal backing, and to continue to play a moderating role toward the regime, the workers, and the population at large. Wyszyński, however, is both aging and ailing, and his departure from the scene would leave a void that no successor could readily fill.

Other Actors

29. Solidarity has set a national example and created a license for the organization of similar interest groups, the establishment of which further dilutes party authority. For example, the organization of student unions and their petition to register as the legitimate voice of Poland's students has been accompanied by the weakening of the country's party-supported official student organizations. Liberalizing pressures have been in evidence in the writers' and journalists' communities. This spontaneous pluralization of the body politic, if it remains unchecked, could pose the most important longer-term threat both to the party and to Poland's experiment. We doubt that the party can eradicate such pressures in the near term. It may, however, be able to temporize on demands for legal registration of new unions. One social group whose demands the regime may not be able to temporize on is the farmers. The petition of Rural Solidarity (which claims to represent one-third of Poland's 3.5 million private farmers) for legal status akin to that of Solidarity could be the focus of the next confrontation in view of Kania's uncompromising stand against such an organization.

The USSR and the Warsaw Pact

30. Moscow has probably made it clear that, while the immediate problem is checking further deterioration, the Polish leadership's basic task must be to begin to reverse the trend. While we believe that the Soviets will not allow the present deteriorating situation to continue indefinitely, we doubt they have established a timetable for Kania. It is their continuing assessment of Polish events

and Kania's reaction to them which will decide whether the Soviets forbear, increase pressure, or use military force.

31. The Soviets retain several options short of military intervention. If Kania is unable to achieve a solution acceptable to Moscow, the Soviets could opt for another change in leadership. Moscow also retains some political pressure tactics not fully utilized. We may see explicit public warnings from Soviet leaders and additional Warsaw Pact summit meetings in which the Soviets urge even a harder stance on the Polish leadership. There are also a number of military measures short of military intervention which the Soviets could undertake to induce additional moderation in Poland and stronger actions by the regime. They might conduct publicized military exercises along Poland's border, engage in small-scale Soviet–Polish exercises inside Poland, or even undertake a limited augmentation of Soviet forces in Poland.

32. The Soviets' reluctance to intervene militarily derives above all from the enormous costs they probably anticipate in eliminating Polish armed and passive resistance and in reestablishing a politically and economically viable Poland. Additional disincentives are the political and economic price they anticipate they would pay in their relations with Western nations, with the Third World, and within the international Communist movement.[14] In view of the obvious Western European interest in maintaining stability in relations with the USSR, the Soviets might conclude that, while the inevitable damage to Soviet détente policies would be enormous, it would not necessarily be irretrievable. They might further conclude that efforts to portray the intervention as "legitimate," as an action undertaken in response to Polish requests with Polish collaboration, and as a limited move vital to the maintenance of politico-military stability in Europe could mitigate the setback to Soviet policies toward Western Europe and exacerbate difference's between the United States and its allies. Another related Soviet con-

---

[14] Another, more immediate consideration is probably the desire to avoid drastic military action prior to the late February congress of the Soviet communist party. Also important in any decision to intervene in Poland will be Moscow's anticipation of any economic costs, which could be considerable. While the Soviets cannot foretell the nature or the extent of resistance by the Polish labor force, they must contemplate the possibility of extended economic disruption as a result of widespread passive resistance and even industrial sabotage. The USSR would have to provide large-scale support for Poland to rebuild political stability and to minimize the effects of its economic shortfalls on trade and economic development elsewhere in Eastern Europe. We cannot predict the scale of Poland's economic difficulties in the wake of an invasion, but, as a conservative estimate of Soviet aid costs, we suggest an overall figure for food, fuel, raw materials, and various subventions to be the equivalent of $10 billion per year. The Soviets almost certainly would not assume Poland's debt service costs to the West, but they could not ask Poland to renounce the debt because of the negative effect this would have on Eastern European creditworthiness. Warsaw would probably declare a temporary moratorium on debt service payments and attempt to arrange rescheduling. [Footnote from the original.]

sideration would be the anticipated U. S.–NATO military response. It is unlikely that Moscow would foresee active Western military opposition. But Soviet intervention would surely alter NATO perceptions of Moscow's willingness to resort to force in crisis situations, and the Soviets would expect new Western efforts to augment NATO's force posture. This is not in itself, however, a calculation which would play a major role in staying a Soviet intervention.

33. Whatever the Soviet perception of such costs, they will quickly fade into secondary considerations if the Soviets see their vital interests threatened. We believe that one or another form of Soviet military intervention is likely in the event of:
- a breakdown of internal order in Poland;
- a frontal assault on the regime's authority, such as a general strike of some duration to which the regime did not respond decisively;
- indications that the Polish regime was becoming unwilling or unable to meet its Warsaw Pact commitments.

34. In addition, we believe that the interplay of conditions such as the following would influence Soviet calculations in favor of intervention:
- the increasingly open display of anti-Soviet attitudes or phenomena in Poland on the part of the public or Solidarity, prompted by perceptions that the Soviets were preventing reforms;
- a marked diminution of the party's leading role in society;
- prolonged continuation of the current instability;
- growing repercussions from the Polish events elsewhere in Eastern Europe.[15]

35. It is improbable that the positions of other Warsaw Pact leaderships will have a decisive effect either in convincing the Soviets to use force or in restraining them. We believe that all Warsaw Pact leaderships in varying degrees oppose the longer term accommodation of the Polish leadership to Solidarity's demands, and feel potentially threatened by the trend of events. The lineup of Eastern European attitudes toward Soviet military intervention would differ, depending on the form that it took or the circumstances under which it was initiated. Eastern Germany and Czechoslovakia—those with the most immediate cause to worry—and probably Bulgaria would be willing to take part regardless of its scale or the form that it took. Moscow is likely to limit East German participation, however, given the history of Polish–German hostility. While the Romanians would not participate in an invasion, the Hungarians might feel compelled to provide a symbolic contingent of troops.

---

[15] Determining the precise Soviet threshold of tolerance is made even more difficult by the likelihood of differences in perception of the situation among the Soviet leadership. In view of the complexity of Polish developments and the competing Soviet interests involved, achieving a leadership consensus on military intervention may involve prolonged debate. [Footnote from the original.]

cause + effect analysis

36. We believe that, barring the type of developments noted above, Moscow will continue to give Kania time, but little additional leeway to maneuver and make concessions. The Soviets will also increase pressure on Kania as necessary to move more decisively to bring the situation under control. This would involve resisting the escalating demands of Solidarity, students, and farmers, moving against dissidents, checking the push for greater democracy in the party, and maintaining the regime's police powers intact. The strategy of the Polish leadership has now in effect been determined in Moscow, and its options for dealing with the protracted crisis have been drastically narrowed. We believe that the Soviets are less hopeful than when Kania won his December 5 reprieve that he can in fact bring the situation satisfactorily under control. The trend is decidedly negative from the Soviet perspective.

V. *The Military Dimension*

Possible Coercive Options Open to the Regime

37. Obviously, the Polish leadership seeks to avoid the resort to force. But it has probably accepted that the limited application of force may now be necessary in implementing a policy which tries to hold the line against further union demands and in underwriting the credibility of its resolve. In early January for the first time the regime used the threat of force cautiously and successfully to break up two small occupations of provincial governmental buildings. Seeking to project both restraint and determination, the regime's hope is that such threats of force will serve to intimidate and restrain, rather than to provoke. We would expect to see a repetition of this kind of coercion at the local level.

38. Because its options for dealing with the domestic turmoil and Solidarity's challenge are narrower in comparison with the October–November period, the chances are greater that the regime will respond with force, probably at Soviet urging, if faced with a major confrontation such as a prolonged general strike or the threat of such a major confrontation. Thus we believe that it cannot afford politically under the present circumstances to exercise the degree of restraint which it demonstrated in the crises of August (when the Gierek regime rode out a massive wave of strikes for three weeks) and of October and November. Again, coercion would be used in a way designed to minimize the escalation of violence. For example, in response to the threat of a general strike we would foresee plant lockouts, the arrest of dissidents, and of some of the more radical Solidarity leaders. In any such showdown, the regime would hope by the measured use of force to avoid violence and bloodshed. But the difficulties of manipulating force in such a tense situation are enormous and the probability of an eruption of violence would be high.

39. If the regime decided to use force against strikers in one or more of the major industrial centers, units subordinate to the Ministry of Internal Affairs (MIA), regarded as the most politically reliable, would probably be committed first. In circumstances where the regime faced multiple strikes in a number of cities, such paramilitary forces would be inadequate because of their limited man-

207

power and geographical availability. In either case, therefore, the regime would have to be prepared to support MIA units with troops from the regular armed forces. (This was the pattern in the 1970 disturbances when the regular police were backed up by regular units of the armed forces using tanks, armored personnel carriers, and helicopters.) Use of the armed forces to control civil disturbances, however, would come only after it was clear that forces of the MIA were incapable of maintaining or restoring order. We believe that Polish authorities would commit the regular military as a last resort in staving off Soviet military intervention.

40. [Two words illegible] predict how regular Army units would behave under such circumstances, especially if they were called upon to fire on Polish workers, and we believe similar doubts prevail in the Polish leadership.[16] In all probability, the responses of different units would vary,[17] but on the whole we believe the picture would be one of disintegration in the armed forces and would be perceived as such by the Soviets. In circumstances in which martial law were declared, and the regular Army deployed before the outbreak of civil disturbances, it might remain intact and loyal to the regime. But we seriously doubt the Army's dependability if large-scale violence were to erupt. Under such conditions we do not believe the Polish Army alone would be capable of containing the situation. The introduction of regular Polish military forces under such circumstances would run a high risk of bringing about the intervention of Soviet forces.

Soviet Military Intervention

41. The Soviets actually began gradually to increase the preparedness of their forces in and around Poland as far back as late summer 1980, when Polish strikes began to pose a political threat to the Gierek regime. The measures taken during the following months included the establishment of communications that might be

---

[16] During the 1970 disturbances many soldiers apparently expressed sympathy with the demonstrators and followed orders only reluctantly. In addition, the use of the armed forces in 1970 had a demoralizing effect on the Army. For these reasons, party and military leaders alike expressed misgivings about using the Army under such circumstances, and the Eighth Plenum of the Polish communist party of February 1971 condemned the use of the military for mass internal repression. During the disturbances of June 1976, Polish Defense Minister Jaruzelski is widely reported to have told political leaders not to count on the Army, that "Polish soldiers will not fire on Polish workers." In the current crisis, a party spokesman stated in November that "the Polish Army will not take part in working out a political solution to the situation in the country." The fact that the national crisis has lasted so long and that Solidarity has stirred such sympathy in the population at large means that similar attitudes are reflected in the armed forces rank-and-file, and possibly in the officer corps. We know that the party and military leadership is monitoring military attitudes closely, and we have indications in some units of widely held support for Solidarity. This casts further doubt on Army dependability if called upon to oppose striking workers. [Footnote from the original.]

[17] For example, the Polish airborne division (garrisoned in Kraków and numbering 3,500) is an elite unit considered among the most reliable of Polish armed forces and could be introduced quickly in any area of Poland. [Footnote from the original.]

used in a military intervention in Poland, mobilization activities in selected units, and field training unusual for that time of year. By mid-November some mobilization activities had occurred in a small number of normally low-strength (category III) divisions in the western USSR. Most of the more ready (category II) divisions in the Soviet Military Districts along the Polish border had engaged in earlier training activity which had brought them to a higher state of preparedness. In late November military preparations were stepped up in the event that a political decision was taken for a movement of forces into Poland. A temporary restricted area along the East German–Polish border was put in effect until December 9, and preparations were apparently undertaken for an unscheduled joint exercise.

42. The introduction of Warsaw Pact forces into Poland was apparently planned to take place under the guise of this joint military exercise with some cooperation from the Polish General Staff. Brezhnev all but confirmed such plans when he told Indian Prime Minister Gandhi on 8 December that the Soviets had planned maneuvers but postponed them because of objections raised by Polish officials. The Soviets presumably believed that introducing troops under ambiguous circumstances would mitigate antagonistic responses from either the Polish population or the West. Moscow's precise intentions regarding the number of troops was not clear. The presumed mission, however, was to use such an exercise (similar to those which took place in Czechoslovakia in June and July 1968) to intimidate the Poles. Moscow may have intended to use its forces to backstop a crackdown by the Polish security forces.

43. The Soviets did not complete the mobilization required to bring most of their divisions in the western USSR to full readiness for movement in Poland. In retrospect, we believe that the November–December military preparations were undertaken in anticipation of a political decision which would determine whether military forces would be moved into Poland. Most of the increased readiness measures have been relaxed since mid-December and Soviet forces are now generally at routine readiness and activity levels. But the recent mobilization-related activities and training of elements of a potential invasion force improve their general state of preparedness and leave them capable of responding quickly to future developments.

44. The size of any Soviet intervention force would depend upon Moscow's assessment of likely resistance from the Polish Army and population. We estimate that, if the Soviets foresaw the possibility of significant, organized resistance from the Polish armed forces, they would intervene with a force of at least 30 divisions. We believe they could ready such a force and activate all of the necessary communications in 10 to 14 days. If the Soviets were to undertake the kind of intervention they apparently planned in November and December under the guise of a joint exercise, we estimate an intervention force of some 20 divisions could be readied within about a week. A substantially smaller force involving some half dozen divisions (or more, depending on the extent to which the Soviets drew on their ready divisions in East Germany and Czechoslovakia) could be readied in about two to three days, but we think it unlikely, given the

possibility of resistance, that the Soviets would actually intervene with such a small force.

45. Under any intervention conditions, Moscow will seek to enlist the backing of the Polish leadership and to co-opt the Polish General Staff. They would probably hope that Polish security forces would take the lead in domestic repression, leaving Soviet forces to concentrate on maintaining order and crushing armed resistance. They would also try to maximize the ambiguities of their move into Poland by utilizing such pretexts as "exercises" in order to minimize the possibility of full-scale, military resistance by the Poles and in an attempt to lessen the international costs. We do not believe that the Polish military would present armed opposition organized under central authority, although isolated units under individual commanders might react to a Soviet move. Such resistance would not provide a serious or prolonged obstacle to Soviet military objectives in Poland.

46. If the Soviets do decide to intervene in the future, we would expect a sequence of preparations similar to what we saw from late November to mid-December. Additional steps that would be taken would include a callup of reservists for a much larger number of divisions, logistic preparations at civilian vehicle parks, military motor transport garrisons, and ammunition depots. Preparations for intervention would become progressively more intense at individual garrisons and more widespread across the force, and probably among East German, Czechoslovak, and possible other Eastern European forces, as the Soviets neared full readiness for an intervention.

47. Soviet forces will soon begin participating in annual multinational and joint forces training exercises. As this training becomes more intense, it could complicate the Polish warning problem by providing the Soviets with an opportunity to disguise preparations for intervention. Despite these ambiguities, however, we believe that the size of the larger intervention forces we postulate, their command characteristics, their geographic scope, the required logistic preparations, and the extent of preparations required will differentiate this activity from normal training and permit us to identify its true nature, especially as the intervention becomes more imminent. The Director, Bureau of Research and Intelligence, Department of State agrees that we would probably be able to detect, and to distinguish from exercise activity, Soviet preparations for an "invasion" of Poland in which 30 or more divisions would be readied to cope with possible significant Polish military resistance; but, he is concerned that we might not be able to distinguish confidently or in a timely manner between the large-scale maneuvers we expect at this time of year and the preparations that would be needed to introduce a substantial number of Soviet divisions (that is 15 to 20) into Poland under the guise of an exercise like the one we believe was contemplated last December.

VI. Conclusions

48. The situation in Poland continues to show a high degree of instability. The pattern of the past months, in which tensions have mounted and subsided in response to events and to the reactions to them of the major actors, is likely to

continue, barring a decisive application of force. There is little prospect over the next six months that Solidarity's demands will abate. On the contrary, the union leadership is determined to press for implementation of concessions obtained in the summer strike settlements and is being increasingly influenced by the more militant elements of its constituency. The regime continues to be in an essentially reactive position, although it has adopted a harder line in dealing with the workers. It can no longer make major concessions to union demands without jeopardizing its own position and increasing the risk of Soviet intervention. The only politically viable response, therefore, seems to be a still tougher policy, which may require the expanded use of force.

49. All Poles share an interest in avoiding Soviet intervention, and therefore in containing tensions. But this has failed to stabilize the union-regime relationship—that is, to give rise to a working relationship which can manage persistent conflict. It does, however, impose a measure of restraint on both sides. It is possible that a pattern of negotiation will develop between regime and unions which will help to subdue the level of tension at least for the next half year if the pattern of haphazard confrontation continues. Both the party and Soviet leaderships can probably tolerate continuing sporadic and isolated strikes, and this in itself is unlikely to require the regime to use massive force against workers or to precipitate a Soviet intervention. In short, the situation could be one of extended, but controlled, conflict. Further, it is possible that under such circumstances the regime could gain the upper hand by pursuing a cautious policy designed to undermine the union's strength.

50. It is difficult to believe, however, that in such a potentially volatile setting, and with the authority of both the party and the union diffused, such a situation can last. Miscalculation by the regime or the union could occur as either pressed its position in an attempt to probe the other side's position. A precipitous increase in tensions—for example, a general strike threat on behalf of Rural Solidarity registration—could occur.

51. We believe that Soviet military activities in November and December demonstrate that the Soviets are in fact willing to intervene militarily. As time passes and if the regime shows no convincing progress in consolidating the party and gaining control of events, the Soviets are likely to conclude that nonintervention options are insufficient. We cannot say exactly when this might be or what specific combination of events might finally bring the Soviets to that decision. We believe that Soviet pressure on the Polish regime will increase and that, if the pattern of domestic confrontation continues, the trend is toward ultimate intervention.

[Source: FOIA release from the CIA, on file at the National Security Archive, "Soviet Flashpoints" collection.]

Document No. 32: Solidarity National Coordinating Commission, "Statement on the Current Social and Political Situation"

circa *February 1981*

Throughout the crisis, the regime and Solidarity battled for the hearts and minds of the population. The Polish authorities, in part responding to Moscow's incessant demands, mounted regular propaganda campaigns designed to blame opposition "extremists" for the country's economic woes and looming political chaos. In this public statement, Solidarity fires back at the most recent spate of charges that the union is not only causing economic hardship but is trying to undermine the power of the state to govern and to protect Poland's international interests. With studied reasonableness, the document argues that the state is at fault because of a history of wasteful policies and a failure to fulfill legitimate popular expectations. The union promises to be circumspect in ordering strikes but reserves the right to guarantee implementation of the August 1980 accords. The authors take pains to reassure public opinion that the current system of government is not in danger, nor is Solidarity questioning the "obligations resulting from treaties of alliance in which the PPR participates," an obvious reference to the Warsaw Pact.

STATEMENT ON THE CURRENT SOCIO-POLITICAL SITUATION

During the past few days, statements and opinions on the NSZZ Solidarity began to appear in public circulation whose tendentiousness and deviation from the truth raise concern. Therefore we deem it necessary to clearly define the position taken by our Union.

1. State and political authorities recently have very critically evaluated the present economic situation in the country. This evaluation is a reflection of broad public feeling. We believe that pointing out the real sources of the current situation and defining responsibility for the policies which lead to economic catastrophe is essential for finding a way to overcome the crisis. The opinion which has recently emerged in the mass media that the collapse of the Polish economy is a result of the workers' strikes is not only untrue, it also proves that there are attempts to conceal the real sources of the crisis. The workers are accused of low productivity and losses suffered by the economy due to strikes, but it tends to be forgotten that the workers' toil has been wasted because of bad policy, arbitrary decisions and extravagance. We strongly declare that it is not the strikes that are leading the country to the threshold of economic catastrophe, but the state policy being carried out against the interests of workers, against the will of the masses, and against the interests of the country. Specifically, it is the workers' strikes that have created conditions for the process of renewal and for overcoming the crisis.

Making use of these conditions assumes a deep-seated economic reform as well as a reform of public life, as has been declared in the Gdańsk Agreement.

Public expectations for state authorities consist of the fulfillment of promises made, not reproaches, reprimands or threats. The establishment of the NSZZ Solidarity, after a period when it was necessary to struggle for its existence, curtailed the strike actions. In October and November, using [the means of] strike readiness and symbolic strikes almost exclusively, we won the registration of the Union without any amendments to its statute as well as unusually important social gains. It is enough to mention the increase in spending on health care, culture and education in the state budget, and the guarantee of improved supplies of medicines.

2. The National Coordinating Committee has stated in several subsequent declarations that our Union has decided to refrain from making new salary demands until a general Solidarity program for worker issues, which would be covered by collective agreements, is specified. This standpoint resulted in an appeal not to declare strikes. Our standpoint is motivated by a difficult situation in the country and by the conviction that it is necessary to create conditions for economic and social stabilization. Therefore, we assume that social agreements will also be implemented by the other side. We expect from the authorities a policy of stabilization, local fulfillment of welfare promises, consultations with the working masses and our Union's representation when making key decisions on economic and social policy. Therefore whether we maintain our point of view depends on the policy of the state authorities. We believe that negotiations are the most appropriate way of assuring the fulfillment of justified worker demands and the protection of social interests. We represent that view in practice, in negotiations such as those that are currently being held in the area of health care. However, we declare that the right to strike as a last resort of union work is an absolute workers' right. We consider it a fundamental guarantee for the implementation of the post-August social agreement.

At the same time, however, being aware of the social consequences of strike activities, we are determined to observe the statutory terms and rights of the Union levels as well as to meet the requirements stemming from the overall situation.

3. The National Coordinating Committee expresses its belief that the systemic order of the Polish People's Republic as well as the social order of the country are not in danger. State and political authorities, who have the constitutional right to represent and protect the international interests of our country, declare that the fulfillment of obligations resulting from treaties of alliance in which the PPR participates and from the international situation is fully guaranteed. Public opinion in our country, including the opinion of union masses, completely shares this view. In this situation we do not see grounds for a broader feeling of danger; we maintain that this creates nothing but social tension.

It is not Solidarity that is introducing chaos and anarchy; on the contrary, our Union is a force for overcoming the chaos and anarchy. It is obvious that in a union of many million [members] there are different views, opinions and concepts. However, we declare that we will not allow the division of Solidarity into good and bad, or interference in the internal affairs of an independent union on the pretext of fighting any point of view.

We express our deep belief that at the moment our motherland has a special need for the harmonious cooperation of all Poles. That is why we are against any attempts at replacing discussion that can promote such cooperation with slanders—but above all with repression. Such activities intensify social unrest and hinder the cooperation between party members and non-party [people] that is currently vital.

We want to strongly declare: our country needs peace.

He who introduces tension, provokes conflicts, or spreads panic does his country no good. The most vital interests, the fate of the nation are at stake. On these grounds, the NSZZ Solidarity declares full readiness to participate in an alliance of reason, sense and national responsibility.

[Source: NCC Secretariat/NCC Documents, November 19, 1980 – February 1, 1981. Translated by Aleksandra Niemirycz.]

Document No. 33: Supplement No. 2 to PUWP CC Politburo Protocol No. 69

February 6, 1981

The minister of trade unions, Stanisław Ciosek, prepared this document after semi-secret talks with a group of Solidarity advisers at the beginning of February. It is a fairly objective record of conversation, lacking the aggressive, ideological tone of so many other internal party and state records. The most important issue being confronted at this time was the status of Rural Solidarity, which would become the next factor in the destabilization of the system.

Information about talks with the advisers of the
NSZZ Solidarity on February 4–6, 1981.

In recent days, in the course of worker contacts with the advisers of the NSZZ Solidarity on ways to resolve social conflicts, problems reaching beyond current conflicts have naturally been raised. These matters include:

1. The arrangement of contacts between the authorities and Solidarity in general categories.

The advisers convey the uniform view that some sort of "code" for the mutual undertakings of the government and trade unions should be prepared; it would specify laws about the trade unions. According to them, discussions on the workers' level could be initiated in the first phase. The intention there is to attempt to find institutionalized solutions so that it is not necessary to incessantly "dash" the local conflicts—especially those that result from Solidarity's non-statutory activity.

2. "Rural Solidarity."

The advisers (Geremek unequivocally expressed this in his speech) believe that a compromise solution to the Rural Solidarity problem ought to be sought—they are prepared to step back from the formula of trade unions and seek solutions which are close to associations of agricultural producers. In connection with the above, they request a postponement of the Supreme Court decision[18]—because that might cause a conflict in which reaching compromise solutions

---

[18] The decision concerned the registration of Rural Solidarity. The court ruled on February 10 that the organization could register as an association but not as a union.

would be difficult. The Church leadership is also interested in such a solution (information from cde. Kuberski).

I propose adopting this motion because the period of two-three weeks (this is probably what is meant) will not be significant for the process of developing Rural Solidarity, while closing the matter by the Supreme Court will not leave scope for negotiations—and the phenomenon of Rural Solidarity cannot be addressed only on a theoretical level because it is already a fact and something has to be done with it.

3. Current conflicts.

The leadership of Solidarity (part of it at least) as well as "moderate" advisers intend to quell local conflicts so as not to provoke any extreme views about the idea of the NSZZ at the CC plenum. They expect that the cc plenary session will propose a formula for the trade union movement which could be "compatible" with the idea of independent self-governing trade unions. My interlocutors fear that the CC plenum will close doors to the construction of compromise cooperation platforms between the authorities and trade unions.

4. Council of Ministers resolution regulating compensation for the period of a strike.

The advisers are very persistently pressing for mitigation of the meaning of this resolution. They have put forward reservations concerning being informed about a decision which has already been made. Their fears are caused by the possibility, as they put it, of an uncontrolled wave of protests organized by local activists and membership masses. In their opinion, the situation in this domain could be dangerous.

The advisers propose that the government press spokesman mention in his statement that faced with growing anarchy the government had to reach for this kind of means in order to calm a dangerous situation in the country. However, the execution of these means will be dependent on developments and will be applied in accordance with the trade unions' leaderships. They do not question the political principle of the resolution itself, they are interested in a public statement that it is not directed against the trade unions.

My interlocutors were: Geremek, Mazowiecki and Wielowieyski.[19] The views they have presented have always been accompanied by the disclaimer that they are not the official positions of Solidarity's leadership. Experience shows, however, that the distance between those views and the official positions of Solidarity is not great.

[19] Andrzej Wielowieyski was editor-in-chief of *Więź,* a Catholic monthly, and an adviser to striking workers in Gdańsk. He later participated in the Roundtable talks and was elected a senator and deputy to the Polish parliament.

The above information contains views of NSZZ Solidarity advisers on important, in my opinion, questions which should be the subject of analysis and on which a position should be taken.

The information was prepared by S. Ciosek.

[Source: AAN, PUWP CC, 1820, pp. 706–707. Translated by Paweł Świeboda.]

Document No. 34: Memorandum of Conversation between Erich Honecker and Fidel Castro

February 28, 1981

Among Warsaw Pact leaders, East Germany's Erich Honecker maintained the most hard-line stance toward the Polish crisis out of concern for its implications for communist authority in his own country. In this one-on-one session with Fidel Castro, he offers an "unvarnished" account of the Polish situation. He raises inter alia the subject of East German assistance to Poland, which includes both economic aid and intelligence information. He also gives a clear idea of the variety of ways Poland's allies sought to apply pressure on Kania during the crisis. Castro, whose overriding interest is in guaranteeing Warsaw Pact support in the face of U.S. military threats against Cuba, asks a question on every observer's mind—whether the Polish army can be trusted. Honecker replies: "For the time being, yes."

Memorandum of conversation of General Secretary of the SED CC Comrade Erich Honecker with First Secretary of the CC Communist Party of Cuba Comrade Fidel Castro (February 28, 1981, Moscow)

The conversation took place in Moscow, in the margins of the XXXVI Party Congress of the Communist Party of the Soviet Union. The following are only the passages relating to Poland.

The meeting occurred at the request of Comrade Fidel Castro. [...]

Comrade Erich Honecker: First I would like to assure you, dear Comrade Fidel, of our complete solidarity. Especially now. The SED and the GDR stand firmly at your side. In regard to your question as to our opinion about the situation in Poland, I would like to say: We have direct, close contacts with the PUWP leadership. Their conduct since December's Moscow meeting[20] does not conform to our expectations. We see the Eighth Plenum of the PUWP CC and the appointment of Comrade Jaruzelski as prime minister as a significant step. However, between you and me, until now there have been no energetic efforts to smash the counter-revolution. Recently I had a personal meeting with Comrade Kania in the neighborhood of Berlin. I had the impression that the Polish leadership is hesitating a great deal. I handed Comrade Kania concrete materials about the activities of the CIA against Poland as well as exact evidence about the plans and activities of the new U.S. administration against Poland and the socialist community. I furthermore handed him extensive materials about the

---

[20] The December 5, 1980, meeting of Warsaw Pact leaders (see Document No. 22).

counter-revolutionary activities inside Solidarity. Comrade Kania said he judged the situation exactly the way we do, but first the party itself has to be consolidated. I pointed out that it is decisive to choose the most favorable moment, not to waste it, to defeat the counter-revolution with military power and in cooperation with all healthy powers, and stabilize the workers' and farmers' power in Poland. These days in Poland there is a double authority; on the one side the party and the government, on the other side the hostile leadership in Solidarity and the clergy. It is good that Comrade Kania agreed to my proposal that direct ties between the party organizations of our districts and the voivodeship committees of the PUWP be continued. This way we can exercise influence. The worst is that the PUWP leadership and the government do not control the mass media—except *Trybuna Ludu* and the army newspaper. All other media are in the hands of revisionist forces. The counter-revolution itself produces newspapers, brochures, etc. It now rudely demands access to television and radio. The situation is extremely complicated. I am in permanent contact with Comrade Leonid Ilyich Brezhnev and with Comrade Husák. We are trying to have the Polish comrades firmly take the initiative themselves to lead developments in a socialist direction. The GDR has provided great material solidarity. We have given the Polish leadership half a billion [Deutsch] marks in exchangeable currency. Polish deliveries to the GDR agreed to by treaty have not come through for as much as 1.9 billion (hard currency) marks. This is how the GDR makes great material sacrifices. We expect that the Polish leadership will act in accordance with the Moscow decisions and its bilateral assurances to us. Very serious is the fact that the counter-revolution can campaign legally. The only positive aspect is the appointment of Comrade Jaruzelski, which creates the possibility of announcing a state of siege at the right moment to smash the counter-revolution.

Comrade Fidel Castro: In case the situation in Poland comes to a head, I hope Cuba will not be forgotten.

Comrade Erich Honecker: As we have in the past, we will always be at Cuba's side.

Comrade Fidel Castro: We are preparing ourselves concretely for Cuba's defense. We will do our part but will need the help of the fraternal countries.

Comrade Erich Honecker: That is clear. Especially because we know the imperialist threats against Cuba. We are trying everything to have the PUWP solve its problems on its own. The events in Poland are a real help for Reagan. If the Reagan administration, independent of the situation in Poland, organizes a new blockade of Cuba, the fraternal countries will not [just] look on. Cuba can always count on us.

Comrade Fidel Castro: Can the army in Poland still be trusted?

Comrade Erich Honecker: For the time being, yes. A considerable part stands firm. But when the crisis goes on longer, this may get worse. We fraternal countries are all standing firm. We have told Comrade Jaruzelski that it would be best if they could settle the situation by their own means. Comrade Kania has told me that they are making preparations for a state of siege. In doing so they rely on the army, the security organs and the militias, as well as the best forces in the party. We have told him that now one cannot yield any further because in that case the last bit of confidence would be lost. Unfortunately in the past couple of days yet another major concession occurred on the part of the Polish leadership to the counter-revolutionary forces among the striking students in Łódź.

The Polish leadership has approved 55 demands of the enemy-inspired students, including that the security organs cannot enter the university area. You do not see something like that anywhere else in the world. I have to describe the situation to you in such unvarnished terms. We operate in constant contact with the leadership of the CPSU and the CPCz as our closest neighbors. About the situation in Poland we have piles of analytical materials.

Comrade Fidel Castro: What do the Hungarians and Romanians say?

Comrade Erich Honecker: On the basis of the Hungarian experience, Comrade Kádár explained in Moscow how the counter-revolution of 1956–1957 was liquidated.

The Romanians are against any further retreat by the Polish leadership in the face of the counter-revolution but they do not want a military commitment. NATO is interfering. If the Polish leadership allows this to go on, we cannot permit the worst to happen. We are prepared accordingly.

Comrade Fidel Castro: We will then need special solidarity, because Reagan threatens us quite openly.

Comrade Erich Honecker: We heed this. Comrade Leonid Ilyich Brezhnev has certainly discussed this in his conversation with you.

We exercise our influence in such a way that the comrades in Poland will solve their problems by themselves. Comrade Kania has promised this. That would be the best solution. At the same time we remain vigilant against NATO interference. When the time comes, we will carry out maneuvers. NATO does this too, by the way. We openly stand up for Cuba's territorial integrity. The communiqué about your meeting with Comrade Leonid Ilyich Brezhnev is being echoed widely internationally. The U.S. will certainly take this as a warning. [...]

[Source: Moscow, 28.2.1981, SAPMO-BArch ZPA, J IV 2/2-1883, pp. 46–52. Translated by Ruud van Dijk.]

Document No. 35: Transcript of CPSU CC Politburo Meeting

March 12, 1981

Three months after the climactic December 5 Warsaw Pact leadership meeting in Moscow, it had become clear that Kania was not following through on his pledge to eliminate the threat to communist rule in Poland. Of all the alliance leaders, the GDR's Erich Honecker was perhaps the most upset about the lack of action, as indicated in this brief description of a conversation he had with Leonid Brezhnev. The Soviet leader commiserates with Honecker but points to the positive development of having Jaruzelski in charge of the government—an assessment he would eventually revise entirely.

[...]

5. On Cde. L. I. Brezhnev's discussion with Cde. E. Honecker.

Brezhnev: The discussion with Cde. Honecker has been circulated and you have had the chance to read it through. The discussion was brief but it carried no small significance for Cde. Honecker. I greeted Cde. Honecker and thanked him for his participation at the congress.[21] In addition, I was interested in how Cde. Honecker thought the congress was going and how the delegates were speaking. He answered that the congress delegates were speaking with great enthusiasm and were talking not only about successes but about difficulties and deficiencies as well.

In addition, during the discussion Cde. Honecker sounded out his unease about the situation in Poland. I said to him that the situation in Poland makes us uneasy, too. In spite of this, I noted that Cde. Honecker had a meeting with Cde. Kania which, of course, was useful. All of us, apparently, are united on the need to get the Polish comrades to implement the most constructive measures for putting things in order in the country and imposing strict stability. Currently Cde. Jaruzelski stands at the head of the government, a good, intelligent comrade with substantial authority.

I told Cde. Honecker also to press Cde. Kania at their meeting to have the Polish comrades carry out more decisive measures in connection with bringing order to the country. Cde. Honecker thanked me for the discussion and enthusiastically invited me to come to the congress[22] at the head of the CPSU delegation. I thanked him for the invitation and said that the Politburo would adopt an appropriate decision about who would lead the delegation.

---

[21] The CPSU Party Congress of February 23 – March 4, 1981, which Honecker was attending when he had this conversation with Brezhnev.

[22] The SED X Party Congress, which began on April 11, 1981.

Gromyko: Poland, of course, worries all of them, Cde. Honecker above all, and that is entirely understandable. It seems to me that Honecker is raising all questions before Kania rather persistently, just as Cde. Husák posed all these questions very firmly.

Rusakov: If one is to speak about Leonid Ilyich's discussions, one can see that all the comrades essentially raised the question of Poland. Of course, the situation in Poland worries everyone. I think that the Polish comrades also feel that concern. They should have responded to that concern by taking more decisive measures. However, after the well-known gathering of leaders of the fraternal countries[23] the Polish friends never realized the need to implement a number of cardinal measures for bringing order to the country.

Cdes. Chernenko, Gorbachev and Grishin also spoke about this matter.

The decision is adopted: To approve the discussion held by Cde. L. I. Brezhnev with Cde. E. Honecker.

[Source: RGANI, Fond 89, Opis 42, Delo 37. Translated by Malcolm Byrne for the National Security Archive.]

---

[23] See Document No. 22.

Document No. 36: Polish Ministry of Internal Affairs Duty Report on Preparations for Martial Law

March 16, 1981

As this document indicates, even before the Bydgoszcz crisis the Polish authorities had already completed many of the most important preparations for martial law. The question they faced now was a political one—whether actually to institute a crackdown. When the regime eventually acted in December 1981, they followed a number of the guidelines and proposals laid down at this time.

[…]

In accordance with instructions from the Comrade Premier [Jaruzelski] on March 15 of this year, a meeting of the MSW leadership took place where recent events in the country were taken into account, and a readiness assessment made in case of the need to introduce martial law. Meeting participants included:

1. Minister of Internal Affairs—Maj.-Gen. M. Milewski
2. Chief of the PA General Staff—Lt.-Gen. F. Siwicki
3. Deputy Chief of the PA General Staff—Maj.-Gen. T. Hupałowski
4. Vice-Minister of Internal Affairs—Maj.-Gen. B. Stachura

The conclusion of the assessment of the state of readiness, in case of the need to introduce martial law, as well as the exchange of views on the current course of the socio-political situation in the country, are stated as follows:

1. The continued persistence of a state of tension in the country requires the continuation of preparations to introduce martial law. The ministries of national defense and of internal affairs, taking into account the experience of the decision games that were conducted, have made further preparations with the aim of increasing the readiness of both ministries for operations in this range. Jointly specified:
   - MND and MSW defense of radio and television objectives, transportation and communications, as well as the larger provisions warehouses;
   - selection and recruitment to sub-units comprised of the Citizens' Police;
   - elimination of particularly dangerous elements from military conscription by the MSW, organization of joint patrols;
   - assistance to the MND in quartering, with military units, the sub-units comprised of the Citizens' Police and the like, successively called up by the MSW.
2. The state of MND and MSW preparations, with respect to legal forms, the use of force and resources, and the introduction of internment operations,

makes both ministries competent in principle to undertake operations in case martial law is introduced. However, this operation cannot be introduced with a positive (for us) evolution of the situation without previously preparing propaganda. As an aggregate of departmental preparations, propaganda still lags behind. An urgent need exists to accelerate work in this sphere. This work could be executed by selected teams of PUWP CC employees, who would make a thorough study of a plan, detailing propaganda preparations and securing the planned operation. The ministries of national defense and of internal affairs would provide essential assistance in this area.

3. In the present situation, it is not necessary to take into consideration the possibility of introducing martial law in defined areas of the country (a province or a number of provinces), because pronouncements by Solidarity would embrace the entire country and would paralyze the effectiveness of preventive MSW operations.

4. In case of the introduction of martial law and the prior removal of particularly dangerous persons for internment, as well as the prepared propaganda operations—anticipating that the course of the situation in the country could be, among others, the following:

First Variant

– devoid of enemy leaders and opposition organizations as well as the whole society as a result of propaganda influence and party activities prepared earlier at places of employment by groups of party agitators (activists)—submit to the orders of the authorities;

– in certain establishments work stoppages, not large, could appear;

– troops and police, after occupying demarcated regions, maintain a passive posture (protective-guarding) and their main effort remains directed at maintaining law and public order;

– positive attitudes of society support abolishing martial law in certain regions of the country.

Second Variant

– in certain regions of the country massive work stoppages appear, as well as the fact of sabotage activities;

– demonstrations and strikes do not go beyond the premises of enterprises;

– troops assume a protective-guarding posture at appointed positions, the KOK actively agitates in the sphere of law and order and also in identifying and eliminating enemy activities;

– the introduction of summary proceedings before common and military courts;

– active party-propaganda actions, supported by ascertained facts about the opponent's sabotage activities, gradually eliminates the negative occurrences.

Third Variant

– immediately after introducing martial law in the entire country, occupation strikes are organized;

- some crews go out on the street;
- street demonstrations together with attacks on party and administration buildings;
- summary proceedings before common and military courts are introduced over the entire territory of the PPR;
- assistance from the Warsaw Pact is not ruled out.

In case a sudden decision is taken to introduce martial law, the impossibility of immediately printing the legal and propaganda documents, for that time, would be a great difficulty. The necessary minimum time for proper deployment of the operation by the MND and MSW is about 7–10 days (from the moment the political decision is taken on the introduction of martial law).

Current preparations for the introduction of martial law are mainly concentrated at the MND and MSW, and to a limited degree at essential departments of the national economy. Work in this area at the MND and MSW is advanced. Both ministries are ready to execute the decisions of the party-government. The preparations, however, do not include such matters as: guarding prisons, freezing bank accounts, provisioning the population, and others. The decision games that were conducted allowed for the analysis of only certain variants of the evolution of the situation in the country after the introduction of martial law.

Taking into account the continued tension in the country, all preparations demand a complex assessment by the party-government leadership. Assignations at the highest levels will assist the MND and MSW, as well as other departments, to execute further ventures guaranteeing the success of the planned operation.

Report prepared by
Deputy Director
First Administration MSW
Col. Jan Wasiluk

[Source: AIPN, MSW II 1412/37a, pp. 5–8. Translated by L. W. Głuchowski for the National Security Archive.]

Document No. 37: Protocol No. 82 from PUWP CC Politburo Meeting

March 25, 1981

At this crucial time, just days after the Bydgoszcz crisis, the Soviets are once more pressing the Polish authorities to introduce martial law. But Kania, as always, is indecisive. Despite Moscow's demands, Kania and his fellow moderates are more concerned that the popular reaction to the Bydgoszcz assaults was much sharper than expected. Among other steps, Solidarity called for a four-hour warning strike to take place on March 27 and a general strike on the 31st. The authorities are further taken aback that so much of the party base has joined Solidarity. At this Politburo session, the leadership again rejects Soviet insistence that the PUWP now has a pretext for taking harsh measures. The warning strike, the largest such action ever under communist rule, occurred on schedule but a last-minute agreement between the government and the union averted a general strike.

[...]

Agenda:

1. The current socio-political situation in connection with the warning strike announced by NSZZ Solidarity for March 27, 1981.
2. Assessment of the current situation in agriculture.
3. Various matters.

Point 1 of the Agenda

Comrade Wojciech Jaruzelski reports about the talk of Comrade W. Namiotkiewicz with the adviser of "S," J. Olszewski, who stated that some in the National Coordinating Commission are turning against Wałęsa, who feels that his position is being threatened. Olszewski proposes to seek a resolution of the conflict through the following: creation of a joint commission of the government and Solidarity to examine events in Bydgoszcz and the issuance of an abolition act including persons arrested up until August 1980.

These are the two most important matters whose undertaking could break the impasse in the talks. They are also putting forward the matter of a security guarantee for the union, which bears no reservation, because at the moment of registration the union obtained a guarantee of security.

He proposes that the matter of abolition be handled by the attorneys. There is a lot of pressure for talks, for resolution of the conflict and avoidance of a strike. There is a letter from a party organization of the work institute "Elwro" regarding this matter (*Comrade S. Olszowski*—this organization is ailing; *Comrade W.*

Kruk—one cannot make an evaluation in such a manner because soon we will be left without party organizations, only the bureaucracy; there are tens of such organizations. I would like to know whether the report of Comrade Bafia[24] is already known and whether we are in a position to prove the details of the evaluation that is included in the PB statement on the 22nd of this month).

Comrade Kazimierz Barcikowski—One should take into consideration Olszewski's suggestions relayed to Comrade Namiotkiewicz. If these matters could be a starting point for further talks, which could result in the aversion of a strike, it would be a success. He proposes: adopting the idea of creating a joint commission, accepting the question of abolition on the basis that it will be handled by the attorneys (*Comrade R. Ney*—I support; *Comrade T. Fiszbach* supports both motions).

Comrade Andrzej Żabiński—One should carefully approach the matter of the commission. We cannot lose the trust of the security service and the Citizens' Police, they were acting under orders. Do not treat it lightly, the atmosphere in the organs is still good, let us not abuse it. Demanding abolition, that is pardoning punishment; stopping the repression against those who were breaking the law prior to August is without precedent.

The PB statement from the 22nd of this month was well received by *aktiv* party members.

Comrade Stefan Olszowski—I propose that in the talks Comrade Rakowski takes note of the suggestion of abolition without taking a position.

Comrade Henryk Jabłońsk—Initially accept the matter of abolition.

Comrade Mirosław Milewski—Demand 1 regarding a mixed commission is important, it is not safe.

Comrade Stanisław Kania—The matter of Bydgoszcz was investigated by a commission of experts, a government commission under the leadership of Minister of Justice Comrade J. Bafia, and now are we to agree to the creation of a joint commission of the government and "S"? Such a commission is going to investigate our people; it is impossible, they will not endure such pressure (Berger, Młodecki, others), it will be they who will inquire into who gave an order. Abolition can be considered conditionally, and it cannot end with August. One cannot agree to a joint commission to investigate Bydgoszcz, this is a matter to be investigated by a government commission.

Comrade Stanisław Kociołek—I think that in the Monday talks Comrade Rakowski should not go beyond the plenipotentiary powers granted by the PB on the 24th of this month. "S" is distributing Bratkowski's letter[25] widely; today in

---

24 Jerzy Bafia, minister of justice from March 1976 to June 1981, oversaw the preparation of a report on the Bydgoszcz incident.

25 Stefan Bratkowski, the chairman of the Journalists' Association and a reformist party member, published an open letter to the PUWP on March 23 accusing party hard-liners of provoking society through tactics such as the Bydgoszcz crisis in order to justify a crackdown.

the Warsaw Steelworks it was read out 13 times. This is an attack on the party; we will see what attitude Comrade Rakowski's interlocutors assume towards his demands. If we make new motions, they will take them as a weakness, the weakness of the PB and the government. I propose not to broaden the mandate granted to Comrade Rakowski yesterday (*Comrade T. Grabski*—could one not say that we will not consider their demands without calling off the strike?; *Comrade S. Olszowski*—it is impossible, but let us confine ourselves to the proposition of Kociołek as well as to consent regarding consideration of abolition; *Comrade A. Żabiński*—we have not arrested any one yet and we are already pondering abolition and amnesty).

Comrade Stanisław Kania proposes to accept and relay to Comrade Rakowski that the PB will not undertake talks in the matter of creating a joint commission and in the matter of abolition. However, he can confirm the guarantee of security for union activity as well as consent to the withdrawal of the Citizens' Police units from Bydgoszcz as long as peace prevails.

Comrade Kazimierz Barcikowski—The situation in the country is bad. "S"'s version was quickly and widely relayed to society regarding Bydgoszcz, which engendered enormous, suggestive propaganda. Meanwhile, nobody believes our version. There are signs of strikes in the entire country. If it comes to a strike, it will be directed against the authorities with the intention of creating substitute structures. We cannot depend on counter-activities. The strike will be a demonstration of the power and organizational competence of "S."

The situation in the party is changing rapidly. Since yesterday "S" has been attacking not only the Security Service and Citizens' Police, but the party and its leadership. The two causes contributing to this are as follows: the statement of the PB on the 22nd of this month regarding Bydgoszcz, and Bratkowski's letter.

The voivodeship committees estimate that soon after its publishing, the PB statement was well received by party *aktiv* members, but soon under the influence of press accounts and others shedding a different light on the course of events in Bydgoszcz, this mood collapsed. Enormous pressure from "S" also contributed to this. Some "S" cells were posing the question outright before the organizations: "Declare what you are for—the PB statement or the truth." Party organizations began to adopt resolutions against the PB statement. Among them were found such organizations as "Elwro," "Dolmel" and the Lenin Shipyard. Organizations of intellectual circles joined the party workers' organizations and together they began to demand the truth regarding Bydgoszcz.

Thus the position of the Politburo from the 22nd of this month on the matter of Bydgoszcz was called into question by party organizations. At the same time demands to convene the plenum are more and more common because "the party is dispersed." This is what Bratkowski's letter has come to, distributed by "S" in millions of copies and disseminated through wire broadcasting centers at work institutes. The letter has become an additional factor undermining trust in the leadership.

In the light of this assessment he proposes:

– to consider convening the Ninth Plenum of the CC for March 30 or between April 10 and 15. The report, almost ready regarding the topic decided earlier, must be solidly reworked and refer to the current situation, indicate the phenomena leading to the disintegration of the party; and refer to the Congress;

– to consider convening the Sejm for the 30ᵗʰ of this month, announce the creation of a Government of National Salvation equipped with additional plenipotentiary forces through the Sejm;

– in an urgent manner, to publish the report of Minister Bafia;

– to bring up Bratkowski's letter at the CC plenum;

– at the conclusion of Comrade Rakowski's talks with "S" to inform the first secretaries of the EC [Executive Committee] about their results.

Comrade Wojciech Jaruzelski—The version of the events in Bydgoszcz presented by "S" caused a shock. The resolutions of party organizations included a negative attitude towards the PB statement from the 22ⁿᵈ of this month and often identify themselves with the assessment of "S." Bratkowski's letter deepened distrust in our position.

Puts forward a motion for an unequivocal declaration of the party leadership towards Bratkowski's letter.

The development of the situation is such that first there was an attack on the security apparatus, now the fire is directed entirely at the party. The Politburo must take action, and learn its lesson. The party is threatened with a serious danger. If worst comes to the worst, then the CC plenum should be forewarned about it.

The Sejm—treat it as a forum for warning society, for taking advantage of all possible means of political activity.

One should immediately work out a scheme for the anticipated development of the situation in the nearest future and have a plan of action for protecting the functioning of life to cover every variant. The elements of this scheme should be as follows:

– the CC plenum reporting the threat to the party;

– the Sejm—with an appeal to the nation;

– staff activity enabling the functioning of national and social life.

Comrade Roman Ney—In light of the meetings held with party organizations in Kraków and Warsaw I can say that as the Politburo we do not have authority in the party. There is a general belief that we are taking responsibility for the state in which we find ourselves, that we are defending our positions. The immediate convening of the plenum, the announcement of elections, the election of the delegates for the congress and setting the time for the congress are necessary. One should also tell about the events in Bydgoszcz at the plenum and explain the matter of the beatings.

Comrade Emil Wojtaszek—reads excerpts of foreign publications with interviews with different radical activists of "S"—i.e. *Lis*: "the main problem in Poland is the breaking of the monopoly of the PUWP; we tolerate the party, but we do not have trust in it."

Comrade Stefan Olszowski—In our propaganda one should emphasize the main thought, which is that only the party can be a stabilizer of the political situation.

Upon my recommendation Comrade Klasa talked with Comrade Bratkowski regarding the matter of the letter and attempted to persuade Bratkowski to issue a statement that the letter was not a public [document]. Bratkowski would not consent. I think that the party should take action against Bratkowski.

If it comes to a general strike, under no condition can one allow the seizing of the PR [Polish Radio] and television building.

Comrade Andrzej Żabiński thinks that the incident in Bydgoszcz was only a pretext to inflame the situation. One should take into account that the next region of confrontation may be the Katowice voivodeship. One should strive for the polarization of positions in the party itself. Bratkowski's letter is close to the context of the information [found] in monitoring Radio Free Europe. One should deal with the letter at the CC plenum.

He thinks that one should strengthen the control of voivodeship newspapers, they are ceasing to be the tool of the EC. One should also, for financial considerations, limit television programs and limit the number of the newspaper editions.

Comrade Henryk Jabłoński thinks that one should urgently publish the report of Comrade Bafia, convene the plenum for March 30, and subsequently the Sejm. It is necessary to set the date of the plenum for June–July.

Comrade Józef Pińkowski—having presented its version of events "S" used tapes which acted more suggestively than written texts. Perhaps we should also employ less conventional means in our propaganda.

Comrade Zdzisław Kurowski—This time a general strike will be used to replace the organs of authority. "S" is already disseminating special instructions on the matter. Counter-actions against the strike will have little effect. One should take advantage of all possibilities for talks, and shock society through the following:

– describing the dramatic economic situation, which will worsen even further if it comes to strikes;

– directing a message to the nation;

– decisively executing a strike prohibition in designated areas of the economy and administration;

– ensuring the functioning of social life under strike conditions;

– securing national and party facilities.

The attack on the party and its leadership is intensifying. The resolutions against the PB statement from the 22nd of this month are coming mostly from those organizations which are always against the central authority.

Bratkowski's letter is a reflection of the off-center tendencies in the party. And at the plenum one should take action not against the name, but against the phenomenon.

Comrade Tadeusz Fiszbach—The events in Bydgoszcz worsened the state of the party. The situation in the market also has an enormous influence on mood.

In the Gdańsk voivodeship we introduced controls on many goods such as butter and cheese.

One observes great fear in the face of a general strike, but if it is announced, everyone will strike, no [attempts at] persuasion will help. One is also considering the possibility of "S" adopting, as a form of pressure, prolonging the readiness for a strike instead of an actual strike. There is much nervousness among student circles. We are losing the support of various social groups.

The statement of the PB from the 22nd of this year was rejected by many organizations on the grounds that the PB prejudged the matter before the end of its investigation of the events in Bydgoszcz. Some are emphasizing that they want to believe that Comrade Kania and Comrade Jaruzelski were absent from that session and therefore the statement was able to be adopted. If the state of emergency is to be declared, there is a fear that it might be only a paper document without any practical meaning. More and more clearly a division is being drawn within the party, as in "S", between the advocates and opponents of renewal.

He proposes that the plenum be held between April 15 and 20 and that a decision be made regarding the congress, which should be held no later than June or July.

We think that the conflict in the background of the events in Bydgoszcz should be resolved through compromise. A confrontational solution will lead to further isolation of the party and will be an outright retreat. "S" has issued instructions on how to take over and replace the authorities in times of a general strike.

The matter of Comrade Lis—meetings of the PPO have been held. Lis denied stating what the PPA alleges. He thinks that the party should not become involved in economic matters. The opinion of Comrade Kacała about Lis whom he met during the strike and the talks in Ustrzyki was positive.

Comrade Władysław Kruk—The majority of party organizations are healthy, not sick. But they feel an enormous need to express their opinions. Only one organization in the Lublin voivodeship is questioning the statement of the PB from the 22nd of this month. However, all others are categorically demanding an explanation through a government commission for what happened in Bydgoszcz. "S" is very suggestively explaining this using tapes whose content is making a great impression. Listening to these tapes people are convinced that the Citizens' Police beat people; they are changing their position and questioning our version. People ask where Kukułowicz came from and what role he played.

I think that, having made a decision, the PB has pondered all its consequences.

A prompt convening of the plenum is necessary as is the convening of the Sejm session and an appearance by the prime minister, because people still trust him. If we do not convene the Sejm ourselves, the deputies will force us to do it anyway. Nervousness and tension is being conveyed to the representatives of the army and security services. If it comes to a general strike, the economic administration will have no say in it, it will be brushed aside unless it concedes to the strike; the administration is indeed in a tragic situation. There is the threat of a strike in schools. I thought that the Bydgoszcz incident would be localized, but I see that it is otherwise.

Bratkowski's letter is being widely distributed. Everybody latched onto the division in the Politburo; there is a widening suggestion that "Kania and Jaruzelski" will get rid of those people.

Comrade Stanisław Kociołek—The authority of the CC and PB is strained. There are many setbacks and active party members would like to have a success. So far, the leadership has managed to avoid the worst crisis even though it is constantly being pushed towards the edge. The leadership completed an evaluation of the government's activity, and it accomplished the change of prime minister. How is it that everyone supports the new prime minister and his 10-point program, but on the other hand they are ready to strike at every nod by "S"?

The PB received instructions regarding individual talks within the party; it was correct on the assumption that the situation in the party will improve. But the situation is otherwise. Therefore, I suggest an exchange of party membership cards as well as submission of an ideological, programmatic and political declaration by every member. I propose to consider this suggestion.

He thinks that one should take a position on Bratkowski's letter from the broader view of its position as expressed, among other ways, in the article in *Życie Warszawy*. It seems that the line of division in the leadership is pointless, but at the same time is capable of producing many results.

The general strike will be a general trial of the organizational efficiency of "S", an opportunity to call up its forces and ready itself for elections and taking over authority. MKZ–Mazowsze has already sent detailed instructions on how to take over power.

We should prepare ourselves for winning the general strike. It may be worth it for a group of comrades to go to Hungary and examine their experiences under such circumstances.

Comrade Stanisław Kania shares the view that the Bydgoszcz incident is a pretext. The dominating tendency among "S" today is to strive for power. Whether the Citizens' Police was beating people in Bydgoszcz or not, it is not a matter for the Politburo. We defend the legitimacy of the decision to remove [people] from the room by force.

At the moment the fundamental and most difficult issue is to make the party aware of the fact that we are facing a most serious crisis.

The fundamental issue is the attitude towards the massive general strike which is threatening us. We put together our motions on the assumption that we would be able to stop the strike, that we would be able to ensure the functioning of social life—food delivery, energy, and the operation of communal services. A group of comrades under the leadership of Comrade M. Jagielski is working to limit the consequences of the strike. We also concluded politically that we could not make concessions, nor withdraw before any demand by "S" to call off and make the voivodeship authorities responsible nor before the demand to register

Rural Solidarity. Under such a political assumption we consciously made a decision regarding the strike without seeing another way.

We must convene the plenum; it will be bitter for us. We should immediately work on a report, strongly indicate in it the threat, personify the phenomena and anti-party tendencies, and indicate the lines for strengthening the party. The harm caused by Bratkowski's letter is obvious.

Convene the session of the Sejm, announce the threat to social development. The Sejm should be held after the second or third day of the strike. I propose the plenum for March 29 of this month.

Point 2 of the Agenda

The Politburo considered and took a note of the evaluation of the current situation in agriculture.

Point 3 of the Agenda

After familiarization, the Politburo approved the following:

– a plan for the composition of the motion commission for the Ninth CC Plenum with the recommendation to introduce Comrades S. Olszowski and J. Waszczuk;

– a plan for resolution at the Ninth Plenum of the CC;

– a memo regarding a quick propaganda reaction in conflict situations;

– a memo regarding the convening of the voivodeship councils of party *aktiv* members.

Recorded by: Zbigniew Regucki
Bożena Łopatniuk

[Source: Tajne Dokumenty, pp. 310–317. Translated by Małgorzata Gnoińska for the National Security Archive.]

Document No. 38: Transcript of CPSU CC Politburo Meeting

March 26, 1981

Poland's worsening economic condition was a constant source of worry for the Kremlin. Previous crises in Poland in 1956 and 1970 also had their source in economic troubles. The situation was particularly intractable because the socialist camp was already stretched thin and found itself severely limited in its ability to bail Poland out (see, for example, Document No. 17). The only other evident solution was to acquiesce to aid from the West, which would inevitably increase Poland's dependence on the capitalist world—a conclusion supported by analyses prepared in the West. Included in the discussion below is some useful basic economic data.

[...]

5. On the results of negotiations with the delegation of the Polish People's Republic.

Chernenko: Cdes. Baibakov, Garbuzov, Arkhipov and Alkhimov held negotiations with the deputy chairman of the Council of Ministers of the PPR, Cde. Jaruzelski. The Polish side made a request for deliveries of raw materials for light industry, for an additional delivery of oil, metal, cellulose and other goods. There is a proposal to give approval to the PPR for an additional delivery in 1981 of chrome ore, sheet rock, asbestos and other materials, as well as a certain quantity of cotton and barley.

Arkhipov: We give Poland a limited amount of raw materials because we simply cannot give any more. In particular, we are unable for now to give a positive answer regarding the processing of Soviet raw materials in Poland.

Regarding the condition of agricultural affairs in Poland, Cde. Jaruzelski reported that the plan for 1981 is 20 percent lower than for 1980. Things are especially bad for the Poles with respect to coal. But coal, as is well-known, is an export item in Poland and is a source of hard currency. Instead of the 180 million tons anticipated in the plan, they will extract 170 million tons under good conditions. Meat production will decrease by 25 percent, sugar by one-and-a-half times. Instead of 1.5 million tons they will produce 950,000 tons, maximum.

There is a question now about rationing the supply of bread and flour in Poland.

As far as the financial situation, Poland's credit liability, mainly to the capitalist countries, is 23 billion dollars. Of this, 9 billion was received under state guarantees. The remaining credits the Poles obtained from private banks. There are 400 such banks. Currently, our Polish friends are facing the fact of having to purchase various products from abroad in the amount of approximately 9.5 billion dollars. All of this will be taken care of through credits. Exports amount to

8.5 billion dollars total. In every way possible, the Western countries are putting off a decision on the question of allocating credit to Poland. Currently, they have to pay 1.5 billion dollars. This is mostly interest on credit. They are asking us for 700 million dollars. Of course, we cannot find that kind of sum. We are currently supplying Poland with oil, gas, iron ore, and so on without any delay.

During the discussion, our Polish friends asked whether they should declare a moratorium on credits or join the International Monetary Fund and request additional credits from the Western countries. Of course, either case would be a concession to the Western countries. It will have no economic effect. The Poles are not unanimous in their opinion on these questions. They are asking us in addition to give them cotton and synthetic fibers. We decided to proceed with a certain increase in deliveries of cotton and synthetic fibers.

Gromyko: The Polish comrades stressed the acuteness of the issue of imports because they cannot pay off these goods. But one should note that they do not attach great importance to raw materials deliveries from the Soviet Union, which is characteristic of them. They regard this matter as somehow trivial. But in reality, you know, it so happens that their cotton comes entirely from us, the ore is all from us, the oil is also ours.

Arkhipov: We supply Poland with 13 million tons of oil at 90 rubles per ton. If one considers that the world price per ton is 170 rubles, then we receive from the Poles 80 rubles less per ton. We could sell all that oil for hard currency and the earnings would be colossal.

Cdes. Andropov, Ustinov, Kirilenko and Grishin also spoke on this question.

The resolution is adopted.

[Source: RGANI, Fond 89, Opis 42, Delo 38. Translated by Malcolm Byrne for the National Security Archive.]

PART FOUR

Search for a "Polish Solution"

Document No. 39: Transcript of CPSU CC Politburo Meeting

April 2, 1981

Soviet frustrations with the Polish leadership bubble to the surface in this record of an important Politburo discussion. Brezhnev relates a March 30 conversation with Kania in which he tells the Polish premier that his colleagues at the recent Polish Ninth CC Plenum were not only right to be critical of Kania and his Politburo allies, they should have "taken a cudgel to you. Then perhaps you would understand." The group then discusses and agrees with a Polish request to have Andropov and Ustinov meet with Kania and Jaruzelski at Brest, on the Soviet–Polish border (see Document No. 43). At this stage, Kremlin concerns are still very much on the increase over whether the Poles are up to handling the crisis with the necessary severity. Gromyko describes information the Foreign Ministry has received that Jaruzelski is "completely crestfallen and does not know what to do next," a situation he laments as "terrible." Andropov adds that Jaruzelski "has finally gone limp and Kania has recently begun to drink more and more," which he in turn terms "a very sad phenomenon." Furthermore, Gromyko raises a basic question about the reliability of Polish security forces, urging that the Soviet military determine whether they would be sufficiently loyal if ever ordered to act.

[…]

5. On the situation in Poland.

Brezhnev: We are all deeply alarmed about the further course of events in Poland. Worst of all is the fact that our friends listen to and agree with our recommendations but do practically nothing at all. And the counter-revolution is advancing on all fronts.

The members of the Politburo are familiar with the contents of all the previous discussions with the Polish leaders. I will speak briefly about the most recent telephone conversation with Kania which took place on March 30.

Kania reported on the PUWP CC plenum and in addition complained that they were roundly criticized at the plenum. I immediately said to him, "They acted correctly. They should not just have criticized you but taken a cudgel to you. Then perhaps you would understand." These were literally my words.

Cde. Kania admitted that they are acting gently, and that they should be more strict.

To this I said to him, "And how many times have we tried to convince you that you must take drastic measures and that it is impossible to compromise endlessly with Solidarity? You speak repeatedly about a peaceful path, not understanding or not wishing to understand that this 'peaceful path' you claim to be making has cost you in blood. Therefore it is important to draw the proper conclusions from the criticism at the plenum."

Our friends managed to avert a general strike. But at what cost? At the cost of successive capitulations before the opposition. Kania himself admitted in a discussion with our ambassador that the new compromise was a big mistake.

Now much depends on how events will unfold in the coming days. In particular, will our friends carry through the measures we agreed upon through the Sejm, which, as was reported today, is being postponed from the 2nd to the 6th of April? Will all these measures be adopted in full? Do they have sufficient determination and strength to put these measures into practice?

Of course, we must continue our work with our friends and seek out new ways to exert influence over circumstances in Poland.

In particular, I think it would be worth it to meet the wishes of our friends halfway and allow Cdes. Andropov and Ustinov to travel to Brest to meet with Cdes. Kania and Jaruzelski. This will allow us to make a detailed examination of the situation in the country, assess our friends' intentions, and restate our position.

We still have in reserve the option of a new meeting of the Seven[1] on the Polish question at the highest level.

We have a Commission on Poland.[2] Perhaps the comrades from the Commission, who are following events in that country, would like to say something?

Andropov: I believe that the proposals articulated by Leonid Ilyich concerning further steps on Poland and the assessment of the situation there are completely correct. In fact, the point now is how to exert more influence and greater pressure on the leadership of our friends. I believe that the proposal concerning a trip by Cde. Ustinov and me to meet with Kania and Jaruzelski is a correct one. In accordance with the exchange of views at the Politburo and with the decisions taken by the Politburo earlier, as well as with the discussions Leonid Ilyich had with Kania, we will carry out the necessary work, and will convey to Cdes. Kania and Jaruzelski all of our claims, proposals, advice, etc.

Ustinov: It seems to me that we must indeed meet with Cdes. Kania and Jaruzelski, the more so because both Cde. Kania and Cde. Jaruzelski are requesting this meeting. We must express all of our claims and give advice in accordance with the discussions Leonid Ilyich had with Cde. Kania.

Leonid Ilyich states correctly in his proposals that we should keep in reserve the option to convene the seven member-states of the Warsaw Pact. But now we must take all necessary measures so that our Polish friends will act independently.

Gromyko: Allow me to inform you briefly about what we are hearing through the Ministry of Foreign Affairs. There is a great deal of information on Poland. However, it must be said that the USA, FRG and other countries are watching the situation in Poland closely and are greatly distorting the true state of affairs. Of course, the American and West European information about the state of affairs in

---

[1] The "Seven" are the other members of the Warsaw Pact, excluding Poland.
[2] See Document No. 2.

Poland is tendentious in nature. It presents the "fairness" of Solidarity's demands and the anti-socialist forces in Poland, and the inability of the Polish leadership to resolve its internal problems. In addition, a great deal is said about the Soviet Union as if in a tone of warning that the Soviet Union, should not involve its armed forces in Poland's affairs. But this matter is clear. Bourgeois propaganda has always taken a hostile position with respect to the Soviet Union and now it is supplying this information, as I have already said, in a tendentious spirit.

I want to say that Kania and Jaruzelski's condition is not the best. There are even suggestions that Jaruzelski is completely crestfallen and does not know what to do next. This is terrible, of course. The fact that the PPR leadership went back on its word in negotiations with Solidarity is also very bad. Even the Polish leaders themselves are saying that the most recent agreement with Solidarity was a mistake by the Polish leadership.

As far as relations with Rural Solidarity, it is essentially already legalized. If this question is transferred for review to the Sejm committee headed by Szczepański,[3] the non-party member, then one can say that the solutions will of course benefit Rural Solidarity. How might the situation in Poland be assessed after the CC plenum? I think we would not be mistaken if we said that there was no improvement whatsoever. On the contrary, there has been a further worsening because the leadership is moving backwards. But as Leonid Ilyich has already said, Kania is raising the question of having Cdes. Andropov and Ustinov travel to Brest for an exchange of views with Cdes. Kania and Jaruzelski. I believe that it is necessary to accept, especially because it presents the possibility to convey everything to the Polish friends in a private meeting. This meeting, in my opinion, will be a kind of intermediate stage, and it must be exploited fully. If, as they say, they are going to proceed with a partial introduction of emergency measures, then we must ask them whether they are sure that the Army, the Ministry of Internal Affairs and security organs will be on their side. I think that it would be proper to carry out a profound analysis by our military of how things stand in the PPR armed forces, and whether the Army represents a vital force and can be relied upon.

The CPSU CC Politburo must have a clear perception of the array of forces in the PPR. This is essential for us to know. The Polish command reports that the Army will fulfill its duty. Is that really the case? In any situation, we should proceed from the need to convey to the Polish comrades the necessity of taking more harsh—I would say emergency—measures for introducing order, and that a further retreat by them would be completely unacceptable. To retreat any more is entirely impossible.

Ustinov: According to the military, the following is where things stand. Today at 20:00 [8:00 p.m.] the military leadership is meeting, together with Cdes.

---

[3] Jan Szczepański, eminent sociologist, served as chairman of the Extraordinary Committee for the Observance of Public Agreements.

Kulikov, Kryuchkov[4] and others of our comrades. As far as the Polish army, as Cde. Jaruzelski reports, it is ready to fulfill its duty. But if one is to speak candidly, then we must keep in mind that Kania and Jaruzelski will hardly seek a confrontation, having in mind the conflict in Bydgoszcz. The results of that conflict showed that one had only somehow to wound two people from Solidarity and immediately the entire country rose up; that is to say, Solidarity was able to mobilize its forces quickly. Of course, there is still some hope now that the army, the security organs and the police will act as a united front, but the further things go, the worse it will be. I think that it will be impossible to avoid bloodshed. It is going to happen. And if one is afraid of that then, of course, one will have to continuously surrender one's position. And that is how all of the gains of socialism could be lost.

I also think about another question—should we not also take certain economic measures? How do our Polish friends see this now? We help them, we divert from ourselves and our friends and we give to Poland, but the Polish people know nothing about this. No Pole knows for a certainty that Poland receives all of its oil, cotton, etc. from us. In fact, if one were to add up all of this carefully and see what kind of help the Soviet Union provides to the Poles, if one were to talk about this help on television, radio and in the press, then the Polish people, I think, would understand from whom they receive this basic economic aid. But not one Polish leader has appeared among the workers and spoken about this aid.

As far as the Polish leaders, I believe it is difficult to answer the question who among them is better. Earlier, we thought Cde. Jaruzelski was a steadfast figure, but in fact he has turned out to be weak.

Brezhnev: That is why it will be necessary for us to clarify everything: What is the situation in their Politburo and who is capable of doing what?

Andropov: I fully agree with you, Leonid Ilyich, with respect to the analysis you have given of the situation in Poland. In fact, Solidarity is now beginning to appropriate one position after another. If an extraordinary congress is convened, it cannot be ruled out that it will be completely in the hands of the Solidarity representatives, and then they will seize power in their own hands without shedding any blood. We must really speak to the Polish leaders once more at a private meeting, of the kind Leonid Ilyich spoke about here, concerning the adoption of strict measures and about not being afraid that this might even lead to bloodshed. You know, instead of strict measures they push so-called "political regulation" before us. We speak to them about taking military, administrative and judicial steps, but they continuously limit themselves to political measures.

In addition, we must seriously pose to our Polish friends the issue of forcing Solidarity to answer for the situation in Poland. In fact, how are things taking shape now? Economic chaos, confusion and all the shortages of food products

---

[4] Vladimir A. Kryuchkov was deputy chairman of the KGB and head of its First Main Directorate, for foreign intelligence.

and other things have arisen as a consequence of strikes by Solidarity. But it is the government that answers for it. The result is an entirely absurd situation. And no member of the Politburo or the PPR leadership has spoken up or communicated to the workers that the blame for the economic shortfalls and dislocation belongs foremost to the leaders of Solidarity. In the PUWP Politburo Cde. Kania must recommend uniting the resolute members of the Politburo and depend on them.

Brezhnev: We must tell them what the introduction of martial law means and clarify everything for them plainly.

Andropov: Correct. We must recount specifically that the introduction of martial law signifies the institution of a curfew, limitations on movement in city streets, the strengthening of protection for state and party establishments, enterprises, etc. Under the influence of pressure from the leaders of Solidarity, Jaruzelski has finally gone limp and Kania has recently begun to drink more and more. This is a very sad phenomenon. I think that we have enough reasons to have a discussion with Kania and Jaruzelski. Of course, we must obviously hear them out.

In addition, I want to say that the Polish events are also having an effect on the situation in the western provinces of our country. In particular, in Belorussia Polish-language radio and television can be picked up clearly in many villages. I must say in addition that in several other regions, particularly in Georgia, spontaneous demonstrations have broken out, groups of noise-raisers [*krikunov*] congregate in the streets, as happened in Tbilisi not long ago, and utter anti-Soviet slogans, etc. We must also adopt strong measures internally.

Ustinov: As far as the Army, their situation has worsened somewhat. The point is they replaced a significant share of their veteran units with a call-up of new recruits, most of whom sympathize with Solidarity. In this way the Army is becoming weaker. We believe it is necessary to retain the veteran units in the Polish Army and not to go through with their discharge. However, the Poles do not want this. Obviously, we will have to speak with them about it.

Grishin: I believe that the proposals Leonid Ilyich has articulated are entirely correct and should be adopted. Cdes. Ustinov and Andropov should go to Brest.

Ustinov: The meeting may take place on the border—either on our side or the Polish side. That will be made clear. The most combative workers in the PUWP Politburo, it seems to me, are Cdes. Olszowski, Grabski and Barcikowski, but they are in the background.

Andropov: I think that for now we should not expand the number of participants at the meeting but keep it limited, as Cdes. Kania and Jaruzelski mentioned.

Brezhnev: When can we inform them of our decision?

Andropov: I think that we should tell them about it today.

Brezhnev: Good. Then we shall consider this proposal adopted.

All: Correct.

The resolution is adopted:

1. To approve the proposals put forward at the Politburo session by Cde. L. I. Brezhnev concerning the situation developing in Poland.

2. To take under advisement the report of Cdes. Gromyko, Andropov and Ustinov on the situation in Poland and the measures being taken by MID, the KGB and the Ministry of Defense in connection with conditions in Poland.

3. To agree to the request of the Polish comrades to arrange a meeting of Cdes. Kania and Jaruzelski with Cdes. Andropov and Ustinov at Brest.

[Source: RGANI, Fond 89, Opis 42, Delo 39. Translated by Malcolm Byrne for the National Security Archive.]

Document No. 40: CIA Alert Memorandum, "Poland"

April 3, 1981

For the second week in a row, the CIA warns that a Soviet invasion may come within a matter of days. Without providing evidence, the authors of this Alert Memorandum state bluntly: "We believe that the Soviet leaders have been convinced by the evident impotence of the Polish party and government that military intervention is necessary." They point to a number of preparations that Moscow has made—although those details have been blacked out in the document—and conclude that an invasion would now be feasible, but the basis for asserting that the Kremlin had decided that an invasion is "necessary" is not spelled out.

Alert Memorandum
Poland

We believe that the Soviet leaders have been convinced by the evident impotence of the Polish party and government that military intervention is necessary. They have set preparations in motion and would have the capability to move in considerable force within 48 hours. We believe it likely, however, that they would want to have stronger forces than they could move that quickly and that it would take about another seven days to have the 30 or so divisions needed if the Poles were to resist. We do not know whether they have reached a final decision to act, but this decision could come at any time and the decision could be to take the Poles by surprise. If this should be the case, there could be a move this weekend.

The situation in Poland remains highly volatile and marked by great unpredictability. While there has been at least a temporary reduction in tension following cancellation of the general strike scheduled for last Tuesday, pressures from militants within Solidarity for additional negotiations and for further government concessions are strong. The conciliatory posture of the Kania–Jaruzelski regime could be viewed—and probably is by hardline elements in Warsaw and Moscow—as manifesting a lack of political will to halt the disintegration of communist rule in Poland.

The Soviets have taken a number of preparatory steps for possible intervention in Poland. [One line excised]

[Half page excised]

Information acquired through April 2 indicates that the Soviets now are capable of intervention with a force of 12 to 20 divisions with little further warning. Whether the Soviets believe such a force is adequate is known only to them. Should Moscow decide on a larger force of 30 divisions or more, an additional preparation period would be required. [Half line excised]

[Source: FOIA release from the CIA, on file at the National Security Archive, "Soviet Flashpoints" collection.]

Document No. 41: East German Report of Discussion with Marshal Viktor Kulikov

April 7, 1981

Warsaw Pact Commander-in-Chief Viktor Kulikov acted as one of the main Soviet points of contact with the Polish leadership during 1980–1981. He visited Poland many times and held innumerable meetings with political and military officials alike, overseeing general military planning and a possible intervention, as well as applying sustained pressure on Kania and Jaruzelski to crush the "counter-revolution." Kulikov had strong opinions about the crisis and about the many personalities he confronted in Poland. In confidential conversations such as this with his East German counterparts he felt comparatively free to discuss his views.

Perhaps the most significant passage below is Kulikov's strong insinuation that while the goal should not be to use military force because "considerable international complications would result," the Poles might secure military assistance if they cannot resolve the crisis themselves. "[T]he Polish comrades... have to try first... If they cannot do so alone and then ask for help, the situation is different from one in which troops had been deployed from the outset."

Report
regarding a confidential discussion with the Supreme Commander of the
Combined Military Forces of the Warsaw Pact countries on April 7, 1981,
in Legnica (PPR) following the evaluation meeting of the joint
operative-strategic command staff exercise "Soyuz-81"

In accordance with the instructions of the General Secretary of the SED Central Committee and the Chairman of the National Defense Council of the GDR, Comrade Erich Honecker, and on the basis of the tasks as given by the Minister for National Defense, Comrade Army General [Heinz] Hoffmann, Comrade Lieutenant General [Heinz] Kessler, and Comrade Lieutenant General [Fritz] Streletz, had a confidential discussion with the Supreme Commander of the United Military Forces of the Warsaw Pact countries Comrade Marshal of the Soviet Union Kulikov on April 7, 1981, following the evaluation meeting by the joint operative-strategic Command Staff Exercise "Soyuz-81."

Comrade Marshal of the Soviet Union Kulikov began with thanks for the greetings communicated from Comrade Erich Honecker and Comrade Minister Hoffmann and emphasized that he had obtained authorization for the discussion from Politburo member and Minister for Defense of the Soviet Union, Comrade Marshal of the Soviet Union Ustinov.

Comrade Marshal of the Soviet Union Kulikov continued:

He had been in the PPR now for a month already and, due to personal cooperation from the leadership of the Polish party and government was able to obtain a picture of the situation in the PPR.

For the duration of his stay, he had been in constant contact with First Secretary of the Central Committee of the PUWP Comrade Kania, as well as Chairman of the Council of Ministers and Minister for National Defense of the PPR Comrade Army General Jaruzelski. Usually, the bilateral meetings took place without witnesses in an open, party-minded atmosphere. Due to this it was possible to explain openly and directly the point of view of the Soviet comrades to the leadership of the party and government as well as to the army leadership of the PPR.

For the past four weeks, the Soviet side has placed an array of specialists in Warsaw, e.g. members of the State Planning Commission, the organs of committees for State Security, the General Staff of the Armed Forces and of the Department of Rearward Services [*Bereich Ruckwartige Dienste*] of the Soviet Army. They have all received instructions from Comrade Brezhnev to help the Polish comrades.

All of the work that Marshal of the Soviet Union Kulikov and the other Soviet comrades in Warsaw have conducted in the past weeks is based strictly on the results of the consultations with the general and first secretaries of the fraternal parties in Moscow.[5]

Marshal of the Soviet Union Kulikov has continually reported on the activities and the situation in the PPR to Comrade Marshal of the Soviet Union Ustinov, who in turn periodically has informed General Secretary of the CPSU Central Committee and Chairman of the Presidium of the Supreme Soviet Comrade L. I. Brezhnev.

The extension of the Soyuz-81 exercise came about explicitly as a result of the requests of Comrades Jaruzelski and Kania. They wanted to utilize the exercises to strengthen their position. Simultaneously they hoped to exert a positive influence on the progressive forces in Poland and to show Solidarity and KOR that the Warsaw Pact countries are prepared to render Poland help all around. Thereby a certain pressure would also be exerted upon the leadership of Solidarity.

It was of great political significance that Comrade Minister Hoffmann and Comrade Minister [Martin] Dzúr [of Czechoslovakia] participated in the "Druzhba-81" joint exercises of the Soviet Army and the Polish Army on PPR territory. With that, proletarian internationalism in action was demonstrated for friend and foe.

Overall, Comrade Kania and Comrade Jaruzelski assess the situation correctly. They view the causes for the crisis, however, as being in the political, ideological and economic spheres, particularly in the mistakes that were made in the past; primarily in mistakes in party work, in the neglect of ideological work and

---

[5] A reference to the December 5, 1980, leadership meeting. See Document No. 22.

in work among the youth, as well as in other spheres. A realistic evaluation of the counter-revolution in Poland from a class standpoint is unfortunately not to be found with either. They do not see the entire development in Poland as a socio-political process with profound class causes. They also do not see that Solidarity is increasingly gaining power, and has the goal of terminating the leading role of the party. The counter-revolution in Poland is being carefully planned, orderly prepared, and supported in many ways both by the FRG and the USA. The goal of the counter-revolutionary machinations in Poland in particular is to bring the GDR, the ČSSR, and the Soviet Union into a difficult situation so as to shake violently the entire socialist bloc.

Up till the PUWP Central Committee Ninth Plenum, the work proceeded more or less normally during every meeting of Comrade Kulikov with Comrade Kania and Comrade Jaruzelski. It was frankly explained to the Polish comrades how the work should continue to proceed, to which they all agreed.

Meetings with Comrades Erich Honecker, Gustáv Husák, and János Kádár had made a lasting impression on Comrade Kania.

Before the Ninth Plenum the Polish comrades were made aware that it was absolutely necessary to present clearly the general line of party work before the Central Committee, to define and fix the phases of future work and the ways the Polish party and government leadership wish to settle the situation. It should be made clear how the battle against Solidarity and KOR can be led offensively and how a proper relationship towards the Church could be produced.

The course of and results from the PUWP Central Committee Ninth Plenum prove, however, that these hints and suggestions that were agreed upon before then, were not given the necessary attention. The Ninth Plenum took the decision to arrive at stabilization of the situation in the PPR through military means. The statements, however, lacked objective conditions.

There was no unity within the Politburo, although it still formally existed after the Ninth Plenum. The Gdańsk party organization demanded a report regarding the fulfillment of the Central Committee's decisions. Since the decisions until then had not been fulfilled, the party leadership was to be dismissed due to incompetence.

Negative forces were to establish a new Politburo. Consequently, Politburo member and Secretary of the PUWP Central Committee Comrade Grabski spoke up, emphasizing that the Politburo should not capitulate and that he would not resign. His determined and positive appearance brought a turning point to the meeting of the Central Committee. A vote of confidence in the Politburo was held. There was, however, considerable criticism of the performance of the Politburo leadership.

One worker who came before the Plenum spoke better than all the leading party functionaries. He brought attention to the fact that everyone is waiting for instructions from above. Since the situation in every region is different, the lower party cadres must show more initiative and not constantly wait for instructions from above.

The demand was stated once again at the Ninth Plenum to convene a party conference soon, to begin with electoral meetings in the local organizations, and to convene a meeting of the Sejm in the coming days in any case.

Comrade Marshal of the Soviet Union Kulikov had spoken with Comrade Kania for that reason, and he had to concede that the goal of the Ninth Plenum had not been achieved.

After the Ninth Plenum of the Central Committee Comrade Kania declared surprisingly that:

- the party is too weak to lead an offensive against Solidarity;
- many party members are organized within Solidarity, and defend its ideas;
- an open confrontation, an open attack through the organs of the party, government and instruments of force is not possible at this point;
- while it is true that there are a number of "bridgeheads," they are, however, not sufficient for an open counterattack against Solidarity and KOR;
- while the balance of power has changed now in favor of Solidarity, three to four months ago it still seemed to be considerably favorable, and it seemed that it would have been good for certain offensive measures to have been conducted at this time.

Comrade Kania further stated that the Polish Army in the present circumstances can only fulfill its tasks in the interior of the country with great difficulties. The organs of state security would have little success fighting offensively, either.

Up until the Ninth Plenum, Comrade Kania and Comrade Jaruzelski had always agreed with the estimate of Marshal of the Soviet Union Kulikov that the Polish Army and the security organs were prepared to fulfill any assignment given to them by the party and state leadership.

Following the Ninth Plenum, however, Comrade Kania took the position that they could not rely on the army and the security organs, and was not certain whether they would uphold the party and state leadership in a critical situation.

Comrade Marshal of the Soviet Union Kulikov tried to dissuade Comrade Kania from this view, showing him positive examples from the Polish Army, and underlined that the Soviet comrades were of the opinion that the army and the security organs were prepared to end the counter-revolution upon the order of the party and government leadership. Comrade Kania did not share this opinion.

That had generally negative consequences. The very next day Comrade Jaruzelski also defended this view that the army and the security forces were not prepared for internal deployment, and that one could not rely fully upon them. This position of Comrades Kania and Jaruzelski is their own invention. Comrade Kulikov said to Comrade Jaruzelski: "You have now broken off the branch upon which you sit. How will things go for you now?"

Due to the view of the Polish party, state, and army leadership, the subordinate generals and admirals up to [the level of] division commanders immediately joined their superiors in their estimate. Even those commanders who had previously affirmed to Marshal of the Soviet Union Kulikov that they and their troops would follow any order of the party and state leadership, now swore that at once that they could not rely upon 50 to 60 percent of their soldiers and non-commissioned officers. Following the Ninth Plenum, the commander of the air-land division in Kraków also advanced the view that he could only rely upon 50 percent of his personal forces.

It was also subtly brought to Comrade Marshal of the Soviet Union Kulikov's attention that it could even be possible that, in the event of an invasion by other Warsaw Pact troops, certain units might rebel.

In this connection, Marshal of the Soviet Union Kulikov emphasized and made clear that one could not lead an army or make policy with sharp appearances, boot-heels clicking and a good posture, but that instead one needs a realistic evaluation of the situation and a clear class position.

The view of Comrade Jaruzelski that the Polish party and state leadership had won a strategic battle in Bydgoszcz was also incomprehensible for Comrade Kulikov. In order to correctly evaluate the situation, one must understand that Comrade Kania and Comrade Jaruzelski are personal friends and lay down the course of the party. Comrade Jaruzelski is the theoretical brain who lays the direction for further work.

Regarding the health of Comrade Jaruzelski, Marshal of the Soviet Union Kulikov called attention to the fact that he is currently stricken by the flu and is physically and mentally exhausted. The estimate by Foreign Minister of the GDR Comrade [Oskar] Fischer, was totally correct, even though there were some who did not want to admit it.

During the last conversations with Comrade Jaruzelski one could notice that he did not always have control over himself. He always wore darkened eyeglasses, even on official occasions, in order to conceal nervous eye movements.[6]

Marshal of the Soviet Union Kulikov concluded that Comrade Jaruzelski is very self-confident, and that he is not expecting to be removed at some point because he assumes that the people trust him. How the situation should develop after the 90 days agreed to by Solidarity, he did not say.

A part of the Politburo is for Comrade Jaruzelski and supports him completely. He acts extremely liberally and therefore enjoys a reputation across broad segments of society.

The Soviet comrades believe that Comrade Jaruzelski is not the man to change the course of events. Until now he has made great concessions in all areas, for instance with respect to:
- the events in Bydgoszcz;
- work among the youth;
- Russian instruction in school as well as;
- the Catholic Church.

---

[6] The generally accepted view is that Jaruzelski suffered eye damage from exposure to glare from the snow while confined in a Soviet labor camp during World War II.

He has very frequent discussions with Polish Cardinal Wyszyński and hopes for the support of the Catholic Church. Wyszyński also holds Comrade Jaruzelski in high esteem, which is evident from many of his statements.

One must admit frankly that the Polish United Workers Party is currently weaker than the Catholic Church and Solidarity.

No one knows yet exactly how many members Solidarity has. One estimate is from eight to ten million, of which one million are supposed to be party members.

On April 10, 1981, a meeting of the Sejm is to be convened. One should not count on any fundamentally new questions. There are two papers on the economic situation provided by Comrades Jagielski and Kisiel.[7] Afterwards, Comrade Jaruzelski wants to give an evaluation of the situation in Poland. The adoption of decisions on limiting the right to strike, censorship and the utilization of mass media is also on the agenda. In any case it would be desirable if the Sejm were to make decisions that would set specific limits on the counter-revolution.

Leading Polish comrades unfortunately believe that they can solve all problems through political means, hoping especially that everything will clear up on its own. One cannot share such a view. It must frankly be stated that the moment to act was not taken by the Polish party and state leadership.

Altogether one has the impression that Comrade Kania and Comrade Jaruzelski do not wish to use force, in order to remain "clean Poles."

Both fear utilizing the power of the state (the army and the security organs) to restore order. They argue formally that the Polish Constitution does not provide for a state of emergency, and that Article 33 of the Polish Constitution only refers to the national defense. Although Marshal of the Soviet Union Kulikov repeatedly called to their attention that in that kind of situation Article 33 on national defense could and must be used, both remained unwilling to make such a decision.

All the documentation for martial law was prepared in close cooperation by Soviet and Polish comrades. This cooperation proceeded in an open and candid atmosphere. The Soviet comrades did not have the impression that the Polish generals and officers were concealing anything from them. Nevertheless, this documentation remains only on paper for it has not yet been implemented.

Marshal of the Soviet Union Kulikov tried to make it clear to Comrades Kania and Jaruzelski that they do not need to fear a strike. They should follow the example of the capitalists in reacting to strikes. Since Solidarity knows that the party and state leadership of the PPR fear a general strike, they are utilizing this to exert pressure and implement their demands.

A difficulty exists in the fact that a great part of the workers in Poland are also independent farmers and would not be greatly affected by the strikes, for they would be working in their own fields during this time. The size of the well-organized working class in Poland is small.

---

[7] Henryk Kisiel was deputy prime minister and chief of the planning commission.

In the countryside, current production is limited to what is necessary for one's own needs, which means that only private fields are cultivated. How national food supplies will develop no one knows.

Comrades Kania and Jaruzelski estimate that the greatest economic support by the capitalist countries comes from France and the FRG. The USA drags its feet when it comes to aid.

The sooner the phase of obliterating the counter-revolution begins, the better for the development of Poland and for the stabilization of the socialist bloc collectively. Not only Comrade Kania but also Comrade Jaruzelski, however, lack determination and resoluteness in their work.

Half a year ago, Comrade Jaruzelski had announced at meetings of commanders that he would not give any orders to deploy the army against the workers.

Marshal of the Soviet Union Kulikov made it clear to him that the army would not be deployed against the working class, but rather against the counter-revolution, against the enemies of the working class as well as violent criminals and bandits. He did not answer the question in a concrete manner. Marshal of the Soviet Union Kulikov hopes that Comrade Jaruzelski will revise his standpoint. Although Minister Jaruzelski combines all power in his hands, he does not wield it decisively. Since the Poles, being devout Catholics, all pray on Saturday and Sunday, the weekend would present itself as an opportunity to take effective measures.

However, at this time the Polish Army remains in the barracks, and is not allowed on the exercise grounds, and therefore does not conduct marches—for fear of the people (in reality, of Solidarity).

Upon the suggestion by Marshal of the Soviet Union Kulikov that Polish Army columns be permitted to drive through big cities in particular as a demonstration of power, he was told that this would only unleash more criticism.

On April 12, 1981, 52,000 Polish soldiers were to be dismissed. The Soviet comrades suggested to the Polish Army leadership postponing the dismissal until April 27, 1981. They did not agree and the dismissal was set for April 12, 1981. It was stated that five battalions comprised of 3,000 men were always ready to accomplish any mission. That would be sufficient. A suspension of the dismissal would only create a negative mood within the army.

Among the leading cadres of the army, the following things are currently notable:

- The chief of the General Staff, General Siwicki, makes a helpless impression in decisive matters, and waits for orders from above.
- He is always winding himself in circles. At first he was proactive but increasingly displays an attitude of surrender.
- General Molczyk,[8] who is seen as a positive force, is always kept in the background by the Polish comrades.

---

[8] Eugeniusz Molczyk was deputy minister of defense.

- The chief of the Main Political Administration, Division General [Józef] Baryla is a loyal comrade, but does nothing and hides behind the orders of Minister Jaruzelski.
- The chiefs of the Silesia and Pomorze military districts, Division General [Henryk] Rapacewicz and Division General [Józef] Użycki follow in the wake of Minister Jaruzelski.
- The most progressive soldier at this point is the chief of the Warsaw Military District, Division General [Włodzimierz] Oliwa.
- The chief of the Navy, Admiral [Ludwik] Janczyszyn, first was in favor of Solidarity; suddenly, however, he is taking a different standpoint. This is not seen as honest. The leadership of the security organs confronts sizeable difficulties since it receives no support from the party and state leadership.

Within the rank-and-file, occurrences of resignations and capitulations are spreading in the face of difficulties.

The reported situation notwithstanding, the Soviet comrades are of the view that we should continue to support Comrade Kania and Comrade Jaruzelski, for there are no other alternatives at this point.

Comrades Grabski and Kisiel are currently the most progressive forces within the Polish leadership. They do not, however, succeed with their demands.

Comrade Barcikowski who is the second secretary within the PUWP Central Committee, is a comrade without a particular profile. His statements and his over-all appearance during the PUWP Central Committee Ninth Plenum prove this.

Comrade Olszowski also does not live up to expectations.

Comrade Pinkowski, the second-in-command to Comrade Jaruzelski, should be released from his duties, but remains in office.

Central Committee member and Minister of Internal Affairs Comrade Milewski, who holds a clear position on all questions, and is prepared to shoulder responsibility, impressed Comrade Marshal of the Soviet Union Kulikov in a positive way.

The greatest share of the intelligentsia is reactionary and supports Solidarity. For example, the director of the Institute for Marxism/Leninism, [Andrzej] Werblan, should be dismissed for his reactionary views but he remains in his position.

Now more than ever, we must exert influence upon the Polish comrades using any and all means and methods. The situation in Poland must be studied thoroughly and demands constant attention. An assessment must be based on the fact—and one has to face this truth—that civil war is not out of the question.

Marshal of the Soviet Union Kulikov finally stressed once again that the common goal should be to solve the problem without the deployment of allied armies into Poland. All socialist states should exert their influence to this end.

The Soviet comrades assume that unless the Polish security organs and army are deployed, outside support cannot be expected, for otherwise considerable international complications would result. Marshal of the Soviet Union Kulikov emphatically brought it to the attention of the Polish comrades that they first have to try to solve their problems by themselves. If they cannot do so alone and then ask for help, this would be a different situation from one in which troops had been deployed from the outset.

As far as possible deployment of the NVA is concerned, there are no longer reservations among the Polish comrades. There were increasing public musings as to how long the Soviet staffs and troops would remain in Poland.

If the Polish comrades were prepared to solve their problems on their own, the Soviet leadership organs and troops could be withdrawn. Except for empty words, however, nothing concrete has been done. Presently the counter-revolutionary forces are regrouping.

He does not know how much longer Marshal of the Soviet Union Kulikov and parts of the staff of the [Warsaw Pact] Unified Armed Forces as well as the other organs of the Soviet Union will remain in Poland. For now, no order to withdraw will be given since one should not relinquish positions that have been seized.

According to the wishes of Comrade Kania and Comrade Jaruzelski, the Soyuz-81 exercise should not be officially terminated on April 7, 1981, but rather continue for another few days or weeks. The Soviet comrades, however, took the view that this was not possible and would create international complications. It only proves that the Poles think that others should do their work for them.

Regarding international aid in the suppression of the counter-revolution, both Comrade Kania and Comrade Jaruzelski spoke with great caution.

Comrade Kulikov strongly emphasized again that this discussion took place with the approval of Comrade Minister Ustinov. He has conveyed everything that is known to him as a communist and as the supreme commander of the Unified Armed Forces because he has complete faith in Comrade Lieutenant General Kessler and Comrade Lieutenant General Streletz, and is convinced that the substance of this conversation will be communicated only to Comrade Erich Honecker and Comrade Minister Hoffmann.

In conclusion, he asked that his most heartfelt greetings be conveyed to General Secretary of the Central Committee and Chairman of the National Defense Council of the GDR Comrade Erich Honecker, and to Minister for National Defense Comrade Army General Hoffmann. At the same time he extended his thanks for the generous support provided during the preparation and implementation of the joint operational-strategic command-staff exercise, Soyuz-81.

The conversation lasted two hours and was conducted in an open and friendly atmosphere.

[Source: BMZP, AZN 32642. Document provided by Tomasz Mianowicz (Munich) and translated by Christiaan Hetzner for the National Security Archive.]

Document No. 42: Brezhnev's Speech to CPCz CC Politburo

April 7, 1981

Leonid Brezhnev's visit to Prague on the occasion of the XVI Congress of the Czechoslovak communist party came as a surprise to virtually every outside observer. No other Warsaw Pact leaders were expected to attend, and the elderly Brezhnev had not addressed a foreign party congress since 1975. Naturally, his presence prompted widespread speculation about his reasons for being there, which may have included a desire to remind the Poles of the outcome of the Prague Spring of 1968, the last major socio-political outbreak in the Eastern bloc. Although he referred to those events explicitly in his public remarks to the Congress, his main emphasis was on nuclear weapons, not Poland, which also puzzled many experts. But in his private comments to the CPCz Politburo, reproduced below, he spoke more directly about the Solidarity crisis, which he described as "the matter which is disturbing us all first and foremost." Nonetheless, his language remained moderate as he reiterated that for the time being it would be left to the Poles to resolve their own problems.

[…]

I am sincerely glad that I have the opportunity once again to meet with you. It is always pleasant to see old friends again. It is all the more pleasant when they are healthy and of good cheer.

Your congress is interesting—considerable and at the same time principled, substantive and self-critical.

I think that you have built a reliable basis for successful work in the future. You have an action program. Communists and workers are resolved to accomplish the plans of the party.

I know that you also have difficult problems. Do not consider that, however, to be only your privilege.

The socialist states entered the 1980s stronger in all aspects. That is an irreversible reality. But the tasks which are facing us are more difficult than before. For all of us the main front is the economic one. And that is where everything is focused on the need to increase production efficiency, improve the level of management and learn to economize better. We can say that this is the common result of our conferences.

It is good that we are approaching the solution of the problem of economic intensification from a uniform viewpoint—from the viewpoint of the maximal exploitation of production potential by each fraternal party and at the same time of unifying our efforts in the production and scientific and technological areas.

If we judge Czechoslovak–Soviet cooperation just from this viewpoint, we can rightly express satisfaction. I have evaluated our relations more than once.

They are indestructible, firm, founded on the unshakable foundations of Marxism—Leninism and proletarian internationalism. I especially want to stress that we highly regard the relations which have been created between the leaders of our parties, and also our relations with comrade Husák.

[...]

Now, to the matter which is disturbing us all first and foremost—the situation in Poland.

I will not speak here about the facts of the situation in that country; you know them as well as we do. The situation, it may be said without exaggeration, is critical. This concerns both politics and the economy as well. However the latter is the result of the former: incorrect policies have also brought the economy to the verge of collapse. To the extent that the actions of the opposition, that is Solidarity and the counter-revolutionaries and enemies of socialism who inspire it, are vigorous and well-thought out in terms of organization and propaganda, to the same extent the actions of the PUWP leadership and Polish government are indecisive and powerless.

You know, comrades, that on March 4, after our congress ended, we met with representatives of the Polish leadership and once again we told them directly that the situation is becoming dangerous. We recommended quite emphatically that they finally take decisive action against the counter-revolution.

After that, in March I had several more talks with Comrade Kania by telephone during which I presented the same ideas and I pointed out new facts arising from developments. And recently, in April, we had some contact with the Polish leadership.

We strongly recommend that the Polish authorities pursue an active and offensive course in internal policy; we directly, boldly and plainly made clear to everyone the situation in the country, its causes, and ways out of the crisis proposed by the party and government in the interests of the people. At the same time it is especially important to show with actual examples the destructiveness of the actions of those who are sowing anarchy, aggravating strikes and undermining governmental authority.

We strongly recommend that the Polish comrades actively make use of valid legal norms and if necessary introduce new ones (by declaring a state of emergency) in an effort to isolate and suppress the apparent counter-revolutionaries, the leaders of the anti-socialist campaign who are being directed by imperialist forces from abroad.

In our opinion all that does not have to mean bloodshed, which is what Comrades Kania and Jaruzelski fear. On the contrary, continuing to make concessions to the hostile forces could lead to shedding the blood of communists, honorable patriots of socialist Poland.

What has been said, of course, does not preclude but on the contrary assumes contact and work with the working masses that are currently in the ranks of Solidarity, as well as with a certain part of the leadership of that organization, since it is far from homogeneous both in the center and especially in the localities. Our friends must above all endeavor to expand the mass basis of their policies and, in support of these, unite patriots in whose hearts lies the fate of Poland.

We are having talks with the Polish leadership roughly along these lines. I have been telling them that there is still a chance to act decisively against the forces of counter-revolution by gathering and mobilizing the healthy forces in the party and by making use of instruments of state power such as the public security forces and the army.

Comrades Kania and Jaruzelski have agreed with their words that it is no longer possible to retreat further, but in reality they continue to retreat and are not taking decisive measures against the enemies of socialism. Take for example developments after the provocation in Bydgoszcz, which was provoked by Solidarity. Impressions are rather gloomy. Our friends succeeded in averting a general strike. But at what price? At the price of further capitulation. Kania himself now recognizes that they made great mistakes and he blames Rakowski, but the latter is losing control.

It is difficult to say now how events will develop further. Given the present tactics of the PUWP leadership it is hardly possible to expect that the pressure of the anti-socialist forces will diminish. Of course that disturbs us all, all members of our community. The Polish comrades are preparing to undertake something at the upcoming session of the Sejm. We will see what comes of that.

In my opinion, our common obligation is to help the Polish communists to take a stand against counter-revolution. They still have opportunities to do that, if the leadership only demonstrates sufficient political will.

As far as I know, comrades, we assess events in the same way and therefore we can influence the Polish comrades and so work in the same direction. It is not out of the question that developments will require a further meeting of the leaders of the fraternal countries on the Polish question. We will not decide on that now.

The crisis in Poland will of course have negative long-term consequences. We must all learn appropriate lessons from it.

For example, one such fundamental question as this: How did it happen that within a few months a country was, in a word, thrown into chaos, the economy was on the verge of collapse and anarchy reigned? Whenever this question is addressed, what is usually mentioned is the continuation of private farming in the countryside, the activities of dissidents, the influence of the church, the diversions of Western intelligence agencies. That is without argument. But, to be sure, forces hostile towards socialism were in Poland even earlier. What has enabled them to emerge? It is obviously the erosion of relations between the party and the working class.

All socio-economic policies of the former leadership were basically calculated to achieve a leap forward with the aid of Western loans. Indeed they succeeded in some respects in modernizing industry. But what sense is there if the new factories are fully dependent on raw products, materials and assembled products which must then be obtained with hard currency?

Furthermore whole plants for prestigious production, for example color television sets, were bought from the West.

And when it was necessary to repay the loans, they found no way other than to place this burden primarily on the working class. Living conditions for workers have worsened in recent years. The party began to lose its main societal support. And that enabled the enemies of socialism to engage in a struggle for power.

Capitalists will not voluntarily assist in the building of socialism—that is the truth of which you all must be clearly aware. If they provide us with loans, if they trade with us, then the best case is that they are applying market principles, and the worse case that they are pursuing purely political objectives.

When Polish representatives explain why it is difficult for them to take the offensive against counter-revolution, they openly say—we are dependent on the West.

That is the greatest lesson for the socialist countries. All of them ought once again to assess the extent of their indebtedness abroad and do everything to prevent it from increasing and approaching a dangerous limit.

[…]

These are some thoughts which I wanted to share with you. Once again, I repeat: our and your party congresses have again shown a complete agreement of opinions and viewpoints between the CPSU and CPCz and the inseparability of our bonds. And we will continue to work in this direction.

[Source: SÚA, A ÚV KSC, PÚV 2/1981, vol. 2, Ad inf. 1; published in part in the Cold War International History Project Bulletin, *Issue 11 (Winter 1998), pp. 69–71. Translated by Oldřich Tůma.]*

Document No. 43: Transcript of CPSU CC Politburo Meeting

April 9, 1981

On April 4–5, Soviet leaders Yurii Andropov and Dmitrii Ustinov held a secret meeting with Kania and Jaruzelski in a railroad car near the Polish–Soviet border. According to Soviet Gen. Anatolii Gribkov, who accompanied the two Poles to the aircraft that would take them to the rendezvous, Jaruzelski particularly was in a state of alarm, believing that he might be abducted to the Soviet Union as Dubček had been in 1968, but with the possibility that he might never return to Poland. This was not Moscow's intention, however, and the meeting took place as planned.

The atmosphere was intense. Andropov and Ustinov used the opportunity to harangue the Poles about their inaction, and tried to force them to sign a document committing them to enact martial law by a certain date. Despite his evidently depressed condition—he repeated a request to be relieved as prime minister—Jaruzelski joined Kania in refusing to sign. The discussion also included a reference to introducing foreign troops into Poland. The two Poles utterly rejected the idea but there is no indication in this account who raised the subject. If the Soviets did, it might undercut the argument that Moscow never intended to use force in Poland. Given the intense pressure the two Kremlin envoys applied at this meeting, Andropov's characterization of their purpose as being simply to "listen attentively... and provide appropriate explanations" is almost Orwellian.

[...]

3. On the results of the meeting between Cdes. Yu. V. Andropov and D. F. Ustinov with the Polish friends.

Chernenko: In accordance with the decision of the Politburo, Cdes. Andropov and Ustinov met with Cdes. Kania and Jaruzelski. Perhaps we will listen to the comrades.

Andropov: D. F. Ustinov and I, in keeping with the agreement with the Polish comrades, went to Brest; our meeting took place in a train car near Brest. The meeting began at 9:00 in the evening and ended at 3:00 in the morning so that it would not be discovered that the Polish comrades had been away.

The problem that was put before us was to listen attentively to the Polish comrades and provide appropriate explanations, as agreed at the Politburo session.

The general impression from our meeting with the comrades was that they were in a very tense state, they were nervous, and it was clear that they were exhausted. Cde. Kania said straight out that it was very difficult for them to handle these matters. Solidarity and the anti-socialist forces were pressing them hard. But in addition, they declared that since the XXVI CPSU Congress conditions in Poland have moved toward stabilization. Kania said that they held an election meeting in most of the local party organizations and it is important to note that not a single person on the slate of candidates belonged to Solidarity; that is to say, all our candidates passed through to the congress. Then, Cde. Kania was obliged to say that subsequent events, in particular the warning strike and the events in Bydgoszcz, showed that the counter-revolution is stronger than us. They were especially fearful of the warning strike, and even more of a general strike, and were doing everything they could to avert a general strike.

"What tasks stand before us?" asked Cde. Kania. Above all, the renewal of trust on the part of the people and party, the mending of economic life, and the elimination of strikes and work stoppages at enterprises. Of course, the Polish comrades have no experience with these negative manifestations, and therefore they do not yet know what methods to employ, and are [merely] shuffling from side to side. As far as the introduction of troops, they said straight out that this is impossible. It is just as unworkable to introduce martial law. They say they will not be understood and they will be powerless to do anything. The comrades stressed in the discussion that they will introduce order by their own means. They have in mind that the IX Congress, for which they are preparing, will not allow Solidarity to advance their candidates as delegates. From party organizations, good workers are being chosen as delegates for the congress.

In the discussion, Cde. Kania also noted that the Polish people are very sensitive about honest communications. For example, they announced the congress, then they acted as if they were going to postpone the congress, and then they said once again that the congress would proceed. And so this kind of delay in the timing of the congress had a strong impact on the situation in the country in the sense that trust in the party was shaken even more. In our turn, we said firmly to the Polish comrades that the enemy is attacking you; he has the advantage; you are on the retreat and have wasted time. Back in September 1980 you could have given the enemy a serious fight. But you did nothing, took no steps at all, either of a political or, even more, an administrative nature. We particularly underscored that it is impossible to oppose military-administrative measures with political ones. It is necessary to combine all approaches wisely.

As far as martial law is concerned, it would have been possible to introduce it a long time ago. In fact, what does it mean to introduce martial law? It would help you break through [*slomit'*] the pressure from the counter-revolutionary elements and all the rowdies, and put an end once and for all to the strikes and to anarchy in economic life. A draft document on introducing martial law with the help of our comrades is ready and these documents must be signed. The Polish comrades say: How can we sign these documents when they have to be approved by the Sejm, etc.? We said that passage by the Sejm is not needed; this is a document you will not act upon when you introduce martial law, but now you, personally, Cdes. Kania and Jaruzelski, must sign it so that we know that you consent to these documents and that you will know what has to be done during martial law. If it becomes necessary to introduce martial law, there will not be time to work out measures for introducing it then; those measures must be prepared in advance. That is the point.

Then, after our clarification, Cdes. Kania and Jaruzelski said that they would look over and sign the documents on April 11.

We asked further what Cde. Jaruzelski's speech to the Sejm would consist of. Jaruzelski said a great deal and he spoke inarticulately. He explained that he will speak about the prohibition on strikes for two months. We asked what "two months" means, and why only for two months. Two months will pass quickly and then strikes will begin again. You make a lot of promises to your workers but then you do not fulfill them and thereby create undue grounds for mistrust of the government and the PUWP.

Now there is an especially serious question at hand about the introduction of broad political measures. Take, for example, the explanation of the issue that you have shortages of bread and other food products. Why does this happen? Because truly incessant strikes are throwing the entire economy into disarray; that is why there are shortages. A huge number of billions of zlotys is lost with every strike, but the workers do not know this and everything is blamed on the government; the government, the party CC and the Politburo become the guilty party while the instigators and the organizers of the strikes stand on the sidelines and, do you see, look like the defenders of the workers' interests. And if, we said, one examines this on its merits, then the ultimate guilty party for all economic difficulties is Solidarity and the strike organizers. That is the point. Therefore, why is it impossible to bring all this to the attention of the workers?

In your country they speak a lot about the creation of a National Front for the Salvation of Poland. These conversations take place in a number of regions. The idea is to include in this National Front for the Salvation of Poland veterans of the revolutionary movement and military leaders such as Rola-Żymierski[9] and others. It would have been possible to make note of that as well. Or for example, now in the FRG there are discussions about giving Silesia and Gdańsk, as territories attached to Poland, back to the FRG. Why not make proper use of that issue as well? I think the people could be rallied around such questions.

We said that in our country there are no objections to the creation of a National Front for the Salvation of Poland. But this front should not substitute for the party and government.

In particular there is the question of the struggle to rally the party and to unify the nation. Much has been said about the unity of the party. We also want to encourage you to take all necessary measures to rally the party and create unity in the nation. Which measures to take is something you yourselves know better. But there are many issues. We have already named them for you, and around them it would be possible to rally the nation and unify the party. The Polish comrades talked about bringing three workers into the Politburo. They quoted Lenin

---

[9] Michał Żymierski, who used the *nom de guerre* Rola, rose to command the Polish People's Army during World War II, then served as defense minister until 1949. After a period of political banishment followed by rehabilitation in 1956, he remained an active figure, becoming a member of the PUWP CC in 1981.

who proposed bringing workers into the Politburo. We said there was no such idea that workers should be in the Politburo. But if there really is such a need in your country, you can include them, but it does not have to be three, it could be one worker. Maybe some number of workers could be elected to the CC; that is, these are all measures that would contribute to rallying and unifying the party. For example, you talk about introducing workers into the Central Control Commission. That is not a bad idea. Of course, it would have been possible to do that.

Further, carrying out other measures, such as speeches at party gatherings of qualified, well-prepared comrades, would also promote party unity. We gave our own examples of how we, right up to the members of the Politburo, have given speeches at party meetings. They agreed with these proposals.

Further, we said you do not have to take it upon yourselves, comrades, to enact puffed up programs, only moderate programs—but be sure to fulfill them. All Politburo members must speak at major enterprises. Now, Cde. Kania is going to Gdańsk. And not only Kania but Cde. Jaruzelski and all the other Politburo members and candidate members should go to other cities to speak at enterprises, among the workers. That is, it is necessary to speak against the organized Solidarity group, contrasting it with your own solidarity. Why is Solidarity so strong? It is strong by virtue of its demagogy. It demagogically promises the workers higher salaries and, as you see, it succeeded. The union also manages to defend the workers and it builds its own authority by announcing a strike when you arrest several workers or other Solidarity officials. We said directly to Kania that every day you retreat and retreat, but it is necessary to act, it is necessary to assert military measures, to assert emergency measures.

Now there is the separate question of the conduct of the Sejm. What is Solidarity doing? It is currently busy cultivating every member of the Sejm. It proposes to the worker-members of the Sejm that they deliver highly specific speeches in the Sejm directed against the PUWP and the socialist order. One has to smash these plans of Solidarity. For example, why do the members of the Politburo not bolster the deputies of the Sejm and acknowledge that they are responsible for these members of the Sejm, and prepare them for their sessions? This is how far things have gone. For example, a telegram came to a worker-member at the PUWP plenum which said that he should speak at the plenum according to the instructions he had been given. This worker's speech at the plenum was delayed, that is, he did not want to speak. Another telegram followed, which said, "For some reason we did not hear your speech." This worker again did not speak, the plenum ended and he received the following telegram: "You might not want to come back." You see that here Solidarity terrorized and frightened this worker. That is how Solidarity behaves.

With respect to support for the Politburo. On whom can it rely? The army in their country consists of 400,000 persons, 100,000 in the Ministry of Internal Affairs, and 300,000 reservists. Thus, a total of 800,000. Kania said that tensions have relaxed somewhat and they have managed to avert a general strike. But how much this quieting down will suffice is hard to say.

What are they going to do after our meeting? One has to say that they are going to do something. For example, Kania is going to Gdańsk. Cde. Jaruzelski is reworking his speech to the Sejm. But one must say that there are many differences of opinion between Kania and Jaruzelski on certain questions. Cde. Jaruzelski again requested that he be relieved of his post as premier. We generally clarified for him that it is essential for him to remain in that post and fulfill with dignity the responsibilities that have been entrusted to him. We emphasized that the enemy is building up his strength in order to seize power.

On the other hand, other Politburo members, Cdes. Olszowski and Grabski, are taking a rather excellent position, more firm than the leadership. It is necessary to work with them. Specifically, they are proposing to organize an underground Politburo and to carry out their work. It seems this idea occurred to them as a result of recommendations made to them by Cde. Zhivkov. I do not know if this is true but they say that Cde. Zhivkov passed along such a recommendation to them. We must also draw the conclusion that if the leaders of the fraternal parties are going to make such recommendations to our Polish friends then we, of course, will gain nothing from this but will only lose from it.

Suslov: Perhaps we should prepare some information for the fraternal parties.

Gromyko: But under no circumstances should we refer to the fact that there was a meeting.

Andropov: It is entirely impossible to talk about the meeting.

Ustinov: Yu. V. Andropov has said everything very well. Therefore I only want to briefly state the following. First, that the beleaguered condition of our interlocutors is really striking. But it seems to me that, notwithstanding that, we have to preserve this duo, Kania and Jaruzelski, and strengthen our relations with them. The point is there are disagreements in their Politburo. Most of all, of course, the strikes upset them, they are very afraid of them. We asked them why they changed their decision on Bydgoszcz. As is known, they did not want to compromise over the Bydgoszcz conflict, then they did compromise. They tried to persuade us that the threat of a general strike hung over them. Further, we said to them why do you pay the workers during strikes? They said that Solidarity demands it. In this way you are being led by Solidarity, we answered them. They have made no decision on Rural Solidarity but effectively they have already acknowledged the existence of this organization.

Yurii Vladimirovich and I emphasized especially firmly the matter of the need for unity in the Politburo. There is no need, as they claim, to bring three workers into the Politburo. That will not strengthen the Politburo. As for the CC, workers should be included there, but according to normal and established procedure, as is done in accordance with party statutes. We told our Polish friends it is particularly necessary to work as needed with the deputies of the Sejm. Further, they hold so-called internal network teleconferences. These are in essence open telephone conversations. Everything they say is immediately known to a wide circle, including officials from Solidarity. What about the method they are using to conduct these conferences? We gave as an example how Leonid Ilyich constantly talks with the secretaries of the Obkoms, Kraikoms and CC's of union republics, but with each he talks in specifics, corresponding to the circumstances of the given region.

In order to dispel their fears concerning the introduction of a state of emergency or martial law, we gave the example that in many countries as soon as an uprising flares up or some kind of turmoil begins, they introduce a state of emergency or martial law. Take Yugoslavia. Demonstrations occurred in Kosovo. They instituted martial law and no one said a word about it. Why the Poles fear instituting a state of emergency we do not understand.

Yurii Vladimirovich has spoken well concerning the plans for introducing a state of emergency. We said that they must sign the plan that was put together by our comrades.

Further, I said to them directly, as we agreed at the Politburo, what will happen in Poland, will the pot boil over [*zavaritsya kasha*], and in what sort of economic state will she find herself? Right now Poland receives all its oil at about half-price from the Soviet Union. It also receives cotton, iron ore and many other goods. And if it no longer receives any of this, what then? Why is such a fact not made clear, why does it not reach the mind of the workers? This is indeed a heavy weapon. You must talk about this to the workers, and to Solidarity as well. Currently, Solidarity is entrenching itself in the largest factories. You must take these factories away from Solidarity. You have good factories in your country, where the workers stand up for the leadership. For example, the television production factory. You can and should support the trade associations and conduct active work with them. Jaruzelski then told me once more that he can no longer work, he has no strength, and he pleaded to be released.

Zimyanin: In Bulgaria at the congress we met with Grabski. This discussion has been circulated, the comrades are familiar with it. From that it is obvious that the situation in their Politburo is truly very difficult. There is no unity, and Yurii Vladimirovich and Dmitrii Fedorovich said correctly that they must work toward strengthening unity within the Politburo.

Resolved:

1. Approve the discussions held by Cdes. Yu. V. Andropov and D. F. Ustinov with PUWP CC First Secretary Cde. S. Kania and Chairman of the PPR Supreme Soviet and Defense Minister Cde. W. Jaruzelski.

2. Instruct the CC Politburo Commission on Poland to follow attentively the development of conditions in the PPR and, as needed, to prepare appropriate proposals.

[Source: RGANI, Fond 89, Opis 42, Delo 40. Translated by Malcolm Byrne for the National Security Archive.]

Document No. 44: Transcript of CPSU CC Politburo Meeting

April 16, 1981

After the extremely tense meeting at Brest (see Document No. 43), where the strain on Jaruzelski in particular was strongly in evidence, the Soviets decided to lighten their approach somewhat. At this Politburo discussion, Brezhnev advocates maintaining pressure but not pushing the Poles to a point where they "build up their nervousness" and "lose heart." Evincing some frustration at the difficulty in finding a solution to the crisis, Brezhnev appears to gently chide the Commission on Poland for not yet producing a set of promised proposals. In calling for a strategic look at the issue, he implicitly acknowledges the possibility that resolving the situation will be a long-term proposition.

[…]

2. On the discussion between Cde. L. I. Brezhnev and PUWP CC First Secretary Cde. S. Kania (by telephone).

Brezhnev: Yesterday I talked on the telephone with Kania. The notes of the discussion have been distributed, and the comrades apparently have familiarized themselves with them. Therefore, I will be brief.

From the conversation with Kania it is apparent that after the session of the Sejm our friends were somewhat encouraged. They gained more confidence in themselves. That by itself is not bad.

But it is impossible not to see that conditions remain as before—extremely complex—and the present lull is clearly short-term. It was in this spirit, as you saw, that I spoke with Kania.

In general, it is very important for us now to maintain the proper tone in our relations with our friends. On the one hand, there is no need to aggravate them unnecessarily, nor to build up their nervousness so that they lose heart. But on the other hand, we should exercise constant pressure in a tactful manner to turn their attention to the errors and the weaknesses in their policies, and to advise them in a comradely way as to what they should do.

Comrades Andropov and Ustinov held an extremely useful meeting with Kania and Jaruzelski. We should clearly continue this practice until the severity of the crisis subsides. Perhaps we should think about holding a similar confidential meeting in the near future, this time with the participation of Cdes. Suslov and Rusakov.

Our Commission, I know, is meeting constantly and discussing what needs to be done. They have promised soon to convey certain impressions and proposals.

Along with this very important work, we should also continue to prepare a broader, so to speak, strategic analysis, which will allow us to step back from events and evaluate a more long-term perspective on the development of events in and around Poland.

And lastly, I wanted to ask the opinion of the comrades as to whether we should inform our closest friends of the discussion that has taken place. They are all very uneasy about the situation in Poland and it will be important for them to know about the actions we are taking.

If there are no objections, we will do so.

Andropov: The discussion was very pithy.

Chernenko: This discussion conveyed clear and precise orders to the comrades from the PUWP leadership, and in addition Leonid Ilyich responded approvingly concerning certain of their measures. That is very good.

Ustinov: The Polish friends received comprehensive instructions.

Tikhonov: Now it is very important that they put these instructions into practice.

Brezhnev: I think that we clearly should inform the leaders of the fraternal parties about our conversation with the Polish leaders.

The members of the Politburo support this proposal.

The decision is adopted:

1. To approve the telephone discussion by CPSU CC General Secretary Cde. Brezhnev with PUWP CC First Secretary Cde. S. Kania.

2. To consider it expedient to inform the leaders of the fraternal parties of the socialist countries about the content of the discussion with regard to the exchange of opinions that occurred at the CPSU CC Politburo session.

3. To instruct the CC Department to prepare an informational text on this question.

[Source: RGANI, Fond 89, Opis 42, Delo 41. Translated by Malcolm Byrne for the National Security Archive.]

Document No. 45: Extract from Protocol No. 7 of CPSU CC Politburo Meeting

April 23, 1981

Moscow's inability to hammer out a solution on Poland continues to be evident in this Politburo discussion. One week after Brezhnev called for a more strategic, or long-term, approach, the Commission on Poland apparently finally came up with a set of proposals that are the subject of this session. The analysis of Poland's internal situation shows several things. The Kremlin understood that Solidarity was not a monolithic institution and that Wałęsa was a relative moderate among its leadership. Their fear at this stage was that extremists would take over the movement and force matters to a head. In a similar way, they worried that pro-Solidarity members of the PUWP might try to take power from within by getting their allies promoted to leadership posts. There is some talk in this document about more hard-line leaders who could replace Kania and Jaruzelski but those individuals are acknowledged to be in the minority and their approach to ending the crisis is too blunt for the Soviets.

Several proposed measures win approval at this session. The most interesting one is to "exploit to the maximum" Polish fears of a Soviet invasion. The possibility that the Kremlin deliberately exaggerated the threat helps to explain why various Polish officials, including Jaruzelski and CIA informant Ryszard Kukliński, believed that such a move was likely, if not inevitable.

[...]

On the Development of Conditions in Poland and Certain Steps from Our Side.

1. To agree to the considerations contained in the note by the CPSU CC Politburo Commission on the Polish question (attached).
2. To confirm the plan of measures for providing aid to the PUWP leadership for the organizational and ideological strengthening of the party (attached).

* * *

On Point VII, Prot. No. 7

[...]

On the Development of Conditions in Poland and Certain Steps from Our Side.

The internal political crisis in Poland has become protracted and chronic. To a significant degree, the PUWP has lost control of the processes under way in society. At the same time, Solidarity has transformed itself into an organized political force, which is capable of paralyzing the activity of party and state organs and virtually taking power into its own hands. If the opposition is not yet ready for that, then more than anything it is due to their concern over the possible introduction of Soviet troops and hopes of achieving their goals without bloodshed and by means of a creeping counter-revolution.

At the Sejm session on April 10, the Polish leadership did not risk raising the matter of decisive actions against the anti-socialist forces. It evidently cannot and in essence does not wish to depart from the line adopted for overcoming the crisis by political means.

It is true that in Cde. Jaruzelski's report to the Sejm there was a series of proposals in the spirit of recommendations, which our side has continuously articulated to the Polish comrades. However, they were not laid out in a way that would be binding but in the form of appeals or aspirations. The compromise nature of the report is explained above all by the fact that it was adopted calmly and did not provoke the confrontation our friends had feared.

Surveying the results of the Sejm, as its first success—albeit a minor one— Cde. Kania and his associates are now becoming somewhat more active in their endeavors to shore up the authority of the party. They have made speeches at a variety of major industrial enterprises, and they held a meeting with worker and peasant members of the PUWP CC. The regular CC plenary session is set for April 25. Documents are being prepared for the PUWP Ninth Congress, which must be held before July 20 of this year. Certain measures are being taken within the government with the goal of somehow restoring order to the economy.

At the same time, it is evident to all that the lull after the session of the Sejm was short-lived. The adversary has approached it for tactical reasons, while continuing to build up his forces to deliver new blows against the party.

Solidarity as a whole and its separate parts are preparing for the next round of blackmail of the authorities by raising various primarily political demands. Signs of stratification that have appeared among the leadership of this trade union have not yet provided grounds for counting on essential changes in its overall orientation. Even if it came to a split between Wałęsa and the extremists from KSS-KOR, Wałęsa himself and the Catholic clergy standing behind him have no intention of alleviating the pressure on the PUWP. One also cannot rule out that the extremists might seize control over Solidarity, with all the consequences that would flow from that.

Recently, a new tactical arrangement has become increasingly defined, around which a mixed bag of opposition elements is effectively uniting. Realizing that Poland's geopolitical position is depriving them of the possibility of infringing on the country's participation in the Warsaw Treaty Organization and the principle of the leading role of the communist party, these forces have evidently decided to corrupt the PUWP from within, to bring about its rebirth, and in this way to seize power "on legal grounds."

As the work of the PUWP CC Ninth Plenum demonstrated, opportunistic elements have already succeeded in taking control of some PUWP local party organizations and, with their help, beginning to put pressure on the party leadership. They will, without a doubt, continue this subversive work, having tried to turn the forthcoming Ninth Congress into the principal battlefield for [taking] power.

In these conditions, the need again arises to weigh our attitude toward the policies of the Polish leadership, and to determine more precisely which forces can ultimately be relied upon to defend the achievements of socialism in Poland.

On the right flank of the PUWP CC there are politicians with revisionist tendencies—Fiszbach, Werblan, Rakowski, Jabłoński,[10] etc. Ideologically, they are close to certain leaders of Solidarity, and they speak out for rebuilding Poland's socio-economic structure primarily on the Yugoslav model. In the area of politics they favor a "partnership" of various political forces, which coincides with "Eurocommunism" and the social-democratic ideas of pluralism.

These figures rely on support from the segment of the party organizations that falls under the influence of Solidarity. One cannot rule out the possibility that under current conditions they may bring many of their allies to the PUWP congress and exert a fundamental influence on the formation of ruling organs of the party. Apparently, they will try to carry out certain changes in the PUWP leadership as soon as the next PUWP CC plenum.

On the left flank stand such communists as Grabski, Żabiński, Olszowski, Kociołek,[11] etc. The statements of these comrades on an ideological level are closer to our own positions. They express the mood of that segment of party membership which is consistently for socialism, for friendship with the Soviet Union, against revisionist distortions, and which demands decisive actions against Solidarity. Behind them stand, basically, old party members who were trained in the school of war and class struggle during the first stages of the creation of people's Poland.

Unfortunately, the representatives of that orientation by no means constitute a majority. One gets the impression that they see a way out of the crisis through a frontal attack on Solidarity, without considering the current correlation of forces. In addition, they do not see the possibility of an improvement in conditions without the introduction of Soviet troops. This position objectively leads to their increasing isolation in the party and the country. Efforts of no small significance will be needed (if it will even be possible) to get them elected to the congress and installed in the leading organs.

Comrades Kania and Jaruzelski, in point of fact, occupy centrist positions. Under complex circumstances after August of last year, they became spokesmen for those in the party and the country who favored resolving the acute problems that had arisen by means of a dialog and agreement with Solidarity. The recent

---

[10] Tadeusz Fishbach, Andrzej Werblan, Mieczysław Rakowski and Henryk Jabłoński. (See the Main Actors glossary.)

[11] Tadeusz Grabski, Andrzej Żabiński, Stefan Olszowski, Stanisław Kociołek. (See the Main Actors glossary.)

period has shown that Kania and Jaruzelski, while declaring the need to preserve the achievements of socialism in Poland, pursued this course passively, with vacillations and frequent concessions to Solidarity. They show insufficient determination and hardiness in the struggle against the counter-revolutionary forces. In their view, adherence to socialism is intertwined with the nationalist idea that was already widespread under Gierek; that is, that "a Pole can always come to terms with a Pole." From this comes not only an unwarranted submissiveness to the demands of Solidarity but a panicky fear of confrontation with [the union], and a dread of the introduction of Soviet forces.

At the same time, Kania and Jaruzelski advocate friendship with the Soviet Union and fidelity to Poland's obligations to the Warsaw Pact. Both of them, especially Jaruzelski, enjoy authority in the country. Currently, there are virtually no other figures who would be capable of exercising party-state leadership.

With respect to the above, it would be expedient to proceed from the following:

Continue to provide political support to Cdes. Kania and Jaruzelski, who, notwithstanding their well-known vacillations, come out in defense of socialism. At the same time, continually secure from them more consistent and decisive actions in the interests of overcoming the crisis on the basis of preserving Poland as a socialist country friendly to the Soviet Union.

Urgently recommend to our friends in the first place that they achieve unity and stability within the PUWP leadership, defending those comrades who have become the main object of attacks by the opposition and the enemies of socialism (Grabski, Żabiński, Olszowski, Kociołek and others). In turn, help these comrades realize the need to support Cdes. Kania and Jaruzelski, to be more flexible, and not to openly oppose slogans of "socialist renewal." It is important that they strike the enemies of socialism, not confusing Solidarity as a whole with the hostile forces existing in that organization.

Turn the attention of the Polish leaders to the need to prepare well for the PUWP Ninth Congress. Get them to fight for the appropriate representation of healthy forces at the congress, and to carry out active work in that direction with the party organizations of major enterprises.

Recommend to the Polish comrades that they bind Solidarity in every possible way to the resolution of questions of production, and that it is necessary to limit [the union's] political activity. With this aim in mind, hasten the adoption of laws governing economic reform and trade unions.

More actively exploit the noticeable stratification of the Solidarity leadership, unmask the anti-socialist and antinational activity of KSS-KOR and their leaders, and achieve the isolation of these counter-revolutionaries. Take decisive measures against attempts to produce a wave of anti-Sovietism in the country.

Impel the Polish leadership continually to take care of the army and organs of the Ministry of Internal Affairs, their moral-political stability and their readiness to honor their duty to defend socialism. It is necessary to support the leadership of the Ministry of Internal Affairs, and [Mirosław] Milewski personally, and not to dissociate themselves from the actions of the police in the protection of law and order.

Exploit to the maximum the factor, clung to by the counter-revolution, which is connected to concerns on the part of the internal reaction and international imperialism that the Soviet Union might introduce its forces into Poland. In foreign policy statements, underscore our resoluteness, as expressed by Cde. L. I. Brezhnev at the CPSU XXVI Congress, not to leave Poland in distress and subject her to harm.

Considering the PPR's exceptionally difficult economic situation, continue to provide whatever help possible, and simultaneously intensify propaganda to the maximum on these matters so that every Pole will know how much the country depends on Soviet aid and support.

In addition to these general proposals, we suggest, in accordance with our instructions (P1/VIII of March 12, 1981), a plan of measures to provide assistance to the PUWP leadership for the organizational and ideological strengthening of the party.

[...]

* * *

On Point VII, Prot. No. 7
Top Secret

Plan of Measures to Provide Aid to the PUWP Leadership for the Organizational and Ideological Strengthening of the Party

In May–June 1981 send a working group of the CPSU CC Department of Organizational-Party Work to the PPR for consultations on matters regarding preparations for the PUWP Ninth Extraordinary Congress.

The CPSU CC Department and the departments of organizational-party work, propaganda, and foreign policy propaganda of the CPSU CC are to analyze drafts of theses for the PUWP congress, of the PUWP statutes and of other documents, as well as the progress of organizational preparations for the congress, and submit suitable proposals to the CPSU CC.

In April–May 1981, receive the delegation from the PUWP CC Organizational Department that was provided for in the plan of inter-party relations for 1981.

Make plans to invite working groups of leading workers from PUWP CC departments to the USSR for consultations that the Polish comrades are interested in conducting.

In accordance with the Polish leadership's wishes, dispatch delegations of party workers to Poland in May–June 1981, through local party organs. In the first instance, make plans to send delegations from the Leningrad, Ivanov, Smolensk, Donetsk, Zaporozhe, Lvov, Kharkov, Cherkassk, Grodnensk and Mogilev obkoms[12] of the party.

In case of confirmation of an appropriate request from the PUWP CC, study further the question of receiving workers from PUWP middle and lower echelons (up to 500 persons) for short courses at the CPSU CC Academy of Social Sciences as well as at the Moscow, Leningrad, Kiev and Minsk higher party schools.

The CPSU CC Department of Organizational-Party Work and the CPSU CC Department are to hold a conference in May–June 1981 of representatives of appropriate CPSU obkoms and gorkoms[13] on urgent matters regarding relations between CPSU and PUWP local party organs.

In April–May 1981, by agreement with the PUWP CC, send to Poland a group of responsible workers from central councils of branch trade unions, headed by the secretary of the VTsSPS,[14] to become familiar with the state of affairs in the Polish trade union movement and to study on location the possibilities of providing political support for the branch trade unions and of intensifying the cooperation of Soviet trade unions with them.

Instruct the Komsomol [VLKSM] CC to propose a plan of measures by May 5, 1981, to strengthen our influence on the situation in the youth movement in Poland.

The Union of Soviet Societies of Friendship and Cultural Ties with Foreign Countries, the Soviet Committee of War Veterans and the Committee of Soviet Women are to continue fulfilling agreed upon plans of action with related Polish organizations and providing them with necessary assistance.

Taking into account the complex circumstances in the PPR creative unions, the unions of writers, journalists, composers, artists and cinematographers of the USSR are to carry out exchanges with them through party organizations.

In May 1981, send to Poland a group from USSR State Committee on Television and Radio (the leader will be Committee Chairman Cde. Lapin) for consultations on Soviet broadcasting into the PPR and for refining plans for cooperation in 1981.

In April–May 1981, the editors of the newspapers *Pravda*, *Izvestiya* and *Trud* are to send to Poland for a period of up to 10 days a group of publicists (one person each) to prepare materials, including denunciations, on the activities of the anti-socialist forces.

[Source: RGANI, Fond 89, Opis 66, Delo 3. Published in Teczka Susłowa, *pp. 28–48. Translated by Malcolm Byrne for the National Security Archive.]*

---

[12] Oblast, or regional, committees.

[13] Municipal committees.

[14] All-Union Central Council of Trade Unions.

Document No. 46: Message from Ryszard Kukliński to CIA

April 26, 1981

Usually, Polish Col. Ryszard Kukliński's secret messages to the CIA during the Polish events were filled with hard intelligence on military preparations or the intentions of senior Soviet and Polish officials (see for example Document No. 21 from December 4, 1980). At times, however, he was quite emotional, as in this communication in which he describes feelings of dismay about Poland's situation that have percolated up the ranks of the Polish General Staff. Implicit in the bitter remark by a general (whose name has been deleted from the source document) that "the Americans sold us out to the Russians" is the noteworthy point that many Poles—even in high office—looked to the United States for help in saving their country. Kukliński was by no means alone in this respect, but even he betrays a certain unease about Washington's commitment to support Polish independence.

The story of how Kukliński communicated to the CIA—here he uses a code name for his chief handler in Washington—is fascinating. After the December 4, 1980, message, the Agency gave him a sophisticated electronic transmitter to replace the need for "dead drops," which were both dangerous and time-consuming. Dubbed "Iskra" (meaning "spark," which was also the name of Lenin's pre-Revolution newspaper), the device was the size of a pack of cigarettes and could send short bursts of data to the U.S. embassy in Warsaw from any nearby location. The problem was that it repeatedly broke down, as it did when Kukliński tried to send the message below. This was understandably frustrating given the urgency of the circumstances, but also because Kukliński, as he later readily admitted, was not particularly technically savvy.[15]

Dear Daniel![16]

After returning from Sofia with some senior officers from the General Staff, we reflected on the hopeless—in military terms—current situation in Poland. In this depressing atmosphere, one of the most dedicated generals who openly proclaims the need for deep political changes in Poland [...] hurled a bitter accusation at your country, maintaining that "the Americans sold us out to Russia." Without their silent approval, he said, the 'comrades' would not act so boldly. We are profoundly desperate but we hope that General [...] is mistaken! [We

---

[15] Interview with Kukliński at the National Security Archive, September 1997, and as described in Weiser, *A Secret Life,* pp. 181, 215, 229–230.
[16] "Daniel" was the code name for David W. Forden who became Kukliński's CIA case officer in June 1973. (Daniel was Forden's son's name.) See Weiser, *A Secret Life,* pp. 68–82.

hope] that the information which he generously sends to you will continue to be properly utilized.

We Poles are deeply aware that for freedom we ourselves must fight, even if we had to pay the ultimate price. In addition, I continue to believe that the assistance your country gives to all who are fighting for this freedom may speed up the attainment of such a goal.

Thank you for your latest, cordial letter.
With heartfelt greetings,
Yours, P. V.[17]

[Source: Originally published in Polish in Tygodnik Solidarność *50 (325), December 9, 1994. Partial translation by Magdalena Klotzbach for the National Security Archive. Further translation from Benjamin Weiser,* A Secret Life: The Polish Officer, His Covert Mission, and the Price He Paid to Save His Country, *(New York: PublicAffairs, 2004), p. 239. Copyright 2004 by Benjamin Weiser. Reprinted by permission of PublicAffairs, a member of Perseus Books, L.L.C.).]*

---

[17] "P. V." stands for "Polish Viking," a code name Kukliński gave himself, beginning with his first communication to U.S. officials in August 1972, and occasionally thereafter. See Weiser, *A Secret Life*, p. 18.

Document No. 47: Transcript of CPSU CC Politburo Meeting

April 30, 1981

After another high-level Soviet visit to Warsaw, the Kremlin leadership meets to dis-cuss the results, and finds more reason for worry. Although Mikhail Suslov sounds a self-congratulatory note about the utility of these bilateral meetings, the Poles con-tinue to make what Moscow views as intolerable concessions to the opposition. High on their list of concerns during this period is the "horizontal movement" within the PUWP which aimed at promoting more democratic procedures at all levels without interference from the central authorities. As CPSU ideology chief, Suslov was par-ticularly upset at this stark departure from Leninist doctrine, as indicated below. For his part, Brezhnev gives voice to a feeling of not just frustration but outright distrust in Kania and Jaruzelski that is growing among the Soviet leadership.

[…]

2. On the results of the negotiations between the CPSU delegation and the PUWP leadership.

Brezhnev: As you know, several days ago, following our decision, Cdes. Su-slov and Rusakov left for Warsaw. Also part of the delegation was USSR Ambas-sador to Poland Cde. [Boris] Aristov.

In accordance with instructions, the CPSU delegation held a discussion in which members and candidate members of the Politburo and members of the PUWP Secretariat took part from the Polish side.

I think that the first conclusion that comes out of the information from the comrades is that we acted properly in sending such a delegation to Warsaw at a time when the Polish comrades were preparing for their plenum and congress.

I think that in the future we should also not preclude the possibility that indi-vidual Politburo members or a group of members could go [on such a visit], or do as Cdes. Andropov and Ustinov did by meeting somewhere outside Warsaw or Moscow. The value of that kind of thing is undisputable.

And now we give the floor to Cde. M. A. Suslov, who will inform us of the results of the discussions with the Polish comrades.

Suslov: Our negotiations with the PUWP leadership showed that the Polit-buro decision concerning our delegation's trip to Poland was very useful and timely. L. I. Brezhnev's discussions with Kania and also the discussions held by Cdes. Andropov and Ustinov during their meeting with Kania and Jaruzelski at Brest have played a big role in stabilizing conditions in Poland. For our part, we sharply criticized the actions of the Polish leadership with respect to Solidarity and the anti-socialist elements, their indecisiveness on this matter, and their at-tempts somehow to smooth over the situation and not focus on the main questions. We expressed ourselves critically with respect to the so-called "horizontal structures." We particularly emphasized the need for a decisive battle with Solidarity and its reactionary right wing, headed by KOR, which in fact wants to turn Solidarity into a political party.

Andropov: The Polish friends, Kania in particular, support the "horizontal structures," and that will lead, as you know, to the collapse of the party.

Suslov: Unquestionably, the "horizontal structures" will sow complete discord within the organizational structure of the PUWP and be utterly at odds with Leninist organizational principles for the construction of a Marxist–Leninist party. Cdes. Kania and Jaruzelski took part in these discussions along with members of the Politburo and the secretaries of the Gdańsk and Katowice voivodeship committees. They all deeply thanked the CPSU CC, and especially L. I. Brezhnev, for their constant concern and assistance.

Brezhnev: I believe they are now holding a plenum.

Suslov: Their plenum ended early this morning. As far as our advice about not excluding Olszowski, Grabski and other comrades from the plenum, they went along with it. Our criticism has a particular influence on the Polish leadership, especially on matters related to preparations for the congress and on other matters. Of course, the Polish leadership should have a certain amount of trust in us, and there should also be a degree of trust on our part. True, for many it is impossible to believe what they promise they will do, but in any case we should in some way support and encourage them on certain questions.

Brezhnev: In general, we have little faith in them since although they listen to us they do not do as we advise.

Rusakov: I must say that L. I. Brezhnev's meeting with our Polish friends had exceptional significance. In addition, the discussions held by Cdes. Andropov and Ustinov played a big role, as did the regular telephone conversations with Kania—all of these played their own positive part. I am sure that the situation in Poland would have been significantly worse if these discussions had not taken place. Their plenum ended today at 5:00 in the morning. Very sharp criticism was leveled at the leadership, particularly at Cde. Kania. After the plenum there was a conference of voivodeship committee secretaries at which Cde. Kania was subjected to sharp criticism.

Brezhnev: If the comrades have no more proposals, then we may be able to adopt the following proposals.

First, to approve the activities of our delegation during their visit to Warsaw.

Second, to instruct the Commission on Poland to continue to follow actively the events in the PPR, and from time to time to inform the CC Politburo, and if necessary raise appropriate proposals during the course of events.

Third, Cdes. Suslov and Rusakov propose to support the request by Cde. Kania and Cde. Jaruzelski concerning the use of PPR enterprises that are not running at full capacity. I think that it is necessary to instruct the USSR Council of Ministers to examine this question.

And finally, it is proposed also to inform the leaders of the fraternal parties of the countries of socialist cooperation about the negotiations in Warsaw and prepare the next set of information for the CPSU party *aktiv*.

All: Agreed.
The resolution is adopted.

[Source: RGANI, Fond 89, Opis 42, Delo 42. Translated by Malcolm Byrne for the National Security Archive.]

Document No. 48: Informational Memorandum from the L'vov District Secretary to the CPUkr Central Committee

May 7, 1981

A major source of worry within the socialist camp throughout the crisis, as with similar periods in Hungary in 1956 and Czechoslovakia in 1968, was the prospect of the unrest in Poland spilling over into neighboring countries (see also Document No. 61). This was certainly on the minds of local officials in Ukraine, then a Soviet republic. In this report to the republic-level Central Committee, the head of the L'vov party district passes on the comments of a Polish security official who is dissatisfied with the shape of events in his own country. The decision to elevate this conversation to the CC, from where it could well have been sent to Moscow, is a sign of how seriously the threat from Solidarity was taken by regional authorities.

Informational Memorandum

On April 16, 1981, a meeting took place with someone in whom we have confidence, a colleague from the PPR state security organs, who informed us of the following: the situation in Poland remains complicated and incomprehensible. The PPR population is under stress from the confusion and the difficult economic conditions. The population wants a firm, authoritative leader, both on the party and government sides.

At present, Jaruzelski is politically active, while not taking into account the opinion of the PUWP Politburo. He also maintains ties to Solidarity unions and the counter-revolution. Our source said that there is a possibility that Jaruzelski has long held negative positions and that his proposal to choose Kania as first secretary is in the interests of his [Jaruzelski's] own line, which increasingly appears to be a negative one. Meanwhile, Kania criticizes the errors of the previous party leadership in his speeches without proposing anything in its place.

There is no unity in the PUWP leadership, not one man from the leadership who could take any kind of firm line. Regarding Wałęsa, some are of the opinion that his position is not so reactionary, but no one from the PUWP leadership is seriously involved with him in order to make use of his positive qualities in the interests of socialist Poland.

The Church's activization is noticeable as it persistently draws in the whole population, including PUWP members, authoritative workers, and the young.

In the cities there is a tendency towards the glorification of Jaruzelski with the aid of posters, radio, and television. He is presented as the head of the Polish government, but not as the head of socialist Poland.

Food, which is rationed, is not always available, so ration cards are not re-deemable *[ne otovarivaiutsia]*.

There is a directive through the Special Departments to prepare special groups of loyalists for possible underground or partisan activities. Such groups are based on two border brigades with a supply of necessary weapons.

Peasants have driven up *[vzvintili]* food prices. One kilogram of meat costs 500 złoty and a half-liter of sour cream costs 120 złoty.

The arrival of provisions from the USA will only begin in July, although the so-called American aid is widely touted.

Deputy Head for Intelligence of the Seventh Border Detachment
Col. Lt. O. P. Donchak
April 12, 1981

[Source: TsDAGOU (Ukraine), Fond 1, Opis 25, Spr. 2235. Translated by David Wolff for CWIHP.]

Document No. 49: Memorandum of Meeting between Leonid Brezhnev, Erich Honecker, Gustáv Husák et al, in Moscow

May 16, 1981

This richly detailed record presents at length the arguments of the key proponents among the Warsaw Pact leadership for replacing Poland's Stanisław Kania and Wojciech Jaruzelski. East Germany's Erich Honecker, along with Czechoslovakia's Gustáv Husák, took the unusual step of asking their Soviet counterparts to meet to discuss the crisis. Although Brezhnev begins with a sharp critique of the situation in Poland, neither he nor his colleagues at the session, some of whom are members of the Politburo's Commission on Poland, are ready to take such drastic action, in part because they do not agree with Honecker and Husák that the hard-liners they favor are suitable replacements. Once again, more calls are made to apply pressure of all kinds, but five months would pass before Moscow acted to oust Kania.

Participating in the meeting on the Soviet side were Comrades [Nikolai Aleksandrovich] Tikhonov, [Andrei Andreevich] Gromyko, [Konstantin Ustinovich] Chernenko, [Dmitrii Fyodorovich] Ustinov, [Yurii Vladimirovich] Andropov, [Konstantin Viktorovich] Rusakov, and [Georgii Khosroevich] Shakhnazarov.

Comrade Leonid Ilyich Brezhnev opened the meeting with the remark that this gathering is being held at the suggestion of Comrade Erich [Honecker], to exchange mutual views, appraise the situation, and draw conclusions.

We must, as he said, proceed from the fact that the situation in Poland has further deteriorated. The party is not just being attacked by Solidarity. It also finds itself in a process of dissolution, created by internal contradictions. At present this process is self-limiting due to the fear of external intervention.

The information before us, concerning the preparations for the PUWP Party Congress [to be held on July 14–18, 1981], is negative. With the election of delegates to the party congress, not only are new people becoming involved, but hostile forces as well. The Tenth Plenum [held on April 29–30, 1981] approved a very weak draft for a [party] program. Thereupon, Solidarity published a document containing enemy nationalist positions, and Kania did not call them to order.

Kania spoke briefly before the party *aktiv* in Gdańsk, like Gierek back in those days, that Poles can always come to an agreement with fellow Poles. Consequently, the events in Otwock[18] are a disgrace, which encourages new anti-socialist acts.

---

[18] In a rare incident of violence by the population during the Solidarity period, a police station was burned and a policeman almost lynched in early May 1981 in the small town of Otwock in central Poland, southeast of Warsaw.

Recently, our Comrades Andropov and Ustinov met privately with the Polish comrades in Brest, and gave them recommendations on a whole number of concrete matters.[19] To prevent these matters from remaining in a narrow circle, Comrade Suslov traveled to Warsaw to talk things over with all the comrades from the Politburo one more time.[20] We have delivered this information to you.

Verbally, they assented to our suggestions, but in reality the situation further deteriorated. The Polish leadership is panicking from fear, they stare, as if hypnotized, at Solidarity without taking any concrete action.

The PUWP can still rely on the Polish Army, the security organs, and the party *aktiv*, but Kania continues to be indecisive and soft; they are not prepared to take a calculated risk. Some comrades believe that [Stefan] Olszowski and [Tadeusz] Grabski are men on whom one can rely. We must grasp, however, that a change of leadership can also have negative repercussions. We see no real personality who can assume command. We see the danger even that [Miecyslaw] Rakowski could assume this position. For us there is no other way now than strengthening the present leadership and bringing pressure to bear on the healthy forces.

Comrade Viktor Kulikov worked out plans for several options to be implemented in case of emergency. To strengthen our influence over the mass media, we have sent the chairman of the Committee for Radio and Television, Comrade Lyapin, to Warsaw.

To stimulate party relations between the municipality and voivodeship committees, eleven delegations headed by the first municipal secretaries will travel to the voivodeships in May/June.

The youth organization is also intensifying its relations with the Polish youth, in order to exercise greater influence. For the time being, though, the opposition still wields its influence on the PUWP. That is why we must bolster our influence on the healthy forces. On the other side, imperialism is attempting also to exert influence on Poland economically, and to gain control of the economy, leading to a weakening of our community. Due to the absence of coal shipments from Poland, for example, the economies of the GDR and the CSSR have fallen into a difficult position. We have provided the Poles with assistance amounting to four billion dollars.

The situation is at present so grave that we must elaborate a number of options for a resolution. It would be useful to draft a joint analysis and in doing so spare nothing. We must deliberate on what has to be done. At stake is the fate of Poland.

Then *Comrade Erich Honecker* spoke. Comrade E. Honecker agreed with the statements made by Comrade L. I. Brezhnev and underlined the full agreement of our parties. Then he proceeded:

[19] See Document No. 43.
[20] See Document No. 47.

1. Recently the Politburo of the SED CC, with great attention, familiarized itself with the report on the result of the discussions between the delegation of the CPSU and the PUWP. The [CPSU] delegation, which was headed by Comrade Suslov, stopped in Warsaw. Our Politburo agreed fully and completely with the assessment of the situation in Poland and the conclusions drawn from it. It articulated its displeasure with the fact that the leadership of the PUWP was apparently not prepared to see matters as they really were, and then draw the necessary conclusions.

2. I would not like, with all due earnestness, to conceal our deep concern over the most recent developments in People's [Republic of] Poland. From all discussions and material before us, it follows that the PUWP finds itself in the stranglehold of the counter-revolution. Solidarity [members within the party] obviously took the renewal of the PUWP propagated by Kania into their own hands. According to the information before us, over 60 percent of the elected delegates to the Extraordinary Party Congress at this point are members of Solidarity. Among them there are few workers. A large portion of the delegates is part of the scientific-technological intelligentsia. It is already foreseeable that the planned Party Congress raises the danger of the PUWP being transformed into a social-democratic party that works closely together with the Church and the leadership of Solidarity with the sole goal of leading a process of renewal, in the spirit of the goals of the counter-revolution, to its victory.

3. The CPSU, the CPCz, and the SED have given the PUWP leadership a lot of good advice. Comrade Kania and Jaruzelski have agreed with them. Unfortunately one must state that they not only have not implemented it [the good advice], but rather encouraged the enormous process of degeneration in the party and state apparatus through their actions. Now there are already statements in the Polish mass media demanding a democratization of the Polish Army and slandering the organs of the interior, party and state. One must look with open eyes at these things, and recognize that the fate of socialism in the People's Republic of Poland, with all its consequences for Poland and all of its allies, is at stake. Wałęsa declared publicly in Gdańsk on 7 May 1981 that Solidarity is prepared to take over the government's authority in Poland at a given time.

4. In weighing all the details, one can only doubt the sincerity of a large portion of the members of the state and party leadership vis-a-vis their alliance partners. The pressure exerted upon Poland by the imperialist powers, above all the USA and the FRG, is supposed to prevent the healthy forces from taking measures against the counter-revolutionary forces. Comrade Kania uses this for his argument that all matters should be solved politically, repudiating Leninist principle that the party must be prepared to utilize all forms of combat to destroy the counter-revolution and guarantee the socialist development of the People's [Republic of] Poland.

5. At the Moscow conference, all realized that the developments in the People's [Republic of] Poland were not just a matter for the People's Poland, but an

affair of the entire socialist community. From all of this, no conclusions were drawn by the leadership of People's [Republic of] Poland. What followed is a complicated situation, not just for Poland, but for the entire socialist community.

Let us take the middle and long-term consequences for the GDR.

Politically: The GDR is located as you know in the center of Europe—we have German imperialism in front of us, and would possibly have a capitalist Poland behind us. The CSSR would find itself in a similar position.

Today already we must wage the battle on two fronts—we have to deal with the FRG and Poland.

I would only like to mention the role of the West German mass media and the large stream of agitation and slander that pours in as a result. The West German television broadcasts its daily programs on Poland, most of all, to influence our people.

Economically: As per [trade] agreements, we must receive from Peoples' [Republic of] Poland per year 1.9 million tons of bituminous [hard] coal by direct route and 3 million tons by diversion, hence 4.9 million tons altogether. In actuality we received 1.1 million tons in 1980, and, in the first quarter of 1981, 1.2 million tons [less than the amount that had been set].[21]

A large portion of our imports and exports to and from the USSR is transported through Poland. That comes out to be 10 million tons of goods per year.

It must not be forgotten that the Soviet Group of Forces in Germany communicate via Poland. But Comrade Ustinov is even a better judge of that.

Now, regarding some information that our comrades recently received during talks with Polish comrades.

From May 12–14, a delegation from the Berlin district leadership was in Warsaw. They reported:

1. The situation in the party organization is not unified but very confused.

2. From the rank-and-file (science and production center for semiconductors "Cemi," housing construction collective combine) there is a pronounced hatred of the old and new party leadership. This concerns in particular the contradictory behavior and decisions of "Rural Solidarity."

3. Among all the comrades there are bitter words regarding the destructive information in the mass media. What the party secretaries defend is revoked, placed into question, and discredited in television programs and press publications. (Good comrades not only feel deserted in their struggle to implement the party line, but also betrayed and even stabbed in the back.)

4. The base organizations [Grundorganisationen] are not familiar with the documents decreed at the Tenth CC Plenum for the preparation of the Party Congress. In the election campaign, they occupy themselves primarily with "settling" the mistakes of the past and with procedural matters regarding the nomination of

---

[21] The bracketed phrase was added in hand by Honecker.

candidates to the leadership, delegates to the municipal and city delegation conference, as well as to the Ninth Party Congress. (As a rule, the election assemblies last 8–10 hours, most of which is spent on procedural matters.)

Among the cadres there is great uncertainty about the future and the coming work. No one knows whether he will be reelected or elected to the municipal or city delegation conference. On May 13, four of the seven first municipal secretaries were appointed as delegates to their own conference. About 50 percent of the secretaries of the municipal leaderships were not chosen to be delegates.

Eighty percent of the members of base organization leaderships are new cadres, chiefly young, inexperienced comrades. The number of Solidarity members in the party leadership has rapidly increased.

5. Our impression of the personnel:

The first secretary of the Voivodeship Committee, Comrade Stanisław Kociołek, is an upstanding communist, who appraises the situation in the country realistically and demonstrates an internationalist attitude. He repeatedly expressed clear positions on the CPSU, the SED and the CPCz in public.

Unlike Politburo candidate and CC Secretary Jerzy Waszczuk, he stated repeatedly that he could not imagine the Ninth Party Congress taking place without the participation of the fraternal parties. He repeatedly emphasized that the situation in Poland would only be mastered when the party was built up anew upon the foundations of Marxism–Leninism and internationalism.

Of the seven secretaries of the Warsaw Voivodeship Committee, two so far have been chosen as delegates to the city conference (Kociołek, Bolesławski— 2nd secretary). Two secretaries have declared from the outset that there is no chance that they would be elected as delegates. (Cde. J. Matuczewicz did not run as delegate for the conference from the "Rosa Luxembourg" concern on May 12, 1981.) The chances of the three other secretaries are uncertain.

6. The talks with the first secretaries of the municipal leaderships of [the Warsaw districts] Mokotow, Praga North, and Żoliborz reflected the lack of unity in the party.

While the first secretary from Mokotow (a graduate of the CPSU Party School) stated a clear position on the situation, its causes, and the activities of the counter-revolution, an unprincipled social-democratic attitude could be seen on the part of the first secretaries from Żoliborz and Praga North. Their main topics were the causes of the "mistakes" and the guarantees against future repetition. Based on the "feelings of the masses," the independence and sovereignty of Poland, and the honesty of the party and of the whole society was to be guaranteed.

While visiting a construction site for a new bridge over the Vistula, we found the slogan "Down with the dictatorship of the CPSU—Long live Lech Wałęsa" on a barrel.

The first secretary from Praga North did not say anything that was party-line, when we addressed this anti-Soviet statement as well as the anti-socialist event at Katyń. All in all, the cadres are becoming used to anti-socialist statements, writings, slogans and other machinations. No one thinks about measures to take against the counter-revolutionary intrigue.

7. The statements of Politburo candidate and CC secretary, Comrade Jerzy Waszczuk, in the presence of Comrade Kociołek (1–1/2 hours), were extremely vague. The fundamental political questions were not clearly addressed. An attempt was made to justify the capitulationist attitude of the leadership when we mentioned it. Questioned about the participation of foreign delegations at the Ninth Extraordinary Party Congress, he answered evasively. Essentially it was answered in the negative. (We do not know how the Party Congress proceeded. There may be provocations, which would be very unpleasant for the fraternal parties.) Comrade Kociołek explicitly spoke out in favor of the participation of the fraternal parties. Otherwise, holding the Party Congress would be inconceivable. Comrade Kociołek repeatedly stressed that there cannot be a second Fourteenth CPCz Party Congress[22] in Poland. Therefore the remaining days must be used to guarantee the correct composition of the Party Congress. In relation to this he expressed his opinion on the creation of a clear personnel structure. It was clear from his remarks that he knew of the statements made by Comrade Mikhail Suslov and supported the implementation of the recommendations given there.

8. Comrade Kociołek beseeched the Berlin District leadership of the SED to take thorough advantage of the various possibilities to influence the Warsaw party organization in the next 30 days in order to consolidate the party and prepare the Party Congress in an internationalist spirit. A corresponding proposal of Comrade Kociołek was strictly rejected by Kania. It seems advisable to implement this offer to work with the Warsaw party organization, and to extend further the existing personal contacts with Comrade Kociołek.

– The head of the SED CC International Relations Department, Comrade [Gunther] Sieber, had a discussion with his Polish counterpart, Comrade Waclaw Piątkowski, on May 14, in Berlin.

Comrade Piątkowski is a candidate member of the PUWP CC and since 1977 has held the position of head of the CC International Relations Department. Previously, he was the PPR's ambassador to the FRG for over 8 years. He is 60 years old and possesses a command of the German language without an accent. Piątkowski was a partisan during World War II in the area around Lublin, and, during the Soviet Army's invasion of Poland, became a regular member of the 1st Polish Army, with which he advanced to the River Elbe. During wartime, he was employed as a scout in reconnaissance due to his language abilities. Through the cooperation between the GDR embassy in Warsaw and the PUWP CC International Relations Department, Piątkowski is known as a class-conscious comrade

---

[22] A reference to a Czechoslovak party (CPCz) congress planned for September 9, 1968, in Prague—two years ahead of schedule. Liberal reform proponents were expected to advance their agenda significantly at the congress, a prospect that may have influenced the other Warsaw Pact member-states to time the invasion of Czechoslovakia for late August.

devoted to the party, who assumes internationalist positions and has an unambiguous relationship to the Soviet Union.

Responding to a question on the present situation in the PPR, he stated:

The situation is more dangerous and graver than is generally assumed. The Poles are in such a state that they not only betray their own interests and their own country but have brought the socialist community of states the gravest difficulties, and endanger world peace.

The unprincipled degeneration of the party has progressed far, the contradictions are getting ever more critical. What is going on in Poland, and where developments are heading, cannot be read about in the party newspaper, but rather learned about most clearly from the broadcasters "[Radio] Free Europe" and "Deutschlandfunk [Radio Germany]" and other foreign centers.

What is the situation in the Central Committee apparatus?

Answer: I am actually no longer head of the International Relations Department. My retirement has been arranged. After the Party Congress in Kampuchea, to which I am still going, I must retire.

Was that your own decision?

Answer: No. Although I am 60 years old, I feel intellectually and physically able to continue working for the party in these difficult times. But my opinions and my attitude do not agree with our present leadership, and so it came to retirement, which I however only see as temporary.

Is it the same for other comrades as well?

Answer: Absolutely. In the CC a commission was formed which would make a thorough study of the entire apparatus according to different criteria. Among others, whether the comrade was an industrious worker in his development to this point or not. Those who have ordered this (Kania), cannot so much as once correctly pronounce the word "industrious worker" and do not know at all what industrious work is. The main criterion is, however, the unconditional support of Kania's policy. This policy I can no longer support or reconcile with my conscience. That is a betrayal of the party and of Poland. Kania is incompetent. He possesses neither political knowledge nor political stature. He is a spineless tool, who conforms to opinion polls, without political principles.

Jaruzelski is a hollow dummy, who mostly flatters himself, as he plays prime minister. Nothing good can be expected from him.

What is the situation among the first secretaries?

Answer: At the last meeting with the first secretaries and the CC department heads, more comrades came forward against the policies of Kania. Among them was Wrocław First Secretary Comrade Porębski. He enumerated to Kania how many opportunities to change the situation have come and gone since August 1980. After this speech he no longer has a chance to run for his office again and now wants to resign. Other comrades came forward similarly, and face the same question.

How do you appraise the party program?

286

Answer: It is possible to get something out of the party program if it is interpreted in a Marxist–Leninist fashion. Given the current situation and the balance of power, however, it will become a program of revisionism and social democracy.

Would a new leadership in this position be able to change the revisionist-right course and put an end to the developments?

Answer: I think so, but there is not much more time for that. I estimate that at most another 14 days remain before the opportunity for such a change has passed.

In your opinion, which people could assume the leadership of the state and the party?

Answer: I believe absolutely that Olszowski is the man who can do that and who wants to. Grabski is also very strong, and the two of them are on very good terms with one another. The first secretary of Warsaw, Comrade Kociołek, is a capable person too, with great political experience, whom one must keep in mind. I must, however, say once again, there is but little time left for such thoughts.

What went on at the Tenth Plenum?

Answer: In my opinion, Rakowski exposed himself as an overt traitor. He made a motion to demand the Soviet Union publicly state their policy west of the River Bug. Kania remained silent on this. Olszowski replied sharply to that and brought about the motion's collapse.

Comrade Piątkowski repeatedly indicated that the revisionist-right development in the party, state and economy had advanced much farther than the most negative formulations of the program show.

– Some time ago, the first secretary of the Frankfurt/Oder SED district leadership met with the first secretary of the Voivodeship Committee of Gorzów. He reported that in the voivodeship, according to instructions that the comrades should not participate in the warning strike (March 1981), everything was done in this direction. Hence, 65 percent of the workers did not take part in the strike. Then, however, everything was called off. Those who went on strike received full wages. There was a very negative reaction from those who followed the call of the party and did not go on strike.

– From the head of the PUWP CC Security and State Organs Department [Michał Atłas] our comrades in Warsaw learned that the deployment of the police in Bydgoszcz was seen as timely in connection with the provocative demonstrations planned there [March 1981]. The nationwide warning strike announced by Solidarity immediately after the incident in Bydgoszcz frightened the leadership so much that they were ready to concede everything. The government then also capitulated in the negotiations with Wałęsa, although at the Ninth Plenum a mandate for negotiations had not been debated or decided upon. One result was that the deployment readiness of the police and state security, which was relatively good beforehand, has been dealt a great blow since.

This appraisal is confirmed by information such as the following:

The Solidarity leadership in Białystok has announced a warning strike for the May 19, Polish radio reported. The decision was justified by the brutal actions of the militia against a disabled person. Solidarity demanded the immediate dismissal of those militia men who directly took part in the incident, as well as an investigation into other members of the police organs. The local militia chief has already stated that both policemen are being relieved of their positions.

A further report stated: at a three-day national meeting of representatives of 16 large-scale combines, theses on a law on worker self-government were formulated. Among other things, it was suggested that a second chamber of the Sejm, a chamber for self-government, be created, whose members would be elected democratically.

During the envisaged new election of the Sejm, they want to depart from previous practice and vote for lists—meaning the PUWP—Solidarity, National Front, among others separately.

What are the resulting conclusions?

1. The role of the party must be fortified. That means
– purging the party;
– utilizing all means of combat and not allowing the enemy to gain further ground.

2. The present leadership of the PUWP is pulling the wool over our eyes. For us the question now is, who can take over the leadership?
– Comrade Olszowski
– Comrade Grabski
– Comrade Kociołek
– Comrade Żabinski

3. Comrade Jaruzelski has stated that he is prepared to relinquish his post. Accordingly we can comply with his request. The only thing that needs to be clarified is who should take over his office.

4. I am not for a military intervention, although the allies have that right as stipulated in the Warsaw Pact. It would be correct to create a leadership which is prepared to impose a state of emergency, and which takes decisive action against the counter-revolution.

Comrade Honecker handed over a list of the members of the PUWP CC, which shows their present position according to our information. The results are:
– 51.4 percent of the CC members might have a positive attitude;
– 41.4 percent have a negative attitude;
– 7.2 percent are wavering.

Comrade Gustáv Husák:

I agree with the statements made by Comrades Brezhnev and Honecker. We are also greatly concerned about developments in Poland, about the PUWP and about socialism in Poland. There is plenty of evidence of negative developments; I need not repeat them.

It is now a matter of being able to aid the healthy forces in Poland. For that reason, the CPCz is publishing the documents from its party congress in Polish, and distributing them in Poland.

Tangentially, I would like to mention a tragicomic story: when Kania was with us in the CSSR, he asked me to autograph a brochure on the conclusions of the events of 1968 before he departed.

We also publish a trade union brochure on the conclusions of events in 1968. Comrade [Albin] Szyszka, head of the branch trade unions, but also other representatives of the branch trade unions, have appeared well in principle. They are, however, supported only weakly by the party.

We are now also organizing three hours of Polish-language radio programs every day, in which we comment on Polish events from our perspective. At the same time we are strengthening our relationship as partners with the voidvodeships, printing flyers and posters which criticize Solidarity. Unfortunately, though, our actions are not coordinated with others and therefore have a relatively scant effect.

It will be bad if the Polish communists lose their perspective and do not know how to continue.

As for the comrades whom one can rely on, we also think of such comrades as Olszowski. We also have close relations with Grabski. Our ambassador is expanding his activities here as well. But these and other comrades have great difficulties in becoming elected as delegates to the Party Congress. With the exception of Kania and Jaruzelski, the possibility exists that others will be elected into the leadership.

It is absolutely possible that a stalemate could develop at the Party Congress, with neither the present leadership nor the Right achieving a victory.

The healthy forces think that it would be difficult to fight friends and former friends, but Kania and Jaruzelski are capable of being manipulated. Public order is disintegrating more and more, and it is possible that a Social-Democratic or Christian Democratic party may develop, disguised with socialist slogans. The Poles have drawn no conclusions from their conversation with Comrade Suslov.

In our estimation, "Rural Solidarity" is more dangerous than "Wałęsa-Solidarity," because it is oriented to the West. The anti-Soviet currents are very strong, which are restrained only out of fear of Soviet action. Of the 3 million members of the PUWP, 1 million are estimated to be positively disposed, but poor or very little work is done with them, and more and more good communists are leaving, or being forced out. They say openly that the politicians look to the left but go to the right, and thus the good Communists see no prospects.

Olszowski, himself, said that he did not know how to continue since the Politburo was giving ground to increasingly stronger pressure from the right. Jaruzelski is incapable and gives ground.

There are already 7,000 civil servants in the army who are members of Solidarity, and the influence of Solidarity is growing in the organs of the Ministry of Internal Affairs and in particular in the mass media.

Żabinski is losing the ground beneath his feet and fears not being elected, which would mean the end of his activity.

We will support every option:

A new [Warsaw Pact] consultative meeting, like the one held in December [1980], would strengthen the healthy forces in Poland. Until now they have not brought much, they have only promised much. The main question remains how to successfully strengthen the healthy forces, which are not few.

At present a hysterical situation exists, difficult for the good comrades, and therefore we must aid them, we must support them.

We support the proposals by Comrades Brezhnev and Honecker, but have, however, no illusions about the selection of delegates to the Party Congress.

Comrade Kápek, first secretary of the CPCz district leadership in Prague, who was with a delegation in Poland, said, however, that it has become impossible to approach the masses. It is only possible to speak to a narrow circle.

Once again, Kania is constantly disappointing [us]. As for the postponement of the Party Congress, that is very doubtful. Olszowski is afraid of the Party Congress, for whoever will come forth against the present leadership is thrown out of the CC [*fliegt aus dem ZK heraus*]. They are disappointed by Kania and Jaruzelski. Olszowski and Grabski take a positive position, but are they the people to lead Poland out of its present situation?

Have they got enough courage, do they have sufficient experience? The question remains then, with whom to work, whom to support? There are a million good communists, but they are scattered, they live like partisans.

If Kania can now carry out his policy of horizontal structures, the healthy forces should also formulate their tactics.

An advisory meeting could be the impetus for a change, but the elections, which are going on at present for the preparation of the Party Congress, are under the influence of Solidarity, and it is very difficult to say how the Party Congress will turn out.

When Kania was in Prague, he stated that he supported convening the Party Congress in order to call it off shortly before the date. But you cannot trust Kania. Moreover, he already has his hands tied.

In a discussion with church leaders, they said that the Catholic Church in its history has found itself in different situations, but it has never allowed the condemnation of its own clergymen.

Comrade Brezhnev said that different options are being formulated as to how the positions of the good communists can be strengthened. The enemy acts always with greater force. We, however, pay too much heed to diplomacy and protocol. The Polish comrades want contact with us, and we must fortify these contacts.

As for the CSSR, it is true that the West is intensifying its propaganda, however, it meets with no response. The Polish events arouse dissatisfaction and anger in our people. There is no danger that the masses support it.

At this point, Comrade Tikhonov interjected the remark that this situation can change, though.

Comrade Husák: The atmosphere in the CSSR is good. We are preparing for elections, holding election assemblies, and we have no fear that the Polish events could have an effect on our country.

Comrade L. I. Brezhnev: What Erich said is correct—something must be done before the Party Congress. The appraisal of Kania, and of a necessary change in the leadership is also correct, though the main question is "how" to do so.

Comrade Gromyko: After the Poles had just arranged with Leonid Ilyich to postpone convening the Party Congress, they convened it without consulting with us and merely informed us about their decision.

Comrade Erich Honecker asked the question whether the Party Congress could be postponed. I think that, although it would be good, it is not realistic. Surely, we cannot have great hopes, since Kania and Jaruzelski exercise idle, unprincipled capitulation. We must therefore work with the healthy forces, though none can say how influential these people are.

Comrade Tikhonov: We all have the same appraisal, the facts correspond. We also have information. Solidarity has even now formed a militia. What is going to happen? An intervention in the present international situation is out of the question, so the opposition of the healthy forces must be actively supported, but these healthy forces have no outstanding leader.

The healthy forces must appear strong, they must meet to prepare for the Party Congress. If at present horizontal structures appear in the foreground, then the healthy forces must create their own structures. The healthy forces must be visible, since they are presently not active in the mass media. [The idea of postponing the Party Congress is not unrealistic. The Polish comrades told us as well that the meeting of the Sejm could not be postponed. Afterwards they did exactly that.][23]

Comrade Andropov: It is surely not possible to find an array of decisive measures to resolve the problems. Therefore we must act in several directions. The postponement of the date of the Party Congress is not realistic, there I have the same evaluation. They speak, promise, but do nothing. Comrade L. I. [Brezhnev] had a very thorough discussion with Kania. It is then a matter not only who to replace, but also how to do so. According to our information, the balance of power stands at roughly 50–50. But the question remains, who will seize the initiative, who will convene a plenum? In my opinion, this way is unrealistic.

The Party Congress is the crossroads where either the party takes the Marxist–Leninist path or it disintegrates. Consequently, the healthy forces must use the Eleventh Plenum to fight the battle.

Four or more good comrades are also well spirited, but we do not know whether it [leading the party into new directions] will work. We know that for example 26 voivodeship committee secretaries, members of the CC, have already been dismissed as secretaries.

---

[23] Honecker added the bracketed text by hand.

Kociołek is a serious man.

Żabinski is distantly related to Gierek.

We must not forget also that there is a rivalry among the three.

On June 10 we will have the names of all Party Congress delegates, then we will know more, see better.

Comrade Ustinov: I am in agreement with the statements made by Comrades Brezhnev, Honecker, and Husák. Everything points to the failure to formulate lengthy principled proposals. It is now a matter of fighting for every healthy man. We must all support the healthy forces.

It is certainly difficult to postpone the Party Congress, but one should remember that it also means that the Sejm cannot be adjourned, but then it will have worked, though.

It was said correctly that Kania was not living up to our expectations, but who shall take over the leadership? The Eleventh Plenum is on the daily agenda.

Perhaps a state of emergency should be imposed, if even just partly.

Comrade Rusakov: A postponement of the Party Congress is no longer possible. The delegates from the factories have already been elected. On May 30, the delegates from the voivodeships will be elected. Until then, nothing more can be done for the healthy forces.

We also have information that enraged anti-Soviet forces are appearing.

Rakowski wanted Olszowski and Grabski voted out of the Politburo, but we were able to achieve their continuation in the Politburo.

On May 18, comrades from our Central Committee will travel to Warsaw to hold discussions with the comrades from the PUWP Politburo and bring them to Marxist–Leninist positions. The comrades from the SED are also exerting their influence on the Party Congress documents.

We are intensifying criticism of events in Poland in the press and on radio. It is very important to come forward unambiguously because there are some, like Rakowski for example, who try to hide behind the CPSU.

Our delegations, which have traveled to Poland, were well prepared and armed with well-composed information. That is the way we can usefully support the healthy forces.

At that point *Comrade Erich Honecker* began to speak. He stated his agreement with the observations of Comrade Ustinov to consider precisely the possibility of a postponement of the Party Congress and of throwing all force now into preparing for the Eleventh Plenum as well as possible, proceeding from what is known of the situation to formulate all essential options.

To conclude the meeting, *Comrade Brezhnev* determined that the exchange of opinions was useful, even if there is no light in sight with regard to a positive change. The comrades are right when they stress that it is essential to employ all levers of pressure. It would undoubtedly be better to postpone the Party Congress or cancel it shortly before its meeting, as Kania had promised at the time, but that is scarcely possible at this point.

The worst would be if the Party Congress took an openly revisionist position. The central matter remains, therefore, that the present leadership cannot be depended upon; we see, however, on the other hand that there are no real potential candidates to replace them. We must think of how we will find suitable people and prepare them for extraordinary situations.

For the time being we have the ability to exert economic pressure, since we are the main supplier of petroleum and other raw materials.

We must now task comrades to form operational contacts with comrades in the PUWP in Poland.

We will inform Comrades János Kádár, Todor Zhivkov, and Fidel Castro confidentially of this meeting.

Comrade Husák's question whether a publication will follow, was answered in the negative.

Should information reach the West, a possibility excluded by the Soviet comrades and Comrade Erich Honecker, it will be denied.

[Source: SAPMO-BArch ZPA, vorl. SED 41559. Published in Michael Kubina/ Manfred Wilke, eds., "Hart und kompromisslos durchgreifen:" Die SED contra Polen. Geheimakten der SED-Führung über die Unterdrückung der polnischen Demokratiebewegung *(Berlin: Akademie Verlag, 1995), pp. 270–285. Translated by Christiaan Hetzner.]*

Document No. 50: CPSU CC Letter to the PUWP CC

June 5, 1981

After months of mounting frustration at their inability to get through to Kania and Jaruzelski, the Kremlin decided to raise the stakes by presenting this formal communication to the entire Polish leadership. Its effect was amplified by recollections of a similar letter to the Czechoslovak leadership in July 1968 just before the Soviet-led invasion. In its sweeping portrayal of the dangers facing the PUWP and Poland itself, the letter points to the particular threat posed by the upcoming Polish party congress which Moscow fears will be used by "forces hostile to socialism" to undercut the party and reduce Soviet influence. Whether the Kremlin passed discreet signals to hard-liners such as Tadeusz Grabski, or whether they simply took their cue from the letter, the congress featured an overt attempt to oust Kania from office (see next document). But the move failed when other senior party members rallied to support the first secretary against what they perceived as patent outside interference in Polish affairs. Kania's resulting boost in standing thus was a further blow to Moscow's attempts to force the Poles to get tough on the opposition.

"THE OFFENSIVE OF ANTI-SOCIALIST FORCES THREATENS OUR JOINT SECURITY"

Dear comrades, the CPSU Central Committee is writing this letter to you feeling deeply concerned about the future of socialism in Poland and about Poland as a free and independent country.

Our action is dictated by the interest which we entertain as party members in the affairs of the party of Polish communists, the entire fraternal Polish nation and socialist Poland as a member of the Warsaw Pact and CMEA. Soviet and Polish communists fought side by side against fascism and have been linked throughout the postwar years. Our party and the Soviet people have helped their Polish comrades to build a new life. We cannot remain unconcerned about the mortal danger which now looms over the Polish people's revolutionary achievements.

We say this openly: Certain trends in the development of the Polish People's Republic, especially in the ideological sphere and with respect to the previous leadership's economic policy, have already aroused our concern for several years.

In complete accordance with the spirit of the relations existing between the CPSU and the Polish United Workers' Party, we discussed these subjects with [Polish] leaders during talks at the highest level and at other meetings. Unfortunately, these friendly warnings and some profoundly critical statements made within the PUWP itself were not taken into account and were even ignored. As a result, a profound crisis has arisen in Poland which has spread through the country's entire political and economic life.

We have fully understood the changing of the entire PUWP leadership, the efforts to overcome certain grave errors connected with the violation of principles of socialist construction with the object of restoring confidence in the party on the part of the masses, above all the working class, and the strengthening of socialist democracy.

Since the first days of the crisis we believed that it was a matter of importance that the party oppose in a determined manner any attempts by the enemies of socialism to take advantage of the difficulties which had appeared to further their long-term aims.

However, this was not done. Continual concessions to anti-socialist forces and their demands have led to a situation in which the PUWP has been falling back step by step under the pressure of the internal counter-revolution, which has been supported by imperialist foreign centers of diversion.

A CRIMINAL PLOT AGAINST PEOPLE'S POWER

The situation has not only become dangerous but has led the country into a critical situation. It is impossible to assess it differently. The enemies of socialist Poland do not conceal their identity nor, especially, do they conceal their intentions. They are waging a struggle for power and are already in the process of achieving it. They have been gaining control of one position after another. The counter-revolution has been using Solidarity's extremist faction as a strike force. By deceiving them, it has involved workers who have joined a vocational trade union in a criminal plot against the people's power. A wave of anticommunism and anti-Sovietism is developing, imperialist forces are making increasingly bold attempts to interfere in Poland's domestic affairs.

The serious danger which looms over socialism in Poland also constitutes a threat to the very existence of an independent Polish state. If things came to worst, if the enemies of socialism were to achieve power and if Poland ceased to enjoy protection from the socialist states, the greedy hands of imperialism would immediately be raised against it. Who would then be able to guarantee the independence, sovereignty and borders of Poland as a state? No one.

Comrades, you recall the meeting of the leaders of fraternal parties of countries belonging to the socialist community held in Moscow on December 5, 1980.[24] On March 4, 1981, talks took place between the Soviet leadership and the PUWP delegation to the CPSU XXVI Congress. On April 23, 1981, a CPSU delegation met the entire Polish leadership.[25] Both during these meetings and

---

[24] See Document No. 22.
[25] See Document No. 45 for the Kremlin discussion of Poland on this date.

during other contacts, we expressed our growing concern about the activities of counter-revolutionary forces in Poland. We have mentioned the need to overcome confusion in the PUWP ranks, protect its cadres from enemy attacks in a determined manner and protect people's power with all party members' bodies.

In particular, attention has been drawn to the fact that the adversary has gained control over the mass media, most of which have become the instrument of anti-socialist activities and have been used to undermine socialism and break up the party. Attention has been drawn to the fact that the party has not won the battle as long as the press, radio and television work not for the PUWP but for its enemies.

ONE POSITION AFTER ANOTHER IS BEING SURRENDERED

We have strongly emphasized the need to strengthen the authority of the law and order organs and the army throughout the country and to protect them from the ambitions of counter-revolutionary forces. Allowing attempts at slandering and breaking up the security services, the militia and later the army as well to almost succeed practically implies that the socialist state will be disarmed and abandoned to the mercy of class enemies.

We wish to stress that on all the issues broached, S. Kania, W. Jaruzelski and the other Polish comrades expressed agreement with our viewpoints. But in fact everything has remained unchanged and no modifications have been made to the policy of concessions and compromise. One position after another is being surrendered without taking into account the documents of the latest plenums, which note a counter-revolutionary threat.

So far, no measures have been taken in practice to counter it, and the organizers of the counter-revolution are not being directly named.

Recently the situation within the PUWP itself has become a cause of particular concern. There is not much more than a month left before the congress. Nevertheless, it is increasingly the forces hostile to socialism that are setting the tone of the election campaign. It is not unusual for individuals chosen at random and openly preaching opportunist viewpoints to enter the leaderships of local party organizations and to be among the delegates to conferences and congresses.

This cannot fail to prompt concern. As a result of the many manipulations of revisionists and opportunists—enemies of the PUWP—experienced activists entirely devoted to the party and with irreproachable reputations and morals are being passed over.

The fact that the elected delegates to the imminent congress include only a very small number of communists originating from the workers environment is also deeply disturbing. The course of preparations for the congress is being complicated by the so-called "horizontal structures" movement, which is the tool for dismantling the party the opportunists are using to promote people indispensable to them at the congress and to guide its proceedings in a direction favorable to them.

One cannot rule out the possibility that during the congress itself an attempt will be made to deal a decisive blow to the Marxist–Leninist forces in order to bring about their elimination.

ALL KINDS OF ANTI-SOVIETISM

We would like to say in particular that in recent months the counter-revolutionary forces have been actively spreading anti-Sovietism of all kinds with a view to eliminating all the results of both our parties' activities and reviving nationalist and anti-Soviet feelings in various sectors of Polish society. These slanderers and liars stop at nothing. They claim that the Soviet Union is allegedly "plundering Poland," and they say this without taking into account the fact that the Soviet Union has given and is still giving vast extra material assistance during this difficult period. This is said of a country which, through its consignments of oil, ore and cotton, at prices 1.5–2 times lower than world prices, is in effect supplying the principal branches of Polish industry.

Respected comrades, in addressing you via this letter we have in mind not only our anxiety at the situation in sister Poland and at the conditions and future prospects of Soviet–Polish cooperation. Like the fraternal parties, we are no less concerned at the fact that the offensive of the anti-socialist forces, the enemies of the Polish People's Republic, is threatening the interests of our entire community, its cohesion, its integrity and the security of its borders—yes, our joint security.

Imperialist reaction is supporting and stimulating the Polish counter-revolution and does not conceal its hopes of changing the European and world balance of forces in its favor in this way. Imperialism is actively using the Polish crisis with a view to slandering the economic system, ideas and principles of socialism. It is being used for new attacks on the international communist movement.

Therefore, the PUWP not only bears a historic responsibility for its country's future, its independence and progress and for the cause of socialism in Poland. A huge responsibility for the shared interests of the socialist community also rests on you, comrades.

MOBILIZING ALL HEALTHY FORCES

We consider that there is still a possibility to avoid the worst and avert a national disaster. Within the PUWP there are many honest and resolute communists, ready to fight actively for the ideals of Marxism–Leninism and for an independent Poland. In Poland there are many people devoted to the cause of socialism. The working class, the working people—even some of those drawn by deception into the enemies' intrigues—who will, when all is said and done, follow the party.

It is now a matter of mobilizing all of society's healthy forces with a view to countering the class enemy and combating counter-revolution. This demands first and foremost revolutionary will from the party, its members and its leadership—yes, its leadership. Time does not wait. The party can and should find within itself the forces to reverse the course of events and to restore them to the right path even before the congress.

We would like to be sure that the Central Committee of sister Poland's Communist Party will be equal to its historic responsibilities.

We would like to assure you, dear comrades, that during these difficult days, as always in the past, the CPSU Central Committee, all Soviet communists and the entire Soviet people are in solidarity with your struggle. Our viewpoint was clearly expressed in Comrade L. I. Brezhnev's statement to the XXVI CPSU Congress: "We will not permit any attack on socialist Poland and will not abandon a fraternal country in misfortune."

[Source: FBIS, Daily Report—Soviet Union, Vol. III, No. 111, June 10, 1981, (FBIS)-SOV-81-111).]

Document No. 51: Transcript of PUWP CC Politburo Meeting during Break in CC Session

June 10, 1981

This brief Politburo session takes place during a break in a larger Central Committee meeting, at which hard-liners were attempting to remove both Kania and Jaruzelski on the strength of the recent CPSU CC letter (see the previous document). Addressing the Politburo, Kania places himself at the disposal of his colleagues in a gesture aimed at preserving leadership unity—and no doubt his own position. At the time, the so-called horizontalist movement had gained strength and appeared to be in a position to split the party. The discussion that ensued is notable for its candor. In the end, most of the members circled together and rejected Moscow's apparent designs, forcing the Kremlin to recognize that the hard-liners had lost this round. This record shows that Kania and Jaruzelski were hardly the passive and ineffectual leaders the Kremlin seemed to believe. In fact they were capable of highly effective political action under extreme pressure, holding off Soviet and hard-line challenges for months while trying to broker a viable compromise with the opposition.

[…]

Cde. Stanisław Kania: Steering the country out of crisis requires unity in the leadership. Today the division in our leadership is a fact. I am aware of my responsibility. The matter concerns me and therefore I am at your disposal without waiting for the vote results.

Cde. Henryk Jabłoński: I think that we should think about and take a position on the motion tabled by Comrade Najdowski and Comrade Rybicki.

Cde. Stanisław Kania: I do not believe today is precisely the moment to explain oneself in detail.

Cde. Tadeusz Grabski: Comrade Kania, this function cannot be performed without the trust of the allies. I thought that you were going to convene a session of the Politburo yesterday. Without the changes in personnel everything will proceed for the worst. You do not have the confidence of the allies, and without it you will not be able to do anything. This is a fundamental matter. We are all submitting to elections.

Cde. Wojciech Jaruzelski: In the situation that has developed, I submit my resignation as a member of the PB.

Cde. Mieczysław Moczar: I also submit my resignation as a member of the PB.

Cde. Mieczysław Jagielski: I submit my resignation as a member of the PB, especially since I had a certain incident in my life.[26] I also submit my resignation as vice premier.

---

[26] Jagielski may be referring to a recent heart attack.

Cde. Stefan Olszowski: Let us think coolly, without emotions. I harbor a bad opinion regarding the statements of both Comrade Grabski and Comrade Barcikowski. The Soviet Union decides Poland's fate, but the party's fate is decided by the nation. We must lead the party towards the congress; this is our great responsibility. We will either proceed together or we will fall apart a month before the congress.

Cde. Andrzej Żabiński: The effectiveness of our actions, mine included, has constantly fallen short. I have always defended the position of the Politburo without, however, being certain whether it is susceptible to change or not. For example, even regarding the matter of releasing the members of the CIP. We did as much as we could in the Bureau. The CWPP [Communist Workers' Party of Poland] letter alarmed me very much. I am of the opinion that in order to lead we should have the support of the party base and of the allies. I see that the latter's support is also close to becoming exhausted. I will submit to a vote. Today's CC plenum was prepared somewhat loosely, for which we will bear responsibility. Before the Politburo all documents should be approved. Comrade Kania, constant concessions have caused distrust in the party apparatus and among the party *aktiv*.

Cde. Henryk Jabłoński: We are responsible for the country's fate and nobody will exempt us from it. This same CC plenum pushed us towards settling accounts. This is how it was at the central level and in the voivodeships. Today we must not give up so easily. In the party and in the country, people are very worried that it will come to a head. Individual resignations from the Politburo now will be interpreted as a protest against the letter of the CPSU. It is another matter if we evaluate ourselves as a whole. You comrades still have a lot to do, you are young. As long as the ship sails, it is we who should be on board.

Cde. Roman Ney: We found ourselves in a very difficult situation, between a rock and a hard place. If today we make a hasty decision, the party will fall apart. I believe that the congress offers a great opportunity and we should push to convene it. Another decision in this situation would be suicidal. I appeal to those comrades who have submitted their resignations today to hold off until the congress.

Cde. Zygmunt Wroński: I am listening to this discussion with trepidation. I am convinced by Comrade Jabłoński's argument. We must hold our guard and we must not submit our resignations. Let us consent to being evaluated individually.

Cde. Tadeusz Grabski: The resignation of Comrade K. Barcikowski was a mistake. I declare that I do not intend to run at the Ninth Congress. I have already arranged a job working for Comrade Jaruzelski.

Cde. Stanisław Kania: Let us not behave like a bunch of anarchists.

Cde. Tadeusz Fiszbach: I would like to call your attention to the fact that the composition of the current CC plenum is not representative of the party. I could naturally submit to the assessment of this audience, but I would like us to think about what will happen beyond this conference room and how the party will react. In Gdańsk, the party *aktiv* and members of the party do not imagine that any changes in the party leadership can take place. I declare that nobody else will be up to the task which Comrade Kania and Comrade Jaruzelski are to fulfill.

Cde. Gerard Gabryś: We must stick together till the end and today we must not submit any resignations.

Cde. Józef Masny: What happened today at the CC plenum is tragic. A heated discussion will flare up in the party. We will be accused of lying since until now we have been saying that there is unity in the Politburo, and meanwhile what? I read the letter as a warning that our guarantees may be withdrawn. It caused a shock. I am in favor of all members of the PB submitting to confirmation.

Cde. Jerzy Waszczuk: We should submit to confirmation by secret vote.

Cde. Mieczysław Moczar: I want to express a fundamental remark to Comrade Grabski to the effect that he brought a squabble from the Politburo before the entire forum of the Central Committee. Until now no such custom has existed.

Cde. Kazimierz Barcikowski: I will not withdraw my resignation. I cannot withdraw it since I am convinced that the members of the CC set upon the Politburo and before its session the Central Committee was "directed" by appropriate comrades.

Cde. Tadeusz Grabski: These are insinuations; do you have any proof?

Cde. Zygmunt Wroński: Comrade Barcikowski, you should present concrete facts because the Politburo should know about this.

Cde. Stefan Olszowski: We should absolutely withdraw all resignations and subsequently submit ourselves to confirmation by secret vote so that we can lead the party to the congress.

Cde. Kazimerz Barcikowski: Comrade Grabski presented a motion regarding the rebuilding of the PB; perhaps he could submit a proposal for a new group.

Cde. Wojciech Jaruzelski: I became premier under particular circumstances. I did not live up to the tasks. These four months have ruined 40 years of military service. At the same time I am serving as minister of national defense. It is physically unbearable. Therefore I do not see myself serving as premier. And there is another matter—the trust of the allies. I feel that this trust was almost withdrawn—it is not only the mention of my name on the list, but still other signs. I can only withdraw my resignation as a member of the PB and ask to be granted some other minor function in the military.

Cde. Kazimierz Cypryniak: I think that what happened today at the plenum should be evaluated critically. In this worst period when the most important matter is party unity, the situation in the leadership has entered into an unfavorable state. We should remember that if someone leaves the Politburo, then a certain faction will follow him. I propose submitting a declaration that the Politburo as currently constituted has decided to guide the party until the Ninth Congress.

Cde. Stanisław Gabrielski: The double-dealing of some of the comrades present here terrifies me. One heard something entirely different from them at the Ninth CC plenum. Today the ones who speak the loudest are those who do not have any moral right, such as you, Comrade Waszczuk. The most important thing is to lead the party to the congress.

Cde. Zdzisław Kurowski: The situation in the party is very tense, a wave of letters is coming in. We are at an impasse. It is true that we are the leadership without the support of society, without the support of the allies or a segment of the party. We harbor bitterness, but common sense should take precedence. We must adopt a motion to submit to confirmation by secret vote.

Cde. Władysław Kruk: I second what Comrade Gabrielski said and I want to state that we are behaving irresponsibly. After all we are not thinking about who will lead the party even for these four weeks. I, too, had, and still have, many remarks regarding the work of the Politburo, but I never thought that it would come to what has taken place at today's plenum. I am appealing to your common sense.

Cde. Tadeusz Fiszbach: I would like to note that the motion for submitting to a confidence vote was reported to the Politburo by the following comrades: Prokopiak, Najdowski, Łabuś; in other words, those who have lost the trust of their regions anyway.

Cde. Kazimierz Barcikowski: Will Comrade Grabski withdraw his motion?

Cde. Tadeusz Grabski: I will not withdraw the motion because you already convinced me once at the Sixth CC Plenum not to submit the motion regarding an examination of Comrade Gierek's evaluation.

Cde. Stanisław Kania: I have considered all the elements and I propose that everyone submit to confirmation.

Cde. Kazimierz Barcikowski: But Comrade Grabski's motion proposed at today's plenum still remains to be examined.

Cde. Tadeusz Grabski: Advise [me], how can I withdraw my motion regarding Comrade Kania?

Cde. Mieczyław Moczar: If you have made a blunder, Comrade Grabski, then you must be able to get out of it.

Cde. Tadeusz Grabski: I have had enough of your moralizing, Comrade Moczar.

Cde. Stanisław Kania: I propose that the Politburo submit to confirmation, and I want to state that I would like to distance myself from the proposition on confirmation.

Cde. Władysław Kruk: I would like to know with whom I will be working in the Political Bureau. I want to work with Comrade Kania and Comrade Jaruzelski.

Cde. Stanisław Kania: While concluding, I would like once more to propose individual voting for members of the Bureau and at the same time I will submit my resignation as well as the resignations of Comrade Barcikowski and Comrade Moczar at the plenum.

Cde. Władysław Kruk: If such a situation develops, let comrades such as Grabski and Waszczuk lead the party.

Cde. Stefan Olszowski: I propose that Comrade Jabłoński make an appearance at the plenum and present the motion regarding confirmation of the PB members. Then we could openly vote down the motion.

Cde. Mieczyław Moczar: In the situation the nation finds itself now we are trapped.

Cde. Stefan Olszowski: Comrades, do you want Solidarity to take power?

Cde. Henryk Jabłoński: Every hasty move will divide the party.

Cde. Kazimierz Cypryniak: Comrade Jaruzelski currently has the most authority among the PB members, therefore he must not resign from the post of premier. At the most, he can consider appointing a vice premier who would later serve as premier.

Cde. Mieczysław Moczar: It is a pity that Comrade Grabski is not withdrawing his motion.

Cde. Stefan Olszowski: Common sense must prevail.

Cde. Tadeusz Grabski: Then what kind of formula should I adopt?

Cde. Stanisław Kania: After all, the question here is not about a formula since Comrade Grabski's motion, submitted at the plenum, is already a fact and it is difficult to change it.

Cde. Tadeusz Fiszbach: If the first secretary submits his resignation, then there is no point in a confirmation.

Cde. Zdzisław Kurowski: I propose that we all submit our resignations and let Comrade Kania assemble a team with which he desires to work until the time of the congress.

Cde. Wojciech Jaruzelski: Perhaps Comrade Grabski would like to consult the people he referred to regarding the motion?

Cde. Tadeusz Grabski: It was only my opinion and my motion.

Cde. Stefan Olszowski: Comrade Jaruzelski cannot resign now since it will complicate the situation. The same applies to Comrade Kania.

Cde. Stanisław Kania: You cannot deprive me of the right to resign.

Cde. Mieczysław Moczar: Whatever logic there was it was buried today and this creates sadness.

Cde. Tadeusz Fiszbach: I propose that Comrade Kania state at the plenum that he submitted his resignation, but that the Politburo did not accept it. Let the CC plenum take a position.

The motion of Comrade Fiszbach was adopted unanimously. The session ended at this point (it lasted one hour and 50 min.). The Politburo approved, by circulating it, a memo regarding meetings with members of the central party authorities.

Recorded by Zbigniew Regucki.

[Source: Tajne Dokumenty, *pp. 401–405. Translated by Małgorzata Gnoińska for the National Security Archive.]*

Document No. 52: Memorandum from Ronald I. Spiers to the Secretary of State, "Polish Resistance to Soviet Intervention"

June 15, 1981

Publication of the June 5 Soviet letter was yet another cause for alarm in Washington that Moscow might be close to an invasion of Poland. In this context, the question naturally arose how the Poles would respond. The State Department's intelligence unit, the Bureau of Intelligence and Research (INR), offered this fascinating take. Virtually all Poles would resist such a move, this memo states, except those who were loyal to the Soviets or wanted above all to prevent bloodshed. But the analysis then leaps to the conclusion that the leadership could therefore be expected to join the population in resisting with military force. Apparently, INR based its assessment in part on the outcome of the June 9–10 plenum in Warsaw, which demonstrated surprising unity and support for Kania and Jaruzelski within the party against strong Soviet pressure. But instead of seeing that the Polish leaders' rationale for imposing martial law could be to comply with Moscow's demands (and their own inclination) to crush the opposition and reassert party control, the memo's authors believe that the Warsaw leadership would use martial law "not to suppress the labor movement but to maximize deterrence" against intervention. INR was not alone in this judgment. The CIA produced a similar analysis at the end of June and again in July.[27]

June 15, 1981
Secret/Noforn

To: The Acting Secretary
From: INR Ronald I. Spiers
Subject: Polish Resistance to Soviet Intervention

Poland's first line of defense against Soviet intervention would be to try to deter it with a show of national unity, which would imply maximum resistance. The Poles might resort to a declaration of martial law and deploy Army units around key points, not to suppress the labor movement but to maximize deterrence by preparing defenses against attack. If the Soviets invaded, much would depend on the state of readiness, deployment and initial actions of Polish air and ground forces, but the Polish Army would not long be able to prevent occupation of Warsaw even if the authorities ordered a maximum resistance effort. Even if

---

[27] See "Polish Reaction to a Soviet Invasion," CIA Intelligence Memorandum, June 30, 1981, available in the collections of the National Security Archive. See also the discussion in MacEachin, *U.S. Intelligence and the Polish Crisis*, pp. 134–135.

Polish leaders decided at the last moment not to try to fight, they would probably not be able to turn off widespread resistance by Army units and the populace.

I. *Deterring Intervention*

The basic tactic of Kania and Jaruzelski in the period immediately ahead is likely to be an increasing accent on national unity. This implicitly threatens the Soviets with widespread and costly resistance to any military intervention. This line is already coming through in some official Polish commentary on the June 9–10 plenum. Solidarity's Wałęsa also appears to be playing it.

Since national unity would be clearly challenged by a resurgence of labor tension, the regime will probably move quickly to remove some of the major outstanding bones of contention with Solidarity. Jaruzelski has already, for example, announced the firing of Justice Minister Bafia, whose removal was demanded by Solidarity in connection with the March 19 police beating of union activists in Bydgoszcz. Wałęsa and other Solidarity moderates are likely to lend their efforts to defusing potential flash-points. The Church can also be expected to work to this end.

II. *Martial Law as a Possible Deterrent*

As tensions mount, Jaruzelski might additionally invoke a state of emergency or some variant of martial law in order to gird the nation against a threatened Soviet intervention.

In late March, it appeared the Poles were thinking of imposing martial law had Solidarity carried out its threat of a nationwide general strike. The Soviets seemed poised to intervene in a supportive role had Polish forces proved unable or unwilling to control the situation on their own.

A declaration of martial law now, however, would be different; it would be intended to prevent civil disturbances from developing, thus depriving the Soviets of this pretext for intervention. It would also keep the Polish armed forces in a heightened state of alert, thus enabling them to react more quickly against a Soviet move.

In the present context, the Polish Army's reliability as a deterrent to the Soviets presumably would be much greater than as a suppressor of Polish workers. While a declaration of martial law nevertheless would risk creating some internal tension, to the extent the Church, Solidarity, and the populace understood it to be directed against the Soviets, they would probably support it.

III. *The Nature of Resistance*

The Polish armed forces are the second largest in the Warsaw Pact. They include 340,000 men in the services, 90,500 militarized security forces and 670 combat aircraft. The Army is deployed predominantly on Poland's western borders and is therefore not well positioned to meet Soviet troops coming in from the East.

There would be widespread resistance by the Polish Army to a Soviet or Warsaw Pact invasion. (The Poles have probably made some contingency plans.)

This would be particularly true if resistance were ordered by the Polish General Staff, but many units would probably resist on their own, although in a less organized fashion. The Soviets do not have officers serving with the Polish forces and they appear to have had little success in increasing their control over the Polish military.

The Polish regime might at the last moment prior to invasion attempt to turn the resistance off. Some leaders might be motivated either by pro-Soviet sympathies—especially on the part of some strategically placed members of the military and security forces—and others by a real concern for the Polish lives which would be lost. To the extent the Polish regime is able to maximize its deterrent posture prior to a Soviet intervention, however, it will also have mobilized the nation and armed forces to resist such a potential Soviet move. It therefore seems unlikely that it could turn off all resistance and at least some units would probably fight.

There is also evidence of contingency preparations by at least some branches of Solidarity. Plans include armed resistance, industrial sabotage, general strikes, occupation of factories, protection of union leaders, and appeals to the patriotism of members of the armed and security forces. The existence of such planning appears in some cases to have been deliberately leaked.

[Source: FOIA release from the State Department, on file at the National Security Archive, "Soviet Flashpoints" collection.]

Document No. 53: Transcript of CPSU CC Politburo Meeting on Brezhnev–Kania Conversation

June 18, 1981

Brezhnev's mounting exasperation with Kania comes across clearly in this report from the Soviet leader to the Politburo.[28] Brezhnev admits that he avoided speaking with Kania for several days but finally could no longer put him off. It did not take long for him to lose patience with Kania's descriptions of his attempts to parry the opposition, and he proceeded to lecture the Pole repeatedly on the need for more decisive action. If he failed to move swiftly, Brezhnev warned, "you will destroy... the Party itself." After each point, Kania's response was essentially the same, to agree completely and promise to do better.

[…]

12. On Information from Cde. Brezhnev concerning a conversation with Cde. S. Kania.

Brezhnev: As you know, for a long time I have not wanted to speak with Kania, but he has tried intensively to have such a conversation: from Friday all the way to Monday he telephoned daily. Therefore, by Tuesday, June 16, it was no longer proper to avoid a conversation, and I contacted him as specified with the members of the Politburo. I conducted the conversation in accordance with the issues that were discussed with the members of the Politburo.

After mutual greetings, Kania began with an expression of thanks for the letter from the CPSU CC that was sent to the PUWP CC. He said that they considered the letter a new manifestation of the CPSU CC's concern for the fate of socialism in Poland, and for our mutual relations. The impact of this letter, in Kania's words, was great and useful.

Kania spoke further about the plenum[29] and the decisions taken there. And again he underscored the impact of our letter on the mood of the participants at the plenum. Kania himself declared at the plenum that the CPSU CC has the right to react in this way and there are sufficient reasons for reacting exactly so.

As far as the course of the plenum, Kania said, there was much criticism. The discussion at the plenum was sharp and principled. All the speakers at the plenum approved the CPSU CC letter. Criticism of the Politburo and the PUWP

---

[28] For Kania's version of the conversation, see the PUWP CC Politburo transcript for June 18, 1981, in *Tajne Dokumenty*, pp. 406–414.

[29] The PUWP CC Eleventh Plenum held on June 9–10, 1981. See, for example, Document No. 51.

leadership as a whole was also considerable. The question was even posed of a vote of confidence. The plenum by a majority vote decided not to permit changes to the composition of the leadership before the party congress. Kania affirmed that he and the comrades who spoke at the plenum were disposed to conducting the congress as a congress of a Marxist party. Additional mobilization and activation of PUWP members is continuing in the struggle with anti-socialist forces.

Kania also recounted briefly Jaruzelski's presentation at the Sejm. He stressed that the issue there was about a firmer rebuff of the counter-revolution.

Here I could not abide this and I said to him: Comrade Kania, how many times have I talked to you about this from the very beginning of all this delay? I have said to you all along that it is necessary to respond with deeds, not words, to counter-revolutionary actions.

Kania agreed with this. He noted that after the plenum there were fewer enemy actions and fewer provocations. Even Wałęsa said they will have to make their case differently.

In a word, Kania believes that conditions for the party struggle have improved and that now the important thing is to bring order to the mass media. They have decided to remove the director of the CC department of press, radio and television, Klyass, from his post. The decision has been made to release the chairman of the television committee and several editors. There will be other such decisions as well. And they have begun the trial of Leszek Moczulski.[30]

On the subject of Moczulski, I said to him: Comrade Kania, how long are you going to mess around with this Moczulski? At one point he was under arrest, then you let him go. Now you are beginning another trial. What next?

Next, said Kania, we will try him according to the law and put him in prison once again. He will get what he deserves.

In Kania's words, their [party] conferences have begun to go better, in a healthier atmosphere. And here the influence of the plenum and the CPSU CC letter [was felt]. The party conference in Kraków went particularly well.

They will also rectify the situation with the workers' representatives at the congress so that the congress is a Marxist–Leninist one. They will adopt a course aimed at strengthening discipline in the party and in state institutions, and at strengthening unity.

I told him that was very good. Everything that we want to tell you about the situation in Poland, about our alarm over the fate of the PUWP and the cause of socialism, all of that is expressed in the CPSU CC letter. I see no need to return to it again. Probably even you understand that. I will only say, I continued, that the policy of granting endless concessions to the counter-revolution has conclusively demonstrated its own bankruptcy.

If you do not try for a turnaround in political circumstances before the congress, you will destroy the congress and the party itself. By your own hands you

---

[30] Leszek Moczulski headed the Confederation for an Independent Poland, an illegal political party. He was imprisoned in mid-September 1980.

will surrender power to the adversary. That is the situation today. And it is time at last that you understood it. I say this to you as a comrade.

Kania fully agreed with this.

In addition, I told him the following. A great many correct remarks were heard at the plenum. They also appear in the plenum's resolution. But the important thing, you know, is not words but deeds, and practical work. You yourself, Stanisław, remarked that it was necessary to begin to take action literally tomorrow. We shall see what becomes of that. It is long since time for you to act.

In my view, I said to him, a question arises in connection with the plenum that is of no small importance. They told me that there were many speeches on various levels containing criticism of the Politburo for its indecisiveness in the struggle against anti-socialist forces. Is that so, I asked him.

It is so, Leonid Ilyich, Kania answered. There was very serious criticism.

That's right, Comrade Kania, that is a serious symptom which by all appearances reflects the mood of a significant portion of the party masses. And it would be extraordinarily dangerous if someone were to try to settle personal accounts on those grounds.

On the eve of the congress, I said, it is especially important to ensure the efficiency of the Politburo as a collective, representing the headquarters of the party and holding forth on a clear, Marxist–Leninist basis. That is what I wanted to say to you in reply. It is necessary to ensure unity in the Politburo. And then, I repeat to you again, it would be very dangerous if someone, on this pretext, on the pretext of providing criticism, tried to settle personal accounts.

Here Kania said: "Leonid Ilyich, I did not fully understand you."

I repeated once more, in the same words, the inadmissibility of settling personal accounts. After this, Kania said that he understood, that he had written it down and that they would do everything he had been told.

Kania affirmed that he would do everything in his power to fulfill our wishes. To which I answered: "Your actions will tell." On that, I brought things to an end with him.

As you see, the conversation was not substantial in terms of [length of] time, but was rigorous in content. That is probably how it had to be. Let the comrades think about it. I think that Kania was correct on one point here. That is that the CPSU CC letter truly had a positive influence on the healthy forces in the party and on a certain improvement in the entire atmosphere. Perhaps in the end they will begin to reflect and act more decisively. As they say, we shall live and we shall see.

Do the comrades have any questions or comments? If not, then let us approve the discussion.

All: Agreed.

[*Source: RGANI, Fond 89, Opis 42, Delo 44. Translated by Malcolm Byrne for the National Security Archive.*]

Document No. 54: CIA National Intelligence Daily, "USSR–Poland: Polish Military Attitudes"

June 20, 1981

This CIA appraisal discusses one of the crucial questions relating to a possible invasion of Poland: the reaction of the Polish military. Previous crises in Hungary in 1956 and Czechoslovakia in 1968 had proven the unreliability and even hostility of local armies. Kania and Jaruzelski both told Warsaw Pact Commander Kulikov that they did not trust the army in particular (see Document No. 41). Polish plans for martial law thus deliberately placed most of the responsibility for securing the country in the hands of the MSW rather than the Polish army. On another topic, relying on sources in the Polish intelligentsia, this report provides a scenario in which Polish resistance to an invasion would produce a minimum of 600,000 casualties—and allegedly many more in the calculations of Soviet intelligence. The report goes on to say that, according to sources, most senior Polish officers were offended by the June 5 CPSU CC letter (Document No. 50), which bluntly warned of outside intervention if the Polish authorities did not swiftly put their house in order. As a result, military officers attending a Polish CC meeting a few days later threw their support entirely behind both Kania and Jaruzelski.

At the end of this analysis are remarks about the relative lack of criticism over Poland in the Soviet press. This belied the continuing barrage of Soviet condemnation of the Poles behind the scenes, in the form of inter-party communications such as the June 5 letter and regular criticism at meetings and during telephone conversations between Polish and Soviet leaders.

[…]

USSR–Poland: Polish Military Attitudes

Sources [half line excised] *said on Thursday that most of the senior Polish military command is now alienated from the Soviets and fully supports the Kania–Jaruzelski team and that the Polish military is likely to resist any Soviet invasion.*

The sources, members of the intelligentsia, who reportedly have good access among Polish leaders, also said that Polish authorities have now begun to calculate the size of a possible Soviet invasion force and the number of casualties that might result from such an operation.

Conjecture on an Invasion

[2–3 words excised] sources believe that at least 50 Soviet and Warsaw Pact combat divisions and additional support units would be needed to invade, and the Polish leaders reportedly estimate there would be a total of 600,000 to 800,000 Polish and Soviet casualties. The authorities allegedly also believe that Soviet intelligence services calculate the cost in lives at a much higher level. There is no other evidence that the Poles have begun to discuss a possible invasion.

We believe that some Polish troops would resist a Soviet intervention, but [2–3 words excised] sources reportedly think it is likely that larger units up to division size would fight. They explained that senior-level Polish officers were alienated from Moscow because of the letter the Soviets sent to the Polish Central Committee.[31] They think the military clearly indicated at last week's Central Committee plenum that it would not support any other leadership team in Poland.

Military officers who are members of the Central Committee did support Kania during last week's meeting, and party organizations within the military this week pledged support to the Jaruzelski government. Kania attended one of these meetings and pointedly thanked the "comrades in uniform" for their invaluable support for the party and its line of renewal. This support, he said, was of "great political importance."

Soviet and East German Commentary
Soviet media commentary and East German activity suggest that Moscow and its allies continue to reserve judgment on how to deal with the Polish party congress planned for next month. Comments by East German officials suggest they have no illusions about rallying opposition within Poland to the renewal process. Although the East Germans are intent on reviving their campaign of making contacts with party officials in Poland, the aim apparently is only to be kept informed on developments there.

The current lack of a sense of urgency among senior officials in East Berlin suggests that the East Germans do not anticipate a Warsaw Pact intervention before the congress. [3 lines excised]

The Soviets have reprinted notably strong criticism from other East European media of the Warsaw regime's failure to act firmly against "counter-revolutionaries," but have confined their own recent commentary to attacks upon "extremists" within Solidarity and some elements within the Polish media. Moscow has refrained from direct attacks upon the Polish leaders, and has even accorded Kania and Jaruzelski moderately favorable television coverage.

Moscow may be refraining from strong attacks in order to preserve the option of attempting sooner or later to restore a working relationship with the Polish leaders. They may also fear that a shriller media campaign would inflame anti-Soviet sentiment among the Polish population, and possibly alarm Soviet citizens as well.

A Soviet Central Committee plenum will probably be held on Monday. The Central Committee normally convenes at this time of year, and Poland is likely to be a prime topic. [2–3 words excised]

[Source: FOIA release from the CIA, on file at the National Security Archive, "Soviet Flashpoints" collection.]

[31] The CPSU CC letter of June 5, 1981. See Document No. 50.

Document No. 55: Information on Andrei Gromyko's Talks with the PUWP Leadership,

July 3–5, 1981

In this report to the Warsaw Pact allies, the Soviet leadership details Foreign Minis-
ter Gromyko's talks with Kania and Jaruzelski on the eve of the important Extraor-
dinary Ninth Congress. Although they point out that the meeting "will appear as a
friendly official visit," it was yet another stern lecture on the need to hold firm against
the "counter-revolution." In addition to generalities, to which the Poles dutifully nod
agreement, Gromyko adds specific instructions for how the plenum's elections to the
party leadership should play out. He insists that no "revenge" be taken against any-
one who has been critical of the party for offering too many concessions to the op-
position, and that no-one "with extreme revisionist and opportunistic convictions" be
elected to the CC. His reference by name to hard-liner Tadeusz Grabski in the former
category is tied to Grabski's attempt to have Kania removed from office during the
recent June plenum. In that forum and at this meeting, the CPSU CC's June 5 letter
(Document No. 50) provided the basis for criticism of the current Polish leadership.

[…]

Guided by concern about the situation in the PUWP on the eve of its Extraor-
dinary Ninth Congress, the CPSU CC Politburo took the initiative for a trip to
Warsaw by Cde. A. A. Gromyko in order to conduct talks with S. Kania and W.
Jaruzelski. The Polish comrades agreed to this proposal.

Both sides have agreed that publicly this trip will look like a friendly official
visit. (As you know, the communiqué was published on July 6.)

On July 3–5, conversations took place with S. Kania and W. Jaruzelski as
well as a one-on-one talk with S. Kania. Cde. A. Gromyko based his conversations on the contents of the letter from the CPSU CC to the PUWP CC of June
5 of this year as well as on respective statements by Cde. L. I. Brezhnev in his
meetings with the Polish leadership and his talks with S. Kania about which we
have already informed our friends previously.

In the talks with S. Kania and W. Jaruzelski, it was emphatically emphasized
that the CPSU CC considered it to be the main task to turn the forthcoming plenum into a plenum, in the course of which, the ranks of the party would be tight-
ened based on Marxism–Leninism and the party armed with a fighting program
that will allow it to overcome the crisis. The cause of maintaining and strengthening the socialist social order in the PPR as an independent, unified socialist
state and firm member of the socialist community demands that during the plenum and the ensuing activities of the PUWP the counter-revolution and all the
forces which aspire to subvert socialism in Poland or, at a minimum, try to turn
the country's development towards social democracy or even capitalism will be

decisively rejected. It was important, A. A. Gromyko stated, to demonstrate the power of the Marxist–Leninist party of communists at the plenum, because the counter-revolution, which has raised its head, will not easily surrender.

There was no attempt by Kania and Jaruzelski to challenge these views and conclusions. They repeated several times that they would do everything to assure that the plenum would be implemented as "the plenum of a Marxist–Leninist party" and that "the leadership would be Marxist–Leninist." Of course, the plenum will answer this question. But for our part, we emphasized this position in a vigorous and principled manner.

During the conversations in Warsaw, Kania was warned not to take the road of revenge with those comrades who had criticized the current leadership of the PUWP at sessions of the CC and at other times [as well as] its policy of unending concessions to the anti-socialist forces. It was also made clear that people with extreme revisionist and opportunist convictions could not be elected to the Central Committee or to the Politburo. It was openly stated that it was necessary to assure the election of Comrade Grabski into the leadership and not to allow the election of Rakowski.

Cde. A. A. Gromyko emphatically pointed out that the matter of the composition of the PUWP's leading organ, the question of what this composition would be like, was of course intrinsically connected with the level of confidence in it by the CPSU CC and the Soviet leadership. During the talks, much attention was given to the other matters of principle which had been raised in the CPSU CC letter to the PUWP Central Committee: among them the question of strengthening the leading role of the party, maintaining the principle of democratic socialism, increasing the influence of the PUWP over developments in Poland, the ideological education of party members, the necessity of a vigorous intensification of the fight against the counter-revolution and anti-socialist forces, controlling the mass media etc.

Cde. A. A. Gromyko stressed that not only political but also economic relations with Poland would be developed in consideration of what Poland will look like. It was stated that we helped and will help our friends, not our enemies; our people would not allow anything else. The interlocutors received these statements and showed understanding; but they were taciturn.

In this connection, Cde. A. A. Gromyko directed their attention to the repeated advice which Comrade L. I. Brezhnev, the CPSU CC, and the leaderships of the other fraternal parties had given the Polish leadership, but which had thus far not been implemented.

S. Kania and W. Jaruzelski affirmed that Poland was and would remain a socialist state and that the party, despite the difficult situation in the country, would not permit the government's authority to be taken over by anti-socialist forces. The struggle would be hard and complicated, they declared, but they did not doubt the final victory of the PUWP. According to S. Kania and W. Jaruzelski, international issues would be debated at the plenum in the proper spirit, which accords with the principles of the foreign policy of the countries of the socialist community.

As a result of the talks conducted in Warsaw, there was reason to believe that the CPSU CC letter to the PUWP CC, as well as the influence of the other fraternal parties on the Polish leadership, will have an impact on the plenum and its course.

It has, of course, been considered by the CPSU CC that S. Kania and W. Jaruzelski previously promised to consider the advice of the fraternal parties but did not take decisive measures. Nobody can vouch that even this time they will not act in a similar fashion. In any case, the Warsaw talks allowed [us] once more to draw attention emphatically to the principles of the CPSU CC letter and to warn of the disastrous consequences of continuing the previous course. Without doubt it was important to do this before the PUWP Ninth Plenum.

The CPSU CC is of the opinion that the PUWP is facing a complicated and difficult struggle at the plenum and in its aftermath in leading the PPR and the Polish United Workers' Party out of the dangerous crisis. We believe that our parties should continue to use all measures to influence the PUWP leadership and constantly support the Polish communists in order to achieve a reversal in the developments in this country.

[Source: SAPMO-BArch, Berlin, DY 30/J IV 2/202/550. Obtained by Tomasz Mianowicz (Munich) and translated by Christian F. Ostermann.]

Document No. 56: Report to HSWP CC Politburo with Verbatim Transcript of July 21 Telephone Conversation between Kania and Brezhnev

July 22, 1981

---

*This apparently verbatim transcript of a Brezhnev–Kania telephone call shortly af-
ter the PUWP's Extraordinary Ninth Congress was delivered to Hungarian leader
János Kádár by a Soviet representative in Budapest. Kádár was about to travel to
the Soviet Union to meet Brezhnev, where Poland was certain to be a major topic
of discussion. Brezhnev opens the call by congratulating Kania on his reelection as
first secretary of the party. It is an ironic moment given that the Kremlin had probably tried to have Kania ousted at the June 9–10 plenum. Kania, naturally, plays
along. In more moderate tones than in previous communications (see, for example,
Document No. 39), the Soviet leader admonishes against further "capitulations"
and warns that "the whole struggle is still ahead of you." Kania in turn promises
somewhat outlandishly to "seize the counter-revolution by its throat," although in
reality the political divide within the Polish leadership, preserved by the congress,
all but ensured that no dramatic action was likely by either side. Typically, Brezhnev used the informal "ty" when addressing Kania, while the Polish leader used the
more respectful "vy".*

REPORT

Comrade János Kádár received Comrade Valerii Musatov, the chargé d'affaires
ad interim of the Soviet Embassy in Budapest, at his request on July 22, 1981.
Comrade Musatov reported that Comrade Stanisław Kania phoned Comrade
Leonid Brezhnev on July 21 while the latter was on holiday in the Crimea. The
following conversation took place between them:

S. Kania: Good morning, Comrade Leonid Ilyich.

L. Brezhnev: Good morning, Stanisław.

First of all, I would like to congratulate you on the occasion of your re-elec-
tion to the post of first secretary of the PUWP CC.

I closely followed the work of the congress. It was a difficult congress. What
is your assessment of it?

S. Kania: You are right, the congress took place in a difficult situation. But after all, it created conditions for development. There can be no doubt about that. I
wonder whether Comrades Grishin and Rusakov informed you about the course
of the congress.

L. Brezhnev: I read all the reports coming from Warsaw during that period.
I followed with interest the television coverage of the work of the congress.

S. Kania: You probably know how the congress received Comrade V. V. Grishin's speech. The delegates applauded every remark referring to the Soviet Union and supported the idea of friendship with your country and our solidarity in the struggle for the principles of socialism. It made the proper impression.

The congress adopted good resolutions. This holds especially for the rules and regulations of the party which your comrades helped us with. In other documents, however, the wording may not be perfectly correct. Nevertheless, we hope that we will be able to amend them when they are put into practice. Unfortunately, some comrades whom we would have liked to see on the Politburo did not get [appointed] to it. I am thinking of Comrades Żabiński and Grabski. Grabski obtained few votes in the secret ballot. In my opinion he had committed a number of mistakes and therefore he lost the votes not only of the revisionists but also those of the reliable comrades.

The present composition of the Politburo will fully ensure that we will work more effectively in the future. Comrade Milewski, minister of internal affairs, became a member of the Politburo. We plan to give him the post of administrative secretary of the Central Committee. You probably know him well.

L. Brezhnev: I have heard about him but I have never met him in person.

S. Kania: Foreign Minister J. Czyrek became a member of the Politburo and the secretary of the CC. We elected two comrades who had previously been doing lower-grade party work to the posts of secretaries of the CC. These are Z. Michałek and M. Woźniak. The former will deal with agricultural issues and the latter with economic ones. We hope that Michałek, who used to work as the director of a major state farm, will be able to help us in reshaping the village structure.

The composition of the Politburo is good, all in all. It is made up of reliable people.

L. Brezhnev: If that is the case, then it is good.

S. Kania: We managed to elect all the people I had wanted into the controlling organs. There were 18 candidates on the list of Politburo members, of which 14 had to be elected. Those I did not consider suitable dropped out in the secret ballot.

Comrade Rusakov was quite afraid that Rakowski would get into the leadership. I promised him that this would not happen. It was not easy to fulfill this as they wanted to elect Rakowski even to the post of PUWP CC first secretary. However, it all fell through and I am satisfied now.

Economic circumstances are, indeed, terrible in Poland. Due to the shortage of market supplies the possibility of rioting is most likely. We are short of a number of products, including even cigarettes. We spoke in detail about all this to your delegation, which we met yesterday. We informed the delegates in detail about the economic situation of the country. They promised to report this to you.

L. Brezhnev: We are examining everything closely here in Moscow.

S. Kania: Comrade Jaruzelski and all the members of the Politburo send you their best regards.

L. Brezhnev: Thank you. Give my best regards to Comrade Jaruzelski and the others.

S. Kania: We are now going to draft a specific plan for further action, which will have to be more aggressive.

L. Brezhnev: That is right. Thank you for the information. I would like to give you my own opinion. We think that the congress was a serious trial of strength for both the party and you personally. It clearly cast light on the extent of opportunism and of the threat represented by the opportunists. If they had been given a free hand, they would have diverted the party from Leninism to social democracy. Besides, they behaved in a malicious way and launched a campaign of slander.

In spite of this, the final outcome of the congress and the fact that the highest party authority chose you for the post of first secretary, create a reliable basis for resolute and consistent measures for the solution of the crisis and the stabilization of the situation.

The most important thing is that we do not waste time. People must feel right away that the leadership is in reliable hands.

I was informed that Solidarity is threatening a strike which is to be organized at your airline company. You have to show them that times have changed. There will be no more capitulations. Don't you agree?

S. Kania: I absolutely agree.

L. Brezhnev: After all, the whole struggle is still ahead of you. It is not going to be an easy fight. The counter-revolution—the danger of which we have already talked about several times—does not intend to lay down its arms.

I would like to believe that, holding together the party *aktiv* and all communists, you and your comrades will be able to halt the course of events, fight the enemies of socialism and defend the achievements of socialist Poland.

In such circumstances, Stanisław, be assured that you can rely on our solidarity and support.

The Soviet people express their pleasure at your election as leader of the party and they will follow attentively further happenings in Poland. This is natural as everything that is going on in your country is close to the hearts of the Soviet people. The development of Soviet–Polish economic, political and other relations will advance according to how events in Poland are settled.

Taking the opportunity of your phone call I invite you to visit us. You could take some rest and, naturally, we would then have the occasion for a more profound discussion. I wish you, Stanisław, strength and health.

S. Kania: I thank you for all that you have said.

L. Brezhnev: I always say openly and sincerely what I think.

S. Kania: I know what you expect from us. You are absolutely right to say that we have to mobilize all our forces in order to take the offensive. We understand that. I assure you that I will do my best to eliminate difficulties. We shall seize the counter-revolution by its throat.

L. Brezhnev: I wish you and your comrades success in this.

S. Kania: Thank you for your invitation for a holiday. I have practically no time to rest. I have already told all my comrades that I would not go on holiday. Yet, I might travel to you for a couple of days so we could talk.

L. Brezhnev: I will meet Comrades Husák and Kádár in the next few days.

S. Kania: If you agree, I would let you know the date of my arrival later, when I can see more clearly.

L. Brezhnev: I understand that you have a lot of work to do. The resolutions of the congress have to be carried out.

S. Kania: Leonid Ilyich, I wish you a good rest and gathered strength. Not only Soviet communists, but all of us need this.

L. Brezhnev: Thank you for your kindness. I cannot, however, free myself from work even during my holidays. Just before your call I was talking on the phone with the leaders of Georgia, Kazakhstan and the regional leaders of Rostov, Volgograd and Stavropol. And it is the same every day.

S. Kania: Nevertheless, you should find some time for a rest.

L. Brezhnev: Thank you. Again, I wish you success, Stanisław. Good bye.

Budapest, July 22, 1981

[Source: MOL, Department of Documents on the Hungarian Workers' Party and the Hungarian Socialist Workers' Party, 288. f. 5/832. ő.e., pp. 20–24. Published in the Cold War International History Project Bulletin, *Issue 11 (Winter 1998), pp. 84–85. Translated by László Beke.]*

[handwritten: ...ear... → strategic use of ambiguity "uses of ambiguity"]

Document No. 57: Notes of Solidarity National Coordinating Commission Conference in Gdańsk

July 24, 1981

In the period after the Ninth PUWP Congress, the Solidarity leadership continued to face fundamental questions about what direction the union should take and what means it should use to achieve its goals. These revealing notes of the first day of debates at the conference describe some of the issues being discussed, such as whether to support self-government in the factories, and, even more importantly, whether to press for Polish national sovereignty or remain a member of the Warsaw Pact. While PUWP critics often accused the party of having no strategic vision, the same might have been said about Solidarity's leadership in these uncertain times. These notes also convey an interesting suggestion of the dynamics of NCC debates.

The Socio-Political Situation in the Country.
Workers' Self-Government.

[handwritten: but taken in Debate - no little debate]

Introduction to the discussion by *A. Celiński.* He says that so far the Union has only addressed its demands to the authorities, leaving the method of meeting these demands to the government. Solidarity was afraid to include the proposal for restructuring the state in their program. Facing the monopolistic position of the ruling party and fearing internal divisions, Solidarity did not want to take any responsibility for the situation in the country. Meanwhile, it was forgotten that the "political game" is based on economic issues. The government did not make any decisions that would allow it to overcome the crisis, which, in Celiński's opinion, was an element of the game as well as a result of the government's weakness. Therefore, the original concept failed due to an unjustified faith in the authorities and a belief that they also want reforms. The Union's demands did not get through to anyone.

Celiński believes that at the moment society is very rebellious; anyway, in the area of awareness encouraging such feelings would be a mistake. So far, too much attention has been devoted to emotions, which the NCC should have subordinated to a reasonably established hierarchy of tasks. According to Celiński, emotional attitudes also reveal themselves in the Union's press, in which too many of the "obsessed" are employed—those who were silent before August 1980 and who are now trying to "compensate" for that silence. Society accepts their publications with eagerness because they alleviate the stress that accumulated before August. However, it is necessary to assume some hierarchy for Solidarity's tasks and to undertake concrete actions. Otherwise, in case of a collapse, it will be difficult to answer society's question: "What have you done?" So far, a kind of dogma about the NCC's infallibility has existed, and failures have been blamed on the mistakes of particular

319

individuals; scapegoats have been sought. Meanwhile, rules of action need to be established. For a long time we blamed the system's flaws on people's mistakes but after September, after their removal [from office], it turned out that they acted with iron logic.

According to Celiński, the Union is self-governing, but it lacks independence because the timing of each of the four most serious conflicts so far has been determined by the authorities. The Bydgoszcz provocation proved the existence of centers striving for confrontation within the authorities, but the organizers and co-ordinators of the provocation have not yet been held responsible. So far, the Union has avoided confrontation thanks to society's consolidation around Solidarity's leadership during the crisis, the mediating activity of Church and its hierarchy, and the lack of another acceptable political conception for the country. However, the Union is becoming weaker after every crisis. After each crisis, personal disputes emerge among the leaders about strategies for overcoming the crisis, despite the fact that these ideas do not differ greatly. Celiński says that although in the past he was against revealing what went on inside the NCC, he now thinks that the motives behind the decisions that have been made should be open to the public. The activity of the Union's leadership declines after each conflict; the authority they have gained is wasted. And so, for instance, after the Bydgoszcz conflict no one managed to show society what, in Celiński's opinion, was most important—that Solidarity and not the authorities was the sole factor responsible for the future of the country.

Celiński says that the economic apparatus of the country and, to a lesser extent, the apparatus of the state and party administration are falling to pieces. The separation of the "party masses" from the PUWP leadership has put an end to the communication of orders. Unfortunately, this process is not being accompanied by the internal organization of Solidarity. A vacuum is emerging in society because neither the Union nor the authorities have any program around which the society could organize.

In the nearest future, says Celiński, one should expect an increase in conflicts based on workers' self-government and the food issue as well as elections for national councils this December. On the electoral law and issues of prices and wages—here, aside from the conflict between the authorities and the Union, conflicts will also arise between branches within Solidarity. Then he asks J. Kuroń to take the floor.

J. Kuroń states that the hitherto existing system of authority in Poland has ceased to exist; the government is unable to rule. The government does not have a democratically elaborated program and cannot appeal to anyone because the Sejm also does not represent society. A revolution, in which the existing order has been overthrown and no attempt has been made to construct a new system, is occurring. Solidarity cannot create it. Such a system must be constructed by the whole society, hence mass demands for a political party. Kuroń brings up Bujak's statement at the Mazowsze WZD—Solidarity is like a sailors' union on a sinking ship. It cannot fight for higher wages or increased food rations. It has to think about what to do to save the ship. First it has to think and make a decision on the issue of the utmost importance: whether Solidarity should give up its role as a trade union and take power. Does it want to be a trade union or a political party? Yesterday it was said in this room that we want to abolish censorship. But then we should start at the foundations, demand full democracy and eventually abolition of censorship. However, says Kuroń, the revolution taking place must limit itself because the USSR will definitely get involved if it decides that its military rule in Poland is being threatened. Discussion on whether they will or will not enter can only be speculative. Anyhow, it should be remembered that it can only be verified empirically. If we decide not to overthrow the authorities, we should not take measures that are important only with respect to the maximum goal. It is not worth "overthrowing the government with an elbow," just by accident or as if through oversight. Such risks must not be taken, especially because survival in itself may also be a way to realize our maximum goals.

Kuroń believes that calling for a [new] party is based on the conviction that it is needed for [carrying out] political activities. There are two party models: the Leninist style, which strives for totalitarian power, and a party which strives for free elections. Kuroń is against a totalitarian system. He believes, however, that it is still too early to demand free elections and create multiple political parties right away. So, since the Union does not want to overthrow the system, it is necessary to support the movement for self-government initiatives, the only force capable of introducing a credible program for overcoming the crisis.

Solidarity cannot retreat from the struggle for self-government's right to determine the guidelines for reform. This movement should develop with the support of self-government initiatives clubs, while appeals to the government will hardly have any results because the government is paralyzed. Kuroń adds that aside from the theory about the authorities' weakness, on which he has based his statements, there is an opinion that the authorities are strong and are fighting the Union in order to reintroduce "the old system" through hunger. In his opinion that view is wrong but it is not worth engaging in polemics because both theories boil down to [the conclusion] that the government does not govern.

L. Wałęsa repeats that it is necessary to establish a continuously working Presidium in Gdańsk that would consist of about seven people.

S. Wądołowski reads aloud the draft NCC statement on workers' self-governments.

J. Milewski (voluntary secretariat of the Network) moves that the NCC authorize the Network to elaborate a draft unified Solidarity statement on the complex economic reform, entrust it with organizing that task, delegate its representative to each meeting of the Network, and also concede the status of the "NCC branch" to the Network. The NCC should also begin to cooperate with the NSZZ RI Solidarity at the highest level. He adds that the basis of the Network are the Union's basic cells, i.e. FC's [Factory Committees] which distribute announcements from Network meetings among the workers. In Milewski's opinion, the absence of objections from 208,000 union members from leading enterprises in the country amounts to authorization for the Network.

M. Gil (Lenin Steelworks, NCC representative for the talks on self-government) states that a broad propaganda campaign among the Union members is necessary. They should be informed about the relationship between the unions and self-government; it is necessary to explain that an authentic self-government is a self-government which, among other things, appoints and dismisses directors and sets guidelines for enterprise development. We need to take a position on the government's draft law on self-government. They should also be informed about Network activity. He notes that the government's draft laws on enterprises and self-government will be discussed in the Sejm on Tuesday. The NCC inevitably must take a position on these drafts. He emphasizes the flexibility and union-like quality of the Network and considers it necessary to define relations between it and the NCC.

A. Gwiazda suggests expanding the draft declaration to include an announcement that the Union will protect all initiators of and participants in the self-government movement. He says that Solidarity's attitude toward self-government has always been positive; however, the process of its formation had to be slowed in order not to let us get into the "government's channel" and to prevent the break-up of the Union.

Solidarity fights for workers' rights and authentic self-government is in their interest; therefore it must be supported. But the self-government movement has to develop outside the Union so that when necessary Solidarity can defend it with all its strength. It is worth using the Network, which is flexible and has its own strength [to gain] support from the crews working in large enterprises. Including the Network in the Union's structure as was proposed by Milewski would mean the NCC would have to accept each stance and would overly hinder the activity of the Network.

S. Wądołowski reads aloud the information from Jelenia Góra's delegate that since July 23 there has been a censor's ban on the Network.

Pałka (Łódź) says that social discontent will probably increase. Such dissatisfaction may partially turn against Solidarity which is not taking any concrete measures in the economic sphere. The Union should have some emergency action plan, which would take into account that kind of possibility. Otherwise, it will find itself in the same situation as the old trade unions found themselves in August. Pałka believes that, in that case, it would be possible to establish strike committees that would not go out on active strike, and that would allow the emergence of self-governments. Should the government attempt to counteract, a strike may prove necessary, even a general one. A scenario for such a strike is necessary. It might also happen that after a series of brief conflicts the government will impose its solutions on society because there will simply be no other solutions within reach. Society should be mobilized to supervise the reform, he continues, because more time is needed for self-governments to act. Although he has nothing against the Network, which has taken an interesting stand, he believes that the Union should validate its concept with the support of its statutory structures and should not formalize extra-statutory ones such as the Network. He adds that in Łódź self-governments are being established outside the Network structure. They should be created based on regional structures.

J. Krupiński (Olsztyn) shares the view that the Network is not fully representative of the national economy; it lacks representatives from small enterprises. It is necessary to establish a good model quickly because at the moment the government is establishing pseudo-self-governments consisting of a director, a PPO representative, and a representative of the old CWS [Conference of Workers' Self-Government]. When speaking about the Union's strategy it is important not to omit the enemy's strategy, which, in Krupiński's opinion, amounts to the development of a chronic disease. Currently one should divide authority among the NCC members; create an optimistic administration at the NCC; persistently execute previous decisions, having set the program of activities, which would anticipate future moves by the authorities and take into account the possibility of failure; provide information widely about the motives underlying Solidarity's current conduct, outside the Union as well, because it also needs support from there; provide Solidarity members with the maximum number of seats in the NMC, NVC and Sejm in the forthcoming elections; determine whether a Union member who is a member of the Sejm can simultaneously perform Union functions. Krupiński also concludes that the act of registering cases of economic sabotage and waste should be centralized. Then perhaps we may get to know what mechanism is operating here. High treason, as Gwiazda says, is not unlikely.

J. Stępień (Kielce) recalls the history of workers' self-government in Poland. Among other things, he states that in the binding decree on enterprise councils from 1945 there is a reference to democratic, adjectival [sic] elections with voting for lists. The structure of self-government could be based on that decree and, while teaching people how authentic elections for workers' councils based on voting for lists should look, one can demand the same change in electoral law for the National Councils.

S. Jakubowicz: The CSPS considers it necessary for the NCC to take a stand on the issue of self-governments. The most important thing is who exercises power at an enterprise, i.e. who appoints and dismisses the director. That is the key problem of economic reform. Leaving this squarely in the hands of the minister makes self-government a fiction. Official propaganda, which uses the argument of collective ownership to attack the Network, produces only, in Jakubowicz's opinion, a smoke screen that hides that key issue. Moreover, the government's draft law says that the minister may relinquish these rights in enterprises he selects; therefore it is not a matter of ideological principle but of maintaining power.

According to Jakubowicz, the laws of 1945 and 1956 Stępień mentioned may have been progressive in those days, but today they are of no use. Therefore, for example, in 1956 it was determined that the workers' council would render opinions on candidates for director, and that is unacceptable. Because the government does not want to talk to Solidarity, the only way left is to exercise pressure on the Sejm. We should oppose passage of the government's draft. The Union should also exhort the social movement in favor of reform since it is unable to elaborate a draft itself.

While emphasizing the Network's successes and the results of its work he suggests supporting principles in the Sejm on which the draft law on social enterprise, elaborated by the Network, is based (see AS No. 19, p. 308), but without treating the issue in terms of prestige, i.e. "this draft or none." This view accords with the Network's standpoint.

A. Gwiazda demands that the NCC oblige the RA's and FC's to support self-government initiatives because some FC's are suspicious of that idea. He emphasizes that self-government is indissolubly tied to the reform because its task is to introduce reform in the economic sphere. Solidarity does not have executive authority either in matters of self-government or reform but it can influence social awareness through giving its support. In Gwiazda's opinion, one should proclaim oneself in favor of the system of proportional elections for lists especially because attempts are being made to create self-governments according to the [following] key: director-1, PPO-1, USPY-1, sectoral unions-1, Solidarity-1. The Union may impose an electoral law and this law will settle the line for self-government, the goal of which will be to seize economic power. Gwiazda emphasizes that self-government should not be a consultative body, or—as anticipated by the original concept—an entity blocking decisions unfavorable to employees. Self-government should rule. Therefore, it must have the freedom to decide, among other things, about financial issues such as taking out and distributing loans. We must decide how to win over these authorities for self-government. One possibility is to put pressure on members of parliament.

W. Frasyniuk (Wrocław, Lower Silesia) supports Wałęsa's idea to have the NCC approve cooptation of a few persons into the Presidium. He agrees with Kuroń that the revolution must constrain itself. The Union must be a guarantor of democratic electoral law but it should not take over power. However, as citizens, we have the right to fight for power.

To date, the Union's methods [i.e.] inspecting and issuing opinions on government activities and involving its authority in that [task], in Frasyniuk's opinion, require a change. We must come out with our own initiatives, such as the Network's program. Also, while speaking about self-government, we cannot forget about the draft law on enterprises. We should turn to the FC's to allow the crews to become familiar with the government's draft laws on self-government and enterprises, and with the draft law on social enterprises. The Network should be recognized as the Union's branch, and the CSPS should be at its disposal; that is because it is a valuable initiative "from the side," while the NCC faces so many other problems. Because, as demonstrated by the discussion, the draft declaration on self-governments presented by Wądołowski is incomplete, Frasyniuk proposes delegating a group to edit a new text.

J. Rulewski says, among other things, that he has the impression that currently it is 1917 and Lenin is urging establishment of the Workers' Councils and seizure of power. He considers the speeches by Celiński and Kuroń to be against the Union's interest. Kuroń wants to curtail Solidarity's activities. A Soviet invasion, in Rulewski's opinion, will not happen in Poland. The USSR, if it is forced to, would rather turn off our taps. Self-governments, he continues, will guarantee the sovereignty of enterprises, but there will be no sovereignty for the country if changes are not made in the Sejm. When talking to the Network as chairman of the NCC working group for economic reform, he agreed that the Founding Committees of self-governments would be created. However, one should remember that for economic reasons self-government will have to lay off workers. This may lead to conflicts within the Union. One cannot create self-government without having determined the shape of the entire reform. Lately, the Union has taken advantage of its advisers' voices too infrequently. If we keep settling economic issues by way of voting at public rallies, then, Rulewski says, "I will emigrate from this country." He emphasizes that, according to Balcerowicz's idea of reform, self-government is in sixth place; in first place they put political conditions, foreign trade, etc. First of all, reform of the Sejm, the National Councils, and so on is needed. The idea of self-government is, in Rulewski's opinion, a mixture of Western democracy and Eastern ideology. And mixtures are dangerous because they are explosive. The idea of self-government was given to the Union not by the Network but by *Trybuna Ludu* which used to announce theses and provoke discussion—within Solidarity, too.

There are doubts about the term "trade union," Rulewski continues. Solidarity is not a trade union but an opposition social movement. He accuses Wałęsa of publicly stating different theories on television. This causes confusion. At the moment it is not clear whether Solidarity can go on strike over censorship issues because its status is unknown. It should be defined, and theses on strategy and programs should be formulated. The Union should set guidelines for reform, but it is too early to take over economic power. For that reason he suggested the Founding Committees of self-governments in order to prepare to take over power, and during that time to elaborate the main directions for reform.

A. Sobieraj (Radom) supports Pałka's speech and demands the establishment of a self-government or commission to prepare its introduction.

J. Kropiwnicki (Łódź) is wondering whether it is more important for the government to make a mess of Solidarity or to improve the economy. If we assume the latter, then we should decide under what conditions the Union wants to negotiate with the government. Solidarity has the advantage: it is the sole credible social institution and only this institution can tell society that there really is shortage of food (if that is the case) and also convince society of the need for a price increase, which has caused trouble for several governments in this country. Currently there are three ideas for compensating for a price increase and the Union has not taken a stance on any of them. It is obvious that 100 percent compensation does not make any sense. Kropiwnicki stands in favor of compensation that would offset an increase in income (not payments) for those with the lowest salaries. It should be taken into account that those who work hardest will object to it. But a good system of compensation is not enough in exchange for a price increase; Kropiwnicki believes that we should win more.

Economic reform is a good bargaining tool. Society will have to tighten its belt [while] the Union has to explain what the future gains will be. But in exchange for that, guarantees for Solidarity's participation (with a veto right) in social supervision over reform are needed.

According to Kropiwnicki, self-government is the only chance to appoint directors based on qualifications and not on political loyalty. We should support the Network's initiative and start to propagate materials instructing people on how to establish self-government. We should also overcome resistance among employees to assuming responsibility for the enterprise.

Kropiwnicki also says that he has seen the program of the Polish Labor Party distributed within the Network and signed by J. Milewski. He has also heard that it [the party] will be built with the support of the Network. Because the Network is asking for the right to represent the Union, he turns to Milewski for a response.

J. Milewski states that this is the author's text and it should not be linked with the Network. He adds that the political vacuum existing in Poland should be filled; the question is when.

After the lunch break, *K. Modzelewski* takes the floor. He says that Rulewski's opinion that the issues of self-government and reform can be settled only after full state and national sovereignty is attained is an ideal for all Poles. It is easy, says Modzelewski, to skin a polar bear, but only when the bear is dead. Meanwhile, Rulewski cannot point out what kind of rifle should be used to shoot the bear—how that ideal can be realized.

The comparison used by Bujak, continues Modzelewski, requires minor correction. When the ship is sinking the sailors are usually not inclined to establish a trade union. Moreover, we have a paralyzed and mute captain on our ship, but any attempt to throw him overboard would result in an attack by bombers flying over the ship. In this situation the sailors have to save the ship anyway. So far the assumption has been that Solidarity is not taking joint responsibility for bringing the country out of the crisis, believing it to be the government's responsibility. In other words, we do nothing while "the ship is sinking and the larders get flooded." This has to change, otherwise people will start throwing stones at us. The Union should adopt a program for overcoming the crisis through self-government, which does not mean it assumes responsibility for directly governing, including through self-government. Solidarity is indeed an opposition socio-political movement that emerged as a trade union and it must remain as such. It would be impossible if it assumed the role of administrator of an enterprise or the country. Therefore self-government has to be independent of the Union. We should avoid Yugoslavia's mistakes which are the argument propaganda uses against the Network. Propaganda speaks about social injustice, [i.e.] that the employees of small and weak institutes will be wronged. The Yugoslav system, in spite of its many merits, has led to situations like that. However, Modzelewski thinks that a strong trade union like Solidarity will be able to promote principles that will alleviate the negative consequences of a self-government system.

The NCC's resolution on self-government's reform is necessary, and should consist of reform of the economy and industrial and regional self-government. This is the key issue. We have to say clearly that Solidarity can afford a conflict in defense of self-government. So far, secondary conflicts have been imposed on the Union. This is also a threat right now—against the background of laundry detergents or cigarettes. We must somehow show the people that market shortages are a result of the functioning of the whole economic and political system, and that the developing self-government movement is a solution for overcoming that situation.

Modzelewski agrees with Krupiński that Solidarity's weapon is that the authorities need it for the announcement of a price increase. Only Solidarity will be able to appease protests against the increases. Receiving only financial compensation in exchange would just prolong the crisis. Modzelewski demands that Solidarity, in exchange for appealing to the Union masses to accept measures that will decrease living standards (a price increase, layoffs), will get: a timetable for reform, a guarantee of social supervision over it and acceptance of the self-government system, and access to the mass media, at least according to the terms and conditions of the January 30 agreement of this year. The same arguments that were used against Yugoslavia when Tito was the "watchdog" are being put forward against the Network [i.e.] that self-governments mean anarcho-syndicalism, collective ownership, etc. The desire to maintain the nomenklatura is being concealed here; that is, the privilege of the party apparatus to fill positions with their own people. The nomenklatura is against professionalism, it precludes reform. It also has to be explained to society that the post-August crisis is a result not only of mistakes by the group ruling in the 1970s, but particularly a result of the central and peremptory system of control over the economy. In the face of threats, when the fate of the Union and the country lie in the balance, we have to decide even before the National Congress how to fix the decision-making system of the Union. At present, in Modzelewski's opinion, no entity exists with a mandate from the Union's members that could continuously make decisions. The Union must consolidate. For that reason, an entity should be established that would operate continuously in Gdańsk until the Congress.

J. Onyszkiewicz thinks that pressure should be exerted on the Sejm. However, one should decide what to do if it proves ineffective, since there is no mechanism for dismissing members of parliament. Power within the party is vague; many accidental [sic] people reach the CC. The government's role has begun to increase. One result will be that the authorities, although still having no one to get their message across to, will respond more quickly and exploit delayed reactions by the Union on different matters. Therefore, Solidarity also currently needs effective executive power.

B. Lis is of the opinion that on the issue of creating self-government one should apply any available means of pressure. However, one should think over the tactics of applying pressure. In Lis's opinion, an active strike, as suggested by Łódź, would result in the introduction of a state of emergency because in practice this means the seizure of power. We should elaborate long-term tactics, which would be based on pressure but also on an attempt to reach agreement with the authorities. Besides negotiations we could, for example, invite members of parliament from the Sejm commission dealing with self-government to the next NCC meeting. In addition, the propaganda for self-government which is being put out by the Union's press should be better organized, because so far every region "writes whatever it wants." That propaganda is supposed to prepare society for the struggle for self-government. Lis emphasizes that before self-government is created, guarantees for laid-off workers should be obtained because self-government will have to make reductions [in force]. It should also be defined who is responsible for an enterprise's bankruptcy—the director or the self-government.

Lis gave a positive answer to the question from *Rulewski* whether employees of an enterprise can strike against a self-government they have elected.

Szeglowski (Słupsk) demands the immediate establishment of self-government Founding Committees because, in his opinion, they will free the Union from the burden of issues which they should not deal with. He also emphasizes the necessity of obtaining access to the mass media.

K. Sobierajska (Legnica, Lower Silesia) believes that the Union's task in creating self-government is to provide support to the Founding Committees.

Z. Bujak declares that one has to have a high opinion of our authorities to believe that they are able to disorganize anything on purpose. The executive mechanisms of the authorities—information, decision making, and organizational monopoly—which were undermined in August, were shattered in the Bydgoszcz conflict. Therefore the authorities, who have no control over anything, cannot intentionally destroy anything. One should realize what the NCC can give to the country and what it cannot. It can convey authentic public feelings and expectations to the government; it can also set guidelines for solving individual problems such as: economic reform through self-government, the reform of social life through democratic elections for national councils, or directions for improving the […] housing situation. On the other hand, the National Commission cannot afford to create mechanisms for accomplishing these goals. Therefore a vacuum appears after their definition. The lack of an executive mechanism prevents the Union from implementing the settlements on access to the mass media; law-abiding behavior, independent cooperatives and national councils are not being established. Nevertheless, the Union should not try to create such mechanisms because then it would be imitating the party; one could compare it to ignorant Bolsheviks who in 1917 tried to create completely new structures having no idea about economic mechanisms. He is against affiliating Solidarity with any social initiatives such as the Network. Self-governments must operate alongside the Union. In the future, self-government will probably be the Unions' opponent in talks concerning the program of an enterprise, etc. Solidarity's task will be to work out a position in the confrontation with self-government.

Bujak is in favor of the well-tried method that has been consistently used by KOR since 1976. The method assumes presenting the authorities with accomplished facts, which have to be be accepted. KOR did not seek registration—it simply emerged; Solidarity was first created, then it fought for registration. Self-government should also be established first, not start with the struggle over a law.

Śliwiński (Szczecin) asks what will happen if self-government proves to be a failure and demands that the whole Union not be involved in the issue but that action originating from the lower ranks be taken, with Union support.

Waszkiewicz notes that self-governmental reform will require the elimination of unions. The army of several hundred thousand workers at these institutions will resist this reform at any cost.

328

A. Wielowieyski (CSPS) believes that Solidarity is a trade union, however, a very special one, because it operates in a country ruled by communists. It fights for the fulfillment of general social demands, and in the West political parties deal with that issue. Therefore, as a result, Solidarity is an opponent of the authorities. It does not aim to fight with the authorities, but by exercising pressure it tries to solve issues important to the whole of society. It may happen that on this ship—perhaps not a sinking one but one that is tossed by the storm—we will have to let someone else take the helm because the helmsman sometimes lets it slip from his hands. He thinks Rulewski's accusations toward Wałęsa are nonsensical. The sequence of the Union's tasks should be the opposite of what Rulewski suggested, i.e. self-government and the national councils first. However, Solidarity should not be directly involved in administration.

Self-governments, in Wielowieyski's opinion, have a very difficult task. Under the system of central planning they will be faced with many obstacles. We should not delude ourselves with the hope that self-governments will take care of the entire reform for us, and that their activities will bring immediate results. Even in small enterprises self-governments will be challenged with basic problems. We should not forget about other elements of economic reform. Wielowieyski believes that the NCC's declaration on self-governments should not be in the form of a loud proclamation, about which so much has been said. Issuing such proclamations is a symptom of a declarative mania for writing. They usually do not contain anything new. We are threatened by the devaluation of documents issued by the NCC. Making reference to the clubs for self-governmental initiatives, mentioned by Kuroń, Wielowieyski claims that they are needed to enliven people, but such discussions should be concentrated on the Workers' Universities that are already operating, which will strengthen the Union. People of different beliefs should participate in them. Kuroń's initiative, originating from one circle, may, according to Wielowieyski, lead to the dissolution of the Union.

L. Wałęsa says that for the first time he sees the real National Commission and that he is satisfied with it. He believes that shorthand notes of the debates should be published (except for yesterday's discussion on the issue of printing) in order to restore the NCC's authority among the Union members.

[…]

[Source: Tygodnik Solidarność, *No. 19, August 7, 1981, (special insert, pp. 1–16).*
Translated by Aleksandra Niemirycz.]

Document No. 58: Record of Brezhnev–Honecker Meeting in the Crimea

August 3, 1981

In the wake of the troublesome Ninth PUWP Congress, Brezhnev and his Kremlin colleagues felt a certain amount of relief that the "rightist forces" did not make more dramatic inroads into the Polish party hierarchy. The loss of some hard-liners such as Tadeusz Grabski was substantially offset by other changes in the top ranks of the PUWP. Still, there was major cause for concern in the socialist camp, as this conversation with the GDR's Erich Honecker makes abundantly clear. Brezhnev tries to put a positive spin on developments but generally agrees with Honecker's conclusions that the party emerged considerably weaker from the congress. It is possible that Brezhnev and Gromyko were simply mollifying Honecker, who always felt the most threatened by the Polish events, but whether or not that was the case it is notable how much more attentive of their allies the Soviets had become by the late Brezhnev period as compared with earlier phases in their relationships.

[…]

Cde. L. I. Brezhnev: […] A gigantic concern for all of us is of course the situation in Poland. Recently we have discussed Polish affairs with you and Comrade Husák in detail. We have every reason to say: the CPSU and the SED carry through a unified line in the interest of overcoming the Polish crisis and in the interest of the stabilization of the situation in this country. That also applies to the extraordinary Ninth party meeting of the PUWP. The work with the Poles in connection with the party meeting was not useless. By carrying out an entire system of measures—started by my telephone conversations with Kania and Jaruzelski, the dispatch of party delegations to the bases, to the direct appeal of the CPSU CC to the PUWP CC, we could hold the Polish leadership to not letting themselves be used by the revisionists. We have saved the centrists from a further slide to the right. The most important is, however, that the real communists have regained self-confidence, that they have seen that they can rely on us fully. The party meeting has of course not brought a radical change for the better in the situation of the party and the country. But that was not to be expected. The crisis in Poland has shaken society deeply. The people are confused, a considerable part has come under the influence of demagogues and crybabies from Solidarity's counter-revolutionary wing.

At the same time there is reason to conclude: the rightists have not succeeded in forcing the party onto a social-democratic road, to seize the leadership. The party meeting confirmed what could already be seen at the Eleventh Plenum of the PUWP CC: the majority of the party supports Kania and Jaruzelski; for them there is no alternative right now. Their position was strengthened, which makes it possible to act bolder and more decisively.

I have given you the record of my telephone conversation with Kania from after the party meeting.[32] I recently sent him a telegram in which I posed sharp questions to him: about the scandalous spread of anti-Sovietism; about the demand of Solidarity to introduce group ownership in the socialist plants; about the danger of the creation of a new mass party—a so-called party of labor etc. Apparently overcoming the crisis in Poland will require long term efforts. We all will need to exert influence on the Polish leadership, to urge upon them consistent, offensive action against the forces of anarchy and counter-revolution.

We receive information that the situation is not improving. For example, "hunger marches" are being held with participation of women and children. I think that I will have a very frank conversation here on the Crimea with Kania and Jaruzelski. I plan to ask them, how should Poland develop? As a socialist country—that is one matter, on a social-democratic road—that is another matter. In my telegram to Kania I have also pointed to these questions.

The composition of the new Politburo of the PUWP CC is not definitively clear. But there are people there one can rely on. Also, Erich, let us work patiently and steadfastly in the direction of securing a necessary change in the situation. Diverging from the prepared text I would like to say that the Poles will ask for economic assistance, for credits and food supplies. Of course they will also report on their party meeting. One has to understand that our own economic situation is very strained, we are very squeezed by the problems. In our leadership we have a group—Comrades Suslov, Andropov, Gromyko, Ustinov, Arkhipov, Rusakov belong to it—that concerns itself with the situation in Poland every day. Possibly we will give the Poles some help—depending on what they will have to show for themselves, what will become clear during the talks.

The events in Poland clarify a lot. What in the past could only be foreseen has now been confirmed by hard and bitter experience [...]

Cde. E. Honecker: [...] We both agree that the Polish events aid the confrontation course of the U.S. This was also confirmed by the recent debate in the U.S. House of Representatives. In regard to the developments in Poland a steady coordination between us is especially important.

Our Politburo has recently received the report of the SED delegation which, led by Comrade Felfe, participated in the PUWP's Ninth party meeting. We came to the conclusion that this party meeting reflected the complicated situation that exists these days in the PUWP and the PPR. In our view it became very clear, that the Marxist–Leninist forces within the PUWP are in the minority and that they were incapable of preventing a further slide to the right. Apparently the healthy forces are still too weak politically and ideologically as well as organizationally to produce a change for the better. The rightist forces were able to influ-

[32] See Document No. 56.

ence considerably the political statements and the elections for the central party organs in a revisionist way.

Cde. L. I. Brezhnev: That is correct.

Cde. E. Honecker: Through the letter of the Central Committee of the CPSU and the attitude of a number of brother parties from socialist countries the worst was prevented. In this sense—and here I agree with you—our common attitude has led to definite results. But the party meeting has not discussed or decided upon concrete solutions through which Poland would be led out of its political and economic misery and the advancing counter-revolution would be smashed.

Cde. L. I. Brezhnev: Right.

Cde. E. Honecker: Our delegation returned with the impression that the PUWP is a torn party, incapable of fighting and increasingly losing its Marxist–Leninist nature. As the analysis shows, the rightist forces have expanded their positions in the Central Committee, Politburo, and Secretariat of the Central Committee. More than 40 percent of the members and candidates of the Central Committee belong to Solidarity, three are members of KOR. Things go so far that an adviser of KOR (H. Kubiak) even joined the Politburo and became a Secretary of the Central Committee.

The counter-revolution led by Solidarity undertakes activities for the undermining, destruction, and take-over of the power of the state on a daily basis, thereby exploiting the economic difficulties. This includes also the "hunger marches" (with the participation of 10,000 women and children) that they have carried out recently under slogans hostile to socialism in Kutno, Łódź, and other places. Our citizens could watch all this on Western television.

The chance at the party meeting to single out Solidarity as the real culprits for Poland's economic misery was not made use of. Instead, only the members of the old leadership were held responsible for this. With this the capitulationist course was justified and continued. The new retreat in the case of the strike threat of LOT [Polish Airlines] is also evidence of this.

Now the enemy tries to stir up the general dissatisfaction and achieve through pressure further division of power, early elections for the Sejm, and the strengthening of capitalist structures. The party meeting produced neither a clear short-term nor a long-term program. The revisionist forces often talk about the new Polish socialism model that should radiate internationally. We cannot underestimate the possibility that the Polish disease will spread.

Cde. L. I. Brezhnev: That is a correct appraisal.

Cde. A. A. Gromyko: The appraisal is correct and sober.

Cde. E. Honecker: Evidently we must, as you have noted already, live with Kania for a certain period. Perhaps it would be useful to agree how we could integrate Poland more closely with our community. It would be possible to take certain correct statements from the party meeting, for example in Jaruzelski's speech, and use them to strengthen the power of the people, to push back the enemy, and strengthen our alliance.

I submit to you, comrade Leonid Illyich, the proposal that the CPSU, the CPCz, the SED, and eventually other brother parties in close cooperation continue to promote the emergence of a reliable, battle-ready Marxist–Leninist leadership in the PUWP. We will use all our contacts to this end.

Cde. L. I. Brezhnev: When did you, Erich, most recently have contact with Kania?

Cde. E. Honecker: That was still prior to the Polish party meeting. After that I had contacts with other comrades. Comrades of our Politburo were in Poland (i.e. Comrade Naumann in Warsaw). We had intensive contacts with at least 15 voivodes.

Cde. L. I. Brezhnev: Respond to me please, Erich, on a delicate question: Can Kania master the situation? Do you personally have confidence in him?

Cde. E. Honecker: No. I do not have confidence in him. He has disappointed us and never kept to his promises. Only recently in a meeting of the Politburo with the First Voivode Secretaries most of them criticized Kania, because he does not reach for decisive measures.

Cde. L. I. Brezhnev: Was this meeting before the Ninth PUWP party meeting?

Cde. E. Honecker: No, after the party meeting. We know this from Polish comrades. Poland is a matter for our entire movement. It would be good for our socialist community and the repression of opportunism, if we came together in the near future to discuss political and theoretical questions that arise from the development in Poland for the communist world movement, for the convincing propagation of real socialism.

Cde. L. I. Brezhnev: Do you have in mind in this regard a meeting of the First Secretaries of the fraternal parties in the Socialist community?

Cde. E. Honecker: Yes.

[…]

Cde. L. I. Brezhnev: I would like to return once more to the meeting proposed by you, Erich, between the General Secretaries of the fraternal parties of the socialist community regarding Poland. It seems useful to me to return to this question later, that is, after our talks with Kania and Jaruzelski and with consideration to the results of these talks. Let us see how Kania will act after these meetings.

Dear Erich, I would like to express my satisfaction with our talks, with the discussion of important questions of our common work. I hope that this will promote a solution to important questions concerning our cooperation.

[*Source: Bruno Mahlow, Moscow, Aug. 3, 1981, Working Protocol No. 17/81 of the Politburo session of Aug. 18, 1981, SAPMO-BArch ZPA, J IV 2/2/A-2419. Published in: Michael Kubina and Manfred Wilke (eds.), "Hart und kompromißlos durchgreifen:" Die SED contra Polen 1980/81: Geheimakten der SED-Führung über die Unterdrückung der polnischen Demokratiebewegung (Berlin: Akademie Verlag, 1995). Translated by Ruud van Dijk.*]

Document No. 59: PUWP CC Assessment of Public Attitudes toward Solidarity

August 17, 1981

This document records an attempt by the PUWP Central Committee to assess Solidarity's position, forecast the union's actions in the coming weeks, and propose steps to counteract them. It is useful partly as evidence of how the party tended to view the crisis. The description of the current state of affairs is substantially accurate but is typical in its tendency to see things through an ideological prism.

Forecast of anticipated public feelings and conflicts with the NSZZ Solidarity and other politically opposed groups in the course of the next few months, prepared with reference to the situation on August 17, 1981. Conclusions and proposals for counteraction.

I. *Forecast of public feelings.*

Decisive influence on public feelings could be exerted currently by:

1. *The continuously worsening market supply of basic products, especially in large urban agglomerations.*

This is the fundamental cause of decreasing discipline and productivity. To an ever larger extent, welfare determines consciousness and consciousness has a diminishing influence on welfare. All organizations lose out on this: the party, the government, trade unions, Solidarity, and the Church (however, the government loses the most and the Church the least).

The above threatens further anarchy in [social] life, hunger demonstrations, etc. Faced with the present danger in the field of improving market supply, the creation of a state-wide national salvation front is possible. Social control commissions could be a prelude to that (with the participation of not only the trade unions).

2. *The collapse of the current rationing system* and a plan for lowering food rations resulting from that, in the public view, prove the government's ineptitude.

Opposition forces are taking advantage of this to show the authorities' inability to take the country out of the crisis.

Recovering credibility for the government without openly pointing out mistakes and settling accounts with those responsible for this mess and, as can be expected, without specific compromises (e.g. concerning changes of rationing rules in relation to food producers), will be very difficult at this stage.

3. *The government's plan for a price increase.*

Society seems to be prepared for the price increase—this does not guarantee, however, the success of this operation.

334

The increase must be based on the authority of, and trust in, the government, and if that is insufficient, it must be backed up by the trust and authority of other social forces (in practice, that of the party, the Church, and Solidarity.)

However, in the case of the Church and Solidarity, the above has to do with the necessity of reaching political compromises along the "something for something" pattern.

Linking the price increase with the whole series of measures aimed at taking the country out of the crisis is to be considered (the problem of trust and credibility).

4. *Economic reform.*

The waiting period before reform works against it and increases indifference and even distrust among the society. Reform will not succeed if the society is not convinced that it is a correct reform.

Distrust is associated with an expected fall in living standards and expected lay-offs, especially in the administration. The latter issue is particularly burdensome for the administrative authorities whose apparatus is currently paralyzed (this is the main cause of the government's low effectiveness).

5. *Harvest action.*

Currently, this is the most significant social, economic, political and propaganda action in the country. For the authorities, this is a fundamental test of their ability to manage the country. Failures in this field (wasting food, disarray in the area of purchasing food products, etc.) might have incalculable and irreversible social, economic, political and propaganda effects. An awareness of this should be the basis for undertaking extraordinary activities by the party and the government during this time and in the field of food collection activity.

6. *Speculation.*

[This is] a very delicate social problem with economic, social and moral consequences. The government's counteractions meet with public support, also because it constitutes an example of the expected decisiveness of the authorities in the face of a troubling pathology.

The fight with speculation should be extended and become part of the decisive activities of the authorities against crime and incidents of law-breaking.

These activities should be used for building the authorities' reputation.

7. *The forthcoming anniversaries of the outbreak of war* might be an opportunity to provoke anti-Soviet feelings, especially against the background of the so-called Ribbentrop–Molotov Pact, the entry of Soviet forces onto the territories of the old Republic [of Poland] and Katyń. In particular, school, student and academic circles, select combatant, nationalist and opposition (CIP) groups can be susceptible to these feelings.

II. *Forecast concerning the NSZZ Solidarity.*

The dramatically worsening social situation has accelerated the discussion about the strategy and tactics of the union.

As a result of the NCC session on July 26, 1981, as well as that on August 10–12, 1981, a program which will most probably be specified at the forthcoming union congress began to appear. It is a program for the "socio-political opposition movement which emerged as a trade union." (Definition formulated by K. Modzelewski at the NCC on July 24, 1981.)

It [the program] is based on an assumption that "a revolution is underway in Poland." It is in a phase which is being stimulated so as not to affect the Polish *raison d'état* and not to provoke a general confrontation between the authorities and Solidarity.

In the current phase of "stimulated revolution," a political vacuum has emerged as a result of the paralysis of the present power structures which, "being separated from the society are not able to manage the country."

In this situation, Solidarity assumes the responsibility "to fill this vacuum directly (J. Rulewski's concepts) or indirectly" by putting into effect their own version of self-governments, presently at the institute level, then at the regional (national councils) and central level (J. Kuroń's concept).

In an appeal to the members of the union and the whole society on August 12, 1981, the NCC accepted J. Kuroń's concept and stated that Solidarity supports the establishment of self-governments. "The reform should also cover regional self-government, transforming national councils and the Sejm into authentic social representation through democratic elections..."

The view that self-governments can be introduced only by a strong organization prevailed in the discussion. It was decided that Solidarity is sufficiently strong at present to preserve control over self-governments. It was stated in the appeal that "...with the support of self-governments and trade unions, it is necessary to establish institutions which would ensure that working people have an impact on the socio-economic policy of the state." The self-governments would therefore not exercise power individually, but with a leading force in the society, which would in reality be constituted by Solidarity.

The NCC backed the accelerated method of introducing self-governments to the factory with support of the so-called "active strike," based on "continuing production and distribution under the supervision of strike committees," which would constitute the foundation of self-governments (initiative of G. Palka).

The NCC announced a modified version of the "active strike" in its appeal of August 12, 1981, in which it calls for working on eight work-free Saturdays, so as not to give them over to the authorities, "...but to ourselves, and immediately introduce the principle of self-government in this dimension... Founding committees of self-governments or institute commissions are to prepare a detailed report on the production surplus, which will be entirely devoted to filling the most pressing supply shortages... "

The government bears the costs of this political experiment because it should provide employees with "...compensation for working on work-free Saturdays ... as much as for days which by law are considered to be work-free."

The union will use a different method for introducing regional self-government, because this is an operation which exceeds the official and legal competences of a trade union.

336

Most probably J. Kuroń's concept will be favored, which comes down to initiating Clubs of Self-Government Initiatives, which would prepare regional self-government in cadre and organizational terms under the indirect patronage of Solidarity.

J. Kuroń's intention does not indicate that these Clubs could be the foundation for a political party; however, such a suggestion seems natural.

Solidarity's initiatives leading to the establishment of a self-government system in Poland do not relieve the union of exerting pressure on current representative organs.

The participants at the discussion in the NCC recommended in particular:
– the need to appoint those people in the representative organs who show "awareness and good will;"
– the necessity to use working contacts for shaping organizational and cadre changes "so that they are most advantageous for the society;"
– carrying out intensive and organized activities in order to introduce possible changes in the electoral law of the representative organs at all levels and to introduce economic reform.

In the phase of the "stimulated revolution," Solidarity activists do not anticipate the need to transform themselves into a political party and directly assume power. They reserve to themselves the role of a driving and controlling force that stands above the authorities and political parties.

They do not exclude, however, "...the second bloody phase usually caused by hunger demonstrations..." (J. Waszkiewicz).

In this situation, direct assumption of power by the union is expected.

"Just in case, our union must prepare itself for direct actions such as assuming responsibility for food rationing, but especially for controlling the situation..."

It is doubtful that it will do so by name other than its own.

Due to the above, it should be noted that:

1. The union is under strong pressure caused by the current socio-political situation. It favors extremist forces which by taking advantage of public feelings have transformed Solidarity into "a socio-political opposition movement."

We should expect a weakening of Church influence without Wyszyński's authority and a constructive program proposal. Calling for restraint and order can prove insufficient for the youth who dominate Solidarity and increasingly pay attention to KOR's concepts which aim at further politicizing the union.

2. The union undertakes the very difficult initiative of introducing self-government in [work] institutes. This initiative bears the risks of:
– a loss of control over institutes in favor of self-governments, which do not have to identify themselves with the union;
– the formation of internal contradictions within the union, which is dangerous during the course of the congress;
– the necessity of taking patronage over unpopular decisions of the self-governments (e.g. concerning laying off some crews);
– the development of tensions between small and large institutes.

The NCC is aware of these dangers. However, it is not prepared to overcome them; hence, we should avoid the danger of blaming the government for the failures of Solidarity in this domain and aim at urgently passing legislation which would comply with the principles of the socialist system.

3. In the face of Solidarity's self-government action we should expect lower engagement by the union in other actions. If any are undertaken, it will be either under compulsion or in order to turn the attention of the authorities away from Solidarity's main field of activity (e.g. "action milk" or "coal for peasants" which are meant to prove the government's ineptitude).

However, this does not relieve the government from activities aimed at raising social discipline and strengthening the law. Nevertheless, this should, to a larger extent, concern street demonstrations and the illegal distribution of antagonistic political publications.

4. The activities of Solidarity are based on a conviction that the union enjoys total support from society and the government is weak and incapable of taking action. As a matter of fact, the union still enjoys public support (especially after the appeal on August 12, 1981), but it is already lower and has strings attached.

This could be the reason for the stumbles—especially in the unpopular activities which the union cannot avoid at this stage.

The activity and efficiency of the government which would secure the so-called "political vacuum" is the most serious danger for the union. There are increasingly favorable circumstances for that. The NCC expects that just as the union, the government will begin to act on the basis of accomplished facts; however, it is not prepared to avoid such danger: " … during this period, the government may undertake pushing forward certain solutions. We can block them, we can protest, but if we do not have a real instrument to pressure the government, after a series of short-term conflicts, we will have to accept the government's solutions…" (from the discussion at the NCC, July 24–26, 1981).

5. It must be stated that the line for political resolution of the crisis, accepted at the PUWP Ninth Congress, is beginning to have its initial effects, which are strengthening the party and the government.

These facts, which Solidarity makes [others] aware of, might push union activists to extreme actions. We need to take them into account and be prepared for them.

We should not expect a general confrontation with the union before its congress. However, later on it may be unavoidable, especially against the background of self-governing and more precisely against the background of self-governments' political control.

III. *Forecast concerning politically hostile groupings associated with Solidarity.*
   The Solidarity social movement constitutes a base for many political movements.
   1. *Political groups (KOR, CIP and IUS) associated with Solidarity.*
   – KOR functions within the union and is gaining increasing support from NCC activists.

KOR, extreme in its purposes, proposes more moderate methods of action than the pragmatic supporters of J. Rulewski who suggest directly taking over power.

This supposed moderation of J. Kuroń and K. Modzelewski allows them to gain large support within the NCC.

Thanks to that support, they have succeeded in diverting the current course of the union to [forms of] self-governing.

KOR activists do not support transformation of the union into a political party because they realize that this could lead to the dissolution of the movement and a weakening of KOR's influence on society. They intend to manage the whole union while being its only "political club."

- The CIP in the above-mentioned meaning is KOR's competitor when it comes to the struggle for influence in the union.

In practice, CIP's significance is minimal and no radical increase in the influence of that group on the union should be expected. Solidarity, aware of the dangers associated with the CIP, will not cut itself off, however, from the line of support for the politically repressed which is being promoted by KOR.

The union, however, will not risk confrontation with the authorities against this background (the withdrawal of support for the "radial march" by the NCC is an example of that).

This does not mean, however, a lack of "moral" or perhaps also financial support for the CIP.

- The Independent Union of Students—in practice and in moral terms—takes advantage of the union's support and of its extreme forces in particular.

Most likely because of that the IUS is increasingly taking political stands.

On the other hand, attention ought to be drawn to the fact that the NCC has inconsiderable possibilities for interfering in IUS matters. It results from the fact that the IUS enjoys the hidden support of some IFC's, even against the will of the NCC. An example of that is maintaining the "radial march" (suspended after the appeal of Archbishop Glemp) against the position of the NCC.

Due to the September anniversaries, a significant revival of the IUS should be anticipated, especially spurring anti-Soviet feelings, distribution of anti-state publications, and organization of street demonstrations, marches, etc.

Due to the above, there could emerge a necessity to suspend the activity of the IUS and a need to deal with extremist student elements within the framework of the university and the NTiSW Ministry authority.

At the moment, an attack at the weakest link of the opposition carries a series of far-reaching consequences which in the long-term could prove beneficial for the authorities.

2. Certain political groupings are forming in the union itself, independently of the movements associated with Solidarity.

This is not yet a mass occurrence but it is more and more probable. Difficulties in the implementation of self-government can generate and accelerate political orientations in the union.

On the basis of:

– Workers' Solidarity—the socio-democratic movement is most clear.
– Farmers' Solidarity—Christian democracy.
– Tradesmen's Solidarity—liberal-democratic movements.

With this in mind, attempts to create the Polish Labor Party (the so-called secret bomb for the PUWP), the Democratic Party and Peasants' Party should be expected.

These attempts are not yet officially supported by the leadership of Solidarity, but members of the leadership are among the initiators of these parties. For example, Jerzy Milewski, a member of the NCC, is an initiator of the PLP [Polish Labor Party].

There is the possibility that political parties will emerge based, for example, on PAX[33] or on centrifugal movements in the PUWP after the Ninth Party Congress, rather than on the union.

The emergence of political pluralism would be supported by Solidarity if it did not take place at the expense of its unity. Given that such a threat cannot be ruled out, there is a centralizing tendency in the NCC. The idea of self-government supported by the union does not exclude, but even presupposes, the existence of many political parties.

Therefore, it ought to be presumed that in the future the union will return to this concept, even if only to weaken the "domination of the PUWP."

The above-mentioned analysis does not take into account the international aspects of this problem.

Conclusions:

1. With the worsening market situation, the possibility increases of uncontrolled social movements that would weaken the position of all the forces in the state.

This could incline all significant organizations to cooperate so as not to allow a further deepening of the crisis.

The National salvation front with the participation of Solidarity and the Church may be organized for the purpose of such cooperation.

In the future, it could be transformed into a reformed FNU (this is significant for the forthcoming elections for national councils and the Sejm.)

2. In the current socio-political situation, a general confrontation with Solidarity (the socio-political opposition movement) should not be expected.

This does not exclude, however, the possibility of conflicts on a smaller scale and a general conflict with other unions, e.g. CIP, IUS.

3. In a more distant perspective it seems impossible to avoid confrontation with extreme elements of the NSZZ Solidarity.

---

[33] "Pax" was originally a Catholic, pro-regime political society. Beginning in 1947 it was headed by Bolesław Piasecki who, before the war, was the leader of an extreme nationalist party. In 1979, Ryszard Reiff took over the society, and adopted a pro-Solidarity position (for example, voting against martial law in the Council of State).

Cooperation with the union, which is currently necessary, should take place under conditions of strengthening the party and government according to the principles determined by the tone of discussion at the Eleventh Plenum of the PUWP CC.

4. The fundamental strength of the authorities lies in their legal and unquestioned character. In connection with the above, the authorities should concentrate on their strengthening and the use of the instruments of law.

5. The demonstrated resoluteness of the government is conducive to the strengthening of order. It should be backed up by effective action—above all, this requires conclusion of the reform of the central administration.

6. The action of collecting and storing foodstuffs must be an organizational success for the party and government.

7. In case of the formation of political parties, the principle of warning their initiators of a violation of Art. 84, point 3 of the PPR's Constitution should be adopted (the CIP sent program declarations to the authorities and understood their silence as consent for action).

Socio-Vocational Department
PUWP CC

Warsaw, August 18, 1981.

[Source: AAN, PUWP CC, 2258, pp. 95–107. Translated by Paweł Świeboda.]

Document No. 60: Information on Brezhnev Meeting with Kania and Jaruzelski on August 14, 1981

August 22, 1981

After the PUWP's Extraordinary Ninth Congress in July, the Kremlin held out slim hopes once more that Kania and Jaruzelski would take advantage of their political momentum and move firmly against Solidarity and its allies. One month later, a clearly incensed Brezhnev berates the two Poles for their "complacency" and warns them that it may already be "too late" to save socialism in Poland. In blunt language, he calls for "extreme" actions to suit the circumstances, and proceeds to lay out a series of specific examples, even as he insists that the ultimate decision on what to do is up to the Poles themselves.

[...]

On August 14, 1981, a meeting took place in the Crimea between CPSU CC General Secretary and Chairman of the USSR Supreme Soviet Cde. L. I. Brezhnev, First Secretary of the PUWP CC S. Kania, and PUWP CC Politburo member and Chairman of the PPR Council of Ministers W. Jaruzelski. Cdes. A. A. Gromyko, K. U. Chernenko and K. V. Rusakov took part in the discussion.

The CPSU CC attached great significance to this meeting with the Polish leadership.

At the beginning of the discussion Cde. L. I. Brezhnev expressed serious apprehension about where Poland was going. We had hopes, he said to Cdes. S. Kania and W. Jaruzelski, that after the Congress a certain change in the course of events would be detected. In fact, the situation continues to get worse and the counter-revolution is intensifying its pressure.

All the steps the CPSU and the Soviet Union have taken in the course of the Polish crisis have been dictated solely by a concern for the interests of socialist Poland. Cde. L. I. Brezhnev proposed with complete frankness, as befits communists, to speak a little about Polish matters.

Cdes. Kania and Jaruzelski recounted in some detail the situation in the country and in the party. They acknowledged the validity of the feeling of alarm over the fate of socialism in Poland that the leaders of the CPSU and other fraternal parties are experiencing.

The Polish comrades underscored the positive influence of the PUWP Extraordinary Ninth Congress, after which, in their words, "the party was able to act more decisively." The PUWP leadership calls the new composition of the CC manageable. "Currently, a process of consolidation of the PUWP is underway... An example of this is the Second Plenum of the party CC, where the speeches were notable for their high standard, their principled character, and their sense of confidence," remarked Cde. S. Kania.

Regarding the PUWP's struggle to find a way out of the crisis, Cde. S. Kania stated in particular: "Today, no one will say any longer that the party does not see the path toward overcoming the crisis. The PUWP has a program and today it has the initiative."

Cdes. S. Kania and W. Jaruzelski attempted to show that the line they have adopted fully responds to the peculiarities of the Polish conditions and provides a basis to talk about the first successes on the path toward political stabilization. As proof that there is a turning point in the situation, they cited the work of the PUWP CC Second Plenum, the agreement with Solidarity at LOT Airlines, the avoidance of street disturbances in Warsaw, and other facts.

The Polish leaders guaranteed that all direct speeches against the people's authority would be dealt an impressive blow. However, their statements evidently do not presuppose a decisive and direct confrontation with their political adversaries or with the counter-revolution at the present time. Cde. S. Kania said: "We aim at all times to use the most decisive measures against the counter-revolution. However, that will be possible only under conditions that guarantee the support of the population."

Cde. S. Kania noted with satisfaction the situation within the organs of state security and the army, which, "despite difficulties, are in a very good state."

Speaking about Solidarity, Cde. S. Kania said that "society and the working class are beginning to turn away from Solidarity, and its leaders do not want it to be perceived as a destructive force."

Solidarity called for a period of no strikes for two months, and for working on eight free Saturdays." It is well-known, however, that Solidarity intends to distribute the work product from those Saturdays through its own channels.

Having spoken about the difficult situation among the mass media, Cdes. S. Kania and W. Jaruzelski talked about a series of organizational measures and cadre changes that have been carried out in order to improve the situation with the press. By the way, it is well-known that up till now only the newspaper *Żołnierz Wolności* has taken a firm position, and even *Trybuna Ludu* permits ideological vacillations.

Cdes. S. Kania and W. Jaruzelski gave special emphasis to Poland's difficult economic situation. In their understanding, this is precisely where the fundamental reason may be found for the prolonged political crisis.

They acknowledged that the difficulties in the economy are related above all to the debt with the West and the destructive activities of extremists from Solidarity. "Poland's foreign debt," said S. Kania, "is spreading like an avalanche... The capital is not giving us any gifts. We are granted credits at very high interest—up to 20 percent."

Cde. L. I. Brezhnev thoroughly and with a wide-ranging use of facts, demonstrated the growing danger of the situation in Poland. He focused the attention of the Polish leaders on the danger to the socialist achievements of the Polish people. Meetings with the leaders of a series of fraternal parties in the Crimea confirmed that we are all alarmed at where Poland is heading. The ranks of the party have become thinner. Its leading role has been roundly undermined. Solidarity runs most of the major enterprises and raises insolent political demands. Anti-socialist forces have become even more aggressive and are preparing an assault on the position of the PUWP.

The economy is suffocating under the weight of the debt. In place of an efficient production rhythm, delays, meetings and strikes are taking place. As a consequence of all this, workers' living standards are going downhill. The collapse of worker discipline, the absence of a clear economic concept, and the disorganization of the economic life of the country by Solidarity are sinking the economy.

In the ideological sphere, the enemies of socialism act with impunity and spread slander against the PUWP, the people's state, and socialism.

With regard to information, which the Polish leaders addressed during the discussion, Cde. L. I. Brezhnev in a sharp and precise fashion, dwelled at length on the political meaning of recent events in Poland. In particular he stressed that the danger which threatens Poland is a danger from the right. Loyal communists and Marxist–Leninists who are currently not involved in party work are an important reserve for the party and must be defended. Attention to this matter, Cde. L. I. Brezhnev underscored, under current conditions is a criterion of party spirit.

On the whole, he said, however the results of the Ninth Congress are assessed, one thing is clear: it did not by itself bring about radical changes in the course of events. The adversary not only maintained the initiative for himself but is intensifying his blows, while the party and the people's authority continue to retreat.

It is impossible to stop the enemy without a struggle. Enough of concessions, we have nowhere to retreat any longer. But at the same time one must say as loudly as possible to all the people that the main cause of today's troubles in Poland is the criminal activity of the ring leaders of Solidarity. Why not say directly that they specifically bear responsibility for the current difficult situation with food supplies?

There is no sense, said Cde. L. I. Brezhnev, that the Polish comrades are prepared for confrontation. It is always described as nothing but "bloody," and it is declared that it must be avoided at all costs. We are actually talking about a political confrontation, which is already going on. It is already being imposed by the adversary. Why, as far as bloody confrontation is concerned, one may well occur if one does not go all the way in a political confrontation to the full restoration of the leading role of the PUWP.

Events are already spilling out into the streets. It could easily be the case that under these circumstances blood will flow no matter what. And it might be even worse than if you took preventive measures, measures for administrative order—sufficiently harsh [ones]. It has never happened that a revolution defeated a counter-revolution without a fight, without employment of force.

No one is opposed to acting reasonably. But the anti-socialist forces are not about to answer in kind. All signs indicate that they are developing a new frontal assault on the party and on socialism. That is why hopes for defending socialism through persuasion without using all the possibilities of power are illusory. Sooner or later, communists must engage in a direct skirmish with the enemy.

We are afraid it may be too late, however: you know, the class enemy is now trying to penetrate the army and the security organs to deprive you of your last means of support. To put off confrontation is to play into the enemy's hands and give him the chance to strengthen his position even further. Now, after the congress, the time is more or less favorable for you, but you know it may not last long.

The insidious scheme of the anti-socialist forces has taken shape with sufficient clarity. With the aid of strikes and threats on their part, these forces are holding the party and the government in a state of constant tension in order not to allow the possibility of stabilizing the situation. At the same time, they are shifting the main emphasis to the demand for workers' self-management, infusing it with some kind of anarchist-trade unionist meaning, up to and including the concept of "group ownership" of enterprises and the means of production.

To yield here would mean to destroy the economic foundation of socialism. In fact the issue is "self-government," which could eventually lead to a variation on a genuinely capitalist path [of development]. But in parallel, it is undermining the political system. They are demanding that elections be expedited for the Sejm and national councils, and they threaten to create a so-called labor party.

Now, as we understand it, noted Cde. L. I. Brezhnev, there is still the possibility of mobilizing all adherents to socialism and deliver a blow to the counter-revolution. But to do that, one must put an end to complacency. The Polish comrades themselves have stressed more than once in various speeches that the situation has become extreme. So this means that the measures being taken should correspond to the circumstances, which is to say—extreme.

Cde. L. I. Brezhnev underlined the thought that, shifting to decisive actions, the Polish friends have a firm basis for counting on the rather broad support of the population which has been tired of anarchy and chaos and is afraid that Solidarity might place the country before a national catastrophe.

During the discussion, other considerations were also expressed as to how to take control of the situation in the country, including concerning active work with trade associations, influencing public opinion in the country, necessary economic measures, suitable work in connection with holding the Solidarity congress, and so on.

Speaking of the situation with the economy, Cde. L. I. Brezhnev expressed the conviction that the crisis in Poland is above all of a political nature, and that the key to stabilizing conditions in the economy is [to be found] precisely in politics and in the struggle with the opponents of socialism. Will you be able, he said, to reestablish your position in political life, return the mass media to your own control, confirm the authority of the regime—gradually these improvements will appear in other spheres as well. Soviet–Polish relations, stressed Cde. L. I. Brezhnev, depend on the further course of events in the PPR. Will Poland be socialist and will there be internationalist relations? Will [Poland] follow another path? Will the character of relations change, along state, political and economic lines? It is important that not only political figures understand this well, but the general Polish public as well. In addition, we proceed of course from the assumption that Polish communists will go to any lengths to prevent the class enemy from placing the country in the capitalist camp.

In connection with the discussion of possible measures to take in the upcoming period, Cde. L. I. Brezhnev said: "What exactly should be done in the nearest term? Of course, the Polish leadership must decide." But we are convinced: the time has come to go boldly into battle. For that one must rouse the whole party, uniting them on a Marxist–Leninist foundation. Among other concrete steps, Cde. L. I. Brezhnev identified drastic measures against the instigators of street demonstrations and unrest, a campaign aimed at making every Pole aware that it was not the mistakes of the PUWP but the subversive work of Solidarity and the ringleaders of the counter-revolution, and the strikes, that are the main cause pushing the country toward chaos, ruin and starvation. Apparently, it is necessary to reject categorically the demand to transfer enterprises to the ownership of individual collectives; not to allow the creation of new parties under any circumstances; not to enter into early elections for the Sejm; and to conclude the legal proceedings against [Konstantin] Moczulski with a conviction for his hostile actions.

That is the minimum that is dictated by today's circumstance. The necessary measures to take on a wider scale have been talked about more than once. All of these, undoubtedly, retain their urgency.

Cde. L. I. Brezhnev directed the special attention of the Polish leaders on the fact that imperialist reaction, together with Peking, are attempting to turn the PPR into a source of additional tensions in the international environment. In addition, they are gambling on the threat of Soviet interference and pretending to be the champions of Polish independence. One must counteract these lines and clarify for the Polish people that the real danger to its national existence comes from imperialism—our common enemy. In particular, it is necessary for each Pole to understand that the credits extended by Western banks and governments are by no means a gift but a commercial transaction for which it is necessary to pay enormous interest. For Poland this is bondage.

During the discussion, bilateral economic relations between the USSR and the PPR were touched upon. Proceeding from the difficult situation in Poland in the economic sphere, Cde. L. I. Brezhnev informed the Polish leaders that the CPSU CC and the government of the USSR had made the decision to carry over the repayment of Polish debts to the Soviet Union from all earlier extensions of credit to the following five-year plan. [The USSR will also] supply the PPR with additional raw materials for light industry as well as certain popular consumer goods and promote the fuller utilization of Polish industrial potential.

At the same time, Cde. L. I. Brezhnev reminded that the USSR and other fraternal countries are doing much to help people's Poland get out of this misfortune. From our side, Poland was only recently given aid in the amount of about 4 billion dollars. However, unfortunately the situation in the PPR's national economy continues to worsen. This also has an effect on the fulfillment of the Polish side's obligations toward the Soviet Union and other socialist countries which is painfully felt by sectors of our economy [*khozyaistvennye zven'ya*], especially those working in cooperation with the PPR.

During the discussion, Cde. L. I. Brezhnev stressed with particular force: now, all of us have no greater wish than that socialist Poland will eliminate the threat of counter-revolution more quickly, recover from the disease that has struck it, and return to normal life. I want to hope, declared L. I. Brezhnev, that comrades Kania and Jaruzelski will do everything that is necessary. He expressed the wish that the deeds of the Polish leaders will not be at variance with their words. As far as the Soviet Union, the PUWP's leaders, and communists, will always encounter firm support. And we will be allies and brothers in the future as well.

Comrades S. Kania and W. Jaruzelski thanked the CPSU CC general secretary for his advice, thorough analysis of conditions, and fraternal assistance. The Polish leaders expressed the thought that their course is "the line of agreement but also the line of struggle." "We will do everything," they declared, "to defend socialism in Poland."

Among the concrete issues posed by the Polish leaders was the request to send to Poland a group of workers from USSR Gosplan headed by Cde. Baibakov. Consent was granted for this. The Polish comrades proposed the idea of convening a special session of the CMEA [Council on Mutual Economic Assistance], where measures for joint assistance to Poland might be discussed. They were told that they should address that question to the CMEA.

The CPSU CC Politburo full endorsed the results of Cde. L. I. Brezhnev's discussion with Cdes. S. Kania and W. Jaruzelski. The CPSU, adhering to the policy toward Poland agreed upon with the fraternal parties, is examining this major new political action as a contribution to the common efforts aimed at achieving a breakthrough in the situation in Poland for the benefit of socialism.

[Source: SAPMO-BArch, ZPA, J IV, 2/202–550. Translated by Malcolm Byrne for the National Security Archive.]

Document No. 61: Transcript of CPSU CC Politburo Meeting

September 10, 1981

Two days before this Soviet Politburo meeting, the first Solidarity national congress issued a message of support to workers throughout the socialist bloc, along with a similar communication to Poles around the world proclaiming their status as not just a labor union but a nationwide civic movement. Reaction by communist authorities was sharp. Jaruzelski likened the actions of the congress to "a declaration of war." Even Western governments feared the union had gone too far in inciting the powers-that-be. Brezhnev's response, which is almost as harsh as Jaruzelski's, appears below. The general tenor inside the Kremlin is notably angrier than at many earlier sessions, conveying a feeling that events have taken a serious turn for the worse. Brezhnev is loathe even to speak with Kania anymore, while others call for tough action against the "hooligan elements" who are "mocking" Moscow. Ever cautious, the group settles on publishing a series of pointed articles in the press, including orchestrated rebuttals by groups of Soviet workers, and transmitting another letter to the Polish leadership (Document No. 63).

[…]

9. Exchange of views on the Polish question.

Brezhnev: Yesterday I familiarized myself with the "Appeal to the Nations of Eastern Europe,"[34] which the Polish Solidarity congress adopted. It is a dangerous and provocative document. It does not contain many words but they all strike at one point. Its authors wanted to stir up sedition in the socialist countries and rouse up groups of various kinds of apostates.

I think that we cannot limit our criticism in the press about this impudent prank. What if the collectives in our major enterprises—such as, let us say, the Kirov factory, Magnitka, Kamaz and others—delivered a rebuff to these demagogues? A letter from them to the Solidarity congress would probably be hard to keep quiet. The more so since we will set aside a fitting place for it in our mass media.

If the comrades agree, let us instruct the Polish Commission to pick three or four industrial collectives and help them to prepare a skilled rebuke to Solidarity.

Gromyko: The situation in Poland is always getting worse. If one can say so, there is not much left of the authorities. The position of the PUWP CC and the Council of Ministers is diminishing every day. As far as a conversation with Cde. Kania, perhaps we really should not speak with him now since there was a conversation not long ago.

As far as a lever such as a telephone conversation, it should not be excluded for it is not a bad means of applying pressure.

---

[34] Originally, "Appeal to the Working People of Eastern Europe" ["*Ludzie Pracy*"].

Brezhnev: Frankly, there is no wish to speak with Cde. Kania now, it seems to me, and no good will comes from it whatsoever.

Chernenko: There were conversations at one time, good instructions were given, a discussion took place in the Crimea. But what was the use? Cdes. Kania and Jaruzelski are doing things their own way.

Grishin: They themselves do not deny now that they are surrendering position after position.

Zimyanin: I want to tell the Politburo what publications are being planned in connection with the Solidarity congress. One can say that the congress demonstrates the further worsening of conditions in Poland. As is known, they turned to the parliaments and people of several countries including socialist ones with their program of "renewal." Therefore, appropriate articles are being prepared following the line of our press and TASS. The actions of the Solidarity trade union will be exposed in these materials. I consider Leonid Ilyich's proposal to be perfectly correct—to give several collectives from major, leading enterprises the possibility to speak out. We will also try to prepare for this.

Tikhonov: We will have to respond somehow, and respond concretely, to these pranks by hooligan elements that are taking place in Poland and against which the government is taking no measures at all. You know, apart from the fact that they are defiling memorials to our wars, they are drawing various kinds of caricatures of the leaders of our party and government, and are insulting the Soviet Union in every way possible, and so on. To put it another way, they are laughing at us. It seems to me that we can no longer keep silent and that we must make a protest to the Polish government in connection with this, either through state channels or other channels. In my opinion, it is completely impossible not to react.

Gromyko: We must think about this carefully. This is about a country that is friendly to us.

Gorbachev: I consider that Leonid Ilyich has made a perfectly correct proposal in connection with having the collectives of major enterprises speak out in the pages of the press and expose Solidarity's actions.

Grishin: We must organize these articles both in *Pravda* and in other newspapers. We will take steps to have such collectives as "ZIL," "Hammer and Sickle" and other major factories prepare articles.

Brezhnev: I think that it would be possible to instruct the USSR MID and the CC General Department to prepare a draft presentation for the government of the Polish Republic in connection with the hooliganistic pranks of the representatives of Solidarity against the Soviet Union. Simultaneously, as the comrades have already said here, we must run articles in the press using various materials exposing Solidarity's actions and the decisions of its congress.

[...]

[Source: RGANI, Fond 89, Opis 42, Delo 46. Translated by Malcolm Byrne for the National Security Archive.]

Document No. 62: Protocol No. 002/81 of Meeting of the Homeland Defense Committee[35]

September 13, 1981

The Homeland Defense Committee (KOK) was established in 1959, linking the military, security services and the state economic apparatus to provide coordination for planning the national defense. The chairman of the committee was the prime minister, the members included the deputy prime minister for planning and the economy, the ministers of foreign affairs, defense and internal affairs, the chief of the General Staff and a representative of the PUWP CC Secretariat. This was the only state institution authorized to provide input into plans for martial law. No other institution, not even the Politburo or the Council of Ministers, was formally apprised of the state of preparations. At this important meeting, the military and MSW finally announced that the technical preparations for martial law were complete. Although those factions supported a speedy crackdown, the decision to proceed was delayed once more.

The deliberations were led by the chairman of the Homeland Defense Committee, Comrade General Wojciech JARUZELSKI—in accordance with the established agenda, as in point 2 of the matter under discussion in the protocol.

The participants at the meeting included Committee members and those invited, detailed in point 3 of the matter under discussion in the protocol.

On points 1–5 of the agenda, i.e. the following matters:

1) the current state of security and public order in the State;

2) guiding thoughts on the activities of the State at the time martial law is in force;

3) the state of readiness for activities of selected institutions after the introduction of martial law;

4) the stage of normative-organizational preparations connected with the introduction of martial law, as well as ventures pertaining to militarization and civil defense;

5) the safeguarding of martial law through propaganda.

The speakers in the discussion included:

Point 1—the current state of security and public order in the State (presented by the minister of internal affairs, Comrade General Czesław KISZCZAK);

---

[35] The translator thanks Kzrysztof Persak in Warsaw for his help in transcribing the handwritten Polish original.

[Section missing] specific assignment of the internal affairs department under the conditions of the current socio-political and economic situation in the country, as well as at the time martial law is in force.

Point 1 and Point 2—guiding thoughts on State activities at the time martial law is in force (presented by the chief of the General Staff of the Polish Army, Comrade General Florian SIWICKI);

Comrade Mirosław MILEWSKI—who emphasized the importance of the conclusions arising from the information put forward with regard to points 1 and 2. He pointed out the need to conduct an appraisal on the contingency of introducing martial law to examine the effective influence of martial law in stabilizing the political situation in the country.

Point 3—the degree of readiness by selected departments to conduct activities after the introduction of martial law (presented by the vice chairman of the Council of Ministers, Comrade Andrzej JEDYNAK);

Comrade Stanisław KANIA—who emphasized that the information presented is not precise on the essential range of problems regarding the functioning of the national economy at the time martial law is in force, mainly with regard to three mutually conditional arrangements: first—the feasibility (reserves) pertaining to the provisioning of the population and the continuation of industrial production; second—the energy system, particularly in assuming communal needs (lighting and heating); third—the consequences as a result of restrictions on international trade.

The chairman of the Homeland Defense Committee, Comrade General Wojciech JARUZELSKI—who, in the context of the currently existing large-scale stoppages at the purchasing center for agricultural products, indicated that under the circumstances arising from the introduction of martial law it is necessary to carry out appraisals concerning the continued delivery of provisions needed by the non-agricultural population.

Comrade Kazimierz BARCIKOWSKI—who proposed considering the purpose of introducing, at the time martial law is in force, the so-called tax on provisions in place of the current mandatory deliveries of agricultural products.

Point 4—the state of normative-organizational preparation connected with the introduction of martial law, as well as ventures pertaining to militarization and civil defense (discussed by the secretary of the Homeland Defense Committee, General Tadeusz TUCZAPSKI);

– there was no discussion on this subject.

Point 5—the safeguarding of martial law through propaganda (presented by PUWP Central Committee secretary, Comrade Stefan OLSZOWSKI).

Comrade Stanisław KANIA—who called attention to the need for a comprehensive examination of the prospects pertaining to the guaranteed continuity of work by radio and television, including taking into consideration the reliance on reserves in electric energy at the time martial law is in force, and also pertaining to the organizational-technical problems connected to the possibility of jamming the reception of radio broadcasts transmitted by foreign centers of enemy propaganda.

Chairman of the Homeland Defense Committee, Comrade General Wojciech JARUZELSKI—who pointed out the need to select, from all the measures connected with the safeguarding of martial law through propaganda, those which should take effect immediately, owing to the evolution of the socio-economic and political situation in the country.

Comrade General Florian SIWICKI—who provided information on the ability to guarantee the supply of radio information through short-wave (with a nationwide reach) by taking advantage of radio transmitters, such as R-102 and R-11O—in case the stationary transmitters of Polish Radio and Television are immobilized.

After discussing matters subject to resolution by the Homeland Defense Committee—the following persons spoke:

Comrade General Czesław KISZCZAK—who emphasized that the political opponent, among other things, through a varied system of protest actions, voting, and announcing programs, aims at confrontation on their own terms; simultaneously resorting to centers directed at the systematic destruction of activities by state administration and PUWP cells. He concluded on the need to intensify party and governmental activities in the direction of taking control of the crisis in the country's economy, which threatens to sharpen present difficulties during the winter period and, among other things, he concluded there was a need to set in motion mechanisms enforcing work discipline, as well as serving to guarantee consistent deliveries by agricultural producers.

Comrade General Czesław PIOTROWSKI—who justified the need pertaining to militarization that embraced the coal mining enterprises, the energy system, and natural gas. He emphasized the economic and political aspects of eventual militarization, as well as the need to take measures in this matter at the right time—principally being ahead in relationship to the time martial law is introduced.

Comrade Kazimierz BARCIKOWSKI—who pointed out the harmful occurrences in the party, including the sluggishness of party organizations in entertaining essential activities—recommended, in detail, the normative and organizational-planning preparations connected to the introduction of martial law (together with bringing to the provinces normative acts and plans of action) in a way that would allow for the possibility to activate the operations connected with it within 36 hours. He also emphasized the need to detail statutes affecting: the optimal choice of the moment to introduce martial law, and the foreseen social reaction of the decision concerning the introduction of martial law; the aims and ways to realize the policies of the party and the government at the time martial law is in force, including the matters connected with economic reform and strengthening the state and the political structures (together with the introduction of the currently prepared governmental and statutory acts; ventures in the sphere of stabilizing the situation in the country and finding a way out of martial law.

Comrade Mirosław MILEWSKI—who underlined that in the present difficult situation, the country's political authorities and the state may act on the principle of relying on the powers of the departments of national defense and internal affairs, whose conceivable erosion would indicate an inclination of social leaning to the benefit of the political opponent. He characterized the essential role of the optimal time factor most optimal from the point of view of introducing martial law, and also pointed out the need to firm up immediately apparent preparations connected to that state. These preparations, to shake public opinion, should also indicate that the behavior of the authorities are the result of the continuous implementation of the policy of renewal, and are occasioned by the need to systematically defend the state, weakened as a consequence of the destructive activities of the opponent, including the extremist powers inherent in Solidarity.

Comrade Stanislaw KANIA—who brought attention to the need for maintaining strict secrecy of all discussions at the meeting on matters concerning martial law, asserted the need to unravel difficult socio-political and economic problems in the existing critical situation—with our own forces and in a way that will ensure the guaranteed well-being of the nation and guard the territory of the Polish People's Republic, as well as frustrate imperialistic calculations to entangle the USSR and other socialist states by worsening their internal and external conflicts. Sanctioning in general the prepared normative and organizational-planning solutions concerning martial law—labeling it a state of class war, which in the fullness of time cannot fulfill the basic system of social life—he indicated that the aim of its introduction should be to introduce a transformation in Solidarity that would lead in the direction of a trade union with socialist characteristics. Emphasizing the need for the energetic continuation of preparations connected to the eventual introduction of martial law, he pointed out the primary role of the department of internal affairs in this area, which, besides applying measures to paralyze enemy activities, should also support adopting positive undertones that influence the growth of social awareness in the direction of sanctioning the political line of the party and the government. He noted that the eventuality of introducing martial law demands fulfilling a genuine assessment of the ability to guarantee the essential needs of the population at the time martial law is in force—above all, in the area of provisions, as well as electricity and heating, keeping in mind that the return to a normal state of affairs will not come in a few days or weeks. He emphasized that the importance of preparations [word unreadable] continuing functioning of the propaganda system for the period before martial law is introduced, as well as during the period it is in force. He remarked that the decision about the eventual introduction of Martial Law would be taken in the fullness of time. However, further preparations in connection with the introduction of Martial Law should be carried out intensely, whereas current readiness plans in this area ought to surpass very realistic preparations. He underlined that preparations connected with Martial Law cannot in any way be in opposition to the current endeavors of the party and the government. The point of departure for an assessment of the present situation should be to proclaim the changes occurring in the public consciousness, which is characterized by growing criticism towards "Solidarity," while in the party there is an increasing will to defend socialism. He pointed out the need to adopt in the near future a "great political offensive" based on the actions of the apparatus and administration, the activities of operational military groups in the field, the proper functioning of laws and authority largely in the direction of liquidating the state of anarchy, making corrections to the situation in the market, [and] finalizing [word unreadable] statutory regulations, new legal norms with respect to trade unions, higher education, and economic reform. He emphasized the need to find the means to secure party organizations for difficult political activities. He noted the need to reexamine the present state of storing arms and explosive devices (in armories and in production), as well as finding the means to ensure maximum effect for its protection.

The chairman of the Homeland Defense Committee—who, stressing the highest range of political matters discussed at the meeting of the Homeland Defense Committee, also characterized the essence and difficulty of the current phase of confrontation with the political opponent, and emphasized that the problems presented at the meeting of the Committee present the clearest review of the situation and allow for precise directions for further actions. He underlined the meaning of the past for a clearer appreciation of the conditions developing in the socio-political and economic situation in the country, as well as our own forces and those of the allies, including the political forces of the opponent. He pointed out the precise meaning and the necessity to settle internal problems with our own forces, as well as the support for our endeavors by the political and economic activities from the neighboring socialist states, about which enemy elements, those inherent in Solidarity, should be thoroughly convinced. He emphasized that the essential strategy of current activities should be the unmasking of the endeavors of enemy forces, appealing to undecided forces on the side of socialism, neutralizing elements in the opposition camp, as well as taking full advantage of public support for the political line of the party and the government, including also the kind of measure for eventual political action by the authorities like the introduction of martial law. He remarked that the main determining factor, based upon taking a justified decision in the matter of martial law, concerns, above all, the passage of time to introduce it, as well as its objective (subject)—it means the kind of choice and subject that under no condition will [it] be assessed as a provocation from the government side, but rather in sufficient measure will explain to society exactly this kind of necessity on the part of the authorities. Assessing the actual state of preparations for the eventual introduction of martial law, he generally underlined the correctness of the proposed solution—indicating also the attainment of a higher stage of readiness from the perspective of the departments of national defense and internal affairs, and naturally a relatively lower stage of readiness in the economy and state administration. He called for the confidential continuation, on a higher level of advancement, of all further indispensable preparations concerning the eventual introduction of martial law, such that indispensable normative and organizational planning has to be deposited at the level of the Citizens' Police Provincial Committee. Assessing the propaganda preparations, he indicated a need for their intensification, as well as the confidential adoption of offensive propaganda activities to serve, among other things: the unmasking of the essential objectives of Solidarity, and revealing its responsibility for the harmful occurrence that came into being last year in the social life and the economy of the country; reiterate to society the problems of accounting for the errors of the most recent period; strengthen the authority of the leading cadre and provide it with support to carry out actual assignments. He pointed out the need for a profound unraveling of the tactics of so-called "strike action," as well as to work out appropriate methods and means of resistance. He recommended undertaking indispensable ventures to block the paralysis and functioning of radio and television; distributing personal weapons to a select group of political and state workers; effective resistance to adventures and violations of mandatory laws; resistance to economic sabotage; [word unreadable] theft, primarily social, especially in the Polish State Railways; tightening state frontiers, particularly the coastal borders. He proposed accepting the preparations made to date regarding martial law, with advice to guarantee security and secrecy, the indispensability of their intensity of support regarding the findings as a result of the discussion and the current developments in the country, including a recommendation to achieve permanent readiness for every circumstance for the eventuality of introducing Martial Law—the Homeland Defense Committee accepted the proposals on this subject. Moreover, the Homeland Defense Committee accepted a proposal, put forward by the secretary of the Committee, to withdraw from the paramilitary organs the [role of being the] "decisive establishment defending the Polish People's Republic."

3. Members of the Homeland Defense Committee: Comrade General Wojciech Jaruzelski; Comrade Kazimierz Barcikowski; Comrade Stefan Olszowski; Comrade Mirosław Milewski; Comrade Andrzej Jedynak; Comrade Janusz Obodowski; Comrade General Czesław Kiszczak; Comrade General Florian Siwicki; Comrade General Tadeusz Tuczapski.

Persons invited: Comrade General Zbigniew Nowak; Comrade General Michał Janiszewski; Comrade General Bogusław Stachura; Comrade General Władysław Pozoga; Comrade General Adam Krzysztoporski; Comrade General Jerzy Skalski; Comrade General Antoni Jasiński; Comrade General Mieczysław Debicki; Comrade General Czesław Piotrowski; Comrade Colonel Bronisław Pawlikowski; Comrade Colonel Zdzisław Malina; Comrade Colonel Tadeusz Malicki; Comrade Walery Namiotkiewicz.

The first secretary of the Polish United Workers' Party Central Committee, Stanisław KANIA, took part in the meeting.

Secretary of the Homeland Defense Committee

General Tadeusz TUCZAPSKI

[Source: Sejm Commission on Constitutional Oversight, Warsaw. First published in Andrzej Paczkowski and Andrzej Werblan, "'On the Decision to Introduce Martial Law in Poland in 1981,' Two Historians Report to the Commission on Constitutional Oversight of the Sejm of the Republic of Poland," CWIHP Working Paper No. 21, November 1997. Introduced and translated by L. W. Głuchowski.]

Document No. 63: CPSU CC Communication to the PUWP CC, "Intensifying Anti-Soviet Feelings in Poland"

September 14, 1981

The idea to send this protest note to the Polish party originated at the Soviet Politburo's September 10 meeting (Document No. 61). Hoping to duplicate the impact of the influential June 5 letter (Document No. 50), the Kremlin gave vent to growing indignation at signs of anti-Sovietism in the country which the note alleges is approaching the level of "hysteria." Using specific examples such as Solidarity's appeal to East European workers and the desecration of Soviet war memorials, and adopting an anxious tone reminiscent of Moscow's attitude towards Hungary in 1956, the note stops short of explicit threats but makes it clear that the limits of Moscow's toleration are close at hand.

Circulated by order of Cdes. S. Kania, W. Jaruzelski to PB Members, Deputies, Secretaries
September 14, 1981

The Central Committee of the Communist Party of the Soviet Union and the Government of the USSR are forced to draw the attention of the Central Committee of the Polish United Workers' Party and the Government of the PPR to the intensifying anti-Soviet feelings in Poland, and the unrestraint which has reached dangerous dimensions.

The facts prove that inside the country a licentious campaign against the Soviet Union and its foreign and domestic policy is being carried out openly, broadly, and without any consequences. The evidence unquestionably demonstrates that these are not solitary, irresponsible incidents by hooligan elements but a coordinated activity by the enemies of socialism with a clearly political character. The main goal of this campaign is to slander the first country of the councils in the world and the whole idea of socialism, spur a feeling of hostility and hatred toward the Soviet state and Soviet people among the Poles, break up the ties of our nations' brotherhood, and as a final result—pull Poland out of the socialist camp, [i.e.] eliminate socialism in Poland.

Anti-Soviet feelings penetrate deeper and deeper into various spheres of the social life of the country, but in particular into ideology, culture, and the system of higher, secondary, and primary education and upbringing. The history of relations between our countries is vulgarly falsified. Unrestrained propaganda against the Soviet Union is led through various publishers, with the help of cinema screens, theater and festival stages. It is openly heard in the public appearances of KSS–KOR, the "Confederation of Independent Poland" and Solidarity ringleaders in packed halls.

The first round of the congress of this new "trade union" became in fact a tribunal from which licentious slanders and defamations directed at our country were delivered to the whole of Poland. The passing in Gdańsk of the so-called "Appeal to the Nations of Eastern Europe" was an outrageous provocation. Anti-Soviet elements continue to maltreat the monuments of Soviet soldiers, hundreds of thousands of whom gave their lives for the freedom and independence of the Polish nation; they defiled the tombs of the defeated. Threats also began to appear toward the soldiers of the Soviet Armed Forces who guard the western frontiers of the socialist community of which the People's Republic of Poland is also a part.

Anti-socialist forces aim to cause an atmosphere of extreme nationalism in Poland which clearly would have an anti-Soviet edge. Simultaneously, the scale, intensity, and degree of hostility of the current anti-Soviet campaign in Poland are gaining the features of an anti-Soviet hysteria that is evolving in some imperialist countries.

Therefore, a question unavoidably emerges among us: why is it that no decisive steps have been so far undertaken on the side of the official Polish authorities to interrupt the hostile campaign against the USSR with which the People's [Republic of] Poland is tied by friendly relations and allied obligations? Such a standpoint contradicts even the Constitution of the PPR which contains the principle of strengthening friendship and cooperation with the USSR. We are not aware of even a single case of a particular instigator of anti-Soviet provocation who would meet sharp resistance from the authorities and would be punished. Moreover, one can say that in order to hold assemblies, the state's facilities are easily made available; they have open access to the mass media, they are given the possibility to use technical means, despite the fact that it is known in advance what all of this will be used for.

Not just once have we turned the attention of the PUWP leadership and the government of the PPR to the increasing wave of anti-Soviet feelings in Poland. It was discussed during the meetings in Moscow in March and in Warsaw in April of this year, and we clearly talked about it in the letter of the CPSU CC on June 5 of this year. It was also discussed in August during the meeting in the Crimea. Each time we were assured that an end will be put to the instances of anti-Soviet feelings. However, reality proves the opposite situation.

We will not hide the fact that all this causes a feeling of deep anxiety among the Soviet people. There is a never-ending flow of letters from party organizations addressed to the CPSU CC, in which Soviet communists and non-party people express their lack of understanding for the causes of the arrogance and freedom which characterize the anti-Soviet propaganda in a neighboring, brotherly, socialist country. The Soviet nation which suffered enormous losses in the name of the liberation of Poland from fascist occupation, and which gave and continues to give your country disinterested assistance, has a full moral right to demand an end to the unbridled anti-Soviet feelings in the PPR.

The CPSU CC and the Soviet Government believe that further toleration of any kind of anti-Soviet instances will harm Polish–Russian relations enormously and is completely contradictory to the allied obligations of Poland and to the vital interests of the Polish nation.

We expect that immediate, radical and resolute steps will be taken on the side of the PUWP Leadership and the Polish Government to break this sinister anti-Soviet propaganda and these hostile activities toward the Soviet Union.

[Source: AAN, PUWP CC, 1827, pp. 85–87. Translated by Paweł Świeboda.]

Document No. 64: Information on the Brezhnev–Kania Telephone Conversation

September 15, 1981

The day after receiving Moscow's protest note over the course of events in Poland (see previous document), Kania called Brezhnev to discuss it. This record of the conversation includes only the Soviet side but it is useful for illuminating Brezhnev's state of mind. The aging leader barely restrains his anger, responding to Kania's initial remarks with the dismissive statement, "It seems to me that you are still in the grip of an illusion." "[Solidarity's] preparations for the seizure of power are being carried out in practice, including the military sphere," he warns, likening union tactics to those used by fascists. He calls it "painful to talk about the raging anti-Sovietism that has engulfed Poland," and asks rhetorically, "How can you reconcile yourself to moral and physical terror against communists?" Characteristically, he addresses Kania with the informal "ty". Yet despite his exasperation, Brezhnev continues to refrain from making direct threats, reflecting his own sense of caution and reluctance to employ more extreme measures.

[…]

Hello Stanisław! I am told you want to talk with me. I am listening.
(After information from S. Kania)

I have listened carefully to you. It seems to me that you are still in the grip of an illusion.

We dicussed the situation in Poland with you and Wojciech [Jaruzelski] in the Crimea about a month ago. Back then there were already more than enough reasons for concern. And since then, in our opinion, the situation has become even more alarming. I will speak frankly: Sometimes you wake up and wonder who is the master of the situation in Poland, and has power already changed hands there? The leaders of Solidarity act too freely not to ask oneself this question.

Solidarity's Congress and the entire atmosphere surrounding it prove that Solidarity openly aims at [assuming] the role of a political party, anticommunist in nature. The results of the first round of the Congress, in our opinion, are a declaration of political war against the PUWP and socialist power.

This, of course, is no congress of workers. Even according to Solidarity's data, they make up only 25 percent. Almost a quarter of the delegates are representatives of the counter-revolutionary organizations KSS-KOR and the "Conference of Independent Poland." The participants in this gathering are not interested in the workers' interests, but in driving the PUWP and the government to its knees.

At the Congress, as we know, the question was raised of removing from Solidarity's statutes the clauses regarding the leading role of the PUWP and recognition of Poland's international alliances. But you know, these are clauses in your constitution. This means that attacks have begun on the constitutional bases of society.

Poland has become too small for Solidarity. It is trying to transmit its subversive ideas to neighboring countries and to intervene in their internal affairs. This is the only way to evaluate the "Appeal to the Peoples of Eastern Europe," adopted by Solidarity. There are few words in this document, but they all hit the same mark. The authors would like to cause confusion in the socialist countries and agitate among various groups of renegades. I do not know how you are planning to act regarding this provocational trick, but we consider it essential that it receive the rebuff it deserves.

Solidarity is not limiting itself to slogans and appeals. Preparations for the seizure of power are being carried out in practice, including in the military sphere. Leaks from the West show that "battle groups" attached to Solidarity have the goal of terrorizing Communists and patriots. These are the habits of fascists, who created units of storm-troopers. The same information [source] shows that Solidarity is starting courses for pre-conscripts to the Polish Army. How can one reconcile oneself to this? Indeed drafting those who are stuffed with anti-socialist and anti-Soviet prejudices could quickly demoralize the army.

Solidarity is taking one position after another under its control. Without following any procedures [iavochnym poriadkom], legally appointed enterprise leaders are being removed. Solidarity runs the show in more than half of the major factories be creating so-called "organs of self-management."

In the countryside there are cases of arbitrary seizure by individuals of lands [belonging to] state farms and cooperatives. Solidarity reacts bitterly to criticism of its activities in the media and is working towards full control of them [the media].

It is painful to talk about the raging anti-Sovietism that has engulfed Poland. How can you ignore this? How can you reconcile yourself to moral and physical terror against communists and all those who wish to work honestly? The opposition puts forward the demand to speed up elections to the Sejm and popular Councils ever more like an ultimatum. The final goal is the destruction "by peaceful means" of the economic and political bases of the socialist order.

I will not speak of many other no less alarming facts. They should be as well known to you as to us. It is understandable why at the last plenums, including the third, many members of the new Central Committee spoke about the situation with great trepidation and demanded from the PUWP leadership not only strong words, but also decisive deeds.

One can understand this. The loud leaders of Solidarity openly announce that their organization is already the leading force in society.

In general, everything indicates that counter-revolution is tearing power from the PUWP grip.

In the Crimea, you, Stanisław, and Jaruzelski said that you "always kept in mind the use of the most decisive measures against the counter-revolution." Where are these measures?

You said that you [ty] had an appropriate contingency plan for the introduction of a state of emergency or martial law. When will even some part of this plan finally be realized?

The growing activity and assertiveness of the anti-socialist forces in [your] country are incomparably [greater] than how the party and government leaders are acting. How can you allow this?

We ask you to tell us, the leadership of a fraternal party, the CPSU, what are you planning to do?

Practically speaking, there is nothing for us to add to those recommendations made to you [vy] for overcoming the crisis in the June 5 letter and during the meeting in the Crimea on August 14. These recommendations and advice remain in force.

Then as now, we are convinced that leaving ever bolder Solidarity challenges unanswered means opening the gates of counter-revolution. In our view, one must mobilize the party without delay for a decisive, uncompromising fight against counter-revolution. And when the fate of socialism is in question, one must not limit oneself to only one form of battle.

I think it is important to emphasize once again that, in the present complicated situation, events in Poland raise the question, increasingly critically for the socialist commonwealth, of guaranteeing security in Central Europe. If Solidarity runs Poland, who will guarantee the inviolability of the vitally important commonwealth arteries passing through Poland, including strategic communications? How will we, members of the Warsaw Pact, be able to guarantee retention of the results of World War II secured by well-known political and international legal acts?

I want to emphasize once again, Stanisław, that the fate of socialism in Poland and the outcome of the political battle going on in your country deeply concern all fraternal countries.

In the present situation I ask you in the name of the Politburo to have the PUWP Central Committee leadership answer our questions so that we can clearly picture your plan of action, at least for the immediate future.

What you have said is interesting, but does not change the general picture. I ask you to treat what I have said to you today more attentively.

[Source: SAPMO-BArch, ZPA, J IV, 2/202–550. Translated by David Wolff for CWIHP.]

362

Document No. 65: Message from Ryszard Kukliński to CIA

September 15, 1981

On September 13, two days before this secret message from CIA informant Ryszard Kukliński, the Homeland Defense Committee (KOK) held a key meeting to finalize plans for martial law and review the level of preparation of the security forces (see Document No. 62). It seemed once again that a crackdown was imminent and Kukliński duly notified U.S. intelligence, providing the additional specifics he had learned. Ironically, the message was initially delayed because he was forced to deliver it via dead drop after his CIA-supplied "Iskra" transmitter malfunctioned. He then unwittingly deposited the note (hidden inside an old glove covered in grease and dirt) at the wrong location.[36]

In a way, the second part of Kukliński's message was more ominous. At the KOK meeting, Minister of Internal Affairs Kiszczak had announced that Solidarity had somehow learned about the plans for martial law. The day before, a Polish counterintelligence officer had visited Kukliński without explanation and warned him to be wary of leaks. The writing on the wall was becoming apparent, and in this message Kukliński passes along the bad news that he will no longer be able to communicate on a daily basis. Before long, he began preparations to escape the country, which he finally did with his family in early November.

During an extraordinary session of the KOK on Sunday, in which Kania participated for the first time, no political decision to introduce martial law was made. Basically, all the participants were in favor of martial law. There is a belief that Kania was surprised by the course of the session. Without questioning the inevitability of such measures, he reportedly said, precisely, "confrontation with the class enemy is inevitable. This means a fight by political means, but if that fails, repression may be applied." Recording the session was forbidden. During the KOK session, Kiszczak declared that Solidarity is informed in detail about our plans, including operation "Wiosna" and its code name. Here I must explain that this is a code name for the operation and not the signal to initiate it. The associated officials do not know that code name; therefore, there will be no problem determining the group of suspects. The MSW was ordered urgently to establish the source. The first steps have been taken. Everyone from the operational administration, except for Szklarski[37] and me, has already been excluded from the planning. Yesterday, Szklarski and I had a visit from an officer from the EC [Executive Committee]. He spoke about how to prevent future leaks. Right now, Jasiński[38] has taken command of planning at the national level. For the time being, Szklarski has removed himself. Since this morning, under Jasiński's direction, we have begun

---

[36] Benjamin Weiser, *A Secret Life*, pp. 256–258.
[37] Gen. Wacław Szklarski was Kukliński's direct superior.
[38] Gen. Antoni Jasiński was a deputy chief of the General Staff.

working—with the participation of a PUWP CC representative, the KOK Secretariat, and Pawlikowski[39] from the MSW—on the central plan for administering the surprise introduction of martial law. The document is still in draft form. I am unable to provide specific details. (I proposed a break from work in order to send this cable.) Generally speaking, there are proposals to introduce martial law on a Friday night followed by a work-free Saturday, or on a Saturday night followed by a Sunday. That is when factories will be closed. The detention operations would begin around midnight, six hours before the proclamations of martial law on radio and television. In Warsaw, about 600 people will be detained by about 1,000 policemen, using their own private cars.

The same night, the Army will block the most important parts of Warsaw and other major cities. Initially, the operations are supposed to be carried out only by the Interior Ministry forces. In order to "improve the troops' situation," i.e., to relocate entire divisions in the vicinity of major cities, a separate political decision is expected to be made.

This will take place only after the major resistance centers flare up. It has not been ruled out, however, that divisions which are stationed far from the areas of their future operations could begin their relocation from the moment of the imposition of martial law, or even earlier, e.g., the 4th Mechanized Division needs about 54 hours in order to move in the vicinity of Warsaw.

*   *   *

Due to the investigation in progress, I have to stop providing daily information about the situation. I ask you to use data provided by me cautiously because I think my mission is nearing its end.

That data could easily reveal its source. I do not oppose the idea—and that is even my wish—that information provided by me serve the cause of those who struggle for Poland's freedom with their heads up. I am also ready to pay the highest price, but we can accomplish something only by action, not by sacrifice.

Long live Free Poland! Long live Solidarity, capable of bringing freedom to all oppressed nations.

Jack Strong[40]

[*Source: Originally published in Polish in* Tygodnik Solidarność *50 (325), December 9, 1994. Partial translation by Magdalena Klotzbach for the National Security Archive. Further translation from Benjamin Weiser,* A Secret Life: The Polish Officer, His Covert Mission, and the Price He Paid to Save His Country, *(New York: PublicAffairs, 2004), p. 257. Copyright 2004 by Benjamin Weiser. Reprinted by permission of PublicAffairs, a member of Perseus Books, L.L.C.).*]

[39] Col. Bronisław Pawlikowski.

[40] Kukliński's CIA handlers instructed him to use this code name when communicating with them. See Benjamin Weiser, *A Secret Life* p. 23.

Document No. 66: Letter from HSWP CC Signed by Kádár to PUWP CC via Kania

September 17, 1981

As a sign of concern over the crisis emanating from other corners of Eastern Europe, Hungary's communist leader, János Kádár, in the name of the party CC, presses Kania on the question of why the Poles have not yet resolved their situation. Kádár, a moderate particularly on the question of outside intervention, is worried about the relationship among the members of the Warsaw Pact. But his letter also shows that he is not acting entirely on his own initiative. The Soviets are clearly coordinating pressure on Warsaw from all sides. Only Romania chooses at this point not to follow Moscow's lead.

[…]

Budapest, September 17, 1981

To the Central Committee of the Polish United Workers' Party
For the attention of Comrade Stanisław Kania, First Secretary
Warsaw

Dear Comrades,

The Hungarian communists and our working people are paying close attention to the extraordinary events in the Polish People's Republic which have been going on for over a year now. Public opinion in our country has been very concerned with the work of the Extraordinary Ninth Congress of the PUWP and people welcomed its resolutions on socialist development, the necessity of the persistent fight against anti-socialist forces, and Poland's commitment and her responsibility towards our alliance system.

Despite justified expectations and hopes, the events of the period since the party Congress have proved that it was not the followers of socialism, but its enemies who took the offensive and sought confrontation and the seizure of power. This fact has been stated and acknowledged by you, the leaders of the Polish party and the Polish State, and by other factors concerned with the welfare of the country and the people.

The traditional friendship that binds the Hungarian and Polish people and also our Parties together, our common socialist goals, as well as the collective responsibility for the maintenance of peace and safety in our countries, prompt us to express repeatedly our deep anxiety for you in the present acute situation. We are also urged to do so as we are receiving questions from our own people—expressing sincere concern and sometimes even impatience—which we find more and more difficult to answer. These repeated questions tend to ask where Poland is heading, how long will it take for the escalation of forces and action to destroy the socialist system, what Polish communist and Polish supporters of socialism are doing, when they are going to take resolute action to protect the real interests of the Polish working people and the common interests of our nations.

We were all astonished by the atmosphere of the congress of the trade union Solidarity: the series of anticommunist and anti-Soviet statements, the unrestrained demagoguery of ringleaders by which they mislead and deceive masses of workers who want to remedy mistakes but not to do away with socialism. In fact, your Politburo and the communiqué of September 15 dealing with the character of the Solidarity congress came to the same conclusion. It is obvious that definite steps must be taken to repel an attack which disregards and imperils the achievements of the Polish people attained by blood and sweat, which, in the difficult situation in Poland, announces a program of devastation and anarchy instead of social reconciliation and constructive programs, which foully abuses the ideas of freedom and democracy, denies the principles of socialism and keeps on stirring up uncontrolled emotions, instead of enhancing common sense and a sense of responsibility.

Dear Polish comrades,

The provocative message of the Solidarity congress directed to the workers of socialist countries is nothing other than the propagation of the same unrealistic, irresponsible demagoguery on an international level. It is evidently a step suggested by international reaction forces to divide and set the people of socialist countries against one another.

The Hungarian people highly appreciate their socialist achievements obtained at the cost of painful experiences and exhausting work. The ringleaders of Solidarity cherish vain hopes. The Hungarian workers flatly reject the blatant provocation and any undisguised effort to intervene in their domestic affairs.

The greatest concern of our party and people is now the activity of counterrevolutionary forces in Poland which is directed not merely against the Polish working class and the vital national interests of the Polish people, but towards a weakening of our friendly relations, our multilateral cooperation and the system of our alliance as well. Their continued activity would definitely have an influence on the security of the community of socialist countries. It is in our and all European nations' basic interest that Poland not be a source of an escalation of international tension but should rather stay a stabilizing factor in Europe in the future.

Comrades,

Since the outbreak of the crisis, the HSWP CC has several times expressed its opinion concerning the events in Poland, as it also did so in the Extraordinary Ninth Congress of the PUWP. Whilst stressing the maintenance of our earlier standpoint, we think that an even more urgent task is to curb counter-revolution by way of joint action taken by forces of the Polish communists, true Polish patriots and forces that are ready to act for the sake of development. Only action and consistent measures can create the conditions for the successful execution of tasks specified by the Congress.

We are certain that in Poland today the supporters of socialism are in a majority, that they can count on the Polish working class, the peasantry, the loyal youth of the intelligentsia and on realistically minded powers of the society. The protection of the achievements of socialism is the most fundamental national interest of the Polish people today, which is, at the same time the international interest of forces fighting for peace and social progress.

Hereby we declare our belief that if the leadership of the PUWP shows a definite sense of direction, being aware of its national and international responsibility, and if the PUWP calls for immediate action in the spirit of the PUWP Politburo declaration of September 15, then the union of Polish communists and patriots and their active campaign will still be able to drive back the open attack of anti-socialist forces and to defend the achievements of socialism attained during a decade's work. Then Poland too, will have the opportunity to start out, having successfully resolved the present severe crisis, toward socialist development, that is, on the way to real social and national prosperity.

The supporters of socialism in Poland—amongst them the international powers of socialism and progress—can rely absolutely on the internationalist help of Hungarian communists and the fraternal Hungarian people in their fight to protect their people's power.

On behalf of the Central Committee of the Hungarian Socialist Workers' Party
(signed) János Kádár

[Source: MOL, Department of documents on the Hungarian Workers' Party and the Hungarian Socialist Workers' Party, 288. f. 11/4400. ő.e., pp. 120–123. Published in the Cold War International History Project Bulletin *Issue 11 (Winter 1998), pp. 85–87. Translated by László Beke.]*

Document No. 67: Excerpt from CPSU CC Politburo Meeting Regarding Brezhnev–Kania Conversation,

September 17, 1981

As this brief report shows, Kania continues to provoke exasperation not only in Moscow but also among most of his erstwhile allies, who are incensed at his "intolerable liberalism" and favor subjecting him to "severe pressure." For East German leader Honecker, only Kania's resignation and replacement by hard-liner Stefan Olszowski will suffice. Brezhnev, who appears reluctant to impose unilateral decisions on the rest of Moscow's partners, indicates that more information on the views of the other socialist leaders is needed before arriving at a conclusion.

[...]

8. Telegram from the Soviet ambassador in Berlin of September 15, 1981 (Spec. No. 598).

Brezhnev: Concerning my telephone conversation with Cde. Kania on September 11, 1981, which we agreed upon at the last Politburo session, I sent information to our ambassadors for their use in apprising Cdes. Honecker, Kádár, Zhivkov and Husák.

The ambassadors fulfilled this assignment and reported on the results. The leaders of the fraternal parties completely agreed with what was said to Cde. Kania in the telephone conversation, and consider that Cde. Kania is displaying an intolerable liberalism and should be subject to severe pressure.

In a conversation with Cde. Pyotr Abrasimov,[41] which he, as you know, described in a telegram, Cde. Honecker put forward this proposal: to gather in Moscow with the leaders of the fraternal parties, to invite Cde. Kania and tell him to submit his resignation, and in his place as first secretary of the PUWP CC to recommend Cde. [Stefan] Olszowski.

In this connection, I would like to advise what our position should be. Of course, it is hard for us now to make a simple decision on this question. We do not yet know the opinion of the other comrades, the leaders of the socialist countries. That must all be mulled over in detail.

Perhaps we will instruct the Foreign Ministry of the USSR, the Ministry of Defense and the CC Department[42] to examine the questions contained in the tele-

---

[41] Soviet ambassador to the GDR.

[42] This refers to the CPSU CC Department for Ties with Communist and Workers' Parties of Socialist Countries, often referred to in Russian as simply *"Otdel,"* the Department.

gram, and taking account of the exchange of views at the Politburo to prepare and deliver the appropriate proposals to the CC.

If there are no objections, then perhaps we will now adopt this decision.

The members and candidate members of the Politburo indicated that Leonid Ilyich's proposal is completely correct and should be adopted, except that the KGB should be included among the agencies instructed to consider these matters.

The proposal is adopted.

[Source: RGANI, Fond 89, Opis 42, Delo 47. Translated by Malcolm Byrne for the National Security Archive.]

Document No. 68: Report to the HSWP CC Politburo by the Hungarian Ambassador to Warsaw

September 18, 1981

The day after Hungarian leader János Kádár signed a letter to the Polish Central Committee (Document No. 66), Hungary's ambassador to Warsaw delivered it to Kania. His lengthy report on the ensuing conversation is highly revealing of Kania's attitude toward the crisis and how to resolve it. The ambassador's description reveals a much more decisive and resourceful character than the irresolute and inept figure Moscow was increasingly disposed to see. Kania's argument is straightforward: Poland's problems arise from widespread social discontent that affects millions of Poles, not just a few counter-revolutionaries. To put down such a broadbased opposition would inevitably require force against the general population to an unprecedented degree. That in turn would trigger the introduction of outside military forces in order to augment Poland's inadequate resources, which would "set back the development of socialism by decades." Kania clearly comes across as a loyal communist who fundamentally opposes Solidarity and is committed to pursuing the "physical annihilation" of "the enemy," yet is restrained by an awareness of the precariousness of the situation and by an aversion to causing major bloodshed.

Report to the Politburo

On September 18 in the morning, Stanisław Kania, First Secretary of the Central Committee of the Polish United Workers' Party, received me at my request. Following the instructions from home, I handed over a letter in the presence of comrade István Pataki, associate of the Department of Foreign Affairs of the Central Committee of the Hungarian Socialist Workers' Party, addressed to the CC of the PUWP, written by comrade János Kádár on behalf of the HSWP CC.

As a verbal addition, I referred to the circumstances leading to the creation of the aforementioned document, namely those factors in the process of events in Poland, which rendered the letter timely. I referred emphatically to the changing mood of public feeling in Hungary, to the fact that though our standpoint remained the same, the situation had considerably changed again. I confirmed that we invariably support the efforts taken by the PUWP to promote socialist development, furthermore that we welcome the decisions taken by the PUWP Politburo, but that we regard the turning of words into deeds and consistent work as the most important tasks today.

Having read the letter, comrade Kania explained in his answer that correspondence was the usual way to maintain relations between our parties. He thought it natural that the letter signed by J. Kádár reflected great concern which had, in fact, solid ground after the congress of Solidarity in Gdańsk. The statements, appeals and decisions made there, were definitely not casual ones in the development of Solidarity. Extremist elements have acquired decisive influence in the organization, in its policy and program. It became clear for the leadership of the PUWP that to negotiate an agreement with this faction of Solidarity was out of the question. The solution could be either a radical change in their attitude—that is, they would have to take up trade union functions—or the disablement of their activities.

Although leaders of the party have no illusions, we must take into consideration that it is not merely counter-revolutionary forces which we are facing, but also the millions of the Polish working-class, for it is in this sphere where Solidarity is active. It includes hundreds of thousands of party members as well. Solidarity did not grow from counter-revolutionary efforts but from large-scale and nationwide social discontent. Here comrade Kania referred to J. Kádár's wording, namely that "we could do more harm to ourselves than the enemy."

The leadership of the PUWP analyzed the situation and came to the following standpoint: regarding basic principles they were determined not to back down. In their opinion the central question in the existing situation was: "who will defeat whom[?]" The most important question to be answered by the Party was: how and by what means could they find a solution? This was also the topic of the session of the Politburo on September 15 and of the subsequent two-day voivodeship meeting of First Secretaries. Awareness that these processes must be put to an end and that counter-revolutionary aspirations must be stopped is getting stronger in the whole of the Party. They see it as a positive sign of party members' political and ideological maturity.

Different measures are being prepared which do not exclude the adoption of even the most drastic measures. S. Kania even made remarks concerning preparations for the introduction of martial law, which was in an advanced stage. The Homeland Defense Committee had had a meeting in the last few days under his leadership which had the same issue on its agenda. The aim of introducing martial law is to break the power of Solidarity and to isolate its leaders. The plan concerning the persons who were to be isolated and even the method of their isolation is ready. The consequences of these measures have also been realistically assessed. "There is no doubt," comrade Kania said, "that this action would provoke today a widespread national strike and it would certainly bring the masses out on to the streets too. In that case, however, force would have to be used not against hostile elements but against the masses." "Hungarians," he added, "have already experienced such events. In Polish recent history there was Poznań, Gdańsk and Radom, when not the enemy, but the masses on the streets had to be confronted. These were localized events at that time. Now, however, it would assume nationwide proportions."

Polish communists have assessed their forces. For such action their resources would be insufficient and thus the support of allied forces would be necessary. The consequences of this would, however, set back the development of socialism by decades. They expect—and they have got reliable information on this—that a part of the imperialist forces would capitalize on the direct intervention of social-ist countries. Thus they want to tie the hands of socialist countries to modify the Yalta Agreement and win a free hand over Cuba, Angola and over other regions of the world. Nobody must think that the Polish leadership lacks courage; how-ever, it requires circumspection and a sense of responsibility to take steps.

There are several ways to overcome difficulties. The more prepared they are for the above possibilities, including also the use of administrative means, the less likely it will be to [have to] adopt them in practice.

Today the most important task is to win over the masses, to supply them with information and to make them realize that they are being manipulated by the en-emy. The objective of the Party leadership's policy is to be on the offensive po-litically and in addition, to supplement this by adopting repressive administrative means. This is the actual Party line followed and approved by the leadership. The reason why this policy has been chosen is that they have assessed not only the forces of the enemy, but their own forces, too. Public feeling has changed re-cently and criticism of Solidarity has become sharper and the Party's "cautious" policy is seen as justified. A new process has got under way. The number of peo-ple abandoning Solidarity is on the rise. Even *Pravda* reported it from comrade A. Siwak's press conference, who is a member of the Politburo of the PUWP and vice president of the Sectoral Trade Union of Building Workers. "You live here, among us," comrade Kania said to me; "now judge the situation of the Party." A couple of months ago there were several dangers threatening the Party and its unity. To anyone who regards matters from an unbiased point of view, it is obvious that the Party is doing everything right. After the Extraordinary Ninth Congress, the Party gathered strength, changed its face and, despite apprehension amongst many, the new CC has proved its strength in the latest plenary meetings. It is true that quite a few party members joined Solidarity which makes concen-tration of efforts difficult, yet, it is true that, all in all, there is a positive process taking place in the Party.

"As concerns the mass media," he went on, "some very unfavorable tendencies emerged, although it is undeniable that we have managed to bring these to a stop. The leadership believes that positive changes have begun in this field as well."

Legitimate reservations towards the army may also exist and there are still some dangerous trends. In spite of this, the army's effective force is firm and the army command has not received any warnings indicating a deterioration in the situation. State security organs and the police are reliable too, though earlier there was a real danger that Solidarity would gain ground in police circles. We managed to quell radicalism here too and the danger of liberalization is no longer imminent.

It is beyond doubt that Solidarity shows an overtly counter-revolutionary at-titude, but it must be also seen that the congress contributed to the "ripening" of the situation and to a certain clear-sightedness in its own way. The leadership of the party will definitely take advantage of this opportunity.

In his train of thought comrade Kania repeated that it was necessary to put up a political fight, combined with the application of administrative means. He also warned that civil riots were to be avoided, for they could not overcome such a situation on their own. Thus the whole party is expected to pull itself together and assume its former identity. A resolution has been passed requiring party members to leave Solidarity. The approval of such a resolution would have been unrealistic before. In comrade Kania's opinion it also proved that the party is able and ready to fight. The party *aktiv* is being prepared and given military training as well. (Comrade Kania added that weapons were given out only during drills and they could not be taken home.) These measures are not only of a defensive character, but they are also meant to influence the political attitude of the party members. The revealing nature of propaganda will become more marked. Further personnel changes are planned in the press. Compliance with the law is required in all state institutions. Even implementation of repressive action was put on the agenda. Dozens of people have been brought to justice. As a consequence of these measures, the situation is expected to change within a couple of days.

A key issue today is the topic of workers' self-government. The resolution of the third plenary meeting on this matter was, as is known, rejected by Solidarity. Yet, they insist that the Sejm confirm in its session next week, the resolution brought by the third plenary meeting. It seems anyway very probable as, from the point of view of the party, Sejm members' attitude has been positively influenced by Solidarity's attack.

To illustrate that the party leadership is no longer willing to withdraw, comrade Kania referred to the curbing of street riots, the repelling of the attacks on the directors of LOT [Polish Airlines] and Huta Katowice [Metallurgical Works in Katowice], as well as to the prohibition of the latest issue of the weekly newspaper *Solidarity*, and to the thwarting of the so-called "star-processions" demanding the release of political prisoners. He also referred to the failure of the earlier press strike organized by Solidarity. He also touched upon the threat of strikes at the radio and television, but at the same time he emphasized that they were prepared for such events and were determined not to retreat.

The verdict brought by the Warsaw Voivodeship Court concerning Moczulski's release, might well give cause for anxiety, yet it should be remembered that the Supreme Court of Justice annulled the verdict the same day, so Moczulski and his associates were not actually released even for a minute. It all goes to show that if necessary, the leadership is resolute and ready to act, while it does its best to avoid mass demonstrations. This is not a policy of retreat but one of a sense of responsibility.

The situation of the national economy and the issue of market supplies invariably pose a serious problem which could well grow to be a potential source of trouble. The previous year's poor potato crop badly affected pig breeding which is one of the reasons for the current shortage of meat supplies. For peasants it is no longer worthwhile selling their livestock for national currency. Circumstances required that meat and butter rationing be temporarily suspended in the villages. Comrade Kania pointed out that, for the first time in many years, they have managed to accomplish a considerable rise of prices in basic articles of consumption, including bread and milling industry products. It still remains, however, a burning issue that the supply of goods is far from equal to the amount of currency in circulation. Taking this into consideration they are planning a large-scale price increase of tobacco, alcohol and petrol.

Regarding the activity of the Polish Catholic Church, comrade Kania said that the previous afternoon, along with comrades Jaruzelski and Barcikowski, he met Cardinal Prince Primate Glemp, Cardinal Macharski from Kraków and Dąbrowski, the Secretary of the Episcopacy. They raised a number of questions on behalf of the PUWP, including well defined demands as to the recommended attitude to be adopted by the Church. They also criticized the practice that had developed lately, namely the celebration of "open" masses outside church buildings and the demand for compulsory introduction of religious education in schools. The Cardinal Prince Primate offered to act as a mediator between the party leadership and Solidarity which was, however, flatly refused by comrade Kania. As a result of the negotiation the leadership of the Church agreed to prevent KOR from exerting influence on Solidarity. Though they have no illusions, still, in comrade Kania's opinion, they managed to get the Church to adopt some of their most important arguments.

In his summary comrade Kania pointed out that they had followed the policy outlined by the Ninth Congress. He added that in an emergency they would employ other means as well, but at the same time they are careful not to take such steps that would irretrievably bring forth the intervention of their allies. Still, he did not exclude the possibility of such an event. In the course of his latest talk with comrade Brezhnev, comrade Kania said, "the fight against counter-revolution claimed 16,000 victims after 1945. There is a fundamental difference between those times and the present. In the past counter-revolutionary forces used to flee to and take refuge in the woods, while nowadays they do so in the factories, where working class to them symbolizes the woods." Comrade Kania was of the opinion that the enemy has to be isolated first of all politically, which is a precondition of its subsequent physical annihilation.

Finally, comrade Kania asked for his kind regards to be conveyed to comrade János Kádár.

At the end of the meeting, having thanked comrade Kania's for his briefing, I promised to pass all his comments to the leadership of our party. The meeting lasted approximately 75 minutes.

József Garamvölgyi
Ambassador

[Source: MOL, Budapest, Department of documents on the Hungarian Workers' Party and the Hungarian Socialist Workers' Party, 288. f. 11/4400. ő.e., pp. 128–134. Translated by László Beke.]

Document No. 69: PUWP CC, "Instructions on the More Important Activities of the Party, Organs of Power and State Administration"

September 18, 1981

This lengthy set of instructions sent initially to the PUWP CC Secretariat, but affecting both party and government, comprises a comprehensive offensive by the party aimed at stunting the activities of Solidarity and other opposition elements and promoting the country's current leaders as the true champions of the Polish people. The directives cover all aspects of public life. On the political front, the party and government are to remove Solidarity members to the extent possible, particularly from key posts. In the economy, sanctions are to be imposed on anyone trying to impede economic performance, while the authorities take steps to improve deliveries of essential goods and reorganize the rationing system. The instructions envision a major propaganda move designed to blame the opposition for everything from economic hardship to social chaos while selling the government's image as the primary source of progressive reforms and societal advancement. In many of these ideas the hand of the Kremlin is evident. As other documents show, Moscow regularly harangued Kania and Jaruzelski to take an aggressive, all-encompassing approach to the crisis that targeted all levels of society. It is now clear that by this time the approach also incorporated a variety of preparations for the ultimate imposition of martial law.

Instructions on the more important activities of the party, organs of power and state administration.

The current political and socio-economic situation of the country, and the course and assessment of results of the first part of the NSZZ Solidarity National Congress session require the party, the Sejm, the PPR government, and the organs of local authorities to undertake decisive political, organizational, and legal-administrative actions aimed at defending socialism—in the name of securing the interests of the working class and the socialist state—in accordance with the policy resolution of the Extraordinary Ninth Congress of the PUWP.

I. *Within the sphere of party activity.*
   1. Inform the *aktiv* and all members of the party about the socio-political situation caused by the proceedings and resolutions of the first part of the NSZZ Solidarity Congress and determine assignments for party organizations and levels. Meetings and consultations of the PPO's devoted to this matter should conclude by taking a position in the form of a resolution or decision.

Responsibility: VC Executives
Time-frame: by September 30, 1981

375

2. Conduct talks with party authorities of all levels who are members of the NSZZ Solidarity and party member-delegates to the First Congress of Solidarity who hold executive positions in the union. The aim of these talks should be self–determination of the aforementioned comrades and the introduction of a trend to leave the NSZZ Solidarity.

Apply statutory sanctions against party members who give political support to the decisions of the NSZZ Solidarity First Congress.

> *Responsibility*: CPC and VPCC, VC Executives
> *Time-frame*: by September 30, 1981

3. Order the employees of Voivodeship, Municipal, District, City-County, and County Committees to leave Solidarity should such incidents take place.

> *Responsibility*: VC Executives
> *Time-frame*: by September 25, 1981

4. Conduct talks with the leadership cadre covered by the *nomenklatura*. As a result of these talks, an increase in discipline among the leadership cadre should be achieved in relation to the execution of tasks resulting from the party's policy and the government's directives. Self-determination in the current situation, especially in the context of problems of the political struggle taking place inside institutes or institutions.

> *Responsibility*: CC Departments, VC Executives and remain-
> ing organs
> *Time-frame*: by October 31, 1981

5. Determine the list of positions within the ministries, offices of the central state administration, the judiciary and prosecutor's office which cannot be held by persons who accept or support the political line of the NSZZ Solidarity First Congress. Depending on the situation, conduct disciplinary talks or make specific personnel decisions.

> *Responsibility*: the PPR government, Prosecutor General,
> voivodes and presidents
> *Time-frame*: by October 15, 1981

6. Establish *aktiv* groups for the voivodeship committees, first degree party organs and Institute Committees in order to:

a) conduct political struggle; edit leaflets, communiqués, news bulletins, posters, the work of the radio systems; take part in meetings and assemblies;

b) actively and decisively fend off the symptoms of hostile propaganda in the cities, neighborhoods and work institutes.

In accordance with propositions accepted during consultation, the voivodeship staffs of the VDC should organize training for *aktiv* groups.

Responsibility: executives of all levels and FC's; voivodeship staff of the VDC
Time-frame: immediate effect

7. Hold sessions of the PUWP, UPP and DP Cooperation Commissions at all levels to determine a joint and uniform platform for political cooperation.

Responsibility: PUWP VC
Time-frame: by September 28, 1981

8. Consistently apply the method of official protests of party organizations and organs, and organs of state and economic authority with regard to resolutions, statements, and activities of the union which violate the Statute of the NSZZ Solidarity and systemic principles of the state.

Responsibility: PUWP CC, PPR government, party organs and organizations, state offices, and social organizations
Time-frame: immediate effect

9. Recommend to members of parliament to participate only in the deputies' meetings organized by the Front for National Unity in order to strengthen the authority of the Sejm and to protect the deputies from attacks coming from Solidarity.

Responsibility: CC Bureau for Sejm Affairs, Voivodeship Deputies Groups
Time-frame: immediate effect

10. Organize meetings of the Polish People's Army with party organizations in order to have them present the threat facing the Polish *raison d'état* from the side of the malevolent political opposition. These meetings should be linked to the anniversary of the creation of the Polish People's Army.

Responsibility: CC Organizational Department, The Main Political Board of the PPA, VC Executives
Time-frame: by October 12, 1981

11. Support the activity of sector and autonomous unions in the sphere of securing workers' basic interests through the party and the state and economic administration; create socio-political conditions for the quantitative development of these organizations and the integration of actions.

Responsibility: CC, VC Departments, organs of the first degree and the FC.
Time-frame: immediate effect

12. Recommend to party organizations and members to boycott any kind of activities and resolutions which do not fit in the framework of the NSZZ Solidarity Statute.

Responsibility: VC Executives, organs of the first degree, FC's
Time-frame: immediate effect

II. *In the field of propaganda and mass media activity.*
1. Launch a propaganda offensive in the press, radio and television, which should:
– prove to society that the party aims to resolve the crisis by political means, and that it is organizing to that effect an agreement with all constructively functioning social forces;
– show the government's actions aiming at the introduction of economic reform, overcoming market difficulties, and implementation of a program to overcome the crisis;
– demonstrate that the NSZZ Solidarity came out of the Congress as a political force clearly oriented toward the West. In this context, reveal Solidarity's ties with bourgeois and anti-Polish centers of diversion (sources of financial aid, links with activists, etc.) and emphasize that Solidarity's program has created conditions for the concentration and joint activity of all forms of political opposition in the country;
– show that at this stage of Solidarity's development it is the leaders and experts who decide about the ideological and political image of the union while the workers' masses have been cut off from ability to influence its [Solidarity] program and activities;
– document and present to the public all facts concerning the dissolution of the economy and steps toward the collapse of the state structure. Show society that the worsening market situation is the result of the destructive activity of Solidarity;
– demonstrate the economically and socially destructive activity of the Peasants' NSZZ Solidarity due to boycotting of food supplies and tax evasion, etc.
– present the threat of anarchy and elements of terror spreading across the life of the country, and simultaneously call for respect for order and discipline;
– present biographies, activity and links of selected Solidarity activists and their advisers with centers of ideological diversion, including members of Peasants' Solidarity.

Responsibility: Departments: Press, Radio and Television, Ideological-Educational Activity, Social-Vocational and Administrative CC
Time-frame: immediate effect

2. Organize a general propaganda campaign on two issues:
a) popular support for the Politburo declaration in the largest work institutes, important socio-professional circles, social and youth organizations, press, radio and television;
b) provoke condemnation for the provocateurs of the anti-Soviet campaign.

Responsibility: all departments of the CC, PUWP Voivode-ship Committees
Time-frame: September 18–25, 1981

3. Complete an assessment and verification of the leadership cadre of party newspaper editorial offices in accordance with the decision of the Ninth Congress and the Second Plenum of the CC.

Responsibility: Press, Radio and Television Departments of the CC
Time-frame: by September 25, 1981

4. Hold consultations with chief editors and PPO executives of the editorial offices of party newspapers and radio and television to discuss methods of fighting the political opponent in the mass media.

Responsibility: Press, Radio and Television Departments of the CC
Time-frame: by September 26, 1981

5. Determine the status of a party newspaper journalist and the government's means of information, radio and television.

Responsibility: Press, Radio and Television Departments of the CC
Time-frame: by November 30, 1981

6. Demand, with immediate responsibility, observance of the principle of the legislative act on censorship of persons printing and distributing leaflets, posters, communiqués, etc. hostile to socialist Poland, her allies, and the PUWP.

Responsibility: Ministry of Internal Affairs, Prosecutor General, state and economic administration
Time-frame: immediate effect

7. Present in the Party press, radio and television the facts and motives of particular persons and groups withdrawing from the Solidarity union.

Responsibility: Press, Radio and Television, Socio-Vocational, and Organizational Departments of the CC, and Voivode-ship Committees of the PUWP
Time-frame: immediate effect

8. Hold sessions of the Central Lectors' Group and conduct a lectors' action in the 207 largest work institutes and 100 chosen counties [*gmina*] concerning the following subjects:
– self-government of the institute;
– current directions of the political struggle;

– the representative system of the PPR and goals for improving it;
– Poland's foreign policy under conditions of a socio-economic crisis.

> *Responsibility*: CC Department of Ideological-Educational
> Activity
> *Time-frame*: by October 1, 1981

9. Prepare the inauguration of a new year of party training at the central level and in local branches; broaden party agitation and train the *aktiv* in four thematic blocs, i.e.:
– Marxism–Leninist theory;
– knowledge about the party;
– crucial ideological-political problems in light of the resolution of the PUWP Ninth Congress;
– the outline of PPR history.

> *Responsibility*: CC Department of Ideological-Educational
> Activity, Voivodeship Committees of PUWP
> *Time-frame*: by October 30, 1981

10. Develop a broad propaganda campaign in the mass media and develop forms of "small" propaganda portraying the anti-socialist image of certain Solidarity activists and experts.

> *Responsibility*: CC Departments of Ideological-Educational
> Activity, and Press, Radio and Television
> *Time-frame*: immediate effect

11. Expand the information system of the party by covering the Organizational and the Ideological-Educational Departments of the CC, and the first level party organs with the current information system. Prepare periodical information for members of the central party authorities and delegates to the PUWP Ninth Congress.

> *Responsibility*: Organizational and Ideological-Educational
> Activity Departments of the CC
> *Time-frame*: immediate effect

III. *In the area of respect for the law and public order.*
1. Establish voivodeship centers for order and public security under the chairmanship of the VC first secretaries composed of: the voivode, the head of the SB VHCP and his deputy, the voivodeship prosecutor, the president of the Voivodeship Court, and the head of the VDC Staff for the operational coordination of political and administrative activities.

> *Responsibility*: CC Administrative Department, first secretaries of the VC
> *Time-frame*: by September 25, 1981

2. Activate the methods and expand the scope of the legal struggle with all aspects of antagonistic anti-socialist and anti-party activity, taking advantage of the expanded competences of the penal-administrative councils.

> *Responsibility*: Administrative Department of the CC, voivodes, presidents, heads of the VHCP, voivodeship prosecutors
> *Time-frame*: immediate effect

3. Activate the functioning of the Voluntary Reserves of Citizens' Police. Begin to train groups of the party *aktiv* within the framework of that organization.

> *Responsibility*: VC Executives, voivodeship heads of the Citizens' Police
> *Time-frame*: immediate effect

4. Create an atmosphere of public condemnation for all kinds of expressions of anarchism, hooligan incidents, vandalism, and violations of personal security, while at the same time utilizing swift and effective means of repression.

> *Responsibility*: CC Administrative Department, Ministry of Internal Affairs, Ministry of Justice, Prosecutor General, and relevant local authorities
> *Time-frame*: immediate effect

5. Undertake decisive actions (also legal) which would aim at the elimination of any kind of incidents of uneconomic management and wastefulness, as well as sluggishness in all public service institutions.

> *Responsibility*: ministries, voivodes, organs of policing and justice
> *Time-frame*: immediate effect

6. Consistently and effectively apply legal instruments to all those who carry out agitation and exert pressure on individual peasants on the question of tax evasion, withholding the sale of livestock and agricultural goods, as well as taking over communal lands.

> *Responsibility*: voivodes, presidents, directors, prosecutors, and heads of all units
> *Time-frame*: immediate effect

7. Create a legal basis that would enable factories to withhold salaries of full-time trade union activists who carry out anti-system activities and withhold financing of whole trade union organizations, whose activity will have an anti-state character (in the new trade union bill).

> *Responsibility*: PPR government, CC Bureau for Sejm Affairs
> *Time-frame*: by September 30, 1981

8. Terminate talks with the NCC and regional boards of the NSZZ Solidarity on issues beyond problems of trade unions.

> *Responsibility*: ministers, voivodes and presidents
> *Time-frame*: immediate effect

9. Subject the contacts of the NSZZ Solidarity representatives with capitalist countries to thorough control. Ban travel abroad for those who have caused political damage to Poland while abroad. Take full control over the influx of financial resources from abroad to the NSZZ Solidarity.

> *Responsibility*: Foreign and Administrative Departments of
> the CC; Foreign Ministry and Ministry of Internal Affairs
> *Time-frame*: immediate effect

10. Conduct talks with representatives of the Church hierarchy at all levels on the subject of the situation in the country and principles of joint action with the state (on the basis of guidelines).

> *Responsibility*: CC Administrative Department, Office for
> Religions, voivodes and presidents
> *Time-frame*: by October 30, 1981

IV. *In the field of economic activity.*

1. Launch an extensive education [campaign] among party members on the question of economic reforms and workers' self-government with consideration given to local situations (reported upon by directors of institutes).

> *Responsibility*: PPR government, CC departments of the
> economic sector
> *Time-frame*: immediate effect

2. Organize expert groups on economic reform and workers' self-government in the voivodeship committees and larger local party organs which would perform consultative-advisory functions for party and economic organizations. Their activity should also be conducive to undertaking initiatives in work institutes.

> *Responsibility*: voivodeship committees of the PUWP
> *Time-frame*: by September 25, 1981

3. Conduct talks with the leadership of the main boards of the PES, the Association of Accountants in Poland, the Scientific Society of Organization and Management, and the CTO on the matter of arranging courses and consultations by these organizations in the area of economic reform.

> *Responsibility*: Industry, Construction and Transport, Trade
> and Finance Departments of the CC
> *Time-frame*: by September 25, 1981

4. At the initiative of PUWP members active in the STA–CTO, hold a meeting of the CTO Chief Council to determine the tasks of the STA and MD CTO associated with organizational and consultative activities. [These activities would be] aimed at including the STA engineer-technical cadre in active work related to preparing enterprises for the introduction of economic reforms and the establishment of workers' self-government. Similar meetings should be organized at the initiative of PUWP members active in voivodeship departments of the CTO.

> *Responsibility*: Industry, Construction and Transport Departments of the CC and VC
> *Time-frame*: by September 25, 1981

5. At the initiative of party members active in women's organizations, hold a plenary session of the National Women's Council with the participation of representatives of party and state authorities, with the aim of presenting the government's position associated with overcoming the socio-political and economic crisis. Aim at gaining the approval of women's circles for the introduction of economic reform and establishment of workers' self-government. Similar meetings should be organized with voivodeship women's councils.

> *Responsibility*: Social Organizations, Sport and Tourism Departments of the CC and VC
> *Time-frame*: by October 15, 1981

6. Recommend to ministers and voivodes that they organize obligatory training of the staffs of ministries, associations, voivodeship offices, and the institutes' leadership in the area of economic and employee self-government reform.

> *Responsibility*: PPR government
> *Time-frame*: by September 30, 1981

7. Announce the government's timetable for stabilizing particular segments of the market and resolutely make more effective the organization of supplies and sale of articles covered by rationing (above all, determine the timing for covering needs fully, for example flour-based products and bread, fruit and vegetable products, potatoes, etc.). Presentation [should be] made for example in the Sejm.

> *Responsibility*: PPR government
> *Time-frame*: by September 24, 1981

8. Put in order the system of rationing foodstuffs and industrial products in the country.

> *Responsibility*: PPR government, voivodes and presidents
> *Time-frame*: by October 1, 1981

9. Prepare plans of action in each voivodeship which would aim at:
– accumulating winter reserves (potatoes, vegetables, fruit, etc.);

- maximal accumulation of resources for the agricultural-food processing industry;
- organizing winter supplies for workers;
- improving the quality of foodstuffs being produced;
- activating the development of breeding and purchases of livestock as well as the purchase of milk;
- activating the production of market products;
- improving the functioning of trade, purchasing centers and other service institutions in urban and rural areas.

The above-mentioned problems should be given high attention in the activity of all party organs and organizations, offices and national councils as well as institutions for public and social control.

There should be information in the mass media about the initiatives undertaken on these issues and their positive results.

PUWP CC Secretariat
Warsaw, September 18, 1981.

[Source: AAN, PUWP CC, 4762, pp. 177–190. Translated by Paweł Świeboda.]

The pope and Jaruzelski meet at Belweder, Warsaw, June 17, 1983. John Paul II was a figure of major political and symbolic importance during the Solidarity period and thereafter.
(http://www.geocities.com/ wojciech_jaruzelski/zyciorys4.html)

Polish Primate Józef Glemp and Jaruzelski hold one of a series of meetings during the Solidarity crisis.
(http://www.geocities.com/wojciech_jaruzelski/foto-ms.html)

Members of the Soviet leadership greet Jaruzelski at the airport in Moscow as he arrives on March 1, 1982, for his first visit to the Soviet capital since declaring martial law. Left to right are Defense Minister Dmitri Ustinov, Jaruzelski, Leonid Brezhnev, Konstantin Rusakov and Foreign Minister Andrei Gromyko.
(http://www.geocities.com/wojciech_jaruzelski/ mockba.html)

Jaruzelski and Wałęsa meet in Warsaw, March 10, 1981, shortly before the Bydgoszcz crisis.
(http://www.geocities.com/wojciech_jaruzelski/ zyciorys4.html)

Lech Wałęsa addresses strikers from the gates of the Lenin Shipyard, Gdańsk, August 1980. (Unknown photographer, photo provided by Barbara Bednarek, KARTA Center collection)

Solidarity activists Jan Rulewski, Jacek Kuroń and Janusz Onyszkiewicz during their internment in Warsaw, 1982. (Unknown photographer, KARTA Center collection)

After the declaration of martial law, ZOMO militiamen face off against demonstrators who have placed Solidarity stickers on their shields. (Unknown photographer, KARTA Center collection)

Jaruzelski announces the imposition of martial law to a nationwide television audience, December 13, 1981.
(http://www.geocities.com/wojciech_jaruzelski/zyciorys4.html)

Interned Solidarity activists Karol Modzelewski, Henryk Wujec, Andrzej Gwiazda and Adam Michnik in the Białołęka district of Warsaw, 1982.
(Unknown photographer, KARTA Center collection)

Members of the Politburo elected during the PUWP's Extraordinary IX Congress in Warsaw, July 14-19, 1981. To Jaruzelski's immediate right are Stanisław Kania and Kazimierz Barcikowski; to his left are Zofia Gryb and Stefan Olszowski.
(http://www.geocities.com/wojciech_jaruzelski/zyciorys4.html)

Stefan Cardinal Wyszyński, Poland's primate and leader of the Polish Catholic Church till his death in May 1981, was a central player during the crisis.
(photo: Tomasz Abramowicz, KARTA Center collection)

Jaruzelski and Stanisław Kania confer during the critical Fourth Plenum of the PUWP CC, held October 16-18, 1981. Kania submitted his resignation as party first secretary at the session, and Jaruzelski was elected to replace him.

Tanks deployed near the entrance to the Lenin Shipyard in Gdańsk following the declaration of martial law.
(Unknown photographer, National Commission of the NSZZ "Solidarity" in Gdańsk—collection of the Coordination Bureau of the NSZZ "S" in Brussels)

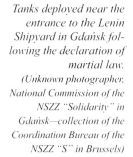

Solidarity's Mazowsze (Warsaw) branch convenes a general assembly at Warsaw University of Technology in early December 1981. The union's increasing size, organization and activism were sources of alarm for Polish authorities.
(Unknown photographer, KARTA Center collection, from the archive of the Photojournalists' Unit of the NSZZ "Solidarity" Mazowsze Region)

PART FIVE

Final Preparations

Document No. 70: Czesław Kiszczak's Notes for October 5 Politburo Meeting

October 4, 1981

These notes describe the state of the Ministry of Internal Affairs' preparations for implementing martial law. Minister Czesław Kiszczak needed this information for a presentation to the Politburo on October 5. The notes show very clearly the extent of the measures prepared by all branches of the Ministry, including lists of writers and artists who could be enlisted for support after the introduction of martial law and the operation to take over Solidarity. Kiszczak may have thought that the political decision would have been made at the upcoming Politburo meeting, but it was postponed for another two months. An interesting aspect of this item is that it is a working document, not a formal memorandum, a rather rare archival find, especially after so many years.

[…]

Assignments:

1) Lists of persons from the academic and cultural worlds, mainly non-party, with clean political slates, leaning in favor of the people's authority—even if not fully identifying with it or having critical opinions towards it—with considerable authority in society, who can provide hope that if needed they will be ready to step forward publicly for the benefit of social common sense. They will also be able to join different official bodies and organs, which are projected to be created.

For all persons indicated above, a few characteristic words, and this formulated in the lists. Underline names especially worthy of attention.

List or link names susceptible to central groups or provincial groups.

At the beginning of the list (as per the first and second versions) provide a summary of how many persons are at play.

This assignment [to be] fulfilled by the Third Dept., personally to Col. Walczyński, to whom all other comrades are sending the data in their possession.

The Minister is eager that this assignment be executed for tomorrow (Oct. 5), but the current directors assert that this will be very difficult. If this is not possible, then present summary data on Oct. 5, and indicate a date certain when the complete data will be available.

2) Lists of journalists on whom the party and Government leadership can rely completely. Underline the names of those who are ready to go for everything [*pojść na wszysko*] and take up all subjects recommended to them. Moreover, indicate the journalists who will be ready to take action against the current APJ

[Association of Polish Journalists] authorities. In this area, have it in mind to "dispatch" some of the APJ's "wild ones"[1] with different missions and delegations to dollar zones, so that by their absence from the country greater freedom for maneuver can be attained, and attempts can be made to create splits.

Provide numerical data concerning supervisory and local ranks on October 5; [or provide] the summary data if need be on that day, and the complete data when available.

3) A list of honest and trustworthy priests, who could be utilized for positive actions. The aim would be to show society and the Church authorities that not all priests think alike and that there are different opinions in the Church. Call attention to priests who would be ready to join different social bodies that support the authorities. Underscore the names of priests who can be counted on absolutely.

This assignment will be carried out by the Fourth Dept.

4) A list of honest writers and artists prepared according to the outline for the list of journalists. The aim is to secure influence over the creative community.

This assignment is being carried out by the Third Dept., also on October 5, even if in a preliminary way.

5) List honest film makers who could counter the Wajda[2] clique and his cabal.

Also carried out by the Third Dept.

6) A list of members of PAS who are complying with the above ideas and outlines.

Fulfilled by the Third Dept.

7) Look over and harness, in relevant lists, members of the senates of individual schools. There should be two lists: one positive, and a second list of "wild ones" who need to be disposed of.

8) Assessments and lists of individual editorial boards for periodicals, and also radio and television editorial boards. Report which editorial boards need to be restrained or liquidated at present or at an appropriate moment, under this or that pretext.

Carried out by the Second Dept., supervised by Gen. [Władysław] Pożoga.

9) An assessment of the situation in the prosecutor's office and the courts—what is it really like in these organs? Point out persons who will eventually need to be removed from these organs.

Cde. Starszak explains that the Ministry of Internal Affairs does not have an operational interest in the prosecutor's office and courts; therefore it is difficult to objectively assess this circle.

---

[1] Denoting the most radical of the independent journalists.

[2] Andrzej Wajda was the renowned director of such films as *Ashes and Diamonds* and *Man of Marble. Man of Iron,* a film about the rise of the Polish reform movement, which included scenes from the strike at the Lenin Shipyard, won the Golden Palm at the Cannes Film Festival in 1981.

After the discussion, the Cde. Minister acknowledged that we will omit the prosecutor's office. We will carry out the assessment of the courts based on information from the Investigative Bureau and Investigative Department of the VHCP.

10) Carry out verification of persons who are supposed to be incorporated under operation "Wrzos."[3] Selection is necessary so as to limit the number of persons who will need to be isolated. Have in mind that with some persons preventive-cooling-off talks may be sufficient. In case of need, isolate those who are the most dangerous.

Determined that Comrade Pawlikowski, in agreement with Comrade Ciastoń, will plan and send to the field the code applied with regard to this question.

Inform the comrade minister, without delay, what kind of change in numbers occur pertaining to operation "Wrzos." Report on Wrocław, maybe someone will even go there and familiarize himself with the situation on the spot.

Execute an assessment of the isolation areas—have the proper places and centers been chosen? Penal facilities placed as far as possible from urban centers and large concentrations of people are desired.

Also execute an assessment of the kinds of cadre work at these penal facilities, if they are worth trusting completely.

Assess the state of readiness to begin operational work at these penal facilities, where they will be isolated within the framework of operation "Wrzos."

Plan a proposal regarding "S" activists who would be able to replace the extremist group regarding what is possible in a political confrontation, or regarding the groups that should be placed in isolation within the framework of operation "Wrzos." For every regional headquarters of "S" there must be a replacement group that does not include any "frantic" [members]. Proposals indicated must be formulated in writing—besides the RA, also take into account large factory and enterprise administrations, as well as certain administrations of larger "S" cells (for instance "Ursus," FSO, the Warsaw steelworks, the Waryński Enterprise).

For tomorrow (October 5), provide numbers where we have already prepared these replacement groups.

Executed by the Third Department. Gen. Ciastoń supports the Second Department.

11) Consider operations that will lead to the creation of groups in "S" that declare themselves in favor of a different "S."

12) Assess whether at this moment or after designated operational activities have begun there are provinces where operation "Wrzos" would not be needed at all, and which conceivably could be excluded from martial law.

13) Assess the state of matériel and essential measures during the period of confrontation (water cannons, tear gas, and so on). Consider what the USSR, GDR and ČSR fraternal ministries could lend or deliver to us in this area.

[3] "Heather"—the code name for the operation to intern leaders of Solidarity.

Comrade Jedynak will present this problem to Comrade Zaczkowski [commandant of the militia].

It is necessary to be aware that fire-arms, should they even be necessary, are a last measure.

14) Consider the question of forming compact units of ZOMO, as anticipated in the plans, in such a way as not to alarm the opponent.

Executed by Comrade Pawlikowski.

15) The analytical group at the MS, which is now not determined, should strengthen its forecasting efforts and elaborate a vision of how the opponent will act. Results of the work of the analytical group must be produced in a few days.

16) Create personnel files on opponents who up to now have not been investigated and about whom there is a lack of important information.

17) It is imperative to intensify operational work and quickly build up the number of reconnaissance sources. In one of the KWK [*kopalnia węgla kamiennego*—coal mines], of 8,000 personnel at this moment there were only 2 such sources, and there should be no fewer than 30–50 of them there. Considering current conditions it is necessary to yield to sources of operational reconnaissance. Take advantage of ASS opportunities and, in doing so, begin appropriate discussions with Gen. Poradko and Col. Ogonowski.[4] Detail from there right away whoever is needed and available.

Expand the practice of creating residencies.

18) Initiate the creation of operational groups that will undertake active work in large enterprises, conveying the atmosphere of particular industrial centers (for instance in Warsaw: "Ursus," FSO, and the Warsaw steelworks).

19) Will it be necessary to direct some staff from "W" Section,[5] RKW[6] and others to these groups? In general, this is about setting up operational contacts and servicing sources of individual identification for the maximum number of employees.

Comrade Pożoga thinks that it is necessary first to check whether there are people with operational training in these Sections.

Gen. Jedynak will discuss this subject with Gen. Stachura.

20) Accelerate regionalization in the organizational structure of the Ministry of Internal Affairs; where possible, introduce it now and create regional SB operational groups that will be engaged in expanding and activating individual reconnaissance sources.

21) Focus attention on leading "S" activists.

22) Widen the circle of party-social activists who can be armed and linked up with operations previously undertaken. Engage the PUWP VC for these operations.

---

[4] Officers in Army intelligence.

[5] The section responsible for monitoring the mails at post offices.

[6] *Radio Kontrwywiad*—Radio Counterintelligence.

23) Enlist more quickly our retired SB and Citizens' Police functionaries who are medically fit for work.

24) Operate more actively in such a way as to lead the opponent "down the garden path" in situations that will place [him] in a difficult or compromising situation; in particular demonstrate that he is irresponsible, quarrelsome, and is leading the country to ruin.

25) Contribute to the effort to make a few appropriate pronouncements in the final part of the second round of the "S" Congress; after the Congress, include a few pronouncements on television and radio, which while generally positive for "S," will still judge certain problems and events critically. Different related ventures and steps are also imperative.

26) Consider operations using leaflets and other printed material ridiculing or compromising certain "S" ventures and their "activists" (for instance, that [Jacek] Kuroń punched [Jan] Rulewski in the mouth at the Congress). Consider other possibilities.

27) In relation to the fact that Rulewski will seek a strike in Bydgoszcz, shortly after the Congress begin appropriate active operations with regard to him, demonstrating his irresponsibility in particular. [One] might take advantage of the juxtaposition of events: Bydgoszcz 19 March 1981, R[ulewski] scratched up, and the attempted assassination of the pope.

28) The minister's PB pronouncements summing up the "S" Congress.

29) Appoint a team to prepare a very revealing pronouncement by the minister at the next CC plenum. Illustrate the security situation in the country from the perspective of the opponent's activities. Show that the party and the Government are doing everything to stabilize the situation, but that the opponent piles everything onto the authorities.

Moreover, prepare material for the minister for replies to anticipated questions.

Comrade Starszak will prepare particulars about what we did in the most recent period: detentions, searches, arrests, cases, and the like (statistical details in a variety of shapes and arrangements; among other things: what has been challenged, especially, hostile publishing houses, duplicators, leaflets in institutional glass-cases, which are emptied of enemy materials).

30) Consider distributing appropriate witticisms compromising the opponent.

[Source: IPN, MSW II, 199, pp. 7–12. Translated by L. W. Głuchowski for the National Security Archive.]

Document No. 71: Notes of Brezhnev–Jaruzelski Telephone Conversation

October 19, 1981

At the Fourth PUWP plenum from October 16–18, a major leadership change took place as Kania stepped down as first secretary and Jaruzelski replaced him. In this telephone conversation, notable for the vast difference in the way the two leaders address each other, Brezhnev warmly congratulates the new Polish leader, who nevertheless admits to considerable reluctance in accepting the position. The Soviets had finally had enough of Kania's reluctance to clamp down and believed that Jaruzelski was the best hope for getting the Polish leadership to act forcefully. In addition to his long record of loyalty to Moscow, Jaruzelski enjoyed a relatively high reputation in his own country. But despite his unusually powerful position—simultaneously holding the posts of party first secretary, prime minister and defense minister—he continued a policy of extreme caution at first. The Kremlin soon began to harangue him with increasing intensity in the absence of any signs of willingness to crack down on his part. Behind the scenes, though, and to a degree unbeknownst to Moscow, he began very soon to lay the groundwork for martial law.

The Kremlin

L. I. Brezhnev: Hello, Wojciech.

W. Jaruzelski: Hello, deeply esteemed, dear Leonid Ilyich.

L. I. Brezhnev: Dear Wojciech, we have already sent you our official greetings, but I wanted also to congratulate you directly on your selection as PUWP CC first secretary.

You acted correctly, having agreed to this decision. There is currently no one in the PUWP who can make use of his authority the way you can; the results of the plenum also to speak to this. We understand that very difficult problems stand before you. But we are convinced that you will master them and do everything to overcome the serious ailment that has befallen your country.

I think that right now, as it seems to me, the most important thing for you is to select reliable assistants for yourself from among the numbers of committed and staunch communists, rally them, set in motion the entire party, and instill in it the spirit of struggle. This, in the literal sense of the word, is the key to success.

And of course it is important, without wasting time, to move on to the decisive actions you have laid out against the counter-revolution. We hope that now everyone, both in Poland and abroad, will feel that events in the country are proceeding differently.

We wish you good health and success!

W. Jaruzelski: Thank you very much, dear Leonid Ilyich, for your greetings and above all for the faith you have shown in me. I want to say to you openly that I agreed to accept this post after a great internal struggle, and only because I knew that you support me and that you are in favor of this decision. If this had not been so, I would never have agreed to it. It is a very heavy and very difficult situation, under such complicated circumstances in the country, that I now find myself as prime minister and minister of defense. But I understand that it is a correct and necessary situation, if you personally believe it is.

L. I. Brezhnev: Wojciech, we have believed it for a long time. We have spoken about it for a long time to our friends.

W. Jaruzelski: And that is why I agreed. Leonid Ilyich, I will do everything, as a communist and a soldier, to make things better and to strive for a turning point in conditions for our country and our party. I understand and fully agree with you that now one of the decisive moments is at hand—the selection of the leadership both of the party and the government. And especially for that reason I have postponed the resolution of the question of cadres till the next plenum, which we will hold in several days, in order to think things through thoroughly, to consult, and in order for this to be an all-encompassing decision and not simply a series of discrete cadre steps.

L. I. Brezhnev: The cadres are very important, both in the center and in the provinces.

W. Jaruzelski: And it will be necessary to resolve this question in the provinces as well. Of course, this has to occur in parallel with the strengthening of the party in the sense of activating the struggle. In the appropriate circumstances, one must employ decisive actions in order to give battle where there is confidence in success.

I am going now to a session of the Military Council of the Armed Forces at the Ministry of Defense. I will assign the appropriate tasks there as well. We will incorporate the army broadly in all areas of life in the country.

Yesterday, after the plenum, I had a meeting with the first secretaries of the oblast committees, and I told them not to take offense that we will be including people from the armed forces in the elaboration of certain processes, and that we will expand meetings of the officer corps with the working class in order to have a direct influence on the workers and to isolate them from the influence of Solidarity. Of course, we are not changing our general direction in the sense that, while fighting for the healthy forces of the people which have lost their way and gone over to Solidarity, and attracting them to our side, we will simultaneously strike the adversary and, of course, strike him in such a way as to produce results.

Today I met with your ambassador. I will try to discuss certain questions with him in more detail, and I will seek your advice on matters which he will probably report to you.

While informing you of all the decisions we have taken, we will report at the same time on how we reached one or another decision.

Right now, the most complicated situation in our country is in the market. In this connection, there are many strikes and protests. Some of these are organized by Solidarity, others are simply spontaneous. This greatly complicates the implementation of measures that must be taken, and it complicates our work since the mood in society is apathetic. But we will try to do everything possible to improve the situation.

This is what I wanted to inform you about at first.

Once again, thank you very much for your kind words.

L. I. Brezhnev: I again wish you, Wojciech, good health and success.

W. Jaruzelski: Thank you. Good-bye.

[Source: RGANI, Fond 5, Opis 84, Delo 596, pp. 33–35. Translated by Malcolm Byrne for the National Security Archive.]

Document No. 72: Transcript of CPSU CC Politburo Meeting on Rusakov's Trip to Eastern Europe

October 29, 1981

In this discussion, the Politburo mulls over the growing realization that Jaruzelski is proving to be just as passive as his predecessor. They decide that they may have to summon him to a meeting. Another growing problem is the need to provide economic help to Poland which is exacerbating shortages in other sectors. Konstantin Rusakov, a member of the Politburo Commission on Poland, offers a fascinating account of a recent visit to several Eastern European countries where each party leader has made clear his disappointment over Moscow's decision to cut back on oil deliveries for the sake of Poland. The GDR's Erich Honecker was especially outspoken, prompting a mix of reactions at this session. The Poles, meanwhile, have also been asking for military support. But both Andropov and Ustinov are unequivocal that there can be no question of introducing Soviet troops into the country.

[...]

2. On the results of Cde. K. V. Rusakov's trip to the GDR, ČSSR, HPR and BPR.

Brezhnev: All the comrades present here know that at the instruction of the CPSU CC Politburo Cde. Rusakov left for the GDR, Czechoslovakia, Hungary and Bulgaria to inform our friends on several matters, in particular on the measures we have taken and will take in connection with the Polish events.

Cde. Rusakov went to those countries and reported to the Politburo on the results of his travels in a note, which you have.

Perhaps Konstantin Viktorovich has something to add to what he put in his note. In that case, please do.

Rusakov: I held discussions with the leaders of four fraternal states, as instructed by the Politburo. The talks dealt with two questions: the first question related to Poland. In my note the course of the discussions with the leaders of the fraternal countries on the Polish question is laid out in detail. One can say that all the leaders of the fraternal parties are unanimously in agreement with us regarding the measures we are taking with respect to Poland, and also with respect to the situation that has unfolded in Poland. In a word, one can say that on this there is total unanimity of views.

During the course of the talks the leaders of the fraternal countries broached economic questions as well. The main question concerned a cutback in supplies of fuel, especially oil. Cdes. Kádár, Husák and Zhivkov, even though they said that this would be difficult for them, nevertheless treated our proposal with understanding, and responded to our request by saying that they would find a solution to the situation and would accept what we proposed. For the sake of further

395

clarity, I asked the comrades the following question: may I report to the Polit-buro that you agree with the point of view I expressed? The comrades answered, yes, you may.

My conversation with Cde. Honecker took a different shape. He immediately said that a cut in oil supplies would be unacceptable for the GDR; that it would cause serious damage to the national economy and the GDR as a whole; that it would strike severely the GDR economy; and that we [*sic*] would be utterly un-able to make ends meet. He even declared that they could not accept this and asked for a written reply from Cde. Brezhnev to two letters they had sent. In this way, the question became very complicated and it was essentially never resolved. Cde. Honecker again produced as proof that they provide us with bismuth and uranium, that they maintain a Group of Forces, and that things are becoming es-pecially complicated because the Polish People's Republic is not supplying coal, which is supposed to be coming from us. In this regard, as Honecker put it, the German people's living standard is dropping significantly and we do not know how to explain it. They will have to review all plan targets.

Brezhnev: I think that we should approve the discussions Cde. Rusakov con-ducted with Cdes. Honecker, Husák, Kádár and Zhivkov, and in our subsequent practical work take into account the impressions expressed by our comrades on the Polish question.

As you know, we decided to limit oil supplies to our friends. They all took it with difficulty and Cde. Honecker, for example, as you see, is still waiting for an answer to the letters he sent us. The others are not waiting for a reply, but in their hearts, of course, they are hoping that we might somehow change our minds.

Perhaps we should somehow say to our friends at our next meeting that we will take all measures aimed at fulfilling and over-fulfilling the plan for oil, and we hope that we will succeed. In that case we could amend our draft plans for fuel supplies, but under no circumstances, of course, allowing them to believe that we are reversing our decision.

It is apparent that Cde. Tikhonov will once more have to examine this ques-tion attentively and, if the smallest possibility arises to alleviate tensions, to sub-mit suitable proposals to the CC.

Gromyko: I would like to say in relation to Poland, that I just had a conver-sation with the ambassador, Cde. Aristov. He reported that the one-hour strike was highly impressive. At many enterprises, Solidarity was essentially in charge. Even if someone wanted to work, he could not because Solidarity extremists pre-vent those who want to from working, threaten them in every possible way, etc.

As for the plenum, as Cde. Aristov reported, it proceeded normally. They elected two additional secretaries. At the Sejm which begins its session on Oc-tober 30, they will table a question on limiting strikes. What shape that law will take is hard to say, but at least attempts are being made by means of the law to limit strikes. Cde. Jaruzelski's speech at the plenum was, I would say, not bad.

Brezhnev: I do not believe that Cde. Jaruzelski has done anything construc-tive. He does not seem to me to be a brave enough man.

Andropov: Jaruzelski has essentially done nothing new, even though some time has passed. [Kazimierz] Barcikowski and [Hieronim] Kubiak are a major obstacle in the Politburo. There have been discussions about this, and it was even advised that Barcikowski and Kubiak be removed from the Politburo. However, Jaruzelski essentially refused to take this step. He explains this by saying that he does not have cadres who could replace these officials.

Everyone pricks up their ears at the question of who the next premier of Poland will be. Jaruzelski obviously looks with favor on Olszowski and Rakowski. Of course neither one is suitable to be premier.

Brezhnev: Even [Helmut] Schmidt in one of our discussions let the cat out of the bag that a very dangerous situation is being created in Poland and that this situation might complicate and influence my visit to the FRG, which might not occur.

Andropov: The Polish leaders talk about military aid from the fraternal countries. However, we must firmly stick to your line—not to introduce our troops into Poland.

Ustinov: In general, one must say that it is impossible to introduce our troops into Poland. They, the Poles, are not ready to receive our troops. In Poland there is currently a demobilization of those who have served their tour. They are sending the demobilized units home so that they can put on civilian clothes and then return and serve another two months. But during that time they undergo treatment by Solidarity. Jaruzelski, as we know, organized operational groups consisting of approximately three people. But these groups have done nothing so far. Obviously, a meeting is needed with the Polish leadership, especially Jaruzelski. But who will meet with them is also a question.

Rusakov: Tomorrow the Sejm opens. Before it will be the question of granting the government its own version of extraordinary powers to decide a series of questions. Jaruzelski, really, would like to come to Moscow. In that regard, it will be necessary to prepare for this question.

Brezhnev: Who will prepare the material for the conversations with Jaruzelski?

Rusakov: I think that we ought to instruct the Commission on Poland to prepare material for a possible discussion with Jaruzelski if he expresses the desire.

Brezhnev: Have we sent meat to Poland, as we decided to do? And have we informed Jaruzelski?

Rusakov: We have informed Jaruzelski. He gave the figure of 30,000 tons.

Arkhipov: We will send meat to Poland from our state reserves.

Brezhnev: Are there any improvements in the receipt of meat in the allied fund from the republics after my telegram?

Arkhipov: So far, Leonid Ilyich, there have been no improvements in the receipt of meat. It is true that not enough time has passed. But I talked this over with all the republics and I can report that measures are being taken everywhere that would enable the fulfillment of the plan for meat deliveries to the state. In particular, such measures have been worked out in Estonia, Belorussia and Kazakhstan. Ukraine has not yet issued orders to the provinces.

Chernenko: But we circulated our telegram to all the provinces.

Arkhipov: We will have the data by Monday. At that point we will report on where things stand.

Gorbachev: Leonid Ilyich, your telegram played a large role. Above all, all the republics and provinces are seriously reviewing measures that would help fulfill the plan. In any case, according to the data we have as a result of telephone conversations with provincial and district committees and the Central Committees of the communist parties of the union republics, this question is being discussed at all the bureaus [*na biuro*]. On January 1 we will provide a summary on the receipt of meat.

Brezhnev: I still think that even though we gave Poland 30,000 tons of meat, our meat will hardly help the Poles. In any case, we have no clear idea of what is to come with Poland. Cde. Jaruzelski is not showing any initiative. Perhaps we should prepare for a discussion with him.

As far as discussions concerning oil supplies, the GDR is especially troubling to me. In general, I want to say that the socialist countries took our proposal hard. If not directly, then in their soul they are unhappy with this decision. And some, as can be seen from Cde. Rusakov's presentation, are directly expressing their dissatisfaction. Cde. Honecker is especially dissatisfied. He says openly that this decision is unacceptable for them, and he even asks for a written reply. What kind of decision we adopt I simply do not know.

Andropov, Suslov, Kirilenko say that one must agree with the statement you have just made.

Arkhipov: Difficulties with fuel continue to arise in our country. The miners are under-producing by 30 million tons. How can that be offset? The petroleum industry will not overfulfill their plan, therefore it is necessary to compensate for that 30 million tons somehow. Beyond that, we are short 1.5 million tons of sugar, which has to be bought, and 800,000 tons of vegetable oil, which one cannot live without.

As far as an answer to Honecker, I think that the proposal Cde. Rusakov introduced is appropriate. We must confirm that we cannot change the decision that was conveyed to Cde. Honecker.

As far as the uranium supplies Cde. Honecker refers to, that uranium supplied by the GDR does not solve the problem. It constitutes in all only 20 percent of the total we expend for uranium. Cde. Honecker also does not take into account that we are building nuclear power stations for the GDR. That is a major activity.

Rusakov: I want to say also that the Poles are asking us to maintain the levels of oil and gas supply that are in effect this year.

Arkhipov: We are conducting negotiations with the Poles and believe that we should maintain economic relations with them according to the principle of balanced plans. Of course, that will lead to a significant decrease in oil supplies to the extent that they do not supply us with coal and other products. However, if everything is all right then in our calculations, we will include supplies of oil in the amount we are currently providing.

398

Baibakov: All the socialist countries are now feeling us out. They are taking their cue from the GDR and watching to see how we deal with the GDR. If Honecker manages to achieve a breakthrough, then they will try as well. In any case, no one has yet provided written responses. In recent days I have had discussions with the chairmen of the state planning agencies of all the socialist countries. They all want to retain the same overall quantities of oil supplies broken down by this year. Several are proposing substituting other energy sources for oil.

The decision is adopted:
1. To approve the discussions of Cde. K. V. Rusakov with Cdes. Honecker, Husák, Kádár and Zhivkov.
2. To ask the Politburo Commission on Poland to prepare the necessary materials for a possible discussion with Cde. Jaruzelski.
3. To instruct Cdes. Tikhonov, Rusakov and Baibakov to examine further the question of oil supplies to these countries taking into account the exchange of views at the session of the CC Politburo.

[Source: RGANI, Fond 89, Opis 42, Delo 48. Translated by Malcolm Byrne for the National Security Archive.]

Soviet bloc resources stretched v. thin!

how fragile a system

Document No. 73: Extract from Protocol No. 37 of CPSU CC Politburo Meeting

November 21, 1981

Jaruzelski's election as party first secretary in October naturally gave rise to hopes in the Warsaw Pact that changes would finally occur in Poland. But once again the Kremlin came to the conclusion that the Polish leadership had no major measures under consideration. The following message to Jaruzelski, occasioned by his request for a meeting in Moscow, contains a list of Soviet concerns and more urgings for prompt action. The reasons for the Kremlin's unease are familiar, but are sharpened here and there by developments such as Jaruzelski's recent meeting with Archbishop Glemp and Lech Wałęsa, which Brezhnev conditionally approved but which raised further questions of political control. Despite the Soviets' rekindled disappointment, Brezhnev adopts a tone that is far more courteous than in his previous conversations with Kania. Here he ends with the very formal invocation: "Esteemed Wojciech Władysławowicz!"

On the reception of the PPR party-state delegation in the USSR and the oral communication of Cde. L. I. Brezhnev to Cde. W. Jaruzelski.

1. Confirm the text of the oral communication of Cde. L. I. Brezhnev, which he instructed the Soviet ambassador to convey to Cde. W. Jaruzelski (attached).

2. Acknowledge the expedience of receiving a PPR party-state delegation in the USSR, headed by Cde. W. Jaruzelski, on December 14–15, 1981.

Confirm the composition of a Soviet delegation at talks with the PPR delegation: Cdes. L. I. Brezhnev (head of the delegation), M. A. Suslov, Yu. V. Andropov, A. A. Gromyko, N. A. Tikhonov, D. F. Ustinov, K. Yu. Chernenko, K. V. Rusakov.

3. For the CPSU CC Department, the Foreign Ministry of the USSR, KGB of the USSR, and Gosplan of the USSR, prepare the necessary materials for negotiations with the Polish party-state delegation, including a draft communication for the press.

For the CPSU CC Department and the Foreign Ministry of the USSR, introduce proposals for organizational measures related to the reception of the Polish delegation to the USSR.

* * *

Regarding Point 21, Prot. No. 37
Secret

Warsaw
The Soviet Ambassador

Visit Cde. W. Jaruzelski and, referring to instructions, convey to him the following oral communication of Cde. L. I. Brezhnev:

Esteemed Comrade Jaruzelski!

We have examined attentively your proposal to visit Moscow as the head of a party-state delegation which would also include the leaders of allied PUWP parties, and we are in agreement with it. As for the dates, the visit could take place on December 14–15 if, of course, that is convenient for you.

At the same time, insofar as there is still time before the meeting, I decided to convey to you via Cde. [Boris] Aristov my impressions on urgent questions regarding the situation in Poland, which remain the subject of our serious unease.

I am not revealing secrets by saying that your selection as first secretary of the PUWP CC was met here with great hopes. We took into account that earlier in the struggle with anti-socialist forces you, as chairman of the Council of Ministers, apparently were constrained by the lack of political decisiveness on the part of the party leadership. Now this impediment has disappeared. The Fourth PUWP CC Plenum made a direct connection between the change in first secretaries and the need for urgent measures for the salvation of socialism in Poland.

When I congratulated you over the telephone, I was pleased to hear that the trust you sense from our side played a definite role in your agreement to accept this responsible post as leader of the PUWP under such critical circumstances. I said this to my comrades and our hopes intensified that in you we would find someone of like mind and an ally in one of the most acute areas of the struggle with imperialism, which Poland has become.

You recall that in that telephone conversation I expressed the hope that there will be a feeling both in Poland and abroad that events in the country are proceeding differently. We then spoke about decisive preconditions for a turnabout in circumstances, and you agreed that you must select reliable assistants for yourself from among the numbers of committed and staunch communists, and set in motion the entire party, having instilled in it the spirit of struggle, and without wasting time launch aggressive actions against the counter-revolution.

Obviously, the core question now is the question of the struggle for the masses. However, the impression is being formed that a turnabout here has not yet materialized. The anti-socialist forces are not only acting as boss at many major industrial enterprises but they continue to spread their influence to ever wider segments of the population. Not a day goes by without the leaders of Solidarity and the counter-revolutionaries making openly inflammatory speeches at various gatherings directed against the PUWP and socialism, and stoking nationalist passions. A direct consequence of that hostile action is the dangerous growth of anti-Sovietism in Poland.

It appears to us that it is now necessary to mobilize the whole party for the struggle for people's minds, go into the very midst of the people with a precise and clear program for getting out of the crisis, and convince everyone of its correctness. In other words, take up your work anew to win the trust of the workers, as the communists did during the years of the establishment of people's power. Regular meetings by leading PUWP officials and the *aktiv* with labor collectives would have a significant impact in this regard, especially at major enterprises—and not just in the capital—which the enemy has succeeded in transforming into his own bastions. And of course the struggle for the masses will not bring the necessary results if genuine party leadership is not secured by the mass media and if, as before, the adversary is able to build up his hostile propaganda without difficulty.

I would like to broach another subject. Recently, much has been written and spoken in Poland about your meeting with [Archbishop Józef] Glemp and Wałęsa. Some call it historical and perceive in it the start of a turn away from chaos toward social tranquility. As we know, the Politburo and PPR government assessed the results of the meeting positively.

We understand, of course, that having put forward the creation of the Front of National Accord as a key issue, you are pursuing a series of tactical goals—chiefly broadening the base of social support for the authorities and creating divisions within the leadership of Solidarity. But how far down the road of agreements can one go without the threat of losing control of the situation? In fact, the class enemies will surely try to assign a political content to the "Front of National Accord" that would reinforce their idea, as a minimum, for dividing power between the PUWP, Solidarity and the Church, with the resulting dismantling of socialism. One may not doubt also that they are using their current influence over the masses to obtain a majority in the upcoming elections for the national councils and to lay the ground for the legal seizure of power in the country.

From that, it seems to me, a clear strengthening of the leading role of the PUWP in the "Front of National Accord", and recognition by its members of the PPR Constitution, of socialism and of Poland's international alliances, acquire fundamental importance. Will this be done in the Front's Charter and other documents? And this is the main thing—will it be guaranteed in practice? How do you propose to hold elections for local organs of authority, taking account of the existing risk that the party will be defeated?

There is another fundamental question associated with this. In many conversations from our side one thought has constantly been stressed: we are not opposed to agreements. But the main thing is that not everything has to be reduced to agreements: alongside measures for winning over the broad national masses and various political forces, decisive actions are necessary against the open enemies of the people's system. You agreed with this formulation of the issue and spoke yourself about your intention to fight for the workers and at the same time to strike the class enemy.

But now the impression is being created that only the first part of this dual formula is being relied upon. We know that you have people in the party leadership who have great hopes for the continuation of Kania's bankrupt course. It would be dangerous to yield to their arguments. Now it is absolutely clear that without a decisive struggle with the class enemy it will be impossible to save socialism in Poland. The essential question is not whether there will be a confrontation but who will initiate it, by what means will it be carried out, and who will retain the initiative.

I would like to stress: when we speak about confrontation we have in mind that it assumes a struggle to attract to the PUWP those laborers and workers' masses who are under the influence of Solidarity, or who take a passive stance, and who are waiting to see who prevails.

You and I, Wojciech Władysławowicz, have both been through war and know that strategy in a conflict is above all a function of time. This is entirely related to the acute situation that has now unfolded in Poland. The leaders of the anti-socialist forces, who have gradually been preparing here and there, even out in the open, for a decisive clash, are trying to delay it until they have an overwhelming preponderance on their side. In particular, they are placing high hopes on the fact that there is about to be a new call-up for the army which Solidarity has worked on. Doesn't this mean that by not taking firm measures against the counter-revolutionaries right now you are wasting valuable time?

The key issue, moreover, is to isolate the open enemies of socialism. Until that is done, everything will continue as before. Furthermore, an openly counter-revolutionary organization like the "Confederation for an Independent Poland" is recruiting new allies and essentially acting legally. Obviously, this became possible because the party is effectively losing control of the organs of the judiciary, as evidenced by the entire history of the case against Moczulski and other KIP leaders.

I want to confide in you my thoughts about one other urgent matter. Obviously, any act in defense of socialism demands above all an energetic struggle for the Marxist-Leninist character of the PUWP and an increase in its effectiveness. After the Fourth PUWP CC plenum one could detect signs of life among the party organizations. As we understand it, the Politburo's letter to the primary party organizations was used to serve this purpose. It is important to stimulate this work and not to allow local communists to fall once again into passivity and throw up their hands. But for that to happen party members must first of all be convinced that words will no longer be detached from deeds and that the leadership intends firmly and consistently to put into practice the solutions they have adopted.

The strengthening of the PUWP depends on a clear line with respect to the various trends within its ranks. Several of your colleagues affirm that there currently exist three directions in the party: left, right and center. They advise cutting off the left and right, and delivering an equal blow against each of them. This is dangerous advice. Who are they calling "leftists" or "thick-headed"? Communists, who stand solidly on Marxist–Leninist positions, by no means negating the need to correct the mistakes and distortions that have been permitted. And who are the rightists? They are people who are advocating revisionist views and in the end are closing ranks with Solidarity. It is clear that any actions taken against steadfast communists would be suicidal for the PUWP as a communist party. And it is just as clear that until you get rid of the revisionists including among the party leadership and those who seek to continue the earlier capitalist line, they will remain a heavy burden for you to bear.

I think that these thoughts also provide a key to the resolution of pressing personnel issues. I am sure that working with the comrades who are referred to as "leftists" and giving them support you will find precisely in these people solid backing in the struggle to surmount this crisis.

Esteemed Wojciech Władysławowicz! Putting before you several questions that are worrisome to us and giving you my thoughts, I am naturally placing in parentheses a number of problems that could be discussed in a private meeting.

[Source: RGANI, Fond 89, Opis 42, Delo 27. Translated by Malcolm Byrne for the National Security Archive.]

Document No. 74: Polish Ministry of Internal Affairs, "Supplement No. 2: Planned Activity of the Ministry of Internal Affairs"

November 25, 1981

This document was prepared less than three weeks before the declaration of martial law. It is a supplement to a larger study, "Assessment of the Present Situation in the Country as of November 25, 1981," and deals specifically with measures the Ministry would take during a crackdown. After considering several possible scenarios, the document lists options for handling the opposition. Of most significance historically is Scenario 3 (see Document No. 36), one of several potential consequences of martial law. The very last sentence—"The assistance of Warsaw Pact forces is not ruled out"—is important for what it may reveal about Polish expectations in the event of violent popular resistance (see also Document No. 82).

Secret, for Special Use
Single Copy

Supplement No. 2
Planned Activity of the Ministry of Internal Affairs

1. Taking into account the current course of events in the country as well as the need to discipline society and reinforce the execution of power, it is necessary to introduce a legislative act (without the introduction of martial law) on extraordinary means of action. The latter act foresees, among other things:

– a heightened responsibility for public goods which one is accountable for, including a prohibition on using factory goods for purposes not associated with the duties being carried out;

– an extension of the rights of workplace managers to give orders to employees, including [where this] exceeds their area of responsibility;

– attaching conditions to the rights that apply to strike actions such as the requirement for prior exhaustion of compromise approaches to settling arguments, pursuing secret ballots and receiving approval from a higher trade union organ;

– a complete prohibition of the right to strike in certain units of the national economy and [certain] institutions as well as authorization from the Council of State to introduce a prohibition on strikes and protests for a predetermined period, in part or all of the territory of the state;

– a limitation on the right to hold public meetings (also trade union meetings). Legal use of direct enforcement is provided for in order to disperse public meetings. The latter means may be used in case of illegal seizure of a building (apartment);

– the introduction of a curfew, a ban on artistic, entertainment and sports events as well as on public collections (except carried out by the Church), suspension of activities of selected associations as well as a limitation on post, telecommunications, personal and cargo traffic with foreign countries;

– an expansion of censorship of selected publications and a ban on leaflet-poster type propaganda;

– authorization for the voievodes to turn to the military for assistance in certain situations of danger to the public order;

– a transferral of cases concerning certain violations of law into the domain of military prosecutors and courts.

Passing the above legislation as well as its implementation will allow the government of the Polish People's Republic as well as the organs of state administration and units of the public economy to take special actions aiming at strengthening the national economy, preventing anarchy and hindering the activity of counter-revolutionary forces. They will also lead to an increase of social discipline and public order as conditions necessary for eliminating the consequences of the crisis, which threatens the normal functioning of the state and the vital needs of the people.

The legislative act will create conditions for the gradual (selective) introduction of bans and orders (limitations of citizen freedoms and assignment of obligations) on part or all of the territory of the country, depending on how the situation develops. Authorization to introduce certain degrees of limitations will also be given to the territorial organs of the authorities and the state administration (voievodes and mayors of voievodeship cities).

The passage of the act and its subsequent introduction will undoubtedly cause various social repercussions, both positive and negative. It will certainly strengthen the morale and attitudes of the party members and all advocates of the socialist system so as to participate in the defense of the state. On the other hand, it will stimulate greater activity by extremist and anti-socialist elements in the direction of destructive actions, for example by calling for a general strike and other things.

2. If the application of the act on extraordinary measures in the interest of protecting citizens and the state is not effective, the introduction of martial law will be necessary. The extension of preparations of the Ministry of Internal Affairs in case of the introduction of martial law has been stipulated in relevant documents.

Among the fundamental tasks which will determine the efficient operation of martial law and which ought to be carried out at the moment of its introduction, or several hours in beforehand, are:

a) the internment of persons who threaten the security of the state—which is the principle endeavor. Two variations of implementing this operation are being considered:

Option 1

– the internment of particularly dangerous persons in the main centers of the opposition such as Warsaw, Katowice, Szczecin, Wrocław, Bydgoszcz, Gdańsk;

406

Option 2
– the simultaneous internment of all specified persons in the entire country. Internment would cover 1,500–4,500 persons. The feasibility of this operation will be determined by the course of events.

The most effective factor to ensure the successful conclusion of the operation would be if it came as a complete surprise to the adversary. It is only possible if the operation is carried out sufficiently in advance of the introduction of martial law.

The operation can also be carried out as a response to the specific activity of the adversary, although its impact would be limited.

It is assumed that the internment operation would be accompanied by the public use of telecommunications and preventive warning conversations with less sinister persons as well as seizing the initiative in the branches of Solidarity by people with moderate views (replacement structures—work is in progress on this question).

b) the remaining important endeavors are:
– the introduction of censorship of postal and telecommunications correspondence as well as control of telephone conversations, especially in the public network;
– the introduction of limitations on: cross-border traffic, changes of residence, the activity of selected associations, the freedom of movement and activity of personnel of diplomatic missions from capitalist countries, and correspondents from capitalist countries; [actions] to make it impossible for Polish citizens to enter diplomatic missions of the capitalist countries;
– the withholding of armed weapons as well as radio broadcasting and broadcast-receiving equipment from certain citizens;
– the extension of protection over 441 sites of the national economy by Polish armed forces and protection of over 891 sites, mainly of the food-supply sector, by the Citizens' Police (CP);
– the protection and defense of sites of the central authorities by the Ministry of Internal Affairs and Defense Ministry forces;
– the mobilization of maneuver units of the Citizens' Police (CP), rural outposts of the CP, MFG and VMU MSW—a draft of about 46,000 reserves has been planned;
– engaging some selected VRCP members, including combined sub-units, in operations.

Some of the aforementioned endeavors will be carried out with the participation of the armed forces. Those questions have been agreed upon with the Ministry of Defense and an action concept has been jointly worked out.

The introduction of martial law may, among other things, cause the following development of events:
Scenario 1
– subordination of political and socio-economic organizations to the demands of martial law with the simultaneous possibility of a limited strike action and restricted hostile propaganda activity.

Scenario 2

– in some regions of the country, mass strikes are organized with a tendency to extend beyond the workplace. Sabotage activities take place.

Scenario 3

– a general labor strike, some workers go into the streets, there are street demonstrations and attacks on party and state administration buildings, as well as those of the Citizens' Police and others. This leads to harsh intervention by the CP forces and the military. The assistance of Warsaw Pact forces is not ruled out.

[Source: IPN, MSW II, 1022, Appendix No 2. Translated by Paweł Machcewicz.]

Document No. 75: Memorandum from Alexander Haig to President Reagan, "U.S. Assistance Program for Poland"

December 1, 1981

The Reagan administration was acutely aware of Poland's dire economic circumstances and the importance of aid from the West. Just a week before this message to the president from the secretary of state, Washington had authorized a $30 million donation of basic foodstuffs to the people of Poland. Here, Haig states his belief that "our entire tradition and security interests dictate prompt action." He proposes immediate additional aid worth $100 million and a longer-term multilateral program of up to $2.5 billion. The administration follows up with promises of aid but the imposition of martial law forces a reassessment of policy options. On December 23, Reagan institutes an economic embargo against Poland but exempts humanitarian aid directed towards "the Polish people" rather than to the regime, while in January the administration announces it will attempt to help Poland avoid defaulting on its loans to Western banks.

The Secretary of State
Washington

December 1, 1981

Memorandum for: The President
From: Alexander M. Haig, Jr.
Subject: U.S. Assistance Program for Poland

In my memorandum of November 13, I expressed concern that democratic forces in Poland would be unable to preserve and consolidate their increasingly impressive gains without additional U.S. assistance. Since then it has become even clearer that Poland is on the verge of potentially catastrophic economic crisis—the sort of crisis that could demoralize and discredit the democratic forces and lead to the re-imposition of an inflexible Soviet-style communist dictatorship. In my opinion our entire tradition and security interests dictate prompt action to avert such an outcome and to reinforce a process that has already placed Moscow on the diplomatic, political and economic defensive and could eventually undermine Soviet control throughout Eastern Europe.

As a result of Wałęsa's public call for U.S. aid and private messages from Pope John Paul II, I am confident that our assistance can be presented and implemented in a way that not only minimizes the risk of Soviet intervention or counteraction but enhances the already formidable power of Solidarity and the Church. Among other things, a meeting between you and Wałęsa could be utilized to demonstrate the fact that we are backing a struggle for national self-determination and political liberalization against a failing communist regime. Wałęsa has indicated that he is thinking along similar lines. He has told Ambassador Meehan that Solidarity's ability to secure U.S. aid could decisively affect the outcome of current negotiations over the reform of the Polish economy and the redistribution of political power.

The Poles have just approached us with an urgent request for $200 million worth of corn, soybean meal and other commodities. Our experts say that $100 million in corn and soybean meal will allow them to carry their livestock and poultry industries through the next three months. Absent such assistance, which only the U.S. can provide in a timely fashion, the Poles would be forced to engage in large-scale distress slaughtering which would further complicate their already massive mid- and long-term economic problems.

As a first step, therefore, the Cabinet Councils on Economic Affairs (CCEA) has decided that we should proceed on a $100 million program in emergency food assistance for Poland through a sale of Commodity Credit Corporation-held corn. Sales financed by CCC dollar credits could be made on appropriately long repayment terms. No immediate legislative action would be required for these sales, nor would there be any budgetary impact. I have talked to John Block and he is eager to help resolve the Polish food crisis. We are working together on solutions to several technical problems involved in a sale of surplus CCC corn. In addition, he feels that emergency assistance [must] be combined with a larger assistance effort addressing Poland's food needs over the coming year.

Accordingly, I recommend that, as a second step, you authorize me to begin consultations with our allies soon on a multilateral aid effort for Poland totaling $2–2.5 billion, of which we would expect the U.S. share to be approximately 25 percent, all in agricultural commodities. Such a U.S. contribution, of which the $100 million in emergency food assistance should form a part, would enable us to meet substantially the recent Polish request to purchase $740 million in agricultural commodities. This figure approximates Polish purchases of agricultural commodities from us in past years and appears to reflect their genuine needs. As part of our effort, U.S. and other Western private banks would be expected to do their share to prevent a total breakdown in the Polish economy. U.S. leadership in the multilateral process is essential to the success of this initiative. Our assistance would be conditioned on Polish implementation of—and adherence to—a credible economic stabilization and reform program. State and Treasury, which represent the U.S. on the Polish Creditors' Commission, will continue to monitor and assure compliance with the details of these preconditions. Poland's decision to rejoin the IMF will help assure that our conditions are met and our loans eventually repaid.

If my consultations show that there is allied interest in building a multilateral aid package, I will report to you what the U.S. contribution should be and our further recommendations. Any large U.S. contribution would require a supplemental appropriation for funding.

Recommendations

1. That you endorse our efforts to implement quickly the CCEA decision to provide a $100 million emergency assistance program for Poland from sales of CCC-held corn financed by long-term credits. We are moving forward rapidly on this.

Approve _____ Disapprove _____

2. That you authorize me to begin consultations with our allies on a $2–2.5 billion multilateral assistance package, of which we would expect the U.S. contribution for Poland to be approximately 25 percent.

Approve _____ Disapprove _____

[Source: FOIA release from the State Department, on file at the National Security Archive, "Soviet Flashpoints" collection.]

Document No. 76: PUWP CC, "Excerpt from Motions at Meeting with CC Members on November 27, 1981"

December 2, 1981

In this document, members of the Central Committee, the party's mid-level decision-makers, present a list of proposals to the leadership. The options provide an interesting window into their thinking and priorities. In the 1970s and 1980s, the top party circles in Poland were far more moderate than the middle and lower levels, and this document duly reflects the position of the hard liners who believe, for example, that martial law should be introduced immediately. Point 16 is a curious one, showing a more self-interested side of the members of the Central Committee who, like members of parliament, argue that they should be eligible for certain "perks," such as the ability to buy vodka and candy without coupons.

[…]

Excerpt
From motions at meeting with CC Members on November 27, 1981:

1. Include tasks for a maximum cap on expenses for the administration, the military, the public prosecutor's office, etc. in the 1982 plan.
2. Executive regulations are still lacking for the act dated September 25, 1981, which was in itself a "fatal compromise"—this results in it not being realized properly.
3. Erroneous decisions are also being taken at plenary assemblies of the CC. One should work out a mechanism that verifies decisions of the CC Plenum.
4. If possible, one should quickly work out a conception for elections to national councils in order to issue an initiative in this regard.
5. One should head off an internal squabble in the party, for which the main threat is opportunism on the Right (Bratkowski, Szumowski, Lamentowicz and others).
6. One should isolate the rightist, liberal-democratic faction in the party.
7. Stop the march towards "a mad democracy." Up till now we have been placing our own cadres by means of our legislation.
8. A state of emergency should be imposed immediately.
9. Under the possible imposition of a state of emergency, consider whether we will be able to find suitable means for guaranteeing the attainment of the intended goal.
10. One should suspend discussion regarding drafts of certain legal statutes, i.e. the Code of Work, in light of the fact that the assumptions of these acts do

not take into account the current political struggle. They should not be advanced.

11. Push for an end to the trials of CIP leaders and consider whether or not the judicial composition should be changed.
12. Relay to the public prosecutors and military courts that the most threatening kind of crime is political crime.
13. Define our position towards the Front of National Accord, formulating with great accuracy the conditions under which we will approach this understanding (we define them, they should not be defined with regard to us).
14. Verify the [loyalty of the] party apparatus, including in the CC and the EC, and direct them to go to the workplaces.
15. Teach a lesson to those liable for the irresponsible conduct regarding changes in the price of gas, including the minister of chemical and light industry, by repealing those changes (arrange a television appearance, but make a decision anyway).
16. The members of the CC, just like the deputies, should have the possibility of purchasing certain goods without coupons, i.e. candies or vodka, in "Konsum" buffets when they come as part of delegations to Warsaw (just like the deputies).
17. Consider the possibility of NSZZ Solidarity having access to Polish Television [TVP].
18. Moreover, it was proposed on the second day of meetings of the CC Sixth Plenary Session that the following motions be defeated:
    1. Immediately impose a state of emergency (extraordinary means);
    2. Introduce the military to influential cells regarding the functioning of socio-economic life and the judiciary;
    3. Postpone the decision regarding a price increase for alcohol for January 1982.

[Source: AAN, PUWP CC, 4762, pp. 174–176. Translated by Małgorzata Gnoińska for the National Security Archive.]

Document No. 77: Notes of Meeting of the Presidium of Solidarity's National Coordinating Commission in Gdańsk

December 2, 1981

Although only a partial document, this record of an NCC Presidium meeting gives an important explanation for what transpired inside Solidarity just before martial law. Contrary to information provided by Jaruzelski and Kiszczak that the Union was preparing an attack against the authorities at this time, these notes show considerable hesitation and uncertainty on Solidarity's part about how to proceed. While radicals in the organization were pressing for action, moderates were appealing for calm. It is clear that by now the authorities were gearing up for conflict, and sought to create a pretext for a crackdown by depicting Solidarity as aggressive and irresponsible.

[…]

The goal of the meeting was to prepare the standpoint of the Presidium of the NCC and its opinion on the current situation to be presented at the meeting of the Presidium of the NCC and chairmen of the RA's on December 3 in Radom.

L. Wałęsa says that "the Union is a huge hanging baton," but the need is to undertake decided and wise actions, and not to use hot [social] feelings. Solidarity is being involved in politics, while typical trade union activities are being neglected. Establishing the Clubs by Kuroń was a political mistake and is dangerous for the Union, because "we will get divided, and the authorities will take advantage of that."

G. Pałka states that society expects the Union to assume an attitude towards essential issues (price rises, elections, diminishing food allowances—rations), therefore one cannot confine oneself to the "basic work." He is in favor of suspending the right to strike for FC [Factory Committee] besides striking for the Union's safety.

Professor A. Stelmachowski discusses the up-to-date policy of the authorities and states that the Union should sharply react to the recent provocations (beatings in Chorzów, surprise raid against WOSP), categorically refuse participation in the National Reconciliation Front and start preparations in case the Sejm passes the law on extraordinary full powers for the government. For that purpose, one should start talks with members of parliament or even take the action of dismissing members of parliament by means of their voters.

S. Wądołowski reports on the course of negotiations of the Radom MKR with the authorities (see: AS No. 55, p. 001) and states that the government side was holding talks "not in a serious way."

W. Frasyniuk says that "the PUWP behaves like a wounded animal in a rage." He calls for a clear definition of political demands.

K. Modzelewski states that the idea of the law on extraordinary measures results from the logic of the system's operations. The so-called provisional system arrangement for the year 1982 will cause an avalanche of strikes in enterprises, whose workers will suffer the costs of somebody else's decisions, so the authorities provide the only remedy that they know: one consisting of repression. Beside that, the apparatus cannot act and gets destroyed in a democratic environment, so they try to revoke the former status by any means. Modzelewski thinks that one should—under penalty of a strike—demand publishing the law on the state of emergency, whose draft has not been revealed so far. However, the strike can be proclaimed only after formulating a positive program. He suggests mobilization of all the Union's cells before future actions and considers the possibility of taking such steps as taking over the orderly functions in enterprises by workers' guards.

J. Merkel draws attention to the weakness of self-governments, which operate satisfactorily in 10–20 percent of enterprises. An active strike, due to organizational issues, is only possible for a very short time. He thinks that on behalf of all the workers' crews, a few persons employed in key positions of essential importance for the enterprise could go on strike, which would avoid problems connected with payment for the strike. A referendum on issues of self-government, reform and prices for basic foodstuffs can also be a tool for pressure on the government.

Z. Bujak speaks in favor of political solutions. If a general strike is proclaimed, it should only last for a couple of days, and then it can be continued by arms factories. That should cause a clinch which will result in a political settlement at the top level, which will allow the holding of elections, appointment of a new government, SCNE [Social Council for National Economy], and the Social Supervisory Board of Radio and Television. He states that purely trade union activities are "ineffective without settlements at the power level."

Att. Siła-Nowicki appeals for a sense of responsibility for the fate of the country, which must be shown by Solidarity, since the authorities are lacking it. A situation in which the Union is fighting the government, and the government is fighting the Union, is lethal for the country. He warns against a general strike, which would be an attempt to overthrow the government, and would threaten a civil war. On the other hand he considers an active strike to be an illusion. He thinks that the Union should first and foremost get involved in training its members.

He points out that Polish legislation does not provide for a state of emergency; only martial law can be introduced.

K. Maruszczyk notes that talks with the government are effective only when pressure is exercised at the same time. Solidarity—in his opinion—should get back to the trade union position, and not relieve the government of making economic decisions but defend Union members against the negative consequences of these decisions.

J. Waszkiewicz states that the "placard war" undertaken by the Union is slowly entering into a confrontation scenario, since it brings the conflict out into the streets. He considers the pacification of WOSP as a warning that the same means will be used should the Union decide to occupy broadcasting stations.

J. Kuroń thinks that in its declaration the Presidium should name the facts which resulted in breaching the agreement, define the basic tasks of the Union, which the Union will not abandon, and formulate a positive program. In his opinion the Union cannot accept elections from one list, price reform without economic reform and passage of the law on emergency measures by the Sejm.

A. Wielowieyski appeals for maintaining the peace and self-control in order to avoid confrontation. He notes that Poland is located in a determined geopolitical structure and the case is to maintain this "system of unstable balance."

Summing up the discussion, *Professor A. Stelmachowski* says that in the declaration there must be a protest against the events of recent weeks which led to the breakdown of foundations for a national agreement and the announcement of consideration of the issue of a general strike at tomorrow's meeting of the Presidium of NC and chairmen of the regions.

The debates ended after 23:00, some of the participants stayed longer to edit the declaration.

Ed. by M. Zielińska, W. Józwiak

[Source: AS. "Biuletyn Pism Związkowych i Zakładowych," *No. 57, 30. XI. – 2. XII. 1981, p. 02. Translated by Aleksandra Niemirycz.]*

Document No. 78: Solidarity NCC Presidium, "Position Taken by the Presidium of the National Coordinating Commission and Leaders of the NSZZ"

December 3, 1981

Solidarity's NCC Presidium promulgated this important statement at the end of a dramatic session in Radom on December 3. Two days earlier, a large police force had stormed the Firefighters' Academy in Warsaw where cadets had been on strike and arrested the entire group. The incident, although not bloody since the cadets' decided not to resist, provoked anger among many Solidarity members. Partly as a result, the Radom meeting featured loud demands by some Presidium members for extreme responses. More moderate voices, such as Wałęsa, managed to delay full consideration of proposals such as setting up a provisional government, and the final statement of the session was relatively muted in tone. Still, the document contained some tough language about the unacceptability of the regime's actions against the firefighters, and in other situations. Of particular note was a demand for democratic elections to People's Councils at all levels, the first time such a proposal to change the system had appeared in an official Solidarity document. Thus, this statement— along with recordings of the Radom session (made surreptitiously and illegally by a NCC member collaborating with the Security Service)—became prime pieces of "evidence" for the authorities as they constructed official justifications for introducing martial law.

The position of the NCC Presidium and chairmen of the RC NSZZ Solidarity on December 3, 1981 (approved by the NC on December 12, 1981).

1. The party-state authorities have used the negotiations with the Union as well as the idea of social agreement to mislead the society. Talks on the key Solidarity demands (control over food supply, regional self-government, economic reform, compliance with the law, access to mass media) have proven to be fruitless. The government surprised the Union by submitting to the Sejm a draft of the so-called provisional system arrangement, which undermines basic interests of the working people. During the negotiations the authorities intensified anti-Union repressions, which were most strikingly manifested in the beating of the picketers in Chorzów and the Citizens' Police attack on the Firefighters' Academy in Warsaw. The justifiable students' strike is being deliberately protracted by the authorities, who torpedo attempts to solve the Radom conflict. Moreover, the Sixth Plenum of the PUWP CC decided to force the law in the Sejm on extraordinary measures, keeping the content of the law, which may determine the country's fate, in secret, without the nation's knowledge. Talks on the national agreement have been used by the government as a shield to conceal preparations

for the attack on the Union. In this situation, further negotiations on the issue of national agreement have become pointless.

2. Regardless of whether the law on extraordinary measures will authorize the government to put civilians before a military court, ban gatherings and restrict traveling, or only to annul the right to strike, it will not be introduced in any other way than through terror. It would amount to an attempt to subdue the society through force. Therefore, the Union will respond to the Sejm's potential passing of the law on extraordinary powers for the government with a 24-hour-long universal protest strike in Poland. In case the government takes advantage of the power granted to it by the Sejm to use extraordinary measures, the Union cells and all [workers'] crews should inevitably initiate a general strike.

3. The so-called provisional system arrangement for 1982 maintains in practice the old system of managing the economy, while burdening the enterprises and their crews with financial responsibility for decisions, which will remain in the hands of central organs. This amounts to voiding the reform and laws on self-government and enterprises which have already been passed by the Sejm, with the simultaneous bankruptcy threat of many enterprises or lay-offs and wage reductions. Together with the provisional arrangement dramatic price increases planned by the government are to be introduced. The society will have to pay for a reform which does not exist. The Union will not agree to price increases without economic reform. We will defend the working people from the consequences of such price increases, factory shutdowns, lay-offs, and wage reductions in accordance with the statutory goals of the trade union and with the use of all statutory means.

4. National agreement cannot be equivalent to introducing the Union to a repainted [przemalowane] FNU, which the government is striving for. Such decoration with the Solidarity badge of the state authorities' old facade, which led the country to collapse, would not alleviate the crisis, but could only deprive the Union of its independence and credibility.

5. The Union will not retreat from the following demands:

a) abolition of any anti-Union repression by the authorities;

b) submission to the Sejm of a draft law on trade unions in a version prepared with "Solidarity's" representatives;

c) the government's retreat from the so-called provisional system arrangement, agreement with the Union, and then implementation of economic reform based on self-government of enterprises;

d) democratic elections for People's Councils of all levels (including voivodeship councils ahead of time) and subordinating regional administration to them. We will not agree to voting on only one list as [was done] in previous years;

e) respect for the Union's control over the economy, including especially food stocks—keeping them secret from the nation is unacceptable;

f) granting the Social Council for National Economy competences which would allow real influence on government decisions and control over the social-economic policies of the state;

g) access to radio and television for the Council, Solidarity, Church, and other centers of public opinion.

These are the minimum conditions for national agreement, which will facilitate a joint, effective battle with the crisis. We are in favor of such an agreement.

[Source: "Tygodnik Solidarność," No. 37, December 11, 1981, p. 3. Translated by Aleksandra Niemirycz.]

Document No. 79: Report on the Committee of Ministers of Defense Meeting in Moscow

December 1–4, 1981

At this last Warsaw Pact meeting of its kind before martial law, disagreements surfaced among its members. Jaruzelski did not attend the session, sending his deputy minister, Florian Siwicki, instead. The Polish leader asked that the final communiqué include phrases describing the dangers of the situation in Poland, his purpose essentially being to frighten Polish society by showing that the Warsaw Pact supported his position and might be inclined to step in militarily. However, the Romanian representative declared that he could not agree to the additional language, while the Hungarian minister indicated he could only sign the communiqué if there were unanimity within the Pact. In the end, no final communiqué was issued.

[…]

Between December 1–4, 1981, the 14th meeting of the Committee of Ministers of Defense of the Warsaw Pact member-states took place in Moscow under the chairmanship of Marshal D[mitri] Ustinov, minister of defense of the Soviet Union. The participants at the meetings included all the members of the defense ministers' committee, except Army General W[ojciech] Jaruzelski, defense minister of the Polish People's Republic. The Polish People's Army (PPA) delegation was headed by Col. Gen. F[lorian] Siwicki, chief of General Staff and deputy national defense minister of the PPR. Each point of the agenda was discussed in the following order.

1. *Analysis of the state and developmental tendencies of the armed forces of the aggressive NATO bloc.*

The head of the Chief Directorate of Information and deputy chief of the USSR General Staff, Army General P. I. Ivashutin, in his introductory speech, thoroughly analyzed the current state of the international military and political situation. It was consistent with the appraisal made at the XXVI CPSU Congress as well as the congress of fraternal socialist states.

PPA Chief of Staff Col. Gen. Siwicki said in his speech, among other things, that the complex socio-economic situation in the country might produce, in the near future, serious disturbances in arms and military procurement for the PPA as well as for the armies of the alliance. He then spoke about the significance of the state of the army's political morale. He noted that as a result of the situation in the country, fundamental changes were introduced in party and political work. More time had been spent on it. The quality of party and youth meetings had improved, including the intensity of individual discussions. At this time, in party

420

and political work, almost 60 percent of the [political training] is dedicated to explaining party and government policies. [He added] that these policies are aimed at bringing the country out of its complicated situation as well as to unmask the enemy activities of those opposed to socialism, especially "Solidarity's" extremist circles.

At the end of his speech, Gen. Siwicki said that "at least once a month, at the meetings of the Military Council, an assessment on the state of the military's political morale is conducted, which, at this moment, appears to be satisfactory. Thanks to this effort, the PPA successfully resists the attacks of the class enemy and plays an essential stabilizing role in the life of our country, despite the fact that the conscripts entering its ranks, who found themselves under the negative influence of Solidarity, preserved their own ideological and political character."

Gen. Siwicki said that the PPA activists support the party and state apparatus. He considers the defense of the socialist states, the snappy battle with manifestations of counter-revolution, to be his duty, to be his highest goal.

With regard to the situation in the PPR and its development, alarm was registered during the discussions concerning that point of the program in the speeches by the defense ministers of the USSR, Bulgaria, the GDR as well as the commander of the Unified Armed Forces.

2. *On the state and development of the air forces.*
A report will be given by a representative of the USSR Ministry of Defense.

3. *On the progress of the resolution passed at the 3rd and 6th meetings of the Committee of Ministers of Defense of the Warsaw Pact member-states on the subject of improving the command system of the allied armies.*
Information to be delivered by representatives of the PPR and Romanian ministries of national defense.

4. *On the program for the 16th Meeting of the Committee of Ministers of Defense.*
Draft to be presented by the chief of staff of the Unified Armed Forces of the Warsaw Past member-states.

The draft resolutions put forward on this point were unanimously accepted.

At the conference, the draft information text to the press, radio and television concerning the work of the 14th meeting of the Committee of Ministers of Defense was prepared for approval.

Before discussing the matter of the draft text, a supplement concerning the reaction to the situation in the PPR was put forward, which was sent by Comrade Jaruzelski to the Committee of Ministers of Defense with a request that it be attached to the text for the mass media with the following content: "The Committee of Ministers of Defense has expressed its alarm at the development of the situation in the PPR, resulting from the subversive activities of the anti-socialist forces, who are making it more difficult to fulfill the allied obligations of the armed forces of the Warsaw Pact member-states and result in the necessity of taking suitable steps aimed at ensuring the common security in socialist Europe."

Regarding this supplement, Minister of National Defense of the Romanian Socialist Republic Lieutenant General C[onstantin] Olteănu did not express his consent. And he demanded that the text with the contents agreed upon before the meeting of the Committee of Ministers of Defense be accepted. The remaining defense ministers supported accepting the supplement.

A closed session of the Committee of Ministers of Defense, including only members, took place next, at which it was proposed that the Romanian defense minister and, if necessary, others who need to do this, consult about the problem mentioned above with their own political leadership.

On the draft supplement, I reported to you, honorable comrade general secretary and president, on the telephone on December 2, 1981, and I asked for your agreement.

After the consultations had taken place, Minister of Defense of the Hungarian People's Republic Army General L[ajos] Czinege, reported that the Hungarian side had agreed to the supplement only in the event of full agreement by all the defense ministers.

During the evening of December 3–4, 1981, the draft supplement was changed several times and its final text contained: "The Committee of Ministers of Defense expressed its alarm at the worsening situation in the PPR. The subversive activities of the anti-socialist forces, behind whom stand the aggressive imperialist circles, have a direct impact on the fulfillment of the allied obligations of the armed forces of the Warsaw Pact member-sates. Solidarity was expressed with the PUWP's battle, with all Polish patriots against counter-revolution, with the battle to bring the country out of its crisis. As a result, it was underlined that the Polish nation can rely completely on the support of the socialist sates."

During the early morning hours, on the last day of the conference, another closed session of the Defense Ministers Committee, including only members, took place, at which it was agreed that the prepared text for the mass media will not be supplemented; but that, apart from this, information will be published in the press by the defense ministers of all the countries, with the exception of the Romanian Socialist Republic. This course of action was agreed upon by all the defense ministers except the Romanian. Further details were to be talked over after the protocol was signed.

After the session ended, another session of the defense ministers committee, including only members, took place, where Comrade Ustinov familiarized them with the substance of Comrade Jaruzelski's request. He asked that in the current, very complicated, practically climactic period the Committee of Ministers of Defense express its displeasure with regard to the situation in the PPR and express its support for the present Polish leadership.

The chief of the PPA General Staff spoke next. He said that the situation in their country had deteriorated greatly, that the Front of National Unity could be organized and that the party was disintegrating. All this was utilized by enemy forces supported by the "West."

In this battle the Polish leadership needs support. Dissolving the firefighting school was a minor success, to which the counter-revolution responded with very sharp demands to isolate further the party and to weaken the state authorities. It wanted to show its strength and to demonstrate that the entire Polish nation was following it. The Solidarity leadership turned to the Sejm so that it would overturn the decision of the government on dissolving the firefighting schools and show a vote of no-confidence in the government. Otherwise, they threatened to introduce strikes, including a general strike. It was also counting on an increase in the wave of discontent with the state of provisions, especially before Christmas.

For the above-mentioned reasons, Comrade Jaruzelski asked that the diversionary claims of the "West," according to which the PPR did not have the support of its allies, be denied. Comrade Siwicki expressed his conviction that supplementing the text for the press would be a cold shower for the counter-revolution and, at the same time, support the battle by the Polish leadership against reaction. He then asserted that the PPR still had enough power to resolve the situation. This was not about any concrete military steps but about moral and political support for the PPR's party and state leadership.

Comrade Ustinov asserted that the complex situation in the PPR was known and understood by us. That was why such moral support could be helpful and would not indicate the threat to use force. His outlook received the consent of the remaining members of the Committee of Ministers of Defense, with the exception of the Romanian minister of national defense.

The Hungarian defense minister asserted that he would give his consent to supplement the text for the mass media, but only if all the defense ministers agreed. The Hungarian side did not quite understand who was supposed to be helped, because after closing the firefighting school 20 counter-revolutionaries were arrested and then let go. Comrade Czinege turned to Comrade Siwicki with the following questions: Why does Comrade Jaruzelski not turn to the first and general secretaries of the fraternal parties with the request, since it was a political problem? Why did they not resolve the situation themselves? And who ought to be supported if they [Polish party] are always on the retreat? He also added that if they [Polish party] resisted, even the counter-revolution would behave differently.

Comrade Siwicki said that they had a few scenarios planned against the counter-revolution. There is a scenario to ban strikes, to limit the freedom of citizens, to introduce military courts, and a plan to establish order in the country.

Further in the discussion, Comrade Czinege again asserted that the Hungarian side will give its consent only in the event that all the defense ministers agree. Given that two defense ministers would not give their consent, the discussion to accept the supplement ended.

After the discussion, a sharp exchange of views followed between the defense minister of the Hungarian People's Republic and the chief of the General Staff of the USSR armed forces, Comrade [Nikolai] Ogarkov, who asserted that the Hungarian comrades possibly forgot about 1956 and the bloodshed that occurred at that time. Drawing attention to this was seen by Comrade Czinege as an insult to Comrade Kádár and himself, and he voiced his astonishment as to how a marshal of the Soviet Union could come up with such a declaration. Comrade Ogarkov added that the Soviet comrades did not want the kind of bloodshed in the PPR that had happened in Hungary, and that was why they supported every effort to resolve the crisis in Poland.

In the talks with Comrades Ustinov and [Viktor] Kulikov, a suggestion emerged about the suitability of raising matters in connection with resolving the situation in the PPR at the meeting of the highest representatives of the communist and workers' parties of the Warsaw Pact member-states.

The 14th meeting of the Committee of Ministers of Defense ended with the signing of the protocol.

In his final speech, the chairman of the conference, USSR Minister of National Defense Marshal of the Soviet Union Ustinov underlined the significance of the concluded meeting for the strengthening of the defense capabilities of the Warsaw Pact member-states. He thanked the members of the Committee of Ministers of Defense for their participation in the conference and gave the last word to the minister of national defense of the Czechoslovak Socialist Republic, who will chair the 15th meeting of the Committee of Ministers of Defense in 1982 in Prague.

In my speech, I voiced my conviction that the 14th meeting of the Committee of Ministers of Defense added to the strengthening of unity and friendship, and to a deepening of cooperation between the fraternal armies. I thanked the chairman, Comrade Ustinov, for organizing and leading the conference. I underlined the strong feelings of the Soviet people for our nation and the decisive role of the Soviet Union in our common struggle, measured to ensure the defense of socialism and peace. I ensured all the members of the Committee of Ministers of Defense that during the preparations and execution of the 15th meeting of the Committee of Ministers of Defense in 1982 in Prague, we will take advantage of all experiences, most of all from our Soviet friends, for a prosperous conference proceeding.

[Source: Sejm Commission on Constitutional Oversight, Warsaw. First published in Andrzej Paczkowski and Andrzej Werblan, "'On the Decision to Introduce Martial Law in Poland in 1981,' Two Historians Report to the Commission on Constitutional Oversight of the Sejm of the Republic of Poland," CWIHP Working Paper No. 21, November 1997. Introduced and translated by L. W. Głuchowski.]

Document No. 80: Protocol No. 18 of PUWP CC Politburo Meeting

December 5, 1981

During a long and extraordinary discussion, the Polish Politburo deliberates over the grim state of affairs in the country. Jaruzelski later describes the atmosphere as "funereal." The population is viewed as largely against the current leadership, Solidarity is a "total movement," which makes the situation worse than in previous landmark crises in 1956 and 1970, and the opposition is seen as poised to take over power—legally. The Politburo mostly still opposes a military solution but is forced to consider a variety of extreme measures including disbanding the PUWP. Ultimately, the leadership grants Jaruzelski the power to make the final decision on martial law. Summing up, Jaruzelski states that it is "a horrible, monstrous shame for the party that after 36 years in power it has to be defended by the police. But there is nothing else left ahead of us."

[…]

Agenda

1. Evaluation of the current situation, prognosis for further developments and conclusions resulting from it [the evaluation].
2. Various matters.

On point 1 on the agenda.

Information presented by Cdes. *Cz. Kiszczak* and *S. Ciosek.*

Cde. S. Ciosek—there are a series of grave tensions facing the line authorities—"S" [Solidarity]. The talks began at "S's" request. We did not agree to discuss subjects such as: law and order, territorial self-government and elections to national councils. "S" demands discussion of matters related to: 1) exclusive and uncontrolled access to the mass media; 2) legal ratification of political changes; 3) economic reform. Consent to reform depends on consent to the first two conditions. Therefore, structural transformation is the price for consent to economic reform. Since the Presidium session in Radom,[7] "S" has completely resisted further talks since it considers them fruitless given that the government declared a provisional economic undertaking with respect to carrying out repressive actions when it was decided at the Seventh Plenum to accept a law on the use of extraordinary measures. ["S"] believes that this law cannot be introduced without terror. That is why ["S"] is threatening a 24-hour warning strike, and in the event [the

---

[7] A pivotal meeting of Solidarity's NCC Presidium on December 3–4. See Document No. 78.

law] is introduced, a general strike that would last until success [is achieved]. "S" is highly critical of the temporary arrangement saying that it means erasure of the reform, that it jeopardizes the interests of the working people, and that ["S"] will not agree to a price change without reform.

They announced that they will not join the Front of National Accord [FNA] as they consider it a repainted FNU.

"S's" minimal program addressed to the authorities is the following:
– an end to repression;
– consent to draft "S" into the military and CP [Citizens' Police];
– withdrawal of the temporary arrangement;
– democratic elections to national councils at all levels, including in advance, to the NVC;
– union control over the economy and especially foodstuffs;
– a grant of broad authority (super-government) to the Civic National Council;
– a grant of full access to mass media for the Civic National Council.

These are the main conclusions of the Presidium declaration which are to be presented and approved at the NC [National Commission] session on the eighth of this month, during which we should expect a further sharpening of "S's" position. Hence, this is a program of open political opposition, which has nothing in common with a trade union and which openly aims at a change of regime and takeover of power.

During the coming days we can expect:
– a mobilization of "S" membership masses to support the leadership's resolution;
– signs that the membership masses are more radical than the leadership.

Cde. Czesław Kiszczak—the new elements of the situation are:
– intensified attacks by extreme "S" forces on the party and the government with the aim of taking over power. Resolutions passed by the Presidium deliberating in Warsaw and Radom, which included regional chairmen, prove that. Very radical resolutions were passed at the meeting of the Gdańsk region in the Lenin Shipyard on December 1. Wałęsa's recent speeches are especially bellicose and aggressive (regarding the Social Council for the National Economy, access to mass media; for the first time he said that "confrontation will not happen without bloodshed"). The tone of other leaders' speeches was equally aggressive and on the order of an ultimatum. They blackmail us with the threat of a general strike (Bujak, Rulewski, Kuroń). They use catchy slogans that their takeover of power will allow for stabilization of the situation and a speedy improvement of social conditions.

Premises concerning a sharpening of the course by the "S" extremists:
– paralyzing the idea of the FNA;
– intimidation of society, the Sejm, and government (against the possibility of approving the law on extraordinary measures);

426

– cementing of the union, but mainly of the leading "S" cells;

– confidence that the USSR will not intervene and that it will be possible to communicate with it over the heads of the party;

– Wałęsa's egging on—"if he does not take a tough course then he will no longer be the president;"

– the true aim of the extremists to take power;

– the testing of society's reaction to the sharpened course.

Local administrations and party organizations are being paralyzed more and more.

Confrontation with the authorities in the countryside is assuming different forms. The Independent Farmers' Solidarity union allies with Solidarity in the cities as well as with other groups such as the Clubs of the Self-Governing Republic.

In academic circles the party is paralyzed, the IUS and "S" are very active.

The Church is very reserved with respect to the FNA. Glemp and Wałęsa met today.

From the evaluation of these facts it appears that the enemy is hastening the dismantling of state structures and a takeover of power.

In this situation it is necessary to act in a way that would make it impossible for the adversary to accomplish his program.

He suggests:

– with respect to legislative work: accelerate passage by the Sejm of the law on extraordinary measures (there is a fear that many deputies, under pressure, may vote against that law);

– pass a law on trade unions;

– consider ways to dismantle Solidarity cells in those factories and enterprises where their activity is especially aggressive, and to ban self-government in these factories and replace it with party-nominated self-government until a law is passed;

– decentralize decisions on procedures in case of the occupation of public buildings;

– consider de-legalization of the IUS as an unequivocally hostile organization; strengthen disciplinary activity toward students and cadres;

– within the framework of the law, increase repression against illegal groups, the CIP; arrest leaders of other anti-socialist groups;

– take decisive and preemptive administrative and [other] appropriate actions to secure the radio and television;

– in case of a general strike, introduce martial law throughout the country.

Cde. Hieronim Kubiak—in addition informs about a school strike in Lublin and about [the fact that] the voivode of Lublin signed an agreement which contradicts political directives and his own first declaration. The signed agreement grants program, management and consultative authority to the social council, *de facto* recognizes two illegal organizations (the Independent Scouts' Union and the Federation of Polish Youth), and fully yields to "S's" demands with respect to the academic history curriculum.

The voivode has abused his competences by signing such an agreement. After discussion with him, he declared that he is ready to publicly annul the agreement and resign from his post.

"S" considers the Lublin agreement to be an example worth spreading.

Conflict […] in Radom—as a result of discussions, only one moot point remains—Professor Hebda's removal (they suggest he take 3–4 weeks of vacation). Our instruction is unequivocal—we will not remove Professor Hebda.

Cde. Włodzimierz Mokrzyszczak—the practice of removing party organizations from factories is increasing. Another form of attacking the party is "S's" refusal to cooperate within self-governments whose members include party people.

"S" is already actively preparing for elections, they are training agitators.

Pressures to come to a reckoning are not weakening within the party. Concrete and imposing actions are necessary on this issue. The PPO complains about weak direct links between the upper levels and members. They want individual contacts in small groups and not big meetings. We should use delegates of all levels for such contacts.

After the latest "S" resolutions there is a threat to the idea of the FNA. The Church's stance is also ambiguous. It will back the stronger one.

What do party members expect, what do they demand?

– persistence in enforcing legal responsibility with respect to everyone equally, no matter their affiliation or position;

– the establishment of party workers' council groups (if necessary they should be secret).

Directors of enterprises should be expected to precisely fulfill their responsibilities.

Immediately send *aktiv* groups to large factories (not only to 207).

Publicly condemn every violation of the statute by the "S" union.

Try to introduce a party representative in factories where workers' self-government has not been elected yet, even if he has to resign from his party functions.

Reach every party member with all decisions and any information regarding economic reform.

Use recordings of "S" leaders' speeches in a propaganda campaign.

Cde. Tadeusz Porębski—suggests collecting opinions on a provisional economic undertaking in large factories as there is talk that a provisional economic undertaking [represents] a break-down of the national economy.

He is against dividing the law on extraordinary measures into two parts.

The situation in the voivodeship—we cannot count on the reaction force of the party in large factories. At the moment, the party is the party committee [instancja], the *aktiv* and some of the masses waiting for what will happen next. In Wrocław, we can count on 2,000–2,500 people ready for anything out of 45,000 party members. The phenomenon of leaving the party is still taking place and the main cause given is fear and uncertainty about tomorrow. This phenomenon may increase. There are also other motives for returning [party] identification cards— a lack of faith in the party and whether it can take the country out of the current situation. But one can also observe an attempt to consolidate the ranks, especially among the senior *aktiv*, in order to organize conspiratorial activity. The threat of provocation lies underneath. These 2,000–2,500 people who are ready for anything are only the left wing of the party, who are Marxists by intuition and belief. In the report there is an orientation toward the middle. We should demonstrate more decisive support for the *aktiv* on the left; this is a matter of principle. Every energetic activity by the authorities will strengthen that *aktiv*. Every concession causes a weakening of that *aktiv*; this should be taken into consideration.

Under current conditions, the slogan about cadre review is not good.

We need to realize the fact that gaining society's trust in the party requires 3–4 years. Society will become more trusting when we effectively resolve vital issues.

We can forget about our hopes for the collapse of Solidarity. We can take action in this direction but we cannot hope that it will lead to quick results.

Hitherto, we had three options for resolution of the situation:

– negotiations—compromise to end the conflict—a new increase in tensions;
– the idea for national reconciliation which, in the light of recent developments, is clearly fading;
– forceful actions.

I support the "carrot and stick" [*pałka i gołąbek*, literally cudgel and dove] method on legal grounds. The slogan of reconciliation alone is not enough nowadays; it is seen as our weakness. Therefore, a definitive act both for reconciliation and order is necessary. We need a different program if the force option is to be chosen; very class-like, socially accepted (a total struggle against speculation and theft, among other things).

We also need to know how we are going to act under conditions of a general strike, which seems to be inevitable.

At the last session, I said that the families of military personnel and CP [Citizens' Police] officers are secure in case of an extraordinary situation, but that the families of *aktivs* are not secure. We need to take care of that. I suggest the withdrawal of *aktivs* from factories; militarize and professionally retrain them and then they will defend themselves and their relatives.

Cde. Tadeusz Czechowicz—a conclusion can be drawn from the meetings that society does not believe the government and vice versa.

He suggests:

– obliging government representatives to frequent meetings directly with workers' crews in factories;
– organizing a meeting of representatives from 100 chosen factories to discuss basic matters related to an economic review and how the weight of the reform will be distributed;
– carrying on the ideological discussion in two phases; the first would be a discussion on reports in large factories and collection of remarks and motions as well as experiences, and the second would be their theoretical generalization during a plenary discussion;

– in our propaganda making use of the fact that the idea of the FNA is very appealing among women. Questions arise during meetings about the make-up of the initiative group;

– holding talks with representatives of our club and our allies to secure Sejm approval of the law on extraordinary measures;

– holding a teleconference with the first secretaries of the VC today.

Cde. Zofia Grzyb—supports the motions presented by Cde. Kiszczak. In relation to the necessity to prepare for a general strike she suggests immediately:

– taking weapons away from factory guards (they are mainly members of Solidarity);

– securing special production (e.g. the Walter Institute in Radom);

– strengthening security forces and the CP (there are many open positions at the local police headquarters in Radom);

– ensuring the security of the party *aktiv* and its families. The *aktivs* in the factories are asking when they will be provided with support, and if simultaneous action by *aktivs* and security forces is possible. The *aktivs* are asking if it is possible to isolate especially active and dangerous representatives of the extremists in advance;

– in relation to students' strikes—considering drafting them into military service;

– when necessary and possible, appointing press spokesmen in the voivodeship and local committees.

Cde. Florian Siwicki—informed about the course of the Committee of Defense Ministers' session of the Warsaw Pact member-states in Moscow.[8] About Polish matters at the session—great apprehension. Criticism of the party and authorities for weak counteraction. Concern about further developments. It was emphasized that the situation in Poland weakens the defense abilities of the WP (transit is more difficult, anti-Soviet propaganda, disruption of deliveries to which Poland is obligated). More radical forms of struggle with the counter-revolution were suggested. The methods used so far will not bring results and may lead to a larger tragedy.

He supports all motions raised by Cde. Kiszczak. The situation is special. "S" revealed its intentions and decisiveness in its attempt to take over power. It set its directions and agenda of actions.

And if that is the case, then we also need to fix our intentions and work out a plan of action against "S", including radical ones anticipating their actions. This cannot only be a counteraction from which we would retreat. We should also move to anticipatory actions. Starting today, begin artillery propaganda preparation of society.[9] Make counter-revolutionary activity openly known, make them realize what a tragedy it can lead to and that those who do not take this into account will bear the consequences.

[8] See Document No. 79.

[9] In other words, prepare the way with a "barrage" of propaganda.

Confirm to a greater degree the implementation of the Fourth CC Plenum resolution in the form of both agreement and battle, that is—both the unification of patriotic forces and the simultaneous fight with our enemies. Strengthen the party on that platform; win over those who are straddling the issues.

He suggests convening a session of the Sejm as soon as possible and implementing the law on extraordinary powers for the government. He is against the division of the law into two parts. He suggests not broadcasting the entire session of the Sejm; the session should be restricted.

Cadre review—one can conclude from the suggestions of the Military Operation Groups that many people in the administration at lower levels should be replaced. This should be selective and peaceful but apparent. This will strengthen the influence of the authorities.

Cde. Stanisław Opałko—in large factories 90 percent of the crews are in "S"; often first secretaries of the FC are in it as well. Party members are intimidated. It is difficult to convince them to destroy anti-party and anti-state flyers and posters. He suggests giving consideration to dissolving party organizations which are taken over by "S".

In Tarnów, "S. W."[10] members continue to occupy a building demanding the removal of the voivode from his post simply because he has worked in the party apparatus before.

The FNA—he feels there is no need to prolong the discussion. If "S" refuses to join, then work without its participation.

People demand concrete information about the enemy and their activity.

The party *aktiv* is intimidated. "S" creates squads of 20 people that are armed and act with absolute obedience and discipline. Therefore we should modify the plans of the [CC] Organizational Department to correspond to the current situation (regarding self-defense).

We should immediately take care of social matters in the factories. Many workers did not receive protective clothing and shoes for a long time because there was no one to take care of it.

The party organizations in many factories have not held meetings in months. The situation is similar in the countryside.

People ask why we do not bring an end to school and student strikes.

At the meetings there are voices demanding a separation from Wałęsa's begging appeal for help to those abroad.

People still bring up the issue of settling accounts.

We should quickly begin preparations for self-defense of the *aktiv* and their families, and defense of party and state buildings.

Cde. W. Jaruzelski—what actions does Cde. Opałko suggest in the Tarnów voivodeship and with which forces? How [can we help] and what kind of help is needed? What can he [the voivode] do on his own?

---

[10] *Solidarność Wiejska*, Rural Solidarity, later renamed Solidarity of Individual Farmers (*Solidarność Rolników Indywidualnych*).

Cde. Stanisław Opałko—suggests discussions with those occupying the building.

Cde. W. Jaruzelski—we will not get far if we count on the military taking care of everything while the party only calls for radical measures. Did the VC draw conclusions regarding the party organizations which did not meet for months?

Cde. Zbigniew Messner—paralysis of the party is a result of the overall situation in the country. People are dispirited by the economic situation and the increasing impertinence of the adversary. There is a complete lack of action in the basic party cells. If it were necessary to dissolve them for that reason, then many would have to be dissolved. There are also active people who are ready for a great deal but they look to the leadership. Nonetheless, this is a normal reaction for a Marxist party. The Fourth and Sixth CC Plenums gave the party a big push. If we spoil that, then the party will fall apart and a new one will be formed based on forums. Therefore, we must persistently enforce the resolution of the Fourth Plenum regarding self-proclamation, beginning with the CC members. The delegation from Katowice wanted to demand at the Fourth Plenum the removal of all "S" members from the CC.

We cannot have delusions that society is ready to support us. The average citizen has a highly critical attitude, is anti-state and anti-Soviet, and wonders why the authorities who have warned multiple times about the unrelenting defense of socialism are not doing anything.

If we persistently act within the framework of constitutional rights, we can win over the part of society that is tired of anarchy and lawlessness.

Reform—the economy needs the introduction of reforms, this is not in doubt. But under war conditions (the existence of controls, weak procurement, and an imbalance in the means of production) we should approach it carefully. There is the threat that in the first quarter basic industrial branches (metallurgy) will break down.

Cadres—this is not the time for verification. Many cannot handle the pressures anyway and leave on disability or early retirement.

The situation in higher education—the IUS forces are significant. If we want to break down students' strikes with force; then in many cases it will be necessary to expel students together with provosts and cadres. The situation is similar with the high school system.

He supports Cde. F. Siwicki's and Cde. Cz. Kiszczak's motions in their entirety—act preemptively, introduce martial law if necessary; we should not be ashamed, we cannot passively watch the system fall apart because in a few weeks there will be nobody who can introduce martial law and nobody who might be interested in it.

Cde. Marian Orzechowski—assumption—no matter what we do, "S" will persistently aim at accomplishing its goal. New, aggressive slogans have appeared in "S's" propaganda.

Our strategic goal is to defend socialism. But it is not possible to achieve that without the trust of a part of the working class and without retaining the party as an instrument for accomplishing that goal.

The substance of our actions after September had a political nature; this was at odds with the adoption of forceful solutions. For many months the state did not use enforcement measures with which it is legally and constitutionally empowered. By doing so we acquired doubts about the state's ability to offer peace and security for its citizens. The dismantling of the party that is taking place is a result of such behavior. The consequence of this within the party is a misunderstanding of the substance of the Sixth CC Plenum resolution (the law on extraordinary measures) which is recognized as a violation of social agreements.

The strategic goal of the adversary is clear. But how do we assess his actions during the coming days? What are his weaknesses and strengths? Why can we draw the conclusion that consolidation around extremist forces is taking place (as we know about the NCC Presidium session in Radom)? Do we have a full assessment of the enemy's forces, plans and means for the coming days? A majority of society supports Solidarity.

Dangerous points for us are:
- a full-time "S" *aktiv,* which is ready for anything and which incites itself and its surroundings; these are young people who create irrational moods among society;
- the CIP—an assault and counter-revolutionary force, ready for anything, the basis for establishment of "S" squads;
- the IUS—in April this year it was still a weak organization but today it is a massive force able to bring students into the streets.

The majority of the working class does not back us, but it does in part.

Therefore we are standing at the Rubicon—we will either overcome it or we will have to maintain the status quo.

In that connection, we should accentuate the following slogans in our propaganda and actions:
- we want to rescue the state as it is, which Solidarity wants to destroy;
- we want to do anything to avoid civil war, which "S" is aiming for;
- the Front for National Reconciliation is a strategic slogan, which is accurate in every situation.

We have to anticipate the enemy's actions on a global scale; on the scale of voivodeships, with our own forces as well.

Neutralize the CIP and IUS, and rid Solidarity of its leadership at the center. These will be the first of those preemptive actions. When undertaking them we should predict how "S" will react to them as a whole. How are we going to react if "S" calls a general strike? To what degree can we count on the security forces and the CP ("S" is directing destructive activities in those circles). Which *aktiv* in the party can we count on? How large is it? Cde. Porębski mentioned that in Wrocław he counts on 2,000–2,500. I think that we can count on one-third of the party membership, but they need to feel a force behind them.

Self-determination—it's about time functional party members left "S" since it is clear that it is a political party. Dangerous views are surfacing that at the bottom ranks party members and "S" will reach agreement if the CC and NC do not set upon each other.

We also need to know how internal allies will react to our actions. We cannot count on them; our tougher actions are not in their interest.

Cde. Stanisław Ciosek—Wałęsa and his advisers are already saying loudly that confrontation is inevitable. They warn that the "S" NC which meets in Gdańsk will go farther than the Presidium in Radom. Wałęsa is also threatening that he will go his own way. However, this is an illusion. They are counting on the resolution on extraordinary measures not being approved by the Sejm. They are preparing to place huge pressures on the deputies. At the same time they are looking for compromises based on the "three" (1/3 of us and 2/3 of them).

The weak points of "S" are:
– miscalculating society's reaction;
– counting on the West;
– weak operational-technical preparation;
– not taking our resistance into consideration.

Cde. Czesław Kiszczak—what is Solidarity planning to do?
– break further talks and divert responsibility onto the party and the government;
– prepare a general strike;
– establish self-governments to substitute for temporary authority, and hasten elections to the Sejm (in May);
– escalate attacks on the authorities with the motto "no support for Jaruzelski's government," and attack Cde. Olszowski for his appearance at "Ursus;"
– ten TV programs on economic reform [presented] in a way that will completely discredit the authorities;
– prepare cadres to take over power;
– introduce to the Sejm a draft election procedure;
– assure the USSR the minimum of interests in Poland—their guarantee is Solidarity and not the party and government;
– not allow passage of the resolution on extraordinary measures;
– attack the Sejm (Stelmachowski: half the Sejm are "leading officials with soft bellies").

Roughly, these are "S's" plans for the nearest future.

Cde. Kiszczak's answer to the question of whether the security service is able to perform the tasks it was assigned: Yes, it is able to; however, it is under great pressure from the adversary, who deceitfully says, "the MI and CP are good, only the parasites need to be removed." The apparatus is ready to perform assignments except for special cases. The action at the Firefighters' Academy, where nobody resigned despite awareness of the dangers, supports [this assumption].

Cde. Hieronim Kubiak—the party's line since the Ninth Congress is correct. Even if a forceful confrontation takes place we do not have anything other than this line. This line is attacked so strongly because it was and is correct. It is expressed by a poster war, starvation marches and various modes of discrediting

time as benefit

the party and the authorities; all of this is meant to cut society off from the party. We were attacked immediately for the FNA initiative because it was aimed at society. That is why we have to continue this line persistently.

However, why did this line prove ineffective? Because:
– we fought too long for this line inside the party;
– we took over the adversary's tactic—small steps in defense of socialism.

This is how we lost a lot of time, which the adversary has taken advantage of. It is beneficial that the adversary has revealed himself; he does not pretend anymore; he attacked all axioms of the system's stability and openly talks about upheaval. Therefore, it will now be easier to attack the adversary.

We should not concede anything right now, especially the regulation on trade unions, which can hasten the process of corrosion of trust in "S" among the lowest cells. We also cannot give up on the regulation on extraordinary measures. Hence, according to the Sixth CC Plenum both these regulations [are] parallel. We cannot have delusions—"S" extreme [resort] to force will react with force.

As a correct line, the line of the Ninth Congress makes it possible to maintain the party and the *aktiv*. All necessary staff actions should be taken to protect the *aktiv* and their families.

General strike—if it takes place, we will not be able to survive long. That is why I believe that when a general strike is declared, [we] should reach out for state constitutional rights and declare martial law.

Cde. Stefan Olszowski—we have wasted about ten days again. We assumed that both resolutions would be in the Sejm around December 5–6. This was our grave mistake. The situation is dramatic as never before. Confrontation is inevitable (perhaps already in January).

He suggests introduction of both regulations—on trade unions and on extraordinary measures. We have to act lawfully, within the entire scope of the law, as a lawful government.

Detailed consultations between the first secretary of the CC and the allies are indispensable.

A special group for cadre matters should be convened.

For some time, stop official price fluctuations.

Meet with the first secretaries of the VC in the next few days.

Cde. Marian Woniak—the economic situation is very difficult. There is a threat that beginning in January 1982 meat rations will fall to 2.9 kilograms; there is no soap or detergents on the market. If western loans are cut off, where will we get, beginning on January 1, 1982, 400 million dollars that is needed to start industrial production?

Based on TGO[11] motions we need to change immediately those regional authority cells which must be at our disposal.

---

[11] *Terenowe Grupy Operacyjne*—Local Operational Groups—were military groups deployed in the countryside.

Cde. Stanisław Kociołek—the *aktiv* together with the military were directed at the [work] establishments. *Aktiv* groups for political work (destroying flyers, attaching posters) and for self-defense are being formed.

In connection with strikes in universities we should exert strong pressure on those leaderships which supported the strike—the Church provided a certain support and "S" provided full [support]. The semester is lost. Provosts from Warsaw universities do not respect the recommendations given by the mayor of Warsaw although they improvise in the role of mediators. The use of enforcement in the universities would be impossible at the moment. It is better to let the strike "decay"—it does not enjoy society's sympathy.

The Mazowsze region is enforcing strike readiness in response to the action at the Firefighter's Academy.

The market—supplies of household articles are catastrophic; speculation is out of control.

The party—a lot of potential strength is still embedded within it. I do not fully agree with Cde. Kubiak's opinion. The theory of an easy approach was a mistake; [i.e.] the practice of dismantling the party from the right wing and from the position of horizontal liquidation and from the position of horizontal structures liquidation by people such as Lamentowicz or Iwanów. There is one possible orientation—Marxist–Leninist, which will take all conditions into consideration—an orientation against the recidivism of social democracy. Politburo members should define their views on party consolidation and the party's left [wing]. This is necessary.

Counting on reconciliation with "S" has proved to be a delusion. "S" rejected the idea of an FNA. [The idea] should still be current; it is an idea in favor of perspective.

He calls for immediate commencement of preparations for introducing martial law and especially for preparing the party to act under those conditions. It is an urgent matter.

Cde. Jan Główczyk—he supports approval of the law on extraordinary measures which would unfortunately take place on the anniversary of the December [1970] events. He supports all other motions raised by Cde. Kiszczak. He believes that Wałęsa is playing an independent role. At the same time we should direct our propaganda in a way that will blame the adversary for the results of introducing the law. He suggests talks with the Church; make them understand all the results.

He suggests preparing emergency methods for managing the economy.

Confrontation is the axis of politics; it is unavoidable. If we do not find courage, its costs may be high.

Remember about security not only for the party *aktiv* but also for trade associations.

Cde. Jan Łabęcki—understood S. Kociołek's presentation as contrary to the resolution of the Ninth Congress. If we undermine this line, then which one should we concentrate on?

He suggests suspending price and apartment fee increases at this time.

In justifiable cases, replace incompetent and unreliable representatives of the administration.

"Zero" hour is approaching. "There are calculations of injustices in the Motherland...," now we need to put these aside. Begin consolidation of the party around the resolution of the Ninth Congress, to defend socialism. A large role is given to the Politburo, but how is it [arrayed]—is it divided or not? We cannot even suggest that. We have a great responsibility for the system, for peace in Europe.

We need to have a plan of action ready for "zero" hour. The opposition will not let it go. It has revealed its goals. We should skillfully take advantage of this, polarize social sympathies. The extremists have hidden out in large factories. This is the new quality of the situation. Party lines are melting in these factories. We need to estimate who else we can count on in these factories. The use of force will cause a division of society. The FNA—this is our argument, do not retreat from that. I have changed my mind regarding the possibility of a division in "S".

Some sort of extraordinary solution for the economy could change the situation, something like the July Manifest. Confrontation is inevitable (*Cde. M. Milewski*—what does Cde. Łabęcki have in mind when talking about a plan of action for "zero" hour?).

Military upheaval, that is what I have in mind. Military upheaval with [all the] marks of the sole authority. Perhaps also the dissolution of the party and the creation of a communist party; but these are only theoretical assumptions.

Cde. Mieczysław Rakowski—we are facing a choice for a new strategy that will decide the future of the country. This cannot be decided by one person but by the whole collective which governs the country. This requires a uniform view. The leadership group does not have a uniform view on that strategy. I am attacked myself by both "S" and a segment within the party.

I will engage in a polemic with Cde. Kociołek. I believe that our policies since the Ninth Congress cannot be characterized as concessions with respect to "S". We did not concede in many matters—resolution no. 199 RM,[12] the strike in Lubogór; we did not concede on the matter of access to the mass media for "S", neither on the matter of the strike at the WSI,[13] in Radom, nor in Żyrardów. There were also defeats but they were not of a decisive nature. The aggressiveness of "S" is among other things a response to our actions. Therefore we cannot say that we only have a series of defeats in our column. We also cannot remain in the world of illusion, e.g. our evaluation of the situation in the trade associations. They are sick, just like the whole party.

The possibilities for a policy of reconciliation have already been exhausted. Our partner considers the fight with us to be his program. We believed that we

---

[12] Resolution 199 of the Council of Ministers (RM—Rada Ministrów) concerned extra pay for work in the coal mines on Saturdays.

[13] *Wyzsza Szkoła Inzynierska*, College of Engineering.

would force him into limited co-responsibility. "S" does not want that. Dividing Solidarity into extreme and moderate lines is a mistake. Such a division does not exist. The "S" leadership forces really believe that they can take over power. They conclude that the USSR will not enter [Poland] and that it will accept their guarantees. The "S" leadership moved from a masked union and social movement to an opposition party with counter-revolutionary features. It picks arenas of confrontation that are not comfortable for us (elections to councils, the Sejm, party organizations in factories, foodstuff control). The concept of a Civic Economic Council is a concept backed by the Church which indeed means a counter-revolutionary government with Czartoryski, Wielowieyski and Stelmachowski.[14] We cannot agree to that.

I am afraid that the next phase of the counter-revolution will be the use of force by the adversary. It is an inevitable process. I have brought this to our attention before. The squads, which always appear at the culminating point, have already surfaced on city streets. This is a new qualitative fact. At the moment calling for respect for law and order is pointless. This does not work with these groups. A considerable part of society is split in two—it covets order but at the same time it does not come out against those who violate it. We are losing day after day. The opposition will not give up the fight. It has already launched certain mechanisms.

The fact that the opposition has revealed itself is a new and favorable [development] for our case. We should take full advantage of that. We can expect that during the coming days drastic actions will be taken against us. At the same time we have to enforce the idea of national reconciliation.

For the coming days and weeks, work out a few directed political slogans and a document that will clearly take "S's" slogans into consideration in our presentations and publications. The resolution approved by the "S" NC Presidium in Radom is a shock to me. It does not leave any room for compromise and brings us to a new phase.

The second direction of operations are force centers. The leadership should establish a few working groups which will immediately prepare concepts for action, including political ones, for "zero" hour, so that there is no improvisation. We need to know which social forces will support us. The guiding idea for this concept should be:

– defense of the state;

[14] Paweł Czartoryski was a professor of history and law. Andrzej Wielowieyski was a journalist for the Catholic monthly *Więź* and secretary of the Warsaw Club of Catholic Intelligentsia (KIK). Andrzej Stelmachowski was a law professor at the University of Wrocław and University of Warsaw, and president of KIK. All three were Solidarity members. Czartoryski and Wielowieyski's familes were also part of the old nobility, so the implication is that the Civic Economic Council would be under the influence of the aristocracy and the Church.

438

– defense of the endangered survival of the nation;

– implementation of the goals of the Ninth Congress and of economic reform.

In the near future, implement necessary changes in the administrative cadres (do not touch the technical one).

The law on extraordinary measures—even if it is passed by the Sejm, it will be by a slight majority. Then there will be the claim that a rump parliament passed a law for the party. Such a law should not be passed after giving it [all that] attention; it should be done instantly. Talks with deputies are pointless, the majority of them are under pressure and they are simply afraid. Therefore we need to decide which actions to take.

Cde. Kazimierz Barcikowski—agrees with the general assessments presented so far. He suggests:

– calling a conference of VC first secretaries for December 8;
– holding a session of the Commission for Cooperation of the Party and Political Parties to present our assessments;
– guiding the resolution on trade unions through to approval by the Sejm (it is not fully agreed upon, differences relate to military matters and the period for which strikes should be banned);
– after approval of the resolution on trade unions implementing the resolution on banning strikes;
– a resolution to delay elections.

Approve the resolution on trade unions and the Teachers' Charter at the Sejm session on December 11–12. Call the next Sejm session for December 17 and approve resolutions on the ban on strikes and on the delay of elections to national councils at that session.

The resolution on extraordinary measures—it would make sense to implement it only when bans resulting from the resolution on trade unions prove unsuccessful in this matter. We should expect that Catholic deputies and social democrats in the Sejm will oppose the resolution; we also do not know how the UPP will behave (Strużek made critical remarks). The majority of our club will vote in favor of the resolution but non-party deputies and those related to them—we do not know how [they will vote]. In this situation, the resolution may be approved by a slight majority, but it might also be rejected. This would be a great defeat for the party and the government.

Cde. Józef Czyrek—in the past, all sorts of crises were solved not by the expansion of democracy but by the extraordinary strengthening of authority, by the introduction of dictatorship. In 1956 and in 1970 we were able to control the situation without that. Today this is not going to happen because we are dealing with a total movement that believes it can take over power legally, that is confident of support from the West, and that even counts on agreement with the USSR. This movement, being a composition of various political and ideological forces, has assumed the status of a national movement. This makes [an attempt to] break it more difficult. This movement discounts and deepens the economic crisis (this is a new feature); it continues in the feedback with the international situation.

What should we do in this situation?

- work out a plan to avoid civil war;
- defend the idea of the FNA, even without the participation of "S";
- use a double tactic—the force of argument and the argument of force;
- act in support of consolidation of the party, engage in major work with the party base centered on the resolutions of the Fourth and Sixth CC Plenum;
- make society realize that if "zero" hour comes, neither the party nor the authorities will bear responsibility;
- prepare all political structures including the party for working under martial law conditions;
- prepare a plan of action for the period following martial law;
- secure political and economic relations with allies.

The socialist states expect us to take the initiative and prove to be persistent in the fight against the adversary.

The expectations of the capitalist states differ depending on their interests in Poland. On the one hand we should stimulate their interest in stabilizing the situation in Poland but at the same time we should secure our economic interests.

If the use of extraordinary measures takes place, try not to let it adversely affect our interests abroad; try not to let it cost us much.

Cde. Jerzy Romanik—agrees with all motions. There is no hope left for reconciliation among society. Party [representatives] in factories are intimidated. Everybody expects decisive action; the sooner the better. Coal miners talk about it in meetings, even those from "S". My factory executed a plan on November 26; sixty percent of the self-government consists of party members. Perhaps in such factories the confrontation should take a different course. Everybody is aware that we will not achieve anything through legal measures.

Cde. Albin Siwak—supports Cde. M. Rakowski's motion regarding the establishment of special groups. [Siwak] does not agree with [Rakowski's] assessment of the situation in the trade associations; there are weaker and stronger cells, just as in the party.

In relation to anticipated developments, he believes that the CC structure should not include "S" members (Arent, Ciechan).

He supports the opinions and motions of Cdes. Siwicki and Kiszczak unequivocally.

From the most recent meetings in the field:

- there is definite approval for an action at the WSOP in Warsaw;
- [there is an] increased effort by the "S" canvassers to torpedo the regulations on trade unions and on extraordinary measures, and to dismiss party organizations from factories;
- there are voices [in favor of] dismantling those PPO's that implement the "S" line;
- in reasonable cases, replace field administration;
- expand VRCP units and train them with weapons;
- [there is] criticism of student strikes and high school youth.

Cde. Mirosław Milewski—the action at the Firefighters' Academy was carried out perfectly. You cannot always assure positive results without any injuries when acting decisively. Our entire repressive action is based on the fact that we assume we can respond in a similar way to every "S" action. By employing repression hastily we could create effects for which we are not prepared.

We need to be aware that the introduction of martial law in any form will affect everyone. We will need to make sure to defend the state and nation, even at the cost of ourselves or our dear ones. Therefore we need to prepare mentally for both the external and internal consequences and effects. We need immediately to make the governments of the capitalist states and the communist parties aware of the "S's" program, its objective of confrontation and its adventurism.

Currently, we need persistently to carry out actions resulting from the resolutions of the Fourth and Sixth CC Plenums. Do not make it seem as though the situation is very tense [or that we are] waiting for "zero" hour. And if it comes then, what is next? We cannot exclude the possibility that the time and place of confrontation will be chosen by the adversary. During the coming days, the tension level may fall, but do not let that deceive you.

We agreed at the last PB [session] that the Sejm will convene on December 4–5 and that both resolutions will be considered. Yesterday we found out that the Sejm will convene on December 12 and 17 and that the resolutions will be considered separately. What will the CC members think about that? We are late again and because of that, among other things, the law on extraordinary measures has no chance of passing.

He agrees with all proposals and motions raised by Cdes. Siwicki and Kiszczak. The explanation for our actions: the defense of a socialist state and nation, and security for citizens in winter.

Cde. Kazimierz Cypryniak—the fight for the system has entered the final phase. Every attempt to strengthen authority will meet resistance. The adversary has concluded that the balance of forces is to his advantage.

He agrees with all motions by Cde. Kiszczak and Cde. Porębski.

Confrontation is inevitable and we must prepare for it. For a year and a half we have been saying that we want to solve the crisis through political means and that the *aktiv* is acting on this assumption. Some have left party principles altogether in their desire to provide themselves with minimal security. Acceptance of the theory of the inevitability of confrontation means triggering other activities in the party. Establish groups that will work out ways and means of action in extraordinary situations, namely:

– leading the party under extraordinary conditions;
– making approaches toward Solidarity;
– planning for a positive reaction to society.

Give the law on extraordinary measures a voice among society.

Cde. Florian Siwicki—every comrade has emphasized that confrontation is inevitable, that time is to our disadvantage and that we should look for various options that would gain popular support for us. This is contradictory because it has been set aside again for later.

If we are to accept the theory that confrontation is inevitable, then we should have a plan of action that anticipates developments.

It is proposed to convene the Sejm on December 17 and approve two resolutions: for a ban on strikes and for delaying elections to councils. This proposal needs to be reconsidered as it also contradicts the entire discussion and the motions.

Cde. Wojciech Jaruzelski—one can sense a general convergence of the key evaluations, an awareness of the threat and danger, and the resulting conclusions in the comrades' statements. The crisis has reached its peak. The counterrevolutionary forces have bluntly revealed their intentions. We must make use of this fact.

We have spoken bitterly about the situation in the party, that this is the last chance to save at least that part of it which is able to act and which is identified with its legacy. We must strengthen the party at every level according to the criteria for [achieving] readiness to fight with the enemy.

In the nearest future we need to act in a way that will allow us to join the confrontation imposed by the adversary from the best vantage point. Not even one step backward. Do not waste any opportunity to confirm the decisiveness and determination of the party to defend the principals of a socialist state. We need to define in which situations we can immediately act offensively; we need to confirm our determination.

[An example of] such a situation is the decisive defense of the party in the factories. The party should defend itself as a political force. Unfortunately, the working class does not defend it. How did this happen? Now is not the time to evaluate that. Therefore, decisively demonstrate a readiness to defend the place and role of the party in a socialist factory.

The CC organizational and administrative section will prepare a concrete plan of action and present it on the seventh of this month.

Immediately publish the analysis of the State Council regarding the party's right to act in factories.

Intensively develop preparations for extreme situations.

Immediately use materials from the NC Presidium in Radom in the media.

Gain social approval for public statements regarding the imminent danger to the state and nation. Make the party and society aware that the party is carrying out a second revolution and that only the party is able to fight with the evil that harasses society. The party is defending the class interests of the working people at this historic point.

Cadres—protect the party and administrative apparatus and remove those who are incapable and compromised. The majority of the administration work honestly and generously. Make decisions based on the TGO proposal (to be prepared by Cde. M. Janiszewski).

442

The Church—unfavorable reassessments are being made, which we should take into consideration. This is not a third force but one that is tightly associated with "S".

Colleges—if an extraordinary situation takes place during the course of strikes at colleges, it should be considered by its results. Hold talks at once with provosts and teaching cadres. Make them aware of the unpredictable results of strikes in light of the NC Presidium resolution.

Economic matters—immediately assess the scope of aid and operations in case internal and external supplies are cut off (Cde. M . Woźniak).

Evaluate the situation and anticipate precautions for transport and communications (Cde. F. Siwicki).

Take necessary actions to secure the radio and television.

Use different methods of bringing the military closer to society.

Secure the *aktiv*, families, and buildings. The CC administrative and organizational divisions will define the forms and scope of this protection. But most of all, expect self-defense.

Immediately direct CC and VC representatives to the factories.

Work out the topography of the situation—where is "S" behaving properly and where badly, especially in large factories.

Protect the passing of resolutions in the Sejm. If otherwise impossible, pass the law on extraordinary measures through an extraordinary procedure.

In the nearest future, meet with allies and representatives of trade and autonomous associations in order to make them aware of the situation and the dangers, and to gain support.

Increase appearances of members of the leadership in the mass media.

Through the mediation of government press spokesmen, take an official position on the resolution of the "S" NC in Radom. Develop this subject into a vast propaganda campaign.

Introduce a state of work alarm and 24-hour duty at every level of the party and administrative apparatus.

We will have to make decisions of the highest responsibility. I have enough experience to fight dramatically for what can be saved. I counted on the workers' class instinct. Unfortunately we proved to be too weak and incapable; we did not work to our full ability. We made mistakes in our decisions and assessments. There was good will and [still] is.

It is a horrible, monstrous shame for the party that after 36 years in power it has to be defended by the police. But there is nothing else left ahead of us. We need to be ready to make the decision that will allow us to save what is fundamental.

Part of the *aktiv* lives under the myth of martial law; part of the administration lives under the myth of reform. These myths need to be filled with the substance of an *aktiv* ready to act decisively and [we should] not count only on the force of the military and police and on the fact that martial law and reform will miraculously change everything.

The P[U]WP fought for power. Today one cannot see the will to fight in the party. The party is paralyzed by mistakes and that is its tragedy.

We need to be aware that if we cannot rouse people in factories, then martial law in itself will not change anything. Therefore we cannot give in to the myths. It is most important to know how to rouse people during this extraordinary situation; how to arm the party and trade associations. This is a cardinal matter.

In an extraordinary situation, the initial operations of the military and CP must be followed by actions by the local *aktiv* that correspond to the situation, to necessity and to conditions.

We will not make the final decision at today's PB session. We have considered the concept. Staff work must be continued, and decisions will be made at the optimal time and within a political framework. A concrete decision, the time and place, and the methods will depend on many circumstances—on the adversary's actions and on the support of domestic allies.

Multi-layered action is necessary, not waiting for "zero" hour and the staffs to achieve their goal. We need comprehensive preparation so that the confrontation, if it takes place, will happen at the lowest cost. We need to make it seem, inside and outside the country, that we are acting rightfully and with deep awareness of our responsibilities. Do anything not to [give the impression that] martial law is our operating concept, but that on the contrary we are doing everything to avoid that confrontational state. Society needs to be convinced that even radical measures are there so that a confrontation does not take place, so that two sides are not fighting. Talking about confrontation is a scandalous political and psychological mistake. It is not we who want confrontation but our adversary.

The Politburo familiarized itself with the following materials:
- the plan for implementing assignments resulting from the resolution of the Sixth PUWP CC Plenum;
- the resolution of the State Council regarding legal defense of the actions of political organizations;
- the actions undertaken by the PUWP Voivodeship Committee in Radom;
- the note regarding dates of the Sejm sessions in December 1981;
- the stance of the NC Presidium and the chairmen of the NSZZ Solidarity regional boards agreed to in Radom;
- the declaration of the NC Presidium and chairmen of the NSZZ Solidarity regional boards, which supports the protests in academic circles.

The Politburo approved motions regarding personnel without discussion [*obiegiem*]:
- the dismissal of Cde. Henryk Sobieski from the position of PPR ambassador extraordinary and plenipotentiary to the Republic of Venezuela and the Republic of Guyana and extraordinary representative and minister plenipotentiary in the Republic of Haiti;

444

– the dismissal of Cde. Zygmunt Pietrusiński from the position of PPR ambassador extraordinary and plenipotentiary to the Republic of Ecuador;
– the dismissal of Cde. Janusz Zabłocki from the position of PPR ambassador to the Republic of Lebanon;
– the approval of Cde. Mieczysław Włodarek for the position of PPR ambassador extraordinary and plenipotentiary to the Republic of Venezuela and the Republic of Guyana and minister extraordinary and plenipotentiary in the Republic of Haiti.

Recorded by: Andrzej Barzyk
Bożena Łopatniuk

[Source: Tajne Dokumenty, *pp. 549–569. Translated by Magdalena Klotzbach for the National Security Archive.]*

Document No. 81: Transcript of CPSU CC Politburo Meeting

December 10, 1981

This crucial record, from just three days before the declaration of martial law, begins with the surprising comment by Brezhnev that the topic of Poland was not even on the Politburo's agenda. Another interesting point about this document is that the substance of discussion at first is entirely about Poland's economic needs, which were a critical issue underlying the entire crisis. Eventually, however, the talk turns to the political dimensions of the crisis and how the Soviet Union should respond. Moscow's frustration with Jaruzelski's vacillations remains high, even as the Polish leader appears to be on the verge of ordering the crackdown. Certainly their faith in his fortitude is as low as it has ever been. Here again, the question comes up as to whether the Soviets should resort to armed force. Perhaps nowhere in the available record is the answer more clearly given—by no less important figures than Suslov, Gromyko and Ustinov, among others—that under no circumstances are Soviet troops to be introduced. This seemingly unequivocal stance would have shocked most observers, particularly in the United States, where the unshakable assumption was that Moscow would never allow control of Poland to slip through their grasp. Unless and until the full record of Soviet leadership meetings becomes available, doubts will persist as to whether this was in fact the final Soviet position or a reflection of a desire not to face the ultimate decision as long as there was any hope of an alternative solution.

[…]

I. *On the question of the situation in Poland*

Brezhnev: This question does not appear on our agenda. But I think this session of the Politburo must begin with this question since we sent Cdes. Baibakov and Kulikov on a special mission to Poland to discuss urgent and pressing questions with the Polish comrades. On December 8, Cde. Kulikov provided information on the discussions he held in Warsaw, and yesterday, December 9, Cde. Baibakov reported from Warsaw that he held discussions with Cde. Jaruzelski. From these and subsequent discussions, it was apparent to Cde. Baibakov that the Polish comrades hope to receive additional raw and other materials during the first quarter of next year from the USSR and other socialist countries roughly in the amount of $1.5 billion.

[…]

And now let us listen to Cde. Baibakov.

Baibakov: Following the instructions of the Politburo I left for Warsaw. I met there with all of the comrades with whom it was necessary to talk over the questions I was entrusted with.

First of all, I held a discussion with Deputy Director of the Council of Ministers Cde. Obodowski. In this discussion, the Polish comrades raised the ques-

446

tion of economic aid. I reported on the Polish request in a ciphered message [to Moscow].

It must be said that the list of goods the PPR has included as aid from us consists of 350 items in the amount of 1.4 billion rubles. It includes such goods as 2 million tons of grain, 25,000 tons of meat, 625,000 tons of iron ore and many other goods. Taking into account what we intended to give Poland in 1982, the total amount of aid to the Polish People's Republic consists of roughly 4.4 billion rubles, taking into consideration the requests made by the Polish comrades.

The time is now approaching for Poland to repay its credits to the West European countries. For this, Poland requires a minimum of 2.8 million hard-currency rubles. When I heard what our Polish comrades were asking and how much all of this aid amounted to, I raised the question of bringing our mutual economic relations into balance. Along with that, I noted that Polish industry is falling short of fulfilling its plan by significant margins. The coal industry, which is a fundamental source of foreign currency, is essentially disorganized, necessary measures are not being taken, and strikes are continuing. Now that there are no strikes, coal extraction is still occurring at a very low level.

Or, for example, let us say, the peasants have products; there is grain, meat products, vegetables, and so on. But they give nothing to the state and are adopting a wait-and-see attitude. In the private markets, a rather active trade is being conducted and at very elevated prices.

I said directly to the Polish comrades that more decisive measures must be taken since such a situation has arisen. Perhaps they should introduce something like a surplus-appropriation system.

If one speaks, for example, about grain reserves, Poland harvested more than 2,000,000 tons this year. The people are not going hungry. City-dwellers go to the market in the countryside and buy all the products they need. And these products are there.

As is known, by decision of the Politburo and by request of the Polish comrades we are providing them with aid in the form of the supply of 30,000 tons of meat. Of these 30,000 tons, 16,000 tons have already been redirected abroad. It must be said that produce, meat in this case, is being supplied in dirty, unsanitized railroad cars used to transport ore, in a very unattractive condition. Genuine sabotage is taking place during the unloading of this produce at Polish stations. The Poles utter the most obscene words about the Soviet Union and the Soviet people, they refuse to clean the railroad cars, and so on. It is simply impossible to count all of the insults that pour out about us.

Realizing this situation with the state of the balance of payments, the Poles want to introduce a moratorium on the repayment of debt to the Western countries. If they announce a moratorium, then all Polish vessels in the waters of any state or at the docks, and all other property located in countries to which Poland is in debt will be seized. Therefore the Poles have now given orders to the captains of vessels to leave port and to remain in neutral waters.

Now I will say a few words about my discussion with Cde. Jaruzelski. He confirmed the requests made by Obodowski relating to the supply of goods. Then in the evening, along with the ambassador and Cde. Kulikov, we again visited Jaruzelski. Obodowski and the secretary of the Central Committee of the PUWP in charge of these questions also attended the discussion. Jaruzelski was in a highly agitated state. It felt as though he was under the strong influence of a letter from the head of the Polish Catholic Church, Archbishop Glemp, who, as is known, promised to declare a holy war against the Polish authorities. True, Jaruzelski there and then answered that in the event of an outburst by Solidarity, they would quarantine all hostile elements.

As far as primary party organizations, they have essentially collapsed and are inactive. And concerning the party as a whole, Jaruzelski said that it effectively does not exist. The country is going to pieces and local districts are not receiving reinforcements because the Central Committee and the government cannot give firm and clear orders. Jaruzelski himself has turned into a man who is unbalanced and unsure of himself.

Rusakov: Cde. Baibakov has correctly outlined the situation with respect to the condition of the Polish economy. What should we do now? It seems to me that we have to supply those goods to Poland which are covered by economic agreements, but then this supply should not exceed the quantity of goods we supplied in the first quarter of last year.

Brezhnev: And can we give this now?

Baibakov: Leonid Ilyich, we can only give it from state reserves or by limiting supplies to domestic markets.

Rusakov: The day before yesterday they had a conference of secretaries of voivode committees. As Cde. Arestov [sic: Aristov] reported, the secretaries of the voivode committees did not understand Cde. Jaruzelski's speech at all, which did not give a clear, precise line. No one knows what is going to happen in the next few days. There was a conversation about operation "X". At first, the point was that it would be at night from the 11th to the 12th, then from the 12th to the 13th. And now they are already talking about it being around the 20th. The idea is that the chairman of the State Council, Jabłoński, will speak on radio and television, and announce the introduction of martial law. At the same time, Jaruzelski declared that the law concerning the introduction of martial law can only be invoked after it has been discussed in the Sejm[15], and the next session of the Sejm is set for December 15. In this way, everything is becoming very complicated. The agenda for the session of the Sejm has been published. The question of the introduction of martial law does not appear on it. But in any case, Solidarity knows well that the government is preparing to introduce martial law, and in turn it is taking all necessary measures [in the event of] the introduction of martial law.

---

[15] The Sejm is the lower house of the Polish parliament.

448

Jaruzelski himself says that he is contemplating addressing the Polish people. But he will not talk about the party in his address, but will appeal to people on the basis of their patriotic emotions. Jaruzelski speaks of the necessity of proclaiming a military dictatorship as existed under Piłsudski, pointing out in addition that the Polish people will understand that better than anything else.

As concerns other figures, such as Olszowski, he has recently been acting more decisively and it must be said that at a Politburo session the decision to introduce martial law and to adopt more decisive measures against extremist figures in Solidarity was passed unanimously; no one expressed any objections. In addition, Jaruzelski intends to be in touch with the allies on this question. He says that if Polish forces cannot handle the resistance from Solidarity, then the Polish comrades are relying on help from other countries, up to and including the introduction of armed forces on the territory of Poland. In addition, Jaruzelski refers to a speech by Cde. Kulikov who allegedly said that help from the USSR and allied states for the armed forces of Poland will be provided. However, as far as I know, Cde. Kulikov did not say so directly, he simply repeated words spoken by L. I. Brezhnev at another time, to the effect that we will not leave the PPR in trouble.

If one is to speak about what is being done in the voivodeships, one has to say directly that one cannot feel the strength of the party organizations at all there. In some measure administrative authority is felt. Essentially, all authority is in the hands of Solidarity. What Jaruzelski is saying sounds like he is leading us by the nose since there is no sense of correct analysis in his words. If they do not quickly organize themselves now, then they do not intend to and they will not act against the onslaught of solidarity; there will be no success in improving the situation in Poland.

Andropov: From the discussion with Jaruzelski it is evident that he has not yet made a firm decision on the introduction of martial law and, notwithstanding even the unanimous decision of the Politburo of the PUWP CC on the introduction of martial law we have not yet seen any concrete measures from the leadership. The Solidarity extremists are attacking the leadership of the PPR by the throat. The Church in recent days has also expressed its clear position. It essentially has gone over to the side of Solidarity.

And of course in these circumstances the Polish comrades must quickly prepare to move on "X" and carry out that operation. At the same time, Jaruzelski declares that we will move toward Operation "X" when Solidarity forces us to. That is a very alarming indication, even more so since the last session of the Politburo of the PUWP CC, and the decision on introducing martial law that was adopted there, testify that the Politburo is becoming more decisive; all the members came out in favor of decisive actions. That decision pressed Jaruzelski and he must now somehow extricate himself. Yesterday I spoke with [Mirosław] Milewski and asked him what kind of measures are being contemplated and when. He answered that he did not know about Operation "X" or about a concrete timeframe for its execution. In this way, it turns out that Jaruzelski is either hiding his plan for concrete actions from his comrades or he is simply abandoning [the idea] of carrying out that measure.

Now I would like to note that Jaruzelski is rather persistently placing economic demands before us and conditioning the implementation of Operation "X" on our economic aid; and I would even say more than that, he is raising the question, albeit indirectly, of military assistance.

Now, if one looks at the list of goods our Polish comrades are requesting then we would say directly that serious doubts arise about the necessity of supplying these products. For example what relation to the success of Operation "X" does the supply of fertilizer and certain other goods have? In this connection I would like to state that our position, as it was formulated earlier at the last Politburo section and as Leonid Ilyich expressed it earlier more than once, is completely correct and we should not retreat from it. Put another way, we take a position [in favor of] international aid, we are concerned with the conditions that have taken shape in Poland, but as regards the implementation of Operation "X", that must be wholly and entirely the decision of the Polish comrades; however they decide, that is how it will be. We will not insist on it, nor will we talk them out of it.

As far as economic assistance, of course it will be difficult to do that on the scale they are requesting. Apparently something needs to be done. But again I want to say that the framing of the question about apportioning goods as economic aid carries an insolent character, and all of this is being done so that if later we do not supply them with something they can then shift the blame to us. If Cde. Kulikov actually spoke about the introduction of troops then I consider that he did so incorrectly. We cannot risk that. We do not intend to introduce troops into Poland. That is the correct position, and we must observe it to the end. I do not know how matters will develop in Poland, but even if Poland comes under the authority of Solidarity that will be one thing. But if the capitalist countries fall upon the Soviet Union, and they already have a suitable agreement, with various kinds of economic and political sanctions, then that will be very difficult for us. We must show concern for our country, for the strengthening of the Soviet Union. That is our main line.

Generally, it seems to me our position in relation to the situation in Poland, which was formulated by Leonid Ilyich in his numerous speeches and affirmed by the decisions that have been made today at the Politburo session, has been going through a very thorough exchange of opinions. All this should form the basis of the policy, which we should adhere to in our relations with Poland.

As for communications, which lead from the Soviet Union to the GDR through Poland, we must of course do something and undertake their protection.

Gromyko: Today we have been discussing the question of the situation in Poland very sharply. Very likely, we have never discussed it so sharply before. This is explained by the fact that we ourselves do not know the direction events in the PPR will take. The leadership of Poland itself feels power slipping through its hands. Kania and Jaruzelski, as is known, were counting on the support of neutrals. But now effectively there are none, there are no neutrals. Their position was defined rather clearly: Solidarity showed itself to be a patently counter-revolutionary organization, a pretender to power that has declared itself openly concerning the seizure of the power. The Polish leadership must decide the question: it will either surrender its position if it does not take decisive measures, or it will take decisive measures, introduce martial law, quarantine the extremists from Solidarity, and establish necessary order. There is no other way.

What is our attitude toward the Polish events? I completely agree with what the comrades have been expressing here. We can say to the Poles that we regard the Polish events with understanding. This is a measured formulation and there is no basis for changing it. At the same time, we will have to try somehow to disabuse Jaruzelski and other Polish leaders of their attitude with respect to the introduction of troops. There can be no introduction of troops into Poland. I think that on this score we can instruct our ambassador to visit Jaruzelski and inform him of this.

Notwithstanding the rather unanimous decision of the Politburo of the PUWP CC on the implementation of martial law, Jaruzelski is now taking a vacillating position again. At first he was somewhat heartened, but now he has grown soft again. Everything that was said to him before remains valid. If they exhibit vacillation in the struggle with the counter-revolution and beyond, then nothing will remain of socialist Poland. The introduction of martial law, of course, would impress upon the counter-revolution in Poland the firm intentions of the Polish leadership. But if the measures they intend to enact are implemented, I think one may expect positive results

Now, with respect to the creation of a new party, about which Jaruzelski spoke, I think that it is necessary to say to Jaruzelski directly that there is absolutely no need to create some kind of new party because that would signify a retreat by the Polish leadership and an admission that the PUWP is really not a fighting political organization but an organization that has permitted mistakes. It would be an admission of its own weakness and play into the hands of the Solidarity extremists. Then the Polish population, which feels definite sympathy toward the PUWP in its function as the leading force, will be completely disappointed in it.

I think that we should not allow any harsh instructions now, which would force them into this or that action. I think that we have the correct position here: establishing order in Poland is a matter for the Polish United Workers' Party, its Central Committee and the Politburo. We have been telling the Polish friends and in the future we will tell them [again] that it is necessary to take firm positions and it would be impermissible to relax now.

Of course, if the Poles deliver a blow to Solidarity, then the West in all likelihood will not grant them credits and will not provide any support. This is what they have in mind and this obviously must be taken into account by us as well. Therefore the proposal by Leonid Ilyich is correct, to instruct a group of comrades to review this question and, taking into account our possibilities, provide definite assistance to the PPR.

Ustinov: The situation in the PPR, of course, is very bad. The situation grows more complicated day by day. In the leadership, in particular in the Politburo, there is no firmness, there is no unity. And all this has already affected the state of affairs. Only at the last session of the Politburo was a decision on carrying out martial law passed unanimously. Now everything hinges on Jaruzelski. How will he be able to carry off this decision. So far no one can speak openly about Jaruzelski's actions. Even we do not know. I had a conversation with [Florian] Siwicki. He said immediately that even we do not know what the general is thinking. In this way, the person who essentially fulfills the responsibilities of the minister of defense of the PPR does not know what is going to happen or what actions the chairman of the Council of Ministers and the minister will take.

As for what Cde. Kulikov supposedly said with respect to the introduction of troops into Poland, I can say with full authority that Kulikov did not say that. He merely repeated what Leonid Ilyich and we said about not leaving Poland in trouble. And he knows perfectly well that the Poles themselves requested us not to introduce troops.

As for our garrisons in Poland, we are fortifying them. I, perhaps, am also inclined to think that the Poles will not head towards a confrontation, and only if, possibly, when Solidarity seizes them by the throat will they act.

The trouble is that the Polish leaders are not demonstrating decisiveness. As our comrades correctly pointed out here, we should not impose any of our decisions on them and we should pursue the policy on which we agreed. In our turn, we must ourselves be prepared and not take any actions not provided for by our decisions.

Suslov: I consider that, as is evident from the comrades' speeches, we all have a unanimous point of view toward the situation in Poland. In the course of the entire period of events in Poland we have displayed self-control and composure. Leonid Ilyich Brezhnev spoke about this at the Plenum. We spoke about this in public and our people supported such a policy by the communist party.

We are carrying out great work on behalf of peace and we cannot change our position now. World public opinion will not understand us. We have conducted such major actions through the U.N. for the strengthening of peace. What an effect we have had from the visit of L. I. Brezhnev to the FRG, and from many other peaceful actions we have taken. This has made it possible for all peace-loving countries to understand that the Soviet Union is firmly and consistently defending a policy of peace. That is why it is impossible for us to change the position on Poland we have adopted at the very beginning of the Polish events. Let the Polish comrades themselves determine which actions they should take. We do not have to push them towards any more decisive acts. But we will say to the Poles, as we did earlier, that we regard their actions with understanding.

It seems to me that Jaruzelski is manifesting a certain cunning. He wants to cover his own back with requests which he presents to the Soviet Union. Naturally, we do not physically have the ability to fulfill these requests, but Jaruzelski

Cursory handwriting

will say later, well, I turned to the Soviet Union and requested help but I did not receive this help.

At the same time the Poles declare directly that they are against the introduction of troops. If troops are introduced, that will mean a catastrophe. I think that we all share a unanimous opinion here that there can be no discussion of any introduction of troops.

As far as providing help to Poland, we have provided more than one billion rubles. Not long ago, we decided to supply Poland with 30,000 tons of meat, and 16,000 tons have already been supplied. I do not know whether we can supply 30,000 tons in total, but in any case, it is apparent that in keeping with this decision we must add a certain number of tons of meat in the form of assistance.

As far as the PUWP and the creation of a new party in its place, I consider that the PUWP should not be dissolved. Others here have said correctly that this would be an entirely negative act.

Grishin: The situation in Poland is deteriorating further. Our party line in relation to the Polish events is completely correct. As concerns Jaruzelski's proposal for the dissolution of the PUWP and the creation of a new party, one cannot agree with that. There can also been no discussion of introducing troops. It will be necessary to review the economic questions and to give what is possible to the Poles.

Suslov: It is necessary to expose in the press the intrigues of Solidarity and other counter-revolutionary forces.

Chernenko: I am in complete agreement with what the comrades have been saying here. Really, the line of our party and of the CC Politburo in connection with the Polish events, which has been formulated in the speeches of Leonid Ilyich Brezhnev and in the decisions of the Politburo, is completely correct and should not be changed.

I consider that today it would be possible to adopt the following decisions:

1. Take into consideration Cde. Baibakov's information.
2. In our future relations with the PPR, proceed from the general political line of the CPSU CC on this issue, as well as from the instructions of the CPSU CC Politburo of December 8, 1981, and from the exchange of views at the CC Politburo session of December 10, 1981.
3. Instruct Cdes. Tikhonov, Kirilenko, Dolgikh, Arkhipov, and Baibakov to continue to study questions of economic assistance to Poland, taking account of the exchange of views at the CC Politburo session.

Brezhnev: What is the opinion of the comrades?

All: Cde. Chernenko has formulated all the proposals extremely correctly; they must be adopted.

The resolution is adopted.

[Source: RGANI, Fond 89, Opis 42, Delo 6. Translated by Malcolm Byrne for the National Security Archive.]

Document No. 82: Notebook Entries of Lt. Gen. Viktor Anoshkin

December 11, 1981

The following notebook excerpt is one of the more important pieces of evidence to emerge in recent years concerning Jaruzelski's desire for Soviet military assistance in connection with martial law.[16] Lt. Gen. Viktor Anoshkin was adjutant to Marshal Kulikov during the crisis and accompanied him as a note-taker on his frequent visits to Poland, including on December 11, two days before martial law. The crucial page reproduced below recounts, according to Anoshkin, a conversation between Kulikov and Jaruzelski that day. (The notes reflect Kulikov's recitation of the conversation to his adjutant.) Here, the Polish leader is depicted as trying, apparently somewhat excitedly, to establish whether Soviet military aid will be forthcoming. By Anoshkin's account, after Jaruzelski learns, via Soviet Ambassador Boris Aristov, that the Kremlin's reply is no, he blurts out: "This is terrible news for us!! For a year-and-a-half people have been rambling on about the introduction of troops—and now that's all vanished. Where does this put Jaruzelski?!" The most apparent implication from this entry is that Jaruzelski, despite his intensive efforts in recent years to claim that he wanted above all to prevent a Soviet intervention, was in fact counting on Moscow to send help—albeit most likely in the belief that an internal crackdown would fail.

16:35 I just came from Cde. Aristov who in a very confidential way informed me of the following:
1. Per instructions — called — Jaruzelski
   Milewski and raised the following issues:
   (1) We are asking someone from the party leadership to come here. Who will that be and when?
   (2) Make a statement in our support. Aristov is convinced that a request was sent to the Center.
   (3) Can we count on assistance along military lines from the USSR (concerning add'l introduction of troops)?
   (4) What meas[ures] for rend'ing econ. assistance to Poland [are planned] on the part of the USSR?
   Aristov ← Rusakov: ↓ Rusakov's answers:[17]

---

[16] Anoshkin accompanied Kulikov to the international conference, "Poland 1980–1982: Internal Crisis, International Dimensions," held at Jachranka, Poland, on June 26–28, 1997. He agreed in advance of the conference to bring his notebook to share with researchers, although only a few pages were ultimately photocopied. For additional selected pages and interpretation, see Mark Kramer, "The Anoshkin Notebook on the Polish Crisis, December 1981," *Cold War International History Project Bulletin*, No. 11 (Winter 1998), pp. 17–28.

1. – No one will come;
2. – Measures will be taken;
3. – We will not introduce troops;
4. – Baibakov is preparing an answer;

[The following lines are written vertically up left-hand margin of page:]
This is terrible news for us!!

For a year-and-a-half people have been rambling on about the introduction of troops — and now that's all vanished [*otpalo*]. Where does this put Jaruzelski?!

[Source: Notebook of Lt. Gen. Anoshkin, originally photocopied at the 1997 Ja-chranka conference (see footnote above). Previously published in Cold War International History Project Bulletin, *No. 11 (Winter 1998), p. 19. On file at the National Security Archive, "Soviet Flashpoints" collection. Translated by Svetlana Savranskaya for the National Security Archive.]*

---

[17] The leftward and downward arrows are approximately as in the original, signifying that Aristov's information, i.e. the four points which follow, came from Rusakov.

PART SIX

Crackdown

Document No. 83: Telegram to Directors of Voivode Police

circa *December 12, 1981*

With this document, provincial, or voivode, police authorities learned that preparations for martial law were underway. Among their instructions was to initiate operation "Ring III" which was purportedly aimed at rounding up criminals but in fact targeted Solidarity leaders for internment.

Comrade Commander!

1. The appropriate decisions have been made. Announcement will be made on December 13, 1981, at 6:00 o'clock [a.m.] on the first station on the radio.
2. I am ordering the commencement of preparations and execution of operation "Azalea" on December 12, 1981, at 23:30, and at 00:30, that is one hour later, operation "Fir" followed by "Maple."
3. Where conditions allow, take over regional headquarters, seize documents and disable printing equipment through operation "Fir"—without destroying things.
4. Execute operations related to radio-television buildings according to the plan, at 24:00 on December 12, 1981.
5. I am providing a reminder about maintaining absolute secrecy. Move the execution of operation "Ring III" to 19:00, using it as camouflage and preparation for the execution of the actions indicated.
6. At 4:00 in the morning on December 13, 1981, notify the first secretary of the [provincial] CC, the voivode, the chief of the Voivodeship Military Staff, the plenipotentiary-commissar of the KOK to listen to the premier's speech at 6:00 on the first radio station.

[Source: Jan Draus and Zbigniew Nawrocki, red., Przeciw "Solidarności". 1980–1989, Opozycja w Tajnych Archiwach MSW (Rzeszów: Zarząd Regionu NSZZ "Solidarność", 2000), pp. 133–134.]

Document No. 84: Communication from Czesław Kiszczak to Florian Siwicki

December 12, 1981

This concise document is a formal request from Minister of Internal Affairs Kiszczak to Defense Minister Siwicki to have the military be prepared to cut off radio and telephone communications as a first step in implementing martial law.

Chief of General Staff of the PA
Comrade Gen. Florian Siwicki

I kindly request that the order be issued for the armed forces to be prepared to execute operation "Azalea" on December 12 at 23:30.

In this connection, the concerned commanders of military units are requested to contact appropriate voivodeship commandants of the Citizens' Police.

Gen. of Div. Czesław Kiszczak

[…]

[Source: Jan Draus and Zbigniew Nawrocki, op. cit., p. 133. Translated by Malcolm Byrne for the National Security Archive.]

Document No. 85: Protocol No. 19 of PUWP CC Politburo Meeting

December 13, 1981

The meeting described here was the Politburo's first after the introduction of martial law. It begins with status reports by the heads of all key departments, after which a debate ensues over the next steps to take. One of the central problems at the time was what to do with the PUWP and how to strengthen it. Jaruzelski informs the group about his conversation with Brezhnev who congratulated him for finally acting. The Polish leader then gives instructions for what to do in the next phase, including what rationales to give to Western ambassadors for actions taken by the authorities. He highlights the importance of various propaganda steps to influence public opinion: for example preparing a White Book indicating responsibility for wrongdoing and biographies of key figures to show who was behind Solidarity, and restocking shops to show the authorities' concern for the population. A necessity at this stage, Jaruzelski underscores, is the need to sustain the "psychosis" [psichoza] of martial law.

Agenda

1. The socio-political situation in the country.
RE: Point one of the proceedings

W. Jaruzelski: I suggest that we discuss the tasks which are before us.

Cz. Kiszczak: A meeting of the Presidium took place on December 10 of this year, and meetings of the NCC on December 11 and 12. Solidarity maintained and even sharpened the position taken in Radom. Solidarity is aiming at overthrowing the Constitution, the authorities. It has made preparations for a coup. On December 12 at 20:30, initial preparations were undertaken to introduce a state of war. Currently, their services are completely mobilized. Radio and television were secured overnight, communications blocked. No incidents were recorded. Three-hundred-and-twenty sites were guarded. Border crossings were blocked. Since midnight, the operation of interning individuals threatening the security of the state has been underway. The operation is 70 percent complete so far. Among the interned are: Rulewski, Wądołowski, Pałka, the Kurońs, Kułaj, the Gwiazdas. Wałęsa has been asked to talks in Warsaw. The operation is on-going; there were more troubles in Gdańsk; the operation in Olsztyn has been completed. In Biała Podlaska, 17 out of 20 persons have been interned, in Bielsko-Biała, 98 out of 120, in Chełm 40 out of 52, in Ciechanów 11 out of 13, in Katowice 463 out of 500, in Kielce 176 out of 196, in Konin 27 out of 28, in Radom 82 out of 93, in Zamość 93 out of 114, in Skierniewice 32 out of 33, in Warszawa 196 out of 293. Solidarity buildings have been searched. Documents have been withheld for use during trials. In Katowice, fire extinguishers were used by people to defend themselves. Doors have been blocked in Lublin. The interned defended themselves also in Konin and Bełchatów.

There have been incidents in Jastrzębie. Plutonium has been used in Kraków; a woman has been wounded in Warsaw. Building occupations were broken up in Świdnica, Toruń, and Olkusz; all involved have been arrested. In Warsaw, in front of the offices of the "Mazowsze" region, Chinese, French and Japanese observers, as well as groups of workers from the Warszawa Steelworks have been noticed. At 7:25, leaflets with hostile contents were being distributed. The MSW is going ahead with preventive, warning talks. Talks have been planned with 4,500 people. Talks with Church officials have been held. Bishop Bednorz has supported the decision on martial law and initiated prayers for social calm. Bishop Bareła has issued an appeal for calm. On December 18, on the other hand, they are organizing a march from the Cathedral to Jasna Góra. Bishop Dąbrowski and Father Orszulik want to call a session of the Episcopate of Poland. They are requesting that communications be reopened for its announcement.

Decision: make it possible for the Episcopate to inform the bishops about the date of the Conference of the Episcopate using military communications.

They have asked Stomma about the legality of the current authorities. Stomma said that the authorities are legal until the first session of the Sejm of the Polish People's Republic. In the Lenin Steelworks in Kraków, 7,000 people are on strike on the night shift; city transportation is immobilized. There are attempts to undertake a strike action at the Polish State Railways [PKP], in "Celwiskoza" in Jelenia Góra. There is a need for local, military and police authorities to function effectively.

Decision: after the first day of martial law, local authorities (administrative, military, and police) should receive guidelines for undertaking more decisive and operational actions.

With the passage of time, the situation could become more difficult. A public statement by Wałęsa and by others is needed.

F. Siwicki: stated that the moral-political condition and the ability of sub-units to fulfill objectives were at a good level. Cooperating closely, 90 centers of communication, radio and television throughout the country have been blocked. Two hundred and fifty sites have been taken over, including four airports, telecommunications sites, and state reserves. Units are patrolling the main highways, blocking the main communications intersections, protecting military and civil sites. Tactical forces moved into the areas of large agglomerations at 6:00 a.m. Parts of these units will go into designated zones. A radio network is being developed, as well as emergency facilities (for 27 voivodeships); 50 percent of the armed forces are engaged in the operation; the air force and navy are on a heightened state of military alert. This is what the analysis of the implementation of objectives in the first phase looks like. I perceive the need to broaden political work; backing up officers with reserve officers is needed. Better living conditions and better uniforms should be provided.

Decision: to intensify political-educational and party work within military units executing tasks as part of martial law. Reserve officers should be taken advantage of for this purpose, as well as officers from military schools and central institutions

462

of the MND. Soldiers of these units should be provided with additional winter uniforms; winter shoes should be provided for some sub-units in particular.

We are maintaining close communications with allied headquarters and the Northern Group of Soviet Forces. The bishops' meetings with plenipotentiaries are proceeding successfully; some of them are awaiting instructions. Cardinal Macharski is interested in the content of the martial law files.

The work of the commissar-plenipotentiaries in the districts and the economic organs is proceeding normally. Additional tasks will be passed on to responsible persons.

Decision: ensure more decisive action by the commissar-plenipotentiaries in the regions.

K. Barcikowski: We held talks with Primate Glemp, informed him about the motives for introducing martial law. Our attitude to the Church is not being changed. Glemp received that information in a calm manner. Glemp holds the view that there are a lot of bad people in Solidarity. The Church will follow the development of the situation and will pray for social calm.

Talks with Bishop Dąbrowski and Father Orszulik proceeded peacefully. They questioned the originality of the documents about martial law and made remarks about the legal acts. They were also interested in the way the press will function, including the Catholic press. We asked for a list of Church publications.

Decision: to prepare a concept for reviving publication of the Catholic press after the end of martial law.

They also expressed interest in interned persons, among others Kułaj, Wielowiejski, and Solidarity advisers. They expressed anxiety about the fact that talks with Wałęsa are being conducted without advisers. We have dispelled their fears. Bishop Dąbrowski has offered to cooperate with us.

S. Ciosek: informed about the content of talks with Lech Wałęsa. He quoted Wałęsa's words that if the authorities provide the society with food, they will control the situation. Lech Wałęsa gave his full backing to these solutions, stating that Solidarity went too far. It had been possible to stop. He spoke in critical terms about the activists, about society. In Radom he had no other choice but to make a sharp statement. He was happy to hear that Gierek had been arrested. The speech by Gen. W. Jaruzelski made a strong impression on him; he said he would back it. He stated that if we do not follow the path of renewal, there will be bloodshed in five years, that he is a soldier and he is executing orders. He takes the view that a new man should head Solidarity. He will propose and ensure the election of a new candidate for chairman. He would like to talk to the primate. He takes the view that we should release internees after they have made a loyalty declaration. He is considering the possibility of convening the NCC Presidium.

Conclusions:

1. Cde. Rakowski is proposing to Wałęsa to make his views public. Rakowski's conversation with Wałęsa is currently ongoing.
2. Consider the possibility of a conversation between Wałęsa and Glemp.

3. Wałęsa thinks he will be interned for a longer time. He is under good conditions.

S. Olszowski: the propaganda operation has been worked on for several days. The operational center consisted of: Olszowski, Szaciło, Rakowski, and the heads of the CC departments. The operation was carried out in secret—this is a sign of maturity. At 6:00 a.m., the radio program was broadcast, and at 12:00 noon the television program, which had been a difficult undertaking. Both programs were broadcast from an additional location. Staff recruiting is ongoing; there are problems with passes. There is no Solidarity [representative] at the radio branch on Malczewski Street. Cde. Olszowski spoke with great esteem for the operations of the army, assessing them as masterly. Voivodeship propaganda groups received their assignments. CC employees have been sent to where journals are being published.

At the central level, *Trybuna Ludu* and *Żołnierz Wolności* are being published together with supplements. Only one paper is being published in the voivodeships. Substantive guidelines have been drafted and distributed. There is going to be a shortened radio and television schedule for a few days. If the situation continues to return to normal, we will extend radio and television programs and increase the number of publications. There is a request by the MSW to make available the materials collected at Solidarity's regional headquarters.

Decision: use the materials confiscated from NSZZ Solidarity headquarters for propaganda purposes.

W. Jaruzelski: welcomed Cde. Jabłoński and asked for information about the work on issuing a decree on martial law.

H. Jabłoński: stated that he had held several talks with each member of the Council of State. Difficulties lay in the fact that no draft of the decree on martial law was ready, as is the case in every country, and such a draft had to be prepared. All members of the Council of State spoke favorably about this matter. [Ryszard] Reiff did not agree to the proposition of accepting the decree on martial law. [Stanisław] Marszałek-Młyńczyk was against. The decree was adopted although there was no formal vote.

J. Czyrek: a meeting with ambassadors from the socialist countries has been held. There exists a problem in making comments about these events in the mass media in the West. Reagan has interrupted his holiday. Haig is conducting consultations within NATO. They have taken the position of not reacting to events in Poland because Soviet troops have not stepped in yet. Chancellor Schmidt has not interrupted his talks with Honecker in the GDR. He has called for restraint, stressing that the Polish people are able to solve the crisis by themselves. The French are in touch with the allies and do not perceive any threat. Chancellor Kreisky has stated that the Polish leadership attempted to fend off the biggest threat because there had been no unity among the opposition forces. In the USA, our ambassador was summoned at 1:00 in order to explain the character of the events in Poland. The view has been that it would have an impact on Polish–American relations, especially in the area of trade (also the conclusion of the talks of Z. Madej). Multilateral talks on the issue of credits will be halted. The representative of Great Britain did not have instructions from his government, but expressed the opinion that difficulties could emerge in economic relations. The ambassador of the Federal Republic of Germany stated that he took seriously the position contained in Gen. Jaruzelski's speech. If no blood is spilled, there will not be a sharp reaction from the side of the FRG government. The government of the FRG is in contact with Haig, the U.S. secretary of state. The Italian representative assured that he will present our matters to his government in a well-disposed fashion, the Italian reaction will be full of understanding. Our explanations will improve Poland's position in the West. The Austrian representative responded with understanding to our decisions, stating that, in his opinion, there had been no possibility of agreement with the opposition forces. He said that he was not able to pass this information on to Vienna, that he had no telephones or telexes, which goes against international conventions.

Decision: do not accelerate the reopening of communications at foreign missions in Poland.

Other talks with ambassadors have not brought anything new. We have sent a cable to the governments of the capitalist and socialist countries. We have also sent a cable to the United Nations requesting that the Polish question not be considered in that forum. We have sent instructions to our CSCE delegation in Madrid (on the issue of violating human rights). We have sent a delegation with appropriate instructions to Geneva to the International Labor Organization (on the question of suspending the rights of trade unions). The governments of the socialist countries received our decisions with respect, but also with concern. The address by Cde. W. Jaruzelski made an enormous impression in their countries. They have asked to be constantly informed about the situation. They have asked whether they should evacuate families. The embassy of the GDR has already evacuated the first group of people. Generally, it ought to be said that reactions are moderate, except for the American one. The USA will probably not sell us corn for chicken-farming. Generally, the question of economic aid has been put on the agenda in talks with the socialist countries. Concrete talks will be held.

W. Jaruzelski: Is the Mazowsze region occupying its offices?

Cz. Kiszczak: Yes.

W. Jaruzelski: This is a mistake; they have to leave those offices and we need to hold them.

K. Barcikowski: A session of the Sejm has been planned for December 15–16 of this year, and it now has to be called off. The Presidium of the Sejm is awaiting the decision. This would be a temporary cancellation. I suggest that the premier send a letter to the Sejm. (The Secretariat expressed its consent.) The adoption of the teachers' bill by a decree of the Council of State should be considered.

H. Jabłoński: stated that the teachers' bill could not be adopted through a decree because the session of the Sejm of the Polish People's Republic has not been closed.

H. Kubiak: proposed issuing a statement of the premier, the chairman of the Military Council of National Salvation on the question of adopting the teachers' bill. He stated that the minister of education proposed suspending classes in all schools, including higher schools for the period of December 13, 1981, to January 3, 1982, except for kindergartens and extramural centers.

Decision: call off the session of the Sejm of the Polish People's Republic. Advise of the decision of the Military Council of National Salvation about respecting the principles of the new teachers' bill which will be adopted at the next session of the Sejm. Set extended holidays in schools and universities from December 13, 1981, to January 3, 1982, except for kindergartens and extramural centers.

J. Łabęcki: Consultation within the party is important. Demanding criteria for membership in the party should be established, for example through verification of party members and exchange of party membership cards. Conflicts in the party should be eliminated. Proposed liquidation of the *Rzeczywistość* weekly because of controversial views. The Plenum of the Factory Committee passed a vote of non-confidence in me for ineffective activity in the Politburo. I request the Politburo take a position on this issue. He stated subsequently that an exchange of incompetent personnel should be carried out, shortening the work week in situations where there is a lack of resources, and reviewing the state of Polish teachers—thus erecting a barrier to oppositionists who should not be working in education.

Decision: draft more demanding criteria for membership in the party and consider the possibility of replacing party membership cards. Party members must define themselves, especially if they fill leadership posts. Undertake actions to strengthen the unity of the party and eliminate tensions. Consider the proposal to end the publication of *Rzeczywistość*. Undertake actions on the question of teacher reviews. Take decisive actions on personnel matters. Replace incompetent staff.

M. Milewski: stated that a decision and an intervention were needed for opposition to the decrees. This should be discussed during the teleconference with the first secretaries of voivodeship committees. Act with words and coercive means.

Decision: react decisively towards violations of martial law decrees and orders. Their content should be publicized in the mass media.

A unit should be created in the Secretariat of the CC to avoid duplicating decisions. Internees should not be released without a loyalty declaration. Former prominent persons should be reached with this position. There ought to be no hurry in reopening communications. It facilitates the actions of squabblers. The Austrians have closed the border after two days. A situation has to arise in which people will feel the burden of martial law.

Z. Grzyb: stated that consideration should be given to how to ensure that peasants will bring foodstuffs to purchasing points, and that peasants will supply goods.

Cz. Kiszczak: We do not have any intention of reopening communications.

K. Barcikowski: proposed adopting "Instructions for leading the party under conditions of proclaiming a state of endangered state security" (Sup. no. 1) as a document of the PUWP CC Politburo.

S. Kociołek: advised that city services are working normally in Warsaw. Provisions of bread and milk are being ensured. There are problems with kitchen salt. There are threats of a strike—mainly at Ursus. There might be problems in the Warsaw Steelworks. I suggest considering the possibility of elasticity in the form of troop presence and movements. Two-person positions would be advisable. Work with self-governments should be developed. VDC consultations should be organized and their presence at work ought to be demanded. *Aktiv* groups are in contact with the factories. December 17 of this year could be a big problem.[1] An inquiry ought to be made as to whether anything is in the offing.

T. Czechowicz: stated that where justified, when there is no work for them, women should be sent home on paid leave.

Decision: where justified (lack of work in the factory) women with children should be sent home on paid leave.

Should the boards of the Commission of Party Control expel [members] from the party?

H. Kubiak: A readiness to take strike action has been recorded in 28 voivodeships. Proposes leaving children at home, also the youth; collective leave and gatherings will be avoided. The number of extramural centers will be increased.

S. Opałko: stated that the introduction of martial law had been expected and received with relief. The authorities are gaining respect and society gaining hope for an improvement of the situation. Instructions on the functioning of the party offer the possibility of introducing order in the party. Stated subsequently that teachers who speak in hostile ways against the system should be eliminated from the field of public education (the Czechs and the Germans did that). Those teachers who went on strike cannot educate the youth. A determined opponent of the socialist system cannot be a teacher. The staff is faced with real difficulties. Administrative personnel should be replaced in the name of the highest objectives.

Decision: aim at removing vehement opponents of the socialist system from the field of education.

W. Mokrzyszczak: introduce changes along the lines of the decrees and defend them. The board of the Mazowsze Solidarity region put itself beyond abolition. Check the way the decrees are put into effect in the voivodeships. It ought to be contemplated whether previously adopted work plans, for example at sessions of the CC Commission and meetings, should be put into effect.

Decision: cancel sessions of the PUWP CC Commission, call off some previously planned meetings.

T. Czechowicz: stated that the army should be shown in action.

---

[1] The anniversary of the 1970 shooting of protestors by Polish security forces.

S. Kociołek: said that party work should be carried on but without excessive information in the mass media. What should be done with the 40,000 full-time workers of Solidarity?

W. Jaruzelski: stated that employees of the trade unions are returning to professions they held before coming to work for the unions.

K. Barcikowski: What is going to happen with people from the sector unions when we deprive them of their full-time positions? I suggest not doing that. There remains the problem of paying them.

S. Olszowski: Explore the possibility and then we will discuss this matter.

Decision: consider at a session of the Politburo or the CC Secretariat the further functioning of the trade unions' personnel apparatus, especially NSZZ Solidarity. Consider the possibility of returning full-time trade union employees to the positions they occupied before joining the trade union apparatus.

H. Jabłoński: The general assembly of the PAN is scheduled for December 18 of this year. At the PAN, there might be attempts to pass a resolution condemning the introduction of martial law. Suggests putting off the session of the PAN.

Decision: put off the session of the Assembly of the Polish Academy of Sciences. Convince Professor [Aleksander] Gieysztor of the need to make such a decision.

Z. Messner: said that violations of principles will result in further complications.

H. Kubiak: An interpretation should be suggested and the significance of illegal meetings explained.

Decision: give an interpretation and explain the significance of illegal gatherings.

J. Główczyk: proposes passing on additional information to members of the CC.

J. Romanik: said that not only should information be given to members of the CC, but they should also be approached directly.

W. Jaruzelski: I received a telephone call from Cde. Brezhnev who expressed his warm feelings towards us and stated that we have effectively engaged the fight against the counter-revolution. They were difficult decisions, but appropriate ones. My speech met with high acclaim. I was assured that we could count on economic aid. In the conversation I emphatically stressed the question of economic aid. The timing we selected was the last possible and the optimal one. A bad situation had prevailed beforehand and it would have turned even worse later on. We did not have a better moment: the process of rapidly advancing negative occurrences, attempts to remove the party from the factories, the announcement of demonstrations on December 17, 1981. Also, in Warsaw the creation of facts and preparation of questionnaires containing negative appraisals of the party and the authorities. The decision about martial law was unanimously taken by the Council of State. There is no talk about overthrowing the government. Legally functioning authorities have introduced the means to ensure the state's security. These are arguments for the West. The operation of all forces and instruments has been very effective: the Ministry of National Defense, Ministry of Internal Affairs, Propaganda. Everybody has had an impact. We are at an advantageous moment, which we cannot let pass. The element of surprise and shock will pass. Everyday troubles will now be addressed to the authorities because there is no Solidarity. The rightfulness of these decisions should be made credible. [We] ought to show, on the basis of the materials acquired, what we managed to avoid. A threatening danger has been overcome at the last moment. The shock caused by our decisions needs to be maintained. Announcements made in my speech need to be authenticated, especially as far as internment is concerned. This should be presented at the teleconference. Declarations about punishing the guilty are to be published. Military persons should be appointed as voivodes, directors. A portion of the reserve officers should be subjected to some sort of militarization (this is to be announced at the teleconference). The question of the operative characteristics of the PUWP VC [Voivodeship Committee]. The method of functioning is old; we are waiting, there is no decision. All directors, secretaries of the VC will have to prove themselves. We have to work 24 hours a day, we cannot waste time. Activities must be decisive, efforts that have been undertaken have to be executed. We cannot argue, we have to act. There are too many leadership centers, they should be put in order. Activities have to be operational, coordinated. Active party work has to be conducted, but we should not flaunt ourselves. The military format is obligatory. The manner in which the CC plenipotentiaries are functioning ought to be determined, especially in difficult conditions and in difficult voivodeships. We should not carry out verifications, but operationally solve concrete issues. Party members who are members of Solidarity need to make up their minds. The membership of Solidarity in the administration needs to be more rigorously put on the agenda. The question of a threat remains. Organized party groups should be sustained. An atmosphere of action has to be created in the party and among the activists. People have to feel that they have joined a struggle. Meetings are taking place in an extraordinary situation. Party bureaucraticism is unacceptable. Retirements should be held off, the best people should be kept in the factories. A martial law psychosis, fear and seriousness are to be kept up, together with authentication of the matters that have been announced. Factory radio networks should be utilized more effectively. There should be a distancing from Solidarity.

As far as the problem of the arrested and interned is concerned, it is a pity that we have not done an analysis of the lists from 1976. The point is not to make the same mistakes as when opposition, criminal elements were integrated into the army. Problems resulted from that and the opposition was consolidated. For example, Rulewski should not be kept together with Bartoszewski at the moment. Ways of treating them should be considered, ways of working with them. Advisers should be separated from cutthroats, talks should be conducted with advisers. We will see how things settle with Wałęsa. Siła-Nowicki behaved properly. These issues should be approached selectively. Proposals should be put forward on how to solve these matters. The Central Committee departments ought to be involved in their resolution. The matter should be consulted with the first secretaries of voivodeship committees. The question of the tone of propaganda—it has to make announcements more credible. Show that the commissioner-plenipotentiaries recommended calling off directors, criminals. Fraud has to be attacked as well as millionaires and speculators, bureaucrats, and representatives of the authorities who humiliate us. The White Book is to be used. Biographies of opposition activists should be publicized: those of Kuroń, Rulewski. It is to be shown who stands behind them. Persons of high moral standing should be won over. Party work ought to be conducted in ordinary fashion and large conferences are to be postponed. There should be talks with the PAN chairman, Gieysztor. We should make an effort to get him to understand us better. The question of market provisions. Market provisions need to be improved. Proposals should be prepared on what we want to receive from the allies. Cde. Czyrek should discuss the question of food aid in talks with allies. We should take everything they offer. A clue for how to reach the peasants should be sought. We are not going for compulsory supplies but each peasant needs to sell goods to the state (this ought to be stated at the teleconference).

W. Mokrzyszczak: said that the course of action has to be made more stringent.

W. Jaruzelski: said that we are not changing the course of our policy towards the capitalist countries. The issue of buying corn in the USA is very important, the production of poultry next year will depend on that. Cde. J. Łabęcki referred to his personal matter. Some people will turn red because they made an irresponsible decision on your issue. Tactics should be employed in current activities so as not to endanger our interests. We will not release a communiqué from a session of the Politburo. Giving out information that the Politburo considered certain questions is an old-fashioned activity. There should not be actions like that, except showing what the commissioner-plenipotentiaries have arranged. The decision about accelerated retirement is a bad one. Cde. Janiszewski will transfer this matter to Cde. [Janusz] Obodowski and it should be put on the agenda of the Council of Ministers today. Useful people should be taken advantage of in the current situation.

T. Czechowicz: said that society should be engaged more extensively in the fight against speculation.

W. Jaruzelski: stated that the commissioner-plenipotentiary controls the voivode in the period of martial law. The commissioner must exercise strong power.

T. Czechowicz: Should there be information in the press as to who the commissioner is?

W. Jaruzelski: We will publish the list of members of the Military Council of National Salvation. It is comprised of generals and colonels.

H. Jabłoński: stated that there should be information about what has been done centrally, who has been replaced, how many people have been removed.

Decisions: publish the names of commissioner-plenipotentiaries. Membership in Solidarity within the administration must be treated more rigorously. Party members who belong to Solidarity must define their position decisively. People penalized for incompetence should be exposed in the mass media. Wherever possible, military persons should assume posts (as voivodes, directors); reserve officers ought to be taken advantage of (dress them in uniforms). Personnel should be covered under certain kinds of militarization. A martial law psychosis should be sustained. The abolition factor is to be skillfully used in propaganda. We should carefully prepare for counteracting attempts to organize a demonstration on December 17, 1981. Decision centers in the Central Committee and in the government ought to be clarified for the purpose of joint cooperation and eliminating duplication of effort; some centers need to be combined. There need to be assurances that party branches and organizations function according to instructions about the working of the party under martial law. Higher effectiveness of the Central Committee Secretariat, Central Committee departments, voivodeship committees and branches of the first degree must be obtained. Arrangements are to be made for 24-hour operation of party committees and departments of the Central Committee. The style of party work needs to be changed, party tactics perfected and used for action, not for flaunting oneself in publications. Ensure that information reaches the recipients quickly, especially in the case of central party authorities and delegates to the Ninth Party Congress. Society needs to be approached with appeals to inform regional authorities about negative occurrences and signs of abuse of speculation, the bureaucracy, etc. Dwell on ways to amend rules concerning earlier retirement age. Party action groups ought to be maintained and their tasks determined under new conditions.

The propaganda front is to be perfected. In particular, the intentions of the Military Council of National Salvation should be made more credible through the depiction of concrete acts in the mass media—making changes in administration; the functioning of commissioner-plenipotentiaries; fighting against crime, corruption, speculation, excessive enrichment, and the bureaucracy; informing about disciplinary lay-offs from administrative organs. The army should be shown in action. Factory radio networks ought to be utilized better. In party and propaganda work as well as in the activity of the government and commissioner-plenipotentiaries, announcements made in speeches by the chairman of the WRON ought to be made credible. An assessment of the functioning of the Central Committee plenipotentiaries to the voivodeships needs to be prepared. Appropriate and selective activities are to be undertaken towards internees, so that it does not cause us political damage. On the question of determining the character of future actions towards interned persons, appropriate departments of the Central Committee ought to be engaged. Biographies of the representatives of opposition forces need to be published (Rulewski, Kuroń and others), and materials contained in the White Book used more effectively. Activities are to be undertaken to win support for party activities from people with significant political and moral reputations, who are respected in society. Actions should be taken to ensure better provisions for the market. Domestic possibilities and foreign aid, especially from allied countries, are to be utilized. The question of offering us food aid is to be taken up in talks with representatives of the socialist countries. Negotiations should be conducted with the representatives of the USA on the question of corn supplies destined for the chicken-farming sec-

tor. Supplies of agricultural goods to meet the needs of the population are to be ensured. An address to peasants should be prepared containing an appeal to increase
production and supplies, but also a warning about the consequences of diminished
supplies from the peasants. A system of regular supplies of agricultural goods to the
state purchasing centers is to be established in consultation with farmers, as well as
a system of transferring goods to meet the needs of the villages and means of production aimed at the development of agriculture. The forthcoming tasks of the party in the period of martial law as well as recommendations of the Politburo should
be discussed at the teleconference on December 13, 1981.

[...]

Warsaw, December 13, 1981

[Source: AAN, Przegląd, *No. 50, December 10, 2001, pp. 48–50. Translated by
Paweł Świeboda.]*

Document No. 86: Extract from Protocol No. 40 of CPSU CC Politburo Meeting

December 13, 1981

This document instructs Soviet ambassadors in several allied countries, from Berlin to Ulaanbaatar, to inform their host governments of Moscow's positive reaction to the declaration of martial law. Romania is not included on the list, presumably because of its regular disagreements with the other members of the Warsaw Pact. The message notes approvingly that Jaruzelski kept the operation a closely-held secret. Apparently, the Soviets themselves did not know he was finally prepared to act until as late as the day before. Along with the positive—from the Kremlin's viewpoint, at least—developments of December 13, however, the Soviets felt obliged to mention the reality that Moscow expected to provide economic aid to the Warsaw regime, which the rest of the alliance knew meant an added burden for all.

[…]

Pay a visit to Cde. Zhivkov (J. Kádár, E. Honecker, Yu. Tsedenbal, G. Husák, F. Castro, Le Duan, K. Phomvihane) and, after referring to the instruction of the CPSU CC, convey the following:

"As is well-known to our friends, the Polish leadership introduced martial law in the country, announced the creation of the Military Council for National Salvation and isolated the most extreme elements of 'Solidarity,' the 'Confederation for an Independent Poland,' and other anti-socialist groups.

W. Jaruzelski's address to the people left a positive impression; in it, in our view, the emphasis was properly placed on fundamental issues. In particular, what is especially important is that the leading role of the PUWP and the fidelity of the PPR to its alliance obligations according to the Warsaw Pact were confirmed.

As a condition of the successful execution of the action, the Polish comrades maintained strict secrecy. It was known only to a narrow circle around W. Jaruzelski. Thanks to this, our friends succeeded in catching the adversary by surprise, and the operation is so far proceeding satisfactorily.

On the very eve of the implementation of the designated plan, W. Jaruzelski informed Moscow about it. We conveyed to him that the Soviet leadership views such a decision by the Polish comrades with understanding. In addition, we proceed from the assumption that our Polish friends will decide these matters by themselves.

According to our preliminary assessment, the actions of our Polish friends are an active step to rebuff the counter-revolution and correspond in this sense to the general line of the fraternal countries.

Under these conditions the question arises concerning the provision of political and moral support for the Polish comrades, as well as supplementary economic assistance. The Soviet leadership, as before, will act on the Polish question in contact with the fraternal countries."

Telegraph upon fulfillment.

[Source: RGANI, Fond 89, Opis 66, Delo 4. Translated by Malcolm Byrne for the National Security Archive.]

Document No. 87: Speech by Pope John Paul II Concerning Martial Law

December 13, 1981

The Vatican's reaction to martial law was immediate but tempered. Anxious not to inflame the situation, the Pope kept his initial statement brief, stressing the need to avoid bloodshed and to do "everything possible… to peacefully build the future of the Homeland."

December 13, 1981,

The Vatican

The events of the last hours call for me once again to address everyone on the matter of our shared Homeland with a request for a prayer. I recall what I said in September: Polish blood cannot be shed, because too much of it has been shed, especially during the last war. Everything possible must be done to peacefully build the future of the Homeland. In the face of the coming 600th anniversary of Jasna Góra[2], I commend [to] Poland and all its Compatriots the course which is the Nation's to defend.

[Source: L`Osservatore Romano, No. 12, 1981, p. 1. Translated by L. W. Głuchowski for the National Security Archive.]

---

[2] Site of the monastery and shrine of the Black Madonna. See also Document No. 3.

Document No. 88: CIA National Intelligence Daily, "Poland: Test of Government's Measures"

December 14, 1981

This brief update, prepared the day after martial law, is decidedly sketchy about the previous day's events, which limits the authors in their ability to predict what will happen next. The assumption—accurate, as it turned out—is Solidarity and Polish workers will not submit to the crackdown without a battle. Despite communications black-outs, news soon filtered out of fighting in several cities as workers occupied factories and the union, including Wałęsa who was in custody, refused to negotiate with the regime. Unfortunately, excisions in the document veil additional details about what U.S. intelligence knew in the immediate aftermath of the regime's actions.

Poland: Test of Government's Measures

The Polish Government moved quickly and decisively yesterday to create the legal structure for martial law, but the first real test of these procedures will come today as workers return to the factories. [One word excised.]

The detention of about 1000 union activists, including most of Solidarity's national leadership, may cow some factory workers, but union members are not likely to passively accept defeat. [One word excised.]

Solidarity presumably is attempting to institute contingency plans, including provisions for automatic changes in the leadership as senior members are detained. Union leaders in Gdańsk who escaped arrest have indicated that they are forming a national strike committee and that a general strike would be the appropriate response to the government's action. The strongest response to the government's measures may come from local chapters along the Baltic coast. [One word excised.]

The government, according to its press spokesman, is conducting talks with union leader Wałęsa in the Warsaw area. The regime, hoping that announcement of such talks will prompt workers to take a wait-and-see attitude, would like Wałęsa to make some kind of statement calling on workers to avoid strikes. Wałęsa would be reluctant to do so, however, because he realizes that such an action could damage his credibility. Archbishop Glemp publicly criticized the government for abandoning the process of dialogue but urged the populace not to resort to violence. [One word excised.]

The regime is aware that sit-in strikes may take place today and seems prepared to use force, a move that carries with it the danger of bloodshed and civil war. [One word excised]

[One paragraph excised.]

476

Soviet and East European Reactions

Soviet forces are not actively involved, but Soviet authorities in Poland, headed by Marshal Kulikov—the Commander-in-Chief of Warsaw Pact forces—were aware of the Polish plans. [Half paragraph excised.]

[One paragraph excised.]

Soviet media continue to report selectively but without comment on Prime Minister Jaruzelski's speech and the measures being undertaken. TASS reports that the situation is generally calm in most areas of Poland. [Half line excised.]

[Source: FOIA release from the CIA, on file at the National Security Archive, "Soviet Flashpoints" collection.]

Document No. 89: Memorandum from Lawrence Eagleburger to
Secretary of State, "General Wojciech Jaruzelski"

December 16, 1981

---

*The declaration of martial law on December 13 prompted new interest in Gen. Jaru-
zelski in the United States. He was almost universally considered highly intellectual,
professional and incorruptible. Among many Poles he enjoyed a generally positive
reputation. This biographic sketch supplied to Secretary of State Haig by the European Bureau of the State Department reflects those attributes. The document, which
unfortunately is illegible in parts, goes on to describe Jaruzelski as being both a Polish patriot and a long-time communist, two seemingly contradictory traits given that
the latter implied a strong loyalty to Moscow. In fact, this duality in Jaruzelski has
made it more difficult in later years to determine whether his order to crack down on
Polish society was, as he has said, an effort to help his countrymen by keeping Soviet
armed forces at bay, or, as his enemies insist, the act of a traitor who put his fealty to
the USSR first. The State Department's depiction of him as a "problem solver" with
"a decided preference for action" is strikingly at odds with the Kremlin's perception
of his extreme indecisiveness.*

Secret

To: The Secretary
From: EUR – Lawrence S. Eagleburger
Subject: General Wojciech Jaruzelski

General Wojciech Jaruzelski has spent his entire adult life in the Polish Army.
His reactions to the multifaceted political problems facing Poland are, therefore,
strongly influenced by his professional background.

Jaruzelski has a reputation among Poles for [2–3 words illegible] patriotism.
Nonetheless, he is a long-time member of the Polish communist party, and a former student at a Soviet military academy. During World War II when he was a
boy, Jaruzelski and his family were reportedly detained in a labor camp in the
USSR where his parents and other family members perished. This experience
undoubtedly left deep scars and has much to do with his outwardly stiff and stoic
demeanor.

Jaruzelski is considered to be a brilliant, intellectually independent officer,
who has a decided preference for action. He is a problem-solver. His personal
integrity and apparent willingness to share the hardships of his men have made
him a somewhat charismatic figure, not only within the army but among Poles in
general. He lives in considerable pain from a chronic back ailment and always
wears a brace which may partially account for his rigid bearing and posture.

478

Jaruzelski has replaced many pro-Soviet officers in the Polish Army with officers who are more loyal to him personally. Until the martial law declaration of December 13, moreover, he repeatedly refused to permit the military to be used against the Polish populace.

The declaration of martial law clearly bears Jaruzelski's stamp. It was a carefully planned and executed military operation, taking Solidarity by surprise and neutralizing its top leadership. Although imposing martial law clearly represented a reversal of Jaruzelski's past opposition to the use of force against the Polish population, it is noteworthy that despite the use of overwhelming force, the military seems thus far to have avoided physical violence. It is therefore arguable that Jaruzelski under extreme [2–3 words illegible] felt his action justified [...]

Unlike some of his harder-line military and party colleagues, Jaruzelski was consistently [2–3 words illegible] policy of compromise and negotiation [...] The sine qua non of such an action would be acceptance by Solidarity and others of the party's primacy.

[Source: FOIA release from the State Department, on file at the National Security Archive, "Soviet Flashpoints" collection.]

Document No. 90: Appeal from Pope John Paul II to Wojciech Jaruzelski

December 18, 1981

A few days after his public statement on martial law (see Document No. 87), the Pope wrote personally to Jaruzelski repeating the substance of his earlier declaration. He appeals for an end to activities of the sort that have led to the bitter events in Poland and begs Jaruzelski to avoid further bloodshed. The Pontiff sends copies of the letter to Wałęsa, Glemp and Cardinal Macharski. In a postscript, he tells Jaruzelski that he will also inform the ambassadors to the Vatican of its contents. This includes the American ambassador, but not the Soviet envoy because Moscow has no representation at the Vatican.

December 18, 1981, Vatican

Appeal by Pope John Paul II to the Chairman of the Military Council of National Salvation, Gen. W. Jaruzelski, on the authorities returning to a peaceful dialogue with society and ceasing to shed blood.

The events of the last days, news about killed and wounded Compatriots in connection with martial law introduced on December 13, require me to turn to you, General, with an urgent request and also a passionate invocation to cease operations, which carry with them the shedding of Polish blood.

During the past two centuries especially the Polish Nation has experienced many wrongs, much Polish blood has also been spilt, endeavoring to extend authority over our Homeland. From this historical perspective Polish blood can no longer be spilt; this blood cannot burden the conscience and stain the hands of Compatriots. I am therefore turning to you, General, with an urgent request and also a passionate invocation in order that the matters connected with social renewal, which from August 1980 has been arranged on the path of peaceful dialogue, may return to that same road. Even if it is difficult, it is not impossible.

This right is being demanded by the entire nation. Also demanding it is the opinion of the entire world, all societies who correctly connect the matter of peace with respect for human rights and the right of nations. Universal desires for peace call for this, in order that martial law not be continued in Poland.

The Church is an advocate of this desire. It is getting closer to the Christmas Holidays, which for so many generations has linked all brothers and daughters of our Nation in the presence of the Christmas Eve host. Everything has to be done so that Compatriots do not have to spend this year's Holiday under the threat of death and repression.

I call on your conscience, General, and on the conscience of all those people on whom at this moment the decision depends.

John Paul II

PS: This same appeal was simultaneously personally delivered to Mr. Lech Wałęsa, Chairman of Solidarity, and also personally to the Polish Primate, Archbishop Józef Glemp, for the entire Polish Episcopate, as well as Cardinal Franciszek Macharski, Metropolitan of Kraków. Representatives of Governments simultaneously notified about the present intervention.

[Source: P. Raina, ed., Jan Paweł II, Prymas i Episkopat Polski o Stanie Wojennym. Kazania, Listy, Przemówienia, Komunikaty, *(Londyn: Oficyna Poetów i Malarzy, 1982), pp. 69–70. Translated by L. W. Głuchowski for the National Security Archive.]*

Document No. 91: Protocol No. 16 of PUWP CC Secretariat Meeting

December 19, 1981

While the Politburo meeting on December 13 (Document No. 85) confined itself to reviewing initial reports and taking clean-up action following the implementation of martial law, this session of the Secretariat, held almost a week later, shows Poland's rulers taking stock of the state of the country and plotting their next steps. The task was enormous, as these notes make clear, ranging from resuscitating the economy to re-engaging society, including dispirited party members. Of course, one of the most intractable problems, for which no answer was ever devised, was how to absorb Solidarity and its membership permanently into the communist framework.

Agenda

1. The current social-political situation in the country.
2. Various matters.

While waiting for the arrival of First Secretary of the PUWP CC, Cde. W. Jaruzelski, the Secretariat of the PUWP CC considered various matters.

M. Woźniak: Since Monday, the consumption of electrical energy has decreased by eight percent, the production of electrical energy is also lower. The output of coal-mines has dropped to 470,000 tons (610,000 tons used to be excavated under normal conditions). On Thursday, the output of the coal-mines was 520,000 tons, on Friday 550,000 tons. The turbulence of the state of emergency could have an impact on the output level. Today, on a free Saturday, 3,000 more miners came to work than the day before. Supplies are improving. The purchase of milk is proceeding more smoothly. Things are worse with deliveries to large agglomerations in Łódź. Reserves of coal power plants are larger (60 days, in some for the whole season; only Kozienice has reserves for 6 days). As far as meat is concerned, we will not have sufficient quantities for the November rationing vouchers; rationed candies and sweets will be fully available, we will give sweets to organize Christmas parties. In January, the meat [situation] will depend on one's own purchase. The decision regarding compulsory supplies will have to be taken at the end of January and beginning of February. There are problems with trans-shipments and downloading in ports, e.g. Małaszewicze from the USSR, 30,000 tons of beef, 25,000 tons of rice, half a million pairs of shoes. There are also deliveries of meat through the wide rails. The GDR has swamped us with assistance on a voivodeship-by-voivodeship basis: gifts [packages] for children, butter, fats, they have declared 12,000 tons of food products for Christmas. Apparently, the people of the GDR are organizing collections of money for Poland.

Cde. J. Czyrek: Collections have been called for by the "Solidarity" Organization. They will give us goods purchased with the collected money.

Cde. M. Woźniak: The SED CC sends aid to our members of the CC. The biggest problem is acquiring wheat and fodder outside the framework of the USA's embargo. We are seeking corn from Hungary and Yugoslavia.

Cde. S. Gabrielski: Stated that union membership fees will not be subtracted from the pay list; that the property of the trade unions has been taken over by the state, which was received with understanding by the unions; that health spas are being taken over by the Health Ministry, and vacation homes are being placed under the control of resorts; that there is a directive to employ people working in the trade unions. Solidarity members should be approached in a diversified manner. Social functions of institutes should be revived to the maximum.

Cde. J. Czyrek: Presented Polish issues in the international arena. The situation has developed in a disadvantageous way for us. The USA has launched an offensive under the name of the Polish experiment in ideology with calls for the release of Wałęsa; the ambassador wants to visit Wałęsa. Economic sanctions were announced; the Americans have suspended all economic relations, including 100 million in loans for corn. The USA is pressuring other governments including the USSR. They proclaim that what we did was in fact done by the Soviet Union. The American assessment that Solidarity proved to be weaker has been the basis for those activities. They want to sustain that organization. There are already repercussions. Costa Rica has been mobilized by the Americans at the U.N. The issue of states with a leftist leaning, like France, is more serious. The French government carries out a party and not a state policy. They have prompted a discussion at the CSCE, they have caused a letter from the ILO to our premier with a demand of freedom for trade unions. The French are placing the issue on the forum of the Socialist International. The French have announced that they are suspending deliveries based on loans unless they do not concern foodstuffs. Canada and others will supply wheat to Poland (Canada 1.5 million tons). The government of Sweden has adopted a stringent position, more inconsiderable movements along the lines of the trade unions, and demonstrations. The position of the governments of Western Europe is positive for us; they are not joining the American economic sanctions. However, we can satisfy our economic needs in spite of the U.S. restrictions. The Church has taken a step towards reason and peace. We have handed over that sharp letter to the ambassadors. The Episcopate has withdrawn and adopted a more moderate position, we have prevented a sharp letter from the Vatican. The harsh position of Reagan took place after the visit of [Agostino] Casaroli who expressed himself in favor of assistance for Poland. The U.S. does not take into account the position of the Vatican.

Cde. M. Woźniak: We have fewer resources for $1.3 billion with the full blockade from the West. Interest payments have not balanced out. If we receive resources from the socialist countries, we will give them goods. If we do not settle, there will be difficulties with production in February. There is a different situation in the area of agricultural products.

Cde. K. Morawski: The issues of the trade unions are not to be overestimated. There is a little bit of hysteria from the side of Szyszka (communications). Sector specialists should be involved in order to strengthen the social services.

Cde. S. Gabrielski: Sector specialists feel harmed that their trade unions are subject to legal restrictions (Szyszka).

Cde. W. Mokrzyszczak: Sector specialists need to be assisted, they defended property against Solidarity.

Cde. J. Czyrek: A letter has been drafted as well as a speech, a presentation by the head of the Military Council for National Salvation to all communist parties in the West. The Communist Party of Italy, Spain and Holland will condemn the state of emergency. The Communist Party of France took an appropriate position.

Cde. M. Woźniak: Is it true that against the background of the leaked material some priests read the first letter?

Cde. J. Kuberski: No. Some have posted the letter in [public] glass cases. The primate's letter will be read out tomorrow.

Cde. M. Woźniak: Have not Glemp together with the Episcopate found themselves in the same position as Wałęsa with the NCC?

Cde. J. Kuberski: The Episcopate is under pressure from reactionary forces because Solidarity does not exist. Glemp's sermon from December 13 was received well. The Episcopate submitted a protest that we are over-using the December 13 sermon of Glemp. Eight out of ten from the Episcopate Council agreed with us. What should be done to resist the pressures of reaction? The letter will be a shock in the West. There will not be a communiqué and the position will be moderate. In the Episcopate, there is a lot of identification with our standpoint as well as concern for peace at all costs.

Cde. W. Mokrzyszczak: We are executing the recommendations from December 13 of this year accepted by the Politburo. Point 1—carried out. There is functionality of the authorities. Reserve officers are involved. Cde. Baryła: consider what should be improved, for example Radio Free Europe broadcasts instructions on UKF—deal with it.

Cde. K. Morawski: I can see the *aktiv* on the streets, there is an action of gifts, but there have been three incidents of poisoning the soldiers.

Cde. J. Baryła: The Association of Fighters for Liberty and Democracy should be involved more extensively. There are attempts to insert a clinch between the military and the Citizens' Police.

Cde. W. Mokrzyszczak: Prepare for publication of the Catholic press after the end of martial law.

Cde. M. Woźniak: Should color press[3] not be issued for Christmas?

---

[3] Color press included various kinds of popular publications, not including regular news, which were often printed in color.

Cde. J. Baryła: There has to be special TV programming for Christmas.

Cde. W. Mokrzyszczak: On questions where "S" buildings have not been maintained, the Organizational Department has put forward proposals. Vehement opponents of socialism have to be dealt with during the review. The issue of exchanging identity cards is under consideration. The question of "S" members in the administration has been raised. The self-definition of party members who are members of Solidarity has begun. The matter of party unity has been tackled. It does not work in reality, however.

Cde. J. Baryła: Let the editors of *Rzeczywistość* write for *Żołnierz Wolności*. Certain militarization is being initiated. No soldier raises the matter of Christmas leave. They will receive recommendations to use them after the military service, in party *aktiv* or in the youth apparatus. Courts and Prosecutor's Office are functioning badly, legal matters drag on for a long time.

Cde. W. Mokrzyszczak: The question of decision-making centers. The Secretariat should be convened every day, it should listen and pass forward what is going on at the center. There is 24-hour work at the Central Committee. For 421 employees of the Committee, 214 are in the regions, 24 are ill, 183 are active within the Central Committee; information is sufficient; there is no showing off in the publications. The official standpoint is required and this is what the Politburo is doing. Communication with members of the central party authorities is maintained.

Cde. M. Orzechowski: It is important how members of the Central Committee are behaving.

Cde. J. Urbański: Thirty-four comrades have withdrawn from Solidarity, 14 have said they would stay and there is no data regarding the other 23.

Cde. W. Mokrzyszczak: We are pointing out what is wrong. We have made internments and there is not enough fighting against speculation and striking at the new-rich. VDCs are functioning, there has only been one caveat whether plenipotentiaries can participate in the WKOs. The issue of women has been dealt with, similarly that of the pensioners. Central Committee Commissions have been called off.

Cde. M. Woźniak: Should not a meeting of Central Committee members-miners be held in Katowice?

Cde. W. Mokrzyszczak: Point 21 has been accomplished. On the question of full time apparatus of trade unions—decisions have been communicated. The session of the PAN has been put off. There will be an assessment of the plenipotentiaries. The *aktiv* has not received the release of the interned in Słupsk well. The Voivodeship Committee did not know about that. The CC departments responsible for policy implementation [*merytoryczne*] are being engaged in that effort. The publication of "S" [members'] biographies is inefficient.

Cde. J. Baryła: For example Rulewski during his year-long term has built a house for himself; [this is] getting rich. The Information Department should report on such data.

Cde. S. Zaczkowski: It has been ordered to videotape Rulewski's villa, the value of which amounts to 1 million złoty. A prominent "S" member has built a house within one year. Somebody from the Information Department should request it.

Cde. J. Baryła: A group at Cde. Majka's should be formed to deal with this issue. Show people with authority. Zukrowski had a good presentation. One person with authority should appear on each edition of the daily news, scientists should write; give us some names.

Cde. W. Mokrzyszczak: The question of market supply was undertaken. Point 31—tomorrow there will be material [for discussion] concerning agricultural goods.

Cde. Z. Michałek: *Aktiv* has been sent to the countryside. We are determining who is going to sign the appeal to the peasants.

Cde. M. Woźniak: The most important question now is what is going to happen to the party.

Cde. W. Jaruzelski: The Secretariat is working. We want to discuss the issues of the party, workers' self-government, and problems of the intelligentsia, academic and journalist circles.

Cde. K. Barcikowski: Martial law was received with seriousness. There have been incidents of disregarding that fact. Strike action has intensified. The number of strikes is currently diminishing; the level of tension associated with strikes is falling. Resistance has begun to grow with time. The introduction of the state of emergency was justified by the intention to paralyze Solidarity. The Solidarity standpoint, the suspension of the union, actions towards particular regions have caused "S" to lose its popularity. This does not mean, however, that its members have ceased to act. The attacks of "S" have been broadened to include the Citizens' Police and the army as their targets. There is also verbal propaganda and distribution of leaflets. A portion of "S" activists will want to initiate underground activity. The party and its behavior are the main problem for us. The reactions of the party vary. Party *aktiv* has been prepared in substantive terms. There is a new wave of handing back party membership cards. This concerns workers' and intelligentsia circles especially where police and order-reinforcing operations took place. Instruction concerning the party under martial law—preparatory works are going on, there are changes in the Factory Committees and Town Committees, the issue of party members in the administration who hold non-party positions are being addressed. This is not an easy task considering the [current] situation. The Organizational Department of the CC has approached the First Secretaries of the VC's to urgently present the situation in their party organizations. Cde. W. Jaruzelski has warned against the mood of revenge towards "S" members. We must concentrate on the party; this is what the progress of the reforms and changes in the country depend upon.

Cde. M. Milewski: It is important to judge the strength of the internal and external opponents. There is no assessment of what they are intending to do. There will be attempts to strike. There is the slogan: we must wait out martial law. It is said that we performed the action in a masterly fashion. Leaflets have disappeared everywhere and the party in the institutes has not entered that space.

486

There is a will to listen to [Radio] Free Europe. We have to think about that, also at the VCs. On the one hand, martial law should be consistently executed, on the other, we need to watch what is going to happen tomorrow and beyond. The first thing is to explain that martial law was introduced for the good of the country and socialism, against threats, extremists, counter-revolution and anarchy. Aside from the stick, there has to be a carrot. There are 4,500 internees and arrested [people]; some have been released and new ones interned. Talks have been held with 5,000; 300 have refused to sign the declaration. Eighty-two have been arrested by the Military Prosecutor, 143 by the General Prosecutors. The Słowik trial[4] is being held today. The sentence is going to be announced today. Restrictions, curfew, and a ban on foreign travel have been introduced. But internees are gradually being released, the curfew will be shortened today except in Katowice, Gdańsk, Szczecin, Wrocław, and Lublin. A portion of the internees received better conditions: Wałęsa, Kułaj. "S" turned out to be an organization led by enemies, anarchists. There are extremists in "S", but also a workers' current—a potential ally for the future. We should cut ourselves off from attempts of retaliation. In central offices, in the field of justice affairs, and in prosecutors' offices "S" members have to make a declaration by December 13 on the content of the cde. W. Jaruzelski's speech. They have to turn away from what is hostile and take a position on the principles of the socialist system, the leading role of the party, and alliances. The verification of journalists should not be a witch-hunt. Each party member should have an opportunity to get involved.

People are disoriented, they interpret December 13 as an attempt by the authorities to return to the state [of the situation] before August. The speech by Cde. W. Jaruzelski should be our bible. The breaking up of the second and the third rank of "S" would amount to "to be or not to be" for us. This is about the party showing itself in a certain new role. The ancillary role of the party should find its appropriate reflection. Intentions regarding intimidation and physical terror appear. The *aktiv* should be prepared, student and youth groups should be formed during the school break. People supporting December 13 should be brought under [our] influence. [Taking into account] the statements by regional "S" members, we should aim at winning the support of future Solidarity. Workers' crews which did not go on strike should be presented and thanked. Order has to be introduced. Appropriate provisions have to be secured for Christmas. In the USA our situation is assessed as having prevented a solution by people other than the Poles and that martial law allowed the party to eliminate Solidarity. There are examples of approval for our moves; economic aid has been suspended temporarily and will depend on our approach to Solidarity. In France, Mitterand expressed his personal approach to "S;" there are protest initiatives on the international level. There is a high degree of astonishment in the FRG, but they accept unchanged economic relations with us.

---

[4] Andrzej Słowik, a Solidarity leader from Łódź, was arrested on December 13. He was sentenced to four-and-a-half years in prison.

Cde. W. Mokrzyszczak: Politburo decisions from December 13 are still unfulfilled. The functioning of the party is determined on the basis of instructions for martial law. The Organizational Department is preparing proposals. The matter of exchanging party membership cards should be approached more broadly. Prosecutorial matters are proceeding slowly. Decision along the lines of the CC-government. One of the CC secretaries working on the Staff is assigning tasks in the CC. Why has there not been a statement from the Politburo? Expose crisis speculators and the newly rich. Work with plenipotentiaries. There are complaints about releasing internees.

Cde. W. Jaruzelski: Whose? Explain precisely. We live with generalizations.

Cde. W. Mokrzyszczak: Negative characters are presented: Rulewski, the question of the villa.

Cde. W. Jaruzelski: This was intensely covered on TV.

Cde. W. Mokrzyszczak: As far as the appeal to the peasants is concerned, it is acceptable. Tasks resulting from the teleconference: intensify the work of the *aktiv* and self-defense groups because the extremists are preparing new actions. There is a warning against lower vigilance on the day of the Christmas Eve mass. What about the curfew on January 1 and on New Year's Eve? To what extent will tensions decrease? What about the points of explaining citizens' rights and quantitative changes among party, economy, and administration full-time positions? There is a request for the TV news bulletin to be repeated before noon (*Cde. W. Jaruzelski*—a decision has been made already). There is a proposal for the party schools and courses to be released from Tuesday. It is suggested that self-defense groups be formed as special units of the Citizens' Police (legal protection, white bands maybe with the sign: PPR). A decree about the legal status of these groups should be adopted.

Cde. W. Jaruzelski: What is the scale, the extent? How is it functioning and what is its character?

Cde. W. Mokrzyszczak: There is a battalion in each voivodeship, a company in former district towns; these are mainly older people and a bit of our youth. They are willing to get involved in these matters. They should be selected according to their tasks. In some voivodeships, there are over 1200 of them and in others below 620. Their slogan is: we are defending order.

Cde. J. Baryła: The most important is the battle for large work institutes. The military is functioning well. "S" is reviving. The PPO are inactive; institutes have to be purged twice or three times. Factory radio systems are very quiet, this is unacceptable. Institutes ought to be taken under control, the party should be mobilized. The second shift in the institutes has always been more aggressive. The last TV news bulletin should be shown in the morning. Things can be bad if we do not take control over empty work institutes. The party guard should be to a lesser extent sent to the cities, but should capture already in the institutes. People are working at a fast pace. We have not launched the youth organizations. We should enter work institutes. Operational groups in institutes have been expanded. Some questions at the teleconference do not instill confidence in us:

488

What about the Christmas Eve mass? What about holidays? And nobody is asking about taking over the institutes. Power has to be handed over, but to whom? Not to "S." The work style of some DC's is not good. People are being called for meetings and discussions instead of working in the institutes. Secretaries should not be pulled away. The functioning of the Intraparty Commission should be perfected. Work with the cultural circles; there is nobody to approach and hold talks with academics. We are requesting names of people who we will use for propaganda. There should be a complex program for the holiday period. On the question of the Christmas Eve mass, we should refer to public opinion, bloodshed ought to be prevented.

Cde. J. Urbański: I attended a consultation in Żyrardów. There is a revival and increased confidence. What is one saddened about? The *aktiv* is of the 40's generation, there is a lack of youth. We cannot carry out a revolution without young people. The mood is better. There is a lot of confusion, how to approach the National Reconciliation Front at the bottom level? Three remarks: 1. The phase of paralyzing hostile forces worked out well. 2. We have moved to control of the situation by the party, but this is sufficient. 3. There is the problem of how to get out of this. Conclusions: Complete the instructions for propaganda, why martial law was needed, what socialism has offered: agricultural reform, industry, illiteracy. For many these are slogans. Mistakes and distortions of the [past] decade; return to the harm brought about after August. We have the cadre—give them perspectives. Ask specialists to prepare the program of the National Reconciliation Front. Such problems as social justice, enrichment, and loans should be taken up. The strength of our party should be summed up. Take care of people who are refusing to work. Intensify penetrations of hiding places. There could be caches of weapons and food. The CPCC and VPCC—verification of people is going on, do not neglect explanatory activity.

Cde. S. Zaczkowski: There is no renewal of strikes. There is an announcement about employing workers again. Work with families in their places of residence and influence workers' attitudes toward employment through families. There is a need for increased ideological-political work so that *aktiv* groups can function in the institutes. There are still terror groups. In Gdańsk, the VC Executive said that it considers the ideological-educational activity as secondary. There should be alleviation as far as the curfew is concerned. High mobility in the activity of the party and vigilance should be maintained.

Cde. S. Gabrielski: The issues of the trade union movement in Poland are piling up. The common ideological stance of the unionists—the socialist one. The organizational model—diverse unions. We are reconstructing the unions. The Staff is working on a future model. The future of the youth movement with a socialist character. In academic circles, there are decisions about making the IUS illegal. The "S" declarations of loyalty must be credible. We can win over youth circles through active cadre policies. Make the young people more co-responsible, present the accompishments of the last 37 years, concentrate on pointing out the future, the model of intellectual life. People accept our ideological values, they did not accept the practice. The question of building the party at the bottom level—make it cohesive, break through a certain barrier. A front of social organizations is being launched, the idea of social committees of national salvation.

Cde. H. Kubiak: Allow children to join their parents and parents to join their children on Christmas Eve. We are moving from one attitude to another too easily. We are winning the war. The method of programming peace, which the war is about, must be prepared. We are going to be badly off when the peace begins. There is a vacuum because of the lack of a peace vision. We crushed "S" which interfered with our construction of renewal. The opponent is absent at the moment and what are you doing? What has the struggle been about and what caused the illusions? The most misleading was the slogan of national sovereignty. Underlining the role of the army that is standing above everything. The army functions in the name of the nation, sometimes against our party, but for us in the name of the party. Peace cannot be won otherwise. Propaganda, reaction to the signal—we consider that from the perspective of the source. Industry is returning to normal; this again is a source of propaganda for success. The situation in the stores is improving—we are launching a rumor that we had kept it all in the stores. Do more and talk less about it [...] It is hard to say what the war is about on the basis of the DTV [*Dziennik Telewizyjny*: television news] broadcasts. What we are showing amounts to nothing. The military in the name of the nation. The party serving the military, hiding behind the military. It is hard to find people with reputation because they were always appearing and especially in the schools of higher education environment. While defending organizations which are ideologically close to us we must gain access to the whole of the youth. We will have to intensify repression in the school system. Specific elements of the peace program have to be built. What has been done since August is important. It is important to capitalize on everything they have done until December 13 of this year.

Cde. M. Orzechowski: What is the party like in the regions? It is rudimentary. Is it going to be the party in the shadow of the military, or is it supposed to revive? We have not reached a turnabout, a picking up in the party. The current *aktiv* group does not exceed the one from before December 13 of this year. In the party we can count on action and support of between 15–17 to 40–50 percent. A large segment of the secretaries have raised their heads; however, they do not act, but speak. The divisions from before December 13 are fading. There is a criterion: What should be done? In Wałbrzych, a Marxist–Leninist seminar joined a group of self-defense. Should not the last days have invoked a turnaround? Can one count on the process of self-purification? We are purifying ourselves from those who have actively withdrawn; we are purifying ourselves from them through the CPC. The basic mass of the party is in a state of lethargy. The worst situation occurs in large organizations. For example at the Głogów Steelworks, the secretary of the VC can count on 30 out of 600 members of the PPO. In Legnica, seven people responded to the party's appeal. What is to be done in this situation? Are we able to revive the party through self-purification and verification? Will the society accept a party which has functioned and functions? Will the society accept democratic slogans of the WRON? There are voices saying that this is not going to happen. We have not sensed out the state of the party. Within intellectual circles, these questions are troubling. Would it not be advisable to form a new Marxist–Leninist party, a Polish one, adapting universal principles to Polish conditions? Discussions about changing the name of the party are considered again. We are winning the war, but winning the peace will be more important. Issues raised by Cde. Kubiak should be addressed.

Cde. M. Woźniak: The problem of the party should be seriously considered. There is socialist renewal, but also apathy, indifference and a sharp struggle against the party. There is the Hungarian way. Combine the managerial and social trends in enterprises. Maybe self-government should be suspended everywhere because it carries with it a danger of gathering of enemies. Administrative personnel should be prepared for replacement after a monthly course. There are opportunities to win credibility for the authorities. There is opportunism on the part of economic activists—we should reach out to the youth. The youth has spoken in favor of a model within the party—those who formed the movement of contestation. The party's role in the national councils should be considered. The question of who is preparing personnel should be tackled on an institutional basis. What about self-government?

Cde. J. Czyrek: Cde. M. Woźniak presented on various matters, Cde. S. Gabrielski on the issues of trade unions, Cde. W. Mokrzyszczak on organizational matters and I on international affairs.

Cde. Z. Michałek: The countryside was used for the *aktiv* to reach it. Nobody has reached the countryside for a year. The county *aktiv*, the agricultural services should reach the farms. The results of the purchase of agricultural goods are better. I perceive the Hungarian program on party matters—there have been leadership changes in the party. If we want to make the party more credible, present the Congress program and points of the opponent that this party has always been weak, has many sins and is not credible. This should be said about the new party and about new faces. I have an appeal to the peasants which might be signed by the WRON.

Cde. S. Olszowski: I appreciate the comments, but I am not prepared for discussion on the principles.

Cde. M. Woźniak: Regional members of the CC should be gathered.

Cde. W. Jaruzelski: The discussion was useful; the clock is working faster; assessments must mature; there should be no delays in formulating tasks for the first battle. Think about winning the war, socialism, and avoid downgrading socialism. Do not allow that to happen. We should move into more systematic and regular work. The work has to be operative: the Secretariat, the military, the government, the leadership. Secretaries who are conducting teleconferences are being informed about everything. The Politburo met on December 13. Maybe the Politburo should meet more frequently. It is sufficient to call the Politburo next Tuesday. What is said during the Secretariat sessions reaches Politburo members in the form of information [reports]. Members of the CC are participating in teleconferences. There should be a meeting with the CC members in the regions, or repeat the Rozbrat Street meeting, especially meeting with the workers. Meet with all of them or make two or three groups. The VC's work should be analyzed. In the future, it should be characterized who is working in what fashion. Those who do not keep up with the pace must be replaced. Whoever does not sense out the situation, does not live up to it, does not have the psychological predisposition, is not able to establish contacts, has not carried out the task— good-bye, and we fill the position with somebody else. An assessment should be prepared as to whom we deal with in the VC's (Cde. K. Barcikowski and Cde. W. Mokrzyszczak). Their assessment has largely been erroneous, those voices criticizing us, me.

The *aktiv's* outlook is poor; they are missing preparation and contact with the masses. Our forceful action has paralyzed the opponent, "S," but also the party. At the bottom, many were not doing anything, fear, giving back membership cards, old sins, lack of work with the PPO. Knowledge of the situation was insufficient; we entered the battle without reserves. What is the chance for renewal? Is it possible in the current shape [and form]? We must undertake efforts to revitalize the party. What is [going on] with the party and which party? This must be the main subject of the forthcoming session of the Politburo; collect as many materials and decisions as possible. The fight is ongoing and activity is necessary. The vacuum needs to be eliminated. Are people present in the factories? Demand more from our people, use the radio systems. How to look at poor people? Is it dilatory? How many can you take advantage of and what about the rest? Utilize the HSSS, send its students to the factories where strikes had occurred. We should move away from the position of a tolerant guardian. We are in a deplorable moral situation. How to help these people? What about the armed people? What are people thinking in the work institutes? What are they thinking on the streets—that we know. There should be a data bank with bad and good information, the value of the effort would be greater. The issue of the verification of party members. The Factory Committee secretaries are not always present at the information sessions (relay this to S. Kociołek). Come down lower. There are too many consultations. The rhythm of work must be different. There should not be any work during this time. There is a lot of gossiping in this building. If the party is to preserve its name and form, there will not be space for many people. This subject should be reconsidered in depth on Tuesday.

There is a need for a declaration about what we are fighting for and where we are going. Slogans from the Eight Party Congress have been stolen from us by "S" because it has defied the workers' ideals in order to stage an attack. The question of propaganda—nothing should be overdone. Do not return to the propaganda of Łukaszewicz. Social justice should be introduced on the banners. The party is carrying out a revolution. Rebuild the party while fighting for social justice with the sharks. What have we done on this issue, with those sharks? I am requesting concrete data on these matters, how accounts should be settled. Martial law should be a state of blessing for our society, the party must take care of this—take care of human problems. There will be gifts—the party needs to be involved. This act should have a warm atmosphere and an appropriate reflection should be arranged. On the question of self-government, we cannot afford a mistake, luxury, or suspension of self-government. However, this should be analyzed with Cde. J. Obodowski. When the self-government is decent, [works] with party members—let it function. And when it participates in the strikes as a hostile force—suspend it or liquidate it. In militarized institutes, the draft should be put off. The director's role will increase. The question of sectoral trade unions—what is going to happen with "S"? Cde. Rakowski should work out a plan. The unions are politically homogeneous, pro-socialist, but they will not be anti-Church. People joined "S" because it was against the failures. If the party renews itself, the sectoral [unions] will need to find their precise image. Distancing themselves from "S," from what is unacceptable. We should take into account the fact that this will be a pro-Church, pro-socialist organization. I treat this as a necessary evil. This is one of the options. It has to be announced that the whole Piotrków region is declaring loyalty. Cde. Kubiak—work out the Walasek statement. The question of the youth—move ahead. We have gained people for the National Salvation Front, but they have not been eager to do so. The offensive is cushioned. We had problems in the military before the Congress because "S" was active. With the youth, education, culture—jump ahead. The youth are soldiers who have stayed for the third year of service; they pass the exam; support them in the counties and towns. The question of the Committees for National Salvation. (*Cde. K. Barcikowski*—Declaration and the establishment of Committees; we will not gain many people.) Let it begin, let the names appear.

Cde. H. Kubiak: What is the relation between the Committees for National Salvation and the Committees for National Reconciliation?

Cde. W. Jaruzelski: The same as in time of war. Some things should be accounted for from December 13 of this year. This should be treated in an integral fashion. We only saw the National Reconciliation Front, the *aktiv* felt resigned. There is a danger of inclining in the other direction. The dropped-in opinions—this will be a turnabout. This subject should be considered in-depth among the intelligentsia, so that the intelligentsia will not organize a conspiracy against us. There is an aversion towards the authorities, a low moral level (they looked through their fingers at the emerging fascism and economic disaster, and now they are making noise). We should come out with an offensive program of renewal. We ought to say what troubled us in the past: what was said in Radom, Gdańsk. How does it relate to the past? Żukrowski, Lenart—I would ask Cde. Kubiak for them to gain credibility, so that there are a few voices like that. I have invited the Hungarian ambassador so that a member of the Hungarian leadership who took part in 1956 and in the renewal assists us. On the question of retaliation—we cannot allow that to happen. If somebody does not take advantage of the opportunities, we will use all available means. The "S" members should be the subject of daily verification. The "S" should be divided into the extremists and those who lived through a drama. The case of CIP should be portrayed more forcefully. *Cde. Milewski*—there were to be more materials. Intellectuals would have to dance the cancan in clownish hats in front of the CIP *aktiv*. The MSW is ridiculing itself with these batons on TV. Show terrorized families in the work institutes. Let the Church and intellectuals see this. Demand examples from the voivodeships during the teleconference, and if there are none, then you were not telling the truth. Show on TV how directors had their hands tied and could not fulfill the plans. Give an explanation for the timing of "W".[5] The legal justification of martial law should be prepared with examples and paragraphs, and then published. We must prove to the world that this was a coup on the part of "S;" that the country was led towards ruin. The investigation of the events in the "Wujek" coal mine[6] should be completed. We will release the WRON, the government or the Politburo statement, regrets and warning.

Cde. M. Milewski: The use of weaponry in the "Wujek" coal mine was legal. More voivodeship bulletins should be issued.

Cde. S. Olszowski: How is the printing equipment being utilized? Do the plenipotentiaries of the CC for the VC only feel responsible for organizational matters?

Cde. K. Barcikowski: They went as plenipotentiaries of the Politburo.

Cde. W. Jaruzelski: But what were Cde. K. Cypryniak's recommendations when he dispatched them?

Cde. K. Barcikowski: Cde. W. Mokrzyszczak and I gave guidelines.

Cde. W. Jaruzelski: They are there on behalf of all the departments and should be given guidelines. Attention should be drawn to the excess shootings in films. There should be more truth in the TV news bulletins and less triumphalism. Talk less about improvement of market supply. Show the damage to the economy caused after August.

Cde. S. Olszowski: What about the theaters?

Cde. W. Jaruzelski: Cde. H. Kubiak will think over the question of theaters and make recommendations in this area, especially as far as the opening of theaters for children is concerned.

Cde. J. Czyrek: Make a statement supporting the resolution of the U.N. Security Council with regard to the Golan Heights.

Cde. W. Jaruzelski: The Christmas Eve mass [*pasterka*] should be transmitted on the radio. Think about a TV program for Christmas, and especially about its propaganda and cultural aspect.

Cde. S. Olszowski: Three publications will come out during Christmas.

Cde. W. Jaruzelski: *Rzeczpospolita* will be published on New Year's Day. Bratkowski is hiding. The issues of Christmas should be looked at in a complex fashion. While winning the war phase, we must provide a peace program. Discount the teleconferences.

Cde. W. Mokrzyszczak: On the day of war, there were 421 political workers in the CC, of which 214 in the voivodeships, from Friday and from Monday. One

---

[5] "W" refers to "*stan wojenny*" or martial law.
[6] On December 16, nine miners were killed and 23 injured when security forces crushed a workers' protest.

hundred and eighty-three persons are working. There are four employees in some departments.

Cde. W. Jaruzelski: What are the people doing in the regions? Are they not sitting in the VCs?

Cde. W. Mokrzyszczak: They travel to work institutes and to the countryside. I assume the obligation to relay each matter.

Cde. M. Orzechowski: Should not the students of the HSSS be directed to work institutes that have been unblocked?

Cde. W. Jaruzelski: Yes, send them to those factories and provide [them] with concrete assignments.

Cde. J. Urbański: The PUWP Factory Committee in the Lenin Shipyard in Gdańsk is demanding that the CPCC settles accounts with the PB members. We should deal with the secretary of the PUWP IC—Jakubik.

Cde. W. Jaruzelski: Has Cde. J. Łabęcki recovered?

Cde. S. Olszowski: Cde. Fiszbach and other members of the executive have already recovered.

Cde. W. Jaruzelski: A communiqué should be issued to the press about the meeting of the CC Secretariat stating that the current socio-political situation as well as the resulting conclusions for the work of the organizations and party institutions were discussed.

Cde. K. Barcikowski: I am concerned about the discussions on the formation of a new party. Let us leave such discussions to ourselves. Questioning the party is equivalent to the end of the party.

Cde. S. Olszowski: Members of the study projects should not speak about them.

Cde. K. Barcikowski: This is the result of the famous Warsaw meeting.

Cde. K. Morawski: The decision about the Christmas Eve mass should be announced at the last moment.

Cde. W. Jaruzelski: The issues of the party branches will be left for consideration next Tuesday. Whoever has a different policy ends his activity and puts himself outside the party.

[Source: AAN, PUWP CC, 2260, pp. 389–409. Translated by Paweł Świeboda.]

Document No. 92: Hotline Communication from Leonid Brezhnev to Ronald Reagan Regarding Martial Law in Poland

December 25, 1981

Brezhnev's letter is a reply to a message from Reagan of December 24, in which the U.S. president called the Soviets to task for their role in instigating the crackdown in Poland. Although some in the administration exaggerated Moscow's part and there was a basic unawareness of the behind-the-scenes dynamics between the Soviets and the Polish authorities, the overall conclusion that Moscow had strongly favored suppressing the Polish opposition was of course accurate. Brezhnev's attempts to label the United States as the offender therefore ring hollow, as do other remarks such as his objection to the implication that Soviet-led military exercises were designed to intimidate the Poles; internal Soviet records make clear this was precisely their purpose. Despite the harsh tone of most of the message, it ends with a sign that the Kremlin hopes to resume talks with Washington on other issues of mutual concern, notwithstanding recent Polish events.

To His Excellency
Mister Ronald Reagan
President of the United States of America

Dear Mister President!

Your message sent by the hot line made it all the more pressing to appeal specifically to you, the U.S. government, to stop, at last, the intervention into the internal affairs of the sovereign state, the Polish People's Republic. This intervention, in very different forms, covert as well as overt, has been continuing for a long time.

By signing your recent message you essentially affixed your name to the fact that crude interference into the domestic affairs of Poland is indeed official U. S. policy. We condemned and still condemn this line, which is inadmissible to us.

In an attempt to shield your line from criticism, you cite without any relevance the letter of the Central Committee of our party on June 5 addressed to the PUWP CC. Besides distorting its meaning, you stand out again on the platform of interference, this time into the relationship of two political parties—CPSU and PUWP—between whom, as between other parties of the socialist countries, exist special, absolutely equal and friendly norms and rules of interaction. These rules were not born yesterday or today.

If somebody in the United States does not like the frank exchange of opinions between communist parties, judgments that they share with each other, we should answer firmly: this is the affair of these parties and only theirs. And they did not choose any referee who would impose norms on them.

It is important to emphasize the following moment of principle.

Our party expressed and expresses today antipathy towards those in Poland who are the enemy of the existing regime, who violate laws and the legal order in the country, and plunge it into chaos.

You as a leader of the state and government of the USA come out against the existing state regime in Poland, in other words for the overthrow of this regime. This is not an imagined, but a very real interference into the internal affairs of another sovereign state. And this is relevant not only to Poland. Such attempts are undertaken with regard to the Soviet Union. American officials and you personally have been continuously spreading slander about our social and state order, our internal rules. We want to rebuff this resolutely.

What in the light of these and many other well-known facts remains of your reflections about our supposed involvement in internal Polish events? Nothing remains of them.

In your address you cite a good clause from the Helsinki Final Act, which ends with my signature and the signature of the U.S. President. Yes, this clause, obligating [all] to refrain from any interference in affairs that fall under the category of the domestic competence of another state, reminds us in a very timely way that it is inadmissible for the U.S. to put forth all manner of demands with regard to the introduction of martial law in their country by Polish state organs, in accord with the State Constitution, and to attempt to dictate to the Poles what they should or should not do.

Nobody should meddle with what the Poles and Polish authorities are doing and will do in their own house.

You pretend to decide for the Poles, instead of them, how, and in what way Polish society should evolve. But only the Poles elected the social order in Poland, not Washington or Moscow. Nobody can point out to the leadership of Poland how it should conduct its affairs, by which methods it could better and more rapidly stabilize the situation in the country.

Attempts to dictate your will to other states stand in flagrant opposition to elementary norms of international law. I would go further: they are immoral through and through. And no game of words, related to human rights, can change that.

The Soviet Union rebuffs the pretensions of anybody to interfere with what happens in Poland.

In your address you speak about military exercises near Poland. You apparently want to read what you want into these exercises, linking them to the situation in Poland. But this is a contrived proposition *[vymisel]* without any foundation.

But if we touch on the subject of military exercises, I have a question: How many exercises of the armed forces of NATO countries, including the USA, took place and take place in Western Europe in the vicinity, for instance, of the territories of the GDR and Czechoslovakia? Why could we not present some complaints to the USA in this field? Why could we not assess such exercises as a threat to the Soviet Union and other socialist countries?

Such is the price of your reference to military exercises.

You, Mister President, are hinting that if the Polish affairs keep developing in a direction the U.S. does not like, then it could deliver a blow across the entire range of Soviet–American relations.

But if you allow me to be frank, your administration has already done enough to blow up, or at least undermine, all the positive [steps] that were achieved at such great effort in the relations between our countries under the preceding American administrations. Today, unfortunately, there is little left from that mutually built positive political capital.

What can be said about these hints? Perhaps one should have weighed everything carefully before even making them.

In general one should observe: the tone of your address is not quite appropriate for communication between leaders of such powers as the Soviet Union and the USA, considering their weight and position in the world, their responsibility for the international situation. Such is our opinion.

If there were to be a further destabilization of Soviet–American relations, it would be not us, not the Soviet Union, who would bear the responsibility for this.

I believe it would be much better if the leaders of the Soviet Union and the USA discussed in a balanced and unemotional way the issues that are really vital for people—how to rein in and end the arms race that long ago acquired such a crazy tempo and scale, and how to preserve peace on earth. We advocate putting these very problems at the center of attention of the leadership of our countries and finding reasonable solutions for them. I assume, and I am even certain that the American people need this in no less measure than the Soviet people and other peoples.

Respectfully,
L. Brezhnev

[Source: National Security Archive "Soviet Flashpoints" collection. *Translated by Vladislav Zubok.]*

Document No. 93: Report to HSWP CC Politburo on Hungarian Delegation's Talks with Wojciech Jaruzelski

December 30, 1981

As part of the effort to rebuild after martial law, Jaruzelski asked Hungarian leader János Kádár to help by offering Hungary's experiences following the 1956 Soviet-led invasion, which placed Kádár into power. Earlier in the fall, Polish party propagandists ordered the showing of a special documentary film on the so-called Hungarian counter-revolution which featured scenes of hangings of Hungarian security troops and damage wreaked upon Budapest during the fighting. The point of the special showing had been to raise concerns in the population about a possibly violent confrontation in Poland. Thus, the Hungarian "experience" was already on Jaruzelski's mind. The discussions below with the Hungarians, as described by the leaders of their delegation, offer in-depth remarks by Jaruzelski about the current situation—a fascinating insight into his thinking as relayed to a like-minded and sympathetic audience. Jaruzelski's bitterness towards both Solidarity and members of his own party shows through. He acknowledges the union is a unique organization with several million adherents but disparages it as a source of "indescribable destructive power" whose real goals are shrouded in "myths." He also expresses resentment at local party leaders for not being "active"—an irony given the heavy Soviet criticisms of his own passive behavior.

Report
for the Politburo

At the invitation of Comrade Jaruzelski, the first secretary of the PUWP CC and the leader of the Military Council for National Salvation, and following the decision of the HSWP Politburo, a delegation of the HSWP was sent to Warsaw between December 27–29. The delegation was led by György Aczél, member of the Politburo. He was accompanied by Jenő Fock and János Berecz, members of the HSWP CC. István Pataki, associate of the Department of Foreign Affairs and József Garamvölgyi, our ambassador in Warsaw, took part in the discussions. At the request of the Polish comrades, the Hungarian delegation went to Warsaw in order to provide information on our experiences in our fight against counter-revolutionary forces and our experience in socialist consolidation and the building of socialism. The exchange of opinions also offered an opportunity to assess the political situation in Poland that has arisen since the introduction of martial law.

In the framework of a plenary meeting, our delegation met the members of an operational committee of 10 which comprised representatives of the Military Council for National Defense, the PUWP Politburo and the Polish government. The talks were led by Comrade W. Jaruzelski who analyzed the Polish situation thoroughly and pointed out those areas where they particularly needed Hungarian experience. The delegation held talks with Deputy Prime Minister M. Rakowski, member of the PUWP Politburo and Secretary of the CC Stefan Olszowski, and with Secretary of the PUWP CC Marian Orzechowski. Comrade Jenő Fock had a talk with Deputy Prime Ministers Janusz Obodowski and Zbigniew Madej, furthermore with Secretary of the PUWP CC Marian Woźniak. There were talks also between Comrade János Berecz and Włodzimierz Natorf, leader of the Department of Foreign Affairs of the PUWP CC. At PUWP CC headquarters, Comrade György Aczél took part in a nearly three-hour party assembly where 120 people were present. At the dinner party hosted by Comrade Ambassador Garamvölgyi, we had an informal talk with Kazimierz Barcikowski and József Czyrek, members of the PUWP Politburo and CC secretaries, furthermore with Deputy Prime Minister Mieczysław Rakowski. At the end of the visit, Comrade W. Jaruzelski and György Aczél had a one-hour discussion. This took place after the all-day meeting of first secretaries of the voivodeships and military representatives, where, as Comrade Jaruzelski bitterly remarked, again only the military representatives were active.

I.

Comrade W. Jaruzelski expressed his thanks to the leadership of the HSWP and above all to Comrade János Kádár for the opportunity that the Hungarian party delegation's visit to Warsaw provided them. He said that although he was aware of the significant difference between Hungarian circumstances 25 years earlier and the present Polish situation, as regards political progress he recognized quite a number of similarities and for that reason the Hungarian experiences, proven by developments since then, were of great value to them. He spoke of the situation that came about after the introduction of martial law. In reference to the tasks and action to be carried out, he formulated his words in such a way that they took the shape of questions referring to the Hungarian experiences.

"Today, the most important task in Poland is to get out of the deep crisis, strengthen the people's power and create the conditions of further socialist development. The most decisive and at the same time the most problematic factor is now the situation of the party. The PUWP, as it exists formally, has to be revived; however, a number of difficulties lie ahead. In the course of three-and-a-half decades the party has experienced more crises and does not enjoy the confidence of society. Under extremely complex ideological, moral and political conditions, the party must restore sincere and open relations with the masses as soon as possible."

Comrade Jaruzelski suggested that, although martial law created favorable conditions and the forces of socialism had won the first battle, with respect to potential developments the current activity of the whole of the party and its organs was still alarming. A segment of party members, especially in areas where strikes had to be stopped by military force, feels ill at ease, is inactive and lacks initiative. Others have become far too self-assured as a consequence of the con-

500

ditions and order imposed by the presence of the military. This, too, gave rise to unjustified self-confidence among those people and some party members even had a tendency to take revenge. Taking into consideration Comrade Kádár's often repeated advice, they regard the drawing up of a statement, which could be suitable as a concise political program, to be one of the most important preconditions of political development. At present they are working on establishing a political platform which they would like to make public in the near future.

Counter-revolutionary forces were very well organized within Solidarity. With the introduction of martial law they managed to break the leadership of Solidarity, to interrupt its activity, to paralyze its propaganda campaign and sometimes even to expose it. In practice, however, the several-million-strong base of the organization still exists. Solidarity is a unique organization in the world and it has demonstrated an indescribable destructive power both within the economy and the affairs of state. It is a fact that this organization has become a symbol of dynamism in the eyes of several million well-meaning workers. The real aspirations of Solidarity's extremist counter-revolutionary leaders will have to be revealed by steadfast work, but this struggle is going to be a hard one, for it is in fact a fight against myths.

Furthermore, an aggravating factor is that the majority of Solidarity supporters and the source of its dynamism are the youth, who joined Solidarity in order to knock down the obstacles that thwart and frustrate their aspirations for intellectual and material well-being. Their attitude may be characterized as nothing less than pro-Western and anti-Soviet. All that goes hand-in-hand with the intoxicating feeling of their, hitherto often successful, political fight against the authorities. Therefore, they have to be offered attractive goals and suitable conditions in a political and economic situation which is by far the worst ever.

The other main character of the Solidarity movement is clericalism. The Polish Catholic Church, unlike the Hungarian, did not get exposed in the course of events. What is more, it has gained ground within Solidarity and reinforced its social position through it. While remaining realistic, the Polish leadership is still looking for possibilities for coexistence between the State and the Church. They are maintaining relations with the Church and trying to keep them from deteriorating beyond a minimum level.

Comrade Jaruzelski pointed out that in the fields of ideological work, propaganda and mass communications they are employing administrative measures first of all. Though there is strict censorship they believe, based on the Hungarian experience, that in the course of time they will be able to use more flexible and more efficient means in this field, too.

The present poor condition of the national economy is a major burden. Even without the destruction of the last 15 months the situation would be grave, but now economic conditions have become catastrophic. There is a general shortage of supplies, prices and wages are unrealistic, the supply of energy and raw materials for industrial plants keeps breaking down. To make things worse, the USA has just effected an economic blockade, thus badly affecting the economy, which has developed a cooperative dependence on the economies of the capitalist countries over the past 10 years. In spite of the extraordinary circumstances, economic reform is going to be implemented in a limited form at the beginning of the year. Poland is in great need of economic assistance from the socialist countries and Comrade Jaruzelski repeatedly expressed his thanks for Hungary's prompt economic aid. He also added that it was clear to them that this kind of assistance could be only provisional as the real solution in the long run is undoubtedly the transformation of the Polish economy into a viable economy.

Summarizing his comments, Comrade Jaruzelski underscored that the tasks ahead were huge and that there is presently no organized force in Poland, beyond the armed forces, which could provide reliable support. Only multilateral assistance from the allied socialist countries could bring real support and clean sources. They wish to pursue the line they took when they introduced martial law; they are aware that they are pulling back but have to take full advantage of the opportunities offered by exceptional circumstances.

II.

Our experience and impressions from the intensive formal and informal discussions held with members of the Polish leadership can be summarized as follows:

1. The activity of the Military Council for National Defense is very well organized, the armed forces and police authorities are carrying out their historic duties with commendable discipline. Their actions have stabilized the government institutions, eliminated open and organized resistance and apparently restored public law and order. The indispensable primary conditions are thus in place for socialist consolidation.

2. The favorable conditions created by the introduction of martial law and the stability attained so far are in danger mainly due to a lack of political power, or rather its disintegration.

3. The party is invariably divided and has become less active. party leaders regard the situation created by the army's actions, that is, the so-called "conditions of artificial defense," as natural and this is delaying development of the political offensive. Within the party there are heated debates among the various trends and tendencies and no determined political platform so far. It would seem that there is a mutual understanding that the party must not return either to the position before August 1980, nor to the one preceding December 13, 1981. Consequently, there has to be concordance between the general principles of building socialism and Polish national characteristics. However, in practice, differences of opinion are emerging even in the process of setting the specific tasks and direct objectives. According to representatives of one of the main trends, national characteristics—the role of the Catholic Church, the degree of Polish national consciousness, the situation in agriculture and so forth—have to be given a decisive role. Furthermore, the past 35 years of the construction of socialism have to be fundamentally revised and reassessed. According to the other trend, which is less

perceptible now among the topmost circles of the party, due to the immediate counter-revolutionary threat and highly sensitive national feelings, the balance has to be restored by way of laying a larger emphasis on the general principles of building socialism and on the basic categories of Marxism–Leninism.

4. Hostile forces were successfully disabled, but not liquidated. The enemy's tactics could be now either of two kinds:

a) To go underground and consistently hamper consolidation by staging terrorist acts and sabotage, or

b) To call for the restoration of quiet and order, and so to emphasize the senselessness of continuing martial law, and then to demand its earliest possible cessation.

5. There was a keen and general interest in the Hungarian experience everywhere. We are of the opinion that in this respect they repeatedly took our previous results as a basis and they seem to know little about the initial steps of the hard-won consolidation. When they are about to announce the introduction of harsh measures, they often refer to these results without proper knowledge of these experiences.

* * *

The delegation of the HSWP fulfilled its mission. The exchange of opinions was useful and we are convinced that our fraternal Polish party needs all-embracing and concrete support in the future, too. As far as we could tell, beyond their expedience, our suggestions provided above all moral encouragement and support for the Polish leadership.

We suggest that, depending on the Polish comrades' needs, a similar discussion take place in Warsaw in the near future and that, at their request, a consultation be held in Budapest on the relevant issues.

Budapest, December 30, 1981
János Berecz
György Aczél
Jenő Fock

[Source: MOL, Department of Documents on the Hungarian Workers' Party and the Hungarian Socialist Workers' Party, 288. f. 5/844. ő.e., pp. 14–20.]

Document No. 94: Transcript of CPSU CC Politburo Meeting

January 14, 1982

The following Politburo excerpt consists of two items. The first relates to a meeting of Politburo members with Polish Foreign Minister Czyrek, the second to a letter being drafted to Jaruzelski in response to his request for economic aid. Brezhnev notes that in assessing the situation in Poland one month after martial law, Jaruzelski says that the crackdown has "broken the back of the counter-revolution." Now the time has come to look at the "strategic" picture—how to address the economy and the battle for the hearts and minds of the population, what he terms "a change in consciousness of the masses." Brezhnev compares Poland's situation with those of Hungary in 1956 and Czechoslovakia in 1968. One major difference with the latter is that political "recovery" there occurred rapidly because "the counter-revolution basically did not intrude in the [economic] sphere," whereas in Poland "it is the opposite." He therefore finds it impossible to say no entirely to the Poles' requests for help, for example with oil deliveries, despite the consensus that the Soviets have little ability to make major contributions. Partly because of that, he also sees little choice but to allow the Poles to look to the West and even to China for assistance, despite the understood risk that Poland might become overly dependent on those two sources in the future.

[…]

2. On the results of the negotiations with PUWP CC Politburo member and Minister of Foreign Affairs of the Polish People's Republic Cde. J. Czyrek.

Brezhnev: I think we all agree that the talks held by Mikhail Andreevich [Suslov] and Andrei Andreevich [Gromyko] with Cde. Czyrek were useful. The Westerners, especially the Americans, are acquiring powerful influence in Poland. Under these conditions, it is important to provide constant political support to our friends, and to cheer them on. We cannot allow them to get disheartened and begin to lose what they have achieved with so much effort.

Martial law in the PPR has already been in effect for a month. The preliminary results are available. As Jaruzelski says, they have broken the back of the counter-revolution. However, the tasks ahead are somewhat more complex.

In restoring relative order to the country, the Polish comrades now must resolve problems, one might say, of a strategic nature: what to do with the trade unions, how to put the economy back on its feet, how to achieve a change in the consciousness of the masses, etc.?

The most important question is the situation in the PUWP. Our friends are looking for approaches to this solution. It looks like Jaruzelski's goals are not to dissolve the party or change its name, but to use martial law to thoroughly clean house. Maybe this will produce results.

In general, one is beginning to get the impression that the general has become stronger as a political figure and, as a rule, is finding the correct solutions. Sometimes it seems he is too cautious and more often than necessary acts with an eye toward the West and the Church. But in the current circumstances brutal methods would only destroy our cause. Along with taking tough, harsh measures on fundamental questions, flexibility and circumspection are required. It is not a bad thing that Jaruzelski is studying the Hungarian experience in their struggle against counter-revolution.

We all well understand that the decisive condition for fully stabilizing the situation in Poland must be the rebirth of the economy. In Czechoslovakia after 1968, political recovery occurred rapidly precisely because the counter-revolution basically did not intrude in that sphere. Here it is the opposite.

In this regard a difficult question has surfaced before us. We find ourselves at the limit of our abilities in terms of assistance to the Poles, yet they are submitting new requests. Perhaps we still have to do something, but we can no longer afford major advances.

Of course we have to respond to Jaruzelski's letter, explaining to him in a comradely way what we can and cannot do. Under any circumstances, we must abide strictly by our delivery schedules for the first quarter—the winter months which are the most difficult for the Poles.

A second matter consists of projects that are a matter of political prestige and do not incur additional pressure on our economy, for example collaborating on the construction of the Warsaw metro. It is worth responding to this request and make our participation publicly known.

By the way, the situation with Polish food supplies is not so hopeless. There is enough bread in the country, and it is only necessary to find an approach to the peasants, to motivate them, and to mend, as they used to say in our country, the union between town and country.

The Polish leadership also continues to count on aid from the West. Well, in principle we cannot oppose this, although frankly it is doubtful whether the Westerners would materially support a military government. They will undoubtedly solicit concessions and here special vigilance will be needed.

Jaruzelski poses another question: Can he accept aid from the Chinese? And strictly speaking, why not? In this case, China is isolating itself from the USA with its economic sanctions.

In conclusion, one can say that the Polish question will be at the center of international politics for a long time. Therefore, our Polish Commission will have to work just as actively as it has up till now.

Tikhonov: Regarding the construction of the metro, the Council of Ministers has already prepared suitable proposals and submitted them to the Politburo.

Chernenko: The proposals regarding our participation in the construction of the metro in Warsaw are currently being voted on in the Politburo.

Suslov: The discussion with Czyrek, in my opinion, was highly useful. He himself creates a good impression and views correctly the state of affairs in Poland and the tasks facing the Polish leadership.

Gromyko: I had a thorough discussion, and I would say, negotiations were held with the Polish Ministry of Foreign Affairs. They touched on many aspects of mutual relations between our countries. Of course, the main emphasis was on the current situation in Poland and on mutual relations between Poland and the USSR. The discussion took place under good conditions. Cde. Czyrek posed a number of requests. I replied that they will be examined carefully. As Cde. Tikhonov has already reported, the question of our participation in the construction of the metro has been examined and submitted for review to the Politburo.

Ustinov: Czyrek truly makes a good impression, and the discussions between him and Cdes. Suslov and Gromyko have great significance because all questions were raised.

Andropov: Cde. Czyrek will probably inform the PUWP CC Politburo of the course of discussions he had here, and this will have great significance.

The decision is adopted:

1. To approve the discussions held by Cde. M.A. Suslov and the negotiations held by Cde. A.A. Gromyko with the Minister of Foreign Affairs of the Polish People's Republic Cde. Czyrek.

2. The CPSU CC Commission on Poland and the USSR Council of Ministers are instructed to examine the questions arising from the discussions and negotiations which Cdes. Suslov and Gromyko held with Cde. Czyrek, and when ready to submit suitable proposals to the CPSU CC.

3. Letter from Cde. W. Jaruzelski of January 3, 1982

Brezhnev: I have asked that this letter be distributed. I know that Cde. Tikhonov instructed the appropriate ministries and departments to prepare a reply to Cde. Jaruzelski.

In the letter, as you see, Cde. Jaruzelski expresses deep gratitude for the fraternal help provided by the Soviet Union to the Polish People's Republic. At the same time, he makes a request that the Soviet side confirm the level of deliveries for 1982 contained in the draft protocol on the coordination of plans by both countries for 1981–1985 for oil, benzene and petroleum products. Delivery levels for oil in 1982 are being kept at 13 million tons, for petroleum products at 2.94 million tons. We should realize maximum levels of fuel oil deliveries in the first quarter of 1982.

Further, Cde. Jaruzelski informs us that he has addressed the general secretaries of the communist parties of Bulgaria, the GDR, Bulgaria, Romania and Czechoslovakia with a request for essential economic aid, in particular to supply the domestic market with basic agricultural and industrial goods.

More than once we have dealt with the question of supplemental measures in providing aid to the Polish People's Republic. Right now I have raised the question simply in order to have an exchange of opinions. It is obvious that we cannot refuse the Poles entirely on everything; we have to try to find something and some way to help. Therefore, on the one hand, I ask that the comrades expedite their examination of the questions they are entrusted with, and to submit the appropriate materials to the Politburo. On the other hand, I ask that they try to decide certain positions in the affirmative.

Tikhonov: Of course it is obvious we have to look for more ways to help Poland, although difficulties do exist.

Baibakov: Leonid Ilyich, I would like to pose two issues. The first relates to additional supplies of oil. I have very carefully looked at our oil reserves and there seems to be absolutely no way to find an additional supply of oil for the PPR. It seems to me that we already supply Poland with a sufficient quantity of petroleum products, and that they can get by with what is being allotted to them.

The second question concerns supplies of grain for baking bread. There is bread in the PPR. They did not have a bad harvest this year and state purchases with the better harvest were significantly lower than last year's.

Andropov: They are currently asking for a certain quantity of grain products in order to [be able to] return it in the second quarter.

Suslov: In other words, they are not asking for additional grain but for purposes of restoring it.

Chernenko: The point is to give the Poles half a million tons in the first quarter on a reciprocal basis, so that they can return it the following quarter.

Ustinov: We must pay close attention to this question and see whether this will be possible.

Kirilenko: Of course, it is very difficult for them now to receive any amount of grain from other countries, although they purchased a certain quantity of grain products from Canada.

Brezhnev: If there are no objections, we can adopt the following resolution:

To instruct the Council of Ministers, Gosplan, and the Ministry of Foreign Trade to examine the requests in Cde. Jaruzelski's letter, taking account of the exchange of opinions that has taken place at the Politburo session, and submit suitable proposals to the CPSU CC.

The resolution is adopted.

[…]

[Source: RGANI, Fond 89, Opis 42, Delo 49. Translated by Malcolm Byrne for the National Security Archive.]

Document No. 95: Notes of Polish Ministry of Internal Affairs and Ministry of Defense Meeting on Implementation of Martial Law

January 15, 1982

The swiftness and efficiency of martial law proved that Polish security forces could be relied on to suppress their fellow Poles. (If Soviet forces had been involved, there is still a question how the Poles would have behaved.) This set of notes of a joint meeting of senior officials from the ministries of defense and internal affairs offers an intriguing inside look at how these key agencies saw their own performance. The speakers generally give themselves high marks for the level of preparation, implementation, coordination and commitment to the mission. At the same time, there is a realization of the need to be aware of the political dimensions of their task, i.e. the need to persuade the Polish people of the legitimacy of their operation.

The notes also lay out in some detail the sheer scale of the undertaking. Tens of thousands of troops were available for action and dozens of preparatory exercises on a wide range of tasks took place—forty "large operations" by the Ministry of Internal Affairs alone—beginning in 1980.

In addition to reviewing the events of December 13, this document also deals with the next stage of follow-on operations designed to keep the lid clamped down on society. In some areas, such as communications between ministries, the situation looks encouraging for military planners, whereas major difficulties loom in areas such as maintaining adequate troop levels, given that major reserve call-ups would mean depleting the availability of farm hands across the country. Martial law was suspended in December 1982 but officially remained in effect until July 1983.

Report

of the joint session of representatives of the MND General Staff, as well as representatives of the MSW Staff on January 15, 1982.

On January 15, 1982, a session took place under the leadership of Minister of Internal Affairs Major General C. Kiszczak with representatives of the MND General Staff and MSW Staff.

From the General Staff branch, Comrade Generals F. Siwicki, J. Skalski, A. Jasiński, M. Dachowski, M. Dębicki, E. Poradko, W. Szklarski participated;

From the MSW Staff branch, Comrade Generals B. Stachura, W. Ciastoń, J. Beim, Z. Sarewicz, as well as Comrade Colonels H. Starszak, F. Jóźwiak, B. Pawlikowski.

Comrade Major General J. Skalski advised that the Armed Forces, in the first stage (December 13–January 6), were placed in a state of readiness, [for a] so-called immediate threat of combat. Assigned detachments supported the operations of martial forces pertaining to coercing law and order, as well as ensuring conditions for the functioning of authority.

Troops became familiarized with assignments after receiving the signal. Military operations were conducted under conditions of intense cold and snow. Primary operations relating to guarding objectives were conducted by forces of about 15,000 soldiers. Defense of the Brześć-Poznań, as well as Hrubieszow-Śląsk-Legnica and other lines of communications—connecting about 4,100 km—was conducted by forces of 6,000 soldiers from transport and railway units.

Improvements were also carried out to the operational positioning of all troops, which was tied with the need to move the military into large areas. Sea and air forces were placed in a state of readiness and assigned tasks.

MND forces guaranteed quarters for about 30,000 persons belonging to the Citizens' Police martial forces. Cadres and soldiers executed posted orders with self-sacrifice and commitment through the full acceptance of decisions.

Good consultation [occurred] during the period discussed on cooperation and joint operations with the organs of the [MSW].

On January 5, at a session of the MND expanded leadership group, operations to date [were] recapitulated and new assignments for the second stage [were] decided upon.

In the near future, the Armed Forces will accept full readiness to assist martial forces and ensure the functioning of the administration. In this period, required maneuvers and regrouping of forces [were] executed. In sum, 20,000 soldiers [were] readied, who at any moment can be used for action. Furthermore, the deployment of reliable forces (70,000) prepared for action [was] executed around large agglomerations (Warsaw, Gdańsk, Szczecin, Bydgoszcz, Łódz, Katowice, Poznań, Lublin). To specified regions, it is possible to introduce 40 percent strength [for troops traveling] within 2–3 hours, 10 percent strength up to 13–15 hours, and 50 percent strength in the space of 1.5–2 days.

In fact, in comparison to the first stage operations, the quantity of demarcated forces is greater. With regard to the new disposition of troops, [it was] established that CP forces will fill the gaps occasioned by troop repositioning. The speaker emphasized that information from Military District commanders does not confirm earlier decisions (regarding introducing CP forces in place of the military); on the contrary, they point to decreasing CP forces.

A state of readiness is still [being] continued in the air forces. However, changes are being introduced pertaining to defense of the maritime boundary by transferring defense of that border to the MFG. He expressed the view that the military ought to withdraw from guarding certain MITS objectives. In further declarations, he submitted the following motions, proposing, in order, to:

1) increase the participation of [MSW] forces in martial operations;
2) take over the guarding of certain industrial objectives by MSW forces;
3) take over guarding railways by the [Railway Guards Service] and CP;

4) relieve certain military barracks objectives occupied by the CP. Since the military occupied certain civilian objectives, [the MSW] could occupy them;

5) execute reciprocal services, needs and accounts together with [the MSW].

In conclusion, he discussed the plan for military operations in the second stage accepted by the Chief of [the General] Staff. He emphasized that in spite of expressed opinions here and there, the military did not cut down on their operations, and on the contrary strengthened them.

Comrade Maj. Gen. A. Jasiński discussed mobilization problems of the armed forces, as well as conscripts entering the ranks of Ministry [of Internal Affairs] forces beside the national [armed forces]. He stated that, among others, 24 infantry battalions were deployed, also three battalions and 13 companies to guard objectives. In total, over 15,000 reservists were called up to the armed forces. [This] took place simultaneously during the course of the alert. The organs of internal affairs made a major contribution in preparing the call up of reservists. Operations, in the period discussed, were carried out proficiently and the bearing of persons called up was good. Here, the speaker thanked [the Ministry of] Internal Affairs for their assistance, chiefly pertaining to selecting persons. He appealed for further assistance in this area. Discussing further intentions, he emphasized that the military, until the end of February, does not anticipate liquidating (releasing) deployed units—conceding, however, minor discharges in individual cases (a lottery, for workers). With accepted policy as the backdrop, a motion also surfaced that [the Ministry of] Internal Affairs should not conduct discharges of persons called up to the CP. The MND is not instituting further deployment of units, although they do not exclude the possibility of deploying, for instance, railway units. Next, he discussed the intentions of the General Staff pertaining to discharges and the calling up of a new class [of conscripts], as well as variations for complementing [troop] strength. He advised also that, until the end of February, [MND is] anticipating a call-up of 60 field [labor] companies composed of elements [persons] not employed anywhere and not studying. He expressed the view that, while selecting the above-mentioned persons, the assistance of the organs of [the Ministry of] Internal Affairs will be valuable.

In conclusion, he brought up the matter of soldiers who took part in operations and distinguished themselves at the time of those operations. He appealed to [the Ministry of] Internal Affairs to assist these soldiers upon discharge with finding jobs, as well as getting into college (if need be without exams). Military organs will deliver the questionnaires from these soldiers to the proper CP units.

Comrade Brigadier General E. Poradko discussed a program prepared with MSW representatives of easing certain consequences of martial law. This program constitutes, among other things:

Pertaining to order and security
– easing MSW instructions relating to curfew hours, conveying decisions on these matters to the provincial administrator, and also dispensing penalties for violations of regulations pertaining to compulsory conduct;

– retain the obligation to obtain agreement for temporary visits solely in large agglomerations, and only with reference to persons between 11 and 60 years of age;
– allow the organization of sessions of administrative organs, the PUWP, as well as the allied [political] parties;
– transfer to provincial administrators' decisions on permitting the organization of cultural and sports events.

At the same time, it would be good to tighten controls warning of regulations concerning curfew hours, the utilization of printing enterprises, as well as introducing a ban on wearing badges, for instance [those of] Solidarity, with regard to the latter motion there are objections inside the KOK:

Pertaining to economic matters
– introduce a ban on strikes, as well as a tightening of the reaction to violations of regulations in this sphere;
– introduce mandatory work;
– reflect on the matter of regulating the problem of private mechanical vehicle traffic.

In passing, he advised that directly after introducing martial law, pressure to militarize enterprises was observed; at present an inclination to demilitarize them [is being] ascertained.

Pertaining to telecommunications
– start radio communications on the Baltic coast;
– start telexes in the embassies of socialist countries;
– partly unblock telexes in the country;
– retain restrictions on city-to-city telephone communications;
– retain control of telephone conversations and censorship of posts;
– bring to an end the depositing of radio devices, broadcast-receivers.

Pertaining to the centers of mass media
– start Program Two of Polish Radio;
– after verifying [vetting] employees, start regional broadcasts;
– successively launch certain publications (*Życie Warszawy, Życie Gospodarcze*).

Comrade Maj. Gen. M. Dębicki discussed the state of security in the armed forces during the period after the introduction of martial law, emphasizing that it was very good. No enemy activities were noted on the political scene, nor desertions. This was the result of many months of training operations, as well as eliminating unreliable elements. The speaker emphasized that consultations [were] very good with MSW organs, whose signals [alarms] were utilized by military authorities. In subsequent comments, he stated that in the present situation it is imperative that MSW [special] services and military counterintelligence continue to operate jointly. He indicated that the holding of meetings by representatives of these services at the provincial level would be advisable for conducting an appraisal of the state of security. It would also be worthwhile to begin discussions with meetings of representatives of [special] services at the headquarters' level.

In subsequent comments, he brought up the matter of inspections at military installations and indicated that it would be good to introduce a system to realize such inspections.

In the concluding comments, referring to the matter of discharging the third class [third year conscripts], he suggested recruiting some of those released for work with [the Ministry of] Internal Affairs. He emphasized that the [Army Security Service] organs are ready to deliver to the Ministry [of Internal Affairs] individual sources of intelligence.

Comrade General F. Siwicki commented that demarcation for next movements and force utilization is set for the third part of February. Until then, they should maintain static forces, as well as repeatedly upgrade them in order to enforce more martial law prerogatives afterwards. Notwithstanding the specific positioning of forces, it is still necessary to maintain control over all the important arteries—on provincial borders. Also, [there] should be a more flexible approach to the matter of neighborhood patrols. The fact of the appearance, for instance, of a printed leaflet in some neighborhood should already prompt increased patrol duties starting the following day.

Considering the matter of guarding railway junctions, he acknowledged that this problem should reflect a resolution such that troops could cease guarding and occupy themselves appropriately—with repair work.

Taking a position on the matter of the field companies, he instructed that persons not studying anywhere and not employed be called up to fill [those positions], but not, for instance, the higher class of KOR activists. Calling up 6,000 persons to field companies will not resolve all of the "idling" [*nierobów*] problems. [We] need to prevail upon provincial administrators to profit from the powers resulting from martial law and to call up unemployed persons to work for the national economy.

Recognizing that at the present time withdrawing from the militarization of enterprises is not possible, he asserted that these matters should not be raised at all at the moment. The fact that some enterprise is militarized does not mean, after all, that everyone must work 12 hours a day. During work hours, at these enterprises the directors decide. In conclusion, he emphasized the good work of the financial services. He stated that as far as financial questions go, referring to employees of our ministries—[they] will follow uniform principles.

Comrade Maj. Gen. B. Stachura introduced problems that will be discussed in turn by comrades present at the meeting. Next, he discussed the most important work conducted during the period by our Ministry. He stated that the operations of our Ministry in the sphere presently being discussed began during the second half of 1980. Beginning at that time our Ministry conducted 40 large operations requiring the use of a serious number of forces as well as convoys. The main effort of the Ministry fell during the period of preparations for martial law. The most important operation, just before the introduction of martial law, covered the operation at the Higher Officers' Firefighters' Academy. Over a period from the second half of 1980, the Ministry trained 30,000 reservists and, before the introduction of martial law, called up 20 companies of the VRCP. After the introduction of martial law, [it] conducted operations "Fir," "Azalea," and "Ramses." To realize operations "Azalea" and "Ramses" military forces took part. To emphasize, he credits very good collaboration between the Ministry of Internal Affairs services and the military.

The Ministry called up the Office of Military Censorship. At present, operation "Maple" is being conducted, to which our Ministry attaches much weight because within the framework of this operation talks have been conducted with persons who could stand as the second and third echelon of Solidarity activists.

On account of the introduction of martial law, the Ministry called up 46,000 reservists to the CP and 3,600 to the VMU MSW. At the moment there are problems with these reservists because most of them are farmers who are indispensable to running farms. Forces at the Ministry schools constitute a serious reserve for the Ministry—at the present time reaching a need to begin studies at the schools. The Ministry faces problems as to how it should distribute our forces most advantageously. Ultimately it will be possible to take a position after carrying out an appraisal of the political-operational situation. That is also why, in the opinion of the speaker, totally replacing the military patrols cannot be managed. There will be difficulty for the CP, for instance, in taking over the guarding of objectives like butcher shops or bakeries. This subject should still be studied and settled.

Added difficulty for the Ministry is created by the fact that to billet our forces we are taking a lot of space at hostels and schools, which have to be abandoned in connection with the commencement of operations.

In conclusion, the speaker thanked the leadership of the MND General Staff for assistance and understanding the needs of our Ministry.

Comrade Brig. Gen. W. Ciastoń stated that as a consequence of Ministry operations the strength of the enemy to undertake wide protest actions in the country has been hindered. For instance, at work establishments strike actions [have been] limited to 199 enterprises in the whole country, and strike committees have come into being in only 50 enterprises. Street manifestations arose only in Gdańsk on December 15 and 17. A manifestation in Warsaw has not materialized.

Thanks to the course of action undertaken the structures of Solidarity, both national and regional, have been smashed and its printing base liquidated, and the isolation of top CIP and KOR activists, as well as the extremist activists of Solidarity, has been achieved. Obtaining documents from the addresses of particular [Solidarity] Regional Committees allowed for the compromising of adversaries, as well as Solidarity's "extremes." At the present moment the possibility of organizing mass protest actions are not envisioned, although on January 13 certain actions in Wrocław and Warsaw were noted. Reaction is immediate to activities of this type. Instigators are ascertained and arrested.

Another indication of enemy activities are the flying publishers. In these cases the SB reacts quickly and concretely. For instance, a secret printer was liquidated in Wrocław. Characterizing the situation in particular Polish centers, he emphasized that after December 13 work establishments are functioning normally. The last strike ended on December 28 in Ziemowit. No deliberate instances of vandalism or sabotage [have been] noted. Personnel [are] working normally and Solidarity activists no longer have much influence in enterprises. Nuisances, difficulties and bitterness towards enterprises result against the background of material provisioning, low wages. In intellectual and cultural circles the situation is still unfavorable. The introduction of martial law continues to be treated as an attack on independence and freedom. In spite of this, in these circles absolutely no concrete action has been taken. In student circles attempts to organize strikes [have been] taken, which in some cases were met with the approval of school administrators (in Warsaw and Wrocław). In relation to the mood that reigns among certain educational workers it will be necessary to count on the possibility that the operation to verify cadres may be impeded.

The Catholic Church reacted negatively to the introduction of martial law. After Archbishop Glemp's talks with Premier Jaruzelski, that position was somewhat mitigated. Nevertheless, the Church continues to come out in defense of the interned, of the sector integrating persons in hiding, of opposing verification, and of exerting pressure to repeal martial law.

[Handwritten:] *Comrade Brig. Gen. W. Ciastoń:*

Suspension of the APJ limited the Association's opportunity for activities. [They are] [p]resently conducting verification of journalists [and] [a]ctivating the positions of persons with a positive standing. Against the background of the characteristics mentioned above, the speaker acknowledged that the political situation will have a bearing on:

1) the economic situation, as well as the market;

2) Church initiatives speaking for Solidarity;

3) the existence of real possibilities for illegal activities.

In conclusion, he presented the general outlook of the Security Service with regard to the materializing political-operational situation. He remarked that the economic situation, and also the rise in prices will lead to a strengthening of enemy propaganda and also to calls for massive resistance. Illegal activities by Solidarity could also appear. It appears that these activities are limited mainly to propaganda actions.

So far as the Church goes, as well as intellectual circles, they are bound to rebuild Solidarity as a factor in weakening authority.

Comrade Brig. Gen. J. Beim, assessing the state of security, emphasized that until December 12, 1981, in spite of a series of operations, there remained a constant tendency towards increased criminal offenses. From August 1981, only the number of traffic violations decreased; that was tied, however, to fuel restrictions. During the period from December 13 to December 23, a clear drop in the number of offenses took place; after that period, an increase in criminal offenses committed by recidivists was observed. As far as speculation offenses go—it can be stated that the conditions exist for committing them. [It is] [s]till difficult to quantify how much of an increase has taken place; however, uncovering them has become more frequent as a result of intensified CP operations in this sector.

514

At present, [they are] conducting a regrouping of CP forces. A series of detachments [are] returning to home units. CP representatives executed General Staff decisions in joint operations. From his side, he proposed maintaining the current status of roving units until the end of critical operations. Simultaneously, it would be necessary to take advantage of this period for [obtaining] better supplies from the quartermaster.

He declared himself in favor of considering third year CP soldiers the same as third year [soldiers] in the Armed Forces, and also [considering] those who, after completing service, desire a job with the CP. To perform sentry duties, 13,500 reservists were called up. Because many of them are farmers a need will arise to discharge 3,000 persons. In relation to the matter of the field companies, he declared that he will assist in designating persons for these companies.

In subsequent comments, he considered the matter of guarding certain objectives by the CP as well as railway junctions in case the troops withdraw. He asserted that this would occasion the need for a decrease of about 30,000 in the number of functionaries assigned to patrol the streets. As far as guarding certain butcher shops or bakeries goes, it would be necessary to coordinate this subject. Guarding these objectives could be conducted through normal patrol operations.

He proposed to continue taking advantage of VRCP members for operations at enterprises, and also to call them up for patrol duties. He declared himself in favor of a further call-up of reservists who would replace discharged farmers.

In conclusion, he considered the matter of controlling traffic between provinces in agreement with the system of blockades worked out by the Office of Road Traffic.

Comrade Colonel F. Jóźwiak remarked that calling up reservists occasioned the need to ensure supplies, which had to be utilized under very difficult circumstances. He emphasized that the Ministry's services would not be in a state to execute these tasks if not for the enormous assistance of the MND. For emphasis, he also credits the assistance of the military police, without whom it would be difficult to quarter many units.

Most Ministry forces were housed in MND buildings, schools and hostels. Some of the buildings have already been vacated; however, the Ministry continues to occupy 24 hostels and nine schools, which have to be vacated.

Great difficulties with supplies arose from the fact of having to keep a significant number of Ministry forces mobilized. Added difficulties occurred when these forces switched to spring uniforms. In such a situation it becomes important for military cells in industry to take into account the needs of our Ministry and enable these deliveries to run efficiently.

Comrade Col. H. Starszak, discussing the course of Operation "Fir", emphasized that it ran very efficiently. This was the result of good preparations, which lasted many months. To fulfill the operation, [it was] launched on December 13 at 0:00 [midnight]. Four hours after beginning the operation, 24 percent of the persons expected to be interned were interned; after six hours—39 percent; after [illegible] hours—57 percent; after twelve hours—70 percent. In total, 5,969 persons were detained. Some persons were released for humanitarian considerations, and also after conducting talks and ascertaining that there was a great probability that these persons would not act against the state. With reference to 87 persons interned, arrests applied. At the present time, 4,971 persons remain in internment centers. They are distributed among 24 centers, four of which function as vacation centers.

After describing the social conditions of internees, he discussed the problem of the number of criminal investigations commenced to date, the numbers and levels of penalties dispensed by the courts, as well as the number of verdicts in the proceedings before the *kolegia*.[7] He emphasized that a feeling prevails that court verdicts do not fulfill preventive functions. Examples are often noted of summary justice being repealed and the matter transferred to normal proceedings.

In conclusion, he discussed examples of not-guilty verdicts. To a question by Gen. Siwicki, he advised that the number of not-guilty verdicts before the common courts comes to 4 percent, and before the military courts 20 percent.

Comrade Brig. Gen. Z. Sarewicz advised that as a result of a worsening of the socio-political situation in the country the Second Department [of the MSW], in early spring 1981, undertook complex, long-range operational-organizational activities in defensive operations around communications and RTV objectives. They had as their aim ensuring the continued functioning of these objectives in every situation, as well as creating essential conditions for the fulfillment of fundamental Ministry operations in case of "W".[8]

The following course of action was adopted at the time:

1) strengthening of operational positions at guarded objectives;
2) operational selection of personnel, among other things, with the aim of appointing cadres of trusted employees to fulfill assignments in threatening situations, as well as persons to be removed from objectives;
3) organizing and educating groups of counterparts to undertake independent employment in [sensitive] positions;
4) development of a system of blocking telecommunications signals;
5) development and training of a system of joint operations. In developed operation plans, pressure was exerted towards excluding opponents from RTV and maintaining Program One of television and radio at all costs.

From the beginning, PPA representatives took part in preparations. Already in February of last year, together with the MND General Staff and specifically with its First Administration, [they] selected 167 communications objectives to place under military guard in case of martial law.

Preparations intensified in August in relation to the sharpened internal situation in the country.

---

[7] *Kolegia* were legal bodies, usually composed of party members or local authorities, that had jurisdiction over minor offenses.

[8] "W" refers to *stan wojenny* or martial law.

After developing joint plans, [they] established direct contacts with PPA sub-unit commanders who were selected to secure particular objectives. [The] [e]nabled them, by operational means, to become familiar with objectives, and indicated the most [sensitive] points at objectives requiring specific protection.

Specific plans [were] jointly prepared to control objectives, taking into account the access routes from static posts, signal officers' system of communications with unit commanders, accommodations for sentry changes, and arms and ammunition.

Specific phases of the operation were exercised jointly in a very detailed manner so as to be ready for "W" hour.

During meetings with sub-unit commanders, details of tasks, aims and self-control functions were discussed. Among other things, [this included] the range of rules for applying the pass system in order to hinder access to the territory of objectives by undesirable persons.

In operations to control the communications objectives of PR [Polish Radio] and TV, as well as block telecommunications signals, about 700 employees of Department T, the Second [Department], and other units of the VHCP, among others; 350 Citizens' Police and ZOMO functionaries, and over 7,000 PPA troops were used.

These operations—as we are evaluating them—ended with complete success and provided essential support for the main operations:

- our joint operations featured speed, resoluteness, and significant efficiency;
- RTV and communications objectives—some of them as large as the center at Woronicza Street [in Warsaw]—were seized literally within a few minutes, and in such a way that they were not used by opponents to transmit information about our operation; and at the same time emissions were not disturbed;
- this was possible only as a result of keeping our operations completely secret, in spite of the fact that numerous forces from different departments of the MSW, MND, Communications, and Committee for RTV Affairs were engaged in it.

Of course, there were stumbles, mainly from our side; for instance, communications in four voivodeships were mistakenly disconnected, but they were not evident in the final results.

On the positive outcome of the operation, above all, it rested on very good joint operations with the armed forces at all levels and in all phases of preparation and implementation. Also good were the joint operations within the framework of the Ministry. Morale and enormous commitment deserve special emphasis, as does the discipline of PPA soldiers. Their resoluteness and decisiveness repeatedly turned out to be the fundamental element in the efficient fulfillment of operations at given objectives. The military continues effectively to support the activities of our operational groups, which undertook intense operational work at these objectives, although its role is different at the moment. In particular, cooperation pertaining to a precise fulfillment of the inspection-pass system passes the test. The normalization of the situation in the country, and also in guarding objectives, allows for a gradual withdrawal of troops from these objectives. [They are] considering decreasing the military defense of objectives taken in operation "Azalea." Among other things, [they are] proposing to stand guard over three city-to-city [telecommunications] exchanges (Warsaw, Katowice, Szczecin) and 12 Voivodeship Exchange junction-exchanges, but considering the possibility of decreasing defense by 50 percent. In the remaining communications objectives, PA [Polish Army] units could be withdrawn, and their defense could be performed by a system of mixed (PA and CP) mobile patrols. In RTV objectives the presence of PA units is considered still advisable in view of the preparations to initiate further programming, as well as the continued verification of cadres. In case of the withdrawal or reduction of military forces it is necessary to consider the advisability of creating assigned detachments in the provinces to remain at the disposition of the VHCP or KOK for quick reaction in case of threats at these objectives.

In conclusion, taking advantage of the situation, he imparted sincere thanks to the participating soldiers and officers of the PPA.

Comrade Col. B. Pawlikowski emphasized that the Ministry's mobilization system completely passed the test. It relied on CP sentries. Courier and dispatch operations were suitably organized, and there was high organizational efficiency in setting in motion the mobilization. Important assistance was given by the RMH.

In the course of mobilization—44 regiments and eight mobile battalions of the CP, as well as sub-units (platoons, companies) at CP municipal commands and stations [were activated], supplemented by MSW reserve troops. Altogether, over 49,000 reservists, over 3800 mechanical transports were called up to the Ministry. Around 40 percent of the reservists were Solidarity members.

But it is necessary to emphasize the proper stand of the reservists at the time conscription cards were served on their arrival at their units. Many reported voluntarily after the state of "W" was announced. This testifies to good reconnaissance on the person selected to be called up.

The actual state of the discipline of the reservists is good. [They] acted suitably in blockades of enterprises and in liquidating strike actions.

It is necessary to assess highly the results of the joint operation with MND, which was and is the fundamental condition for the success of destroying the counter-revolutionary forces. It embraces all the problems that interest both ministries, and, lastly, specifically embraces: the exchange of information, common planning of legal norms for the state of "W" and the plan for directing the state, securing the physical basis of the operation—internment and disconnecting telecommunications signals, preparing for our Ministry bases for quarters and subsistence, preparing training grounds for maneuvers by Citizens' Police forces, participation in all Citizens' Police operations (Gdańsk, Katowice, Lublin, Warsaw), participation in patrol duties, and disinformation operations.

A positive appraisal [was given] of Citizens' Police and military joint operation, the form of the cooperation, methods of planning, as well as the state of force readiness and means for operations in the state of "W."

Joint operations should be continued and intensified.

Comrade Lt. Gen. F. Siwicki stated that the military still defends about 130 objectives of provincial importance. At the present stage, we can bring an end to military defense. Withdrawn soldiers should immediately go about their assigned tasks.

In connection with information received, that soldiers are being used for duties at centers where the prominent are interned, he announced a requirement not to engage soldiers for these purposes.

In relation to information about foreign correspondents traveling out of town, he expressed the view that surely it is still too early to allow them also to travel—unless certain higher considerations call for it.

The problem of industrial production for defense needs appears bad and the situation is still worsening. That is why it is not possible to count on it very much. It will be necessary to adopt a regime of thrift, utilize used uniforms, and so on. [We] should take into account existing difficulties, because despite utmost kindness, all requests in this period cannot be fulfilled.

In conclusion, he considered the matter of billeting Ministry of Internal Affairs forces. CP forces must abandon schools and hostels, military forces must return to barracks. The Ministry ought to resolve the problem of quarters not only by taking advantage of all opportunities. There may still be some opportunities in the eastern regions.

Comrade Maj. Gen. C. Kiszczak emphasized that this session has accomplished a profitable exchange of information, as well as decisions.

As is evident from reliable sources, the operations of military units were appraised very highly by Western experts, emphasizing the efficiency of regrouping a large number of forces, as well as the fact that secrecy was successfully maintained for such a serious operation. He pointed out that if the opponent mounts cadre changes in their intelligence units this will indirectly constitute an evaluation of our operations. At the present moment, the opponent is conducting a re-evaluation of the state of political-morale in the military, CP and party, because that condition was estimated as being low until now.

Also, our domestic opponents evaluate our operations very highly, and even with respect. They were surprised by the efficiency of the operation, and that it had been conducted with such small losses.

Both of our ministries conducted the operation efficiently. So far as the Ministry of Internal Affairs goes, it conducted the assigned task in the first stage thanks to the assistance, including material, of the MND. The speaker, in the name of the leadership of the Ministry, expressed thanks for that assistance.

At today's session, a series of proposals were formulated on the matter of alleviating the rigors of martial law. These proposals are valid; however, fulfillment of them will depend on many factors, such as the course of the operation, price changes, whether universities will be reopened, the opponent intensifying conspiratorial activities and the intensification of incidents of diversion and sabotage. Alleviation of strictness must be introduced in such a manner as not to allow the opponent to take advantage of the situation.

The current period will allow for bringing discipline to society. If we do not take advantage of this, we may not have another [period] like this for long.

All instances of violations of martial law regulations must be severely enforced. Ring leaders have to be diligently and severely punished. The situation in this area, as the data indicates, is not good.

Serious tasks stand before us, the accomplishment of which we cannot expect from different institutions. It is a question of destroying the old structures of Solidarity, PAN, and the like, so as to appoint new ones, totally at the discretion of the party. In this area, MSW, SSA and party joint operations are indispensable. In justifiable circumstances, in the field of operations, it is even possible to opt for a division of tasks.

A series of tasks, until now performed by MND, must be taken on by the MSW. However, we are not in a position to take on all of them, and such a need has not even occurred. [We] ought to shrewdly evaluate the situation in the enterprises which MND will cease guarding and which there is no need for us to assume guarding.

The Ministry must execute a regrouping of our forces and means. We will do everything not to turn to the military for assistance regarding quarters. It is necessary to base ourselves at our rest centers; however, should our contingents become exhausted, we will then turn for assistance in facilitating accommodations to military centers.

[We] ought to assume operations during the period in which price changes are introduced and universities reopened. It is necessary to reflect on what to do in order to guard and calm people against irresponsible acts. If the matter of prices and reopening of universities is precisely prepared and introduced, we will have calm until late spring.

As far as VRCP goes—some people must be released (farmers, and the like) and younger ones called up in their place. Observing this kind of practice will indicate that our Ministry is not withdrawing from the operations conducted.

The speaker turned to the SSA organs about also directing their work to uncover illegal activities and relieve tensions.

The proposal to conduct joint military-police inspections on the provincial borders is valid. [We] should also strengthen inspections at railway stations.

The Ministry has cadre troubles and will be grateful for assistance in resolving them by eliminating vacancies with soldiers released to the reserves.

The comrade minister explained that trips to the interior of the country by Western journalists occurred on the instructions of Deputy Premier Rakowski, and the whole matter is being steered by Captain Górnicki.

The speaker gave instructions to recall the military guards [overseeing] prominent internees. In conclusion, the comrade minister sincerely thanked the representatives of the General Staff for providing assistance, as well as for participating in the working meeting.

Comrade Lt. Gen. F. Siwicki, offering thanks for the hospitality, stated that embarrassing praises are being directed at the military. He emphasized, however, that during operations the employees of the Ministry of Internal Affairs were on the front lines.

Meeting began 17:10
Meeting ended 20:20

[…]

[Source: *Bogusław Kopka, Grzegorz Majchrzak, eds.,* Stan Wojenny w Dokumentach Władz PRL (1980–1983) *(Warszawa: Instytut Pamięci Narodowej, 2001), pp. 129–145. Translated by L. W. Głuchowski for the National Security Archive.]*

Main Actors

[Unless otherwise noted, positions listed for each person are those held during the 1980–1981 period.]

Allen, Richard V.: National security advisor to President Ronald Reagan from 1981–1982.

Andropov, Yurii Vladimirovich: chairman of KGB; member of CPSU Politburo; member of Politburo Commission on Poland.

Aristov, Boris Ivanovich: Soviet ambassador to Poland.

Arkhipov, Ivan Vasil'evich: member of CPSU CC; first deputy prime minister; member of CPSU CC Politburo's Commission on Poland.

Baibakov, Nikolai Konstantinovich: member of CPSU CC; deputy prime minister; chairman of Gosplan.

Barcikowski, Kazimierz: Member of PUWP CC; deputy Politburo member until September 1980, then full member; from October 1980, secretary of PUWP CC.

Bartoszcze, Roman: member of the United Peasant's Party until December 1981; activist in Rural Solidarity; participant in the Bydgoszcz strike in March 1981; interned during martial law.

Beksiak, Janusz: economic adviser to Gierek until 1979; from September 1980, member and adviser to Solidarity; in 1981, member of the Programmatic-Consultative Center for Social-Occupational Works attached to the National Commission of Solidarity.

Berlinguer, Enrico: national secretary of the Italian Communist Party.

Borusewicz, Bogdan: member of KOR; among the leadership of the August 1980 strike at Lenin Shipyard in Gdańsk; subsequently on the Inter-Factory Founding Committee of Solidarity in the Gdańsk Region; during martial law, member of underground Solidarity leadership.

Brezhnev, Leonid Ilyich: general secretary of the CPSU from October 1964–November 1982.

Brown, Harold: U.S. secretary of defense until January 1981.

Brzezinski, Zbigniew: national security advisor to President Carter from 1977–1981.

Bugaj, Ryszard: leading member of Mazowsze branch of Solidarity; interned on December 13, 1981.

Bujak, Zbigniew: organizer of the strike in Solidarity with the Lenin Shipyard at the "Ursus" factory in August 1980; from September 1980, chairman of Mazowsze branch of Solidarity; member of the Presidium of National Coordinating Commission; went underground on December 13, 1981 to act as the head of the Regional Executive Commission in the Mazowsze Region; arrested in May 1986.

Carter, Jimmy: president of the United States from 1977–1981.

Ceaușescu, Nicolae: president of Romania from 1974–1989; general (then first) secretary of the Romanian Communist Party from 1965–1989.

Celiński, Andrzej: member of KOR; secretary of the Presidium of Inter-Factory Strike Committee in Gdańsk; subsequently secretary of the Presidium of National Conciliation Committee for Solidarity; interned in the martial law period.

Chernenko, Konstantin Ustinovich: member of CPSU Politburo; CPSU CC Secretary; chief, General Department, CC CPSU; member of Politburo Commission on Poland.

Christopher, Warren W.: deputy secretary of state until January 1981.

Ciosek, Stanisław: member of PUWP CC from February 1980 to July 1981; regional PUWP first secretary from 1975–1980; minister-member of the Council of Ministers in charge of contacts with trade unions from 1980–1985.

Cypryniak, Kazimierz: first secretary of Szczecin Voivodeship Committee from May 1980 to May 1981; from April–July 1981, member of PUWP CC; head of the Political-Organizational Department of PUWP CC from 1981.

Czyrek, Józef: minister of foreign affairs from August 1980–July 1982; from February 1980, member of PUWP CC; from July 1981, secretary PUWP CC; from July 1981, member of PUWP Politburo.

Dąbrowski, Archbishop Bronisław: general secretary of the Episcopate of Poland; chairman of the Legal Commission of the Episcopate; delegate of the Conference of the Episcopate of Poland for relations with the government of the Polish People's Republic.

Demichev, Pyotr Nilovich: Soviet minister of culture; candidate member of CPSU Politburo.

Dobrynin, Anatoly: Soviet ambassador to the United States.

Dolgikh, Vladimir Ivanovich: secretary of CPSU CC; chief, CPSU CC Department of Heavy Industry.

Eagleburger, Lawrence S.: U.S. ambassador to Yugoslavia until January 1981; assistant secretary of state for European and Canadian affairs from May 1981–February 1982.

Fiszbach, Tadeusz: first secretary of PUWP Voivodeship Committee in Gdańsk; signatory of the Gdańsk Agreement; from December 1980–July 1981, member of PUWP Politburo.

Frasyniuk, Władysław: co-organizer of the strike in Wrocław in August 1980; member of Inter-Factory Founding Committee of the Lower Silesia Region; from February 1981, Solidarity chairman of the Lower Silesia Region, member of the National Coordinating Commission and National Commission Presidium; from December 13, 1981, underground chairman of the Regional Strike Committee of the Lower Silesia Region.

Geremek, Bronisław: adviser to the Inter-Factory Strike Committee at the Lenin Shipyard, August 1980; adviser to National Coordinating Commission; chairman of the Programmatic-Consultative Council of Solidarity's National Commission; delegate to Solidarity's first Delegates' Congress and chairman of the programmatic commission; interned for a year beginning December 13, 1981.

Gierek, Edward: PUWP first secretary from December 1970–September 1980.

Gil, Mieczysław: member of Solidarity's National Coordinating Commission.

Giscard d'Estaing, Valery: president of France from 1974–1981.

Glemp, Archbishop Józef: bishop of Warmia; from May 1981, primate of Poland.

Główczyk, Jan: member of PUWP CC; from July 1981, deputy member of PUWP Politburo.

Gomułka, Władysław: PUWP first secretary from October 1956–December 1970.

Gorbachev, Mikhail Sergeevich: member of CPSU Politburo; Secretary of CPSU CC.

Górnicki, Wiesław: correspondent of leading Polish journals; close adviser to Jaruzelski.

Grabski, Tadeusz: member of PUWP CC; from December 1980–July 1981, candidate member of PUWP Politburo.

Grishin, Victor Vasil'evich: member of CPSU Politburo; first secretary of Moscow party committee.

Gromyko, Andrei Andreevich: Soviet minister of foreign affairs; member of CPSU Politburo; member of Politburo Commission on Poland.

Grzyb, Zofia: first female member of PUWP Politburo, from July 1981; Solidarity member until October 1981.

Gwiazda, Andrzej: Solidarity activist; one of the leaders of the Gdańsk strikes.

Haig, Alexander M.: U.S. secretary of state from January 1981–July 1982.

Honecker, Erich: SED first secretary from 1971–1989.

Husák, Gustáv: president of Czechoslovakia from 1975–1989; general (then first) secretary of CPCz from 1969–1987.

Jabłoński, Henryk: member of PUWP Politburo; president of the State Council.

Jagielski, Mieczysław: member of PUWP Politburo from 1971–July 1981; Polish deputy prime minister until July 1981.

Janowski, Gabriel: founding member and deputy chairman of Rural Solidarity.

Jaruzelski, Wojciech: Army general; PUWP first secretary from October 1981–July 1989; prime minister from February 1981–November 1985; minister of national defense from 1968–1983; chairman of the Military Council for National Salvation (WRON) from December 1981.

John Paul II: born Karol Józef Wojtyła, served as Catholic Archbishop of Kraków from 1964–1978; inaugurated pope on October 22, 1978.

Jurczak, Stefan: vice-chairman of the Workers' Commission of the Metallurgists in the Lenin Steelworks and deputy chairman of the Małopolska Region; member of the National Commission of Solidarity.

Jurczyk, Marian: chairman of the Strike Committee of the Szczecin Shipyard and chairman of Inter-Factory Strike Committee Szczecin in 1980; one of the main negotiators and signatory of the Szczecin Agreement of August 30, 1980. From September 1980, chairman of Inter-Factory Regional Committee in Szczecin; from June 1981, chairman of the Board of the Pomeranian-Western Region of Solidarity.

Kádár, János: HSWP first secretary from October 1956–May 1988.

Kania, Stanisław: PUWP first secretary from September 1980–October 1981.

Kapitonov, Ivan Vasilievich: CPSU CC secretary; chief, CPSU CC Organizational Party Work Department.

Kirilenko, Andrei Pavlovich: member of CPSU Politburo; CPSU CC secretary.

Kirkland, Lane: president of AFL-CIO.

Kiszczak, Czesław: Army general; member of PUWP CC from July 1981; minister of internal affairs from August 1981–1990; from December 1981, member of the Military Council for National Salvation.

Klasa, Józef: head of the PUWP CC Department of Press, Radio, and Television from September 1980–June 1981.

Kociołek, Stanisław: first secretary of the PUWP Warsaw Voivodeship Committee from November 1980.

Kowalczyk, Stanisław: member of PUWP Politburo until December 1980; minister of internal affairs until October 1980; deputy prime minister from October 1980–February 1981.

Kruczek, Władysław: member of PUWP Politburo from 1968–December 1980; head of official trade union from 1971–February 1980.

Kryuchkov, Vladimir Aleksandrovich: deputy chairman of the KGB; head of KGB First Main Directorate (for foreign intelligence).

Kubiak, Hieronim: member of PUWP Politburo and PUWP secretary from July 1981.

Kukliński, Ryszard: Army colonel; head of Strategic Planning Office of Polish General Staff from 1976–1981; agent for CIA from 1970–1981. Considered by many to be a national hero who fought for independent Poland.

Kulikov, Viktor Georgievich: Soviet marshal; supreme commander of Warsaw Pact armed forces from 1977–1989.

Kuroń, Jacek: co-founder of KOR; leading adviser of Solidarity.

Kuznetov, Vasilii Vasilievich: candidate member of CPSU Politburo; first deputy chairman of Presidium of Supreme Soviet.

Lis, Bogdan: deputy chairman of Inter-Factory Strike Committee at the Lenin Shipyard, August 1980; signatory of the Gdańsk Agreement; member of National Commission of Solidarity; member of PUWP until expelled in October 1981.

Mazowiecki, Tadeusz: co-founder of Clubs of Catholic Intelligentsia; chairman of commission of experts of the Inter-Factory Strike Committee at the Lenin Shipyard in August 1980; from March–December 1981, editor-in-chief of *Tygodnik Solidarność*.

Meehan, Francis J.: U.S. ambassador to Poland from October 1980–February 1983.

Merkel, Jacek: member of Founding Committee of Solidarity; vice-chairman of the plant commission at the Lenin Shipyard; member of the Presidium of Solidarity's National Commission.

Messner, Zbigniew: from July 1980, member of PUWP CC; from July 1981, member of PUWP Politburo; chairman of Voivodeship Committee from Katowice.

Michnik, Adam: leading Solidarity adviser; member of KOR; editor of independent periodicals: *Biuletyn Informacyjny*, *Zapis*, *Krytyka*.

Milewski, Mirosław: minister of internal affairs from October 1980–July 1981; member of PUWP Politburo and PUWP CC secretary from July 1981.

Moczar, Mieczysław: member of PUWP Politburo from December 1980–July 1981.

Moczulski, Leszek: founder and chairman of Confederation for an Independent Poland.

Modzelewski, Karol: head of the Wrocław Solidarity delegation; Solidarity press spokesman from September 1980–March 1981.

Mondale, Walter F.: vice president of the United States from 1977–1981.

Muskie, Edmund S.: U.S. secretary of state from May 1980–January 1981.

Obodowski, Janusz: minister of labor, wages, and social affairs until July 1981; deputy prime minister from July 1981.

Ogarkov, Nikolai Vasilievich: Soviet marshal; first deputy defense minister; chief of the Soviet General Staff.

Olszowski, Stefan: minister of foreign affairs from July 1982–November 1985; member of the PUWP Politburo; PUWP CC secretary for media information from August 1980–July 1982.

Onyszkiewicz, Janusz: member of the Presidium and spokesman of the Board of the Mazowsze branch of Solidarity; from April–November 1981, spokesman for Solidarity's National Commission.

Orzechowski, Marian: secretary and member of PUWP CC from July 1981.

Pel'she, Arvid Yanovich: full member of CPSU Politburo; chairman of Party Control Committee.

Pińkowski, Józef: prime minister from September 1980–February 1981.

Ponomarev, Boris Nikolaevich: candidate member of CPSU Politburo; CPSU CC secretary; chief of the CPSU CC International Department.

Porębski, Tadeusz: member of PUWP Politburo from July 1981.

Pożoga, Władysław: deputy minister of internal affairs.

Rakhmanin, Oleg Borisovich: first deputy head of the CPSU CC Department for Liason with Communist and Workers' Parties of Socialist Countries; member of the Politburo Commission on Poland.

Rakowski, Mieczysław: editor-in-chief of *Polityka*; deputy prime minister from February 1981.

Reagan, Ronald: president of the United States from 1981–1989.

Rulewski, Jan: chairman of Inter-Factory Strike Committee from September 1980, then Solidarity Inter-Factory Founding Committee in Bydgoszcz; member of the Presidium of Solidarity's National Coordinating Commission from February 1981.

Rusakov, Konstantin Viktorovich: head of CPSU CC Department for Liaison with Communist and Workers' Parties of Socialist Countries.

Schmidt, Helmut: West German chancellor from 1974–1982.

Siła-Nowicki, Władysław: lawyer active with political opposition; adviser to Wałęsa; member of the Programmatic-Consultative Council of Center for Social-Occupational Works attached to the National Commission of Solidarity.

Siwak, Albin: worker; member of PUWP Politburo from July 1981.

Siwicki, Florian: Army general; commandant of Polish forces during the 1968 invasion of Czechoslovakia; chief of Polish General Staff from 1973; deputy member of PUWP Politburo from October 1981; one of the main architects of martial law; member of the Military Council for National Salvation from December 13, 1981.

Słowik, Andrzej: a leading Solidarity activist in the Łódz region.

Suslov, Mikhail Andreevich: full member of CPSU Politburo; CPSU CC Secretary; chairman of the Politburo Commission on Poland.

Thatcher, Margaret: prime minister of Great Britain from 1979–1990.

Tikhonov, Nikolai Aleksandrovich: full member of CPSU Politburo; prime minister from October 1980–September 1985.

Turner, Stansfield: U.S. director of central intelligence from 1977–1981.

Urban, Jerzy: journalist; chief government spokesman from August 20, 1981–1989.

Ustinov, Dmitrii Fedorovich: Soviet marshal; full member of CPSU Politburo; Soviet minister of defense from April 1976–December 1984; member of the Politburo Commission on Poland.

Walentynowicz, Anna: member of the Inter-Factory Strike Committee in Gdańsk; her dismissal in August was a major catalyst for the Gdańsk strikes.

Wałęsa, Lech: electrician; chairman of the Inter-Factory Strike Committee based at the Lenin Shipyard from August 16, 1980; signatory of the Gdańsk Agreement; from September 1980, headed Solidarity's Inter-Factory Founding Committee and subsequently became chairman of Solidarity's National Coordinating Commission; elected chairman of Solidarity at the first National Delegates' Congress.

Werblan, Andrzej: PUWP CC member from 1948; PUWP CC secretary from 1974–July 1981; member of PUWP Politburo from February–December 1980; vice-marshal of the Sejm from 1971–July 1982.

Woźniak, Marian: member of PUWP CC from July 1981; PUWP CC secretary from July 1981–July 1982; from July 1982, member of the PUWP Politburo.

Wyszyński, Stefan: primate of Poland from November 1952 until his death on May 28, 1981.

Żabiński, Andrzej: member of PUWP Politburo from September 1980–July 1981; first secretary of Katowice Voivodeship.

Zamyatin, Leonid Mitrofanovich: chief of CPSU CC International Information Department; member of the Politburo Commission on Poland.

Zhivkov, Todor: president of Bulgaria from 1971–1989; first secretary of Bulgarian Communist Party from 1954–1989.

Zimyanin, Mikhail Vasilievich: CPSU CC Secretary; member of the Politburo's Commission on Poland.

Selected Bibliography

Adamski, Władysław, ed. *Polacy '81. Postrzeganie kryzysu i konfliktu*. Warszawa: Wydawnictwo IFiS PAN, 1996.

Andrew, Christopher M. and Vasili Mitrokhin. *The Sword and the Shield: The Mitrokhin Archive and the Secret History of the KGB*. New York: Basic Books, 1999.

Ascherson, Neal. *The Polish August*. New York: Penguin, 1982.

Baev, Jordan. "Bulgaria and the Political Crisis in Czechoslovakia (1968) and Poland (1980/1981)," *Cold War International History Project Bulletin*, No. 11 (Winter 1998): 96–101.

Barcikowski, Kazimierz. *U szczytów władzy*. Warszawa: Wydawnictwo Projekt, 1998.

Békés, Csaba, Malcolm Byrne, and János M. Rainer, eds. *The 1956 Hungarian Revolution: A History in Documents*. Budapest: Central European University Press, 2002.

Bernhard, Michael H. *The Origins of Democratization in Poland: Workers, Intellectuals and Oppositional Politics, 1976–1980*. New York: Columbia University Press, 1993.

Bernstein, Carl and Marco Politi. *His Holiness: John Paul II and the Hidden History of Our Time*. New York: Doubleday, 1996.

Bingen, Dieter. *Die Polenpolitik der Bonner Republik von Adenauer bis Kohl 1949–1991*. Baden-Baden: Nomos, 1998.

Brumberg, Abraham, ed. *Poland: Genesis of a Revolution*. New York: Vintage Books, 1983.

Brzezinski, Zbigniew. *Power and Principle: Memoirs of the National Security Advisor, 1977–1981*. New York: Farrar, Straus, Giroux, 1985.

———. "A White House Diary," *Orbis* 32:1 (Winter 1988): 32–48.

Byrne, Malcolm, Paweł Machcewicz and Christian F. Ostermann, eds. *Poland 1980–1982: Internal Crisis, International Dimensions, A Compendium of Declassified Documents and Chronology of Events*. Washington, D.C.: The National Security Archive, 1997.

Curry, Jane Leftwich. *Poland's Permanent Revolution: People vs. Elites, 1956–1990*. Washington, D.C.: American University Press, 1995.

Cynkin, Thomas H. *Soviet and American Signaling in the Polish Crisis*. New York: St. Martin's Press, 1988.

Davies, Norman. *God's Playground: A History of Poland: Vol. II—795 to the Present*. New York: Columbia University Press, 1982.

Diskin, Hanna. *The Seeds of Triumph: Church and State in Gomulka's Poland*. Budapest: Central European University Press, 2001.

Dobbs, Michael. *Down with Big Brother: The Fall of the Soviet Empire*. New York: Alfred A. Knopf, 1997.

Dobrynin, Anatoli. *In Confidence: Moscow's Ambassador to America's Six Cold War Presidents (1962–1986)*. New York: Times Books, 1995.

Garthoff, Raymond. *Détente and Confrontation: American–Soviet Relations from Nixon to Reagan*, rev. ed. Washington, D.C.: Brookings Institution, 1995.

Garton Ash, Timothy. *The Polish Revolution: Solidarity 1980–82*. New York: Scribner, 1984.

———. *The Uses of Adversity: Essays on the Fate of Central Europe*. New York: Vintage Books, 1990.

Gates, Robert M. *From the Shadows: The Ultimate Insider's Story of Five Presidents and How They Won the Cold War*. New York: Simon and Schuster, 1996.

Gerrits, André. *The Failure of Authoritarian Change: Reform, Opposition, and Geo-politics in Poland in the 1980s.* Brookfield, Vt.: Dartmouth Pub. Co., 1990.

Głuchowski, L. W. "Poland 1956: Khrushchev, Gomułka, and the 'Polish October,'" *Cold War International History Project Bulletin*, No. 5 (Spring 1995): 1, 38–49.

Goodwyn, Lawrence. *Breaking the Barrier: The Rise of Solidarity in Poland.* New York: Oxford University Press, 1991.

Hahn, Werner G. *Democracy in a Communist Party: Poland's Experience since 1980.* New York: Columbia University Press, 1987.

Haig, Alexander M., Jr. *Caveat: Realism, Reagan, and Foreign Policy.* New York: Mac-Millan Publishing Co., 1984.

Holzer, Jerzy. *"Solidarność" 1980–1981. Geneza i historia.* Warszawa: Wydawnictwo Krąg, 1983.

Hough, Jerry F. *The Polish Crisis: American Policy Options.* Washington, D.C.: Brookings Institution, 1982.

Jakubowicz, Szymon. *Bitwa o samorząd 1980–1981.* London: Wydawnictwo "Aneks," 1988.

Jaruzelski, Wojciech. *Stan wojenny dlaczego.* Warszawa: BGW, 1992.

———. *Hinter den Türen der Macht.* Leipzig: Militzke, 1996.

———. "Commentary," *Cold War International History Project Bulletin*, No. 11 (Winter 1998): 32–39.

Kaliński, Janusz. *Gospodarka Polski w latach 1944–1989. Przemiany strukturalne.* Warszawa: PWE, 1995.

Kania, Stanisław. *Zatrzymać konfrontacje.* Warszawa: Polska Oficyna Wydawnicza "BGW," 1991.

Krajowa Komisja Porozumiewawcza NSZZ "Solidarność". Posiedzenie w dniach 31 III –1 IV 1981. Warszawa: Archiwum Solidarności, 1987.

Kramer, Mark. "Poland, 1980–1981: Soviet Policy During the Polish Crisis," *Cold War International History Project Bulletin*, No. 5 (Spring 1995): 1, 116–139.

———. "Jaruzelski, the Soviet Union, and the Imposition of Martial Law in Poland: New Light on the Mystery of December 1981," *Cold War International History Project Bulletin*, No. 11 (Winter 1998): 5–14.

———. (Introduced, translated and annotated.) "The Anoshkin Notebook on the Polish Crisis, December 1981," *Cold War International History Project Bulletin*, No. 11 (Winter 1998): 14–31.

———. "Colonel Kuklinski and the Polish Crisis," *Cold War International History Project Bulletin*, No. 11 (Winter 1998): 48–59.

———. "'In Case Military Assistance is Provided to Poland:' Soviet Preparations for Military Contingencies, August 1980," *Cold War International History Project Bulletin*, No. 11 (Winter 1998): 102–109.

———. *Soviet Deliberations During the Polish Crisis, 1980–1981*, Cold War International History Project Special Working Paper, No. 1. Washington, D.C.: Woodrow Wilson International Center for Scholars, 1999.

———. "The Soviet Union, the Warsaw Pact, and the Polish Crisis, 1980–1981," paper presented at the conference "From Helsinki to Gorbachev, 1975–1985: The Globalization of the Bipolar Confrontation," Artimino, Italy, April 27–29, 2006.

Kubina, Michael. "Moscow's Man in the SED Politburo and the Crisis in Poland in Autumn of 1980," *Cold War International History Project Bulletin*, No. 11 (Winter 1998): 90–95.

Kubina, Michael and Manfred Wilke, eds. *"Hart und kompromißlos durchgreifen." Die SED contra Polen 1980/81. Geheimakten der SED-Führung über die Unterdrückung der polnischen Demokratiebewegung.* Berlin: Akademie Verlag, 1995.

Kukliński, Ryszard. "The Crushing of Solidarity," *Orbis,* 32:1 (Winter 1988): 7–31.

Lewis, Flora A. *A Case History of Hope: The Story of Poland's Peaceful Revolution in October 1956.* New York: Doubleday, 1958.

MacEachin, Douglas J. *U.S. Intelligence and the Polish Crisis.* Washington, D.C.: Center for the Study of Intelligence, 2000.

Machcewicz, Paweł. "'The Assistance of Warsaw Pact Forces is Not Ruled Out,'" *Cold War International History Project Bulletin,* No. 11 (Winter 1998): 40–42.

Mastny, Vojtech. *The Soviet Non-Invasion of Poland in 1980/81 and the End of the Cold War,* Cold War International History Project Working Paper, No. 23. Washington, D.C.: Woodrow Wilson International Center for Scholars, 1998.

Meehan, Francis J. "Reflections on the Polish Crisis," *Cold War International History Project Bulletin,* No. 11 (Winter 1998): 43–46.

Meretik, Gabriel. *La nuit du Général: enquête sur le coup d'Etat du 13 décembre 1981.* Paris: P. Belfond, 1989.

Michnik, Adam. *Letters from Prison and Other Essays.* Berkeley: University of California Press, 1985.

Michta, Andrew A. *Red Eagle: The Army in Polish Politics, 1944–1988.* Stanford: Hoover Institution Press, 1990.

"More Documents on the Polish Crisis, 1980–1981," *Cold War International History Project Bulletin,* No. 11 (Winter 1998): 110–133.

National Foreign Assessment Center. *Directory of Officials of the Polish People's Republic.* Washington, D.C.: Central Intelligence Agency, August 1979.

Navrátil, Jaromír, ed. *The Prague Spring '68.* Budapest: Central European University Press, 1998.

Ostermann, Christian F. *Uprising in East Germany, 1953.* Budapest: Central European University Press, 2001.

Paczkowski, Andrzej. *Pół wieku dziejów Polski, 1939–1989* [Half a Century of Polish History, 1939–1989]. Warszawa: Wydawn. Nauk. PWN, 1995.

———. "Wydarzenia bydgoskie w strategii walki z "Solidarnością". In *Marzec 1981. Materiały z sesji naukowej,* edited by Adam Bezwiński, 33–42. Bydgoszcz: Instytut Wydawniczy Swiadectwo, 2001.

———. *Droga do mniejszego zła. Strategia i taktyka obozu władzy, lipiec 1980–styczeń 1982.* Kraków: Wydawnictwo Literackie, 2002.

———. *The Spring Will Be Ours: Poland and the Poles from Occupation to Freedom, 1939–1989.* University Park: The Pennsylvania State University Press, 2003.

———. "Playground of the Superpowers, Poland 1980–1989: A View from Inside." In Olav Njolstad, ed. *The Last Decade of the Cold War: From Conflict Escalation to Conflict Transformation.* London: Frank Cass, 2004.

Paczkowski, Andrzej and Andrzej Werblan. *On the Decision to Introduce Martial Law in Poland in 1981: Two Historians Report to the Commission on Constitutional Oversight of the Sejm of the Republic of Poland,* Cold War International History Project Working Paper, No. 21. Washington, D.C.: Woodrow Wilson International Center for Scholars, 1997.

Perlez, Jane E. "Poland '80–'81: Players Do a Surprising Postmortem," *International Herald Tribune,* November 12, 1997.

Rachwald, Arthur. *In Search of Poland: The Superpowers' Response to Solidarity, 1980–1989.* Stanford: Hoover Institution Press, 1990.

Rahr, Alexander G. *A Biographic Directory of 100 Leading Soviet Officials.* Munich: RFE-RL, 1981.

Raina, Peter, ed. *Jan Paweł II, Prymas i Episkopat Polski o stanie wojennym. Kazania, listy, przemówienia i komunikaty.* London: Oficyna Poetów, 1982.

Raina, Peter and Marcin Zbrożek, eds. *Operacja Lato-80. Preludium stanu wojennego. Dokumenty MSW 1980–1981.* Pelplin: Bernardinum, 2001.

Rakowski, M. F. *Czasy nadziei i rozczarowań. Część II.* Warszawa: "Czytelnik," 1987.

———. *Dzienniki polityczne 1979–1981.* Warszawa: Iskry, 2004.

Rolicki, Janusz. *Edward Gierek: Przerwana dekada. Wywiad rzeka.* Warszawa: Wydawnictwo Fakt, 1990.

Rosenberg, Tina. *The Haunted Land: Facing Europe's Ghosts after Communism.* New York: Random House, 1995.

Sabbat, Anna and Roman Stefanowski, comp. *Poland: A Chronology of Events, July–November 1980,* Radio Free Europe Research RAD Background Report, No. 91. Washington, D.C.: RFE-RL, 1981.

———. *Poland: A Chronology of Events, November 1980–February 1981,* Radio Free Europe Research RAD Background Report, No. 263. Washington, D.C.: RFE-RL, 1981.

Sanford, George. *Polish Communism in Crisis.* New York: St. Martin's Press, 1983.

———. *Military Rule in Poland: The Rebuilding of Communist Power, 1981–1983.* London: Croom Helm, 1986.

Staniszkis, Jadwiga. *Poland's Self-limiting Revolution.* Princeton, N.J.: Princeton University Press, 1984.

Stefanowski, Roman, comp. *Poland: A Chronology of Events February–July 1981,* Radio Free Europe Research RAD Background Report Chronology 3. Washington, D. C.: RFE-RL, 1982.

———. *Poland: A Chronology of Events August–December 1981,* Radio Free Europe Research RAD Background Report Chronology 4. Washington, D.C.: RFE-RL, 1982.

———. *Poland Under Martial Law: A Chronology of Events 13 December 1981–30 December 1982,* Radio Free Europe Research RAD Background Report Chronology 4. Washington, D.C.: RFE-RL, 1983.

Sułek, Antoni. "The Polish United Workers' Party: from mobilization to non-representation," *Soviet Studies,* 42:3 (July 1990): 499–511.

Syrop, Konrad. *Spring in October: The Story of the Polish Revolution in October 1956.* London: Weidenfeld and Nicolson, 1958.

Taras, Ray. *Ideology in a Socialist State: Poland 1956–1983.* Cambridge: Cambridge University Press, 1984.

Tischler, János. "The Hungarian Party Leadership and the Polish Crisis of 1980–1981," *Cold War International History Project Bulletin,* No. 11 (Winter 1998): 77–89.

———. *I do szabli... Polska i Węgry. Punkty zwrotne w dziejach obu narodów w latach 1956 oraz 1980–1981.* Warszawa: LSW, 2001.

Tůma, Oldřich. "The Czechoslovak Communist Regime and the Polish Crisis, 1980–1981," *Cold War International History Project Bulletin,* No. 11 (Winter 1998): 60–76.

Wałęsa, Lech. *A Way of Hope.* New York: Henry Holt and Company, 1987.

———. *The Struggle and the Triumph: an Autobiography,* translated by Franklin Philip. New York: Arcade Publishers, 1992.

Walichnowski, Tadeusz, ed. *Stan wojenny w Polsce. Dokumenty i materiały archiwalne, 1981–1983.* Warszawa: Wydawnictwo Comandor, 2001.

Weiser, Benjamin. *A Secret Life: The Polish Officer, His Covert Mission, and the Price He Paid to Save His Country.* New York: Public Affairs, 2004.

Wejdą nie Wejdą. Polska 1980–1982: wewnętrzny kryzys, międzynarodowe uwarunkowania. Konferencja w Jachrance, listopad 1997. London: Wydawnictwo "Aneks," 1999.

Weschler, Lawrence. *Solidarity: Poland in the Season of its Passion*. New York: Simon & Schuster, 1982.

———. *The Passion of Poland*. New York: Pantheon, 1984.

Włodek, Zbigniew, ed. *Tajne Dokumenty Biura Politycznego: PZPR a "Solidarność", 1980–1981*. London: "Aneks," 1992.

Zapis wydarzeń. Gdańsk—sierpień 1980. Dokumenty. Warsaw: NOWA, 1999.

Zinner, Paul E. *East–West Relations in Europe: Observations and Advice from the Sidelines, 1971–1982*. Boulder, Colo.: Westview Press, 1984.

Index

rural self-government, 114, 190
in Szczecin agreement, 66
as threat to socialist system, 345, 491
"The Self-Governing Republic", 23
Shakhnazarov, Georgii, 280
Sieber, Gunther, 285
Sikorski, Jerzy, 80
Siła-Nowicki, Władysław, 105, 415, 469, 527
Siwak, Albin, xlii, 26, 372, 440, 527
Siwicki, Florian, 452
in 1968, xxviii
addresses KOK, 352
addresses PUWP Politburo, 430, 441–442, 462, 512, 516, 519, 521
and martial law
implementation of, xlvi, 460
preparations fo,r 223–225
opposes Warsaw Pact intervention, 140
Soviet views on, 252
at defense ministers' meeting, 420–424
Skalski, Jerzy, 355, 508
Skibniewska, Halina, 107
Słowik, Andrzej, xlvi, 33–34, 487, 524
Sobieraj, A., 325
Sobierajska, A., 325
Sobieski, Henryk, 444
Sobieszek, Lech, 80
Social Council for the National Economy, xliii, 29, 415, 418, 426
Social Democratic Party (FRG), 148
Socialist International, 483
Socialist Union of Polish Students, 106, 114, 173
Socialist Unity Party (SED), 15, 134, 218, 221n., 282, 284, 285, 287, 292, 330, 331, 333, 483
Solidarity trade union (*see also* names of individual leaders)
access to mass media, 55, 67, 72, 73, 327, 328, 417, 425
accused of anti-Sovietism, 186, 206, 366, 432
accused of "terror", 144n., 262, 361, 378, 487, 489, 494
"Appeal to the Working People of Eastern Europe"
awareness of martial law plans, 363
blamed by authorities, 212, 343

debates over proper role, of 320–321, 324–325, 326–327, 328, 329, 335–340, 415, 416
establishment of, xxxii
First National Congress (September-October 1981), xli, xlii, 23, 27, 327, 345, 348, 349, 358, 360, 366, 375
National Coordinating Commission/ National Commission, xxxii, xxxiii, xxxv, xxxvi, xxxvii, xl, xli, xlv, 11, 26, 31, 32, 33, 34, 382, 426, 434, 461, 463
acknowledges Warsaw Pact obligations, 213
conference in Gdańsk (July 24–26, 1981), 319–329, 335–340
disagreements within, xxxvii, xxxviii, 202–203, 226, 414, 484
on Polish crisis, 212–214
Presidium session in Gdańsk (December 2, 1981), 414–416
Presidium session in Radom (December 3, 1981), 417–419, 433, 438, 442, 443, 444
on Solidarity's registration, 101–102
public perceptions of, 28, 343
registration of, xxxii, xxxiii, 12, 101–102, 104–105, 108, 113, 125, 201n., 213, 215n., 226, 328
size of, 105, 108, 184, 201
splits within xxxviii, xli, xlii, xlv, 31, 105, 202, 226, 268, 414
and Warsaw Pact obligations, 213
and work-free Saturdays, xxxi, xxxv, xxxvi, 18, 22, 68, 76, 78–79, 110, 113–114, 184, 202, 336, 343, 364, 482
Solidarność, xxx
Soviet Union (*see also* Communist Party of the Soviet Union), xxvi
and aftermath of martial law, 504–507
agricultural aid to Poland, 172, 199, 398
and anti-Sovietism in Poland, xxxix, xlii, 15, 85, 97, 152, 206, 292, 295, 297, 331, 357–359, 361, 432

armed forces
    Baltic Military District, 64–65,
        136, 138, 165–166, 209
    Belorussian Military District,
        64–65, 136, 138, 165–166,
        209
    Northern Group of Soviet Forces,
        124, 136, 283, 396, 463
    Transcarpathian Military District,
        64–65, 136, 138, 165–166,
        209
    economic aid to Poland, xxxviii, 14,
        39–40, 111, 127, 130, 132, 151,
        182, 199, 205n., 234–235, 242,
        264, 297, 347, 395–396, 446–
        447, 450, 468, 506–507
    used as leverage 21, 27
Gosplan, 32, 347, 400, 507
and importance of mass media, xxxix,
        148, 159, 161, 180, 183, 185,
        219, 402
and military intervention (*see also*
        Military exercises)
    as intimidation, 209, 271
    preparations for, 64–65
    Soviet views on, 21, 253–254, 395,
        397, 446, 449, 450, 451,
        452, 454
pressures on Polish leadership (*see
        under* Jaruzelski; Kania)
and Warsaw Pact strategic
        communications, 362, 450
views on Polish hardliners (*see also*
        Grabski, Tadeusz; Kruczek,
        Władysław; Milewski,
        Mirosław; Olszowski, Stefan;
        Żabiński, Andrzej), 126
Spasowski, Romuald, 82
Special Coordination Committee (U.S.),
        xxxii, xxxiii, 15, 87–90, 162–164
Spiers, Ronald, 304
Stachura, Bogusław, 223, 355, 390, 508,
        512–513
Stalin, Joseph, xxviii
Stanny, Tadeusz, 80
Starszak, H., 388, 391, 508, 515
State Department (U.S.), xxx, xxxi, 36–
        37, 39, 478
    Bureau of Intelligence and Research
        (INR), 26, 304–306

presumes Polish leaders oppose
        intervention, 305
    and force requirements for
        intervention, 209, 210
Štechbart, Horst, 136
Stelmachowski, Andrzej, 414, 416, 434,
        438, 438n.
Stępień, J., 323
Stevens, Ted, 162, 162n.
Strikes, prior to August, 1980
    December 1970, xxix, xxx, xxxiv,
        xxxv, xliv, 2–3, 7, 51, 57, 67,
        68, 72, 108, 142, 191, 207–208,
        208n., 234, 425, 436, 439, 467
    June 1976, xxix, 2, 4, 5, 6, 6n., 72,
        143, 208n., 469
    July 1980, xxix, 47
Suslov, Mikhail, xxxix, xlv, 32, 125, 130,
        265, 281, 282, 285, 289, 400,
        504–507, 527
    addresses CPSU Politburo, 125, 167,
        168, 187, 263, 275–276, 398,
        452–453, 505
    and Politburo Commission on Poland,
        xxxi, 9, 50, 64–65, 123, 180,
        331
    rejects military intervention, 452
Suzuki, Zenko, 164
Szczecin agreement, xxxi, 66–69
    Soviet reaction, 83–84
Szczepański, Jan, 241, 241n.
Szklarski, Wacław, 363, 363n., 508
Sztandar Młodych, 58
Szydlak, Jan, xl
Szyszka, Albin, 289, 484

TASS, xxxix, 349, 477
Thatcher, Margaret, xxxi, 41, 81, 162–
        164, 527
Tikhonov, Nikolai, 280, 291, 396, 399,
        400, 453, 506, 527
    addresses CPSU Politburo, 125–126,
        130, 349, 505, 507
Todorov, Stanko, 93, 120
Trichkov, Krustyu, 98
Trudeau, Pierre, 164
Trybuna Ludu, 63, 219, 325, 343, 464
Trybuna Robotnicza, 180
Tsedenbal, Yumjaagiyn, 473
Tuczapski, Tadeusz, 351, 355, 356

Turner, Stansfield, xxxii, 87, 527
Tygodnik Powszechny, 5

Ukraine, 278–279, 397
Union of Polish Writers, 112, 173
Union of Socialist Polish Youth, 114, 173, 324
United Kingdom, 10, 41, 148, 465
United Nations, 90, 163, 465
United Nations Security Council, 90
United Populist Party, 12n., 115, 377, 439
United States (*see also* Carter, Jimmy; Reagan, Ronald; agency names), xxvi
  economic aid to Poland, xxxix, xxxi, xliv, 39n., 252, 410–411
  rescheduling of Polish debt, xxxiv, xxxvii, xxxix, xli, xliv, 21, 89, 447
  sanctions against Poland, xlvi, xlvii, 39, 39n. 40, 41, 42, 483, 505
  sanctions against Soviet Union, xxxiv
United Strike Committee (*see also* Interfactory Strike Committee), 83, 85
Urban, Jerzy, 527
Urbański, J., 485, 489, 495
Ursus factory, 104, 389, 390, 434, 467, 523
Ustinov, Dmitrii, xlv, 18, 19, 32, 246, 247, 254, 420, 422, 423, 424, 527
  addresses CPSU Politburo 123–125, 131, 168, 187, 235, 241, 243, 263–264, 266, 276, 397–398, 452, 506, 507
  meets with allies, 168, 280–293
  meets with Polish leaders, xxxv, xxxviii, xxxix, 21, 239, 240, 241, 244, 259–264, 265, 275, 400
  and Politburo Commission on Poland, xxxi, 9, 50, 64–65, 123, 331
  rejects military intervention in Poland, 395, 397, 446, 452
Użycki, Józef, 253

Vistula Military Units, xxvi
Voice of America, 192
Voivodeship Committee, 47–48, 63, 69, 106, 109, 115, 116, 118, 180, 182,

276, 284, 287, 291, 375–378, 380, 381, 383, 390, 430, 432, 435, 439, 443, 444, 469, 485, 489, 490, 494
Voivodeship Court of Justice, 101, 102, 373, 380
Voivodeship Defense Committee, 376–377, 380, 467
Voivodeship Exchange, 518
Voivodeship Headquarters of Citizens' Police (*see* Citizens' Police)
Voivodeship Military Staff, 459
Voivodeship Party Control Commission, 376, 489
Voluntary Reserves of the Citizens' Police (*see* Citizens' Police)

Wądołowski, S., 321, 322, 324, 414, 461
Wajda, Andrzej, 388, 388n.
Waldheim, Kurt, 162
Walentynowicz, Anna, xxx, 80, 177, 185, 527
Wałęsa, Lech, xxx, 104, 124, 160, 321, 329, 434, 436, 481, 527
  audience with pope, xxxv, 176
  and August strikes, xxx, xxxi, 7
  and Bydgoszcz crisis, xxxviii
  discussions of Big Three (Glemp, Jaruzelski, Wałęsa), xliii, 30, 400, 402
  discussions with Church leaders, xxxviii, xliv, 36, 427
  discussions with Polish leaders, xxxiv, xxxv, xxxvii, 463
  discussions with U.S. officials, 409–410
  and Gdańsk agreement, xxxi, 79
  interned, xlv, xlvii, 33, 41, 461, 463, 483, 487
  as moderate voice, xxxvi, xxxviii, xlii, xlv, 20, 22, 31, 51, 105, 226, 267, 268, 278, 289, 305, 414
  named leader of MKS, xxx
  reactions to martial law, 463–464, 476
  and Solidarity
    elected leader of, xxxii, 11
    registration of, xxxii, xxxvi, 104
  travels abroad, xxxv, xxxix, 176–179
  and U.S. aid 409
Warsaw agreement, xxxviii, 21
Warsaw insurrection (1944), 51

? strategic ambiguities / ambivalence
re use of force by SU; by Jaruzelski
v.
(incoherent) ambivalence(s) re use of force
> profound
e.g. Nov 8, 80 Jaruzelski speaks out
against martial law (p.14) while a few
days earlier initiating planning for martial
law (p 103)   "uses of adversity"
                 " uses of ambivalence " —>
                      Barancrak on

layout of book
  sections   blk + white
  #'f documents for each party   pictures

  (intro paragraph to each doc —> departure
  (from previous volumes in series ?

  > "limited" "S" coverage
          not so much about S as about
          responses to S

Key questions
      posed / answered
            addressed

      assessment of S both Sur + Polish side were
  IRC repression
right
SU- "S" was a counter rev — partic'ly threats'g
            to commun that had to be dealt w/ decisively

PolishCP was right that not to deal w/ decisively
      until movement had lost steam; shift in
      public mood